Praise for *Alan Lomax*

"The title of John Szwed's objective, detailed, above all loving biography of *Alan Lomax: The Man Who Recorded the World* . . . is hardly an understatement. . . . Mr. Szwed's meticulous and comprehensive book is remarkable for presenting Lomax as a man rather than a legend, an outsider whose day job just happened to be discovering some of the world's most enduring musicians . . . populated with some of the great anecdotes of American music."
—Michael Miller, *The New York Observer*

"It's hard to argue with Szwed's decision to focus on the crucial role [Lomax] played in preserving and championing traditional music and the communities that produced it. . . . In this dense, rich biography, Szwed captures Lomax with all his contradictions intact, refusing to tidy him up."
—Wendy Smith, *Los Angeles Times*

"Szwed admirably captures the efforts of a man who seemed determined to honor what came before him."
—Mark Burman, *The Washington Post*

"Jelly Roll Morton, Zora Neal Hurston, Margaret Mead, Carl Sandburg, Eleanor Roosevelt, and Bob Dylan (on whom Lomax is unfairly blamed for pulling the plug at the 1965 Newport Folk Festival) are but a few of characters that people this entertaining, informative, warts-and-all account of one of the most important cultural figures of the twentieth century."
—*The Atlantic*

"An important and valuable biography and also an interesting slice of American history. Even those who assumed they knew Lomax and his work will no doubt be surprised by what they learn here."
—*The Seattle Times*

"It's the human elements—people like Guthrie, Leadbelly, Seeger, Bob Dylan, Burl Ives, Carl Sandburg, the incomparable Zora Neale Hurston, even J. Edgar Hoover—that give *Alan Lomax* its flavor, color, and, at times, zest."
—*Newsday*

"Szwed, author of Sun Ra and Miles Davis biographies, records a fascinating man who expanded the boundaries of popular music."
—*New York Post*

"[Szwed] unspools a mural of a man bursting with energy, enthusiasm, and notions of what folk songs tell us about the cultures that produce them."
—*The Cleveland Plain Dealer*

"The author expertly weaves together the contradictions of Lomax himself (the overachieving student who all but turned his back on the world of 'straight' academia to follow his passions), while also chronicling a century of political and social change through the prism of song. In an age where most new music is accessible through the click of a mouse, our ancestors (not to mention countless performers) should give thanks that someone with an impeccable set of ears did so much legwork to form our own tastes and enthusiasms. This lovingly presented tome offers the perfect tribute."

—*Record Collector Magazine*

"An invaluable and fascinating resource for anyone interested in the history of American music."

—*Knoxville Metro Pulse*

"A graceful and informative cradle-to-grave study that's a perfect marriage of author and subject."

—Douglas Brinkley, *Texas Monthly*

"But through jazz history John Szwed's new biography, *Alan Lomax: The Man Who Recorded the World*, we see the passion and intimacy that fueled Lomax's life."

—Kolby Yarnell, *Bookforum*

PENGUIN BOOKS

ALAN LOMAX

John Szwed has written biographies of Sun Ra and Miles Davis. He is a professor of music and jazz studies at Columbia University.

ALAN LOMAX

The Man Who Recorded the World

JOHN SZWED

PENGUIN BOOKS

PENGUIN BOOKS
Published by the Penguin Group
Penguin Group (USA) Inc., 375 Hudson Street, New York, New York 10014, U.S.A. • Penguin Group (Canada), 90 Eglinton Avenue East, Suite 700, Toronto, Ontario, Canada M4P 2Y3 (a division of Pearson Penguin Canada Inc.) • Penguin Books Ltd, 80 Strand, London WC2R 0RL, England • Penguin Ireland, 25 St. Stephen's Green, Dublin 2, Ireland (a division of Penguin Books Ltd) • Penguin Books Australia Ltd, 250 Camberwell Road, Camberwell, Victoria 3124, Australia (a division of Pearson Australia Group Pty Ltd) • Penguin Books India Pvt Ltd, 11 Community Centre, Panchsheel Park, New Delhi – 110 017, India • Penguin Group (NZ), 67 Apollo Drive, Rosedale, Auckland 0632, New Zealand (a division of Pearson New Zealand Ltd) • Penguin Books (South Africa) (Pty) Ltd, 24 Sturdee Avenue, Rosebank, Johannesburg 2196, South Africa

Penguin Books Ltd, Registered Offices: 80 Strand, London WC2R 0RL, England

First published in the United States of America by Viking Penguin,
a member of Penguin Group (USA) Inc. 2010
Published in Penguin Books 2011

10 9 8 7 6 5 4 3 2 1

Frontispiece: Alan Lomax in Greece, 1957. Courtesy of the Alan Lomax Archive.

THE LIBRARY OF CONGRESS HAS CATALOGED THE HARDCOVER EDITION AS FOLLOWS:
Szwed, John F., 1936–
Alan Lomax : the man who recorded the world / John Szwed.
p. cm.
Includes bibliographical references and index.
ISBN 978-0-670-02199-4 (hc.)
ISBN 978-0-14-312073-5 (pbk.)
1. Lomax, Alan, 1915–2002. 2. Ethnomusicologists—Biography. I. Title.
ML423.L6347S98 2010
781.620092—dc22
[B] 2010015332

Printed in the United States of America
Designed by Carla Bolte

To
Roger D. Abrahams
and
The Department of Folklore and Folklife,
University of Pennsylvania
1962–1999

CONTENTS

INTRODUCTION

The first time I saw Alan Lomax was in November 1961 at a meeting of the Society for Ethnomusicology, an academic group then too new to have developed its own orthodoxies. They were still debating the definition of music, the meaning of dance, the function of song, all with a sense of wonder and urgency. The founders of the discipline were all there—Charles Seeger, Mantle Hood, Alan Merriam—but the doors were still wide open.

I was a graduate student new to the world of folklorists and ethnomusicologists and eager to connect with them somehow. The big event that night was a concert of African music by the Nigerian drummer Olatunji, who had added to his group some of the members of the Sun Ra Arkestra, and the mixture of the two musics had the scholars puzzled. As the audience filed out, I saw Lomax talking with two men who I later learned were Colin Turnbull and Weston La Barre, not your everyday anthropologists. I knew it was Lomax despite never having seen a picture of him, because his slightly genteel Texas accent drifted to the back of the room. He was big, though I suppose not as big as he looked, in an ill-fitting blue suit, with his collar and tie askew. *Well-dressed enough to be a Bible salesman in Alabama*, I thought, *but missing the mark of a successful academic.* Later, in the high sixties, when I knew him better, it was he who chastised me for my choice of clothing—he told me that government-grants people and highly placed folks of color would not take me seriously. (My one effort at dressing up for something or other amused him, and he said my tan suede jacket and bright tie made me look like a southwestern TV station manager.)

I must have been staring at him that day in the theater, for as he passed me, stepping over rows of seats, he declared as if it were the day's headline, "Pygmies are a baseline culture," and went on his way. He sounded like some nineteenth-century grand theorist speaking from a higher plane, with a scarcely concealed moral program and no sense whatever of then-trendy cultural relativity. Once I had heard him speak at length, I began to wonder what kind of folklorist was this, if that's what he was, with no particular interest in the text of a song or a tale. It turned out that he was speaking comparatively of other levels of art, of humanity—preverbal levels, where bodies interact in front of a cross-cultural tableau, and where art emerges from deeply encoded but virtually nonconscious behavior.

Later, I worked for Alan on occasion, though never for money, as it was understood that he was always short, and I had a day job. He was infinitely patient with the novice, answering questions more fully than was required, with tales of this or that epiphany on the shores or in the swamps of this or that community, of sheriffs with bowie knives who threatened to cut his throat if he ever came back to their county. His stories of working with Zora Neale Hurston were rich and full of his admiration for her fearlessness while doing fieldwork among hoodoo practioners. When I asked him for advice about graduate study, he suggested I drop out and instead do as he had done: seek the company of the very best people in the fields that interested me.

Whenever Alan asked me to join him for lunch or dinner, it was always someplace with well-etched character, though sometimes with marginal food. It might be a bar where the bartender was also waiter, cook, and cashier—"like it used to be." Or a tiny Chinese restaurant where he felt free to order something not on the menu. In conversation, Alan could shift instantly from deadly serious or highly focused to mock folksy or laughing at the absurd, his eyes always a clue as to what was coming. When he called me, usually late at night, it was never just to talk, but because he wanted something—a reaction to a new research project, maybe a suggestion of a name of someone who might work with him on it. Though the request was unspoken, I always knew he was asking me if I would do it. And I wondered how many he had called before me.

Sometimes what he had dreamed up could cost great sums of money, or simply be impossible at the moment. One idea was a plan to sell the television networks on a half-hour prime-time program that featured old people being old people—talking about their lives, maybe sharing secrets, making connections to tradition, performing wisdom and maturity, he said, something like that. He spelled out the details of what would be a kind of homespun reality show. When I cautiously suggested that this would be impossible to sell in the high-profit atmosphere of the media, he pointed to a little vase on the table with a few tired daisies in it and said, "This is not much of a vase, and the flowers aren't much. But if you knew that you could count on finding this vase and those flowers on the table every night for years to come, wouldn't that be something?" He could be hard to argue with.

His enthusiasm was boundless and seemed to grow with age. His drive to celebrate life in all its diversity and to see, taste, and hear everything was astonishing. If you mentioned the blues, he could tell you that Son House was the greatest folk musician in the Western world. Tell him that you were on the way to Trinidad, and he'd say that a man named Nassus Moses who played a one-string fiddle and lived in a hut in the suburbs of Port of Spain was the greatest folk musician in the Western world. And in one sense or another, they always *were* the greatest at something or other.

One night he suggested that several of us go to the Village Gate in New York to see Professor Longhair. It was a bit surprising to hear him praising the brilliance of New Orleans's sainted rhythm and blues pianist, since we weren't aware that he kept up with that sort of thing, but we happily followed him to the club. Since we were late, we squeezed our way in and found seats wherever we could. When 'Fess opened his first set with "Jambalaya," Longhair's rolling, "blues rumba"–flavored revision of Hank Williams's revision of Cajun music, backed by a Crescent City band of beboppers and funksters, I expected a post-gig lecture from Alan about taking creolization too far. But then I felt something brush by my leg, and when I looked down there was Alan crawling on the floor toward the bandstand so as to stay out of people's vision. When he reached the stage he knelt there, his hands on the edge of the stage like a supplicant Kilroy, until the set was over. As he came back to our table, he cried out over the crowd, "Greatest folk musician in the Western world," then followed it up with a letter to the *Village Voice* spelling out the New Orleans piano lineage, how Longhair was the roots of Fats Domino's style, and thus basic to the history of rock and roll, if not the world.

To those who knew Alan's work only from his songbooks he seemed to be the pied piper of the folk, a kindly guide for a nostalgic return trip to simpler times. But he might have thought of himself as spokesperson for the Other America, the common people, the forgotten and excluded, the ethnic, those who always come to life in troubled times—in the Great Depression, in the rising tide toward World War II, during the postwar anti-Communist hysteria, and inside the chaos of the era of civil rights and counterculturalism—those who could evoke deep fears of their resentment and unpredictability. At such times folk songs seemed not so much charming souvenirs as ominous and threatening portents.

Despite having spent most of his life in New York, he never quite seemed to fit the city. He took up too much space, assumed too much, and laughed too easily for a New Yorker. But neither did he seem to fit Texas either. We once shared chili and beer in an El Paso dive, where his beard and sideburns were the event of the evening. Yet he never seemed uncomfortable, for he moved with an absolute assuredness of who he was and where he was at the moment. In that, he was a true bohemian, not a New Yorker or a Texan. But it seems odd to call Lomax a bohemian. His father had aspired to being a hobo, wandering the countryside, but bohemian was something else; it meant belonging nowhere or everywhere. Much of Alan's life in the city was spent in Greenwich Village, among its artists and his dissident neighbors. Most Village residents, after all, came from somewhere else, some small town in the hinterlands, and most of them were happy to say that they had come from nowhere, never mentioning their family and their life before the city. But Alan never denied that he was from Texas or tried to disguise his accent. In his youth he often lived in a state of resistance to his father, but he never rejected him publicly, and in fact often quoted him and identified with his goals. To many in New York, especially in the 1930s and 1940s, a Texan was all the bad things they had left behind somewhere on the other side of the Hudson River—insularity, bigotry, churlishness, and various hatreds and philistinisms. But Lomax would not let them get away with it, and insisted that he be seen as an individual.

I once asked him why he stayed in New York, and he said he could get done in the city in one day what it would take a month to do somewhere else. And before the age of the computer and cell phone, who could deny it? But that was not the whole story—bohemian or not, he had lived in New York longer than anywhere else.

Alan was intense, passionate, in and out of love, dependent on others, but often resistant to them when they got too close. He could get by on little money, live an unsettled life, drift out of his times at one moment, but then come back again, deeply involved. He worked like a dog, driving himself until he fell asleep—in the middle of a recording session, in the waiting room of an office—but only for moments, as life to him was too long not to fill the time with curiosity. He took on more than was humanly possible, and paid for it in frustration over his own incomplete projects. His was a life not easy to live.

CHAPTER 1

From Chisholm Trail to Harvard Yard

It begins like so many other stories—a sensitive, intelligent, and sickly child, kept at home under his parents' close watch, overcomes obstacles to achieve great success. It could be written as an American romantic narrative—but it was tougher and earthier than that, and lingers in some of the lost and forgotten backwaters of America. It might be a western, but it travels to the rarefied air of Harvard Yard, into the heart of the United States government, and across the ocean. It plumbs the depths of the homegrown American character by examining the soul of Haiti, the north of England, and in a near-parody of the Grand Tour, wanders into Franco's Spain and the hard land of the Italian *paisan*.

It begins, then, with a boy in Texas in the first part of the twentieth century, and the boy's father is John Avery Lomax.

Two years after the end of the Civil War, John Lomax was born in Goodman, a tiny Mississippi farming village in Holmes County. By the time John was two, his parents, James and Susan Frances Lomax, had left the chaos of postwar Mississippi and traveled by covered wagon to Texas. There, on the Bosque River, just up the hill from the Chisholm Trail, they settled in Meridian, a small frontier community southeast of Fort Worth, made up of fellow southerners, recently freed slaves, and a few Norwegian immigrants. Like many southerners, the Lomaxes claimed well-to-do ancestors who had come from England and had fallen on hard times. "The upper crust of the po' white trash" is the way that John described his family's place in Texas society—a family of ten surviving by hard work and discipline.

At age six John was already clearing brush and beginning to chop cotton. Soon he was cutting wood and tending the cattle and horses. Though he was never quite a cowboy because their livestock was never that numerous, he nonetheless grew up in the world of working cowhands, since the cattle drives brought them down the Chisholm Trail. Huddled in the brush near their campfires, watching and listening, John was fascinated by their talk, even more so by their songs, and he absorbed their style and manner from an early age. Still, his father and mother were eager to have their children educated, both at home and at school. They subscribed to several newspapers from as far away as New York City, and there were always books in the house—Shakespeare, the English poets, works in Latin. Poetry was taken very seriously, and they all memorized poems and songs, reciting and singing on special occasions. This mix of poetry from the printed page and the poetry of folk songs was never a contradiction to John, since he viewed both as oral forms, and both of them imbued his life and shaped his character. Later, when it occurred to him to turn the cowboy songs he grew up with into books, it made perfect sense.

John's parents tried to have their children take a year of college by the time they were twenty-one, and in 1887 it was John's turn. To pay his way, he sold his horse, borrowed money from his father and a cousin, took a part-time job, and left home to enroll at nearby Granbury College, a tiny country school. By the end of the year he qualified for a teaching license, which he used to get a job as principal and the only teacher in the Preparatory Department of minuscule Weatherford College in Clifton, near Meridian. At the end of the first year, the school paid his way to study bookkeeping at summer school in Eastman Business College in Poughkeepsie, New York, so that he could return to head up Weatherford's newly created Business Department (where, once again, he was the sole teacher). For six years John stayed at Weatherford, teaching twelve to fifteen classes, six days a week, and was paid so little that he was continually in debt, especially as he helped support several of his brothers and sisters. His only real personal expense was a trip he took every summer alone to Chautauqua, New York, where one of America's grandest efforts at mass education was under way. It was a series of performances and lectures, held out of doors in the main, and attended by folks eager to escape the heat and go to the country, where the Chautauqua tents were set up by the lake. There they would see William Jennings Bryan preach, Maud Ballington Booth ("the Little Mother of the Prisons") decry the horrors of the penal system, and Jacob A. Riis describe life in the slums, or they would learn higher mathematics or listen to poetry readings and concerts. Some thought Chautauqua was a godsend (Woodrow Wilson described it as "an integral part of the national defense"), while others saw it as an early sign of the decline of a great country (Sinclair Lewis said it was "nothing but wind and chaff and . . . the laughter of yokels"). For John it was the quickest and cheapest way to get an education, even though he was all too aware that it was not the real thing.

But in the fall of 1895, at age twenty-eight, John arrived in Austin to begin working toward a bachelor's degree at the University of Texas with the financial help of a cousin. At enrollment, he signed up as being several years younger than he was, then took double the number of required courses in an effort to make up for lost time. He did so well in his classes that he was classified as a sophomore even before he ended the first semester. At the same time he was editor of the *Texas University* magazine, writing articles and poetry, and joined the staffs of the student newspaper and the yearbook. By his graduation in 1897—four years of college compressed into two—he had majored in English literature, become deeply involved in campus politics, been acknowledged as a student leader, and moved easily among the faculty and administration. It therefore came as a shock when he was unable to get a teaching job after graduation. Just when he was beginning to lose hope, he was equally shocked to be offered the job of registrar at his alma mater. He accepted the offer, though it was not at all what he had wanted, since he assumed it concerned little more than recordkeeping. But once in the job, he was also asked to handle some of the university's correspondence, to serve as the president's secretary, and to manage the men's dormitory. What's more, to assume this job he was required to continue being a student and had to enroll for a two-year M.A. program. It was a poorly paid, overworked position, but one that would give him more education and immediate respect, so it was hard for him to resist. By age thirty he had become the sole support of his mother, and his siblings regularly sought loans from him. To the world at large, he would soon seem successful, dignified, and scholarly. With his long coats and his Stetson hat and cigar, he was called "Professor" by students and many of those outside the university. It may have been a functionary's job, but he made something of it, and over the years he managed to survive the resignation of an unpopular president who had backed him, and also learned to steer his way through the arcane and fickle politics of Texas. Because he had the role of guiding young students' entry into the university, he became a well-known and popular figure all across the state, one who played a significant role in the lives of most of its future business, educational, and governmental leaders.

At his age, he might have been thought of as settling into the life of an academic bachelor, but his interest in women was pronounced, if well controlled. Most of the women he knew were much younger than him, and were understood to be under his protection at the university. In fact, for five years John had been carrying on an intense if largely long-distance relationship with a young woman of culture and intelligence from the Texas town of Palestine. Shirley Green was John's first love, but a doomed one, as she was dying of tuberculosis, a fact that she revealed to him only when he began to press her about their future. Just before she passed away, she told him that she was encouraging several of her women friends to correspond with him. One of them, Bess Baumann Brown, a kindergarten teacher in Dallas, visited Austin with plans to enter college, and to his amazement showed a strong interest in him. After Shirley died, he and Bess became close and began to talk of marriage.

The University of Texas had from its beginnings been embroiled in state politics, yet John had found ways to handle the shifts and turns that came with it. But when the university's president, George Taylor Winston, whom he had served so faithfully, clashed too many times with the Legislature, he resigned, and John began to feel his future threatened. Once again he began thinking of teaching, and asked for time off to study educational administration at Harvard, the university that provided most of the senior faculty at Texas. When his request was turned down by the administration, John applied again, but Texas would still not grant him leave. Then, in the summer of 1903, at thirty-six years of age, he made an uncharacteristically sudden move, quitting the university to become an instructor in English at its archrival, Texas A&M, where one of his Austin friends had just become president. It meant a cut in pay and a loss of prestige moving down from Austin, but he hoped now at least to have more time for his interest in folk songs and to be free of academic politics.

After nine months of teaching and traveling back and forth on weekends from College Station, the home of Texas A&M, to see Bess in Austin where she was studying, they were married in early June 1904 and then traveled up the East Coast to Harvard, where John attended summer school. When they returned to A&M, they chose a small faculty house as far away from the campus as they could find and stocked it with chickens, two pigs, two milk cows, and a dog. It was not unusual to see a family with a few chickens in the South at the time, but the Lomaxes were supplying much of their own food, as well as selling milk and eggs to the neighborhood.

Suddenly everything seemed to be breaking John's way. When their first child arrived in August 1905, they named her Shirley, after Bess's former girlfriend. When he boldly asked to have the whole year of 1906–1907 off to study at Harvard, the administration agreed, giving him an unprecedented one-third of his salary. Harvard accepted his application and, more surprisingly, awarded him a top teaching fellowship that paid $500.

Harvard meant validation to John, perhaps even revenge on the teachers who had taken his ability, his passion for folk song, and his aspiration to be a first-rate scholar lightly. Now he was in the premier department of English in America, in a group of students that inclued Van Wyck Brooks, Charles Seeger, and T. S. Eliot, another fugitive from the provinces. From his first days on campus John became a favorite among some of the faculty, who were unusually receptive to nontraditional students. The dean of Harvard College, Le Baron Russell Briggs, for example, who taught John's English composition class, made him comfortable writing about things he knew, and welcomed essays on subjects that were far from the norm: lynchings, cattle roping, and all things southwestern. Barrett Wendell, who taught "Literary History of America," encouraged his students to write about the regions of the United States from which they came, and became so excited when John proposed to write about cowboy ballads that he immediately introduced him to George Lyman Kittredge, the preeminent scholar of English literature of his time, a specialist on Chaucer and Shakespeare, and the foremost student of the ballad in the country. Kittredge and Wendell were delighted by the idea that there were distinctively American ballads in existence and that they might still be being created somewhere, and the two professors encouraged John to begin systematic collection of western ballads. They even allowed him to use their names in sending letters across the country in search of song texts, and promised to look for a foundation that might underwrite his research.

John revealed to his mentors that he had earlier assembled a collection of cowboy songs in a "roll of dingy manuscript written out in lead pencil and tied together with string" and taken it to show to one of Texas's English professors. He was told that his songs were "tawdry, cheap and unworthy," and that he should instead devote himself to the best that English literature had to offer. In anger and shame, John said, he waited until night, went behind the dormitory where he lived, built a small fire, and burned up every scrap of his song collection.

John spent days writing hundreds of letters in search of cowboy songs, and still kept up with his classes. By spring 1907, the letters began to pay off and songs started coming in. By then, however, Bess was pregnant again and he needed to go back to work, though he had no luck with his job search. As his final examinations approached he began to suffer from eyestrain and stomach problems and ended up in the infirmary. His professors agreed—against all rules—to grant him his master's degree without completing his exams for what they termed "a nervous collapse."

Back in Texas, he continued to work on his collection, and when a research grant failed to materialize, Professor Wendell helped modestly finance John's work out of his own money. On June 14 the Lomaxes' first son, John Jr., was born. The lack of money was now becoming a problem: both children were sick with various illnesses, John Jr. quite seriously, and Bess was suffering from what she called "a general breakdown." Harvard then offered him a postgraduate fellowship on the condition that Texas A&M would give him a year off at half salary. When the A&M administration refused, Harvard offered him three successive yearly grants for his use during vacations.

In 1909 John convinced some friends in Austin that they should form some sort of organization to gather and preserve local folklore, and he was elected the first secretary of the Texas Folklore Society. At the request of Professor Kittredge, he addressed the meeting of the Modern Language Association at Cornell on the topic of "Cowboy Songs of the Mexican Border." It was a paper written to be read, as was the academic practice, but he delighted the gathering of professors when he began to sprinkle Texas stories throughout his talk. And when he yelled cattle cries across the room, sang songs, and asked the austere audience to join in, he created a sensation that would eventually bring hundreds of invitations for him to speak from all across the country. Now in his forties, balding, paunchy, and wearing a suit, he looked like anything but a cowboy and often drew giggles when he first walked onstage. But he knew how to draw in an audience, recalling his elocution courses, reciting as much as he sang, and booming out southwestern country poetry and ranch songs as if he were an old hand himself.

Then, again to his surprise, he was asked to become the secretary of the University Faculties at Austin. It was still not the teaching position he wanted, but when he asked for time off in the summers to travel in search of songs, the administration agreed. He now had time to finish the book he called *Cowboy Songs and Other Frontier Ballads,* which was published in 1910, with an introduction by President Theodore Roosevelt, appearing just in time to feed a rising interest in American folk songs. It sold steadily and stayed in print for years, helped in part by Bess and John, who promoted and sold copies from their home and at lectures.

When John Lomax began to gather cowboy ballads he joined a tradition that stretched back well over a hundred years. The story of folk song collecting in the English-speaking world begins in the eighteenth century with accusations of a forgery that had international consequences. James Macpherson, a teacher in the Highlands of Scotland, created a sensation in 1790 by publishing a collection of very old poems that suggested Scotland might possess a body of classical literature equal to that of the Homeric poetry of Greece. A few years later, however, suspicions arose that in his *Fragments of Ancient Poetry Collected in the Highlands of Scotland and Translated from the Gallic or Erse Language,* Macpherson was inventing "translations" of nonexistent poems, that there were very few genuine pieces in Macpherson's epics, and that even those were heavily altered by him.

He was not alone in trying his hand at this form of authorship, especially in Scotland, where some writers were driven by the desire to prove that theirs was a much older and more literate culture than that of the British who had defeated the Scots and then annexed them. Right behind Macpherson came Thomas Percy, the son of a grocer in Northumberland, across the border in England, who created a collection of ballads based on an old manuscript collection of poetry, which he claimed to have rescued from the hands of a housemaid, who was about to light the fire with it. He published this collection as *Reliques of Ancient English Poetry* in 1765. Percy, like Macpherson, thought ballads were records of earlier ways of life, but unlike the Scotsman, he found them not particularly valuable as poetry, and so he felt free to alter or improve his ballad texts in order to make them more readable. The book sold well anyway, like Macpherson's, especially among the

German Romantics—Goethe, Schiller, and even Beethoven, who was inspired by it to transform a number of Scots folk songs into lieder.

Years later, Sir Walter Scott was drawn into the debate over origins and whether ballads were pure Scottish products. Having Percy's book as a child, he began heading into the countryside along the Scottish border to collect ballads as early as 1792, relishing the stories of outlaws, murderers, adultery, and abduction. He too sometimes constructed more "complete" versions than existed, aiming for a higher level of literature than what was already there. The ballads in his 1802 *Minstrelsy of the Scottish Borders* were "restorations."

Whether forged or genuine, ballads required some kind of authentication, and the two standards of the times were that there be enough of them to matter and that they be very old. They had to be presented as proper collections, not as random findings. Demonstrating their antiquity required the skills of a philologist or an antiquarian to date the manuscripts on which the ballads had been discovered. To help the dating process along, some collectors "aged" the songs, treating them as fragments that had been found and reassembled by an editor/archaeologist, and made the story of their discovery part of the proof. A manuscript rescued from the fire, found hidden in a wall, or lying on the floor—they were all part of the tale, the romance of the collector-antiquarian. These found ballads were presented to their eighteenth-century audience as sung by bards, not folksingers or poets, for "bard" was a Celtic word, identified with Scotland, Ireland, and Wales, and so were connected to a history that preceded the Acts of Union of 1707 and 1801 that attempted to erase the boundaries between England and these other countries.

The Scots collectors were not acting solely out of nationalistic interest, however. They also sought personal betterment by attracting the attention and the imprimatur of an aristocrat, often an antiquarian himself, to whom the book was then dedicated. Most of the collectors who chose this route had already failed at some earlier occupation, and were using collecting as the vehicle for a second chance. There was little wealth to be gained from ballads, but there was a kind of fame.

In the United States, interest in ballad collecting began in the Northeast, especially in Cambridge, Massachusetts, among those connected to Harvard. In 1855, a thirty-six-year-old James Russell Lowell announced that he would be giving a series of twelve public lectures, the fourth of which was titled "The Ballad," and the audience was pleased to see him rise in defense of America as a literary nation, and of the ballad as an important part of its literature. "The ballads are the only true folk songs that we have in English," he said. "There is no other poetry in the language that addresses us so simply as mere men and women." Then he took aim at the British. "English writers demand of us a national literature. But where, for thirteen centuries, was their own?" His stunning answer was that what the

English call their literature was borrowed from the Celts, from the romances that were written about King Arthur and his court. Not only was he disputing the right of the British to lay exclusive claim to ballads when they were Celtic in origin, but he was also extending his argument westward and announcing his own declaration of cultural independence for Americans. (Lowell's mother, incidentally, was a Scot, who read Sir Walter Scott to him as a child and sang him to sleep with Scottish ballads.)

Seated at Lowell's lectures was the young scholar Francis James Child, who would later become a colleague of Lowell's at Harvard as its first professor of English, and between 1882 and 1898 would publish a series of ten books called *The English and Scottish Popular Ballads.* Child started by gathering together ballads in manuscript and published form like other collectors before him, and then set about categorizing them and putting them in order. The three-hundred-plus ballads in his ten-volume collection were the result of this ordering, and they became the standard for what could be called a folk song from the thirteenth to the nineteenth centuries. For Child, the age of balladry was over, and nothing as fine or as noble could ever be found again in live performance.

When Child retired, his student George Lyman Kittredge replaced him. As with the other academics of his time and before him, it was the words of the folk songs that counted, and the roots of high poetry they saw in them. He had little interest in the actual music of the songs, the instruments that accompanied them, the way they were performed, or even in what they meant to the people who sang them. Collectors from the northeastern United States seldom went out among the people to gather songs, and when they did, they followed the British practice of contacting local gentry or community officials and asking them to locate the singers for them.

In England there was one collector who was interested in ballads as songs, not poems. Cecil Sharp was a musician, not a literary scholar, and for years he collected both the words and the music of songs live from singers in the field, first in England, where he had started the English Folk Dance Society in 1911, and then later in the United States. He spent twelve months in Kentucky between 1916 and 1918, and his collection, *English Folk Songs from the Southern Appalachians,* was published after his death in 1932.

Whether it was the influence of Sharp, or something deeper that Kittredge saw in John Lomax and his cowboy ballads when he came to Harvard as a student, the professor's encouragement of Lomax's recording of music and text was sincere, and gave John the courage to go forward. For Kittredge to accept cowboy songs as ballads was no small thing, for they were not taken seriously at the time. Sharp, for one, had ignored cowboy ballads, remarking that the cowboy had been "despoiled of his inheritance of traditional song."

The history of the early song collectors resonated in John Lomax's life, and he sometimes found himself reliving it. When John asked former president Theodore Roosevelt, a Harvard graduate himself, to write "an endorsement" of his book, he was repeating Percy's and Scott's experiences with ballads in a democratic way. Because he was forced to sell their work to the public to survive outside of university life, John was condemned by scholars, who argued that the composite texts he published were corrupt—the same claims made against Macpherson, Percy, and Scott, even though they were eventually well received by the public. As a folklorist who collected in the field, John also found himself roughing it like big game hunters and bringing back the evidence that he had somehow managed to work his way into one or another of these groups of rural and tough people.

It was all this that led John to take these songs with him when he went to Harvard to study. That roll of cowboy songs he had burned up as a young man back in Texas, and that he had reconstructed to take with him, was part of the romance. The South was suffused with the spirit of Walter Scott, and when Lomax considered giving his ballad book the title of *Cowboy Songs of the Mexican Border*, he was bringing notice to the parallels between the culture of the *vaqueros* and the life of the Scots reivers who robbed and stole on the Scottish border.

When the Lomaxes moved back to Austin, they lived closer to campus, but still kept chickens, turkeys, cows, and a pony, and raised a full garden of vegetables, with Bess cooking on a woodstove. John worked as hard as always, developing an alumni magazine, expanding the involvement of ex-students in the affairs of the school, attending and taking notes at every departmental and university meeting, and fund-raising for scholarships. Still, he made time for lectures, and in 1911 he launched the biggest tour yet, across the country to the East Coast and then up as far as Vermont, speaking at important schools and professional organizations and picking up songs from the libraries and the audiences as he went along. In 1912 he repeated the tour, this time focusing on black music, and even engaging a theatrical agent to coordinate his appearances. In a time before motion pictures with sound, before sound recordings were available in every home, even before serious radio programming, John was taking the lives of cowboys, blacks, and workers of all types into American universities and spreading the message of folklore. Though he was becoming well known on these tours, he fretted that they were often not as good as they should be, and feared that he was becoming a cheap theatrical hustler. Yet he persevered, eventually himself becoming part of the many Chautauquas that were springing up across the country.

The Lomaxes' second son, Alan James, was born on January 31, 1915, at home in Austin. Shirley was now ten and John Jr. eight, and both were handsome, increasingly healthy children and a source of pride. Alan's health, however, was a constant concern, as he was afflicted with asthma and then sinus infections and earaches. He developed slowly and remained underweight for many years. Alan recalled his childhood in that house, where his father attempted to re-create his own childhood home:

> Our house was a two-story building made of soft sandstone that weathered into all kinds of colors. A beautiful red river runs through the town. There are hills with wild wolves, occasional rattlesnakes, and mountain lions. Way back in the hills are sure enough mountain people whom I didn't get to know until later. Right back of our house was a creek with water moccasins and catfish. It was a tremendous place for a boy to venture in with swimming, fishing and camping a hundred yards away. My father always built on the edge of town so there was always plenty of country to run in.

In 1917, two years after Alan was born, the new governor of Texas, James Ferguson, became locked in combat with the university, demanding the resignation of its new president, R. E. Vinson; when that attempt failed, he insisted that Vinson fire seven faculty members whom the governor viewed as disloyal—John Lomax among them. (In his public talks, Ferguson had occasionally singled out Lomax's cowboy song collecting as a symptom of the university's wasteful and frivolous ways.) Then, after threatening to veto the budget of the entire school, Ferguson fired the regents of the university and appointed a new board that was willing to dismiss the president and the marked faculty members who still remained on campus. Throughout this affair, Lomax spent part of what had become his annual lecture tour looking for a job elsewhere. Professor Wendell at Harvard put him in touch with his son, a Boston banker, who managed to have Lomax offered a job as a bond salesman in the Illinois office of his banking firm. John, though he knew almost nothing about banking and was unhappy to be forced into it, moved his family to a house in Highland Park, along the North Shore of Chicago, and got to work.

He turned out to be a good salesman, and with his statewide contacts in Texas and the improving economy at the start of the First World War he was an immediate success. Amid his many sales trips to Texas he found time to do a bit of folk song collecting, even among businessmen he met. Though he was not especially happy in Chicago, it did offer him the opportunity to meet new people, and he found his way into the local journalists' world, where he met a number of writers, including Carl Sandburg, who had just published his first poems and was collecting folk songs for his own book. The two men were on opposite sides of the political divide—Sandburg being sympathetic to various socialist causes, and

Lomax a social conservative—but they were brought together by their common populist and literary passions and became lifelong friends.

Governor Ferguson was eventually impeached for financial irregularities, and in 1919 the Texas Exes—the alumni group John Lomax had spearheaded—asked him to return to Austin to become the secretary of the Ex-Students Association and to help recruit new students to the university. He accepted the post and the family returned to Austin, settling back into their old life of urban mini-farming, John continuing to work for the Chicago firm "on the side" with Bess as his business partner, editor, and financial adviser. "In addition to being a talent scout for the university," Alan recalled, "my father was also a really great teacher. He felt English literature to be more important than folklore, and for years, he read Kipling, Tennyson, Mark Twain and O. Henry to the kids out of the backwoods. He'd often visit his ex-students on his rides around the country, and they all seemed delighted to have him. They'd take him into their libraries and say, 'Look, John, this is what you did for me.' Soon he was behind a big cigar and a glass of whiskey, telling stories."

On January 21, 1922, Bess gave birth to her fourth child, a girl, whom they named Bess, and often called Bess Brown Jr. Whatever schools their children might be attending—and they attended some of the best available—Bess and John saw themselves as their true teachers. John, always the late starter, was determined that they would never suffer his fate of having to piece together an education. Bess knew how to teach young children, and her commitment to the task was reinforced when Maria Montessori visited the United States promoting a new approach to children's learning. Since several of the Lomax children were often sickly, they were kept home much of the time, and the line between education and home was never rigidly drawn: chores, play, all the day's activities were the makings of some kind of lesson or other. A drive in the car could be turned into a songfest or a light opera of their father's spontaneous creation, its libretto semi-improvised and the roles assigned to the children. Evenings were set aside for singing, spelling, math, and reading, and visitors to the house were commandeered into audiences for the children's latest memorized recitations. The children were made to compete with each other, with records kept of who did what first at a certain age. Alan was started on reading as soon as possible, and before his fifth birthday his father had drawn up a diploma stating that he had "successfully completed a course of study in *The Primer* in which is featured the wonderful story of 'The Little Red Hen.'" The diploma declared that Alan was now a member of the "Society of the Primum Primerians." "I was given an absurd notion of my capacities," Alan insisted. "I don't know how I survived. Maybe that's why I still antagonize people. I was pushed ahead of my class although I wasn't brighter than anyone else."

> I've always had an oppressive sense of not living up to family expectations and standards. We were expected to have nothing less than across-the-board, perfect moral conduct. I really never told a lie of any kind until I was over twenty-one. When I was a little boy, I never said good-bye because I knew it meant God Bless You, and I was an atheist. I left all churches when I was seven. I was so bored I couldn't stand it any more, but all of us children were sent to Sunday school.

Once he entered elementary school in Austin, Alan's grades never fell below A's (except in physical education and penmanship), and his report cards glowed with praise from his teachers. He did miss many days of classes when he was sick with tonsillitis, asthma, nasal problems, and earaches. (His infected ears were often lanced without anesthesia, which eventually led to near deafness in one ear by the time he turned thirty-five.) Alan recalled going to elementary school for only two full years: "I've always been afraid of being rejected, and I guess I took it as a rejection that my mother sent me, and so I became too sick to go."

In 1923 John became the focus of a number of controversies involving Texas politics and campus life, particularly for his criticism of the money spent on college athletics. Letters critical of him appeared in the alumni magazine, especially focused on his concern with alumni issues at the expense of undergraduate affairs. When he was replaced as editor in 1925, he quit altogether, at age fifty-eight. But once again he was rescued by the child of an academic—this time by Leslie Waggener Jr., the son of a former president of the University of Texas, who hired him to run the bond department as a vice president of the Republic National Bank of Dallas. His new salary was such that John had an architect design them a nine-room house in Forest Hills, "the house in the woods," miles outside Dallas.

Alan was by now enrolled in the Terrill School for Boys, the most prestigious private school in town, which had classes so small they were virtually tutorials. It was assumed that at graduation each of its students would head to Harvard or Yale. Alan was on the honor roll every month with A's in every subject but Latin. His teachers wrote that he was "superior" in effort and deportment, a model student who won honors in English and finally even conquered Latin.

But John Lomax sought more than the scholar in Alan, and made it clear that he wanted to build him up physically, give him character, teach him to be a man—a Texas man. Alan's constant ear and nose infections left him thin and tired and underweight, yet he signed up for the school's younger students' football team, on which he played end. His father felt that he would also benefit from the same kind of outdoor work he himself had known as a child. So, beginning in the summer of his tenth year and for several years after, Alan was sent off to the Brazos to a ranch in the high hills near Comanche, Texas, owned by Oscar and Stella Calloway, old family friends. Through the hard-baked months of July and August he was to put in a full day's work tending sheep and cattle, making hay, picking cotton, and repairing the roads on the ranch. In the evenings he was expected to read the books that his father sent him, mostly histories and biographies such as *The Life of John Marshall*, and then be quizzed about them in his letters.

But on his arrival Alan became sick with an earache and was kept in bed for several days. Throughout his stay he suffered from hay fever, and he became convinced that his father believed he would never get well and would perhaps even die there. He faced the situation without complaint, hinting meekly in his letters that he hoped his sister Shirley might be allowed to come and visit him. When she failed to appear, he admitted that he missed his mother and wished she could come. His father wrote back that he should not become impatient or dissatisfied—they missed him too, but ranch life was good for him, and, incidentally, he should reread the letters he wrote home before he mailed them and correct the misspellings and mistakes. Alan bore it all as best he could, but it was a rough life for a boy, full of teasing by the hands and daily tests of endurance that left him miserable.

When the end of August came and it was time for Alan to return to Dallas, his father wrote that he could come home only if he promised that he "would no longer swim without an inner tube and would cease diving altogether," and that he should be willing to stay home from school that fall until they felt he was strong enough to return. His mother would teach him at home, and he would continue to do outdoor work and fish and hunt, all for his health. Otherwise, they would have to find him another ranch home where his duties would keep him healthy. "I decided not to die; getting sick hadn't gotten me what I wanted from my mother."

Even at home, Alan was tested physically, and clashed with his older brother, John Lomax Jr. John was a handsome and likable boy, who, according to his sister Bess, should have been the prince of the family: "He was everything Father wanted—he was competitive, frugal, successful, and knew how to make money. He helped Father in endless ways, even becoming a folklorist himself, doing his own collecting, and then financing and producing films on blues singers Mance Lipscomb and Lightnin' Hopkins. Alan may have been puny as a child, but he was intelligent, and it was he who was Father's favorite." Yet he persisted on picking fights with his older brother, fights he could never win. John Jr. spared nothing for Alan's size, and their mother made no effort to stop them, believing they'd work it out sooner or later.

Alan called the first ten years of his life his "mauve decade"—the stifling and rigidly proper houses, with their dark, heavily furnished Texas interiors, blinds drawn exactly two-thirds the length of the windows (in the German fashion, as his father pointed out to him), hiding evil and hypocrisy. Life for Alan did not improve in high school. When Bess was thirteen and daunted by beginning high school herself, Alan wrote her and reflected on his own discontents at her age:

> At thirteen I was a junior at Terrill Prep School, that I went to the movies unattended after I first got a telephoned permission from mother, that we were living in Forest Hills, that I was somewhat vaguely in love with Mrs. Sharpe [a teacher], reading Virgil with a very pleasant and intelligent young man for a teacher and two not very much younger men for classmates who had a habit frequently of cribbing my translation, that I was half-heartedly writing for the school newspaper and annual, and quarter-heartedly participating in the activities of a slowly dying scout troop with a bunch of boys that I saw seldom [and] liked little, that I had lost interest for the time being in leading the school in grades since I had seen the year before that it was easy, that I was greatly interested in sports and pictured myself a football hero more often as I did anything else, that I was at the same time a very clumsy and gawky foot-ball player which may explain my utter contempt for athletes and athletic ideas now, that I did not understand how anyone could in any way be interested in girls or parties. That I wrote a long tedious essay on Poe . . . and got the only A+ in class, that my teeth were being straightened and all the while I was called Chipmunk, that I was very much afraid of a good many boys, that I shrank from any physical pain.

Only Harvard would do for Alan's college education, and in order to ensure that he was accepted, John contacted several people on the faculty, who suggested that Alan apply to the Choate School in Connecticut for his senior year, 1929–30. While it was a considerable social leap for him to a school for the sons of millionaires and the elite—only a few years after Alan arrived, John F. Kennedy would begin his studies there—Alan was accepted, and even given a $2,600 scholarship, enough to cover his tuition and expenses.

Once there, he worked hard and impressed his teachers. One wrote that he was a "very capable and mature *person,* not simply 'a boy' "—this in spite of being a year younger than the youngest member of the senior class. His only problem was his preoccupation with grades: "He expresses real disappointment at anything less that 100%." By the start of the second term his homesickness and the fear that he was not as good as the other boys in his studies left him deeply depressed, and he began skipping meals and staying in his room. The headmaster and his wife became so concerned that they brought him into their home and fed and comforted him. The faculty also encouraged him, especially with his writing, and he was put on the board of the *Choate Literary Magazine.* His only real difficulties came in physics and sports, but even there he was lauded for his unceasing effort and his persistent work in tennis, gymnastics, and football.

Most of the students Alan met that year talked with the ease and sophistication of those raised in the life and culture of the Northeast; as aggressively as he had been schooled, his frontier manners often left him struggling. (He had to be instructed how to use a knife and fork after his first meal at Choate.) By the middle of the year he had developed an intense friendship with one of those students, Michael Bullard, built around long talks about literature, philosophy, and the meaning of life as seen from Wallingford, Connecticut. Over Easter vacation he stayed in Boston with Mike and his sister, a social worker in the tenements.

Whenever he could, Alan spent weekends in New York City. After one of those trips he sent a postcard to his sister Bess describing his stay with some cousins, spending seventeen dollars to see three plays and hear the New York Philharmonic. His parents saw the card and wrote him that they could not afford such expenses. Alan apologized and promised not to spend so carelessly again, but within weeks he was asking for money to go to Boston to visit museums, hear the Boston Symphony, and see a girl from Switzerland, the first "date" he said he had ever had. His father was adamant: they couldn't afford it, and in fact were even canceling a long-planned family trip to Europe that summer for lack of money. In any case, he was too young to be involved with a girl. His mother followed with her own thirteen-page letter that listed each of his cousins who had been a failure because of some girl or other, and contrasted them with those (primarily his brother John Jr.) who had succeeded because of their single-minded devotion to their work. It was his sister Shirley he resembled, his mother said—the flapper, the social butterfly, someone who was unable to control her emotions. Bess, on the other hand, might "perhaps have a better mind" than he. Furthermore, his father had changed his mind and did not want to join his mother and Bess for their planned visit to Choate that spring, "as the trip was ruined for him." His mother concluded by asking him to refrain from using words like "hell" and "damn" in his letters. But Alan was not to be threatened, and wrote back challenging their judgment about him and those to whom they compared him, arguing that it was normal for boys his age to be interested in girls. He clinched his argument by threatening them that he had been "rapidly developing into a homosexual. My view of such matters was morbid and unhealthy." But his new girlfriend had changed all of this. The problem, he said, was that they didn't know him and he didn't know them in any serious way, only superficially. And, by the way:

> Please don't make definite plans for next year until you see me. I have very definite ideas as to what I want to do and as to what I think will be best for me. Mr. St. John [the headmaster] wants me back here next year, but I don't think I want to come back and I don't think it would be best for me. I can't possibly tell you the things I feel or why I feel them in a letter but I can talk them to you when you come.

> This year for the first time in my life I've begin to *think*. I have done some thinking and reading which has changed my idea about life very considerably. They probably won't agree with yours for the simple reason that we are of different generations.

As it turned out, his winter quarter exam grades were not as good as he had hoped, with the worst of them in English, his favorite subject. With graduation approaching, he dove back into his studies and stayed at school to work on weekends.

Headmaster George St. John wrote Alan's parents urging them to let him stay on at Choate for a postgraduate year, especially in light of his young age and his promise. He stressed how well Alan had done and what a great joy he was to them. If he remained another year, he could study advanced English and more French, history, biology, art, and music appreciation, and do so on full scholarship because of his "splendid work." Several of his teachers and the headmaster's wife also urged him to remain, as he was such a pleasure to teach. But his mother had recently become ill, and Alan put the extra year at Choate aside and proposed forgoing college entrance exams to Harvard to stay at home with her in Dallas. He would study Latin on his own, improve his writing, and learn the techniques of poetry, which he said had "brought me to the brink of the greatest enjoyment of my life." A year at home was not an acceptable plan to his father, however, but with his wife growing sicker and his financial problems increasing, they worked out a compromise in which Alan would attend the University of Texas at Austin for his freshman year, where he would also be close to home, and then would transfer to Harvard. He graduated from Choate eighth in a senior class of eighty-two students.

The fall term of 1930 at Texas began badly for Alan. He was bored by his roommate and struggled with a teacher he didn't like, with the result that his grades in English began to suffer. He loathed the fraternity world, and threw himself into writing a daily column, "In the Day's News," for the *Daily Texan*, for which he selected odd events of the world and wove them into an ironic narrative. This got him selected for membership in Scribblers, the writers' group, and by the end of the year his grades made him eligible for Phi Beta Sigma, the freshman honorary society. He wrote a few editorials for the paper, but resigned when the editor refused to publish his editorial against the pope's encyclical opposing birth control.

At the start of the spring term of 1931 he moved to the house of a mathematics professor, where he roomed with Walter Goldschmidt, who would later become one of the leading anthropologists in the United States. Goldschmidt recalled meeting Alan and discovering that he was "frighteningly smart, probably classifiable as a genius," though he also remembered him suddenly exploding one night while studying and crying out, "Damn it! The hardest thing I've had to learn is that I'm not a genius."

The students Alan called his friends set themselves apart from the campus: among them were Charles L. Black, who went on to became a professor of constitutional law at Yale and Columbia, and was a major figure in the *Brown v. Board of Education* Supreme Court case; and Harold Preece, who later became a folklorist, author of western books, a political radical, and a man who dared to criticize Zora Neale Hurston for the conservatism of her racial politics. "Race and culture were central topics of discussion among the students we knew then," Goldschmidt said, "and Texas was at the bottom on those issues at the time."

Music was Alan's entrée into the lives of black people, as it was for many like-minded people his age at the start of the 1930s. Whatever the barriers that kept the black community separated from the white, music was a ticket in for the outsider, and people of color were hardly surprised that whites would be drawn to their arts. Alan first found his way to Austin's black-owned record shops and, hearing the music from the loudspeakers that played the latest songs to passersby, began buying blues and religious recordings, especially those of Blind Willie Johnson, a street singer whose heroically strained voice and descents into false bass were the most passionately intense singing he'd ever heard. He wore out that first Johnson record, he said, carrying it around with him wherever he went: "It wasn't a matter of folklore. It was the way I felt."

He took his dates to the black section of town to visit the home of Ruby, "a woman who played blues guitar and whose husband was a powerful blues pianist. We drank bootleg beer, and listened to the music with the blinds drawn. [She] represented the real South to me."

> In visiting Ruby's place, of course, I was risking expulsion, but in that I was no different from a whole generation of southerners who have gone across the tracks for adventure and for friendly contact with the race they do not wish at all to shun. I was a part of a generation of college students who furtively called at Ruby's little unpainted three room house, and heard the real blues.
>
> I used to try to get Ruby to talk, to tell me how she felt about the town and her life there. She could only throw back her head and laugh long, long, and show her mouthful of gold teeth and tell me, "Lissen, boy, you wants to know too much. You like the man had the finest Jersey cow in the world, give him more milk than any other cow even been heard of. Then he get the idea he want to send that cow to college. But you think she would go up and register. That old cow balk and stay right where she belong. She appreciate herself just the way she was. . . . Now wouldn't you . . . like to send out for more beer? I got another blues you never heard yet."

In late May, his mother died suddenly. "I was numb," said Alan. "It was like a natural disaster or as if fire had suddenly burned up the whole town. I couldn't cry, couldn't express any feeling. I was struck with shock and horror." His father was even more distraught. The Depression had cut into his bond sales, and he had been suffering from various ailments. Following his wife's death he spent much of the summer in bed, with Alan tending to him.

Alan's grades for the first year were A's in every subject except for a C in English in the fall term, which he received before he could transfer to another teacher's class. By then he had met some of the philosophy faculty and students, and he wrote his friend Mike Bullard that he was thinking of staying at the University of Texas because he had been converted to Nietzsche. But his father remained set on his entering Harvard, and began writing his own former teachers, Le Baron Briggs, now dean of Harvard College, and Lyman Kittredge, to ask for their aid in helping Alan transfer there for the fall 1931 semester. The problem was that Alan needed a scholarship, for which transfers were not eligible. So on a visit to Harvard in March, Alan had sought advice from Kittredge, then applied to Harvard and was given the entrance examination. Shortly afterward, Alan received a letter from Henry Pennypacker of the Committee on Admission at Harvard informing him that he would soon receive a letter of acceptance. A few days later he learned that by some creative accounting Harvard had found a way around their rules on transfers' scholarships and that he would after all be awarded $850 toward tuition and board—enough that with some care it would get him through the year.

He entered Harvard with confidence, bolstered by his successes at Choate and Texas, and by having met some of the key faculty through his father. He was admitted as a sophomore, with the proviso that he take one additional course a year in order to assure that he would graduate in three years. By then, Alan had made up his mind to become a philosophy major, especially as he was now at one of the centers of philosophical thought. His teachers included C. I. Lewis, a pragmatist, a philosopher who also had a passion for aesthetics, and one of the leading logicians of the time. The courses Alan took included "An Introduction to Philosophy" and "A Theory of Knowledge," in which he wrote papers on "Theories of Value" and "Bertrand Russell's Lectures on Logical Atomism" and read deeply into George Herbert Mead, whose social philosophy and personal engagement with political issues appealed to him. Alan's adviser was Raphael Demos, a specialist in classical philosophy, with whom he had a yearlong tutorial. Continuing a friendship he had made with a Texas faculty member, Alan also did an informal long-distance reading course with Professor Albert P. Brogan on Plato and the Pre-Socratics. He made a half-hearted stab at campus life at Harvard by getting a goldfish and a white rat as pets for his room and writing odes to them, as well as by attending a Gilbert and Sullivan festival and seeing Aimee Semple McPherson preach at a revival in Boston. He also tried out, unsuccessfully, for the swim team.

He knew his way around, having visited Cambridge and Boston several times, but now he wandered more widely, especially into the ethnic neighborhoods and the slums, poking around in restaurants and shops. He increasingly withdrew from the campus itself, seemingly unimpressed by Harvard's aura. In his letters home, Alan said that he found many of his classmates detached and shallow, and he judged some of the faculty as reactionary and "warped by their environment." His daily life was so finely detailed in these letters that his description of a champagne party with three Vassar girls incited his father to ask him to please exclude "the sordid details of college life." But Alan insisted that he wrote about everything that was happening to him only out of respect and closeness to his father, and even hinted that his grades would be disappointing. In truth his father was sometimes so moved by his observations of Boston life that he forwarded one of Alan's letters to the dean of Harvard and asked that it be considered in the face of his falling grades.

However, his letters soon began to dwindle, and then stopped altogether, leading his father to write Professor Pennypacker and ask him to talk to Alan and give him encouragement with his studies. Pennypacker replied that he would speak to him, and when John heard nothing back he wrote again, and learned that the professor had sent a note asking Alan to come by to see him but had never heard from him. When Alan did begin writing home again, his letters seemed distant and his references to campus life began to fade, while his talk about social unrest and communism increased.

Now his father stoped writing. It was a while before Alan learned that Republic National Bank and Trust Company had started to founder, like other banks in the Depression, and John had been ordered to sell the bank's bonds at any price, to anyone who would buy them. But there were no buyers. Even worse, he had to face associates and friends in Dallas whom he had encouraged to buy these securities, which were now worth only half what they had paid for them. John was forced to accept an unpaid leave of absence that fall. He told no one that he had lost his job, went home to bed in an empty house, and quietly suffered a breakdown that lasted months.

When the seriousness of the situation became clear to Alan, he wrote his father about a summer plan that he and some students at MIT had for selling magazine subscriptions, something his brother John had once done with considerable success. He hoped his plan to follow his brother's example in becoming self-sustaining might cheer his father. The extent of John's needs was becoming a burden in the face of his own doubts about his future in the university. Just before Christmas, he wrote home with another idea that he thought might solve his father's problems and, incidentally, also get him out of Harvard:

> For your own good and happiness I believe that your ballad-collecting and distributing per the lecture platform is the best was to earn money. With your uncanny ability to make friends with anything and anybody and your quiet, friendly way with folk less prosperous in life, and your own intense enjoyment of people and what they've got to say it seems to me that you are made before you start in ballad-collecting. You know more about . . . folk-lore than anyone else. . . . If you think I could help you with it, let me lay off Harvard for a year and help you get it done. We would both enjoy it and I might be able to be of some use to you.

John Jr. had been working for his father's welfare as well, and had encouraged him to let his son make arrangements to get him back on the road lecturing again. John Jr., who had also recently lost his own job in the City National Bank in Corpus Christi when it went into receivership, moved home, offering to be his father's driver if he did decide to go on tour. That plan would enable Alan to stay in school.

In February the Scholarship Committee at Harvard turned down Alan's request for financial support for the following year because of his grades. Though his marks in mathematics and Greek were A's, he had earned only C's in philosophy and physics. He had successfully petitioned to transfer into the physics course out of Professor Kittredge's English class, in which he had a C average, an embarrassment to both himself and his father, but he was still required to attend the class without credit. Kittredge was quoted endlessly by John Sr., but Alan had not found him the lion of American literature that his father remembered. In fact, he thought the professor had cast his father as a "superior inferior" by telling him that he should collect folklore but not analyze it. Alan found himself sitting through Kittredge's class bored and resentful.

Just after midterm exams Alan contracted pneumonia and was sent to the university's medical facility to recover. He asked his father for permission to go to Bermuda for his health over spring vacation, arguing that he could afford it with his magazine earnings. And if that were not possible, he said, he would rent a car and "go to Kentucky and investigate the conditions of the coal-miners there."

Harlan County, in eastern Kentucky, his proposed destination, had become a pilgrimage site for students on the left, much like Mississippi and Alabama would be during the civil rights struggle of the 1960s. Alan was now the head of a student organization at Harvard that was raising money to send the miners food, and he worked his way around nearby colleges, collecting from them as well. In 1931, labor organizing by the National Miners' Union had seriously resumed in Harlan in the wake of the Depression, and a strike had been called. The mine owners, insisting that Communists were behind the organizing, resisted their efforts with armed force, evicting miners' families from company houses and bombing the homes of those who refused to move. If the local press dared to write about the situation, they too were threatened. In April 1931 Theodore Dreiser invited a group of writers and intellectuals to his home in New York City to urge them to help, and the result was the formation of the Writers' Committee to visit Harlan and see for themselves, a group that included Sherwood Anderson, John Dos Passos, and Malcolm Cowley. When they arrived in Kentucky and began gathering testimony, all of them were arrested. In 1932 another writers' committee was organized for an investigative visit and the mission of providing food for those out of work, this time including Edmund Wilson, Waldo Frank, John Hammond, newspaper writers like Mary Heaton Vorse, and newsreel photographers. Many of them were again arrested, but this time the events were filmed and spread across the country by reporters. It was this trip that Alan had proposed to join, but in the end he was unable to go.

When he wrote his father of his spring plans he repeated his wish to go collecting with him in the coming summer. He cheerfully added, "By that time I shall be partially soaked and soaking in theoretical communism. My arguments will then floor you, pin you down, and hog tie you. I shall be able to run Johnny up a tree in theoretical economics and Johnny, I am sure, will be able to run me up a tree in practical economics by means of his hard, hard hand."

He followed this letter with another:

> Dear Father,
>
> This summer you need me to drive you to your lectures. I shall do that gladly. But next summer I want you to help me get a job on a boat—(manual labor preferred) and ship me off to Shanghai, the Mediterranean, or India. I feel the desire to do something with my hands. As I look at these sheltered Harvard professors and the doubly-sheltered Harvard students, I think their life is very warped, that it lacks the exuberance and sharp brief pain that comes from laboring with other men to move a ship or build a ship or somehow fit parts of the world together to be useful. What would I do, I wonder, if a world . . . war destroyed our delicately balanced civilization or if Communism came and abruptly asked me to produce something for my soup and black crust? My environment, if changed, ever so slightly, would devour me.
>
> An epistemologist, a man who knows what terms like "togetherness" & "time" really mean (if they mean anything) would be the first to starve, the last to get a strong woman to help him and to bear him children.
>
> I have learned this year at Harvard to converse with apparent learning on any deep subject; I have learned some of the complicated technique of the game of

philosophy; I have learned to be obscurely witty and superficially profound in company (that is what the present tension-strung generation admires most in conversation); I have even learned to act like a perfect ass on occasion (some bitter people will say that I have needed no practice); But all these things only serve to repress all that is animal and frank in me. These things teach me little about how one can live with the people the world is made up of; I only learn to despise such things. I turn into a pale shadow lively only when intellectual winds blow down the plane of learning. I satisfy none of man's primary needs: physical labor, strong drinks, food, and women. Rather am I becoming so highly conditioned that soon they will all be too strong for my palette? Self consciousness is developed to the point of frenzy, for here one is either stupid, self-conscious, or a man of force (genius).

This is, perhaps, exaggeration, but it is exaggeration to the good. A year ago I would never have believed that I could think thus. There is a reason for this outburst: it is not the entire truth, but at least it is the primary part of it. Last week I saw a Russian picture that showed the reclamation of those "wild boys" who were left fatherless after the war to wander, pillage, and drink of evil in Russia. It was a very simple and beautiful picture, the actors all being non-professional and spontaneous, the motif direct, the directing the best. It was no more propaganda for communism than any Hollywood production is propaganda—one of the American movies that demonstrates the fact that a pent-house and a beautiful woman are just around the corner for us all. This Russian movie was more serious in tone because there were in it people who were very much interested in the success of an ideal. (Perhaps the decline of the west is due to boredom with present ideals. Communism would then come as a stimulant in the veins of a spiritless Europe.) As I watched this movie, I grew more and more ashamed and humiliated. The people I saw there did not spend their time thinking, making, or wishing they could make witty remarks, nor yet were they busy with building a comfortable wall around themselves and the rest of the world; neither were they concerned with the roots of German nouns or the facts of false hypotheticals in logic. They were working intensely, unselfconsciously, eating, drinking, anything, working with an enormous gusto that will probably always be denied to me. They roared with laughter at funny things; they spoke with passion and fought with equal passion when they were wronged; they seemed to live with wine in their veins while mine runs water.

The film he had seen was Nikolai Ekk's 1931 film *Putyovka v zhizn* (*Road to Life*), one of the first Russian movies with sound, the story of homeless youths battling one another in gangs after the Russian revolutionary and civil wars, until they were rounded up and placed in reform schools. Then, after the government failed them, they were taken to the country, placed in communes, and taught trades by sympathetic teachers. It might seem odd that Alan would lecture his father on the importance of a practical education and life among the working classes, considering his summers in the Brazos. But he was in fact attempting to distance himself emotionally from John, and preparing to tell him that he was dropping out of college. When Alan finally informed him that he would not have the scholarship that would allow him to stay at Harvard, John assured him that he was not upset and that Alan could enroll at Texas again.

At one point Alan wrote him that his father's affection for him had become frightening. John replied:

> In dealing with me for the last two years you may not [have] kept in mind at all times:
>
> 1. That I have recently taken a lot of severe blows from life.
> 2. That pain over sleepless nights and growing sorrow over a long period broke my nerves and left me marvelously and mentally only a shell of what I was.
> 3. That the breaking up of my home and constant separation from children is a strain every hour I live.
> 4. That as a result of these conditions and others, coupled with constitutional limitations, I have been volatile, moody, seeing lions by the roadside—a poor excuse for a friend and companion.
>
> As for the direct bearing my state of mind has had as affecting you, I have been unreasonably terrified when something loomed that seemed to becloud your chance of happiness. It was not my wish for your national success, but, as I have told you once, a sort of passion that has dominated me to see you have a chance for healthy and normal mental development that was denied me at a time when youth and desire were joined. And I have as a result have gone off my head and needlessly worried you and worried myself.

He said he hoped never to be a burden to his son, and wished that his health might improve enough that Alan would never have any "duties" toward him. On the other hand, he admitted, he was down to his last savings, and his creditors wouldn't wait. "I wish I might find it possible to spend the rest of my life collecting and recording stuff of all varieties—pronunciations, localisms, vernacular, etc., as well as stories and songs."

Whatever misgivings Alan had about Harvard and Boston, one reason surely must have been that on May 10, he had joined a rally at the offices of the U.S. Immigration Bureau in East Boston. There had been previous demonstrations in Springfield and Boston protesting the threatened deportation of labor organizer Edith Berkman back to her native Poland. Berkman, nicknamed "the Red Flame" by a Catholic priest opposed to strikers and unionization, had been sent by the National Textile Union to organize workers in the factories of Lawrence, Massachusetts, in 1931, where she had been arrested for conspiracy to destroy company property, and was now being held in Massachusetts Memorial Hospital because she had been diagnosed as having tuberculosis. Alan was one of a group of thirty-two people who staged hunger strikes or attempted to speak to immigration commissioner Anna C. M. Tillinghast. Later he said that he expected half of Boston to be there, but instead he found half the Boston police force.

The police told the marchers to disband, but seven refused and were arrested, Alan among them. He had no money for bail, but a classmate, hearing that he had been arrested, showed up at the jail and declared that he'd come for Lomax. The officials assumed that Alan's bail had been paid and let him go. Soon radio news announced that a radical had escaped from prison in a brilliant plot, but Dean Briggs rushed to the jail to explain the situation and pay his bail.

Alan was shocked to be taken into custody merely for speaking out, as he had not resisted arrest. He accepted Dean Briggs's instructions to plead guilty at his court hearing, but he also insisted on arguing that he had a right to try to see the commissioner and that he had done nothing illegal. He was cut off in midsentence and told that he would receive no jail time, but was fined twenty-five dollars for disturbing the peace. Full of anger, that night he spoke from the pulpit at Faneuil Hall about his arrest. Midway through, he realized the farce that surrounded his crusade, and he turned his sermon into a comic anecdote. The *Boston Traveler* wrote about his arrest, describing him as a Harvard student and a radical.

Little was made of the matter at Harvard. No disciplinary action was taken, and the incident never turned up in Alan's records. Still, this arrest would ten years later become the stated reason for FBI investigations when the Bureau became interested in Alan's political activities.

A few weeks later John Lomax and John Jr. were visiting friends in Cambridge during the time when Alan was studying for exams, and seeing the problems Alan faced, John later wrote him, "It is . . . simple truth that you have helped me most through your fine letters. I have dreamed of you and planned for you and reveled in your manifest growth and progress. And every moment loved you and honored you." All that Alan had been through that semester was summarized gently: "In your present situation, because of loss of time through your sickness and also because of the exciting diversions you have recently chosen for yourself, you may consider yourself not ready for the examinations in the difficult subjects you chose at Harvard. I believe you will come out all right."

John and his two sons drove back to Texas together, arguing all the way, with Alan defending his actions as a matter of free speech and an act of "righteousness," but his defense only made his father feel worse, Alan recalled. The two sons kept a log of their trip, and the last sentence, written as they approached Dallas, said, "They know nothing of the future, even ten days ahead. They are homeless, jobless, and have no expectations. Let the curtain fall upon this woeful last scene."

Alan wrote his sister Shirley that "Communism [written with a flaming "C"] + low grades + monetary deficiency will keep me out of Harvard indefinitely. The same probably goes for any other college." His final second-term grades were much the same as those from the first: B's in Greek and philosophy, C's in the rest. He had already applied to the University of Texas for the Oldright Scholarship in Philosophy, making it clear that he had to have financial support, along with a part-time job, in order to attend. Tuition at Texas state schools was small, but he still needed living expenses. His application included a proposal for "an extensive study of animism; then trace through the Pre-Socratics into Aristotle's 'Logic' whatever carryover of the animistic point of view there may have been; then with that in mind, begin a study of the development of European logic." He claimed that it would be valuable because:

> First, it is imperative in the light of the findings of anthropology and the work of Ogden and Richards that an individual, who believes that he can solve problems by thinking about them, investigate the animistic way of thinking, and if he find it different or opposed to the scientific method, discard one or the other. If that is impossible, it will at least be valuable for such an individual to become conscious of this difference in some instances and to know, then, how he is thinking. The value of such self-consciousness is, of course, most obvious in the study of society and ethics; but it may well be valuable to a scientist, too. Second, since Aristotle is more or less the inventor of formal logic, it will throw new light on that subject if he were studied from the point of view of the animistic ideas that were crystallized in the philosophies of his day. Thirdly, it seems to me, will be a most interesting approach to the more moral problems of proof, cause, etc.

Alan's application for readmission to Texas was supported by A. C. Hanford, the new dean of Harvard College, who wrote the University of Texas that

> had Mr. Lomax not had pneumonia during his year at Harvard, his grades would have been higher. Mr. Lomax was regarded by those who knew him as a young man of rather unusual ability, originality, and intellectual enthusiasm. He took courses somewhat more advanced than the average sophomore in Philosophy.

Nothing was said about his politics or his arrest.

A few months later Alan wrote his stepmother of his time in Cambridge:

> A year at Harvard has just run away from me; I really didn't treat that poor nine months very well, what with periods of over affection, cold indifference, and anger, and I really can't blame it too severely for leaving me. We both learned things, mostly what neither of us were very anxious to know; but unless the preachers of the last generation were right, what we learned can do us no harm.

CHAPTER 2

Road Scholars

We were the most powerful nation. Who could tell us any longer what was fashionable and what was fun? Isolated during the European War, we had begun combing the unknown South and West for folkways and pastimes, and there were more ready to hand.

—F. Scott Fitzgerald, "Echoes of the Jazz Age" (1931)

As the Depression spread across the world in 1931, the Lomaxes, like every other family, were hit hard. With no money coming in, both sons continued to plead with their father to return to folk song collecting, lectures, and writing until something else came along. Young Bess could live with her sister, Shirley, he could rent out the house, and then he could be free to travel. John Jr. put all his time to working out a lecture tour for his father that would keep the two of them busy traveling through much of the following year. To cut expenses, he suggested that they camp out as they traveled. The income would not be substantial, but it might be enough to draw his father out of his bed and free him to think about things that he might want to do.

In a burst of enthusiasm John traveled to New York City in June 1932 and convinced the editors at Macmillan that they should give him an advance to edit an anthology of American folk song. A book that drew together all the songs of America was something the times seem to demand; but to also include in it the folk songs of African Americans, properly presented, was an important step in itself. Most white Americans outside of the South did not know this music, and those who did had heard it only through professionally arranged and modified spirituals and folk songs. Lomax proposed not merely to reprint songs from other sources, but with the advance on the book he would also collect them himself in the countryside, record them, and transcribe them accurately from the performers themselves. Macmillan bought the idea, and John began making plans.

The next day he went on to Washington to talk to Herbert Putnam, the Librarian of Congress, and Carl Engel, chief of the Music Division and the man who oversaw the development of the Archive of American Folk Song. The archive had been created at the Library of Congress in 1928, with money provided by the Carnegie Foundation, Andrew Mellon, and other donors. For its first four years it had been headed by yet another student of George Lyman Kittredge at Harvard, Robert W. Gordon, a popular writer on folk songs who had pioneered in making field recordings, and was now living on grants he applied for through the library. John Lomax thought there might be some way that his own ambitious ideas for folk song collecting could be coordinated, if not actually supported, by the Library of Congress.

While they were in the capital, John Jr. got an interview with the newly formed Reconstruction Finance Corporation with the help of Senator Tom Connally of Texas, and a month later they offered him a job. Once he moved to Washington, John Jr. took up his father's cause at the library, suggesting that John Lomax could be of great help to them. The library, meanwhile, had become unhappy with Robert Gordon's work (or lack of it), his failure to raise funds, and perhaps his drinking, though he continued to work there without pay for the time being. Lomax wanted a similar nonpaying relationship with the library to give him the status necessary to raise funds from scholarly organizations. In return, he offered the library the promise of building up an extensive collection of recordings in the archive, an idea that new recording technology had only recently made possible. In addition, Lomax stressed the importance of African American folk music, and with the rapid rise of black popular and country music on commercial records, it was a suggestion that the librarians found interesting. They may have also felt that Lomax was the ideal individual to carry out this work, since conventional academic musicology seemed unwilling and was perhaps incapable of dealing with folk music.

John was scheduled to give a lecture at Brown University, and after they left Providence they headed to Cambridge to pick up Alan at Harvard to join them for the next few months of travel. Between mid-June and mid-August they would drive four thousand miles across the country to the Pacific Northwest, then back to Texas, sleeping outdoors every night except when they stayed with John's friends in university towns. They camped in ballparks, along rivers and lakes, on a racetrack, and in farm fields, sometimes being chased by farmers or bulls, arguing all the way, Alan spelling out the principles of socialism, his father rebutting him, and his brother staying out of it. When John Jr. left them in July, Alan and his father motored on for the next two months, "two bourgeois," as Alan put it, continuing through the night, pausing at national parks and record stores, where they listened to Beethoven and Cab Calloway's "Minnie the Moocher" ("the latter of which we both liked—tremendously").

In the fall of 1932, as wages continued to fall and unemployment rose, breadlines began to appear in major cities. Thirty-four million people were without income, sixteen million without work. When Alan arrived back at the University of Texas in Austin, his father had arranged for him to live in a large apartment over a four-car garage on an estate near the campus; Alan's roommate from the year before, Walter Goldschmidt, now a graduate student in anthropology, moved in with him. Bess Lomax recalled visiting for a few days and seeing that "he was living like a hippie. His apartment had a huge Victrola phonograph, and a pile of classical records. A pot of hot coffee was always on the table. Symphonies were playing, and one student or another was always up conducting. Alan liked to argue with anybody who was willing, and he was never one to follow. Each of the students had some kind of radical position or other, but they were all very different and argued for them passionately. Alan's view was that if you weren't into something in those days, you were just boring. And above all else, Alan didn't want to be boring."

Each new class challenged him, and he tried on every subject as a possible career—playwright, artist, physicist, biologist. He was still deep into philosophy, attempting to find underpinnings for his political passions, and he hid none of it from his father. At one point he wrote him about how he had unified his intellectual and political interests by systematically comparing Plato and Marx. In this same letter he advised his father to "spend your years in folk-song work," and told him how he might also fit into this plan:

> I think now that, unless I go red, I should like to look at the folk-songs of this country along with you and do some research in that field from the point of view of sociology and anthropology. You and I are peculiarly well fitted for a partnership in this task, it seems to me. You have the practical experience in the field and an instinct for what is genuine and whatnot [*sic*]. That experience I believe I can soon begin to supplement by making correlations between the ideas in the songs and their social implications. Why not, for instance, study the relations between the content of the Kentucky mountain songs and the mores, popular in that district, the geographical isolation of the folk, the way they carried over the attitude in the English ballads has affected the ideology of the mountaineers. Why not do the same for the negroes in different parts of the country? You and I and Mr. Gordon, who knows his origins, ought to be able together to do some very valuable work in that field.

There may have been a degree of filial baiting in his letter, but Alan was serious in urging his father to become a full-time folklorist. The problem was that he was not at all convinced that chasing down folk songs was what *he* should be doing in such volatile times, let alone traveling with his father and arguing politics and race with him day after day. At the same time, he also knew that given his father's age and state of health he would not be able to drive long distances, carry the recording equipment, and do the rest of the work that lengthy traveling involved. And without this trip, his father and he and Bess would soon be destitute. Shortly after writing this letter, Alan and his father agreed that they should work together for a couple of months.

Walter Goldschmidt could not believe that Alan was so willing to accompany his father. "He got whisked away . . . his father wanted him to go collect songs. It surprised me because Alan was part of that whole radical movement, [which is] anti-family—there's the element of slaying the father." Said Goldschmidt, "Alan was very snide about his father. Money would never draw him into his father's world . . . but folklore did." Alan also saw the trip as a chance to learn about social conditions in the South, especially those of black people. The family house in Austin was on the edge of the black community, where he could hear singing in church and see people of color on the street every day. "Our cook, Ethel, who had great dignity and force, was my second mother. One of the sorrows of growing up was feeling the distance between us widen." In Dallas, when he was eleven, during the brief period in which his father made good money, the Lomaxes had had a maid—"the prettiest girl I had ever seen except for my big sister"—whom Alan had invited to share his sandwiches and milk one Saturday. "Very pleasantly, very quietly, my mother took me aside and told me that I had made a mistake. Why? I asked. She explained that one didn't sit down and have lunch with Negroes. But I like her, I protested. She's nice. What's wrong with that? My mother said, 'We don't eat at the table with Negroes. You cannot invite her today or tomorrow or any day, because even though she is a very sweet girl, she's a Negro. Now run along and have your lunch.' . . . By the time I was sixteen and in the state university, I had read enough to be certain that my mother had been wrong. And that my whole state, my whole part of the country was convinced of something I could never believe." It was a moment of disappointment in his mother that would resurface in his writings and interviews for the rest of his life.

When Alan finished the term at the University of Texas in May, his father moved into his apartment with him and began planning a collecting project for them, which had over the last few lazy months grown epic in scope. John had received modest sponsorship from the Library of Congress, which included money for food and gas and the use of a car and recording equipment. He had come to see their collecting trip as both a temporary way out of his financial problems and the kind of project he had always dreamed of undertaking but never could afford. Having given up his beloved house in the woods, John would be homeless, bumming across the country, but doing so with noble goals and legitimacy of the highest order.

It had been ten years since John had last done fieldwork, and at sixty-five his age was showing. But he was eager to begin, and he went to work, spending his days writing letters to anyone he thought might be willing to share songs with him and to libraries that might have folk songs hidden in their stacks. In the evenings he began another ambitious venture, courting Ruby Terrill, the dean of women and a professor of Latin at the university. He had met her thirteen years earlier when he was lecturing at East Texas State Teachers College where she was then dean, and she had later been one of Alan's teachers in Austin. She had never been married, and marriage hardly seemed an obvious fit for a man who had already raised a large family and was thrilled to go wandering across the country without a job. There was precious little time for him to get to know Miss Terrill, much less wed her, but he felt the need for someplace to return to, with someone there to represent home, and once he and Alan were on the road he began writing carefully thought out, courtly letters to her.

In the last weeks of May, Alan was out most evenings attending parties thrown by seniors, and on the day after graduation John roused him from a few hours' sleep and they drove off to Lubbock to visit Bess and Shirley in what was to be the first step toward their journey. In June the two of them set out in earnest, and over the next few months they would travel through the South—first across Texas, then on to Louisiana, Mississippi, Tennessee, and Kentucky. Most of their days would be spent among people of color, their nights camping out, like knights of the road. When there was a need to look presentable to a certain class, they would rent a room in a hotel or stay in a rented cabin where they could wash and iron their.lothes. They traveled in a Model A Ford with its backseat removed, along with the wall separating the trunk from the inside of the car. But they traveled light: nothing but a few changes of clothes, two army cots, bedding, and camping gear.

Their first stop was Dallas, to buy a windup office Ediphone that could record voices, but with a thin, faint sound that would later have to be transferred from cylinders to discs at the library in Washington. Two years before, John had approached the widow of Thomas A. Edison about a recording machine. She had loaned him one of her husband's early hand-wound cylinder recorders, but it was ill-suited to the conditions under which they would be working. Now, anxious to try out this new, lighter device, they pulled off the road in Terrell, some twenty miles south of Dallas, when they heard a black washerwoman singing, and asked her to sing for the recording machine. It was intended in part as a test of the equipment, but when she put on a fresh apron and began singing, it turned into a performance:

Healin' water done move.
Healin' water done move,
Soul so happy now,
Healin' water done move . . .

Alan listened to the woman's intensity and seriousness as she sang while scrubbing the clothes, and he had the first of many epiphanies on the road:

> The voice of the skinny little black woman was as full of the shakes and quavers as a Southern river is full of bends and bayous. She started slow and sweet, but as the needle scratched her song on the whirling wax cylinder, she sang faster and with more and more drive, clapping her hands and tapping out drum rhythm with heel and toe of her bare feet, and as the song ended, she was weeping and saying over and over, "O Lord have mercy, O Lord have mercy."
>
> I was seventeen . . . and I was embarrassed. But beneath the embarrassment, I wondered what made her voice soar so beautifully in her simple and charming song of one line, and what sorrow lay behind her tears and her "Lord have mercy."

He would later say that it was at that moment that he became convinced that folk song collecting was important, something he had to do, even if it meant dropping out of college and putting off his last year of study.

Along the Trinity River near Huntsville they stopped at the Smithers Plantation and approached the manager with their plans for collecting songs, stressing that they wanted to hear locally "made-up" songs, not spirituals and pop tunes. That night they were summoned to the schoolhouse, lit only by a single oil lamp. When their eyes adjusted to the darkness they saw that the building was filled with black tenant farmers and their families, sitting there quietly waiting. The manager had assembled a command performance for them. The whole group sang several spirituals, which they duly recorded, and then Alan awkwardly asked if anyone there could sing "Stagolee," a song about a legendary badman, a figure whose celebrated feats he suspected were sung by black men as an allegory to express dissatisfaction with their own lives in America. Protest, even in poetic form, was out of the question in the South, and could lead to beatings, or worse.

A man called Blue was pushed out in front of the group, and he allowed that he could sing that song, if they would let him sing another one first. "Is it a made-up song?" the plantation manager asked. "Well, I reckon 'tis," Alan recalled him saying. "Didn' I make it up dis afternoon in the field, special foh des gen'lmuns?

I reckon it's 'bout the madeupines' song dey is. Turn on yo' machine, young mistah, 'cause I ain't gwine sing it but one time an' I want to git on yo' recort." With one eye on the manager and the other on Alan, he began:

Poor farmer, poor farmer, poor farmer,
They get all the farmer makes,
His clothes is full of patches,
And his hat is full of holes,
Stoopin' down, pullin' cotton,
From the bottom bolls,
Poor farmer, poor farmer, poor farmer,
They git all the farmer makes . . .

As the singer described the sorrowful role of the tenant farmer for several verses more, a giggle started to rise from the assembled workers, which soon turned into a "nervous" roar. The man called Blue stopped his song and began to speak as if he were addressing a letter to President Roosevelt, in hopes these white folks from Washington would pass it on:

> Now, Mr. President, you just don't know how bad they're treating us folks down here. I'm singing to you and I'm talking to you so I hope you will come down here and [do] something for us poor folks in Texas.

Alan remembered this moment as his calling to be more than just a folk song collector. He was also to be a messenger for the masses:

> When the record was over, we played it back and there was immense joy in this group because they felt they had communicated their problem to the big world. . . . They [knew] the machine and they did know we came from somewhere else and they wanted those people at the other end of the line to hear what life was like for them. That's why they were singing for us; they wanted to get into the big network. . . .
>
> That experience totally changed my life. I saw what I had to do. My job was to try and get as much of these views, these feelings, this unheard majority onto the center of the stage.

Prisons held a certain fascination for John Lomax, as they did for most southern men, who had grown up hearing stories of men who were broken by heat and dehydration and the dawn-to-dusk work of the prison farms, or who had simply disappeared, lost in the system, incarcerated "under the jail." Farmers had been the last producers to adopt machinery and industrial methods, and prison farms were even more resistant to change, since they were never short of labor. For black men, such prison work meant a return to slavery. For whites it was the ineradicable mark that signaled trash. Like army bases and lumber camps, prisons were the sites at which men were separated from their wives, mothers, and sisters, the women who kept them in check. Though segregated by race, these men were reduced to a common human denominator and made into servants of the state, plagued by fierce loneliness, isolation, and displacement. There remained nonetheless an awful dignity rooted in a certain body of knowledge that was passed from generation to generation of inmates, and it was that knowledge, that lore, that made some degree of artful living possible. Prisons were a warped mirror of a segregated world, so it was there, among black men—the Lomaxes reasoned—that a degree of cultural purity might still be found. There they might observe a culture unsullied by daily contact with white people, radios, phonographs, and jazz, the corrupting force they feared most, the music that was blazing a modernist trail across America and the world. A proposal written by seventeen-year-old Alan to the Carnegie Foundation summarizes their thinking:

> The Negro in the South is the target for such complex influences that it is hard to find genuine folk singing. His educational leaders, broadening his concepts and thus making him ashamed or self-conscious of his own art; his religious leaders, turning away from revival songs, spirituals, and informal church services to hymns and formal church modes, ranting against any song that has to do with secular subjects; prosperous members of the community, bolstered by the church and the schools sneering at the naiveté of the folk songs and unconsciously throwing the weight of their influence in the balance against anything not patterned after white bourgeois culture; the radio with its flood of jazz, created in tearooms for the benefit of city-dwelling whites—these things are killing the best and most genuine Negro folk songs.
>
> We propose to go where these influences are not yet dominant; where Negroes are almost entirely isolated from the whites, dependent upon the resources of their own group for amusement; where they are not only preserving a great body of traditional songs but are also creating new songs in the same idiom. These songs are, more often than not, epic summaries of the attitudes, *mores*, institutions, and situations of the great proletarian population who have helped to make the South culturally and economically.

The Lomaxes were not the first collectors to look for folk songs behind prison walls. Lawrence Gellert, a northerner with a revolutionary's temperament and a folklorist's zeal who worked so privately that few today have ever heard of him, recorded songs in the Greenville, South Carolina, county jail and surreptitiously collected chain gang songs along the road as early as 1924, coding his notebooks to protect the prisoners from retribution. A slaveholder's son, David L. Cohn, had also visited prisons in the Mississippi Delta in the early twentieth century, sprinkling his observations with texts and descriptions of folk songs and spirituals in his 1940 book *Where I Was Born and Raised.* But no one before the Lomaxes had appreciated the richness of creativity within prison life, and none had sought it out with such dogged persistence.

Nor were the Lomaxes the first to record African American folk songs in the United States. Folklorists Gellert, Howard Odum, and Robert Gordon had all made cylinder recordings of black singers in the 1920s for archival purposes, at a time when most Americans only knew African American music in the form of spirituals or minstrel and ragtime tunes. Commercial recording companies were slow to realize that they could sell records by African Americans, and it was only when the craze for blues reached national proportions that their talent agents began crisscrossing the country in search of material. John Lomax was, however, the first to claim that there was a wealth of distinct forms of black folk song in the land, and to argue for the importance of systematically recording throughout the country. And only he had foreseen that transcripts of those recordings could be gathered together with others in a book that could accurately represent the songs of all Americans.

On June 10 Alan and his father arrived at their first prison, in Huntsville, Texas, only to have the warden refuse them entry, even after John dropped the names of local and state politicians and the president of the University of Texas, and established that he had the imprimatur of the Library of Congress. Undeterred, the Lomaxes went on to an African American school, Prairie View State Normal College, hoping to find some folk music at a convention where seven hundred black teachers from rural districts had gathered. They played the recordings they had made at Smithers Plantation for the heads of the music and English departments, but the response was tepid and guarded. As word spread over the campus about what these white men were looking for, they were greeted with suspicion everywhere they went. Religious songs that had either been arranged or composed were the only music they were allowed to hear. "They were very polite, very pleasant, but our overture to them totally failed. It was partly because our approach wasn't exactly right, I think. We were just a couple of Southerners." Only when they were walking past some of the dormitory rooms could they occasionally hear a few seconds of the secular folk songs they were seeking. One sympathetic professor at the college finally offered to take them to Sunnyside, a black community in the Brazos Bottom, where he introduced them to a family who agreed to help them find singers.

Alan spent the next day sitting under a persimmon tree with a man known as Burn-Down, recording him as he sang blues songs and accompanied himself on guitar. John went up to a house where a group of elders were singing religious songs and sat on the steps writing down the words. That night they drove Burn-Down and his three brothers to a birthday party and dance. Alan went inside to watch, but as the three-room cabin began to fill with dancers, he shyly slipped out the door and watched from outside, realizing that his presence was inhibiting them. He had never seen a rural black dance before, and was astonished by the rhythmic unity of the dancers' moves, their close attention to the beat, even while they each moved in their own distinct styles:

> They were slow-dragging, their big country feet sliding in a heavy one-rhythm over the rough unpainted floor. The whole shack quivered and boomed with this rhythm as if the full Texas moon were beating out the rhythm on the tin roof. The orchestra consisted of one guitarist. He never let the rhythm of the bass strings stop and he kept the trebles always crying out an accompaniment for his harsh young voice. . . .
>
> *A dollar's round and rolls from hand to hand*
> *I tell you,*
> *A dollar's round and goes from hand to hand*
> *The way those women goes from man to man.*
>
> He had enough couplets to last all night. And when he hit off something specially apt, some of the women would break away from their partners and run to the corner where he sat with his guitar and kiss him all over his face.
>
> I wanted to ask a question, but it's hard to begin when you're a Southerner born and bred. It's hard because somehow you have been given the impression that he's another kind of person than you, not quite human.

The following day, July 3, they drove on to Galveston, slept on the beach, then dressed up and treated themselves to breakfast at a resort hotel. The plan for the day had been to record stevedores on the docks, but they had forgotten that there would be no workers there on the holiday. So they instead spent most of the day attending a nearby black church service simply as wayfaring strangers.

On their next visit to a prison—Imperial State Prison Farm, at Sugar Land, just outside Houston—they were granted entry. Some cajoling and the right state officials' names had sufficiently impressed the warden, and they were allowed to record two older prisoners, both of them powerful and dramatic performers, and among the most impressive singers they would hear on their travels. First, in the prison hospital room, they encountered Mose "Clear Rock" Pratt, a man who had spent forty-seven of his seventy-one years incarcerated for stoning three people to death, but who seemed to possess an endless body of songs. He was also something of a folklorist's dream, as he knew any number of variations of individual songs, and was able to make up several new ones on the spot. He never sang a song the same way twice.

The second singer recorded was James "Iron Head" Baker, a sixty-four-year-old trusty whose deep knowledge of songs led John to proclaim him a black Homer. Baker lived his songs, feeling their emotions viscerally, pacing mournful songs like "Old Hannah" as slow as the day he had just spent in the sunburnt fields, or carefully building the drama of "Shorty George"—a song about leaving prison that had once moved him so much that he tried to escape, only to be caught.

What they heard in that prison and those that followed were songs about trains, dogs, foxes, and horses; praise songs of black and white cowboys and legendary supermen like Jody and Stavin' Chain; songs about women who ruled the men around them; deeply personalized ballads; stomp-down dance tunes; and songs of cotton, boll weevils, and the miseries of work—heat, hammers, guards, endless days, iron bars, and the sun. There were none of the sentimental meditations or ancient European ballads that John Lomax was accustomed to hearing from white singers. Indeed, the white prisoner workers they encountered never sang alone or together, and were sullen, withdrawn into their own worlds of tuneless silence.

Rather than face further rejection at prisons, John wrote Carl Engel at the Library of Congress and asked him for a letter of introduction to the prison authorities, one that was as impressively worded as possible. On July 7 they were again allowed entry into a prison farm, this time at Darrington, thirty miles from Houston. They were developing a routine of working as long as the circumstances and the inmates would tolerate it. Their days were filled with meeting resistance at the gate and again inside the prison walls, tending to a recording machine that needed constant watching, keeping track of the short stretches of time that a cylinder could be used, and operating in a general state of tension in the heat and the dust of the farms.

Driving on to East Texas, near the Sabine River that divided Louisiana and Texas, they reached the Big Thicket, the huge, densely wooded, dark and swampy area that gave many of the nearby communities their names: Pineland, Bleakwood, Yellowpine, Live Oak, Pine Grove, Quicksand, Pine Forest. Wiergate was the first stop, a sawmill community built by the Wier Brothers lumber company. In a makeshift bar, Alan recorded "Stagolee" sung and played by a pianist named

Joe Hunter. (A few years later, under the name of Ivory Joe Hunter, he'd write songs that were covered by Elvis Presley and Pat Boone, and would record his own hit records, "Since I Met You Baby" and "I Almost Lost My Mind.") But for John the true thrill of the place was in hearing the cry of a lumberjack as a tree was felled, something he described as "a dirge of the dying pine and at the same time a warning signal." (Alan was annoyed by what he saw as his father's excessive romanticism, and later criticized him for it in an essay published that year in *Southwest Review*, " 'Sinful' Songs of the Southern Negro.")

When daybreak came, Alan followed the woodsmen into the hills, riding the train that carried the sawyers and track crew, observing every step of the logging process and writing down the songs that accompanied each. What particularly caught his attention, though, was the voice of Henry Truvillion, the head of a track-lining crew that laid new rails wherever they were needed to run yellow pine logs out of the woodland and down to the mill. As they tamped down clay and gravel and hammered spikes into ties, Truvillion sang,

I'm goin' tell you somethin' I ain't never tole you befo',
What de ole lady say when she come to die?
Han' on her hip an' de odder on her thigh—
Oh, Lawd,
Have mercy,
Oh, Lawd,
Have mercy

With each "Oh," the men heaved against the long steel crowbars that were used to align the tracks.

Alan borrowed a horse from the camp office, rode deeper into the woods to where the men were cutting down trees, and recorded their call-and-response chants as he watched the physical rhythms that connected each man to the collective effort. Some men resisted singing other kinds of secular songs for him, as they were church members and forbidden to sing the "devil's songs." Others deferred to Henry Truvillion as the only real singer among them. When John later heard the recordings that Alan had made that day, he asked Truvillion to let them record more of his songs, and they spent the last night of their stay on the porch of his house. He was an elder in a nearby church, and he too was hesitant to sing anything but the "sanctified tunes." His wife firmly backed up his objections. But after he heard the playback of the spirituals and was pleased by the sound of his voice, Henry admitted that there might not be any harm in singing some children's songs, and he even permitted Alan to record a few "hollers"—the melodic cries that served as calling cards across fields and yards—once he had closed the door and windows so that neighbors who were members of the church couldn't hear him.

After those three days in Wiergate the Lomaxes drove to Baton Rouge, Louisiana, to pick up a new recording machine they had requested from the Library of Congress, paid for by a grant from the Rockefeller Foundation. The rear of the car was now stuffed with a 315-pound disc-cutting recorder, a vacuum tube amplifier, two seventy-five-pound Edison batteries to power them, a generator for recharging the batteries, piles of aluminum and celluloid blank discs, a mixing board, a loudspeaker, a microphone, and boxes of replacement parts. Like the 1940s crime photographer Weegee, they had turned their car into a studio, and wherever they could they pulled it close to the recording site. If that wasn't possible, Alan dragged the equipment up hills, across fields and creeks, onto front porches, and into houses. This made it possible for them to cut a record "live" in a natural setting, play it back on the spot with the use of a stylus of cactus needles, thorns, or casein knitting needles (made from cow's milk), and check the recording to see if a second take was needed, even while its playback entertained the singers. The sound quality was limited, but oiled aluminum discs had the ability to withstand aging better than any other medium.

It was the first time that most of the singers they were finding had ever seen a recording machine, and their reactions were unpredictable. On hearing his own voice in playback, one man cried out, "Stop that ghost!" Another started his recording by saying, "Hello Mr. Roosevelt," and then just trailed off. When he was told to continue, he said, "I'm waiting for him to hello me back." Many reluctant performers found the machine irresistible and poured forth. While the Lomaxes were now effectively in the recording business, it was a nonprofit, archival version—a subtlety that often escaped the singers, some of whom assumed that as soon as they were recorded they would become stars.

John and Alan were not naïve about the source of whatever cooperation they received among prisoners, and they quickly learned to discern how they were likely to be received. By the early 1930s, penal reform was in the air, with movies like *I Am a Fugitive from a Chain Gang* (1932) and exposés such as John L. Spivak's book *Georgia Nigger* (1932) leading the way. Wardens were suspicious of every outsider, and many prisoners thought that visitors with notepads were reformers or important figures from Washington, and their means to talk or sing their way out of a sentence. When the wardens did not outright reject the Lomaxes' request to enter the prisons, they agreed to it grudgingly, with warnings about the dangers they were risking inside. The guards often stood there while the recordings were being made, intruding into the session, ordering the prisoners about. The Lomaxes sometimes found themselves accidentally or on purpose left alone in a barracks with hundreds of inmates. The guards regarded them with paternalistic humor, if not open hostility. Alan recalled many years later the menace of the black snake whips the guards snapped close to his ears to amuse themselves. And try as they might, it was difficult for the visitors not to wonder what crime had put each of the inmates they met behind bars. While they were visiting the women's prison and listening to young girls angelically sing "If I Could Hear My Mother Pray Again" to their sewing machines, the warden informed them that most of the women were there for murder.

On July 16 the Lomaxes arrived at the Central Convict Sugar Plantation, the prison more commonly known as Angola, named after the eight-thousand-acre plantation in West Feliciana Parish, Louisiana, on which it was built, the farm itself having been named for the area in Central Africa from which so many slaves had come. Surrounded on three sides by the Mississippi River, and thirty miles from the nearest town, it was infamous for its long list of prisoners with sentences that guaranteed they'd never leave alive.

Alan and John stopped at the women's prison first, and when the warden granted them entry they went straight to the dining room where some of the inmates were singing hymns while others played cards. In a letter he wrote from Angola, John noted with some amusement that one of the young women did her best to attract Alan's attention. And, in fact, Alan had all along been doing his best to slip away to talk to the prisoners on his own, asking about their working conditions, where they came from, and the reason for their incarceration. He kept this from his father, for John was already angered by what he considered Alan's exaggerations of the condition of the poor farmers they saw along the road. Alan, he insisted, was disappointed to find out that many of them owned their own land. And now, John wrote home, "Alan seemed to want to set [all the prisoners] free." This was a terse summary of a more serious problem: throughout the trip he and Alan had been arguing about the politics of race and the conditions of the prisons. The twenty-four-hour days they were spending together had heightened the tension between them.

During their four-day visit to Angola, they moved on to the men's prison, where they were shocked to discover that the prisoners were no longer allowed to sing while working in the fields. They had assumed that everyone knew that blacks worked better while they were singing, and to see all of these men toiling in silence was a huge disappointment. But then, just as they were leaving, they encountered one remarkable singer.

He was hard to miss. Huddie Ledbetter, better known as Lead Belly, the self-proclaimed "King of the Twelve-String Guitar," was a powerful presence, bold, outspoken, and, at forty-two, unbowed by his years in prisons. He had earned his name from a life of toughness, from his strength, his badness, and a bullet in his stomach. Though only five feet seven inches tall and 171 pounds, he appeared bigger than he was, and seemed to give off light when he sang. He spoke with confidence, pride, and an undisguised intelligence, none of it part of the standard prisoner's repartee. He moved like a boxer, light on his feet, and had the muscles of having been a lead man on the prison work crews for years. Born in the 1880s on a family farm near Mooringsport, Louisiana, Lead Belly had learned to play an array of instruments while he was still a child, but had settled on the twelve-string guitar because of its volume and the buzzing sound that he said appealed to women. He played with an aggressiveness that suggested Texas Mexican guitar bands and two-fisted juke-joint piano, and sang in a declamatory tenor that, like his guitar, could cut through the noise of street traffic and crowded bars. Singing with his eyes closed, rocking his body as he kept the rhythm with his feet, he seemed to draw inspiration from some distant, undisclosed source, or perhaps just from long memory.

As a young man he had worked on farms and in the oil industry, played in bars and at parties, and for a while performed on the streets of Dallas with the legendary blues guitarist Blind Lemon Jefferson, from whom he learned new songs and the technique of slide guitar. In 1915 Lead Belly was arrested for an assault charge in Marshall, Texas. After his father mortgaged the family farm to pay a lawyer to defend him, Lead Belly was convicted for carrying a pistol, a lesser charge, and then imprisoned on a chain gang for a month. But he escaped after only three days, and under the name Walter Boyd settled in DeKalb, Texas, with his wife, Althea "Lethe" Henderson. Two years later he was charged with the murder of his friend Will Stafford and sentenced to seven to thirty years in the prison at Sugar Land. During a visit to the prison, Texas governor Pat Neff heard him sing a song that Lead Belly had written for him, and Neff became a fan, sometimes even bringing his houseguests to the prison to hear him perform. When Lead Belly was close to the seventh year of his minimum term in 1925, Governor Neff commuted his sentence.

After a year spent as a mechanic and a musician in Houston, Lead Belly returned to his birthplace in Louisiana, where he lived by doing odd jobs and distilling moonshine whiskey. In 1930 he was arrested again, this time for using a knife in what he said was self-defense, when three white men tried to push him off the sidewalk. Since one of the men in the incident was cut badly, Lead Belly was charged with assault with intent to kill. He barely escaped a lynch mob in the local prison, and received a six- to ten-year sentence, most of which he served in Angola.

Performing in and out of prison for years enabled Lead Belly to develop a large and diverse repertory of songs that stretched from church music to blues, folk songs to popular vaudeville favorites. The Lomaxes recorded eleven record sides with him in Angola, three of which were versions of what later came to be known as "Goodnight Irene," and two of which were variations on "Angola Blues." During their talks together, Lead Belly asked John Lomax to help him get paroled so that he could come to work for him, driving his car, cooking for him, washing his clothes, and helping him with his collecting. Although John resolved to get him pardoned so that he could travel with them through the rest of their trip, his enthusiasm cooled when the warden told him that Lead Belly had been sentenced for murder.

The Lomaxes reached New Orleans on July 21 in a rainstorm, and the rain continued for another week. John phoned Bertrand Cohn, one of his old friends from the University of Texas, who got them guest cards at the New Orleans Athletic Club, where they could for the moment live like gentlemen, and where Alan could spend some time swimming in the pool for his health. John had also asked Cohn to find a pair of plainclothes detectives to travel with them to what John called the "jungles of Negroland," looking for ballads of the seamier side of city life. But before they could move into the streets, John was struck with a high fever, and by what Alan described as neuritis, indigestion, sciatica, and the grippe (although it was more likely malaria that both of them had picked up at Angola). His father was in the hospital for over a week, and though Alan himself was feeling ill, he kept going out with his bodyguards, wandering the waterfront, the French Quarter, and the Creole district, stopping people on the street or in bars to ask for old songs. But an eighteen-year-old white man who walked into a black bar with a couple of detectives only encouraged the customers to flee. Finally, at one bar, a man named Billy Williams spoke up. "I knows what you wants," Alan remembered him saying. "You wants to make records of my singin' an' play 'em over de radio en so nobody will ever wanter hear me play again 'cause den ev'body'll know de songs dat I knows an' den where am I at? Des' like you say, dey ain' many of us folks what knows de old songs lef', and dat's what makes my livin'. Dat's the way I sees it—a cole cash proposition, dat loses me money ef I makes any records fuh yuh. Every minute I picks de guitar, every note I sings, us wurth money to me. How much do I git?"

When the new recording machine broke down, Alan went out into the streets alone in a last-ditch effort to salvage the New Orleans trip, dragging his bulky typewriter along to take down the words to any songs he might hear. This time he hired a pimp he had met at one of the bars to steer him through the neighborhood, until his guide quickly ran up bar bills and lost money at pool, and Alan was obliged to pay for them all. Ditching his guide, he set out the next day on his own. With no one to talk to, he paid closer attention to his surroundings and began making notes: he passed a dead man on the sidewalk, watched a fight between lovers, chatted with folks hanging on a corner. The next morning he tried again, and this time, like Blanche DuBois on her first walk down Elysian Fields Street, he heard what Tennessee Williams called a "blue piano" tinkling from a darkened house. He stepped through a wide-open door and at last found a man who really knew "Stagolee." There in the unlit, unlicensed bar, a small crowd drank and joked while a man played an upright in the corner. The pianist struck a deal with him: if Alan made a record that sold, they'd split the profits, and meanwhile Alan could pay for the gin that he and his friends were drinking. The singer launched into the epic of a battle over a milk-white Stetson hat between Billy Lyons and Stagolee, a blue steel .44-toting badman. Twenty stanzas in, the singer became offended by the rudeness of some in the bar, and led Alan and his own friends miles away to another "barrelhouse" where he felt he could get more respect. But after only a minute of singing, with Alan seated on a milk crate pecking away at his typewriter, the owner threw them all out. Finally, in another house along the way, Alan was thrilled to hear the singer finish the last of the forty-one stanzas he knew, where Stagolee winds up in hell, drives the devils away, and rules their evil kingdom by himself.

After a few more days of hearing no French Creole spoken on the streets, and nothing sung but church songs, the blues, and jazz, Alan gave up and mailed a postcard to Carl Engel, saying that New Orleans was now "a barren field for collection. The river packets are gone and with them the singing roustabouts. The police have driven out the 'Hoo-doo' dances. And speaking in Creole is entirely out of style." The recording machine was running again, but before he had an opportunity to use it, he too grew sicker, and was now lying on a cot in the same hospital room as his father.

Once their fevers had broken, they left New Orleans and headed for Jackson, Mississippi. While Alan drove, John kept busy taking notes for a book about his folk song adventures that he planned on writing at some point, or compiling lists of prisoners' nicknames to send back to Harvard to Professor Kittredge, who was interested in naming practices. The Mississippi State Prison Farm in Oakley was the next stop, where they began recording spirituals and hymns at a Sunday service as soon as they arrived. Both men were deeply moved by what they heard: John wrote, "Were it possible for the world to listen to such a group singing, with no vestige of self-consciousness or artificiality, the songs that seem to have sprung full-panoplied with beauty and power from the emotional experiences of a people—I say the world would stop and listen." This was not the music that America had heard from genteel African American traveling religious groups such as the Fisk Jubilee Singers: these were songs that awakened the eschatology stored in the inner ear, and engaged the whole body. This was ritual music with the power to transform both singer and listener. The songs were powerfully choral without being rehearsed, and sung without a leader, and when individual voices rose up from the group, each was unique and well-etched.

So powerful was this music that the machine was not up to recording it, and instead Alan picked out small groups of singers to record separately. Blank record discs were expensive, and before they wasted any of them he auditioned each singer, away from his father's hearing wherever possible, where he could also listen to their stories and their pleas of innocence.

Eighteen hammers fallin', get on line,
There ain't no hammer here ring like mine . . .

Parchman Farm. The name said it all: a sweatbox of a prison, and, like Angola, once the site of a plantation. Prisoners at Parchman were all too aware of its history of slavery. They were still being run into the fields by white men on horses to pick cotton shortly after 4 a.m., and the offspring of the same bloodhounds and German shepherds that once tracked down escaped slaves were ever present to menace and worry them. Yet being situated in the Yazoo Delta, Parchman was also firmly in blues country, perhaps the deepest and richest site of African American folk music in the United States. The Lomaxes reached the farm on August 8 and set up camp. That evening the warden assembled some of the prisoners to perform for them. As Alan later recalled, "When the men finished with work, they were brought out to sing for us, and I heard extraordinarily exciting singers—men like Long Henry, Bat Eye and Tough Eye. They stood in the light of a kerosene lamp with shotguns poking them in the back and sang like mockingbirds."

The Lomaxes' work at Parchman was especially unpleasant, as the exhausted prisoners were resistant to singing during the only times they were allowed to record them—their brief rest at noon, or in the free time they had between supper and lights-out at nine o'clock. Some were suspicious and diffident, others simply regarded the music as amusement for white folks, and in either case they refused to perform. John and Alan worked as if they were under surveillance themselves, which indeed they were, and by the end of the day they were soaked in sweat. Like the inmates, they lay down and drank lemonade to gather strength for the rest of the evening.

It was at Parchman that they first heard "The Midnight Special," sung by a man they knew only as "Lifetime."

If you ever go to Houston,
You know you better walk right.
You know you better not stagger,
You know you better not fight.
Because the sheriff will just arrest you,
You know he'll carry you down.

And you can bet your bottom dollar,
Oh Lord, you're penitentiary bound.

The black folk songs that they had heard until now had always been a certain kind of sacred music, or someone's singing to himself while he worked or walked the streets or sat on a corner curbstone. This was something altogether different. These songs were approached at a deeply personal level, the singers enacting them, inhabiting them, assuming the song's persona through the ever-present "I":

Wake up, dead man, and help me drive my row,
Wake up, dead man, and help me drive my row.
Some in the building, and some on the farm,
Some in the graveyard, some going home.
I looked at Old Hannah, and she's turning red,
I looked at my pardner, and he's almost dead.

The pain and raw humanity of these songs showed the marks of years, or decades, of after-work contemplation of the weight of time. This was as close as twentieth-century people were going to come to the sound of slavery.

Ask my cap'n, how could he stand to see me cry,
He said you low down nigger, I can stand to see you die.

These were not the otherworldly, distanced, impersonal songs of the white balladeers, set deep in the past, but performances that asked the audience to link the singer with the song, to understand it as a naturalism that demanded that the singers draw on their own experiences, use their bodies and their faces to register meaning and sincerity. Alan was powerfully affected by what he heard and saw, and it would be a reference point for the world's music for the rest of his life:

> The people who sang for us were in stripes and there were guards there with shotguns. They were singing there under the red hot sun of Texas, people obviously in enormous trouble. But when they opened their mouths, out came this flame of beauty. This sound which matched anything I'd ever heard from Beethoven, Brahms, or Dvořak. They sang with beautiful harmony, with enormous volume, with total affection. And this was the second stage of my conversion to my profession. I had to face that here were the people that everyone else regarded as the dregs of society, dangerous human beings, brutalized, and from them came the music which I thought was the finest thing I'd ever hear come out of my country. They made Walt Whitman look like a child; they made Carl Sandburg, who sang

> these songs, look like a bloody amateur. These people were poetic and musical and they had something terribly important to say. "Go down old Hannah / Don't you rise no more / If you rise in the mornin' / set the world on fire." I mean, "Volga Boatman" was down the stream from that. So I had found my folks. I had found the people that I wanted to represent, that I wanted to be with. After that I could never have enough and still to this day, I can't have enough of finding and making more avenues.

The next journey—to Harlan, Kentucky—was more of a side trip, a break, where they stayed with Harvey H. Fuson, a lawyer and local collector whom John knew from his 1931 book *Ballads of the Kentucky Highlands*. Fuson took them to visit a blind white farmer named James Howard, who sat in a rocking chair under a tree, singing of life and love in the mountains, accompanying himself on the fiddle. Alan explored the town, looking into the miners' lives and their struggles with the union. Unaware of all of his son's wanderings, John was amused that Alan had gone off with a young girl he spotted standing in front of a cabin—"starry blue eyes, very fair, with wavy hair, neatly dressed, seventeen, a mountain rose just emerging from the bud." Later, Alan wanted to help pay for the girl's education, and wrote Harlan High School about her and received from the principal a copy of her record and a letter that welcomed any aid and help he could give to Pauline Vowell, "a superior student."

Once again they pulled off the collecting trail and tried to focus on the book they were writing, one they planned to call *American Ballads and Folk Songs*. They drove to North Carolina and dug their suits out of the back of the car to consult with four professors at Duke University and the University of North Carolina: Howard W. Odum, Guy Johnson, Arthur Palmer Hudson, and Newman I. White. Their visit was a courtesy call, an acknowledgment that they were venturing onto local folklorists' turf, but they were also seeking the advice and support of academics who were the principal figures in southern folklore. The four men were very different in their understanding of folk song. White and Palmer were literary scholars, students of Professor Kittredge at Harvard, and the songs they had were largely collected by their students. Odum and Johnson were social scientists who viewed the texts, which they themselves had gathered, as part of an overall cultural pattern, a particular way of life. But they also sought to use the texts to argue for a liberal social perspective within the limits of the divided racial cultures of the South. Odum was especially interesting to Alan, as he was the founder of the first sociology department in the South, a political liberal, and an outspoken opponent of lynching. At that moment he was in the process of writing *Southern Regions of the United States*, the book that launched the "new regionalism," the idea that a progressive South could be linked to the rest of the country while remaining culturally unique. He had also just completed writing the Black Ulysses trilogy of novels, which was based on the life of a folksinger named John Wesley "Left Wing" Gordon, from whom he had collected a number of songs.

On the way to Washington to finish their book the Lomaxes also arranged a visit with the governor of Tennessee to get his approval for their work in his state, and then squeezed in short stops at the Memphis Work House and the Nashville State Penitentiary. In Nashville, a prisoner called Black Sampson refused to sing any secular songs, even "an innocently worded levee camp-song," until the warden ordered him to do so. Even then, he first apologized to the Lord as the recording machine turned: "It's ha'd times when a po' man, member o' de chu'ch, has to sing a sinful song. But, oh, Lawd, make it all right fo' me to sing dis."

They reached Washington on August 23, and found rooms in a boardinghouse near the Library of Congress. The recordings they had just made were left with the library, and they settled down to work in an unused cellar room with a small table and some empty shelves. Two weeks later Carl Engel arranged for Alan to discuss their travels in a lecture-and-record performance for the scholars and heads of departments of the library in Coolidge Auditorium. The idea of giving a lecture based on recordings was unprecedented, but to use records to argue that folk songs were deserving of serious study was even more radical. "So, for the first time," Alan said, "America could hear itself, because up to then, *no one* had ever heard these people singing. There had been poems about it, but ours was the first time contact had been made. Well, the Library of Congress gave us a standing ovation." The talk was so successful that Alan was asked to repeat it later. His father was beginning to see Alan's success with folk songs as a means of steering him away from the politics of his friends: instead of returning to the University of Texas the next fall, he could go back to the Calloway ranch to regain his health, and as he wrote Ruby Terrill, he would be away from the "extreme radicals and rebels against society" with whom he had been associating.

After being in Washington a few days John offered himself to the Library of Congress as a consultant who would serve without compensation. Head librarian Herbert Putnam agreed, and appointed him "Honorary Conservator of our Archive of American Folk-Song, incidentally continuing, with our machine, at your own expense, to record and collect material in the field, and while in Washington, assisting in the response to inquiries involving the Archive itself." For this, John would be paid only one dollar a month, but would be able to publish whatever work he did and maintain control over his own recordings. He would have to pay for his own blank discs, however, and the library would have the right to copy any records he had made before his appointment and afterwards. It was much the same arrangement that had been made with Gordon, and if it was a bargain for the taxpayers, it provided no real source of income for him. Still, for a man of John's background and limited finances it was an honor that might with a little luck offer him great possibilities.

Engel's advice to John Lomax before he left Washington was something he scarcely needed to be cautioned about in collecting folk songs, but it at least showed that the librarians were getting the point: "Don't take any musicians along with you . . . what the Library wants is the machine's record of Negro singing and not some musician's interpretation of it; nor do we wish any musician about, to tell the Negroes how they ought to sing."

Within six weeks the songs were assembled for *American Ballads and Folk Songs*, the notes and the introduction written and a foreword by Professor Kittredge added, and the Lomaxes delivered the manuscript to the publisher in New York in October. Macmillan considered it a potentially important work and made its delivery into something of a formal ceremony, inviting Charles Seeger and Henry Cowell, both of whom they hoped would read the manuscript and approve it. Seeger was a precocious composer and scholar who had conducted the Cologne Opera at age twenty-four and become the chairman of the Department of Music at the University of California at Berkeley when he was twenty-six, only to lose the job over his opposition to the First World War. Now he was teaching in New York City at the Institute of Musical Art (which later became Juilliard). Henry Cowell was Seeger's student, who at a very early age had become one of the most important composers in the group known as the ultra-modernists; his composing had been supported financially by Charles Ives, and he had just completed a stint as a Guggenheim Fellow, during which he had gone to Germany to study the folk musics of the world with the comparative musicologist Erich von Hornbostel. But the Lomaxes viewed them as academic musicologists who were likely to misunderstand and meddle with their work. Seeger recalled that "part of the ceremonies was a presentation to us of the material by John and Alan, who was a young man and extremely belligerent once he saw these two highbrow musicians who were going to pass on something they knew nothing about." But as it turned out, Seeger and Cowell were excited by the manuscript and enthusiastically supported its publication.

Macmillan feted the Lomaxes with a cocktail party and a formal dinner, after which Charles A. Beard, the doyen of American progressive historians, introduced them around among the scholarly crowd, and later in the evening they wound up playing their field recordings at the home of George Brett Jr., assistant to the president of Macmillan. Brett was so enthused that he wrote a letter to the Carnegie Foundation suggesting that their work was deserving of financial support.

To promote the forthcoming book and earn some money, John scheduled a tour of colleges and civic groups beginning in November that would stretch across Massachusetts, Connecticut, New York, West Virginia, Pennsylvania, Ohio, Illinois, and Michigan, with stops in between to visit other folklorists and to rummage through libraries in search of songs, all timed to get them back to New York City by Thanksgiving. It was an ambitious travel plan, but John had a publicist's sense of what it took to get attention. He talked and told stories, and Alan sang. Before it was over, Alan thought, he'd become a "singing lobbyist."

Everywhere they went they stirred readers' interests by playing the songs that were about to appear in print. Alan, meanwhile, was getting an education in how to pursue an idea relentlessly and survive on the edge of academia. In Michigan they stayed with Carl Sandburg and his family, and Carl and Alan talked together for hours. Sandburg was fond of young Alan and his father, though he often teased John about his conservative ways, sometimes signing his letters to him as "Carl the Red."

Sandburg had done his own share of hoboing and wandering across the country picking up folk songs and swapping tales. As a reporter, he had documented the lives and poverty of black people in Chicago, and developed a distinctively American leftist brand of political thinking. Alan saw him as a model of what one man could accomplish while not losing his soul. Six years before they met, Sandburg had assembled *The American Songbag* (1927), a collection of folk and folklike songs gathered from people, books, and newspapers and edited and reassembled in his own performances over ten years of heavily attended lectures across the country. He had also recorded some of these songs for RCA Victor, and his publisher, Harcourt Brace, had rushed out a shorter, limited edition of the *Songbag* so that he could copyright the songs he had put on record. The book was geared to the popular reader, with the songs divided into categories such as "The Big Brutal City," and "Road to Heaven." Some reviewers were skeptical and dismissive (Abbe Niles's review was the briefest: "*The American Songbag* is another book by that American songbug, Carl Sandburg.") But it was enormously successful and proved that the country was hungry for a vision of itself in song. The book's organization was an influence on the shape the Lomaxes' *American Ballads and Folk Songs* would finally take.

John Lomax had continued his long-distance and rather quiet courtship of Dean Ruby Terrill back in Austin, and as December came on, he and Alan left for Texas. A very short visit to Miss Terrill resulted in a secret agreement that they would be married if his children approved, and with that, Alan and his father left for Lubbock to spend Christmas with Shirley's family and Bess.

Just after Christmas John was to address the Modern Language Association in St. Louis on the topic of "Songs from Negro Convict Camps." John could be riveting when the audience was with him, what with that resonant voice, the measured phrases, his imposing Texas girth and swagger, the Stetson that he never removed from his head (except when he swept it off in the presence of a lady), his cheap cigars, and his I-alone-have-returned-to-tell-the-tale narrative. Several influential people in the audience became convinced that the work he was doing deserved immediate support. The director of the Humanities Division of the Rockefeller Foundation implied that they might underwrite the whole project. Representatives of the American Council of Learned Societies had also heard him speak, and a few days later they recommended to the officers of the Carnegie Foundation that they financially support the rest of the trip. Carnegie then offered him money, hinting that it might be long-term support that he could channel through a university, say, Texas or Harvard. And all of this came about just as John's money was running out.

The Library of Congress had not had any contact with John Lomax since he had been appointed to his new honorary position four months earlier, nor had they been able to find him, as he had rented out his house in Austin, arranged for his mail to be delivered in care of the university post office, and had shared his travel plans with no one. When they heard of these offers of funding, the librarians became concerned that he was freelancing in their name and might be accepting multiple grants for the same projects. But as it turned out, both the library and Lomax were too optimistic. When the actual offers came in, Rockefeller's was only a disappointing $350, while Carnegie's was $3,000. Both grants were awarded through the Library of Congress, the smaller one paying for an upgrading of recording equipment and the modifications of the new car to carry it, and the larger one covering their travel and living expenses for a year. Despite the modesty of the grants, John was buoyed by them and the successes he had had over the last six months, and began writing to numerous prisons and reformatories—those for men or women, and boys or girls—across the United States asking about songs among their populations, explaining what kind of material he was seeking. But the replies were discouraging, most of them indicating that their prisoners only knew the kind of songs that glee clubs sang.

Now that he was at least semi-officially a part of the Archive of American Folk Song, John felt that he should expand the range of his collecting. In early February 1934, he and Alan headed into southwest Texas in search of songs in Spanish by Mexican Americans. The first stop was San Antonio, where they were looking for *Los Pastores*, the songs and narrations of the Nativity, with the help of rancher Richard Dobie, brother of Texas folklorist J. Frank Dobie. Alan had the idea of recording the *vaqueros* on the King Ranch, but getting permission to enter the 800,000-acre estate proved to be more difficult than entering a country without a passport, and they finally gave up. To salvage the trip, they went on to Port

Arkansas on San Jose Island, hoping to record sea chanteys from fishermen, but with no success, and drove back to San Antonio and then on to Austin. Three weeks had gotten them only a few songs for religious occasions, a few others used for children's games, and a couple of *vaquero* songs.

A lecture tour was set up to carry them into spring, but much of it was canceled when John had to be hospitalized for hemorrhoids at Baylor Hospital. Alan had surgery on his nasal passages at the same time, stayed close to his father in the hospital, and corrected the galleys for the book. When they both recovered, they drove to Chicago and managed to complete the last part of the speaking tour. John had made $750 ($10,160 in today's dollars) on ten public lectures between November and March, enough that he could now promise Carl Engel at the Library of Congress that they would be back on the collecting trail for the rest of the year. Ruby Terrill and John Lomax announced their engagement at an elaborate luncheon at the University of Texas on March 31, and two days later he and Alan were traveling again, this time to Clemmons Prison Farm outside Brazoria and the state penitentiaries at Huntsville and Richmond.

Macmillan began to pressure them to complete their proofreading. The book's publication had already been postponed because of John's delay in correcting the musical proofs, and by then it had been discovered that the transcriber they had hired, a music teacher in Washington, had not been adequate to the job.

But they stayed on the road, and by June they were traveling to the Cajun and Creole areas of south Louisiana. Though it might have seemed like another sidetrack from their original plan, the French Creole–speaking black peoples of rural Louisiana were scarcely known outside the state, and Alan especially was excited by what they might find there. Commercial companies had managed to record some of the singers from that area at the same time that they were recording in other rural areas of the South, and for much the same reason—they were also in the business of selling gramophones, and they wanted to build interest in recorded music by producing records that appealed to each distinctive area of the country. Leo Soileau, Amédé Ardoin, and Cléoma Falcon were among the first French-language musicians to make commercial recordings in the late 1920s in the early style of Cajun and Creole music. But by the mid-1930s many musicians in south Louisiana were already drifting toward country music and western swing, the kinds of music that could be heard in local dance halls. When the Lomaxes heard these records coming out of the jukeboxes and store radios of the area, they knew that they would have to go to homes and worksites to find the older styles they were after. This was to be mainly Alan's project, as his father was now working on his next book, a memoir of his travels and collecting, and Alan knew a little French. With the help of Irène Thérèse Whitfield, a graduate student at Louisiana State University who was herself collecting songs that would be part of her M.A. thesis (published as *Louisiana French Folk Songs* in 1939), they were introduced to singers in their homes and at weddings, with Alan doing the recording and Whitfield transcribing the words. When she was not around, John and Alan went to bars and drinking parties to gather a different type of song.

They started in New Iberia, and stayed overnight at Avery Island, home of McIlhenny's Tabasco Sauce, as guests of E. A. McIlhenny, the owner, and something of a folk song collector himself, as he had gathered Negro spirituals and claimed to know the songs of the Eskimos. Over the next few weeks they would wander through Delcambre, Erath, Kaplan, Indian Bayou, Morse, Crowley, Jennings, and White Oak recording track-lining songs, string bands, accordion-driven waltzes, and songs of failed courtships and lovers who ran away. The appeal of the Cajun area to the Lomaxes was its relative cultural and linguistic isolation from the rest of the country. But among the recordings they made were Anglo-American songs that had been translated into French Creole, jazz tunes, and some African American songs that seemed only a step short of becoming blues.

They did record some very old songs by both black and white singers, and the biggest discovery was *juré*, a song form that Alan first heard from singers in Jennings, Louisiana. The Lomaxes had wondered if there would be songs in French Creole that would be similar to those of African Americans sung in English across the United States. Would there be spirituals or the blues in Creole? In the *juré* Alan witnessed a music similar to the shouts he would later hear on the southeastern coast, especially in the Georgia Sea Islands. A lead singer improvised a line at a fast pace, while the others overlapped him or her with fixed responses that were close to hocketing (individual notes of the melody being alternated among several singers), and the rest of those gathered clapped in polyrhythm (more than one rhythm at the same time). Those who danced to it—whether in church or out—danced in pairs, shuffling across the floor, but carefully avoiding any crossing of the feet, as that was considered the mark of secular dance. Alan grasped immediately that these dances were not European in origin, and once he saw them in other parts of the country he would connect them to common African sources. "These *jurés* are performed in rapid tempo, with powerful accents and syncopations, and with so much overlap between the lead vocal and accompanying parts that polyrhythm is constant. Voices here are played like so many African aerophones [wind instruments], with singers emitting raspy growls and high-pitched trumpet notes in counterpoint against one another. The leader's part is short: the chorus is almost always on the air, creating a canon-like hocketing effect that links these songs to the ancient turn-taking choruses of the African Bushmen and Pygmies."

To see these dances in a small country church was an experience that expanded Alan's sense of what music could achieve, the social forces it could muster, the spiritual realms it could reach. Dances such as these appeared in northern cities in strictly secular form by the 1920s, and music was written for them by jazz pianists such as James P. Johnson. *Juré* would also later turn out to be a part of the beginnings of zydeco, the raucous, scratchy dance music that emerged in the 1950s.

Given the amount of driving they had been doing over the last year, the awful condition of the roads, and the intense weather they had encountered, the Lomaxes had been rather lucky. Every bump in the road threatened the recording equipment, as well as the car. They wore one car out, had a second one stolen (and then returned) in Chicago, and now, as they were nearing the end of their Louisiana stay, this car overturned, spilling battery acid on their clothes and damaging the recording machine, but leaving the two of them unhurt.

That summer in Louisiana was critical for Alan: "I had my first glass of wine, my first shrimp creole, my first full-blown love affair and made my first independent field recordings." The love he was referring to was not a Cajun or Creole, but Becky Machanofsky, five years older than himself, Russian-born, Jewish, a social worker and an avowed Communist from Brooklyn, New York, whom he had met in Austin that summer. She called herself "the ghetto girl," was proud of her urban roots and her radicalism, and missed no opportunity at shocking the bourgeoisie. Walter Goldschmidt said that she claimed to be able to read palms, and she was scathing when some faculty wife would agree to have her fortune told. Alan's relationship with Becky was intense, its fire fed by the passion of shared political ideals, and by a mutual curiosity about the lives of working-class people of the world. They had long discussions about the differences between Cubans, West Indians, and rural and urban African Americans. She shared her dream of returning to Russia after she had gained some useful skill—maybe a medical degree—and they compared their experiences among the poor in cities and countryside. With plans to meet in Mexico the following summer, they continued to write each other once she returned home to Brooklyn, both professing the depth of their love even as their ideological and family interests rapidly diverged. She urged him to break with his father and join her in New York:

> Why do you isolate yourself in the hinterlands to learn what life is? Open your eyes, my love, look around you. Here is work and sweat and labor and laughter, and movement, and love and creation. Look out your window, don't cloister yourself to an old man who wants to make money to marry an intellectualized old maid.

Becky split her time between labor organizing and social work, and was deep in the hothouse of Depression-era New York City politics, but she nonetheless proposed that they have a child without the bourgeois fetters of marriage. Once he was done with his father, his family even, she said, they would be free to work together for a greater cause. Why should he continue on with the pointless enterprise of folk song collecting, the gathering of the shards of dead cultures, when together they could make the songs of a future world? His dream of finding ever more isolated cultural preserves was a fool's errand: the poor were the poor wherever they were to be found, with the same forms of expression.

Her analysis stung him, since he already had doubts about what he was doing, how much of it was what his father wanted rather than his own choice. He'd later say that when he "started to sing Negro worksongs, all techniques of concealed protest and hidden hostility—[he'd] always sung in front of or at the behest of my daddy and so was almost consciously ridiculing and defying him, at the same time as I was publically helping him and publically doing what my mother would have done or would have wished me to do." Still, there *was* something important about what his father was doing, even if the gap between the two of them was growing wider.

Meanwhile, Alan's letters became fewer and fewer, and Becky had begun to be promoted up the supervisory ladder in the world of social work. By the time summer arrived she had made her own vacation plans without him.

CHAPTER 3

The Saga of Lead Belly

Leadbelly was a river, was a tree. His 12-string guitar rang like a piano in a church basement. The Rosetta stone for much of what was to follow.

—Tom Waits, in the *Guardian* (UK), March 20, 2005

The disc recording machine required major adjustments, but once he heard the sound of the improved machine filling the room, John knew the pinched, thin recordings they had done belonged to the past—they seemed like ruins of a dead civilization. He began to regret that they could not rerecord all of the singers they had met. Lead Belly's voice, above all, would have to be recaptured. He promptly wrote the warden and found out that Lead Belly was indeed still in Angola, and John and Alan returned to see him on July 1, 1934. In the meantime, Lead Belly had composed a new song that was addressed to the one man in Louisiana he felt might pardon him, if only he could find a way for him to hear it: Governor O. K. Allen.

In nineteen and hundred and thirty-two,
Honorable Governor O. K. Allen, I'm appealing to you. . . .

Had you, Governor O. K. Allen, like you had me,
I would wake up in the morning, let you out on reprieve.

When the Lomaxes left the prison, they left a copy of the recorded plea with the governor's secretary, as Lead Belly had requested.

A month later, Lead Belly was released from prison, but it was not a song that had gained him his freedom, nor was he pardoned. He was freed under Louisiana's "good-time laws," having satisfactorily served four years, five months, and five days of his six- to ten-year sentence. Alan and his father may nonetheless have felt that they had had something to do with his release, as they continued to refer to their role in his discharge. Lead Belly himself also seemed to believe that his singing and the Lomaxes' help had freed him from jail. Years later he told film director Gordon Parks that "one day [the Lomaxes] took [my records] to old Governor O. K. Allen and played them for him. And what do you know? I'm out of prison again." It was a good story, a very old and maybe even universal story—the victim who saves his life by keeping his captor amused by telling a tale, or riddling, or singing, and it brought attention from the press. Lead Belly came to be seen as having powers denied to men of color, much less one who was a convict. The legend of Lead Belly, if that's what it could be called, was powerfully appealing, and turned up again and again over the years: in a 1936 poem in the *New Yorker* by William Rose Benét, in Tennessee Williams's 1957 play *Orpheus Descending*, and in *Leadbelly*, the biopic directed by Gordon Parks in 1976. And Lead Belly had, in fact, earlier been released from another prison stay, when Texas governor Pat Neff freed him. Audiences who saw him perform later came to know the story of his pardon in Louisiana, or confused it with his release in Texas, and it became the center of the narrative surrounding him.

After Lead Belly left jail he found it difficult to get work and drifted through several towns. Before being freed he had written John Lomax telling him of his upcoming release and again asking him for employment. And now, after seeing nothing promising, he wrote him again at the start of September. Two weeks after John and Alan had returned from Louisiana, Ruby Terrill and John were married, and they left on a five-week honeymoon trip across the country; Lead Belly's letter arrived while they were gone: "If you get there [Dallas] before I do I will be in Kilgo [Kilgore] Texas. But I am looking for you I am going to work for you, your Servan, Huddie Ledbetter." When he didn't hear back, he wrote twice more. Lomax found these letters on his return to Austin and tried to reply, but again they missed each other. When they finally did connect, Lomax wired him on September 22. "Come prepared to travel. Bring guitar." Two days later they met in a hotel in Marshall, Texas, where they agreed that Lead Belly would drive the car and be John's field assistant for two months, and immediately set off for Little Rock.

In the fall of 1934 Alan was at his sister Shirley's in Lubbock, recovering from a prostate infection that turned out to be gonorrhea. With Chris Mansell, his physician brother-in-law, tending to him, he tried to keep it from his father, but he confided in Lead Belly, who had no use for doctors and had his own cure that involved turpentine and other nasty-smelling fluids. Alan wanted desperately for Lead Belly to be his friend, but Lead Belly always kept a certain distance. (Much to Alan's distress, Lead Belly called John "Big Boss" and Alan "Little Boss.") If anything, Lead Belly favored John over Alan, since the two of them were closer in age and each knew exactly where he stood with the other.

Though his affliction kept him from traveling or returning to school, Alan kept busy proofreading the galleys for *American Ballads and Folk Songs* and setting to work on his first piece of writing on folk songs, " 'Sinful' Songs of the Southern Negro," an article that he published later that year in *Southwest Review*, the principal southern literary journal of the time. Oddly, his father was also working on an article with the same title, published that same year in *Musical Quarterly*. Although both articles covered the same territory—the adventures of their previous summer's recording of secular songs in prisons—their point of view was quite different, and neither one repeated any of the examples of the other. John Lomax's article stressed the "naturalness" and "simple beauty" of the "real" black folk songs, while Alan's focused on the circumstances of their recording, and so created a more dramatic narrative. (His article also contained song texts that were considered objectionable to the editors and were cut out.)

During the long late fall days at his sister's, Alan spent his time learning to read music, playing guitar, reading, studying French, and writing letters to find lectures and performances in Texas and Louisiana for his father, Lead Belly, and Carl Sandburg. Sandburg was still traveling from town to town, singing and telling tales. Though not quite a folksinger, he set the songs in historical and social frameworks that made them more understandable to his audiences.

It was Sandburg who first encouraged John to join the lecture circuit, and now he also suggested that Alan might think of doing the same rather than going back to school. Opera singers like Tito Schipa, John McCormack, and Feodor Chaliapin, he said, were getting up to "five grand per night." "It is malicious mischief for me to say I would rather hear you sing Po Lazus than anything Schipa or McCormack have in their whole repertoire or that your father's performance in the present hour is more momentous to America than Rosa Ponselle or John Charles Thomas at two grand per." Sandburg went on to detail what he was being paid by the Redpath Lyceum Bureau to speak and sing on the Chautauqua circuit that was now being staged in ten thousand American communities.

Sandburg developed real respect and affection for Alan, and he proposed that Alan become even more involved in helping get him speaking engagements in the South, for which he'd pay him a 20 percent commission, more if the fees were higher than usual. But there was the wink of the idealist/con man behind the scheme: "I am sure that you and I can never be American business men with straight faces." When Alan taunted him that capitalism had obviously corrupted him, Sandburg responded:

> Of course capitalism has tainted me. So has feudalism and when I am meanest and lowest of all it goes back to systems and isms preceding the alphabet and recorded annals. . . . Unless you need a degree for teaching why do you want

> more university training? I was going to say that you already carry a miniature university under your hat and what you need is a target rather than more javelins.

Alan did find bookings for him and was paid his commissions. A few months later Sandburg wrote him that they should plan to meet someplace where they could "talk about business, poetry, the higher life, and whether the New Deal can possibly mean revolution."

With Lead Belly at the wheel, John traveled to Arkansas, back to Sugar Land, then to Louisiana and Alabama, stopping at as many prisons as they could. Lead Belly's powerful voice, his knowledge of songs, and his own prison credibility served to inspire the prisoners they met. On occasion he even passed his hat and made a little money. Together they recorded over a hundred records. After the day's work, Lead Belly went wherever he wanted, and John, like a worried parent, fretted when he failed to return that night or the next morning. It had become a strange trip, filled with quibbling, recriminations, apologies, reunions, and grudging respect, and Lead Belly was increasingly unhappy: he was anxious about being back behind prison walls, even for short stretches; he missed his girlfriend Martha Promise; and he wanted to drive the car into Shreveport, where he could see old friends. Lomax acquiesced to the latter, and in late October they drove to Louisiana, from where John returned to Austin to await the publication of *American Ballads and Folk Songs.*

The book ultimately contained much more than folk songs gathered from fields and homesteads and obscure sources. There were also songs that most Americans already knew from childhood, like "Yankee Doodle," "Dixie," "Shortenin' Bread," "Down in the Valley," "Amazing Grace," and "Swing Low Sweet Chariot." Some of the texts and melodies came from other collections, the radio, commercial recordings, newspapers and magazines, John Lomax's own family's recollections, and literary sources such as Robert Frost, Willa Cather, and Carl Sandburg. *American Ballads and Folk Songs* appeared just at the point in America's history when its citizens had begun to think seriously about the culture they had developed, and about where they stood among the nations of the world. John's vision of America meant that ballads from England were excluded as not being native, and songs sung in Spanish were left out because of "lack of space," as he said in the introduction. The absence of Native American songs was also noted, but not explained. The Lomaxes placed songs into categories that illustrated their sources ("Songs from the Mountains," "The Great Lakes"), their uses ("Working on the Railroad," "Breakdowns and Play Parties"), their form ("Blues"), and their subject matter ("Cocaine and Whisky," "White Desperadoes"). The selections reflected

John Lomax's view that American ballads largely centered on miners, lumbermen, sailors, soldiers, railroad men, blacks, and the down-and-outs—the hobos, convicts, bad girls, and "dope fiends." There was a male roughness, a focus on work and the outdoors that had never been seen in the songbooks that emerged from the collectors who toiled in the parlors of the local nobility and church rectories in Britain. Lomax aimed to show that not only did America have folk songs, it had even more of them and a greater variety than England.

When the book appeared, folklorists complained that some of the songs were not "real" songs but composite versions, folk songs put together from versions by several singers or from other books, and not what had been sung by individuals. In fact, by using only what they thought of as the best stanzas from the best versions, the Lomaxes had merged songs that seemed similar but which no one had ever sung in quite the way they were presented. It was in part an editor's book, in that what they had produced was a somewhat literary product. The Lomaxes would argue that the distillation and refinement of the songs they had gathered in their field trips was justifiable, because the originals were stored intact on recordings at the Library of Congress and available for study. They did not feel that purity was necessary for the kind of book they were creating. Other folk song collectors also drew on different versions when they sang the songs. In fact, there was a long tradition of texts being edited together, one that ran from Bishop Percy to Sir Walter Scott and to the Brothers Grimm, the very collectors who made folklore popular for a literate audience.

For some, what was more troubling than editing to create the *best* versions was that when John defended this practice for African American songs, he added the justification that they often contained "jumbled and disconnected stanzas." And when he regularized African American dialect in the songs so that it would more easily be understood by non-black readers, he was moving beyond the editor's function to that of the translator's.

In a remarkably open comment in the introduction, John Lomax became one of the first to raise questions about ownership and creativity, and about the role of print and literacy in oral tradition, that were to continue to plague folklorists over the years:

> Although much of the material [in this book] represents actual fieldwork, a considerable portion we "went and took" from indulgent and generous correspondents and, by permission, from collections already in print. The previous collectors in turn picked up the songs somewhere. The real author or authors remain unknown. . . . Worse than thieves are ballad collectors, for when they capture and imprison in cold type a folk song, at the same time they kill it.

While most reviews of the book were positive, praising its scope and the full sense of America it evoked, a few did pull at what they considered loose threads. In *the Nation* Mark Van Doren suggested that it was hardly an American collection, as it lacked the very English ballads and songs of Spanish speakers and American Indians that Lomax had noted were absent. And when John said in his introduction that during his visits to prisons "no case of cruelty was noted," he irritated reviewers who could not accept such a characterization in an era of calls for prison reform. Alan certainly did not accept it—nor in fact did John, who on several occasions sent letters to state governors protesting the conditions in their prisons. But he was not ready to publicly state his opposition to white southern tradition, especially while still needing to stay on the good side of southern prison wardens.

During Christmas vacation in 1934 Alan traveled to Shreveport to meet his father and Lead Belly, to join them in visiting prisons in Texas, Georgia, and North and South Carolina. But Alan came down with the flu and was sick for most of the trip. He stopped to get injections and massages from doctors along the way during the long drive, but he was running a high fever and was so weak that one night Lead Belly had to carry him home in his arms. John had by now learned of Alan's sexually contracted disease. "For Father I continue to be a source of disappointment," Alan wrote his brother-in-law. "Try as he may, he can't help often expressing his respectable resentment of my condition. This, as you can imagine, is not a particularly happy relationship."

On Christmas Eve, Alan, John, and Lead Belly checked into the YMCA in Washington, where they were joined by John Jr. That night Lead Belly and John Sr. performed for the guests of Major Isaac Spalding, a collector of military songs who worked in the Office of the Chief of Staff of the Army. On Christmas morning Lead Belly also performed for journalists, and for the first time was described as a prisoner who had sung his way to freedom. Afterwards, he and the Lomaxes celebrated Christmas together with a small tree and gifts.

John was scheduled to perform once again for the meetings of the Modern Language Association, this time in Philadelphia. Lead Belly asked to go along, and since a few of the songs he sang were included in *American Ballads and Folk Songs*, John thought having him sing would give life to the book. Reporters were there to meet them, and Lead Belly gave his first interview with the black press, the *Philadelphia Independent*, which published it under the headline of "Two Time Dixie Murderer Sings Way to Freedom." Their MLA appearance took place on December 28 at a dinner and "smoker" at the Benjamin Franklin Hotel Crystal Ballroom, where they followed the singing of "Elizabethan Ayres to the Virginals" with a sing-along of sea chanteys before a thousand scholars dressed in evening clothes. Lead Belly passed his hat among the crowd and walked out with a great deal of money. "Smacked of sensationalism," John Lomax sighed, but they were reaching the audience he most wanted to know his work. He took that idea one step further on December 30 when the two of them performed at a Bryn Mawr College tea for Philadelphia's literati, where the hat-passing offended the college's president.

Word of Lead Belly had reached New York City well ahead of them, and the Lomaxes were invited to a New Year's Eve party at the Greenwich Village apartment of Margaret Conklin and Mary Elizabeth Barnicle, where it was understood that Lead Belly would perform for a mix of New York tastemakers, Village intellectuals and artists, reporters, and faculty from Columbia and New York University. Conklin was a part of several East Coast literary circles, having been poet Sarah Teasdale's lover for a number of years and her literary executor after her death. She had met John Lomax the year before at Macmillan, where she was now an editor, and was impressed with the art of the songs he had collected. It was she who introduced the Lomaxes to Barnicle (as she preferred to be called), a popular professor of English at NYU who was well known for her political activities. She had been a suffragette, was active in the labor movement, and had caused a stir when she distributed questionnaires on students' sexual activities to her classes for the feminists Florence Britten and Dorothy Bromley. Barnicle taught folklore and medieval literature, and had just begun using *American Ballads and Folk Songs* in her classes. She had also introduced the book to popular New York singers such as Earl Spicer and J. Rosamond Johnson (the composer of the music to "Lift Every Voice and Sing" and editor of a series of books on Negro folk songs with his brother, James Weldon Johnson).

After Lead Belly left the party, much to John Lomax's chagrin, he headed uptown to Harlem's nightlife and wound up at the Rockland Palace, where Cab Calloway's Orchestra was playing a New Year's Eve breakfast dance. He was back in the Village the next morning, without sleep and hungover, just in time to be interviewed by a reporter from the *New York Herald Tribune*. Calloway, he claimed, had offered him a job with the band, but "I can beat Calloway singin' every time. . . . He don't know nothin' 'bout singin'."

Lead Belly's performance the night before and in the interviews he gave the next day brought out the tabloid mentality latent in even the best newspapers and magazines. The *Brooklyn Eagle* called him "a virtuoso of Knife and Guitar," and *Time* dubbed him a "Murderous Minstrel." But it was the *Herald Tribune* that set the tone for what was yet to come in the Lomax–Lead Belly adventure. It headlined its story LOMAX ARRIVES WITH LEAD BELLY, NEGRO MINSTREL, and tossed in some subheads: SWEET SINGER OF THE SWAMPLANDS HERE TO DO A FEW TUNES

BETWEEN HOMICIDES; SNIFFS AT CAB CALLOWAY; and WHY, HE HIMSELF HAS SUNG TO 2 PRISON PARDONS. The Lomaxes were appalled by the media's treatment, but Lead Belly liked "Sweet Singer of the Swamplands" and used it on his own stationery a few years later.

John and Lead Belly's intertwined careers as performers went spiraling upward quickly in the rush of publicity and public curiosity. Lead Belly auditioned (unsuccessfully) for the singer Rudy Vallee's very popular radio show on NBC, *The Fleischmann Hour*. The CBS radio news program *March of Time* met with them to discuss a feature on Lead Belly that would center on a reenactment of the Lead Belly pardon story, and within three days they had written and rehearsed the show, which broadcast on January 11, 1935. Afterwards the show's producer invited them all home to meet writers from *Time* magazine and the owner of Loew's chain of theaters. Offers were now beginning to flow in, though few with money behind them, and John refused all of those in which Lead Belly was not allowed to ask for donations. More worrisome to John was that Lead Belly had begun to expand and modify his repertoire with pop and jazz songs. The sincerity and charm that he had seen in him when he was in prison was now slipping away and being replaced by showbiz conventions. Even worse, he felt that he too was becoming an entertainer. "Lead Belly," John wrote his wife, "of this moment is the most famous [black man] in the world and I am the most infamous white man."

To John, their relationship was still the same as he had intended it when they started out. On collecting trips, Lead Belly would drive and handle the chores and equipment and talk to those people he wanted to record. John was still booking himself into colleges through people he knew, and when he lectured, he and Lead Belly both sang to illustrate and spark up the performance. John was growing even more uneasy about the attention from the media, since he was still doing scholarly work and was aiming primarily at educated and academic audiences. "Up to now this experiment has been a sort of nightmare," he wrote his wife. "I hate the hard faces of the gold hunters. I despise the female cranks and celebrity hunters." Despite his ambivalence, John had seen the offers being made to Lead Belly after some of their performances; he felt it was wise to suggest to him a contract that made himself his "exclusive manager, personal representative and adviser" for five years, for which Lomax would receive 50 percent of all his earnings. What he was offering was within the usual 40–50 percent range of agents' fees at the time, and since Lomax was more than half of the performance they were doing, it was his contacts that got them work, and he was paying all of Lead Belly's living expenses, he thought it was not an unreasonable proposal. Then, after thinking it over for a few weeks, and taking into account Alan's role in recording the performances, editing the book, and performing with them, he added

Alan to the contract as a partner, recalculating the shares so that each received a third. Lead Belly signed the contract.

Four days later, with Margaret Conklin's help, John signed a contract with Macmillan for a book on black American folk songs based on Lead Belly's life and songs. He was given an advance of $250, half of it to be paid on signing. The deal granted the publisher the right to copyright the material in the book in either John Lomax's name or the company's to protect their rights to the material, so that others might not reprint the same songs in other books. It also stipulated that John would pay $250 to Lead Belly for the rights to use the songs. Lead Belly agreed to the arrangement.

When they were in New York City the Lomaxes stayed with Conklin and Barnicle, while Lead Belly roomed at the YMCA in Harlem. Their contact was sporadic, though John expected to hear from him regularly. He worried about Lead Belly, fearing that he might be moving in bad company, drinking too much, or, worse, getting in trouble with the police. To escape the spotlight and get back to the work he thought most important, he accepted an offer for them all to stay rent-free in Martha Conklin's summer home in Wilton, Connecticut, in an area of small farms where New York artists and intellectuals often retreated. There, in a house once owned by Frances Perkins, Roosevelt's secretary of labor, surrounded by woods and overlooking a stream, without a telephone and the distractions of the city, he and Alan would work on the book, now to be called *Negro Sinful Songs*, with Huddie Ledbetter as artist in residence. But Alan had a different set of interests in mind:

> We retired to the country, and I had the tremendous pleasure and excitement of recording everything Lead Belly knew. Sat there with an old-time aluminum recorder that engraved its images on an aluminum record, and Lead Belly and I worked at what he knew for three or four months. He learned through the way that my father and I felt about his songs, his country songs, that they were great songs. And then he went out and sang them for the audiences that we found, and he found a tremendous reaction to that. So Lead Belly, instead of going through the normal kind of commercial process of having to adapt his material to the standards of what somebody thought would sell, arrived in New York with his whole country background of music intact.

Yet white audiences were not used to seeing real people of color on the stage, and they were unprepared for a folksinger who actually lived the life about which he sang. The songs were unfamiliar to them, and they often couldn't understand what he was saying. Lead Belly's repertoire included the full range of African

American folk song, and some of the performances could startle and disorient those who were familiar with only a narrow spectrum of black emotion and dramatis personae. Alan and Lead Belly confronted these problems, the two of them working on ways to shape how he presented his material. Alan suggested that he talk to the audience the same way he talked to him when he was introducing and bridging the songs, and urged him to expand those explanations and autobiographical settings in his performances. This was no small effort, for he had to put at ease a concert audience and lead them into learning about work gangs and churches, pool halls and dance halls, children's games and gamblers' strategies. Lead Belly would draw on his entire repertoire, from drug songs like "Take a Whiff on Me" to western favorites such as "When I Was a Cowboy," or "Rock Island Line," which was originally a prison gang's woodchopping song that he learned while collecting with John. "We went over Lead Belly's repertory with him. And we helped him round it off into concert form so that when he got up in front of his audience, he sang ballads and work songs and lullabies and children's games and square dance tunes, the whole thing." Alan was attempting to steer Lead Belly toward introducing blacks as people with a culture and a tradition to white Americans, who more often than not saw them as ciphers. What emerged was more than performed songs: Lead Belly was presenting one-act dramas on country dances, work in the fields, and the struggles of men and women to survive.

John and Alan had also begun to learn how Lead Belly thought about his material, how he saw himself performing. Fred Ramsey, a folklorist who recorded many of Lead Belly's songs some years later, described how the singer learned songs:

> We asked Lead Belly how his songs came to be. He stated that he took a melody from any given song, combined it with words of another or of his own free rhyming, and then had the piece he was ready to sing. Some he felt he should change a great deal; others he left pretty much as he found them.
>
> "I just take 'em an' fix 'em," he said. "But you got to keep your mind together." When Lead Belly heard blues singer Bessie Smith's record of "Nobody Knows You When You're Down and Out," he sat very still at first, listening to the introduction and the chorus. By the time Bessie was on her second go-'round, Lead Belly was humming along with her. Then right after hearing the record, he sang it through. But two weeks later, Lead Belly came back, announced that he had "learned" the song, and proceeded to run through it in a style completely his own.

Alan attempted to record every song that Lead Belly knew in multiple versions whenever possible, since he often sang them differently. He also asked him to annotate each song—"annotate" was the word Alan used—and explain its meaning to him. What resulted was an encyclopedia of black American song, from blues to work songs, many of which are even today known to singers only from the Lead Belly versions, such as "The Midnight Special," "Boll Weevil," "C. C. Rider," and "Where Did You Sleep Last Night?" He was also interviewed while he was being recorded to create an oral autobiography to be deposited in the Library of Congress. Alan had heard that Soviet folklorists were writing down the stories of folk artists' lives, in part because they wanted to honor them as artists, but also because they felt that these biographies were the best way to understand the meanings of the performers' songs. But Lead Belly was not an easy interview: "He sang, he was very pleasant socially, but he was also close-mouthed. He'd been through too much, and he'd learned not to talk. But I was his young admirer. We lived together with my father for about six months and I became his confidante. Bit by bit, he told me his story . . . and I wrote his story, which was the first singer biography in America."

When Martha arrived at Penn Station in New York City on January 13 she was greeted by Lead Belly, John (Alan was sick in bed), and a corps of press and photographers, as the New York papers had been carrying the story of her arrival for the past three days (with headlines like SWEET SINGER OF THE SWAMP GRINS ALL OVER AS "BOSS" LOMAX WIRES FOR BRIDE, and HOMICIDAL HARMONIZER AT THE TRAIN FROM DIXIE). When Lomax told the reporters that a marriage would take place as soon as a license could be granted, it was more than a soap opera script he was following, as he had worried that if the two weren't married quickly, Lead Belly might be charged for violation of the Mann Act, the law that prohibited the interstate transportation of women for immoral purposes.

The wedding was set for January 20 in Wilton, timed for the end of Lead Belly's probation, but the Associated Press photographers were so keyed to the story that they arrived five days early. The minister and deacons of the Bethel A.M.E. Church in Norwalk presided, John gave away the bride, and Alan was best man, with reporters from *Time* and the New York and Norwalk newspapers looking on. Afterwards Lead Belly and John rushed off to play a party in Brooklyn given by the editor of the *Brooklyn Eagle,* where the mayor of New York City, Fiorello La Guardia, was the guest of honor.

What John had hoped would be a rural escape from show business was short-lived, as they were now deluged with requests for performances, an increasing number of them for fraternity parties and private gatherings. John tried to handle all the invitations by mail, but finally gave up and began to schedule bookings over a phone he had installed.

It was Tex Ritter, the country singer from Texas, and a friend of John's, who got Lead Belly his first commercial recording contract with the American Recording Company, then the dominant force in popular records, for an advance of $250 against royalties. Art Satherley, an Englishman who pioneered country music recording, was the producer of the session, which resulted in approximately forty songs being recorded in their Broadway studios between January 23 and 25, and two more sessions in February and March. In the end they decided against releasing most of them, and only six songs, all of them blues, and all intended to appeal to current tastes, were issued in Lead Belly's lifetime. Their sales were poor, however, for his relative fame. Lead Belly's songs seemed out of date and too rural to the black record buyers who bought music on the "race" labels on which American Recording Company issued them, while whites, who would never have heard such music before, could not find them in record stores.

It was beginning to be obvious that Lead Belly could succeed only within the college music circuits that John Lomax had been cultivating for several years as a speaker/performer. Most of the academic performances were well attended, some remarkably so, but when they went outside these institutions trouble often followed. Invited to perform for a society wedding, all three of them were treated as servants and told to stay out of the way of the guests. Even some of the college dates could be difficult, as when the president of Hamilton College canceled their appearance after he read one of the New York City newspaper articles on Lead Belly. On his own, Lead Belly could find bars to sing in within black neighborhoods and keep all the money for himself, but he seldom made enough to cover his own food and drink.

Wilton might have seemed a kind of heaven at first—plenty to eat, logs in the fireplace, a snowy landscape away from the rattle and hum of the city—but it turned out to be just a place to sleep for everyone but John. Alan had his own friends in Greenwich Village, and spent whole days commuting back and forth or disappearing for a day or two at a time visiting some girls in New Milford. Lead Belly chafed at being so far away from people of color, and when he could he headed for Norwalk to escape. John, following his own version of Booker T. Washington's plan of self-help and improvement for the Negro, had vowed to Martha to save Lead Belly's earnings so that they could buy a house and farm and be free and independent back in the South. But Lead Belly's vision of himself had been changing those many weeks, and with life in prison receding behind him, he now wanted his money for himself as fast as he earned it.

Even for John, peace was hard to find in the Connecticut countryside. If the phone wasn't ringing from some college or other looking to book them, visitors from New York City tracked them down, or Alan invited people up. In February, for example, they were visited overnight by Aunt Molly Jackson, the spiritual leader of the miners' strike in Harlan, Kentucky (though Alan introduced her to his father as merely a fine example of a mountain singer, without mentioning her union credentials). While John was away in March, Alan recorded her in Connecticut for the Library of Congress, singing fifty-four traditional songs, but none of them political in nature.

The three made many visits up to New Haven to see Professor George Herzog at Yale. Herzog was then something of a rarity: he was trained in music in Europe, but had also studied anthropology at Columbia, and was the perfect candidate for making accurate transcriptions of Lead Belly's singing and writing scholarly notes on the transcriptions. The problem was that Herzog took the task too much to heart, became deadly serious about making the Lead Belly book a model of anthropological musicology, and critiqued the project as the Lomaxes conceived it. To begin with, he disliked the book's title: "Sinful," he argued, did not accurately describe the music. The Lomaxes countered that that was the word that African American church folks themselves used for all secular songs, but Herzog held firm. The notes that he was to write turned into a thirteen-page introduction in which he described the complexity of transcribing black singers' songs on paper and discussed the compromises that had to be made to make them readable by a general audience. But he also claimed that very few of the songs in the book—as few as three—were original with Lead Belly; many of the rest came from white American tradition ("more than half of these melodies and texts have been published in other collections, in some other version"). Some of the guitar accompaniments Herzog characterized as "jazzy," and seemed to come from ragtime and popular recordings. This was very different from the image John had originally had of black prison songs, which he had conceived as being in a state of purity, but his views were changing, and variability and creativity were becoming more important to him. Herzog and John Lomax had lengthy discussions that held up the publication of the book, and in the end most of Herzog's introduction was cut. But in John's introduction, he acknowledged having responded to some of Herzog's criticisms:

> We present this set of songs, therefore, not as folk songs entirely, but as a cross-section of Afri-American songs that have influenced and have been influenced by popular music; and we present this singer, not as a folk singer handing on a tradition faithfully, but as a folk artist who contributes to the tradition, and as a musician of a sort important in the growth of American popular music.

Alan's contribution to the book was a twenty-five-page "character study" of Lead Belly, mostly in dialect, and the annotations, in the form of introductions to the songs that Lead Belly had given him. John wrote a long account of his experiences with Lead Belly, much of which had to be cut. When it was published under the title of *Negro Folk Songs as Sung by Lead Belly* in November 1936, the critical response was good, with raves from James Weldon Johnson, Constance Rourke, J. Frank Dobie, and others, and *Life* did a photo feature. In the *New Masses,* Lawrence Gellert criticized John Lomax for exploiting Lead Belly, accusing him of bribing guards to get into prisons, and in subsequent letters to the editor he claimed that Lomax had passed over the "heart of contemporary Negro folk lore" in favor of a patronizing, romantic view of black life in the South:

> Beyond the doggerel—beyond the nonsense jingles served up for the white man's amusement, lies the heart throb of the Black Folks—the agonized voice of the mass crying out against the peonage, poverty and degradation. The savage brutality of the Law and the lynching mob. And the new attitudes toward all that exemplified by Tallapoosa, Angel Herndon, Scottsboro boys and other vital factors in the lives of the suppressed black masses. A hundred songs current in the Black Belt freshly stamp the glorified images of members of their race who participate in the day to day struggles against their oppressors. But we catch not a glimmer of all this in the Lomax volume.

A few years later, Richard Wright would also discover Lead Belly, and would call the John Lomax prison recordings "one of the most amazing swindles in Amazing history," implying that he had made a great deal of money from them.

Lead Belly, too, was unhappy with some of what John had written about him, especially the accounts of his violence, and hinted at taking legal action. When the attention the book attracted led to offers to appear on radio and film, he thought that Macmillan held all rights to the songs in the book, and so retained a lawyer to help him regain the performance rights. The publisher quickly agreed, eager to indemnify itself against his threatened suits against the content of the book. Lead Belly accepted the offer of ten dollars and the right to sing his own songs in exchange for his promise not to sue the Lomaxes and the publisher for any reason pertaining to the book. But Macmillan was mistaken in thinking it held the rights to each individual song when used outside the book. In fact, it later emerged that Macmillan had not copyrighted the songs properly, and had no rights to them whatsoever. As it turned out, the book sold poorly, never earning out its advance, and was out of print a year later. As John Lomax would later complain, Lead Belly was the only one to ever make any money on the project.

The producers of *March of Time* were so pleased with the radio program they had done on Lead Belly that they proposed another one for their newly created newsreel series, which was designed to compete with *Fox Movietone News* and would be shown between feature films at theaters in 168 cities. The Lomaxes were initially paid $150 to help with the script and to scout locations, with a promise of more. Alan quickly wrote his own script for the filming that emphasized American ideals, but it was largely ignored by the producers in favor of a reworking of the sensationalized *Herald Tribune* "Sweet Singer from the Swamplands" article.

Neither John nor Lead Belly had any control over what was filmed, but by playing the roles written for them, they were seen as approving the accuracy of what was depicted and were permanently typecast by their film characters.

JOHN LOMAX: Have you got a pistol?
LEAD BELLY: No, sir, I got a knife.
JOHN LOMAX: Let me see it.
[Lead Belly Produces a short knife. Lomax examines it and hands it back.]
JOHN LOMAX: What do you do with that thing?
LEAD BELLY: I'll use it on somebody if they bother you, boss. Please, boss, take me with you. You'll never have to tie your shoestrings anymore, if you'll let me—long as you keep me with you.
JOHN LOMAX: All right, Lead Belly. I'll try you.

Production began in Wilton and Norwalk in February 1935, with only one camera, so that many scenes had to be reshot to aid in editing, and in the process some scenes disappeared entirely. In its final version the short film begins with Lead Belly being recorded in prison by John Lomax, who promises to take the recording to the governor. Next, Lead Belly asks Lomax to hire him. The wedding in the Wilton house follows, and the story concludes with Lead Belly's recordings being placed in the Library of Congress alongside the Declaration of Independence, and with "Goodnight Irene" sung by Lead Belly over a close-up of the Declaration.

There was something in the film to upset everyone. Alan detested it, and though John was deeply disappointed, he salved himself with the idea that they had brought a great singer and a great folk tradition to an audience that might never have heard any of it. Lead Belly was the angriest of all for not having been paid for his part in either the film or the radio version. In retrospect, many have assumed that it was John Lomax who forced Lead Belly to emphasize his prison history by wearing stripes for this film, and who insisted that he do so when they performed at colleges. But Lead Belly always wore overalls and a scarf onstage in his early years of performing, and he chose to have a picture of himself dressed this way (along with another one of him dancing in suit and tie) on his stationery after he broke with Lomax. Stripes were the visual identifier of prisoners at the time, and when convicts were characters in stage shows, usually as part of early novelty acts, they were always in striped clothes. Even after Lead Belly left Lomax he wore stripes in a reenactment of the *March of Time* film for two stage shows at the Lafayette and the Apollo in Harlem in the late 1930s, and he was still presented in stripes when Gordon Parks directed the 1976 film *Leadbelly*, which Alan also detested.

In mid-February John left Wilton to be with his wife in Atlantic City, where she was attending a convention. While he was away, Lead Belly took the car to town and upgraded it by buying new tires, wheels, and hubcaps, and put it all on credit without John's permission. When Lomax returned he was furious. Amused by it all, Alan called Lead Belly "a black Uriah Heep," and had to explain to his father that what he really wanted was a car of his own.

John had booked performances for Lead Belly and himself from March 3 through March 15 at the University of Rochester, the University Club of Rochester, Albany State College for Teachers, Harvard, and the Wilbraham Academy, often with several appearances at each. Their long drives together through snowy countryside were increasingly silent, especially as John was not feeling well. When they were touring, Lead Belly often took the car and went off on his own, and though Lomax worried about his losing his voice by singing at black bars on the same day as the college performances, he was more concerned about trouble that he might encounter. When they reached Rochester and settled into their rooms, Lead Belly disappeared with the car and had Lomax wandering the streets in search of him and checking with the police. But Lead Belly turned up in time for the concert. "I found some of my color and been stayin' with them," he said. He had decided that he no longer would listen to Lomax's pleas to stay away from bars and people he didn't know. His period of accommodation was over, and Lead Belly the race man surfaced, demanding to go where he wanted to go and the right to sing for his "own kind" after hours. He also wanted Martha with him on the road, and for her to keep *all* of the money they made.

In Buffalo Lead Belly became even more independent, demanding the money for their performance up front. John felt so threatened that he asked a judge he knew to have Lead Belly followed. A detective took Lead Belly's knife away from him and escorted him to the evening's concert. Somehow John had convinced himself that Lead Belly was on parole and that he was responsible for him, and he feared that he would soon be put back in prison, the tour would come to an end, and John himself would be humiliated. He told Alan that the relationship with Lead Belly was over and that he was sending Martha and Huddie home to Shreveport as soon as they completed their engagement at Harvard. Alan, deeply upset by this news, thought his father was overreacting.

The performances at Harvard were the ones that mattered most to John, and on March 13 they appeared before the Poetry Society of Cambridge at Emerson Hall in the afternoon, and again at Leverett House in the evening for a lecture/concert sponsored by the dean. Professor Kittredge was the master of ceremonies, and Lead Belly, whatever his feelings, came through, reaching deep into his repertoire, banging the guitar strings until they rang like bells, and even dancing before an ecstatic, cheering crowd of six hundred. Kittredge whispered, "He is a demon, Lomax!"

The last night of the tour was March 20 at the Providence Art Club. With Harvard behind him, John refused to go on, and Alan took his place. When John told Lead Belly and his wife four days later that he was sending them back to Louisiana, they were pleased and excited. They said good-bye to their friends in Norwalk and the Lomaxes drove them to the train on March 26.

John and Lead Belly's association had lasted only six months and eleven days, three months of which were spent recording in the field; two months in New York City and Wilton; and less than three weeks on tour. According to John's accounts, they had together earned $1,550 ($24,000 in today's dollars) on the tour, $800 of it from performances, a $250 advance from the book, $100 for the *March of Time* radio show, $150 for the *March of Time* film, and a $250 advance from the American Recording Company. (None of this included Lead Belly's hat passing, which he kept for himself.) Everything earned after January 5 was split two ways, and after February 9, three ways, with a share for Alan. For the first three and a half months after John and Lead Belly began to work together John paid all of Lead Belly's living expenses, but once they were in New York City, Lomax began deducting for cash advances, a new guitar, clothing, food, dentist bills, and the like. There were no living expenses charged the Ledbetters while they were in Wilton, since the two of them had worked as cook, driver, and housecleaners while they were there. As they were leaving he gave Martha $298.94 ($4,600 today), $150 of it split into three postdated checks and the rest in cash, because, he said, that way Lead Belly wouldn't spend it all at once.

Once they were back in Shreveport, Lead Belly began to fret over the money. When he learned that he couldn't cash all the checks immediately, he wrote Lomax about it in a way that John considered intimidating. Lomax then contacted Sheriff Tom Hughes (who was the subject of one of Lead Belly's songs) in Shreveport and told him that he had been threatened, but offered to pay Huddie in cash if that seemed advisable. Lead Belly, meanwhile, had hired a lawyer who demanded his money, and Lomax gave it to him. Next, the lawyer brought up the matter of the recording for the American Recording Company and demanded an accounting. But since the records had sold so poorly, there were no royalties to be paid. Lead Belly then hired a second lawyer to look into his earnings on the *March of Time* film, get an accounting of earnings from the tour, and look into the book contract. Lomax had not been fully paid for the film himself, but he sent Lead Belly the rest of what he was owed for his part. This time Lead Belly thanked him, and proposed that they might now reunite to continue working together. He then hired yet another lawyer, and the letters his attorney wrote to Macmillan had the publishers so concerned about legal entanglements that they put the book on hold until the dispute could be cleared up. Lomax was pressured to settle and finally agreed to a $250 payment to Lead Belly in exchange for Macmillan retaining rights to the songs to protect them from further lawsuits, as well as the voiding of his and Lead Belly's management contract.

Lead Belly wrote John two more times asking him to join him on the road, but John was adamant: their relationship was over. Alan was painfully caught up in their conflict, wanting desperately to find some way to stay close to Lead Belly. He made a quick decision that he would continue working with Lead Belly in whatever way he could, and Elizabeth Barnicle was one means by which he thought he might be able to do so. She welcomed Lead Belly's break with John, and made her own plans for continuing his tours of colleges through her contacts at Bennington, Sarah Lawrence, and other women's colleges. He and Alan would be part of each other's lives until Lead Belly's death fourteen years later, and that relationship would remain yet another source of constant friction between Alan and his father.

CHAPTER 4

Travels with Zora Neale Hurston and Mary Elizabeth Barnicle

With their income limited to what they could manage on the low-rent outskirts of academia, Alan and his father were forced to look for a larger audience than the groups of professors John Lomax had been entertaining at banquets and smokers. They had to develop a style of writing and performance that would reach the average person, the big publishers, and the press. John had his own style: a local colorist who spoke from personal experience, sometimes as a collector, sometimes as a native son. Alan was still trying to find a role for himself, and searching for his own voice, mainly in literature, and that was how he came across the writing of Zora Neale Hurston. He knew of her as an anthropologist who had studied at Columbia University and was making her way in New York City academic and literary circles as the only professionally trained black folklorist in town. Her education, her southern experience, and her race gave her license to challenge what others wrote about the lives and arts of ordinary black people. Hurston sought to reclaim African American folklore from the grotesqueries created by white writers and artists, whether they be slumming modernists seeking primitivist thrills or old-school minstrel men grasping at yesterday's fantasies. But she was equally unafraid of taking on black intellectuals for their out-of-touch pontifications about their own people. Who else would dare mock W. E. B. Du Bois's famous discussion of spirituals as "sorrow songs" in *The Souls of Black Folk*? To her, black religion was serious drama, performance worthy of comparison to opera. Just at the moment when the literati of the Harlem Renaissance were adapting high modernist ideas to African American purposes and Alain Locke was arguing that black culture should be "elevated" through refinement, extension, elaboration, and formalism to bring African American art in line with modernism, she was insisting that black folk culture was already high art. Like Yeats, Kafka, and other "minority" writers whose readers were largely part of the majority, she walked a difficult line. But she walked it with style, grace, and a self-conscious intelligence that astonished and sometimes dismayed her colleagues, black and white.

Hurston had just published her first novel, *Jonah's Gourd Vine,* in 1934 and now was completing *Mules and Men,* a volume of black American folklore and ethnography. Yet, as was often the case with her, she was short of money. Her reputation for flamboyance, infighting, and refusing to step off for anyone had killed her chances for the academic job she once hoped to have at Fisk University, and she was now caught up in an affair of the heart that was going bad fast.

When Alan read Zora Neale Hurston's "Hoodoo in New Orleans," her first-person account of participating in the Afro-Creole occult, he was swept up by her confidence and daring as ethnographer and writer. "Imagine," he'd say, amazed at her description of initiation into a cult, "lying naked, face down on a rattlesnake skin for three days, through, and that hoodoo doctor starts painting a lightning bolt down your back!" What astonished him was the bravery with which she had gone beyond the rules of her anthropological training, becoming one of the folk, embracing their beliefs and dreams, then writing about it with elegance and high affect. She had gone too deep, though, and her identification with her subject kept her from ever telling all she knew. "The oaths of secrecy she swore and the terrifying physical and emotional ordeals she endured in these initiations left their mark on her," Alan said, "and there were certain parts of her material which she never dared to reveal even in scientific publications."

Hurston represented to Alan what was possible for an intellectual of a certain type, and pointed the way toward how he, too, might come to write in a deeply personal and expressive style and still be an ethnographer and folklorist true to his subject. Though she was educated in the kind of careful ethnographic techniques and objective methods of anthropology that had the laboratory report and the scientific monograph as their models, to Alan "she was no reserved scientist but a raconteur, a singer and a dancer who could bring the culture of her people vividly to life. For she opened the way, with sure taste and a scientist's love of fact into the whole world of Negro folk lore."

In the months before they first met, he had been transcribing recordings of songs, tales, and oral history, listening in careful detail to the gentle and subtle nuances of southern speech. He had struggled with turning everyday talk into readable prose, realizing that writing in dialect could seem patronizing or, worse, could make speech seem downright silly. He recalled his first encounter with Hurston's writing years later in a letter to her biographer, Robert Hemenway:

> Lead Belly that all of us who really experienced American folk in those pristine days agreed upon was the extraordinary character of the language, the style, that came to us. The writing, the talk of that time, in middle class circles, was already beginning to be lifeless. Today it has hit a nadir of colorlessness. Moving among the working people with a notebook or a recording machine was to be bathed

> continuously in pungent, strong, growing language. My father's chief pleasure in life were the poets of speech that he had heard. And he made all of his children aware of this and we have always taken great pleasure in it. . . . Therefore when I was introduced to Zora Hurston, who not only appreciated this prose, but who had learned how to turn it into spoken and written prose of her own that was the purest and finest aesthetic quality, I was entranced and dazzled and almost worshipful. I was engaged in my attempt to reach the same peak of excellence and later in my own books of oral history I hope I occasionally achieved it, but when I met Zora she already had mastered the editorial style necessary to transmit the whole plangent sound of black folks' speech onto the page then confused by mistransliteration or the redundancies that no eye can accept.

Early in 1935, Alan boldly took the lead and wrote to ask if she was interested in working with his father and himself in Florida, and later that year she sent letters to both Alan and John suggesting that they meet, and asking, by the way, if she could also be introduced to "brother Lead Belly."

In the meantime, Professor Barnicle had met and become friends with Hurston in Manhattan. Sometimes Zora went downtown to speak to Barnicle's classes at New York University, or Barnicle joined her in Harlem and met friends of hers such as Alain Locke or the pianist and singer Porter Grainger, who recorded her songs and arranged music for several of her theater pieces. Earlier, Barnicle had proposed that she and Alan go to Kentucky on a collecting trip in the summer of 1935, but in the middle of May she came up with the idea that she, Hurston, and Alan go collecting together in the Southeast. The idea was that Alan could get money from his father's grant, Barnicle would finance some of the trip to make recordings for her classes at NYU, and Hurston would use the project to complete the fellowship she had from the Julius Rosenwald Foundation. Hurston planned the trip and picked the areas in which they'd work. Barnicle suggested they also rent a motion picture camera in New York as well as a trailer to haul cots and cooking equipment behind her car, while Zora drove a second car.

In early June, Barnicle and Hurston set out driving south and met up with Alan in Brunswick on the coast of Georgia. They were a strange trio to be traveling anywhere, least of all the South. Alan, who had just turned twenty, was precocious enough, but still very young, and Hurston and Barnicle (black and white, both of them in their forties) were surely two of the freest spirits in America. Yet there was a logic to their relationship: Alan was in charge of the trip, as far as the Library of Congress was concerned, and he had two years of collecting and recording experience. Barnicle brought a knowledge of ballads and folk songs to the project, and would keep copious notes. Hurston's role was to introduce the other two to black culture from the inside and guide them on how to work in the field. It was her region, her people, and she was the trained anthropologist and the experienced fieldworker, even if her approach to collecting was unorthodox. Instead of working with people alien to one's own way of life and reveling in the raw sensitivity that culture shock was supposed to induce, Hurston chose to work with people she had known for a long time, or with whom she could identify, or could at least make feel as though they were old friends. Once, while traveling with Langston Hughes from New Orleans to New York, she had insisted on stopping to collect songs in towns all along the way. Hughes apparently became impatient with hearing the same songs from singer after singer, songs that he didn't think were that good in the first place. "You can't just sit down and ask people to sing songs for you," she told him, "and expect them to be folk-songs and good ones and new ones." She tried as much as possible to be both investigator and subject, participating in the singing, learning the songs as she listened, then singing along with the singers and writing it down later. Zora's personalized approach to collecting was remarkably effective, even if other anthropologists dismissed her results as too subjective, too literary. Her manner in the field impressed Alan, and as the trip went on he too became more involved with the performers.

Zora thought that more could be accomplished if they stayed in black communities. They first located themselves near the eighteenth-century town of Frederica, on St. Simon's Island, a few miles east of Brunswick. It was one of the Sea Islands, and though they were not islands in the strict sense of the word, they were nonetheless separated enough from the coast by inland streams and rivers to give them both a real and symbolic isolation from mainland American culture. The trio rented a shanty with three rooms, a kitchen, front and back porches, and an outhouse. Even when they discovered that the house was filled with bedbugs, they were not discouraged. They stayed up all night on the porch talking excitedly and looking at the stars, then spent the next morning trying to clean up.

Zora let it be known to the community that they wanted to hear singers and listen to tales, and the next evening they found the yard filled with curious folks. They set about recording everything they could: there were discussions and arguments in Gullah, the local creolized speech (which Alan noticed sounded similar to West Indian dialects of English he had heard), and an interview with a man of ninety-two who recalled slavery and Reconstruction times for them, making it the first recorded account of the life of an ex-slave. They recorded hymns, spirituals, and sacred ring shouts similar to the *jurés* Alan had encountered in French Louisiana; the "breakdowns" or "jook" songs played and sung for dancing in tiny country bars, along with the guitar players' explanations of techniques of fingering and tuning; and folktales, children's game songs, and ballads. Though Alan had collected "John Henry" before (it was the first song in *American Ballads and Folk Songs*), for the first time he began to understand the changing meanings and uses of the song, and saw it as music that reached out beyond race to something that was quintessentially American. Its words were so finely fitted to its melody that it could be spoken and still sound like music. It could serve as a ballad, a work song, or an epic; or, understood as a song with veiled references to Shango, the Yoruba deity of thunder and lightning, and his brother Ogun, the god of iron, it could be a song of African cultural persistence or a religious relic. Stories about powerful black men had an enduring fascination in America, and "John Henry" spin-offs like "Take This Hammer" could even serve as a song of organized labor. Alan later fitted new words to it:

And if he asks you what's my Union,
It's the C. I. O.,
It's the C. I. O. [the Congress of Industrial Organizations]

Crossing into Florida in mid-June, the only southern state where the Lomaxes had never collected, they headed for Eatonville, where Hurston had grown up, an all-black town of 350 people near Maitland. Zora suggested that Alan and Barnicle darken their faces with walnut oil so they would not appear to be crossing all of the social lines of the South. When Alan objected that black people would easily spot them as fakes, Zora replied that it was not blacks she was concerned with, but whites, and this simple disguise would be enough to keep them away. The white sheriff of Maitland was neither confused nor fooled, however, and arrested Alan for his part in their minstrel act, but Zora somehow "sweet-talked" (as Alan put it) the district attorney into letting them go.

But troubles with the law did not cease there. As Alan was coming out of a barbershop in a nearby town he was suddenly surrounded by police and put in the back of their Packard car. No one would tell him what he was being charged with, and the car was accompanied back to the station by motorcycle police. Yet once he was booked and placed in a cell, Alan said he actually felt relieved: "My Dostoievskyan weight of guilt was finally lightened. I felt good even though I still didn't know what the charge was. There were no conflicts and no more worries. I'd been found out, and the judge would settle everything." When he was taken to the district attorney's office a few hours later, Zora, who had some local notoriety for her recently published book, was already there, pleading for his release. After Alan explained himself, the district attorney said, "I can't tell you that you can't live there, but I can't be responsible for what will happen if you do. There was an organizer down here from the Workers Alliance a while ago, and as I remember, he was tied to a tree and whipped to death." Hurston promised to take Lomax out of the county immediately. Later, Alan said, "A white man had for once been extricated from trouble in the South by a local Negro, instead of the other way around." But it was not over: later, both Barnicle and Alan were stopped by the police after dropping Hurston off at some friends' house on their way to Miami.

In Eatonville they recorded a few ballads, spirituals, a sermon, and some game songs, and Zora found a singer named Gabriel Brown who they thought was the best they had ever heard, even if he lacked the passion and fire of a Lead Belly. They could scarcely claim to have discovered Brown, for just the year before he had won the National Folk Festival in St. Louis as best guitarist and singer. Nor could he be claimed to be just one of the folk, as he was a graduate of Florida A&M, where he had acted and sung in Hurston's musical *All De Live Long Day* just six months earlier. But after they recorded him, all three of them worked to get him known more widely, and by the next year he was acting and playing in Orson Welles's Federal Arts Theater productions in New York City, making commercial recordings, and appearing on radio, and was later slated to be one of the leads in Hurston's own 1944 play *Polk County*.

Alan wrote his father from Eatonville on June 22 that they were leaving for Lake Okeechobee and the towns of Belle Glade and Chosen, where Zora promised to gather Bahamian dancers for them to photograph. They also hoped to ask the commissioner for the Seminole to help them find singers among the Indians. Belle Glade was a new community built on a tract of drained swampland, an area rich in bean and cabbage production, and when the season was right it was filled with thousands of farm workers who lived in shacks, rooming houses, or their cars, who worked in the fields all day in the semi-tropical humidity and crowded the town at night looking for ways to spend their daily earnings. Farther out in the country, the migrant workers from the Bahamas camped together and nightly danced and celebrated to their own songs and drums.

Hurston would recall that summer in Belle Glade when she described a Florida town in her novel *Their Eyes Were Watching God*:

> Day by day now the hordes of workers poured in. Some came limping in with their shoes and sore feet from walking. . . . They came in wagons from way up in Georgia and they came in truck loads from east, west, north, and south. Permanent transients with no attachments and tired looking men with their families and dog flivers. All night, all day hurrying to pick beans. Skillets, beds, patched-up spare inner-tubes, all hanging and dangling from ancient cars on the outside, and hopeful humanity, herded and hovering on the inside, chugging on to the muck. People ugly from ignorance and broken from being poor.

The three of them stayed in a tourist camp, recording day and night or looking for subjects. It was the sort of town that encouraged secularism, and they recorded several harmonica players, a jook band, some blues, hollers, ballads, and only a single religious song.

Living expenses turned out to be greater than imagined, and Lomax and Hurston quickly ran out of money. Alan had to write his father and complain that he shouldn't have been expected to venture out on a major project such as this with only $117, and that if it weren't for Barnicle using four months of her own salary to support them all, they would have had to quit long before. Hurston tried to eke out a little funding by writing Professor Ruth Benedict at Columbia to ask if the Department of Anthropology would be willing to pay for copies of the records for their archive.

Throughout the trip, Alan felt himself drawn closer to Zora. Her energy, her love of the beauty of the everyday, and her refusal to surrender to racism were irresistible. By now, however, Hurston and Barnicle were clashing over racial ideology and perhaps also the politics of their relationships with young Alan. (Barnicle, at least according to Hurston, was drawn to him, whom she called her "dear boy.") Emotional tensions were underscored by political differences between the two women, and Alan found himself acting as a buffer between them. "Miss Hurston . . . is ambitious, argumentative, and definite," he wrote his father. "She and Miss Barnicle could not understand each other and their continual silent conflict would have been amusing if it had not been so tragic in its implications."

> Miss B. and Miss H. were raging so that I never knew from one minute to the next what was going to happen, what with Miss B. determining hourly to leave for N.Y. and Miss Zora for parts unknown. I finally decided that it was no use trying to hold the expedition together and that B. was the best bet in the long run.

The breaking point came when Zora objected to Barnicle's taking a picture of a black child eating a watermelon. Alan sided with Barnicle and told Zora that she was being unreasonable. Once they reached Miami for a rest, Zora pulled out of the last leg of the trip, the Bahamas, even though it was she who had suggested they go there. Zora was acting capriciously, Alan thought, but he was still devoted to her. In a letter to the Library of Congress about the work they had just completed in the Southeast, he said that "Miss Hurston, who had been, so to speak, our guide and interpreter in Georgia and Florida, who had led us into fields we might never have found alone, who had generously helped us to record songs and singers she had herself discovered, could not, for various reasons, come with us to Nassau; but we felt that until the time she left us, she had been almost entirely responsible for the great success of our trip and for our going into the Bahamas."

Alan continued on with Barnicle by plane to Nassau and then to the other islands by sloop in July. He contacted the newspapers about this part of the journey, and such was the fame of the Lomax name that his trip was reported in newspapers in New York City, Washington, and Austin, each of their articles stressing that he was now working without his father. In one account, Alan was quoted on the rationale for the trip: "Negro Songs there are probably as nearly like those in Africa as any you can find in the Western hemisphere." The rest of the Western world may have thought of the Bahamian archipelago as a tropical paradise, a chain of dreamy green isles floating in a pellucid turquoise sea, but for Alan it offered the chance to view the culture of people of African descent as it might have been in the United States at the end of the eighteenth century.

He was caught up in stories about obeah and other forms of African-derived magic in the Bahamas that he had heard from Hurston, but he and Barnicle never made full contact with the occult. What they recorded instead on Andros Island, in Nassau, and Cat Island were sea chanteys, anthems (the local equivalent of black American spirituals), songs that accompanied "rushing" dances (a sacred dance similar to the shout on the Sea Islands or the *juré* in rural Louisiana), jumping dances (where one dancer at a time performs his or her own steps inside of a ring of drummers and clapping spectators who are waiting their turn), ring dances (similar to jumping dances, except that one couple at a time performs longer and more elaborately inside the ring), and round dances. There were also locally adapted English ballads, folktales that were accompanied by songs, even some songs by Haitian workers, and a few melodies as remembered by an old woman whose mother was African. Alan discovered that some songs had parallels in earlier times in African American history: the anthems of the sponge fishermen were built on an overlapping call and response that was very different from European antiphony. One singer "based" the others with held bass tones in a manner similar to one described by American abolitionists when slaves were first being freed.

Sailing out with the fishermen, he heard the rhythms of work and sea in the bob and pitch of the sailboat, the rattle of ropes on sails, the creak of mast and blocks. He watched as sudden shifts in weather demanded quick changes in styles and methods of work aboard ship. What he heard was different rhythms weaving among each other, some natural, some human-made, and the use of song among these fishermen to organize and reorganize what he called "energy patterns and social [work] roles primarily in terms of tempo, but also of dynamics and pitch. Increase in tempo, and multiple tempos, are the very heart of much of African music."

In spite of being a stranger on these islands, Alan felt liberated by the experience. The people there were open and expressive with him in a way he had never experienced among people of color before. "There were story sessions every night. Or fire dances or sessions of sea chanteys or something. It was just for me, heaven, for a Southerner to actually move freely past the color line which had always held me back."

By the middle of July Alan was again writing his father for money, while Barnicle was asking NYU to support her research and to let her off from teaching in the fall. Alan talked about going on to Haiti, and said he might even stay on if Barnicle had to leave. Meanwhile, he and Barnicle were living day to day, and taking risks everywhere they went. They took a boat to Andros Island, for example, with no plans, no local connections, next to no provisions, and little money. All they knew was that it was the home of the sponge fishing industry and some of the best sailors in the world. They slept in the hold or on the deck, shared a can of pears and some crackers for dinner, and the next morning were dropped off on the beach with their luggage, where a crowd of excited locals gathered around them as if they were exotic flotsam. Hungry, without a place to stay, and with night coming on, they went to the home of the commissioner of the island, and after three hours of talk aimed at convincing him that they were not tourists hustling a cheap vacation, he invited them to dinner and helped them rent a tiny shack for their stay.

Here, on the white sands, near the clear water, with hundreds of brilliant birds singing in the trees, Alan and Barnicle set up their recording machine, and when night came the local folk crowded around to "tell old story with sing"—folktales of B'Rabby and B'Booky intercut with songs, DJ-like. "It was an evening out of long ago, out of the first full, free, simple days of mankind," Alan wrote his father. But his idyll soon came to an abrupt end. In August Alan caught a cold, developed an ear infection, and was in bed for four days, unable to hear anything. The hurricane season had arrived, making every plan tentative. Then, when Alan and Barnicle were taking notes on the sponge fishing industry, the commissioner began to suspect that they were labor agitators, and on their return to Nassau they were ordered to leave the country.

Hurston wrote John Lomax at the end of August that she knew that Alan planned to continue working in folklore after graduation the following June, so she had been pressing him to "see further than the surface of things" in black cultural life. "There has been too much loose talk and conclusions argued at without sufficient proof. So I tried to make him do and see clearly so that no one can come after him and refute him." She said that he talked to her about his father all the time, and she was impressed that Alan respected his opinions. Then, in a thinly veiled reference to Barnicle's influence, she said that he was turning his back "on all urgings to come to New York this fall." What's more, he had repudiated the Communist Party, saying, "It is as my father says. I couldn't, *wouldn't* hurt him *ever again* by refusing to accept his judgment in such matters." In closing, she mentioned that Alan had tried to speak to Franz Boas, the father of American anthropology and her own mentor at Barnard College, but had found him cold. She promised his father to introduce Alan to Boas "in a way to catch his eye."

In September she wrote John again and bluntly warned him that "Miss Barnicle" was trying to separate him from his son, and to keep Alan from returning to school in Texas. In fact, she admitted that she too had once been part of Barnicle's conspiracy:

> When she proposed that I go on this trip with them one of the things she earnestly urged upon me was that I must help her to get this lovely young man out of his stifling atmosphere. He had a backward father who was smothering Allan [*sic*] with fogy ideas both of mind and body. . . . I promised that I would help all I could to persuade him to that end. But Mr. Lomax when I met Allan and he told me his plans and talked about you in the way he did, I just could not find it in my heart to help destroy the boy.

According to Hurston, Barnicle's real interest was her wish to build a reputation as a folklorist on the Lomax name, as well as a certain attachment to "the boy." Lead Belly was another object of Barnicle's efforts, she added, because "she was attracted to him as a man by her own admission," and because she wanted to free him from John Lomax and recruit him into the Communist Party. It was not those Negroes in Norwalk, Connecticut, who had been leading Lead Belly astray; it was Barnicle.

It's not clear how much of this John Lomax believed, for he was fond of Barnicle, but he was worried that Alan might be planning to stay on in New York City with Becky or some other woman. He wrote and reminded Alan that he expected him to go back to Austin for his senior year when the University of Texas fall term began, and warned him against the temptations of New York. And the temptations were many. Since coming back from the Bahamas, Alan had been staying at Barnicle and Conklin's apartment in the Village, dutifully transcribing and cataloging the two-hundred-some records they had made, but he had also been discovering New York bohemia. Strolling the streets of the Village and visiting the bars, it was possible then to run into Dawn Powell, e. e. cummings (Estlin, as he was known there), Djuna Barnes, Delmore Schwartz, Edmund Wilson, Malcolm Cowley, John Dos Passos, and the infamous Joe Gould, who claimed to be writing the history of the world. Alan took to the bohemian life as if he were bred to it. Folk song was catching on with the younger Village dwellers, and the Lomaxes were already well known among them. His open-faced, brash style may have been off-putting to some New Yorkers who styled themselves as understated, aristocratic observers of a bourgeois world from their downtown haven, and his Texas accent signaled wisps of racism, anti-Semitism, and the South that represented the world beyond the Hudson. But Alan treated any rebuffs he faced in the city much as he did those in southern hamlets—as the mores of the folk, data to be observed and gathered by an anthropologist who understood cultural relativism. *He* was the true rootless cosmopolitan and saw beyond their provinciality.

Fieldwork was something you could also do in the city. In early September, Alan and Barnicle began recording Aunt Molly Jackson, the self-proclaimed "pistol-packing Mama" of the coal miners' struggle, in Barnicle's apartment. Aunt Molly was one of the most vocal members of the miners' community in Harlan, Kentucky. She had spoken to the committee that Theodore Dreiser had brought to Harlan in 1931 to investigate conditions, and so impressed them that they invited her to New York City. Threatened by both the police and the mine owners, she took them up on their invitation. (Alan said, however, that Harlan people had told him that "the neighbors had asked her to leave because she kept whiskey at her place and her Saturday night parties were ruining all the men in the territory.")

Though she was a midwife by vocation, it was her ability to move an audience with powerful speech, her colorful and salty language, the huge reservoir of traditional songs she could draw on, and most of all her saw-edged songs with new and politically charged words put to old folk melodies that stuck with those who saw her and led them to give money to her cause, the miners' relief.

I am a union woman, as brave as I can be,
I do not like the bosses and the bosses don't like me.

From her apartment on the Lower East Side she found her way into the homes of the famous and the wealthy in New York City and traveled across the country with her message of the workers' plight.

At a time when most urban dwellers had never heard a singer of folk songs from America's hinterlands, Aunt Molly was a revelation. One of the first groups to pay attention to her was the Composers Collective, a newly formed group on the left (with members such as Charles Seeger, Marc Blitzstein, Ruth Crawford, Earl Robinson, Elie Siegmeister, and Aaron Copland) that attempted to create music for the proletariat, who they assumed lacked an appropriate music for their political situation. Hans Eisler, a protégé of Arnold Schoenberg, had broken with modernist music and joined with Bertholt Brecht, and was something of a model for them. They thought workers' songs, even those like "The Ballad of Joe Hill," were bourgeois products of the past and only put workers to sleep, the way they had always done. "Modern life and its tension demand dissonance," Eisler insisted. Songs like Eisler's choral compositions and marches for workers were complex and hard to sing, however, and so were seldom heard outside of the Degeyter Club, another activist composers' group with which the

Composers Collective was associated, this one named for Pierre Degeyter, the French composer of "L'Internationale." When Alan brought Aunt Molly to sing for the Collective, her stark, unadorned singing was tolerated, at best, by most of the members. But she found their music equally distasteful and retreated to a corner of the room. Charles Seeger had already been exposed to hillbilly music through Saturday night gatherings at the Eighth Street loft of painter Thomas Hart Benton, where Charles and his new wife Ruth Crawford browsed through records or heard amateurish country music played by Benton, composers Charles Ruggles and Henry Cowell, and Jackson Pollock on harmonica. (He'd already smashed his fiddle in frustration.) And now that Seeger heard the music live, it seemed to him even more vital and exciting. He rushed over to Aunt Molly to declare that she was on the right track and they were on the wrong. According to his son Pete, Charles Seeger was also inspired by hearing her say that composers ought to find their own country's folk songs and then use them as a basis for developing an American classical music.

On her first trip to the Northeast, Aunt Molly was quickly sanctified as something of a workers' saint, but a saint who could also sing and compose her own songs. Intellectuals and novelists like John Dos Passos, Theodore Dreiser, and Margaret Larkins wrote about her, unions held her up as a model, and newspapers tracked her closely. But she was soon to become a problem and a bore to many of her acolytes: she picked useless fights with would-be allies; she claimed as her own work songs that she had taken from folk song collections; and she invented incidents that would swell her fame. She was tough, vulgar, funny, bursting with energy, and at times turned her small apartment into a brothel. No surprise, then, that Barnicle saw her as a sister in the struggle and solicited her friendship. She worked to get her talks and performances at Sarah Lawrence and Bennington, and invited her to visit her classes at New York University so frequently that at one point she attempted to get the university to make Jackson her assistant. To raise public awareness of Aunt Molly, Barnicle bought some country-looking cloth and with the help of the theater department had a wrapper, apron, and sunbonnet made of it. She dressed her, gave her a corncob pipe, and invited the press to class. The next day, there was Aunt Molly's picture in the *New York Times* over an article headed "Mountaineer Woman Sings Ballads Here" that described her (without quotation marks) as "a-singin' and a-composin' since she was a tyke of ten."

It's easy in retrospect to dismiss these crude efforts at what was thought of as presenting "authenticity," especially as similar attempts at identity-building were already being manipulated more professionally by the executives of recording companies on what they were now calling hillbilly singers. But there was a deep sense of urgency and sincerity about these folklorists' efforts to present America to itself that set them apart from the commercial calculations of those who aimed only to make money from their creations. Thirty-some years later Charles Seeger would reflect on this moment of innocence among folklorists:

> Put any good "authentic," traditional singer before a microphone or on a platform before an audience not of its own kind, and soon the peculiar requirements of the situation produce the typical traits of exhibitionism. To my personal observation, it took Molly Jackson only a few months after her expulsion from Harlan County, Kentucky, to convert herself, when expedient, from a traditional singer, who seemed never to have given any particular thought to whether anyone liked or disliked her singing, into a shrewd observer of audience reaction, fixing individual listeners one after another with her gaze, smiling ingratiatingly, gesturing, dramatizing "by" words in her songs. Lead Belly was already an astute handler of the nonfolk by the time I met him (about the time he left John Lomax). . . . Since each [the folk and the nonfolk] has now exploited the other for a couple of decades in the large frame of the United States, there must exist few, if any, persons left ratable as 100 percent either folk or nonfolk. The vast population lies between these limits, each individual made up of varying proportions of inhibited or released folkness or nonfolkness.

Barnicle and Alan set about recording Aunt Molly's autobiography, creating a memoir that would include traditional songs, along with comments on their meaning to the singer and the community from which she came. Aunt Molly later asked to be paid for the recordings she had made, even though the Library of Congress at that time did not recompense anyone for recording sessions. When Alan wrote her for permission to use some of her stories and songs in his and his father's 1941 book *Our Singing Country*, she replied that she was writing a book of her own and warned him against using any of them. When they later did reach an agreement, he paid her himself, and her recorded comments were threaded throughout the published book. Yet she continued to try to get more money from him, as she did from others, especially those who had befriended her.

Alan began an ambitious plan for what would have to be done next if folk song was to be taken seriously and he was to survive along with it. Having learned that the Library of Congress wanted to move the Archive of American Folk Song out of the dark and dusty corner in which it sat and open it up to the public, he proposed to his father that the archive could build up its collection by exchanging recordings and song texts with other libraries and then become a distribution center to which all institutions could have access. Records could be distributed to schools at cost, for example, a scheme that would also draw the attention of foundations and government to help with further funding and research. A list of commercial studio recordings of folk songs could be developed, and those recordings would then be added to the library and the public encouraged to hear them. Since John had recently been ill, Alan offered himself for the job: "If you aren't well enough for a while, I could stay on for a couple of months in Washington and proceed in the way you and your superiors thought best." His last year in college could wait. He ended his letter with a reminder of what he could do on his own: "225 records for this summer and if we hadn't been delayed by everything possible at least four hundred."

At one of Barnicle's parties where city folksingers gathered, Lomax met Herbert Halpert, one of her favorite students. Halpert had just graduated from New York University and had taken a job as a recreation worker for the new federally created Works Progress Administration on the Lower East Side, where he was collecting children's rhymes. When he heard the records that Alan and Barnicle had brought back from their southern trip, he was excited by the possibilities that recording offered, of being able to hear a living tradition rather than simply read about it, and he began discussing another trip to the Bahamas with Barnicle and Lomax. Alan, however, was much more interested in learning about the WPA's folklore programs and how he might use their musicians, technicians, and stenographers in his own work. He quickly wrote up a proposal and took it to the New York City office of the WPA, where he sang for the office staff. His plan was to create and coordinate a class in folk music led by a distinguished musicologist such as George Herzog, who would teach musicians how to notate folk music correctly. By working from recordings that had already been made, a body of transcribed music could be put into print. Finally, Alan would create a clearinghouse for the collection and housing of folk songs from everywhere in the country. If the WPA would agree to fund it for a year, he would then send the project on to the Library of Congress to see if they would take it on permanently.

He was about to leave for Washington to pitch his idea to the national office of the WPA when a letter from his father arrived urging him to return to school. He answered by ignoring his father's concerns and instead showing how industrious he had been since he had returned to New York City, giving him the details of his proposal, and gently taking the lead in their relationship:

> I'm going to disobey you straight out and go to Washington where on Monday morning I will expect to hear from you, either by wire or by airmail, special delivery. You and I now have the chance to do something really big, something of lasting value in all sorts of ways both to ourselves, for this country and for folk-songs. The money is crying to be spent. I would suggest that you come on to Washington so that we can march in on the WPA together next week. I have

> already been invited to see the head of it and I think I can put over the first part of the project by myself, provided that the Library (you) will let me make copies of all its records so that they can be worked up by this group of musicians in the Library. I have a chance to get a good job and, although that doesn't seem really as attractive to me as a quiet, lazy year in Austin, still, if in a year I can get the ball rolling fast in the right direction in the field of American folk-songs, I will be glad to spare that year.

But it turned out that there was no job for him in the WPA, and by late September he was back at school in Austin with a schedule heavy in courses in anthropology and philosophy. The book that John had hoped would bring him some income, *Negro Folk Songs as Sung by Lead Belly,* was published in 1936 and sold poorly. Lead Belly himself, meanwhile, had attempted a New York comeback, managed now by a Shreveport gas station owner, but his performances were sparsely attended and were given short shrift by the New York papers.

Alan turned twenty-one in the spring term at Texas in 1936 and sailed through his courses, even as he continued to do some fieldwork close to home. On one weekend venture he recorded the Soul Stirrers, a popular gospel quartet from Trinity, Texas, when they appeared in Austin. As up to date and innovative as they seemed, he heard something much older in their singing. Their lead, R. H. Harris, sang in a falsetto that was a novelty in gospel quartets, but Alan sensed it had origins in Africa. The quartet was in the process of developing a new style, one that used switch leads, two singers taking turns, passing the solo part back and forth like the horn players in the older New Orleans jazz bands. The Soul Stirrers could fall behind the beat and then accelerate back up to tempo, improvising lyrics as they sang. Or they riffed behind the lead singer, rhythmically repeating words or phrases, something that black *sexteto* singers were also doing in Cuba at the time. (Harris would leave the group in 1950 and be replaced by Sam Cooke, a singer who would take them up to the edge of pop music and then leave them to cross over into it as a star.)

It was that spring that Alan met Elizabeth Harold Goodman, an eighteen-year-old freshman from Dallas, a brilliant, beautiful political radical with a cool assuredness and grace that set her apart from other southern women. She was a poet, deep into literary tradition, but driven to change the world and unafraid of the price that the South could extract from a woman like her. Her maternal grandfather was Judge H. T. Lyttleton, a liberal, who had been declared an enemy by the Ku Klux Klan. Her mother had married Michael Harold, who was institutionalized when he was still young after fatally assaulting his brother, leaving his wife and her children—Elizabeth, Michael Jr., and Anne—destitute. While

Elizabeth was in high school she had a child, but the father's family adopted the baby and raised it, and Elizabeth left for college.

Alan fell in love with her and declared that he wanted her with him forever. But John Lomax disliked her from their first meeting, and when he found out that they were planning to be married he was strongly opposed to it, even telling Alan's friends of his disapproval. Alan made sure the two of them did not meet again.

In May Alan was awarded a B.A. in philosophy, summa cum laude, and membership in Phi Beta Kappa. His plan now was to get a fellowship and earn enough money to enter graduate school at the University of Chicago and study anthropology. Meanwhile, he went to Dallas, where preparations for the Texas Centennial were under way, thinking that he could create a barrelhouse where visitors could experience the music and rough life of workers' barrooms, or maybe set up a tamale concession. When he learned that no one was willing to back him for either business, he took off for Saltillo, then the center of intellectual activity in Mexico, ostensibly to study Spanish and do research on Mexican folklore. Elizabeth may have been with him at least part of the time, as he talked about her in letters he wrote to friends, but he never mentioned her when writing his family.

He had no plans, his money was running out, and his attempt to sit in on classes in a local high school to learn Spanish taught him little. He spent most of his time wandering the streets, living on fruit, watching a performance of *Los Pastores*, and practicing on the new guitar his father had given him for graduation. "It is much the nicest gift I ever had," he wrote his father. "It will make me completely free of society and I can wander through the world like a troubadour and care for no man." John suggested that he might be able to help him get work in Washington, but Alan insisted he had to make his way without him: "After all we had been together for three years almost constantly," he wrote him, "and during that time had spent ourselves in numerous fits of unbearable anger and hurt. It seemed to me time to go. . . . I simply had to make some sort of gesture of independence because for months I had been miserably scared of what might happen to me when I stepped out from under the parental roof. I hope you understand."

But by September it was clear that he was going nowhere. He wrote his father from Mexico that all his plans had fallen through, and he wondered if there might still be something for him at the Library of Congress—handling mail, maybe, or filing and arranging the records? "But I'm going to need more money, I'm afraid, than my guitar would be able to give me next year at the University of Chicago."

CHAPTER 5

Honeymoon in Haiti

Haiti in 1936 was no island paradise, no romantic retreat. Tourists were so scarce that any non-Haitian who showed up on a boat was regarded with suspicion by officials. A nineteen-year-long American occupation by the marines had ended in 1934, the United States having been a latecomer to a long list of invaders of Hispaniola, the island that also includes the Dominican Republic. The country was now a shambles of a civil society, whose model for almost two decades had been dictatorship, with forced work gangs, a debased educational system, and legitimized violence from the top.

In addition to the weight of Haiti's history of occupation and struggle, there was also Vodou, the nation's peasant religion, a syncretic lamination of Catholicism and West African and Kongo religions. In the 1930s some elements of Vodou became a focus of titillating excitement and fearful obsession among Americans and Europeans and entered the public consciousness through tabloids, pulp fiction, comic books, films, and stage plays. In the movies, a kind of Vodou hysteria peaked between 1932 and 1936 with *White Zombie, Voodo, The Emperor Jones, Drums O' Vodou, Ouanga* (or *Crime of Vodou*), and *Revolt of the Zombies*. But it was a 1929 book by William Seabrook, *The Magic Island,* that made Haiti a permanent part of American and Western European popular culture. Seabrook, a journalist, traveler, sadist, alcoholic, and friend of the photographer Man Ray and the mystic Aleister Crowley, wrote a scandalous book on Haiti under American occupation that drew on old images of blacks under slavery and white fear of blacks. It was a gaudy, sensationalistic account of outrageous practices of savagery that he claimed to have witnessed.

The zombie emerged at the center of this grim fixation: the visage of the living dead, represented in images and descriptions of tall black men raised from the dead by manipulative priests and sent out against their masters' enemies. For Westerners there were already fragments of this figure in the Greek *daimon,* in black magic, and in the widespread belief in ghosts. But the image of the zombie was far more graphic, with its collective nighttime rituals that involved music and dancing, possession, burial alive, and a vengeful resurrection.

Haiti was of particular interest to a handful of anthropologists, such as Melville J. Herskovits. He had entered the country just as the troops were leaving and picked a small rural community in order to study its economics, religion, and culture, which resulted in the 1937 book *Life in a Haitian Valley*. That work was part of Herskovits's larger plan to understand the adaptation of African peoples to life in the Americas. For his part, Alan Lomax viewed Haiti as a grand site of unrecorded song, the product of a people who were culturally closer to Africa than any others in the New World, and also less marked by the effects of mass communication. He asked the Library of Congress to underwrite a trip there to collect recordings of Haitian music, a genre the archive lacked completely.

By November 1936, the library had approved his trip and appointed him temporary assistant to the archive for a period of five months at a salary of thirty dollars a month, even though he was only twenty-one and had never conducted a research project by himself. Financially, they risked very little: his travel expenses, a recording machine, a motion picture camera, film, blank recording discs, and five dollars a day for living expenses. Nonetheless, they wanted to keep track of him, and asked for regular progress reports. Because relations between the United States and Haiti were still tense, the library also insisted on having a number of letters of introduction prepared for Alan—to the lieutenant colonel of the U.S. Marine Corps, the secretary of state, the American minister and American consul in Haiti, General Calixte and Colonel André of the Garde d'Haiti, and the minister from Haiti in Washington. The letters to the Haitians stressed that he was associated with Zora Neale Hurston, who was already in Haiti and known by local intellectuals and officials of the government. Hurston had applied for a Guggenheim Fellowship in 1935 with a plan to study obeah and magic in the West Indies, extending the work she had done on hoodoo in New Orleans, but this time for a popular book: she wanted to research the role of Moses in West Indian magical practices and build a novel around it. She had applied for a Guggenheim once before, in 1934, but was turned down after receiving negative reports from anthropologists Ruth Benedict and Franz Boas. When she applied the second time she no longer listed herself as being in anthropology but in "literary science." This time she received the fellowship, becoming the first black woman to be awarded one of America's highest honors. After she left for the West Indies she wrote Alan from Kingston, Jamaica, inviting him to bring his recording machine with him and to meet her in the highlands of Jamaica—Maroon country, the home of escaped slaves from the seventeenth century—from where they would proceed to Haiti. Because he was unable to leave then, they made plans to meet in Haiti.

Arriving in Haiti in late September, Hurston spent much of her time finishing

Their Eyes Were Watching God. By November she wrote Alan to warn him off mentioning Vodou or anything that even suggested William Seabrook's book when he came to Haiti, since the country's upper class was still angry with what he had written. She offered him clues as to what to look for in songs and, incidentally, asked him to buy her some stockings ("color light, golden tan, size 10").

Each of the anthropologists, dancers, and researchers who visited Haiti had used the same guides to lead them into the bush to experience Haitian folk culture. (In those days, the "bush" was only a few hundred yards from the main streets of Port-au-Prince.) "Doc" R. H. Reiser, a former navy pharmacist's Mate then supervising the National Insane Asylum, lived with a local woman, had been initiated into Vodou and become accepted among the ranks of the priests of Vodou as a psychic, and acted as a cultural middleman for journalists and social scientists alike. It was he, along with Faustin Wirkus (a marine sergeant left in charge of the island of Gonâve who had proclaimed himself a king, as well as directed *Voodo*, a faked part-documentary, part-fiction film) and a small group of self-selected experts, who were on call for visitors, usually taking them to the same places, sometimes with unpleasant results. Zora Neale Hurston, for example, had been led to a particular *houngan*, or Vodou priest, hoping to learn enough to be initiated as a believer. While she was dancing in a ceremony, she was furious to find that Professor Herskovits's graduate assistant George E. Simpson and novelist and travel writer Harold Courlander had both been guided by a bellboy at their hotel to the same service where she was dancing and intruded into her research. She did not speak to either one of them for the rest of their stay.

Alan left for Haiti on December 10 on the *SS Pastores* with 155 pounds of luggage, arriving in Port-au-Prince on the fourteenth, and he was happy to have Zora guide him in getting settled. With the government wary of American tourists who might be writers or filmmakers, for the first few weeks he had to be careful and count on the kindness of influential locals, who themselves were involved in a folkloric and ethnographic reaction against the imposed culture of the invaders by preserving and understanding local culture. Zora introduced him to Rulx Léon, director of the National Health Service, who promised to set up meetings with the president of Haiti and others so that he could be granted permission to move freely around the country. To defuse suspicions that he was there to study Vodou music, Alan let it be known that he was interested in all kinds of Haitian music, and soon was taken by some local intellectuals to the house of pianist-composer Ludovic Lamothe, the best-known classical musician in Haiti, who played for them pieces he had composed that reinterpreted local Carnival music in European forms, much the way Louis Moreau Gottschalk had done with New Orleans folk music.

Alan felt uneasy about being introduced to Haiti by its bourgeoisie, given that the gap between the upper class and the peasants was so pronounced. He began to resent their supercilious and distorted view of folk culture and was even becoming disillusioned with Zora, who he felt was spending too much time with the elites and not enough living with the folk: "She had become the toast of the Haitian army."

"Zora is hard enough to fathom by herself," he wrote Elizabeth, "and as uncertain and potentially violent as she can be."

> At first I was completely dependent on her and on top of that I was afraid she was falling in love with me. Nothing has happened so far and now I have made some friends on my own and am not so completely dependent on her as I was at first. But God I'll be glad when I breathe my last breath of Port-au-Prince air and get out into the country where there is a little more physical danger involved, but where the issue is simpler—do the people trust and like you or not?

A few days later Zora left for the island of Gonâve to spend Christmas, where she discovered that White King Wirkus was a fake, and then went on to Archahaie, which she had heard was the center of Vodou in Haiti. In March she took a break from fieldwork and returned to New York to visit with friends and work on a novel.

Now left completely on his own, Alan hired an interpreter, guide, and cook named Revolie Polines, who had been working for the Americans before they left. By the end of their first day together, Alan was calling him in his field notes his mentor, professor, and master. Lomax's five dollars a day was expected to cover Polines's pay and provide for both of their expenses—food, transportation, housing, and medicine. For anything else—batteries, rental of musical instruments, refreshments, and pay for performers or for the right to photograph Haitians—he had to submit a request to the library, and by the end of the first week he was beginning to worry about how he could get by on so little money.

One of the first things he and Revolie did was to stop by a concert of a military band in Port-au-Prince on the Champ de Mars, but they soon grew bored and left for the outskirts of the city and found themselves immersed in a rich sonic world:

> Five or six radios going very loud. The further west we got the poorer the houses, the ragged [*sic*] the people, until at last we went in between some little shacks to my man Polines' present domicile with his cousins, exchanged courtesies with two slim and handsome Negro women with red head-rags and then the drum pulled us deeper into the moonlight behind the house . . . to a little thatched shed set up on poles, open on all sides where, by the leaping flame of a little kerosene lamp . . . the tambours were speaking and the vagabonds and whores were dancing.

. . .

> We had not walked twenty yards when we came around the corner of a shanty and saw four couples dancing a slow one-step in the alley-way between a high candelabra cactus fence and the house. Hanging from the fence was an old bicycle tire, burning slow and orange, throwing a golden flame across the dancers and the wall of the shanty. I wish I could tell how beautiful this scene was, how melancholy, how restrained and graceful. The music was click, chatter, tinkle and deep-throbbing thump-thump.

They had wandered into a yard where Ago's Bal Band was playing a wider range of music than Alan had ever expected to find in rural Haiti: "marches, blues, meringues, bals," even one piece in Spanish. When he wrote his first report back to Strunk at the library, he described this band:

> This country is, so far as my experience goes, the richest folk-song field I know. The drumming is intricate and sophisticated. Last night I listened for an hour to one of the native orchestra[s], composed of a pair of bones, a three string guitar, a pair of Cuban cha-chas (or gourds), and a manoumba (a peculiar bass instrument)—a rectangular box, with a circular opening in the side across which are ranged in an iron bar eight inch-wide iron tongues (an octave of them I think) with one hand and beats the box with the other—; each of the instruments had a distinct rhythm which fitted into the rhythmic pattern of the whole, the guitar played the melody and the manoumbas the bass, and the four players sang. It was deliciously lovely.

The dancers to this music moved with angularity and flexibility, and with such sudden shifts of attitude that they seemed to him to turn themselves into cubist sculptures. Alan had seen expressive black dancers in the rural South of the United States, but this was something altogether different: the movement of their hips, their pelvic thrusts and undulating arms responding to the multiple meters of the rhythm, songs that openly expressed sexuality, the casual, rough unison of the women's voices rising over the hand drums. In only a few days he had come to experience firsthand the sharp demarcation between the Haitian *élite* and the *masse*, between the rich and the poor, between those who spoke French and those who spoke Créole, between Catholics and *vodouistes*.

Just after Christmas, Alan traveled ten miles or so northeast of Port-au-Prince to Port Beudet, a small village on the Haitian American Sugar Company's plantation, on the rich land of the Plaine du Cul-de-Sac, to seek an audience with Doc Reiser. Other writers before Lomax mentioned Reiser with gratitude, sometimes exaggerating his importance by calling him a doctor or a psychiatrist, perhaps even alluding to his anomalous connection to Vodou, but never in any revealing detail. Alan, on the other hand, took extensive notes at their first meeting, fearing that if he waited until he knew more he would be too overwhelmed to write it. His first sight of the village was recorded in his notebook:

> The banana and cane plantations are orderly jungles. Something about the banana grove makes it the most tropical thing I have ever seen. Something completely foreign about it to the very nature of this temperate zone. Something exaggerated about the size of its great knife-like leaves—a huge palm with forty feet of its bole buried out of sight in the earth. . . .
>
> The [mental] institution is inconspicuous among the ear-like banana leaves—a lot of low-lying green and white sheds. . . . Here are two hundred twenty inmates and their chatter never ceases—it is like New York without the subway or the excuse to stay awake . . . this world is awake at all hours.

Reiser told him that he had been raised on a farm in Utah, in a family of musicians, and he himself sang and played guitar. He joined the navy, married, and became involved with a famous movie star, he said, which led to his divorce. (Alan noted to himself that this particular detail seemed a little incredible.) After wandering the seas for years, he was transferred by the navy to Haiti, where he at last felt at home and found his calling. He discovered that he had the gift of divining patients' illnesses simply by looking at them. Next, he learned that he was psychic and was able to see the future. Such feats spread his reputation across Haiti, and as word reached the *houngans*, the Voudun priests, they began to seek him out and eventually initiated him. It was a short step to adapting his abilities to possessional states, where under the influences of one or the other of the most extreme of Voudun deities he performed extravagantly. Reiser narrated his account as a grim parade of ghostly patients passed them by, some moaning or weeping, some bent over or walking on their knees, one pretending to read an American magazine, another begging to go home to give birth to her baby. Alan ended his handwritten notes by saying, "I am so nervous I can scarcely write as this scrawl witnesses."

The phantasmagoria that was Haiti had begun to take hold of his imagination, his senses bombarded by the dizzying mix of poverty, sounds, color, smells, and the ravages of malaria that a few years later would be called surreal by André Breton, the father of surrealism, when he visited the island. Alan observed that

> everything is so new here. Food, temperament, culture, landscape, climate. I listen and look, myself enervated in five or six hours and add to that the laziest air in the world inviting to repose and you have the sum of my problems and

a perfect excuse for not writing. . . . God knows I have enough work to try to figure these people out. My former experiences as a collector were mere child's play; here I am up against something. . . . I have to learn diplomacy, how to collect, how to handle a servant, how to beat the tambour, how to dance, how to bargain, how to lie, how to run the new recorder, how to take notes, how to budget and keep accounts, all on top of my personal problems, which have formerly kept me completely occupied. And, God, this world is beautiful, beautiful and strange.

There was the language problem:

This land is literally all folklore, and what's not such is more interesting than the other. People tell me things I want to hear all day long in a language that they all say is very simple but is the most difficult thing I have struck yet. It is a sort of short-hand French. An idea of it in English—"m da flo I nt gay wn own—my dear fellow I want to go down town"—only backwards. My French is very infantile and I have to translate from Creole to French and then to English. Of course, there is one consolation. After one overcomes the first area of difficulty, and where I wallow now, the rest is easy. The language is non-inflective, the grammar is simple though subtle, but the subtleties are "English" enough so that they are not literally impossible. It is twice as hard for me as Spanish, especially because I can't just sit by and absorb but have to talk English and find out what people mean all the time. You can imagine the problems uncountable in transcribing singing in this Patois. One has to invent orthography as one goes along.

The two languages, as he said, were products of the class structure, in which the schools ignored Créole, the Haitian constitution forbade Vodou, and the peasant associations (such as the cooperative work groups and savings societies) were ignored by the bankers. In a very long letter Alan wrote to Charles Seeger, he managed to express what was different about folklore collecting in a society like Haiti:

This is the first place I have ever visited where there were *two* classes, each of which had its language and its culture, completely separated and distinct. The working class, the peasants who sit flat on their buttocks upon the soil, so to speak, are all informants, so far as the folklorist is concerned, especially if he has a lot of radical notions about folklore not being old, necessarily, or cut to fit any special pattern, or the sole possession of a few adepts, but the property of whatever person it has by the tongue. That makes every single peasant I meet here an informant and most of the population is peasant. So I have been buried, snowed under. I wish I had the virtue of the single-track mind, but I am interested in everything I hear.

A novice at Créole, with no help from reference books, the names of dozens of Vodou deities buzzing all around him and subtle interpenetrations of Catholic and Vodou doctrine a theologian's nightmare, he wrote Melville Herskovits for help on what to record, and the professor obliged, also sending him his own notes on Vodou religion.

Whatever the delays he ran into in Haiti and his cultural confusions, by halfway through January Alan had succeeded in recording Vodou songs and drummers, string bands, dance bands, Catholic and Vodou services and prayers (the first recordings ever done in a *hounfort*, the site of Vodou services), and the compositions of M. Lamothe, so many recordings that he had used up most of the blank discs he had brought with him and was waiting impatiently for a new batch to arrive from Washington.

Alan and Revolie set out by bus January 20 to Les Cayes, a city on the south coast of Haiti, where, Alan had been assured, the inhabitants were ruled by "strange gods," if not by devils. It was a venture worth writing about, and as it turned out it would be the only thing he'd ever publish from his Haitian trip. In "Haitian Journey," an impressionistic account for the *Southwest Review*, he described the passengers on the bus, dockworkers loading coffee and singing work songs, and horseback rides to various towns, and told about riddles, game songs, folktales, Mardi Gras songs, and tales of zombies. The article ends at the point where he and Revolie go on to the town of Plaisance, where they recorded RaRa bands that were rehearsing for Holy Week. The sound of drums rippled from one hilltop to another, family and religious bands roamed the streets, bamboo horns called *vacines* hocketed together, the leaders of these groups wearing feathers and wildly quilted suits, twirling batons, and wearing dark glasses. And through it all Alan and Revolie witnessed the counterpoint of the ravages of malaria.

Before he left New York, Alan had asked Elizabeth Harold to join him in Haiti, where they would be married. It was a romantic gesture, and one that also avoided his having to invite his father to a wedding to which he strongly objected. Yet Alan fretted, because he did not know until late January whether Elizabeth would actually be coming, and once she did arrive in early February they had to halt their nuptial plans when they discovered that neither one of them was of legal age for marriage in Haiti and therefore required parental consent. Haitian law also required that banns be publicly announced two weeks in advance. Alan was forced to turn to John for help, though he had yet to tell him that he planned to be married:

> I am in a rather desperate mess and you are the only person in the world who can help me out of it. You, or perhaps an expert forger. The situation is as follows.

> (1) As you know by now—and only an unexpected unrolling of the yarn of fate prevented me from being the first to tell you—Elizabeth is on her way here and we will shortly be married. I was never certain before last night, when her letter came, that she would come at all although I had asked her repeatedly. . . . I had not had time to prepare in advance; or to tell you, myself, as I certainly wanted to. However, I have been so unhappy away from her and I love her so completely and entirely, and am so much more alive and happy when she is near that the temporary embarrassment doesn't count. That largely arises out of the complexities of the Haitian code of civil marriages which calls me still a minor at 22 and demands the consent of my father before it will consent to say its magic formula over me. Therefore, please, if you love me, send me airmail *a statement of your consent, affirmed by a notary and along with this a copy of my birth certificate from Seton,* very official. I know you don't approve of my marrying but please give me a charitable lift out of the hole into which this legal technicality has thrown me. . . . This is a hard letter to write and I can tell you I've spent a good many hours of agony over it in this strange country. And it took all my nerve to carry me over for a while. But now all I feel is joy in the knowledge that I will see Elizabeth in a few hours and that, whatever happens, we will win through. Please send me your love and your blessing and your official consent.

They were married on February 23, following Alan's plea to Estenio Vincent, the Haitian president, to waive the banns. ("I come to you with an unusual request, the granting of which will both facilitate a scientific work, important to Haiti, and make possible the happiness of myself and my fiancée.")

Living in a hut with a thatched roof, awakened in each other's arms by roosters and song, they were at work all their waking hours, often from seven o'clock to three in the morning, eating peasant food, tramping up creek beds and climbing mountain roads, sometimes riding in an old borrowed car painted yellow with scarlet trim ("It was like a great, square-cut, tropical fowl, a fantastic bird with an olive green beak and a black toupee, and it was named Fleur d'Innocence"). Elizabeth (whom Alan now called "Chavella" or "che' Neg' ") learned the rituals and deities, the two of them standing on the edge of the Vodou services, watching the *houngan* prepare a *verver* (a ground painting done with a mixture of ashes and cornmeal) appropriate to the deity addressed in the service, swept up by the music of the drums and voices that accompanied this work, leading to dances of possession where priest or priestess and supplicants are addressed by the sacred. At one point, Alan and Elizabeth let themselves be buried in a grave for a few moments as part of a ritual to protect them from harm. Once they were dug up, they were taken to a grove of trees where a *houngan* captured a tarantula and fed it. Now, they were assured, nothing and no one but God himself could kill them.

Just before Elizabeth arrived Alan had contracted intestinal malaria and was unable to eat or drink much for a few weeks. He was drained of strength for the bulk of the rest of his time in Haiti, and when Elizabeth became sick too, their work began to suffer from lack of money and the authority that money and vitality buy in a poor country:

> In Haiti it is not a good policy to grow weak and helpless and to be broke. My formerly effective arguments could bring no singers before the microphone. I had just enough money to buy a little rum for the crowds that gathered each night at the house to listen to records being made, but not enough to make them all respectful or considerate. Invited into my house they took possession of it. They camped on all the chairs and refused to be moved. They laughed and talked while the records were being made and no threats or wheedling reasons could stop their mouths. Occasionally the gendarmes would descend from the *bouque* and pretend to clear the house, but it was only to occupy the chairs themselves and add more undiscipline to the already boisterous audience. And Revolie grew disaffected, too. Neither he nor they could understand Elizabeth and myself. When a Haitian peasant gets sick he retires into a corner like a dog and is silent. Neither the peasants nor Revolie could see much to sympathize over in the contemplation of a spectral and irritable pair of blancs who spoke laughable Creole and tried to give thunderous orders in voices that now bore no trace of authority.

By March Alan had completely run out of funds when his check from the Library of Congress was held up in the mail. He attempted to borrow twenty dollars from the American consulate in Port-au-Prince, but was turned down by the consul, who caustically suggested he surely could find credit somewhere else, since "you make friends so easily with the natives."

In their last week in Haiti, Alan and Elizabeth tried to crowd in everything they had to complete before they left. When the day for departure came, they delivered their luggage and packages to the boat in the morning, then rode by bus for several hours to Cap-Haïtien in the north to visit the Citadel, built after the Haitian Revolution by Henri Christophe to withstand European invaders. But they misjudged the distance, and by the time they got back to the wharves of Port-au-Prince the boat was pulling out. The owner of an American yacht anchored in the harbor was just arriving in his motorboat and, seeing their situation, offered to take them to the ship. When they caught up with the steamer, they jumped from the deck to a ladder on the side of the boat. The ship's officers didn't speak to them for the rest of the voyage.

Once they reached Washington on April 23, Alan wrote letters of thanks to Doc

Reiser, to Revolie, and to others who had helped them, sending them copies of recordings, promising gifts as soon as he could afford to, and encouraging others to give Revolie a job equal to his abilities. He then set to work organizing his field notes and recordings, all the while managing to keep John and Elizabeth at a distance from each other.

The Haitian materials he had collected proved to be overwhelming. Alan returned from Haiti with more than fifteen hundred recordings—some fifty hours of recorded sound—including the music associated with Vodou, Mardi Gras, Catholicism, old French romance ballads, the work songs of the collective labor groups (the *konbits*), as well as folktales, children's game songs, bands of all sorts, jazz and classical music, and three songs sung by Zora Neale Hurston that had nothing to do with Haiti. Everything was accompanied by notes, drawings, logs, transcriptions, and translations. There was also 350 feet of remarkably fine 8mm color motion picture film by Elizabeth Lomax that showed the making of drums, dances, work, domestic life, and religion. Alan wrote short essays on how drums were made and baptized, interviewed drummers and *houngans*, made notes on the songs and dances of Vodou and Mardi Gras, on the pantheon of deities in the Plaisance area, and on Vodou rituals and beliefs. Because the library wanted a final report on the trip, Alan got help in translating the folk songs he had collected from the Haitian scholar Suzanne Comhaire-Sylvain, author of *Le Créole Haïtien*, and wrote the anthropologist/choreographer Katherine Dunham asking for a Haitian bibliography, but he was never able to complete the full report. In the end, he gave up on his Haitian writing and instead helped his father prepare a new edition of *Cowboy Songs and Other Frontier Ballads*. Later he would say, "It was characteristic of me then to let my father's work come first. That way I could avoid my own needs and problems."

If the library had conceived of this trip along the lines of another straighforward ballad-collecting venture, they would have been surprised at the results. The links between music, culture, and social structure that Alan had rapidly grasped in his fieldwork in the United States by a mixture of insider knowledge, shrewd judgment, and a keen sense of observation were not enough to carry him in Haiti. Nor was four months sufficient time to learn what he needed to know about Haitian peasant life. At one point he wrote in his notebooks that Haitian culture was best left to experts. In fact, no one has even yet produced an outsider's account of Haitian culture that is entirely satisfactory. The doubleness of European and African culture affects every institution and cultural domain in Haiti: two languages, two religions, two medicines, and so on, and yet both of them interpenetrating and operating together by means that are inherently deceptive—as deceptive as a slave needed to be to survive. Such knowledge is not easily learned from the outside.

While Alan was in Haiti, John had written him with a number of suggestions for jobs that might interest him when he returned to the United States, and had become annoyed when Alan failed to respond to any of them. In early April John tried again with another possibility that he thought Alan would not be able to turn down: he had asked Vice President John Vance and others in Washington to have a line added to the library's budget for a clerk to index the folk song materials in the archive, and the House had passed the allocation. Vance had already recommended Alan as the perfect candidate for the job. His temporary job was extended two months, and in June Alan was made assistant-in-charge of the Archive of American Folk Song at the Library of Congress. His father would still be "honorary consultant" and technically his boss, but Alan was to deal directly with Harold Spivacke, the new chief of the Music Division. Spivacke was a musicologist who had been assistant to the classical music critic of the *New York Times*, Olin Downes, and had been serving as assistant to the chief. During Spivacke's tenure the library would expand its chamber music concerts in the Coolidge Auditorium and greatly increase its classical holdings. But he was also a man of wide and adventuresome tastes who had encouraged John Lomax, and had even done field recording in a prison with him.

The archive had no real budget and only a shadow staff before it received the small appropriation from Congress in July, a cautious if somewhat grudging recognition that there was a unique American culture, one that was alive and flourishing even at the bottom of the social ladder. But even with Alan's appointment, it was recognition on the cheap: his salary was $1,620 a year, a bit more than a day laborer's pay, his father was still making only a dollar a month, and the office was still a dusty cubbyhole under the library.

Yet Alan scarcely seemed to notice any of this. With the imprimatur of the Library of Congress, he began moving fast. Before the end of the year he had given a talk on folk song at the prestigious Cosmos Club of Washington and had sung at parties for senators and their spouses. He had given interviews, written short articles on folklore for newspapers, and made plans to gather folk songs from sailors, miners, and lumberjacks in Michigan as a first step in a plan to collect folklore in every state in the country. He spent his days classifying records, listening to songs and typing out their words, and answering a stream of letters asking for bibliographies, recordings, the sources for this or that song, or for suggestions of folk songs that could be harmonized for use in school concerts. He advised parents on how to help their children to have careers as singers, and responded to letters asking for "good airs" to turn into an elementary school alma mater song. There were also letters from sculptors looking for inspiration in folk art, from pageant directors in search of songs, and from Hollywood moguls wanting to hear field recordings for possible movie scores. He also spoke at the annual meetings of the American Library Association and the Progressive Education Association, and at dozens of other educational, entertainment, and folklore-boosting groups whenever he was asked.

Alan invited Lead Belly and his wife to come to Washington in June to record more songs for the library, and to meet some people who might be able to find him work. They drove down to D.C. with Barnicle and her friend Kip Kilmer, son of the poet Joyce Kilmer. The Ledbetters were to have stayed with the Lomaxes in their apartment, but when the landlord got word that they had Negroes as guests he threatened to call the police and, under Washington's segregationist housing laws, have them all put out of the building. The next day was then spent driving around town, trying to find a black hotel or rooming house that would take the Ledbetters in, and a place where they could all eat together, but when the Ledbetters arrived with white people they were turned away again. Lead Belly wrote a song about it, "Bourgeois Blues," to which Alan later added new words (when Alan sang it, it sometimes came out as "Bush-wah Town"):

Tell all the colored folks to listen to me,
Don't try to buy no home in Washington, D.C.
Chorus:
(Lord) It's a bourgeois town, it's a bourgeois town,
Got the bourgeois blues, gonna spread the news all around.
Me an' my wife run all over town,
Everywhere we go, the people turn us down.

The Depression may have flattened the country economically, but not spiritually or ideologically. America at its lowest was rich with ideas, each with the immediacy of potentiality. Every institution, from church to family, school to factory, was put into question, and everyone had an analysis. Some reached back for answers to the beginnings of the country, to a time when democracy had the feel of divine predestination. Others looked abroad, to the upheavals of Europe and the wide-eyed array of revolutionary and utopian ideas being played out against a background of rising fascism. If there was an orthodoxy in America, it was about making one's life count for something, of personal experimentation, of turning social upheaval into a vision of saving a dream. Some, like Ernest Hemingway, thought that the world was worth fighting for, while others thought that it was worth singing for.

When Alan moved to Washington, President Franklin Delano Roosevelt's administration's first efforts to channel social cataclysm into progress were beginning to be felt. New offices, programs, and initiatives were popping up everywhere, and existing departments were being redefined, subdivided, and redirected to new purposes and projects. The first goal was to get every person on relief back to work until the Depression was over, and most of the efforts went toward giving the average worker a job building roads, bridges, post offices, dams, levees, hospitals, and schools. But there was work for the visual artists as well, in raising the spirit of America, and in offering the country a vision of greatness and a future they could glimpse in a poster. Shopgirls, postal workers, riveters, and farmers began to appear in photos and on murals, inspired by similar tributes to Mexican workers portrayed by Diego Rivera. Images of people and the land were used to introduce one part of America to another, and to make the everyday iconic. The artists and visionaries put to work by the government developed their own democratic ideology, such as their notion that the people had a right to the best that had ever been written, danced, painted, or sung—it was a matter of "cultural rights." But just as the high arts would be made available to the folk, the folk arts would be introduced to the cultural elite. Folklore as an activity, as a subject, as a calling rather than an academic study, developed quickly under the New Deal, gripping the imagination of a people becoming aware of how deep and multifaceted their own culture might be. New strands were revealed within the country that were exotic and aesthetically new, but also very old, and they formed a baseline of America that all the artist-workers were discovering. "Everything local and native had been treated as non-art up until this period," Alan said, "or at best inferior to urban and European. Suddenly we opened up the flood-gates. The creativity of ordinary people, engaged in living in ordinary places, came into focus."

They were ordinary people, certainly, but also the very people who were the hardest suffering. Art, for many, was now the basis of a crusade for justice and cultural equality. It was a thrilling moment to be alive, Lomax said:

> The New Deal was the time the American revolution began again. It wasn't just dealing with the Depression, it was dealing with all the problems we had accumulated in the hundred years between the time of the American Revolution and then, through selfishness and greed and exploitation. . . . We knew what the problems were, we had been to school and this was our training . . . there were tens of thousands of us in that city, all related to the problem and given a go-ahead signal, do something. It was made possible by the New Deal. We had the ear of the common man. All intellectuals were involved; everybody was in it. The Roosevelts were marvelous orchestraters. We unionized America, we set the base for integration, we set it free from European snobbery. It was a time of exhilaration, a dizzy feeling. By God! We Americans were pretty marvelous.

The Works Progress Administration was one of the most important parts of this development, a massive corps of unemployed workers being put to work.

Within its ranks folklorists were trained, created, and set to work in the various federal theater, writers, arts, and music projects. Even John Lomax himself would join them in 1936, becoming the director of the Folklore Studies Division of the Federal Writers' Project, a group whose workers across the country contributed to the city, state, and regional guides that were being edited together for publication. They focused on the uniqueness and brilliance of the regional arts and cultures of America, did surveys of folklore in each state, interviewed garment workers, clockmakers, copper miners, and steelworkers, and then produced volumes of oral histories, such as those that came out of the large program of interviewing ex-slaves about their lives before emancipation. It helped that the president and his wife, Eleanor, themselves were interested in folk arts: Franklin liked a good fiddle tune and brought string bands in to entertain friends at his Warm Springs, Georgia, vacation spa. The First Lady was even more involved, inviting folk musicians to the White House and visiting folk festivals in the remotest of regions.

The Resettlement Administration was another home for folklorists, this one within the Department of Agriculture. Its task was to restore health and income to farmers and farm workers who had been devastated by erosion and wind damage, falling prices, debt, and displacement. Much of the farm population was made up of migrant workers, hobos, and sharecroppers, all of them now struggling under the weight of a faltering economy. The Resettlement Administration attempted to deal with these problems by providing loans and debt relief, introducing widespread conservation practices, and the creation of new communities for displaced farmers that would emphasize cooperation and conservation and resist future depressions. Model communities such as Greenhills in Ohio or Jersey Homesteads (now Roosevelt) in New Jersey were set up in several states. "It was [Rexford] Tugwell's idea," Alan said, "that we should begin to build a new kind of community in America over the makeshift communities that had been run up in the factory towns and in shanty towns around the country. He invited artists to come down to help him give these new communities a living culture."

The Special Skills Division was a unit in the Resettlement Administration set up to help train farm people in the arts and crafts to strengthen community ties and to give them the possibility of making some extra income. The division drew together an extraordinary group of artists: filmmaker Pare Lorentz; photographers Roy Stryker, Dorothea Lange, and Walker Evans; painters Jackson and Charles Pollock and Ben Shahn (who would soon also become a photographer). There was also Charles Seeger, recently out of work, and director and playwright Nicholas Ray, back from stints of study with Frank Lloyd Wright in Taliesin West and John Houseman's Group Theatre in New York. Seeger was in charge of music, and Ray was head of theater arts. They often worked together, with Nick traveling to a mining community or a farm town where he interviewed the residents, took notes on their livelihoods and problems, then sketched out a play for them, staging it onsite. Seeger then joined him to create musical settings for some of the plays. Along the way each of them recorded folk songs, folktales, or fiddle tunes, some of which ended up in the archives at the Library of Congress.

Alan met Nick Ray through Charles Seeger, and the two of them were drawn together by their common interests, but also by what each of them uniquely knew:

> When I met Nick in Washington in the 1930's . . . he was certainly one of the most splendid young men in the whole world. He seemed to be the person I'd always dreamed of being. . . . And I think I represented something equally splendid for him, the whole America that he didn't know anything about and I had already explored by then, while he was just beginning, because he was in charge of starting theater in rural America. He was just starting to think what it was about and I had already been to all those places and knew what kinds of music there were. So we could talk immediately about common problems: where he was far ahead of me was in thinking that you could restore or support all of these many American working-class structures with the techniques and the dreams of sophisticated theater people.
>
> I was the only person who had been out there with the Blacks, the Mexicans, the Cajuns, and all the rest. And Nick was one of the people who came and listened and took it seriously. Very seriously, and in ways that I wasn't aware were possible. His colleague Charles Seeger, who was a musicologist, added another level of seriousness in it for me, and we became a sort of trio of cultural workers in the city. So Nick and I were like Damien and Pythias, like brothers. He always understood without having to be told all I was experiencing; and he was feeding me back all the richness of a theatrical tradition and the sophistication of New York, which I didn't have . . . and Frank Lloyd Wright, this whole marvelous monument.

While Elizabeth was away on a trip to Mexico, Alan stayed with Nick Ray and his wife, Jean Evans, in their house in Alexandria, Virginia, and when she returned the Lomaxes moved in with the Rays, sharing expenses. The house quickly turned into a performing space and hostel, their guests frequently including the folksingers that Alan brought to town to work in the library or for some other function. They often spent nights in group singing, or in trying on new identities by attempting to sing in the style of one or another folk hero of theirs. But beyond the world of folk song, houseguests included the theater people who regularly visited Nick and Jean, including Joseph Losey and Elia Kazan. Losey, like Nick, had attended La Crosse High School in Wisconsin and had worked with him in theater in New York City. He directed *Gods of the Lightning*, the play about Sacco and Vanzetti that Maxwell Anderson had written with Harold Hickerson, and had become part of the Federal Theatre Living Newspaper productions in New York, producing political cabaret shows in the city. Kazan was a director and actor in the Group Theatre in New York, and had gone south with Nick on one of his trips, running into Lead Belly on the way. Alan also became close to John Hammond, the wealthy heir of the Vanderbilt family who was deep into Harlem nightlife and the jazz world as promoter and fan. Roosevelt's administration urged cooperation between the different New Deal programs, and there developed unusually high synergy and agreement on their various goals. The Library of Congress archive was expected to reach out to every other governmental group and agency that had overlapping interests in collecting folk songs, especially the Farm Security Administration of the Department of Agriculture, the Writers' Project, the Folk Arts Committee, the Music Project of the WPA, and the Department of the Interior, whose Radio Broadcasting Division freely furnished labor and equipment to make copies of these groups' recordings to go into the archive.

When John Lomax was offered the job with the Works Progress Administration that summer for $3,200 a year, he accepted it immediately. He had always hoped for a full-time job in the archive, but neither he nor Alan had received a salary for the last five years, and since his family had been living on his savings, the rent from their home, and the meager royalties from his books, he could hardly turn it down. He moved his wife and daughter Bess to Washington, where he had found an apartment on Capitol Hill, close to the Library of Congress. Now, with Alan and himself in the same town, and with Bess to help, they could pay more attention to the second volume of *American Ballads and Folk Songs* that he and Alan were preparing, which would ultimately be published under the title of *Our Singing Country*. Alan and Bess found a spot to work on it up in the library's attic, where the sound of the endless replaying of records would not disturb anyone. Huddled together like artistes in America's garret, they shuddered against the winter winds that blew through the cracks, and sweated through the heat of D.C. under the eaves in the summer. Each week Alan and John met with the two people they had asked to be their music editors, Charles and Ruth Crawford Seeger, and with whom they argued over every aspect of the book: what songs should be included, how they should be transcribed, and who the songs were for—teachers, folklorists, musicians, singers, the average American? And how would people use them? What was certain was that the Lomaxes wanted this book to be received as favorably by the academic community as *American Ballads and Folk Songs* had been by the public, and that meant providing more scholarly notes and more accurate transcriptions. As time went on, John and Charles had less of a role, distracted by other duties, and the main work was left to Alan and Ruth, with Bess as messenger, carrying copies of records and the manuscript back and forth on the bus between Silver Spring, Maryland, and Washington.

Ruth Seeger was not a folklorist, nor even a collector or a fieldworker, but a classically trained musician and a brilliant composer, the first woman to receive a Guggenheim Fellowship in composition. But somewhere between her political commitments and her devotion to her young children, she was drawn to folk song, and largely abandoned her ambitions as a composer. She had been a student of Charles Seeger's, who left his wife to marry her in 1932, and they rapidly had three children to raise, and sometimes even Pete, Charles's youngest son from his previous marriage, who occasionally stayed with them. Ruth approached folk music with the zeal of the convert, driven to bring everything she knew about music theory to bear on what most people thought were rather plain melodies. Like Béla Bartók, who found that Hungarian folk songs resisted easy transcription using standard Western notation, she saw that the singers seemed to bring something special to their performances, something that oddly paralleled modernist classical music in its hard-won quality and its resistance to immediate understanding.

Ruth's job on the book was to transcribe the tunes from the records, and she was deadly serious about the task. If traditional methods of music notation were not up to accurately capturing what was on the recordings, then what was to be done? Previous folklorists had elevated the words of the song to the higher position, with music always subservient, but those who believed in the power of recording were confident that the process had captured all the critical information about a particular song—not what the singer intended to sing, not how he would have sounded if he knew the song better, or was younger, or of a different race or class, or came from a town where the song was better known, or knew a better version. The problem, then, was what *was* on the record? What was that word? Was that note a C or a B-flat? Did the singer sigh, or was it a musical note? Was it twelve bars long, or twelve and a half? Ruth pledged herself to find a way to accurately represent on paper what she heard, even if it meant listening to a recording eighty-five or ninety times and wearing it out in the process.

Alan had recorded many of these songs, sitting with people on their porches, or in farm fields, bars, or churches, and he knew what they looked like and how they might have struggled to get the song right. He knew the aesthetic and the tradition that underlay what was recorded, as well as the pain and joy that the singers experienced as they sang. Like a Proust of the folk, he wanted to get all that into the transcription so that it would evoke the experience of recording it. A line was soon drawn between Alan and Ruth, each of them defending his or her perspective, and they argued endlessly over the details and over what they thought the singer might have intended, or whether it mattered. Bess recalled Alan complaining about Ruth's scrupulous transcription: "You tell Ruth that no blues singer God ever made would sing 'redder than rouge'—it's 'redder that ru(by)' with a voice break in the middle—that's why she doesn't hear it right."

"Now, Bess," Ruth would reply, "you go back and tell Alan and your father that I have listened to this song exactly 78 times all the way through [she kept a tally sheet], not mentioning single verses. How many times have they listened to it? Get them to figure it out."

Meanwhile, time was running out with the publisher, and the book was getting larger: Ruth wanted Alan to print multiple versions of the melodies they heard on different recordings, even when the song text was the same; she also insisted on including an eighty-page essay, "The Music of American Folk Song." By 1940, three years into her part of the project, Macmillan began to hold Ruth responsible for the delay in publication, demanding that work on it stop and refusing to print her essay.

It was quickly becoming clear that the archive could not record everything or everywhere in the United States, and that it would have to plan to get as representative a sample of the country's music as it could manage within its resources. This meant continuing to count on collectors to donate their materials. The plan the Music Division settled on was to send Alan out to selected strategic points in the country to collect, and to create a model that could be used to encourage others to do so. Eastern Kentucky was the area that Alan suggested they start with that summer, as the archive had only twenty-two records from the entire state. Just as his request was being considered, the Music Division heard from Harvey H. Fuson, a local collector, asking that someone from the library be sent to record songs that he wasn't able to include in his book *Ballads of the Kentucky Highlands.* A few weeks later a letter arrived from another Appalachian collector, Jean Thomas, looking for the loan of a recording machine to collect songs in the Ashland, Kentucky, area. This local interest and potential support solidified the idea, and the library proposed a two-month excursion into Kentucky, with phonographic and recording supplies, a gas allowance, and five dollars a day for housing, food, and personal expenses.

As he was preparing to go, Alan explained to his employers that the state of Kentucky was geographically and culturally complex and divided into distinct zones, the most interesting of which from a folk song point of view was likely to be the mountain region. On his second trip to eastern Kentucky he would look for singers by means of his new contacts, Thomas and Fuson, but also through Barnicle, who knew the area from previous excursions and would meet Elizabeth and him there. Alan also wrote for help from the state's senators and representatives, the teachers who worked in schools that had been set up by northern philanthropists, and Mary Breckenridge, who pioneered nursing services for the mountain folk. He laid out a plan based on his travels and what he had been reading:

> The shortest and best road to Harlan enters the Shenandoah Valley at New Market, Virginia, runs straightaway southwest through Staunton and Roanoke to Bristol. Then one heads up into the mountains through Gate City to Pennington Gap, and on country roads over the Big Black Mountains into Harlan. There one is in the heart of the mountains that have protected for generations a rich heritage of Elizabethan song, manner and speech, and at the same time have hidden the veins of coal that are leading to the disappearance of this tradition. And so one finds in Harlan and nearby communities the mountaineer—the so-called mountain eagle—and the miner—a modern workingman. Both types have produced folk songs, and Omie Wise [a tragic heroine from a Kentucky ballad of the same name] flows naturally into The Hard-Working miner. Here the mountains have formed culture eddies where one can find the music of the American pioneer, in all degrees of purity, in some isolated spots little affected by nearly a hundred years of change in the "outland," in others acquiring new vitality in the mouths of the miners. From Harlan, Bell, Clay, and Knox, the coal-mining mountains North into Pike and Breathitt, I shall be journeying backward in time and adding to the Archive materials essential to the understanding of the development of American folk-music, material that at present it particularly needs.

Barnicle would join them in September and lead them to the people she had met in the coal camps in Harlan, Pine, and Bell counties over the three or four summers she had spent in Kentucky. The local collectors that the library had urged on him turned out not to be as helpful as they'd hoped, and Alan was concerned that he was not finding enough to justify his trip. The coal camps were disappointments to Barnicle and himself, and when she left for New York to start the fall semester, Alan began to worry. He told Spivacke that he was on his own now and establishing his own contacts, and had made thirty-two recordings of ballads, Baptist and Holiness hymns, feud songs, banjo and fiddle tunes, sentimental hillbilly songs, and United Mine Workers' ballads. Traveling with the five volumes of Francis James Child's *English and Scottish Popular Ballads* and Cecil Sharp's *English Folk Songs from the Southern Appalachians* as guides, he knew what they expected of him back in Washington. But how was he going to do this alone?

Elizabeth was sick, he had the flu, the batteries were wearing out faster than he expected, and he was running out of needles. There were government forms and vouchers to fill out and mail, weekly shipments of the records he'd made, and his checks for expenses were not arriving on time. He'd been dragging equipment up hills and into creek beds. Recordings had been made in hotel lobbies, on front porches, and out of the trunk of the car. He'd fended off noisy bullies threatening the sessions and a jealous sixty-year-old husband with a knife. The rutted country roads were breaking the blank glass discs and shaking the car apart. And local manners demanded that "one has to make friends of the people everywhere one goes and that takes time. They simply won't sing for you until they feel that you are friendly or that you are friends of friends of theirs." What should he do? he asked Spivacke. Move faster, to be able to get something out of every county? Or take his time and cover whatever places he did visit more thoroughly? Spivacke's reply did not make things easier:

> Try to remember . . . that this trip is supposed to be the beginning of a nationwide survey. Please don't prove such a survey impossible by your own actions. Your visit was also supposed to have propagandistic value and bring in more material from others. This might indicate moving about a bit. Remember also our aim to get 300 records by this trip. I realize, of course, that the first two weeks are the hardest and that your rate of production should increase.

Alan's response was to redouble his efforts and to move deeper into the more isolated parts of Kentucky, places like Leslie County, where until two years before there were no paved roads into its county seat, Hyden. He spent two days driving through the road dust, stopping to talk to everyone he saw:

> The young people were so shy that it was hard to find out what their names were, but the oldsters, as soon as they had been made to understand several times that my name was such and such and my station thus and so were very willing to help. From them I learned the name of singers up and down the road—Betsy Napper, a seventy year old banjo picker and buck dancer; Singin' John Caldwell, ballad singer; Old Jim Bolan, the oldest Baptist preacher in the region; Farmer Collett, who lives on Jacks Creek near Roark's store and whose multifarious musical activity extends through harmonica blowing to fiddling; old Granny Space, 87, from whom Sharpe collected thirty-five of his best Kentucky ballads and who in years gone by was at the same time the county's best ballad singer and its gay lady.

At the end of October, Alan told the library that they were ready to come home. Elizabeth had been ill for weeks and had spent most of her time in the hotel, and even Alan admitted that the rural food was getting to him. But Harold Spivacke asked if they might stop by Akron on their way back and record Pearl R. Nye, a former canal boat captain who had already recorded a small portion of his songs for John Lomax four months before. Sick as they were, and tired (and "tired of making records"), they drove north to Akron and for two days recorded the captain's songs, many of them clear-voiced and finely articulated Child ballads. When they reached thirty-nine songs they were all three exhausted, and Alan and Elizabeth left to drive on to Washington. Though it was hit-and-run collecting, and he never returned to record the rest of the six hundred or so songs that Nye claimed to know, Alan arranged appearances for him at the National Folk Festival in 1938 and 1942, and the two of them wrote each other regularly for the next seven years.

At the end of each fiscal year the archive was expected to report to the library on its activities, which the library in turn reported to Congress. There was a standard bureaucratic format for this sort of thing, and Alan always bowed to it in his opening paragraph. In the year ending June 30, 1938, the archive had recorded 1,502 discs, with 143 added as gifts from other folklorists, and so more than doubled the 1,313 records that the archive had already acquired in the previous ten years. But even apart from the quantifiable facts, Alan's annual reports could have been published and read just as they were, as cultural criticism:

> The mountains have always been poor but, so long as that poverty also meant comparative isolation, the tradition of homemade music could survive more or less unchanged. In the last decades, rural music and the mores associated with poverty have found difficulty in resisting the competition of metropolitan intrusions backed by wealth and prestige. This condition is most marked in coal-mining areas. The miners only shook their heads when the titles of the old ballads were suggested, and the ballads recorded were largely fragmentary or sung by the aged or the infirm. In the purely agricultural counties, however, the story was somewhat different. There, where cultural competition was not so extreme and poverty not so marked, it was easier to find banjo pickers and ballad singers. From this point of view, it is interesting to compare the material collected in McGoffin, Morgan and Leslie counties with that from Harlan, Clay and Perry.
>
> The tenacity of homemade music even in the mining area, however, is evidenced in three ways: in the use of traditional tunes by union-conscious mountaineers in the composition of strike songs and ballads, in the tremendous vogue of "hillbilly" and cowboy music and in the resurgence of song-writing in the Holiness and Gospel churches. In Hazard, county seat of Perry County, two blue-jacketed miners walked into our hotel room one afternoon and asked if we weren't "the fellers who were catching mountain music," and then sang two narrative songs that they had made up about the union. In Harlan, Clay, Bell and Johnson counties yet other union songs native to this region were heard.
>
> The "hillbilly" musicians on the air have furnished another outlet for the homemade music of the mountains. Many of them come from rural backgrounds and their hopeful imitators in the hills of Kentucky are legion. The tempos of their square dance tunes have grown faster and their concern with the "mammy" song and the sickly sentimental love song greater, but they also sing some of the indigenous mountain ballads and "blues" and their production of songs is large.

They have been chosen by the producers of commercial programs, to the neglect of many interesting musicians, since the producers look for those who perform in the style of already successful radio artists; but there is a gradual trend toward the absorption of more of the traditional styles into the "hillbilly" broadcasts and this may be one of the important channels through which the homemade music of the mountains can reassert itself.

CHAPTER 6

Doctor Jazz

It might seem odd today, a time when departments of folklore have been dismantled to save a few dollars and the treasures of American vernacular culture are stored in the basements of university libraries, when folk music is the fodder of alternative bands from Seattle to Brooklyn, that a serious person could become an intellectual on the basis of the songs of the forgotten people of modernity, the music of those at the bottom of the greased pole of life. Even stranger that a young Washington bureaucrat could identify with Brer Rabbit, invert the values of the humanities, of government itself, and still become a personage in the capital, welcome in the homes of the country's leaders, even in the White House. Alan had grasped a cultural theme that was running through the times and traced it doggedly, obsessively to its end. He had gone out into the country, followed the road when it turned from tar to gravel, crossed regional, class, and racial lines, and lived among those "real Americans." Like his father, he could spin a homely country ballad or a tired field holler into a chapter of history or a sign of things to come, and there was no audience too marginal or elevated for him to address.

In February 1938, Alan began teaching a short course on folk songs for the Federal Workers School, an after-work program sponsored by the United Federal Workers of America. Every Wednesday at five o'clock he played to the class recordings that he had made in the United States, Haiti, and the Bahamas and discussed their political and social meanings. He encouraged the students to bring their own instruments and sing and play along. A few weeks later, he did a condensed version of his course at one of the union's evening musicales, never blinking as he followed another teacher who enthused about Haydn's Symphony no. 6 and Schubert's Symphony no. 8.

Though such one-shot lecturing opportunities were as close as Alan would ever come to being an academic, he never showed deference to those in the universities. At the end of 1938, for instance, he reviewed *Folk Songs of Mississippi and Their Backgrounds* by the much-revered University of North Carolina professor of English Arthur Palmer Hudson, and went far beyond the scope of the usual reviews of folklore books. As if addressing the Harvard professors who had taught his father, himself, and Professor Hudson, he began by noting that there were now thousands of pages of folk song manuscript piling up in libraries across the country, but little attention was being paid to interpreting their social context and the role they played in the lives of their singers. Hudson had set out to do just that, but when he declared that because Mississippi was dominated by plantation owners of the "same stock," their folk songs had no room for class envy or the "vocabulary of hate," Lomax was aghast. Hudson went on to argue that the unifying principle of southern life was an incipient feudalism in which the "privileges of a superior order were more or less conceded," something one could see reflected in the aristocratic tone and lordly manners of traditional ballads. Alan had grown up hearing all sorts of southern justifications for the evils of human exploitation, but when its folk songs were thrown into a pastoral rationale, it was too much for him to bear. Were "poor white trash" and "rednecks" not part of the vocabulary of hate? What was the proof that the songs were the property of the rich instead of the poor? The professor had told us nothing of the poverty of those singers from whom he had surely collected the ballads. If the ballads were models of life under feudalism, were they not also class weapons, like many other institutions of the South? Why did Hudson's collection stop with the oldest songs, with no sign that song traditions were still alive and developing? Where were the newer songs of the "fiery Holiness minister and his guitar-picking wife, the Negro blues singer, that traveling band of 'hill-billy' musicians, the indigenous union organizer," the "mouths through which American folksong is growing?" And why were there no songs from blacks, or any sign that southern music was the result of the mutual influence of white and Negro folk songs?

A month later Alan headed off to Indiana University, a school then emerging as the new center of folklore study outside of Harvard. In Bloomington in late March, Elizabeth and he stayed with Professor Stith Thompson, another student of George Lyman Kittredge at Harvard, who had also roomed in Alan's parents' house when he first began teaching at Texas, and who, along with John Lomax, was one of the founders of the Texas Folklore Society. Thompson was the premier academic folklorist in the United States, and Alan had interested him in a plan to develop a National Folklore Archive in the Library of Congress, an archive that would go well beyond folk songs to collecting folktales, legends, autobiographies, and other forms of folk art and knowledge. Alan was there to announce his new position in Washington in grand style, by presenting his plan at the first meeting of the newly formed Hoosier Folk Lore Society. Then, with the help of local folklorists and WPA workers, Elizabeth and he spent several weeks in Indiana, visiting towns like Deuchars, Evansville, New Harmony, and Princeton. They focused on collecting Amish and American songs and English ballads, and then looking for survivals of French music in Vincennes, a town that was once an eighteenth-century French fur-trading post.

From Indiana, Alan and Elizabeth crossed over to Ohio for some quick collecting trips in Hamilton and Akron, and to record some of the performers in the Ohio Folk Festival in Cincinnati run by Bascom Lamar Lunsford. But Alan thought the event was of poor quality, "a very sloppily run and stupid hill-billy show masquerading under the title 'folk festival.'" He hoped that Lunsford would direct him to the better performers in the show, but Bascom left before Lomax had a chance to ask him: "He gave me not one scrap of information about who was [a] folk-singer out of the huge drove of yodeling, crooning, Alabama-mooning Kentuckians he had assembled. I was able, however, in the course of the most horrible exhibition of Anglo-American, blond, blue-eyed sentimentalism and musical gaucherie that I have ever endured to single out a few genuine informants."

Part of his misgivings came from having seen the real thing in its natural setting, and resenting its commercialized dislocation. He had himself been part of the staging of smaller events in Washington and knew that better casting and production values were needed for them to be effective. The most successful of these presentations was Sarah Gertrude Knott's National Folk Festival, a four-day production that had moved from St. Louis to Chicago, and was the first to gather together folk and near-folk artists in one place to perform for national audiences. In 1938 the festival moved again to Washington, D.C., under the sponsorship of the *Washington Post,* and it was held there for the next five years in Constitution Hall, owned and operated by the Daughters of the American Revolution. They were eagerly attended by Eleanor Roosevelt, herself a member of the DAR.

In May, Alan attended the festival in Washington and wrote his father:

> It was the usual uncritical hash of everything you can think of and Miss Knott played her ordinary dumb but beautiful role, sweeping across the stage in a long white dress and pushing folk singers around like a professional checker player. All the folklorists, from Miss [Martha] Beckwith on down, spent their time in the lobby wishing that folk festivals had never been heard of; there is a move afoot to attempt to depose or at least demote Miss Knott.

The force behind these early folk festivals was an odd and wonderful Appalachian trio. Sarah Gertrude Knott was a regional actress from a small Kentucky town who had miraculously put together a board of directors that included every major folklorist except the Lomaxes, and had found backers that ranged from major newspapers to state governments. She even managed to enlist President Franklin D. Roosevelt to sing the festival's praises. Bascom Lamar Lunsford was a folk musician from North Carolina, and the real thing as far as folklorists were concerned. (His 1927 "I Wish I Was a Mole in the Ground" is one of the most influential and iconic recordings of folk and "old-time" music.) But he was also a lawyer and a politician, an educated man who had turned the Asheville, North Carolina, Chamber of Commerce's rhododendron festival into the Mountain Dance and Folk Festival in 1928, and since then managed to largely regulate and control who would be certified as a folk performer from the Appalachians. (Blacks, for example were excluded from the Asheville festival.) Jean Thomas had started her professional life as a court stenographer, worked her way into management in professional baseball, had been Cecil B. DeMille's script girl, and was in the nightclub business in New York City before she returned to Kentucky to collect folk songs and organize the Asheville (Kentucky) Folk Festival. Alan crossed paths with all three many times—Lunsford at one point worked for Charles Seeger in the WPA; Knott had ties to dramatists, folklorists, and governmental leaders; Thomas seemed to have already been there wherever Alan went in the southern mountains. The folk festivals, like the recording companies that sent expeditions into the woods looking for hillbillies and blues singers, were potential threats to Alan's vision of turning folklore into national art. And yet he learned from them, and sometimes needed their help.

When he reported to Spivacke on the trip to Indiana and Ohio, Lomax felt that what they had accomplished was "a partial idea of what happened to Anglo-American folk music in the Middle West. Both of these states, however, have been influenced more by currents of cultural migration from the South and less by the intrusion of foreign language groups and by the flow of migration from New England than other Lake States." So before the archive went any farther west with their national collection project he thought it important to look at the Lake States—Michigan, Wisconsin, and Minnesota—because they would give a very different picture from what they had seen so far. "In sounding folk-lore resources of this region, the Archive will be able to record what remains of their once vigorous lumber-jack culture, to explore the musical potentialities of the many foreign language groups of that area (Swedish, Norwegian, Finnish, Gaelic, French-Canadian, etc.) and to observe what have been the results of the moving of these cultures with the Anglo-American matrix." He proposed to record in that area in July and August, since it was not completely accessible in the winter months.

The amount of work he did and the plans he made were astonishing in their breadth and ambition, but at the cost of losing contact with friends and family, so that he often had to apologize to them or complain to them about his lot. To his brother John he once said that his "job, union duties, teaching, radio scripts, lectures, senators, visitors, and Spivacke kept me tighter than I am quite man enough for yet. I hope to God I can manage to ease up a little this summer and stick with something long enough to finish it. But what killed me was working like the devil all day and then having to play, sing, and talk somewhere at night. . . . For *us* life is complicated. Elizabeth and I certainly welcome the relative ease of the road when it comes." Angry at his father, he said, "He makes me wish sometimes that I'd never gone into this folk-lore work, because I'll always be called ungrateful and unnatural if I quarrel with him over matters that do not concern folk-lore."

In June, Alan was given an assistant and a raise to $1,800 a year. George Herzog and Charles Seeger were now consultants to the archive, which helped raised the importance of its work in the eyes of the library. But Alan reacted to the uptick in his fortunes by questioning if he was really worth it. He wrote his father, seemingly apologizing for his success or seeking some kind of reassurance: "The whole thing still seems a little bit churlish and certainly it has come my way too easily. I keep thinking that perhaps the best thing would be for me to let go with both hands and try something else that hadn't been handed me on a silver platter."

From time to time, Alan got calls with suggestions for singers he should record. Nearly all of them turned out to be dead ends, coming as they did from people with no idea of what a folk song was, recommending an older relative or a neighbor for a place on the Library of Congress's shelves. But occasionally he was led to the real thing: Justice Learned Hand, for instance, who collected songs when he was a child, happily recorded for Alan. Or a woman from Philadelphia, Kay Dealy Newman, who called about an extraordinary singer she knew, Jennie Devlin. What she told him sounded promising, and since Devlin had spent much of her life in New Jersey and there was very little in the archive from that state, he thought she could be an important addition. Once he heard her range of songs and listened to her life story, he saw her as a kind of indomitable protagonist from *Moll Flanders* or Samuel Pepys's diaries, or a virtual Dickensian figure. Rejected by her mother as a child, she was cast into indentured servitude, spent most of her life as a domestic servant, and yet had survived and raised a family against all odds. She reminded him of Aunt Molly Jackson, or the Haitian women who were servitors at the Vodou temples, women who were not merely singers of old songs but had learned songs with powerful emotional and social significance in their lives and those of other women. Dealy recalled years later that as Alan was packing up his recording equipment that day, he told her, "Modern folksongs are as important as old ones. All folksongs should be sufficiently collected so that they may be studied, and this race to collect special gems and then tie up the records, etc., is silly. We must show social conditions, not just songs." In the foreword to Katherine Dealy Newman's 1995 *Never Without a Song: The Years and Songs of Jennie Devlin, 1865–1972*, Alan said that Devlin and other women he had recorded over the years belonged to a feminine mainstream that had kept the traditions alive across the centuries. "Indeed, in my lifelong experience in recording folksongs, it is the women who most stand out as the great rememberers."

Somehow the word got around among hardcore collectors of hot jazz recordings that Jelly Roll Morton was living in Washington, D.C. ("where the shows come to die," as Alan would say), and you could see him perform there any night. Morton was the bartender, maître d', entertainer, and part owner of a small low-ceilinged second-floor club over a hamburger joint at 1211 U Street, D.C.'s black Broadway. Once called the Jungle Inn, later the Jungle Club, Morton's place was at the moment known as the Music Box (though on the rare occasions that it was advertised it was also called the Blue Moon Night Club). He held court there, seated at a spinet piano in a room with a kitchen, a jukebox, chairs lined up along the walls, a few booths, and a small oil stove, amid tatters of primitif decoration left over from its days as the Jungle Inn—"All genuine bamboo," he'd proclaim to first-time visitors.

Ferdinand Joseph Lamothe was born in or around New Orleans in 1885, though many have questioned that date as five years too early to be consistent with the other facts of his life. (No birth certificate has ever been found.) His parents were both Creoles, the free people of color whose Haitian ancestors had come to Louisiana after the Haitian Revolution. His father left when Ferd was three, and when his mother remarried he took his stepfather's name, Mouton, and later anglicized it to Morton. Rejecting the bricklaying trade for which he was destined, he began performing as a pianist in Storyville at the very moment when jazz is said to have begun, and there developed a distinct style of piano that drew on everything he had heard, from the folk to the concert hall. From 1907 to 1917 Morton traveled across the United States working in vaudeville as a pianist and singer; while he was in Chicago in 1915 his composition "The Jelly Roll Blues" became the first jazz tune to be published. He moved on to the West Coast, where he married Anita Gonzalez, a Creole woman he had known in New Orleans, and made Los Angeles and the West Coast his base of operations from 1917 to 1923. In 1923 he left, alone, for Chicago, where his band, the Red Hot Peppers, made some of his most popular records for RCA Victor between 1927 and 1928, and where his music was published by the Melrose Brothers Music Company. In 1930, as the Depression set in and the new swing bands gained in popularity, he lost his contract with RCA and cut his ties with the Melrose brothers, who he said had cheated him out of his money. That year he moved to New York City with his second wife, Mabel Bertrand, where they struggled to survive for the next five years.

In desperation, Morton moved alone to Washington, D.C., in 1935 to try his hand at boxing promotion, but like so many other business ventures he had undertaken outside music, it went nowhere. In 1936 he appeared on radio station WOL in Washington, where he hosted a program called *The History of Jazz*. Morton undoubtedly was seeking to promote his own music, but at the same time he had created what just may have been the first radio show on jazz in the United States.

To most of those who stopped by the club in Washington, he was only an aging, failing musician who had run out of luck. But to cognoscenti, he was as close as they would ever come to a founding figure of jazz. Among his visitors was William Russell, an avant-garde composer and a percussionist for a Chinese puppet theater called the Red Gate Shadow Players. Russell, who would become one of the most important figures in the revival of New Orleans jazz in the 1940s, would continue to track Morton's life for the rest of his own, and produce the mammoth *"Oh, Mister Jelly": A Jelly Roll Morton Scrapbook*. Ahmet and Nesuhi Ertegun, the Turkish ambassador's sons, who were destined to be two of the most important figures in the history of the recording industry, dropped in from time to time. Murray Kempton, editor of the Johns Hopkins student newspaper and later one of America's great journalists, was a regular, as was William Gottlieb, a writer for the *Washington Post*, who would later produce some of the most memorable photographic images of the jazz life. Alistair Cooke, a young British reporter breaking into broadcasting by borrowing American folk song recordings from the Library of Congress to use for his series of thirteen BBC programs *I Hear America Singing*, sat with Morton while getting tips on how to play the blues, which Jelly Roll delivered "in that billiard-ball baritone he rolled out for formal occasions." "If you want to play the blues, boy, take it easy," Morton told him. "Just chords, and cut out that picture-show right hand." Finding Morton in such modest surroundings, Cooke said, "was like meeting the President at a shoe-shine parlor."

It was at the suggestion of Cooke that Alan Lomax dropped in. Of his meeting with Morton, Alan said, "He was trying to make a living in this night club in Washington, and there he was the ultimate host. When you came there he always served champagne . . . at his own expense. A bottle of champagne to the distinguished visitor, whoever that was."

Because Alan was focusing on documenting American traditions in their original settings, relatively undisturbed by the emerging commercial entertainment industry, he had not really considered recording someone like Jelly Roll Morton. Alan later made no secret of the fact that when he met Morton he was opposed to all that the musician stood for: "He came [to the library] with some friends . . . who knew him, and said he wanted to correct the history of jazz. He was the 'originator of jazz, stomps, and swing,' and he had been robbed of his music. At that time, jazz was my worst enemy. Through the forces of radio, it was wiping out the music that I care about—American traditional folk music." And Alan and his father had already written off New Orleans as of little interest to folklorists.

Still, this broke and largely forgotten man presented himself with dignity, eloquence, and grace, dressed in an aging but sharp and carefully preserved suit, with a lavish hand-painted tie of silk, matching shirt, socks, and handkerchief, a watch fob and rings of gold, and flashing a half-carat diamond in an incisor when he smiled. "I looked at him with considerable suspicion. But I thought, I'd take this cat on, and . . . see how much folk music a jazz musician knows. The first recording began by [my] asking if he knew 'Alabama Bound.' He played me about the most beautiful 'Alabama Bound' that I had ever heard."

Alan had intended to make only a few records with Morton, but he began to understand that he was face-to-face with what he called a "Creole Benvenuto Cellini."

> I said, "Just a minute." We were on the stage at the Coolidge Auditorium. A bust of Beethoven, and Brahms were up there. We were where the chamber music of the United States was being played. Jelly Roll felt that was just the proper setting for him. . . . He wasn't the least bit awed by that. I ran all the way upstairs into the office of my chief—Chief of the Music Division—and said, "Harold, we have an absolute great jam here. I want to get permission to use fifty blank aluminum discs. I think he'll have something to say." I think they probably cost altogether about $100, maybe $200, to record this man. On the way back down I decided to do a full-scale interview. I was at top-speed. . . . I had a bottle of whisky in my office. I put it on the piano. . . . I sat down on the floor, looked up, and said, "Jelly Roll, where did you come from and how did it all begin?" He then began to play the piano and talk. It came out of nowhere, the fact that he decided to do that. We hadn't agreed on it at all. Sort of half closing his eyes, he gave that immortal definition of his family, and New Orleans.

Lomax had recorded brief life histories before, and had written a short autobiography for Lead Belly based on his interviews with him ("Lead Belly Tells His Story" in *Negro Folk Songs as Sung by Lead Belly*). The idea of oral biography had been discussed by Alan and his father ever since John Lomax had first proposed that interviews with ex-slaves be conducted under government support to create a collective oral history of slavery. Alan had also heard that the Russian folklorists were beginning to write down the autobiographies of folk performers, bringing the singer or tale teller up to the level of importance of the song or the tale.

It was the richness and flow of Morton's story, the nuance of his speech, and the integrity of his narrative that really engaged Lomax:

> As I listened to it, I realized that this man spoke the English language in a more beautiful way than anybody I'd ever heard. He had a totally original style. . . . This man who had been associated with gun thugs, living in this very cruel environment . . . proceeded to speak the most fantastically elegant and sensitive English about culture, and character, and so on. . . . A gravel voice melting at the edges, not talking, each sentence bowling along like a line from the blues, like an eddy of a big sleepy southern river, weaving a legend, and as the legend grew, the back seat of the hall filled with [ghosts of] ladies in crinolines, listening. . . . Basically, he realized that he had been given an opportunity to make his statement in full. There was nothing in front of him but free time. I was at his disposal. The Library of Congress was backing him. Suddenly, he felt that he had the kind of recognition that he, in truth, knew that he deserved. I think that it made a vast difference to him then. He felt in good courage to start writing again, and start running recording sessions.

What ensued was a performance that lasted for over a month, a recitation of Homeric proportions, with Morton accompanying himself on a piano instead of a lyre. It was the longest recording session anyone had ever tried, with Lomax seated on the floor at Morton's feet, a pair of battery-powered Presto disc recording machines behind him so that he could reach back to change the discs—minimizing the breaks and sometimes overlapping what was said on one recording onto the next—but still maintaining eye contact with Morton ("the best position with somebody who's feeling a little bit insecure"). Despite the grand piano and the concert hall, it was still a field recording session in the Library of Congress.

Once they started, Jelly Roll paced his speech with chords on the piano, vamping his way through history, changing keys and shifting into minor as the subject demanded. When he sang he kept time by stomping on the hard floor, every sound overamplified by a cheap crystal microphone on a metal stand. Alan adapted to the epic unfolding before him, and the usual direct field interview questions—"When was this?" "What was his name?"—slowly faded as Morton found his rhythm and Lomax became his audience.

For Alan these recordings were a breakthrough in method:

> I later came to call this process "the cultural system," where people talk their images into a recording instrument or into a film, and suddenly begin to find that they have importance, what they have to say is significant. All that came out of the Jelly Roll interview. . . . This was the first oral history, and that's how it all began on the stage. Jelly Roll invented oral history, you might say.

Alan called these sessions the "Autobiography of Jelly Roll Morton," and later made a series of other recorded interviews he also called "autobiographies." When he first read John Steinbeck's *The Grapes of Wrath* it struck him that he had been working with people who talked like Steinbeck's characters. Recorded interviews such as Morton's were "almost like an analytic interview (only there is no couch). What I had decided on was a twelve-foot shelf of unknown America recording its life in prose. The convict, cowboy, steel worker, and so on." It was also a way of reconstructing the lives of whole communities of people. We may never know precisely why Athens was the great city it was, since its origins are lost in time, but New Orleans—the Athens of the New World, as Lomax often referred to it—was still there, with its deep history and its great talkers, and it might yet be possible to grasp its unique efflorescence. For Morton, it meant putting his story on record, creating history, something he had begun to do on paper. Now he would write in sound the first history of American jazz, and would raise the level of discussion about the music through what turned out to be the first musicological discourse on the music and its originators.

On the evening of March 26, 1938, Robert Ripley had W. C. Handy as his guest on his popular radio program *Believe It or Not.* Handy, a composer and bandleader, was at the time perhaps the most widely respected African American in the United States. He was a partially blind, elderly gentleman who, without possessing any remarkable musical creativity, nonetheless had published "St. Louis Blues," one of the most popular songs in the world, as well as a number of other blues, and had built a successful music business in the face of every conceivable opposition. In 1941 he would publish *Father of the Blues,* an inspirational autobiography that testified to Handy's belief in his country and his willingness to persevere in spite of all odds. The book was enormously successful, driving Richard Wright's *Native Son* off the sales charts, and ultimately was chosen to be distributed to soldiers overseas by the Council on Books in War Time.

Ripley introduced Handy that night on the radio as "the originator of jazz, stomps, and blues." This was all too much for Morton, for whom Handy was a fake, a second-rate, out-of-date musician, and little more than a shrewd businessman who knew how to capitalize on others' music and present himself as a humble, hardworking Negro. Morton wrote to Ripley, *Down Beat* magazine, the *Baltimore Afro-American, Melody Maker,* the *Washington Afro-American,* and the *New York Amsterdam News,* protesting the mantle bestowed on Handy. In his letters Jelly Roll asserted that New Orleans was the birthplace of jazz, and that it was he, not Handy, who had first created jazz in 1902, written the first stomp ("King Porter Stomp") in 1906, and used "swing" in a title ("Georgia Swing") in 1907.

(Morton was a bit more cautious about the blues, and merely pointed out that he had written "New Orleans Blues" in 1905, early enough, in any case, to precede W. C. Handy's claims.) Further, Handy could not play jazz, Morton said, as he was unable to execute "plenty of figure work in the groove ability, great improvisations, accurate, exciting tempos with a kick." What he played were folk songs, hymns, and anthems. Jelly Roll went on to accuse Handy of stealing other people's music and of not understanding the rudiments and origins of the jazz drum set. He also demanded that Ripley provide proof for the claims made on his show. Morton concluded, ominously, "Lord protect us from more Hitlers and Mussolinis."

None of this was of much help to Morton, even if he was more right than wrong in his claims. He was a leftover hero from another age, and almost no one was interested in his self-promotion and corrections of jazz history. But Lomax saw behind Morton's self-possessed mask a great artist who had laid the groundwork for jazz as we now know it and was keenly aware that he was on the verge of disappearing from musical history. "Jelly Roll had been deeply hurt. . . . He occasionally let that slip through, but not very often."

The dustup between these two elder black men piqued Alan's curiosity, and on May 6, just a few days before his sessions with Morton were to begin, he had recorded an interview with Handy. In it he explored the origins of the blues, Handy's inspirations and sources for songs like "Aunt Hager's Children" "Loveless Love" "Memphis Blues," Roll On Buddy," and "Olius Brown." It was a short session, lasting only six record sides, but it was something of a rehearsal for the Morton interview to come.

The Morton interviews continued through much of May and into mid-June, then were interrupted when Lomax went to record Jennie Devlin, and in August traveled alone on a field trip to Michigan, Minnesota, and Wisconsin that would last until November. He first stopped in Detroit, spending some time recording in the Hungarian neighborhood, then he found Sampson Pittman and Calvin Frazier, two black singers from Memphis. There, in the promised land of southern workers who had headed north in the Depression diaspora, he was hearing rural blues and dance music like "Dirty Dozens," "Welfare Blues," and "Cotton Farmer Blues." Then he crossed town to record Serbian diple players. All this he heard in a few days in a single city.

With the help of a professor at Michigan State Teachers College at Mount Pleasant, Alan was given introductions to several lumberjack singers. Another professor from the University of Michigan pointed him toward Beaver Island in Lake Michigan where there were some Irish sailors, one of whom sang for him more than one hundred songs. Although the community had a mixed population of Irish, Native American, Germans, and Poles, he found the island to be "the most purely Irish colony in the United States," with deep and vivid memories of Ireland even though only a few of those alive were born there. Crossing to the northeastern side of the Lower Peninsula, he visited Posen, a town settled by Poles, where ballads were sung in Polish and fiddle tunes from the old country were still played. In fact, something of a revival of older dance forms was then under way in both Posen and Detroit. But at the same time there was a contrary trend, and local bands were all expected to play jazz and American square dance tunes, as well as Polish music.

In Champion and Baraga in the Upper Peninsula he found French ballad singers and attended singing fests that went late into the night. On he went, to Calumet, Charles, Grandville, Marinesco, Munising, Newberry, Greenland, Ontonagon, St. Ignace, and Traverse City, and in more than two and a half months he recorded over a thousand songs on 249 discs. It was a difficult trip, filled with various forms of anxiety ranging from exhaustion to loneliness. Among other things, he learned that he did not like traveling alone. Elizabeth was in Mexico working as a journalist, so he found local girls along the way to keep him company. He was plagued by equipment failure and shortages of money to live on. Buying food and drinks for the people he recorded, sometimes staging parties for them, turned out to be enormously expensive, and he had to beg Washington for more money and advances on his salary.

If Alan had thought that fieldwork would allow him to escape the pressures of Washington, he was disappointed. As a new employee, operating with media that were alien to librarians, he was being closely monitored by the library. He had to submit bills accounting for food, gas, housing, and other expenditures before he could be sent more expense money, and he had to project precisely how many blank discs he would need, and then justify either not using them all or needing more than he asked for. There was also the problem of paying for songs, as the library did not allow for that expense. In explaining why he hadn't produced as many songs as he had projected, he wrote, "Not that this country isn't fertile, but it is stubborn and the people simply can't see why they should sing for me without pay. This is a question we shall have to take up at some length on my return. The proper answer, when you are asked, flatly—'Well, do you get paid for this?' Nothing I have thought of so far seems to be quite adequate." While he was still traveling from town to town in the North, he was also being asked to complete his field notes from the Indiana trip and submit them to the Librarian, and there was pressure to turn in his final report on the Haitian trip. The bureaucracy in Washington was turning the gentlemanly art of collecting into industrialized labor, and at low pay at that.

When he returned from field trips there was a large volume of letter writing to do, as it was Lomax's practice to write each person he had spent time with to thank them, exchange some news, and sometimes make plans for another visit. These correspondences often continued for years, a number of them throughout his lifetime. After catching up with the mail for this trip, he had vacation time coming, though the Jelly Roll Morton recording sessions were still preoccupying him. He and Nick Ray had also sketched out a play on "the growth of jazz," and the two of them went off to Maryland for a week to work on it.

On December 14 the interviews with Jelly Roll Morton resumed and were completed, probably at a different location, since Jelly Roll played guitar on this session. Other interviews with Morton were taken down and recorded by a stenographer. There was also a chronology of Morton's life, a list of New Orleans musicians and their characteristics, details on hoodoo, and thoughts on everyday life in New Orleans. On his own, Jelly Roll wrote out short accounts of his early travels, lists of pimps' names from New Orleans, and the story of the club he managed in Chicago in 1926, the Elite No. 2.

There was a passion for detail in Morton's entire narrative that suggests that he not only feared that his own contribution was not appreciated, but that the importance of New Orleans to American culture was being forgotten. Like James Joyce writing *Ulysses,* Morton set out to immortalize the Crescent City for those to whom it was lost or never known. New Orleans's institutions and community rituals were described, its street life evoked with descriptions of the social clubs like the Broadway Swells and the High Arts; the many parades; the very public and communal funerals, with their wakes and feasts and singing, the processions they called the second line, and the fights that sometimes followed; and Mardi Gras, with its costumes and masked balls. Morton was among the first to describe the rituals and performances of the Mardi Gras Indians.

When Morton laid out his theory of jazz, he noted that "jazz is based on strictly music" and said that it used ideas drawn from operas, symphonies, and overtures: "There is nothing finer than jazz music," he said, "because it comes from everything of the finest class music." When these interviews were first issued for sale on records in 1947, the notes by art critic Rudi Blesh that accompanied them went to some pains to explain that Jelly Roll was attempting to confront the prejudice against non-European-based music that was widespread in 1938 (and remains even today in many music departments and conservatories), as well as to mock the then-popular urge to make jazz more like classical music. Blesh went further and argued that by the 1940s classical music had itself become debased and commercial, and that the only truly serious music of the times was jazz:

> Today, however, the divine right of "serious" music is growing a little thin. One famous conductor performs for animated motion picture cartoons; another plays

> fourth-rate imitations of syncopated boogie woogie in the films; while a Wagnerian tenor, the "greatest of our generation," sings Tin Pan Alley trash on the radio. Today, questions that few dared ask ten short years ago are being asked. Where is the "art for art's sake" of serious music, once so revered, now a saleable commodity of the music appreciation racket? Where in all contemporary "serious" music is to be found the hot, vital, revolutionary creativity of great jazz music? Where else is to be found the devotion that great jazz players, through decades of want and misunderstanding, have given us in their music?

Only days after starting the Morton interviews, Lomax was beginning to dream up ways of bringing Jelly Roll and the music of his era back into the limelight, and he started searching for others who might share his enthusiasm. Earlier that year the *New York Times* music critic Olin Downes had been put in charge of all of the musical events for the World's Fair of 1939, a spectacle that carried unusual weight in a world struggling to pull itself out of the Depression, fending off the onset of war, and desperate for forms of entertainment that were emblematic of better days. Downes was the obvious choice for the job, a hearty, blond popular lecturer and radio personality, and a cheerleader for the composers he admired. His taste in classical music was not the most progressive, but his politics were leftist, and he supported innovative efforts to bring other forms of music into the concert hall and the classroom. Downes himself had conceived of the idea of short operas for radio, and encouraged Kurt Weill to write *Down in the Valley*, a thirty-minute collage of American folk songs. A few years later he and Elie Siegmeister would put together their own version of the Lomaxes' book when they published *A Treasury of American Song*. Now Downes was prepared to bring American folk music into the World's Fair.

Harold Spivacke, his boss in the Music Division, recommended Lomax to Downes as the best person to plan a series of folk performances for the event, especially for the Fourth of July festivities. Nick Ray and Alan set to work together to plan an elaborate production with the title "Yankee Doodle Comes to Town." It was a pageant that would cover three hundred years of New York City's history with a huge stage backdrop that grew and expanded from a dull green wilderness in 1609 to the shadows of giant buildings in the twentieth century. Two choruses representing "The People" and "The Mighty" would grow in size as actors in different sketches left the light for the shadows and then reemerged as members of one or the other group. At times they would represent the living and the dead of the city, at others they would be General Howe's marching army singing "God Save the King," only to be scattered when General Washington's troops appeared singing "Yankee Doodle." There would be Dutch and English folk songs, sea chanteys, pirate songs, American Indian music, and dances.

Behind their proposal was a form of populist modernism, a sophisticated sense of theater for the masses, hinted at throughout and then finally mentioned in the last sentence of their proposal: "We suggest these techniques as a few supplementary ideas, already assuming that we will utilize our experience with Living Newspapers, the Mayerhold [*sic*] technique and with folk plays to the best advantage." "Living Newspapers" was a new dramatic form being used by the Federal Theatre Project of the WPA to engage their audiences through presentations that brought history to bear on contemporary social problems. Actors planted in the audience, spotlights, projections, masking, ramps into the audience, and an offstage voice on loudspeakers that connected scenes and introduced characters were all used to jolt the spectators out of their passivity. Vsevolod Emilievich Meyerhold was an acolyte of Stanislavsky at the turn of the century who had broken with the master and developed anti-realistic and anti–Method acting techniques that attempted to stimulate an audience's imagination more directly and immediately. The "folk plays" that Lomax and Ray had in mind were the regionally based outdoor pageants and plays staged in North Carolina by Paul Green, a playwright who collaborated with black authors like Zora Neale Hurston and Richard Wright and brought them to the University of North Carolina in the 1930s and 1940s, wrote plays for the socialist Group Theatre in New York City, and cowrote *Johnny Johnson* with Kurt Weill. His folk plays were vehicles for social and historical themes specific to the region, but were aimed at working- and middle-class families and were filled with dancers and musicians, dazzling lighting, rich costuming, live animals, military reenactments, and special effects not possible in an indoor theater.

When Alan began to write the proposal for the folk theaters and entertainment on the midway at the fair, he started with food. The restaurants at the fair, he said, ought to serve "authentic food, drink, dance, and music" of the cultures they represented, and the organizers of the fair should have the right to "edit" these concessions and show them the commercial possibilities of a "genuine atmosphere." To frame these traditions, a giant "main street" would offer a re-creation of the French Quarter of New Orleans; a Pennsylvania Dutch tavern; a Haitian house with cooking, religion, "voodoo dances," and "the tempestuous history of this island for dramatic materials"; a western saloon with cowboys, miners, "gambling sharks and gay ladies, serving venison steak and whiskey with saddle nails for chasers"; a Down East fish house with ballads and chanteys; a Mexican patio with tamales, tacos, and tequila vendors with the ballads and religious festivals of northern Mexico and the southwestern United States; a Hawaiian house; an Acadian dance hall with food, music, and dance, but which would also be used to draw parallels to French cultures in southeastern Missouri, western Indiana, and French Canada; an Appalachian square dance hall; and an African American church and juke joint. In all of it, he stressed, these would not be staged re-creations, but lived environments, spilling into the street and the fields around it. Visitors were to join in the cultures, learning to cook and dance and sing and coming to understand the cultural bases on which these arts and crafts were built. And unlike most of the other exhibits at the fair, these would be fun, free of commercial influence, and free of charge.

Alan worked out the details for staging these cultural groups in remarkable detail, especially given that he was far from certain of being hired for the position. For the Appalachian square dance hall, for example, he specified that

> the stage [should be] a raised dais about eighteen feet in diameter leading down by a series of steps to a dance floor that encircles the stage, and around the dance floor, in turn, levels for tables. On the dais-stage, scenes from back country life will be set in the simplest possible fashion. For example, a pot-bellied stove and a big lard can will represent the country store. The actors will make their entrances and exits down the series of steps and through the audience that surrounds and watches them. The stage will serve to raise the performer to the level where all the participants can see him as he sings or acts or dances, even when a dance is going on the floor.
>
> Here as well, a demonstration group of square dancers can perform so that the audience, both on the dance floor and at the tables, can observe them and learn the figures. The action of the drama will be punctuated with numerous dances, and the company of folk performers can step across the narrow well of the dance floor and bring the audience into the action of this play by teaching them the square dances. In this fashion, the folk performers will not feel themselves isolated from their audience; and thus working under conditions to which they are accustomed in their own environment, will be able to unfold for the patrons their own culture in the most natural fashion possible.
>
> I should insist that in the break-down house, there be served corn bread, corn liquor, spare ribs, hominy, green corn, apple cobbler and all the other succulent dishes of rural America.
>
> Each table should be provided with a set of songs that will be sung in the course of the entertainment, and the audience naturally will be encouraged to join in the chorus.
>
> I have in mind at this moment a number of mountain people who could fit into the break-down house very naturally: Aunt Molly Jackson, Sarah Ogan, Pete Steele, Luther Strong, Walter Williams, Uncle Alex Dunford, Crockett Ward, Fields Ward, and many another.
>
> As for the dramatic material, the ordinary mountain square dance can provide plenty of this. Such affairs are beyond the religious pale in most communities because they are often times the scenes of quarrels, desperate fights, and a great

> deal of love-making. Into this picture the whole pattern of back-country speech and culture can be woven and I predict that all of New York will come to the break-down house to learn really how to square dance and sing mountain ballads.

What he was aiming for in this ambitious program was a means of helping Americans redefine the country to themselves and to the world by means of performance. But he also wanted to take these performances into the streets of the fair, both to reach the public and as a demonstration of the kind of popular arts that were disappearing. "Driven into the back woods by the radio and the cinema," he wrote, "popular art has tended to become the monopoly of professional virtuosos and big corporations. The World's Fair can, by falling back upon the ancient techniques of the strolling player, the Commedia dell'arte, the wandering minstrel, the medicine show and the parade, help to bring art participation back to the people and at the same time make the World's Fair the simple and merry people's festival that it was in the Middle Ages." The object was to engage the audience face-to-face, on the same level, in the spirit of street performers. "People come to the fair, despite the educational exhibits, to look at each other, to participate in hard amusements and to do and see things that are outside their everyday experience. They will look at a few wonders of science, but what they mainly want is fun; and they should find it in the streets of the New York World's Fair, free."

In the middle of it all would be the American Folk Theater, a concert hall and educational center for the popular arts. In order to ease audiences into folk culture and avoid the chaos of the typical folk festival, the theater would promote academic symposia and stage carefully scripted concerts that would put folk music in historical and aesthetic context:

> In [folk] festivals a genuine folk singer is forced to compete with a group of sophisticated singers performing folk songs and no difference is made for the benefit of the audiences between the two types of performers. The folk performer, therefore, is likely to suffer, since the audience is more accustomed to citified than countrified singing. An American Folk Theater, however, if it were carefully edited, could present a continuous series of programs covering all phases of American folk culture from the buck and wing to Katherine Dunham, from the mountain ballad singer to the orchestral suite, from the folk anecdote of the academic lecturer to folk tales.

The symposia he proposed—on the musicology of folk songs, on folktales, regional literature, the ballad, and the like—would connect to the performances in the theater, and create performed histories of popular song and of vaudeville. One of his suggestions, a concert that would show the development of black music that "led from spirituals to minstrel music to ragtime to cake walk to jazz," anticipated the "From Spirituals to Swing" concert presented by John Hammond six months later.

Somewhere in this array of performances, Lomax saw a chance for Jelly Roll to finally be recognized for his achievements, and he wrote Downes urging that Morton be given a key position:

> You may not agree with me that the ragtime-jazz-blues-swing tradition is the most important American contribution to so-called sophisticated music, but at least this tradition deserves a great deal of attention at the World's Fair. I have encountered a Negro here in Washington who might fit into the World's Fair program very nicely and who I think could represent this tradition as well or better than anyone I know. His name is Jellyroll Morton. He is well along in his fifties and grew up with jazz as it developed in the tenderloin district of New Orleans and spread up the river to Chicago. . . .
>
> I am recording for the Library all of his compositions, all of the folk tunes he knows along with very full bibliographical material. I think the musicologists of the future will find in it essential material for writing the history of American music. Jellyroll is still a great pianist and a fine singer and he has had wide experience in the organization of orchestras, in arranging and composing. He also knows personally everyone who has ever had anything to do with jazz or swing. He might be the ideal person to put in charge of the World's Fair Jam Session, without which, of course, the World's Fair would be musically incomplete.

In the end, a series of bureaucratic tangles and turf wars resulted in the musical events planned by Lomax either being appropriated by the director of entertainment's office or not being approved at all. The African American juke joint was made a concession for the owners of the Savoy Ballroom, the Dutch Tavern was built and sponsored by the Heineken Beer Company, the Hawaiians were put in the South Sea Islands section, and the theater production was *The Hot Mikado*, a black adaptation of the Gilbert and Sullivan comic opera brought in from Broadway with Bill Robinson in the lead and Whitey's Lindy Hoppers to back him up. Finally, in the cruelest of ironies, it was W. C. Handy who was appointed to organize the black musicians and entertainers at the fair, and who then went on to serve as a musical consultant to the next two World's Fairs in America. Olin Downes resigned in protest over these and other changes made against his wishes.

Lomax continued to work on Jelly Roll's behalf, advising him on copyrighting his music and on the lawsuits he was planning against Melrose Music, ASCAP, and the Music Corporation of America. Then, sometime in the fall, Jelly Roll was stabbed by a customer following an argument in his club. He recovered from the wounds but, added to his other ailments, the injuries weakened him. By November business was so slow that he and his partner, Cordelia Lyle, closed the club; and though Jelly Roll tried playing at a lounge run by boxer Natty Brown on 13th and H streets, N.W., he was dropped after a week for lack of customers.

When Morton talked about his problems with Lomax, Alan suggested he go to New York, where the World's Fair plans still promised some work, and where possibilities for recording and press attention were better. Roy Carew and Lomax helped him pay off his Washington debts, and Morton and his wife, Mabel, headed north in their car on an icy late December day.

John Hammond's "From Spirituals to Swing" concert, which was planned for December 23, was to be an all-black performance for an integrated audience, an event then still rare in New York City. But the bigger impact would come from the concert's program itself, a history of jazz from Africa through black American folk music to pop music in the swing era (Hammond in the concert program notes called swing the "Children's Crusade") to an art of the people, an expression heard more and more in those days. For such an ambitious undertaking, nothing less than Carnegie Hall would do. Hammond was from a rich and elite family (his mother was a Vanderbilt), and he had devoted himself to black causes and especially to jazz since dropping out of Yale. But even he could not afford to pay for the concert himself, and in any case he wanted the imprimatur of a politically progressive group like the NAACP (on whose board he sat) or the International Ladies Garment Workers Union. When neither would support him, he turned to the *New Masses*, a journal for which he wrote music reviews under the name of Henry Johnson. Hammond even did a bit of his own fieldwork (though he worked through a regional talent scout), driving south in his Terraplane roadster with classical musician (and later president of Columbia Records) Goddard Lieberson to sign up for the concert Mitchell's Christian Singers, mouth harpist Sonny Terry (Hammond had wanted Blind Boy Fuller, but Fuller was in jail, so he settled for Fuller's next-door neighbor and sometime recording partner), and blues singer William "Big Bill" Broonzy, who was to fill in for the recently deceased Robert Johnson (who also favored Terraplane autos). Hammond set out to find performers whom he considered authentic—that is to say, who would have never played for white audiences before, or were at least unknown to most whites. He also booked gospel singer and guitarist Sister Rosetta Tharpe, boogie-woogie pianists Albert Ammons, Meade "Lux" Lewis, and Pete Johnson, blues shouter Big Joe Turner, Sidney Bechet, stride pianist and composer James P. Johnson, and the Count Basie Orchestra. With all this talent and with the help of a few recordings of African music, it was a concert that set out to prove that this was a great art, one that stood alongside the great cultural accomplishments of the world's civilizations. More than that, it would show white people that it was blacks who were the masters of this music, and that what white audiences had been hearing as jazz was ersatz and counterfeit.

The concert's program drove home the poverty of African Americans, even those on the stage ("Most of the people you will hear are absurdly poor"), and what the latter had had to overcome to get there ("Jim Crow unions and unscrupulous nightclub performers"). The ads in the program—for the Medical Bureau and North American Committee to Aid Spanish Democracy, a new Clifford Odets play at the Belasco Theatre, Soviet films from the Amkino Corporation, and the Workers Book Shop—left no doubt about the politics of the concert's backers and producers. The concert was an unqualified success (even if *Time* magazine didn't get the African bits and thought that Sidney Bechet and Count Basie had leapt up the "evolutionary ladder from the jungle") and had been oversold, with four-hundred-some members of the audience taking their seats onstage behind the performers. (The next year Hammond would repeat the concert with different performers, adding Professor Sterling Brown of Howard as MC and Joseph Losey as director.)

Alan came up from Washington for the 1938 concert and said he "adored what Johnny Hammond had done in bringing boogie-woogie and [gospel] quartet music and the blues and jazz together in one place." Alan was so excited by what he had heard, he asked Hammond if he could record Albert Ammons, Meade "Lux" Lewis, Pete Johnson, Sonny Terry, and James P. Johnson. The day after the concert Alan, Fred Ramsey, Charles Edward Smith, Bill Russell, and the musicians all went to the Allied Recording Company. Before they began, Lomax encouraged all of the pianists to talk about the music or sing a bit. Lewis explained the origins of his composition "Honky Tonk Train"; Ammons and Johnson demonstrated various blues and boogie-woogie styles; Terry played and sang songs he used to do as duets with Blind Boy Fuller; and James P. Johnson reluctantly agreed to awkwardly sing a few bawdy songs and blues, since Alan seemed to have confused him with another Johnson, a blues singer from Kansas City. (James P. Johnson had accompanied Bessie Smith and Ethel Waters and written a number of stride piano classics; but he had also performed "Yamekraw: A Negro Rhapsody" in Carnegie Hall nineteen years earlier, had written two operas, and in 1938 was working on a symphonic score.) Two weeks later Ammons and Lewis became the first musicians to record for Blue Note Records, the company that a German immigrant named Alfred Lion created just to record them.

Once Jelly Roll was situated on West 145th Street in Harlem, he began to rehearse a band, but he wrote Lomax that the Musicians Union was not anxious to accept him for membership since the numbers of musicians who had come to town hoping to work at the World's Fair were overloading its ranks. Morton was disappointed that the Library of Congress recordings had not done more for him, and Alan promised to come to New York to introduce him to Decca Records executives. But when Elizabeth became ill, their meeting was delayed. In March they met again at one of Morton's rehearsals, and by the end of the month Lomax had managed to get him an audition with John Hammond with the idea of having the Brunswick Company record him. But Jelly Roll was stricken by a heart attack on April 17, hospitalized for three weeks, and advised to give up playing.

Lomax, meanwhile, was trying to interest jazz writers such as Charles Edward Smith to write articles about Jelly Roll in national magazines to increase his visibility. In September 1939 his efforts paid off when Morton signed with RCA Bluebird to record eight pieces with a band that included New Orleans musicians such as Sidney Bechet, Albert Nicholas, Zutty Singleton, and Wellman Braud. The session went well, but Jelly Roll was sick. Frederic Ramsey Jr., who was at the studio, said that Morton "tried to show that he could outdo the younger men, but emotionally he was walking a tightrope. He was doing a brave thing." Lomax then set up a number of sessions for him at General Records beginning in December 1939. The plan was for Morton to record a series of single records that followed the general outline of the Library of Congress sessions, but without speech. They were issued as an album under the title of *New Orleans Memories*. A series of recording sessions in January 1940 would prove to be his last. Morton continued to search unsuccessfully for work, traveling around the country, even going as far as the West Coast, where he died in 1941.

Music pundits have often charged Jelly Roll Morton with being a braggart whose only subject was himself, not considering perhaps that his accounts of jazz history and his own role in it might have been more accurate than not. Lomax, too, has been criticized for taking Morton at his word. Without a doubt Jelly Roll was a man of words, indefatigable in his own defense. But in truth, he did not brag excessively. There are some factual errors in his autobiographical accounts and some overstatements, but considering that he was improvising the history of jazz for recordings that could not be edited, and given that he was speaking to a generation who knew little or nothing about the history of jazz, a music that they as yet didn't understand, his was a generally reasonable, well-considered performance.

Musicians he played with in New Orleans like Albert Nicholas and Omer Simeon said Morton could live up to his talk and that he was the best at what he did. Danny Barker was one of Morton's staunchest defenders, and he became something of his interpreter, often speaking of Morton's presentation of self: "Jelly Roll never spoke of being held back by anyone. He believed in Jelly Roll and was not going to step off for anyone. Those trunks of Hart, Schaffner, and Marx clothes were his armor against those who would deny him and his importance. The diamond in his gold tooth was testimony to his status, that he was good for whatever he asked for, just as the two or three bulldogs he kept with him were marks of the gentleman he laid claim to being. . . . Jelly Roll was outspoken. . . . He spoke up when people weren't speaking up. And he could back up what he said."

His story had convinced Lomax that jazz had been developed within a small community, that it was only a very few talented people who had introduced the music into the fertile ambiance of New Orleans. In a word, they were a folk society. "I realized that Jelly was telling me the history of jazz, because jazz was a neighborhood project. Only a few individuals in this small, sleepy town were involved in evoking the music of jazz out of the broad basis of American Negro folk song. The Downtown Creoles could play their notes, but the Uptown boys had much to teach them. As Papa Big-Eye Nelson told me: 'You had to put the cryin' in your clarinet.' "

Morton saw his mission to be one of correcting music history and elevating this small community of musicians to their rightful place. "There was as yet no serious jazz criticism or jazz history. Jelly Roll was attempting to find a basis for such criticism and history. It was also a time in which the music that had been created first by black musicians was being taken away from them by the 'amusement industry.' Suddenly everyone was calling themselves jazz musicians. He himself had his rights to his music pirated away, and the contributions he made to the orchestration of jazz had been formalized in swing for millions of dollars to be made, while he himself had faded from the picture. It had been done by the tricks and gimmicks of the newly forming public relations industry."

Lomax believed that the changes that occurred in jazz were not just a matter of dollars and cents. "The industry thought it was loving jazz," he said, but loving it as Middle Europeans, as members of an American business culture—as a people raised within a different aesthetic. "The consequence was that they attempted to make changes in the music, beginning with tempos and organizational detail, and wound up with whites replacing blacks in the musicians' chairs. . . . It began as a bit of conflict and irritation and moved on to corruption." It was not so much the corruption of entertainment by commercial enterprise, for New Orleans had always been commercial; but it was rather a forced change in "New Orleanians' Afro-Creole Southern context" when the music reached Chicago and New York and lost its regional quality to become a nationalized music, much as had country music when it was first popularized.

New Orleans provided all the evidence Lomax needed to see what had happened. Jazz music had a pronounced vocal quality to it. "The musicians seemed to be singing through their horns, emoting through them, not merely playing with pure tones as in the European classical tradition" but using moans, animal noises, calls, and children's cries. There was bodily response to the music, among the dancers and the seated audience, and also among the musicians. When Jelly Roll stomped on the floor during the recordings at the Library of Congress, it was his attempt to keep the body within the music, to mark off the differences between European- and African-derived traditions of music performance. The recording process had not only denied the listener a means of observing the age, race, and gender of the performers, it also standardized musical procedures and removed the body in ways that buried style and aesthetic. New Orleans drummer Baby Dodds said that when he recorded with Morton's trio, Jelly Roll sometimes stomped so loud that it sounded as if they had two bass drums. And when he heard Morton's orchestrally oriented piano playing, with the various horns assigned to his left and right hands, Lomax saw Morton as hewing to an ancient African form of musical organization—with multiple leads spread among instrumental voices, with overlapping parts, all of it supported by a strong polyrhythmic sense.

Lomax was also fascinated by the role of the Creoles in the making of jazz. He saw Morton as practicing the Creole tradition of using cultural elements from any tradition that was handy and appealing. The jazz band as Morton understood it was constructed from European and African materials, and Jelly Roll had underlined this multicultural nature of New Orleans. It was French, Spanish, and English, but also African and American Indian. In that sense New Orleans was a Caribbean city.

> New Orleans was the only place in America, socially speaking, where you had many, many independent black musical organizations that played for funerals and for the benefit of the community, marching in the streets from 1860 forward. I think that is the most important thing about New Orleans. The fact that this was a town where the blacks were sticking up for themselves in the street with uniforms and parades, and able to make a statement. As I listened to Morton's story, I realized that I had never heard any American Negro speak of "music lessons." This was a privilege of the Creoles. They kept all they could after the defeat of the Reconstruction period. If they didn't have the vote, they were, as Jelly Roll said, "very organization-minded."

Some have accused Alan Lomax of being a "moldy fig," one of those fans who in the late 1930s and early 1940s regarded swing (and later bebop) as diluting the African American contributions to jazz. Like many of the jazz revivalists at the time, Lomax saw a parallel between folk music and early jazz, both being indigenous, emergent musics of the working classes, and both in danger of becoming corrupted by values imposed from the pop and high arts. He even considered moving to New Orleans and writing "a sort of musical dictionary of all the principal jazz breaks and riffs," locating them on the commercial records on which they were first widely introduced, then connecting them to folk songs and ragtime music that were their original sources. This, he hoped, would be used to show how these elements were different in New Orleans, Chicago, and New York, and how jazz came to absorb and accommodate these differences in its development. But he had also witnessed both sides of the social and economic equation and had seen people with few resources having their own creations appropriated, reshaped, and turned into American popular culture by powerful forces with different cultural assumptions and predispositions. More than merely reflecting his personal taste, Lomax was making a judgment about inequality and the forces at work on the aesthetics of American peoples.

> In just a few years you get the amazing kind of swing from Kansas City with bigger orchestras. But those people were all playing basically unison. The unison principle had taken over from the polyvoiced principle. And it's been that way ever since to the great detriment, I think, of the development of music. . . . I mean, New Orleans gave an incredible vision of new possibilities. And unfortunately the white world couldn't handle them, and so the music went white in various ways until the blacks were then taking off from the whites based on the whites' interpretation of the jazz, rather than from their own. And they thought that these old handkerchief heads down there in New Orleans were nothing, but they couldn't hack that [music]. Nobody has hacked it since. Nobody. There's nothing like it still. Nothing, nothing.

CHAPTER 7

Bohemian Folklorist

In the fall of 1938, at the age of twenty-three, somewhere between recording Jelly Roll Morton and spending a few months collecting songs in the north of Michigan, Alan considered straying from the true path. He had just received a raise that brought his pay to $2,600 a year ($34,017 in current money), but once again even this modest success heightened his concern. He was on the verge of becoming the best-known folklorist in America, but self-doubt haunted him. Was he also on the way to turning into yet another one-dimensional bureaucrat? Was this what he wanted to do with his life, or only what his father wanted? Did he know enough to do this kind of work? So, after only a year on the job, he suggested to Spivacke that in order to continue, he needed to take graduate courses at Columbia University, the birthplace of American anthropology, where the faculty took seriously the cultures of all human societies and where he could learn the anthropological approach to music from Professor George Herzog, one of the first scholars to be called an ethnomusicologist. Once he was back in New York he could also take classes at NYU with Curt Sachs, a European musicologist who promoted the idea of creating archives of world music and whose theories attempted to take account of all the music and dance on earth.

He asked the library to let him work only part-time while he began studying in the spring of 1939. In return, he offered an ambitious plan to record the folk music of New York, and while he was in the city that was home to the music industry he would begin "investigating the extent of American folk song items already recorded by commercial concerns" and create a discography. He would also complete the second volume of folk songs that he and his father were still working on with Ruth Crawford Seeger.

Spivacke was convinced by Alan's sense of mission and recommended to the library that he be allowed to go on half salary from February 1 to June 1; that he have access to a New York recording studio; and that he be given transportation costs and expenses to return to Washington once a month. To help cover what Alan estimated would be $250 for tuition and $600 for living expenses, the library would also ask the American Council of Learned Societies for a tuition grant. The council did eventually award him $500, but it did not arrive in time for him to pay his tuition bills until after the term was over. In the meantime, he applied for loans from various welfare agencies, and Spivacke lent him money on his own from time to time. Alan also got the occasional invitation to sing at parties in Washington for organizations like the Department of Labor and the Colorado State Society. He also performed for gatherings in the homes of senators, and since many of these events were covered by the newspapers, his name was soon recognized around the capital. Alan also sang for labor unions, at the social gatherings of government workers, and at cabarets and local bars; though he was often paid, he refused to call himself a professional singer and sometimes settled for drinks and food.

Alan and Elizabeth moved to New York City at the beginning of February and were put up by friends at several different addresses before they found an apartment in the Village at 124 West 12th Street. While he waited for classes to begin at Columbia he worked full-time for the archive, meeting with representatives of Radio France and the BBC about lending them recordings from the archive for their radio shows. He also began negotiations with Goshen College in Indiana to record more of the Amish music that he and Elizabeth had recorded there the year before. (The Amish were initially resistant because they feared that these recordings would be played on the radio and would be laughed at by the outside world.)

Within days of his arrival in the city Alan joined the widening circle of performers and playwrights who saw the arts as a key to political change, groups like the Theatre Arts Committee, which was formed in 1937 to raise money for the Republican cause in Spain. When he first approached them about working with them, they were in the process of adding musical performances to their schedule, and he became part of their first cabaret. It was held at the YMHA, and was important enough to warrant a feature in the *New York Times:*

> You'll get some idea of what TAC would like to do by scanning this list of compositions and performers: "I Hear America Singing," text by Walt Whitman, cantata setting by George Kleinsinger; Earl Robinson's "Ballad for Americans," words by John LaTouche, sung by Michael Loring and the American People's Chorus; Henry Brant's tone-poem, "The Marx Brothers—Three Faithful Portraits," Morton Gould, composer; Alan Lomax, American balladeer; and the Clarence Profit Trio, in some jazz improvisations, or—to coin a word—swing.

By the end of the year Alan was planning cabarets for TAC, scouting through Harlem with Lawrence Gellert in search of black singers, and doing lecture-performances at Café Society.

At registration for the spring term at Columbia, Alan signed up for three anthropology classes: two with George Herzog, "Primitive Music" and "Phonetics and Technology," and "Invention in Human Culture" with Gene Weltfish, a woman less known for her research in American Indian cultures than for her efforts on behalf of the rights of minorities and women—a commitment that later led to the loss of her job at Columbia after she refused to answer questions when called before Joseph McCarthy's Senate Internal Security Subcommittee. Alan also audited Curt Sachs's class on "Primitive and Oriental Music" at New York University. Elizabeth had become very ill shortly after their move, with what may have been a breakdown, and required nursing that they could not afford. But despite his studies and the constant care that Elizabeth needed, by working overtime Alan made good on his promised projects for the library.

He wanted to visit as many record companies as he could to hear what they had recorded on "race labels" (records aimed at African American buyers) and hillbilly recordings (the name the companies had given white country music), and to ask to have copies of the ones he selected given to the archive. This way he would develop a discography of the best American commercial recordings and organize them by artist, biographical information, title, geographical location, and type of music, "so that the basis would be laid for a really intelligent study of American taste."

Alan first contacted John Hammond at Columbia Records, who assured him that he could get him everything he wanted. RCA also promised to help, and Alan wrote the library to tell them about his successes. This was not the way things were done at the library, however, and Harold Spivacke asked him to let them handle these negotiations: he had already received promises from officials much higher than Hammond at Columbia that they could obtain what they desired. Spivacke informed him that he had also broached the possibility of Alan's producing reissues of commercial recordings for Columbia. But his instructions had come too late, and records were already beginning to arrive at the Library of Congress by the truckload. Spivacke begged Alan to at least listen to the records before he asked for them: there wasn't enough help to unload the trucks, much less to process and store the records in the library. Alan then traveled by train up to Bridgeport, Connecticut, to the Columbia factory to go through their catalogs, and learned that the company had over twenty-four thousand masters of recordings of hillbilly and black music, but no copies of records to be listened to. Much of what he wanted to hear had already been scrapped anyway, he was told. Discouraged as he was, he nonetheless went ahead with the project and worked his way through the holdings of Decca, Vocalion, and Bluebird (the cheaper RCA label), and made plans to listen to the records in Hammond's own collection and those of other New York City collectors.

At the RCA plant in Camden, New Jersey, he talked to special products supervisor R. P. Wetherald and to Frank Walker, who when he was at Gennett Records was one of the first people to record hillbilly music. What Alan found in their Bluebird catalog of hillbilly music and blues was far richer than he expected. Many of the songs on these records were in whole or part the very tunes he and his father had collected in the field, or at least showed the stylistic influence of those field recordings. Far from being corrupted by commerce, many of them seemed quite fresh. He was also surprised to find a number of songs of open protest, apparently recorded without the constraints or censorship of commercial interests.

He met with Jack Kapp and Art Satherley, the hillbilly producers at Decca, a new company that was building a large catalog of old and new ethnic and southern musics. He also talked with J. Mayo "Ink" Williams, the pioneering black producer of race recordings who had worked for Paramount Records. No folklorist before him had ever taken commercially recorded music this seriously: "My opinion is that the commercial recording companies have done a broader and more interesting job of recording American folk music than the folklorists and that every single item of recorded American rural, race, and popular material that they have in their current lists and plan to release in the future should be in our files."

Not satisfied simply to collect recordings, Alan wanted to take up Spivacke's suggestion of producing his own collections of reissued recordings. He had already discussed the prospect with Columbia, and Hammond and he were planning to do a reissue of the late Robert Johnson's music, and were considering new recordings with Jelly Roll Morton. When he approached the Musicraft Record Company to look at their catalog, he also proposed producing albums by Aunt Molly Jackson and Lead Belly. Next, he negotiated with Wetherald at RCA for his father to produce a set of older cowboy songs for commercial release, and for him to reissue three sets of older RCA Bluebird recordings. One of them was to be an album of square dance music, as there was something of a fad for it at that moment, especially in New England and New York City. Alan and Charles Seeger were to pick the records, but when they heard what was available in the catalog they were disappointed, and Alan instead suggested that RCA should record new square dances with some of the groups they already had under contract, with callers added. The Musicians Union, however, had recently blocked the recording of any singers and musicians who were not union members—and none of RCA's cowboy singers were—and the company had already canceled the usual recording expeditions they had been running into the South.

Alan's projects in New York sometimes became entangled. RCA began to use him as their expert to tell them which copyrighted folk songs were actually old songs that should be in the public domain, and therefore free for them to use. This meant that he would have to pore through songbooks and listen to records to track down the words and melodies of pieces like "Oh, Didn't He Ramble," copyrighted in 1902, only to discover that its music was actually drawn from the melody of an old English song, "The Ram of Darby." What must have seemed a simple matter to Alan quickly became more complex when he sent the results to RCA. The company wanted to see more than his opinions: they asked for copies of song texts and recordings to see for themselves that the songs were the same. They also asked him to judge the merits of conflicting stories told by musicians about who wrote what, and soon they were needing more and more versions and better evidence. It was a relationship in which he was expected to act as an intellectual property attorney at the same time that he wanted the company to learn to think like a folklorist.

While rummaging through record stores, Alan stumbled onto a large stash of leftover Paramount recordings that was something of a hidden museum of rural culture from 1922 to 1932—white country performers like Wilmer Watts and the Lonely Eagles, the Fruit Jar Guzzlers, the Blue Ridge Highballers, Cajun singers Soileau and Robin, and black songsters and bluesmen James "Boodle It" Wiggins, Bumble Bee Slim, and Sweet Papa Stovepipe—recordings whose scarcity and antique sonority would one day make them the most prized discs among collectors. Alan asked Spivacke if he could buy 225 of them at fifteen cents each. After this find, he wanted to go out to the Port Washington, Wisconsin, furniture factory where Paramount records were pressed to see if there might still be some more stored there.

It didn't take him long to figure out that it would take a good part of a lifetime to listen to all of the rural recordings, as he had learned that at least seventy-six recording companies had at one time or another operated in the United States. So with the small budget he had, he hired his sister Bess (then in her first year at Bryn Mawr) and Charles Seeger's nineteen-year-old son, Peter, to help him.

Alan had first met Pete in 1936, the year after Charles moved his family to Washington. He was then seventeen, a senior at Avon Old Farms, a Connecticut prep school modeled on a mixture of Eton and social consciousness that encouraged work for the poor and needy. ("It's where I leaned to use an axe," Pete would proudly exclaim.) He went on to Harvard, like all the men in his family, but with the goal of becoming a journalist. By the spring of 1938 he left the school without taking his exams and headed for New York, where his dreams of a career as a newspaperman were quickly dashed by his lack of experience. But he still managed to survive in the city by sweeping up trash at the World's Fair or singing and playing for dances at the Dalton School and for Margot Mayo's folk dance company. (Mayo was a Texan who pioneered folk music in New York and spearheaded the revival of folk dancing and square dancing there in the 1940s.)

Alan became Pete's guide to the city, enthusiastically introducing him to Aunt Molly, Lead Belly, and the rest of the folk crowd. ("When we were walking around New York, Alan would sometimes break out in a ballad at full volume. One day on Park Avenue he just started singing Lead Belly's 'Julie Ann Johnson.' At the top of his voice!")

Pete began working for Alan in 1939: "John Hammond told Alan that they were about to throw out a lot of records at the Columbia plant in Bridgeport, so he went up there and filled a car trunk with hundreds of them. He did the same with the Decca and RCA recordings. He told me to listen to them, set aside the schmaltz, and pick out the best." Then in the fall of 1939 Alan asked Pete to come to Washington with him, where for fifteen dollars a week he would be his assistant and learn about folk music by cataloging and transcribing songs, and continuing the quest to find the best commercial country records. "I picked out about one in ten," Pete said. "He wanted me to listen to banjo pieces such as those by Uncle Dave Macon. . . . Alan was almost completely deaf in his left ear, from an ear infection, and it only made him want to listen harder."

When she could get away from school, Bess also helped out. She recalled going with Alan to a small record company in New Jersey and setting to work in a room filled floor to ceiling with record masters. In a battle against the destructiveness of commercial culture, they had twenty-four hours to hear them all, as the company was destroying the records and melting down the plates used to press them. "We sat there in two chairs with a phonograph and listened to country, race records, anything promising. Alan had to have the best, and nothing but the best. He asked my opinion, and when we both decided to reject a recording, he dramatically sailed it out the window and down an air shaft."

Alan's long trek through the lists of commercial country and blues recordings was finally completed, or completed as far as he could go at the time, and it would be published as a "List of American Folk Songs on Commercial Records" in the *Report of the Committee of the Conference on Inter-American Relations in the Field of Music* in September 1940, and then made available in free mimeographed copies. Of the some three thousand records he had listened to, he selected 350, and those he listened to closely, classifying his choices in an elaborate system of styles ("hill billy in quality," "hill billy with jazz," "modern," "traditional," "revival," "Holiness") and importance ("representative," "fine," "very fine," "important," and "remarkable"). His very small list of "remarkable" recordings included Sleepy John Estes's "Diving Duck Blues" and "Milk Cow Blues," Blind Roosevelt Graves and Brother's "I'll Be Rested" and "Woke Up This Mornin," Memphis Minnie's "I'm Talkin' About You," Elijah Jones's "Katy Fly" and "Mean Acting Mama," Robert Johnson's "Kind Hearted Woman," and J. E. Mainer's Mountaineers' "Back to Johnson City," all of which were African American performances except for

Mainer's, but even that was a blues. What he found gave him hope for the future of American music:

> But I have come away from this listening experience with the certainty that American music, while certain folklore specialists have been mourning its decline, has been growing in new directions to compete with "thick" commercial music, and that it is today in its most "distorted" form in a healthier condition, roving across the radio stations and recording studios, than it has been or ever will be in the notebooks of collectors. No better indication of this can be found in the scores of contemporary ballads and songs, some of them songs of protest, that can be found on this list.

On March 5, Lead Belly fought over Martha with an acquaintance, Henry Burgess, and slashed him repeatedly with a razor. Lead Belly insisted that he was defending her, but the police had their doubts, and he was arrested and placed on Rikers Island, with the bond set at $1,000. He called Alan for help, and Lomax found a bail bondsman who accepted fifty dollars to get him out, and then tried unsuccessfully to get the victim to drop his charges. Alan and Barnicle held benefits at her New York apartment to hire a lawyer for Lead Belly and to find money to support his wife. While trying to find a recording session for Jelly Roll, Alan also got Lead Belly a contract for a record date with Musicraft, a label created to record baroque and early organ music, but whose owner, attorney Samuel Pruner, was also recording the folk music of blacks and soon would become one of the early promoters of bebop. The advance for the recordings went straight "from Huddie's hand to the lawyer's pocket," Alan said.

Lead Belly came to trial on May 4 at a general sessions court, where the charge was lowered from felonious assault to third-degree assault, and the jury voted to convict him. Sentencing was delayed for a few days while the judge examined his prior prison record, and during the wait, Lead Belly walked into a store where a robbery was under way, overpowered the gunman, and held him until the police arrived. His actions got him a lighter sentence, less than a year on Rikers Island, and his "good time" there got his stay shortened to eight months.

Through it all, Alan fell behind with his studies, and at the end of the term was given credit for "attendance only" and dropped out of Columbia graduate school. Spivacke hadn't heard from him for weeks, and repeatedly asked him for news of what he had been doing for the library, reminding him that he was due to come back to work full-time on June 1. Though Alan did not immediately tell Spivacke about Lead Belly and the efforts he had made on his behalf, nor even about leaving Columbia, his work for the library took up so much time that he had little left in which to file reports. He routinely answered mail forwarded from the archive, met with foreign scholars when they visited New York, and advised the National Progressive Education Association on their American regionalism research project, even speaking at their annual meeting in New York City. And he was receiving so many requests to speak on American folklore that he was passing many of them on to Lawrence Gellert and Pete Seeger.

Alan had also begun planning for what he would do when he went back to the archive full-time. There was still more work to be done with Mrs. Seeger on the new folk song book. He corresponded with Vermont folk song collector Helen Hartness Flanders about joining her in collecting in her state, and applied to the Ford Foundation for support. Several trips to Vermont were scheduled for collecting, spread over several different weeks. He also wanted to go back to Michigan to record a lumberjack singer he had missed on the previous trip. Maybe there would also be room for a visit to the Southwest, now paying more attention to the people's lives and the communities in which he and his father had recorded songs. If there was any time left over, he'd spend a week or so with cowboy singers, maybe go into Mexico to see what there was to be done there. He wrote Spivacke with these suggestions, adding that he thought he ought now to begin making recordings good enough to serve as record masters, by using only one side of each disc so as to better preserve the surfaces. Spivacke was astonished by Lomax's ambitious plans and replied that "for the life of me I don't see how you can possibly do all of that in less than a year. . . . Personally, I shall be very satisfied if you succeed in completing a good New England trip this summer."

But at the same time Spivacke himself had been pushing Alan to widen his efforts, urging him to use his connection to John Hammond to become a writer and producer for Columbia Records, even before he left for New York. And in May, Hammond did offer him a contract to anthologize some of the early folk recordings on commercial records owned by Columbia, with the promise that if they did well he could go on to do other albums. But Alan and Hammond had become wary of each other, and Alan was not sure that the work would go so smoothly: "[Hammond] does not completely trust me in the matter of Negro material, but that he'll leave the hill-billy things completely up to me—he's a very impudent young lad, indeed."

In May, Lomax went over to Staten Island to Sailor's Snug Harbor, the retired seamen's home, for two days of recording eighty-two-year-old Captain Dick Maitland singing sea chanteys. The captain's songs turned out to be far older than those already in print, and Alan got him to talk on the recordings about how those songs were used aboard ships of the Black Ball Line and other vessels. He once again recorded Aunt Molly Jackson, this time for a talking and singing biography that took up sixty-one records. As with the Jelly Roll Morton recordings, it went beyond biography to become an ethnography of songs sung in the southern mountains, with her own thoughts about what they meant. Alan was now managing to pay the singers and performers he recorded, a practice the library had not been willing to allow on a regular basis before, and something that no other folklorist was doing.

"As you probably know by the papers," Alan wrote to Spivacke in late May, "I've been asked to play banjo for the King and Queen next week in a very august assembly of performers. Will Dr. Putnam permit it or not?" Eleanor Roosevelt was planning an evening of entertainment at the White House for the visit of King George VI and Queen Elizabeth of England, an event she hoped might encourage solidarity between isolationist American and war-threatened Great Britain. Recalling previous performances of folk music put on by the WPA, Mrs. Roosevelt asked their staff to organize the entertainment for the June 8 visit. It was to be a memorable occasion, and would be recorded, with only three copies to be made, to be placed in presentation folders for the king and queen, the White House, and the WPA archives. Charles Seeger was put in charge, and he quickly organized an evening that must have seemed like something out of the court of Louis XIV, an urban pastoral scene, with the Washington elite and British royalty encountering the likes of the Coon Creek Girls from the *Renfro Valley Barn Dance* radio show in Cincinnati, Nell Hunter and the North Carolina Spiritual Singers, Sam Love Queen's Soco Gap Cherokee Indian square dancers (using steps they had learned from many sources, including black dancers), banjoist Bascom Lamar Lunsford, and a cowboy singer. When Seeger couldn't find a cowboy who could sing, he asked Alan if he would perform some of the songs from his father's collection. But then the program was tinkered with by what Seeger called "the committee who is always hanging around to manage things in the White House [and who] managed to filter in some things that were out of key," namely pop and opera singers Kate Smith, Marian Anderson, and Lawrence Tibbett.

The officials at the Library of Congress were thrilled to have one of their own staff appear at the White House, though Harold Spivacke was worried about Alan's casual attitude toward the occasion: "I should like you to devote all your energies towards this for the next week. You will have to 'open cold' and must therefore be thoroughly rehearsed. . . . I want you to go over big, very big." And according to the *Dallas News*, rehearsing was just what he was doing, in front of a reporter in his apartment in Greenwich Village a day later:

> Young Alan Lomax threw back his head, thrust his fingers fast across the face of his blood-red guitar and sang a low, throaty lament. . . . This was Saturday, in New York City. But as he strummed along, his voice rising in that old song of men who lived in a day that has gone now, you couldn't hear the subway anymore.

> You could hear the wind waving the Johnson grass. You could see, not the bright shabbiness of The Village, but the blue black of a slow dusk. . . . "I'm no singer. I don't claim to be. I hope it goes well, though."

When the evening arrived, Alan was thinking about all those singers who had asked him to let them send a message to the president or Mrs. Roosevelt, messages he sometimes recorded, sometimes wrote out as letters for them. It was how he saw himself on his best days, as the people's messenger. And now here he was in the White House, on the first hot evening of the season, sweating in his borrowed tuxedo in a small dressing room downstairs from the ballroom and nervously fingering the few chords he would need for "The Old Chisholm Trail" and "Git Along, Little Dogies." It was a thrilling but daunting evening for a twenty-four-year-old, sitting at the edge of the source of power, the First Lady praising the performers, the king and queen of England looking small and a little faint in the D.C. heat, a grinning Vice President Jack Nance Garner with his fiddle under his chair, ready to join in with some Texas tunes if the opportunity arose, and five hundred guests. The only problem was, everywhere Alan went in the White House, people were bumping into him and then begging his forgiveness. A polite bunch, he thought, but awfully clumsy. It was only when he walked upstairs from the improvised green room that he understood what was happening: two men—one coming from behind, the other descending toward him—both collided with him at the same moment, then apologized, all the while putting their hands on him. "They told me later that some woman who said she was my aunt had warned the FBI that her crazy nephew was going to blow up the building." The usual protocol was of little help in dealing with a guest who might also be a terrorist.

The incident made enough of an impression on Eleanor Roosevelt that she mentioned it years later in *This I Remember:*

> One of the young men who had been asked to sing some folk songs had been reported to the FBI as a communist or Bolshevik and likely to do something dangerous. The charge was completely untrue and made by someone who wanted to be disagreeable, but when the FBI reported it to the secret service men they had to be true to their traditions and follow the tip through. When the young man came in after dinner he was "frisked" by our secret service men and then by the Scotland yard people, and apparently was so frightened he could hardly sing. I hoped fervently that he would not reach for his handkerchief during the performance.

The source of the trouble was a woman who had contacted the Federal Bureau of Investigation's field office in St. Louis in early June after she read about Alan's upcoming White House appearance. She told them that he had been arrested while at Harvard for "making Communistic speeches"; that "he had lived with a Russian-born Communist while at Harvard," "a Jewess"; he was now married to a member of the Communist Party; and that she had been told that Alan was overheard saying to his father at a family wedding in Dallas ("in effect") that "I am just as much a Communist as I ever was—if not a stronger one, but don't say anything about it for you will only get me into trouble." On receiving the report, J. Edgar Hoover asked the Attorney General's Office to determine if an investigation should be launched. When they failed to reply, Hoover asked again, and this time they took him seriously: the Bureau began a new series of investigations of Lomax that would continue for the next thirty years. Agents in Boston, Austin, Dallas, and Washington were put to work compiling files on his life, and the heads of Harvard University, the University of Texas at Austin, and the Library of Congress were all contacted, along with the Lomax family's neighbors in Austin and Washington and his coworkers at the Library of Congress. The FBI learned little beyond the fact that Alan was the "artistic" or "bohemian" type; that he collected hillbilly songs and cared little for his personal appearance; that he often took the side of the underdog, and once protested to the administration about the beating of a black man at the University of Texas; and that he sometimes brought undesirable-looking people into the archive. But no one they interviewed said he was a Communist.

There was not much that could top an appearance at the White House, but when Alan attended the Third American Writers' Congress a week later—a forum for leftist intellectuals that *Time* labeled a Communist gathering, "a flock of well-shepherded sheep"—he managed to keep the excitement going. Following a talk by Edvard Beneš, the exiled president of the recently overrun Czechoslovakia, he sang at a reception at Carnegie Hall where writers like Sylvia Townsend Warner, Dorothy Parker, Dashiell Hammett, and Thomas Mann were gathered. The next day he spoke on a panel at the New School for Social Research that included the presidents of all three radio networks. But Alan could keep things in perspective, and when the chance to collect folk songs arose anywhere, he was ready. Seeing Langston Hughes, he pulled him away from the buffet table and asked him if he had anything for him. Hughes later sent him a number of texts, including "Dupree," which he had heard in Cleveland. Alan put music to it and included it in the second volume of the Lomaxes' ballads and folk song books, and he thanked Langston, saying that it just showed "who should be collecting Negro folklore."

Unlike most folklorists of the time, Alan never hesitated to ask for help on musical questions. For a young man, an untrained musician, and an advocate of a music that most academics dismissed, he was nonetheless respected by many music scholars. Perhaps it was not surprising, then, that when the newly formed American Musicological Society brought together the world's music authorities for its first International Congress in New York on September 1, there were performances of medieval music scheduled at the Cloisters, Handel at Juilliard, colonial and Federalist period music by Ralph Kirkpatrick at the Metropolitan Museum, a trip to the World's Fair to see *The Hot Mikado,* a visit to Harlem "under the chaperonage of Wilder Hobson to experience American jazz in its natural habitat," but also "an evening of ballad singing by Alan Lomax." And just four months later, he hosted a segment of radio station WNYC's first "Annual Festival of American Music," a ten-day series that included composers Leonard Bernstein, Morton Gould, Henry Brant, Deems Taylor, Earl Robinson, Ralph Kirkpatrick, Wallingford Riegger, Elie Siegmeister, Vernon Duke, Paul Bowles, Roy Harris, and Marc Blitzstein.

By the early 1930s, radio had outgrown its novelty stage and developed the technology to reach across the country to every farmstead, rooming house, and mansion. There were those who grasped that it was the latest in a series of electronic inventions like the telegraph and the telephone that had the potential to knit people together, to create a country in synch with itself. They understood radio's possibilities as an educational force, a powerful means of communicating information and culture. But most of the owners of the first radio networks saw their companies as extensions of the entertainment business, whose profits lay in providing what they thought people wanted to hear and what advertisers would support. It was not until 1934, when the Communications Act was passed and the Federal Communications Commission was created, that the networks began to fear that unless they improved the variety and quality of broadcasting they might become subject to governmental control. RCA hired conductor Arturo Toscanini to create a symphony orchestra, and the Columbia Broadcasting System began developing original radio dramas with writers like James Thurber, Dorothy Parker, Archibald MacLeish, and Stephen Vincent Benét. Under this government-inspired competition, radio rapidly matured into a medium with distinct values and forms and its own auteurs. Orson Welles, for example, came into radio from the theater, and by 1938 his ensemble company was appearing weekly on CBS as *The Mercury Theatre on the Air,* performing adaptations of literary classics such as *The Count of Monte Cristo*. Their notorious production of H. G. Wells's *The War of the Worlds* interwove the new conventions and genres of radio so effectively that they convinced a large part of the audience that an invasion from outer space was under way. Norman Corwin, a writer and director on the same network, was so innovative that he seemed to be creating new directions for radio every week: dramas were built around famous poems or songs (Corwin had already shaped "Ballad for Americans" into a play starring Paul Robeson), and dramatic programs were written that marked news events, such as the bombing of Guernica during the Spanish civil war, almost as quickly as they happened.

President Roosevelt pointed the way for radio to become a national medium by using it to appeal for unity to a nation that was becoming increasingly anxious in the face of world events and the instability of the American economy. His Fireside Chats with the public began with a talk on the banking crisis at the end of his first week in office, March 12, 1933, and continued throughout his years as president. The role he assumed on his program was a mix of kindly patriarch and the nation's teacher. When letters to the president began to flood the White House in response, radio began to be viewed with a new sense of its power and purpose.

In the same spirit, the Library of Congress attempted to convince radio networks to program folk music by demonstrating to them the uses that the BBC and Radio France were already making of American folk music they had borrowed from the archives. Then, during a recording session in May, Alan was approached ("when I was very tired, broke, and dirty") by Davidson Taylor, the supervisor of the *CBS Workshop,* the series that initiated some of the most experimental programming on radio with broadcasts of *The War of the Worlds* and some of composer John Cage's first performances. Taylor offered him a chance to create a season of twenty-five weekly programs of American folk music for CBS's *American School of the Air* as part of a series of shows that had been developed between CBS and the Board of Education of New York City. It would be the most costly production that radio had ever attempted, with four scriptwriters, ten actors, five producers, three commentators, a fifty-piece symphony orchestra, singers, educational directors, engineers, and announcers.

Alan had never been particularly interested in radio, thinking it at best a waste of time and at worst a tool with the potential for fascistic manipulation. But Nick Ray saw its theatrical possibilities and its ability to quickly connect with a large audience, and he encouraged Lomax to listen to what Norman Corwin's radio documentaries were accomplishing:

> I thought this was a joke. I didn't know that anybody could be seriously interested in working on the radio, a pile of crap. Then I heard Corwin's broadcasts and I did a flip, I realized that radio was a great art of the time, there was a way to do it quick and straight. . . . I took the job, partly because Nick encouraged me and said it would be an opportunity. He was always a good writer, he had a sense of theater and drama, so it was with his encouragement that I learned how to write a script.

CBS accepted Alan's outline of programs, and they signed him for the next season, from October to May. He was to be the principal singer, on-air commentator, and the adviser on the script for a program that would reach 120,000 classrooms across the country. Each week, he would present a new musical and social theme: British ballads in America, the gold rush, love songs, lumberjacks, railroads, sailors, the American Negro, the blues. This was exactly the use of the archive that the library had envisioned: the music it had recorded and collected would be the means of introducing all of America to its many parts and regions, while at the same time communicating the government's interest in the vernacular arts of the country. But CBS had an even bigger idea. Alan would sing most of the songs, and the network would commission a series of classical composers to use one or two songs as the basis for new compositions to be premiered on each program—the folk supplying the raw material of art, the popular media helping it reach a larger audience, and the serious artists developing and refining it. That was how culture was supposed to operate in the eyes of the high modernists of the times, and out-of-work composers rose to the occasion. Ruth Crawford Seeger and Charles Seeger wrote compositions, as did Roy Harris, Aaron Copland, Henry Brant, Ross Lee Finney, William Grant Still, Nathaniel Dett, Ferde Grofé, and others, each for a $400 commission. For a song like "Rissolty, Rossolty," Aunt Molly Jackson would sing a Kentucky version:

Married me a wife in the month of June,
Rissolty, rossolty, row, row, row,
I carried her home in a silver spoon,
Hey, gee-wallity, nickety-nollity, rest of your quality,
Nickety, nackety, now, now, now.

Then Ruth Crawford Seeger's orchestral fantasy on the song would follow, after which Aunt Molly and Lomax would discuss a woman's life and work in the mountains.

Incredible as the opportunity was for him, Alan was uneasy with the concept: for one thing, he thought it was old hat, the sort of thing that George Gershwin and Paul Whiteman had tried to do in the twenties, an idea that people who didn't appreciate the importance of folk songs would come up with. He recounted the behavior of one of the composers—Aaron Copland (though not identified in Lomax's text)—when he was face-to-face with the music:

> I recall the day I took all our best field recordings of "John Henry" to one of our top-ranking composers, a very bright and busy man who genuinely thought he liked folk songs. I played him all sorts of variants of "John Henry," exciting enough to make a modern folk fan climb the walls. But as soon as my singer would finish a stanza or so, the composer would say, "Fine. Now let's hear the next tune." It

> took him about a half-hour to learn all that "John Henry," our finest ballad, had to say to him, and I departed with my treasured records. Not sure whether I was more impressed by this facility, or angry because he had never really listened to "John Henry."
>
> When his piece was played on the air, I was unsure no longer. My composer friend had written the tunes down accurately, but his composition spoke for the Paris of Nadia Boulanger, and not for the wild land and the heart-torn people who had made the song. The spirit and the emotion of "John Henry" shone nowhere in this score because he had never heard, much less experienced them. And this same pattern held true for all the folk symphonic suites for twenty boring weeks.

Even the format of the show bothered Alan, for it seemed to him that the producers had decided on it without really knowing him or what he could do:

> They didn't even listen to me sing. They just said, "Come on and start the program; here is a symphony orchestra." They didn't even know if I could carry a tune or not. They should not, with all of the American school children as their audience every morning at 9:30, present somebody that they didn't even audition just because he happened to have a job in folklore.
>
> The whole thing was ridiculous so I took this job only on the basis that I could have guests on the program and could pay them.

"I specified that I could have so and so many guests who would be paid such and such fees and that the Golden Gate Quartet . . . would be hired as the network's staff quartet," Lomax wrote. The Golden Gates were singers from Norfolk, Virginia, who worked on local radio in Charlotte and had recorded religious jubilees and secular pop songs for RCA Bluebird in 1937. John Hammond put them in his second "Spirituals to Swing" concert in December 1939, and shortly afterward they appeared at Café Society in New York. They were polished performers with a far smoother sound than most folk quartets, and Alan was able to work them into his radio shows as both singers and actors. This nationwide exposure he gave them led to their being invited to perform on the broadcast of Roosevelt's inauguration ceremony in 1941, then to make films in Hollywood and tour internationally.

Burl Ives was another of the singers that Alan added to the show, an ex–football player and fraternity boy from Illinois who had dropped out of college, bummed his way across the country singing and doing odd jobs, and who, Alan liked to say, had been sleeping in Central Park since he came to New York. All true, but he had also been studying at Juilliard and NYU, working Greenwich Village clubs, playing small parts in Broadway shows, and, just before Alan's CBS series began, appearing in a role written for him in Rodgers and Hart's *The Boys from Syracuse.* By some people's standards Ives was not an authentic folksinger (one singer accused him of having been "raised in lace drawers"), but Alan thought he could present a folk song convincingly. Burl turned out to be so popular that a year later he was given his own CBS program, *The Wayfaring Stranger,* which was named after a song taught to him by Alan. Lomax was so convinced of his potential that he gave him songs from the yet-to-be-released *Our Singing Country,* making John Lomax furious. As he had done with Lead Belly, Alan helped Burl build a song repertoire in the same sprit that his father and he had created their folk song anthologies, and in the long run his genial manner and taste in songs helped widen the repertoire and style of popular music by adding folk songs to it.

With Ives from the Midwest, the Golden Gates from the Eastern Shore, Aunt Molly from the Kentucky mountains, Lead Belly from Louisiana, Pete Seeger as the young New Englander with the five-string banjo, and himself from Texas, Alan had the beginnings of a repertory company that could cover most of American folk music. "We cut past the fancy ballads. What we had were the songs of occupations, the songs of women, the songs of blacks, the songs of the prisons and we went into every school in the country."

CBS Pix, the network's weekly press release, began announcing Alan's show in the middle of August: "Lomax, 24-year-old assistant in charge of the Archive of American Folk Song at the Library of Congress, explains the purpose is to show that America has an authentic music lore which should be as important and exciting to students as the works of the great masters." A large manual was prepared by Alan and CBS to guide teachers using the program in the classes, and gave them lesson plans and assignments. The program was aimed at children from ten to seventeen, and listeners would be encouraged to make up verses of their own to go with the songs, or to send in any folk songs they knew. No records would be used, and Alan or his guests would sing the songs.

Lomax asked the library for two days a week unpaid leave in order to travel back and forth to New York City. The library would then pay him $30 a week and CBS between $100 and $150, depending on what the show required that week, for a total annual income of about $4,685 ($65,081 in contemporary dollars)—more money than he had ever seen, but it had to cover travel and housing expenses while he stayed in New York, and pay various helpers along the way. After a nervous start at rehearsals during the first week, he got a hotel room in the Village and stayed in the city for seven days. He had woefully underestimated the amount of work involved. Over the last few years he had begun to learn how to write scripts, and he was mastering the techniques of interviewing and recording, so he thought he knew what had to be done. But now here he was, standing alone, audibly nervous in front of a microphone with his guitar in the middle of a huge studio before the Columbia Symphony Orchestra conducted by Bernard Herrmann.

That season started with minimal direction and a straightforward format: an announcer introduced the show, and Alan presented the songs. The singing was the main attraction, and children listening in school were encouraged to sing along with them. The first show's theme was "On the Trail"—songs of the cowboys—and Alan did all the songs: "Git Along, Little Dogies," "The Old Chisholm Trail," "Doney Gal," "The Lone Star Trail." Then the orchestra played "Sheep and Goats Walkin' to Pasture" by David Guion, a Texas composer who had built a small career arranging folk songs and writing compositions drawn from his Texas heritage. The show then ended with an orchestra arrangement of a Mexican love song, "Allá en el Rancho Grande."

The CBS people were happy with the first shows, as was Spivacke and the staff at the library. Alan's father, however, wrote him several withering letters in response to the first few shows, complaining that his speaking voice was ragged, stilted, and unnatural and his choice of singers completely wrong. John's edginess was one of the signs that their relationship had begun to reverse, with Alan now seeking funding for his father's collecting trips, acting as his agent with recording companies, and taking over the lead in editing their new book of folk songs. Neither of them was completely comfortable with his new role.

With his commitments in New York getting longer by the week, Alan now invited guests on his show to come and stay with him in Washington so they could rehearse at home, to help him keep up with his work at the library. His job description at the archive in 1939 read more like a work schedule for an entire staff of researchers and scholars than it did for a part-time worker. He was to answer correspondence; lead recording trips for the archive; plan collecting trips for other folklorists; supervise the cataloging and indexing of records and texts; prepare the annual report; assist in budget planning, grant requests, and press releases; lecture at universities, scholarly gatherings, and congressional groups; write and edit notes for recordings issued by the library; write and appear on CBS's *American School of the Air*; develop plans for the use of folk song in the National Defense Program; interest composers, educators, writers, and theater people in using the archive; convince recording companies that they should be recording American folk songs; and encourage institutions and individuals to donate their recordings to the archive.

Alan had pushed back his trip to Vermont several times, finally settling on November. As he prepared to leave, he received a letter from his local guide, Helen Hartness Flanders, a woman well known for her proprietary ways, who made it clear whose territory it was that he was traversing: "I am recognizing that by November

3, I am letting you come into Vermont to go about as I do, with potential addresses of unknown quantity." Flanders was from a wealthy industrialist's family, had been one of the founding members of the governor of Vermont's Commission on Vermont Country Life, and was the wife of one of the state's most distinguished senators, Ralph E. Flanders. Whatever tension there may have been between the New England matron and the young Texas New Dealer, over the ten days they spent together they managed to gather more than 150 songs, tales, and fiddle tunes in Vermont in the towns of Bennington, Chelsea, East Calais, Quebec, Springfield, and in Orford and Walpole in New Hampshire.

New York hummed nightly with one political performance or another in those days, and such events could always be counted on to fill the biggest concert halls, as they usually featured an incredibly diverse roster of well-known artists. Alan was asked to sing for a benefit shortly after arriving back in town, this one for the Spanish Loyalist refugees at the Mecca Temple on 56th Street on February 25, 1940. One of the most anticipated performers that night was a recent arrival, Woody Guthrie, a wiry little man from Oklahoma with his hat tilted back, his guitar slung behind him, and his voice as dry as the Dust Bowl he sang about. He had been coaxed to the city with a vague promise of a role in the Broadway hit play *Tobacco Road*. It was a long shot, but he was broke and hopelessly stuck in Texas with a family he couldn't feed. Woody hopped a bus to Pittsburgh, which was as far as his money would carry him, and thumbed the rest of the way to New York, arriving just in time to stroll onto the stage, scratch his head, and begin singing a couple of his migrant worker songs, as well as a new one, "Why Do You Stand in the Rain," critical of Franklin Roosevelt's brusque handling of a meeting with the American Youth Congress that month in Washington.

Alan had heard some of the extravagant claims about Woody, but now that he had seen him sing, he too was drawn to the rustic cool of his performance and the ease with which his speech and songs flowed together—like a country opera, Alan said.

> Woody was on the show. . . . He stepped out on the stage, this little tiny guy, big bushy hair, with this great voice and his guitar, and just electrified us all. I remember the first song I heard him sing. . . .
>
> *Come and gather round me children, and a story I'll tell,*
> *About Pretty Boy Floyd the outlaw, Oklahoma knew him well.*
>
> Well, I realized, listening to this song, that I was meeting a guy who was a ballad maker, in the same sense as the people who made "Jesse James," and "Casey Jones," and all the ballads that I spent my life trying to find and preserve for the

American people. I thought they were from anonymous people. Well, here was Mr. Anonymous singing to me.

When Lead Belly followed Woody onstage, it occurred to Alan that he could document and present Woody just as he had Huddie. After the concert he asked Woody to consider coming to Washington to visit the archive and record his songs and autobiography, and later appear on his radio show in New York. Alan's fast talk, his references to "folk" and "folk songs"—terms Woody claimed he'd never heard before—put Guthrie off. Despite his Texas accent, Lomax seemed too eager, too fired up, maybe just another city hustler.

To many who saw him perform that night, Woody looked like the real thing, a southwestern Walt Whitman, or, better still, the missing link to the working classes and a part of American history that would help authenticate their dreams of freedom or revolution. But Alan had no such illusions. He was well aware that Woody had been a radio performer and a reporter in California, that his father was a land speculator and politician, and that only a string of family tragedies and reversals had brought him to where he now was. Though he would sometimes call him a natural, Alan knew that Woody approached his songs and writing as conscientiously as any professional. He could improvise and toss off verses when he had to, but he worked hard at his writing, often deep into the night. He was not a pure product of the country, the passive heir to Anglo-Saxon tradition, but a synthesizer, a bard of a region of the country that was changing quickly:

> Woody came up in a frontier place in Oklahoma, Injun territory, which was new country, in an oil boom. And everything was happening there. The town was full of Injuns, Mexicans, blacks, people from all over the country, and Woody lived in those honky-tonks, and he picked up his guitar, and he learned how to make music that would make sense to all those folks. It was composed of ragtime, hillbilly, blues, of all the currents of his time. He made a new idiom that really represented the opening of this new Western frontier of new highways and power lines and Dust Bowl migrants and all that. It had the sound of movement in it. His guitar has the sound of a big truck going down the highway with the riders bouncing around in the front seat. It was a new idiom.

Alan saw Woody as a self-made intellectual, with the curiosity and critical ability necessary to succeed with a public tired of the usual politics. But he could do so without the canned corn of a Will Rogers, that folksy comedian-philosopher from Oklahoma, on whom Woody modeled part of his persona. Woody was a great talker onstage, sometimes forgetting to sing, maybe striking a chord on the guitar, then launching into a joke or story; or, starting to sing, he might be reminded of a story and leave the song behind.

Guthrie could play the hillbilly to perfection when it suited him. He would claim that he hadn't read *The Grapes of Wrath* or seen the movie, or seem to be as spontaneous as a jazz musician when he had prepared for hours in advance. The highbrow disguised as a primitive was a role that Alan understood and tolerated most of the time, the double disguise of the true revolutionary. Still, Woody could drive those around him crazy with his offstage posturing, sleeping on the floor, refusing to eat at a table, declining to bathe. Once when he came into Alan's apartment and deigned to climb into bed with wet clothes and muddy boots, Alan erupted: "Your lumpenproletariat act is too much, Woody! Grow up!" Guthrie seemed to be driven to test those around him, pushing them to reveal the extent of their belief in him.

After he met Lead Belly that night at the concert, Guthrie became friends with the Ledbetters, often spending the night at their apartment. To Woody, it was Lead Belly who was the real thing, who had been tossed into southern prisons as brutal as concentration camps (which is what Alan called them) and survived them physically and spiritually, who had come out of them whole and laughing and joyous and confident. Lead Belly, for his part, saw Woody as proof that some poor white folks could be decent people and understand the plight of black folks. Woody often defended him to blacks who criticized Lead Belly for working and living with a white man. Both singers came from oil boomtowns in the Southwest and knew many of the same songs, the stories of the cowboys, the epics of the railroad workers, oil riggers, and hobos, the plights of lonely women and men, the ballads of the brokenhearted. They had come up at a moment when the old West was giving way to the new, the country opening up, and like everyone else they had suffered from the fragmentation of a society under the pressure of industrialism. "Their music has grabbed the attention of the world because it sums up the whole country," Lomax said. "It has everything in it: ballads, mountain music, ragtime, jazz, blues, and yet remains a genuine rural folk music that doesn't depart from the canons of that." Lead Belly and Woody were recording just at the moment when the commercialization of all forms of music was beginning, and were among the last performers to come of age without electrical amplification or the demands of the recording studio.

> The guy in back of the glass there, a person who had no knowledge of what the songs actually signified emotionally, was saying, "Oh, put in a little bit more of that, do a little bit more this way. No, no, that's too long. No, speed it up! Slow it down! Stomp your foot harder!" and so forth. Lead Belly and Woody managed to

escape that and brought their pure country style right to town. They liked each other for that reason. And Woody learned from Lead Belly. Some of his best things are based on Lead Belly tunes. And I think they were of enormous help to each other, because they were, aside from Sonny Terry and Brownie McGhee, the only folk singers in the city at the time.

John Ford's film of John Steinbeck's novel *The Grapes of Wrath* opened to a packed house in New York in late January 1940, and continued to pull in audiences for weeks. Taking advantage of the film's success, a folk music benefit was staged for a committee that Steinbeck had formed to aid farm workers. The organizer of the event was Will Geer, an actor who had built his reputation as a Shakespearean in the 1930s, but by 1940 was appearing in *Tobacco Road*, a play that, like the novel of rural Depression life on which it was based, had been a critical failure, a target of censors, but a huge success with its audience, eventually running for over seven years in New York. Offstage, Geer was fiercely active in social causes and union organizing, and did stints in political theater and cabaret, all of which would lead to him being blacklisted in 1951 by the House Un-American Activities Committee and kept out of work until the 1960s, when he returned to win awards for his film acting and his work on the TV series *The Waltons*.

At midnight on March 3, the "Grapes of Wrath Evening" benefit opened on the stage of the Forrest, the theater where *Tobacco Road* was playing, with Geer, Aunt Molly Jackson, Alan and Bess Lomax, the Golden Gate Quartet, Lead Belly, Burl Ives, Josh White, Richard Dyer-Bennet, Pete Seeger, Woody Guthrie (who kept calling it "the Rapes of Graft"), and others performing before a large audience and a curious press. Alan would later proclaim this the moment when the folk revival in America was born.

Before Woody could drift off, Alan finally got him to agree to be a regular guest on his *American School of the Air* radio program and to come to visit him in Washington. For a month that summer, Guthrie stayed with the Lomaxes and the Rays, and Alan took him into the archive and played him records, and talked to him about the folklore of the American people and its importance for the political moment. When Woody agreed to record for him, Alan wanted to use the best-quality record blanks to do it, so they moved over to the Department of the Interior's studios and engaged a professional engineer, Jerome Wiesner. Later Wiesner would travel with Alan as recording engineer, and the two of them began experimenting with innovative recording techniques such as multitracking and editing. (When World War II began, Wiesner became one of the early developers of radar, rising up in the science world until he became adviser to President John F. Kennedy, and ending his career as president of the Massachusetts Institute of Technology.)

Woody recorded for Alan and Elizabeth three days straight until seventeen 16-inch aluminum discs were filled. He sang and played forty songs, talked about his life, and answered questions. It was oral autobiography, but a very different one from Jelly Roll Morton's. Since Alan planned to use the recordings for a radio program called "Dust Bowl Ballads," some of the recordings were sketched out in advance, if not actually scripted, with Alan introducing each day's sessions on the first disc, and then closing out the day's last recording as if a program were just ending. Woody swept through his entire repertoire of blues, ballads, church music, and songs about the migrants who fled west from the drought that uprooted them in the middle of the Depression. Some of the songs were prompted or set up by Alan, and he steered Woody away from some subjects and toward others.

But Alan was not happy about all of the songs that Woody chose to sing. He found some of them "thin," and he may even have taught Woody a few other songs to replace them. Still, he was less of a director than on his sessions with Lead Belly. He sensed that Guthrie was still developing, working out his own creative destiny, and tried to leave him alone to do so. It was not purity of tradition that he wanted from him, but to get him before the public as quickly as possible. Still, there was a vérité feel to the sessions, the songs interspersed with stories of Guthrie's early life, his family, travels, and occupations, with some of his memories evoking strong emotions in him, as well as some humor:

LOMAX: When did you make that one up, Woody?
GUTHRIE: Yesterday up in your office. (laughter)
LOMAX: Where did you come up with the idea of it?
GUTHRIE: Well, I was looking through a magazine here . . .

For the radio version of Guthrie's interview, Alan asked him to write out a few paragraphs about his life that he could use in the script. After a night at a borrowed typewriter, Woody came back with twenty-five single-spaced pages that Lomax said were "a kind of combination of Joyce, Mark Twain, and the musical *Oklahoma* . . . something that I had tried to write myself, and I had dreamed about but there it was, on the paper." He rushed a copy of it off to an editor he knew, who also became excited by what he read.

Alan was aiming to make this the most complete documentation of any singer who had ever lived, and he had no end of ideas of how it should be done. Woody could write out all the songs he knew and he would help him make a book out of them; he told him that he was going to start keeping his letters, and suggested Woody do the same with his; maybe they'd write a folk opera together. Another thought was that Woody, Pete Seeger, and Alan would put together a book of protest and workers' songs drawn from the Lomax collections, the archive's holdings, commercial recordings, mimeographed song sheets from union labor schools in Tennessee and Georgia, and wherever else they could find them. It would be "a testament to an unknown America, the folk poets who had been politically active and still kept their gift for song-making," as Seeger put it. Using Woody's phrase for a title, *Hard Hitting Songs for Hard-Hit People* was completed in rough form by 1940, with a foreword by John Steinbeck and a lengthy autobiographical statement by Woody. Woody also wrote the introduction, since he had lived the life the songs were about, and he and Pete transcribed words from commercial recordings and did the final work of assembling it.

This book would be a triumph for the kind of song collecting Alan had done. The scholar-collectors treated the songs they gathered as nostalgic remnants of a simpler life. They had never stood in the cornfields or sat in the workers' shacks, nor had they come to see the singers they heard as poor people, full of anger and pain. This collection would vindicate Alan's approach by revealing that protest against injustice could be found even among the older singers and the hillbilly and race recordings sold across the South, as well as in the repertoires of the younger folk poets. Still, such songs were not an easy sell: they were not the sort of thing that children sang at camp, or church groups might join in on at a picnic, and the more popular songs from commercial records seemed illiterate when they were written down. Lomax tried repeatedly to get the book published over the years, but no publisher would take it. Moses Asch of Folkways Records finally brought it out in 1967, a tumultuous time when such songs would be framed by other kinds of protest, connecting that moment to an American tradition of resistance and struggle that had been buried by time, neglect, and misrepresentation.

R. P. Wetherald, the recording supervisor at RCA whom Alan had worked with on reissues, offered Alan the opportunity to make a record of himself singing some southwestern songs, but he didn't consider himself a good enough singer and told Wetherald he knew of others who should be recorded instead. Woody Guthrie, for example, was the voice of the Southwest, "the poet of its people," a singer who could bring the characters of *The Grapes of Wrath* to life in music. The popularity of the film and Lomax's recommendation were sufficient incentive, so, without an audition, Guthrie was offered a two-album contract to write a suite of songs based loosely on the film, providing he could get them ready in less than a month. Though the short writing period worried him, what Woody produced was some of the best work he had ever done, songs like "Pretty Boy Floyd," "Dusty Old Road (So Long, It's Been Good to Know You)," and "I Ain't Got No Home." The keystone of the albums—titled *Dust Bowl Ballads*—was "Tom Joad," a song drawn directly from the Steinbeck book, and that Woody finished writing at Alan's apartment one night after hearing the Carter Family's recording of "John Hardy" and seeing how he could fit his words to its melody. Its seventeen verses are a masterly condensation: a six-hundred-page novel had been reduced to fewer than seven minutes in a song. At one point, he collapsed six chapters into two lines:

They buried Grandpa Joad by the side of the road,
Grandma on the California side.

When the recordings appeared in the summer of 1940, the *New York Times* classical music critic, Howard Taubman, wrote of them, "These albums are not a summer sedative. They make you think, they may even make you uncomfortable. . . . The albums show that the phonograph is broadening its perspective, and that life as some of our unfortunates know it can be mirrored in the glistening discs."

At the same time as Alan was producing Woody's records, he promoted two other sessions with RCA for Lead Belly. The songs were to be some that Lead Belly already knew, plus others that the Lomaxes had collected in prisons. The first was titled *The Midnight Special and Other Southern Prison Songs*, and it, like Woody's album, would become one of the first concept albums—songs grouped together around a single subject or theme. Alan also had wanted the Library of Congress to issue its prison field recordings to the public through RCA, but since the library was still leery of competing with commercial companies he decided that a studio recording would be the next best thing. To get the feel of a prisoner singing to other prisoners, Lomax suggested that Lead Belly be recorded with the Golden Gate Quartet. Wetherald discussed it with the Gates after a performance at Café Society, who told him that they knew nothing at all about prison songs—their repertoire was largely based on what they had sung in church. Even though they crossed into popular and blues territory in their club appearances, Wetherald worried that their singing was too polished and formal to be convincing in folk songs. Lomax's answer was that Lead Belly would teach them how to sing it. The Golden Gates, Alan later wrote, "learned these songs from Lead Belly by rote and after the first rehearsal or so were already forcing him to sing his best to keep the lead. The result is *not* complete authenticity, but I believe the nearest thing to it that could be achieved away from the prison farms themselves. There is a growling, surly, unison-based strength in these discs that I have not heard in other records." Lomax's job as producer was to rehearse the singers, supervise the recordings, teach Lead Belly songs (such as "Take This Hammer"), and prepare notes to go with the records, for which he was to be paid a two-cent royalty for each two-sided record they sold. These records were issued on RCA Victor, RCA's principal record label, rather than the cheaper Bluebird, because Alan was able to convince the company that it had a chance for sales to whites.

The second set of songs by Lead Belly, a solo album, was issued on Bluebird, but neither set sold well. It was clear that Lead Belly would never become a widely popular performer, but he remained a favorite for left wing fund-raisers and theater productions. He would be invited to Roosevelt's inauguration, play the Village Vanguard with Josh White, and sometimes turn up in august company, as when the following year he performed at the American Music Festival at Hunter College with Benny Goodman, Roy Harris, Tommy Dorsey, Aaron Copland, and Hazel Scott. But he was still barely making a living.

For much of March and April, Alan was sick with throat infections, but he managed to get through his broadcasts and even become involved in another media project, the formation of a small film company with three of the most socially conscious filmmakers of the time, all of whom were destined to be important figures in the history of cinema—Joris Ivens, Joseph Losey, and Nicholas Ray. They proposed to begin by making three ten-minute films under the Library of Congress's sponsorship, one by each of the directors, with Alan writing the scripts. Ivens was already much acclaimed as a documentary filmmaker in Europe, a master at integrating film and music, and in the United States had made the antifascist film *The Spanish Earth*, and had directed *Power and the Land* for the Department of the Interior. The other two were just finding their ways into the movies, Losey going on to direct such feature films as *Accident*, a remake of *M*, *Modesty Blaise*, and *Mr. Klein*, while Ray would be the director of *Rebel Without a Cause*, *They Live by Night*, *In a Lonely Place*, and many others. The four of them planned to make films about the Holiness Church, spirituals, railroad songs, and music of the Southwest, each of which would be aimed at theatrical release, with their earnings going back into a fund at the library to make future films. They hoped to get the Rockefeller Foundation to give the library a grant for the projects, or the Pan American Union, but after a year of trying they were never successful in raising funds.

Herbert Putnam retired as Librarian of Congress in the fall, and Archibald MacLeish was almost immediately appointed by President Roosevelt to succeed him. MacLeish had been many things: a poet, a lawyer, a playwright, an editor of the *New Republic* and *Fortune* magazine, and he had distinguished himself in all of those roles. He had even done a bit of folk song collecting in Arkansas. Yet the American Library Association raised objections to his appointment because he was not a trained librarian, and some members of Congress objected to his embrace of leftist causes. (The term "fellow traveler" was coined to apply to MacLeish himself.) But President Roosevelt ignored their complaints, since what he wanted was someone he could count on to support his policies and help him reach out to the public.

MacLeish already knew Alan's work before he became head of the library, and he gave him complete support in his activities in and out of the archive. Having written radio plays himself, he was especially interested in Alan's work in that medium. When Lomax was offered a second year of *The American School of the Air*—now under his own subtitle, "Wellsprings of Music," to be broadcast three times a week to what CBS projected to be an audience of fifteen million listeners—MacLeish enthusiastically approved it. These new programs were so successful that the National Association of Music Educators adopted folk songs as a focus for public school teaching, and one program, with Woody Guthrie, won an award as best Music Education Program of 1941. Alan had grown comfortable enough with the program that he even managed to slip his sister Bess in for duets with him when he could get the dean at Bryn Mawr to allow her to miss classes. For its part CBS was so pleased with Alan's work that they offered him a chance to create a second folk song program to run in the same season. This one would be aimed at adults, and would need more sophisticated scripting, so Nick Ray was brought in to write and coproduce, and Clifton Fadiman, a well-known editor, literary critic, and host of a popular radio show, *Information Please*, would be the master of ceremonies—a compromise, as far as Lomax was concerned—to make the show "a commercial possibility." Not all of the guests on the new show could read, so the script and many of the songs would sometimes have to be taught orally—like folklore.

Nick and Alan next worked up a pilot titled "Back Where I Come From" to try out on the CBS summer series *Forecast* on August 19, 1940. "We wrote a script about the weather with all the members of our cast," Lomax recalled. "We had Adam, we had Noah, we had the busboy, we had all the American folklore of the weather in this one show, and it had an all-star cast of the greatest singers in the US." Josh White did a sermon on Noah, Burl Ives did "Foggy, Foggy Dew," and Woody Guthrie sang about the Dust Bowl.

WOODY: Hear you fellas talk . . . you'd think that all the great storms of American history, by George, happened way back yonder. That ain't true. You know, storms've hurt people, they drive people out of their homes and they take their livin' away from 'em—and that very thing's a-happenin' right today, back in the dust bowl where I come from.

CLIFTON FADIMAN: What about this dust bowl, Woody Guthrie?

WOODY: Well, I come from Okemah, Oklahoma . . . now, out in that country ain't nothin' in the world to stop that north wind but a barbed-wire fence . . .

(WIND SOUND EFFECTS)
That dust bowl hit, and it hit like thunder,
And it dusted us over, an' it dusted us under,
Blocked out the traffic, covered the sun,
And straight for home all the people did run,
Singin':
Chorus (entire cast):
So long, it's been good to know yuh . . .

CBS was encouraged by the pilot to offer Alan a contract for a program three times a week, even though they had not been able to find a sponsor. The new series began in August, in prime time, with coast-to-coast broadcasts, featuring many of the performers from his other programs, plus some new ones, like jazz musicians Sidney Bechet and Bunk Johnson. The programs opened with an announcer setting up the topic: "Back where I come from we always say . . ." Then the cast came in with what they might have been saying in their different communities about the subject of the day—travel, for instance:

JOSH WHITE: When a woman's blue she hangs her little head and cries.
WOODY: And when we got mad and slam the door in her face,
We holler back, I'm going so far it'll take a dollar to send me a postcard.
WILLIE JOHNSON (of the Golden Gate Quartet): I'm gonna buy me a ticket just as long as I am tall.
WOODY: Sometimes that ol' road gets littler and littler until it just naturally runs up a tree.
GOLDEN GATES (sing):
Look down. Look down, that lonesome road,
Before you travel on.

From there the cast went on to sing the songs from which each of those lines came, and in between the singers joked and sometimes argued among themselves as they moved from one part of the country to another through radio's magic. The subject might be anything: "Who knows a song about . . . animals, food, workers and bosses, traveling?" Alan would weave a great variety of songs with a certain amount of spoken continuity, and "Nick was behind the glass window telling us to speed it up or slow it down, pointing up cues."

Taking direction was not something for which everyone in the cast was ready, however. Woody especially felt intimidated by Nick's giving him cues, and told him he froze whenever he pointed to him. Nor did he like the idea of anyone having control over what the performers said. So when Nick suggested that Alan drop Lead Belly from the show because listeners would have trouble understanding his southern accent, Woody was furious and quit the show. Alan managed to talk Nick into a compromise of letting Josh White speak Lead Belly's lines in a different voice, while Lead Belly continued to sing on the show, but it was too late—Woody was gone.

The individual programs were now reaching ten million students in two hundred thousand classrooms. CBS had expanded into international broadcasting, adding stations in Canada, Hawaii, and Alaska, and in 1941 began to provide translators to reach twenty-six other nations. To launch worldwide programming, CBS would sponsor in Mexico a global conference of a thousand broadcasters in February 1941, where Alan spoke and gave a demonstration of his program along with talks by Nelson Rockefeller from the Pan American Union, the president of the American Museum of Natural History, and the Mexican ambassador. Alan's reputation had grown to the point that a lecture bureau was acting as his agent for talks and folk song performances. He chatted with Sam Goldwyn about film possibilities, and Mrs. Roosevelt invited him to an evening at Hyde Park. But despite this success and high visibility, *Back Where I Come From* never picked up a commercial sponsor. The program ran for only twenty-one weeks more before it was suddenly canceled in February, 1941. Alan put the blame on CBS president William Paley, who he claimed "hated all that hillbilly music on his network."

CHAPTER 8

A Bourgeois Town

By late summer of 1940 all the talk in Washington was of war. It had moved from possibility to inevitability, and the government was increasing orders for armament and setting up mechanisms for rationing goods essential to combat, while Congress was debating the draft. Thinking that the Library of Congress would soon be ordered to change its priorities, Alan wrote a series of memos to Spivacke with suggestions for the role the archive might play in wartime. He still believed that the American people needed a national discussion on American identity, or what it was supposed to be, and he thought that folk song had already done some of that work for them. All that was needed was to make those songs better known to the public, and the military bases where large groups of men might soon be gathered by the draft would be the places to begin:

> I need not overstress my opinion that "God Bless America" and Kate Smith are both extremely dull and mediocre. They have both been elevated to an artificially astronomical position by the power of mass advertising and the star system. One of our contributions to the integration of the people and, specifically, of the conscripts would be to find and help encourage all sorts of poetry, songs, and talent of all sorts among the conscripts and give it publication or a place to be heard. We can work through the NYA, the WPA Arts Program or whatever other agency will be concerned with the recreational activities of the men to encourage and foster the poets and singers of the camps.

The plan he developed would have the library sending out recording trucks to the military camps to find the talent and record it, and then send the music back out to the camps by record and radio. Word was that Roosevelt would be instituting the draft any day (in fact, he signed the Selective Service Act a few weeks later, in September), and Alan wanted to move quickly to make up songbooks that would be used to ease the transition from civilian life for the new draftees. There would be different books for the West (*West of the Mississippi*), South (*Down in the Valley*),

North (*From Maine to Washington*), and, given the segregation of the armed forces, African Americans (*John Henry*), with each containing twenty-one songs arranged by Charles Seeger for group singing, and chosen for their appeal to men. Each book would feature a different folk hero—Pecos Bill, Davy Crockett, Paul Bunyan, and John Henry—with illustrations drawn from the *Index of American Design*, the WPA's book of regional art styles. But this would only be a first step: why not also have these songs arranged so they could be played by string orchestras or marching bands, and used for radio music and film scores? And why not have them recorded by pop singers like Maxine Sullivan and Frances Langford so that they "would be more useful than they now are in Cecil Sharp's ten dollar treatise on 'English' folk songs of the Southern Appalachians"?

Another proposal from Alan would have Nick Ray and himself produce radio programs for the library in which a roving reporter would travel across the country, stopping along the way and visiting homes where the people struck up a song or told a tale. Or maybe they could send an American reporter to visit a Latin American country and connect the two continents through song and story? Archibald MacLeish loved the idea, and joined in by spinning out his own variations on the theme—foreign reporters could visit American homes and discover what it meant to be American; or members of Congress could tell stories about themselves and the people in their districts and states.

Just before Christmas the Library of Congress announced "A Festival of Music Commemorating the Seventy-Fifth Anniversary of the Proclamation of the Thirteenth Amendment to the Constitution of the United States," a four-day celebration of the abolishment of slavery that included paintings, manuscripts, book exhibits, and music by African Americans. The music committee for the event was made up of some of the country's leading black intellectuals and composers—Henry T. Burleigh, Lulu B. Childers, Alain Locke, William Grant Still, and R. Nathaniel Dett—and what they developed was four nights of performances that boldly declared the richness and depth of African American musical culture. The Budapest String Quartet played works by black composers, and two opera singers included spirituals and works by black composers in their recitals. The third night, December 20, was announced as "A Program of Negro Folk Song with Commentary," and the concert was held in Coolidge Auditorium, a hall that Lomax never tired of reminding people had been built for string quartets and the music that America had inherited from Europe. The significance of the venue was even greater because only the year before the Daughters of the American Revolution had prevented contralto Marian Anderson from performing in their building, Constitution Hall.

The evening's music was deeply moving, with the audience both in tears and in jubilation, sometimes joining in on the songs. But there were also didactic moments when the songs were interspersed with recordings from the archive and talks by Alain Locke, Sterling Brown of Howard University, and Lomax, the one white participant, now being publicly acknowledged as an authority on black folk culture. All of them saw what they were doing as both a cultural event and a political act, since integrated audiences and performances were hard to find in D.C., or anywhere in America. But to break the social codes and to present African American cultural accomplishments "in a dignified manner," as Professor Brown put it, was a milestone.

The concert was in three parts: the first was "Negro Spirituals," with the Golden Gate Quartet opening with "Freedom," a song that would echo into the civil rights movement of the 1960s. The second part, "Blues and Ballads," presented songs like "How Long Has That Evening Train Been Gone?" and "Silicosis Blues" by Josh White, and was interspersed with Sterling Brown talking about racial injustice, under the rather bland rubrics of "What are the Blues?" and "Social Song." The evening's last section was "Reels and Work Songs," with Lomax commenting on juba dancing, Brer Rabbit, and railroad work songs. But just before he introduced the last song on the program, the Golden Gates' "Rock My Soul in the Bosom of Abraham," Alan shifted into elegiac mode, nurtured perhaps not so much by his politics as by what he had seen and heard over those countless miles he had traveled and in those many churches in which he had sat quietly and listened to preachers while he recorded them:

> I hope you will be ready now to listen to Negro songs with different ears. These songs are full of love for people, they are lonely for people and they are full of hunger for gentleness and kindness in this world. These songs rose up out of slavery, out of misery. They jumped up out of levee camps, they sprang from turpentine camps and back alleys. The people became happy and made them up in churches; the people "got high" and made them up at dances; they rose up out of tough people and good people. Some of these people were so mad that they could kill you as soon as look at you and, when some of these people had the quiet blues, they were so quiet you could hear them think for miles around. Some of these people could look past poverty and misery, they could look clear through the darkness and despair and ignorance and see something on the other side. The old folks said, "On the Other Side of Jordan." These songs rose up out of these people without their having to think about it, because they were lonesome for more kindness and goodness and richness than they could find in life right where they were.

"Alan was pretty hard-hitting about what the Negro had to bear in the South," Pete Seeger recalled. "Old John A. [Lomax] was in the audience, getting madder and madder. After the concert, he roared up to Alan, and as their argument grew louder, the shouts were echoing down the corridors. 'You have disgraced the South,' John A. was bellowing, shaking his fist." It was an event that John Lomax would not soon forget, and even a year later he was still complaining about Sterling Brown's account that evening of the death of the great blues singer Bessie Smith, who Brown said—doubtlessly quoting a published secondhand account by John Hammond—had been refused treatment at a "white hospital" after a serious automobile accident in Mississippi, and was allowed to die without medical care. John doubted the story, and wrote letters to various doctors and officials until he confirmed that it was indeed false: Bessie Smith had been attended to by a white doctor passing by the accident and was taken to a whites-only hospital, where she was treated but died from loss of blood. To John what it came down to was that a false narrative had been created that told of the brutal coldness of whites toward their black neighbors, a story too poignant to correct even when the facts were known. This he was not going to tolerate from Alan, Brown, or anyone else. Alan sent Sterling Brown copies of the documents that his father had collected, along with a letter that said his father was "infuriated" by Brown's story. Alan and Brown apparently met to talk about it. But even fifty years later, Alan and almost everyone else was still telling the same story of Bessie Smith's death as an example of racism and neglect in the old South.

At the beginning of 1941 the White House called on MacLeish to organize an evening of folk music in tribute to the troops in the armed services. Alan was sent to talk with Mrs. Roosevelt, and together they quickly organized "A Program of American Songs for American Soldiers" for the East Room of the White House on February 17, with Alan as master of ceremonies and including regulars from *Back Where I Come From* like the Golden Gate Quartet, Josh White, and Burl Ives. Since Alan knew that the president was fond of sailing, he recruited retired seaman J. M. "Sailor Dan" Hunt to open the program by singing sea chanteys unaccompanied. Hunt started strong and filled the room with "When Jones' Ale was New," but when he reached the climax of the first verse he forgot the words. "By that time," Alan said, "the Golden Gate Quartet had fallen into rhythm with him, and Burl Ives and the rest of us were all tapping time, until he came in with the missing line, and then the audience burst into applause. It was the whole show. . . . He was obviously an old guy, and he was trying. That melted the hearts of the admirals and the colonels. For he was one of them."

Wade Mainer and his band followed, playing Appalachian music, Burl Ives sang ballads and music from the pioneer traditions, Josh White played the blues, the Golden Gates performed black sacred music. Finally, a group of black and white recruits that Alan had found in nearby boot camps sang hillbilly and religious songs to wrap up the evening. The guests were a who's who of Washington, including the secretaries of the cabinet and the heads of all of the military. The printed program included words to the songs, and by the end they were all joining in. The day after, Mrs. Roosevelt chatted happily about the evening in her column in the *Washington Daily News*, *Time* magazine stressed the interracial nature of the performances, and Katherine Graham wrote the evening up for the *Washington Post*, with a large photo of Alan accompanying the article. In Washington terms, there were few bigger social events.

The next day MacLeish asked Alan to prepare a memo for him to send to the heads of the armed forces on using folk music to boost morale. The only branch of the military that responded was the air force, which instituted a program to encourage music-making. Throughout the war its bands and choirs were exceptional, and it built up a collection of songs and recordings from all over the world for its troops to sing.

With the war in Europe intensifying, new divisions of the U.S. government were put in place, and plans were being made for shifting national policy to what seemed inevitable. Archibald MacLeish asked Lomax for suggestions on how they could find help in Washington when they began losing personnel to the draft. His response was that of any archivist—a consideration how they might best protect the collection—and he requested that the library make duplicates of all its recordings and folk song manuscripts and then move them to some secure location to preserve them in case of an attack. When MacLeish told him that they had been offered the services of the Music Project of the WPA, Alan asked that Sidney Robertson of that unit might work with them on some joint projects. Alan had heard of her extraordinary background: she had studied with Carl Jung, Ernst Bloch, and Henry Cowell, worked as an assistant to Charles Seeger in the Special Skills Division of the Resettlement Administration, trained as a folklorist in the field with John Lomax and Frank C. Brown, and had carried out her own large-scale recording surveys in Wisconsin and California. (It was Robertson's collecting in Wisconsin that had originally inspired Alan to work there in 1938.) At the moment she was working to get Henry Cowell pardoned from prison in California where he had been arrested on a "morals charge" for homosexuality and in a few months would marry him. Alan thought that she could help complete some of the checklists and bibliographical work that the archive was developing.

Robertson was familiar with the hard work involved in folk song collecting, but she was still amazed at Lomax's commitment and energy. "He'd get so excited about a project that it became the only thing that existed. And we'd find ourselves caught up in his drive. He was once putting on a concert in the Library; and as usual, he was staging it, fussing with the lights, checking the recording equipment, changing the position of the chairs. Archibald MacLeish, head of the library, walked in and Alan yelled over his shoulder, 'Archie, bring that chair over here, will you?' Mr. MacLeish automatically walked across the room and brought him the chair." Alan's friend the anthropologist Margaret Mead said he was like "royalty in action."

Just as Macmillan Press was preparing to finally publish *American Ballads and Folk Songs, Vol. 2,* a horde of new problems surfaced. Edward B. Marks Corporation was threatening to sue the Lomaxes over their use of "Allá en el Rancho Grande" in the first volume of their folk song book. Though they had gotten the song from J. Frank Dobie, who confirmed that it was "traditional," there was enough legal activity circling around it that Macmillan insisted that John go back and check the copyright status of every song in the new book. Next, the publishers announced that because manufacturing costs had risen, they were going to have to raise the price of the book to a prohibitive level unless the Lomaxes agreed to a reduction in their royalties. Then, at the last minute, the book's title was changed by the editor, retaining the old title as a subtitle. *Our Singing Country: Folk Songs and Ballads,* "collected and compiled" by John A. Lomax and Alan Lomax, with Ruth Crawford Seeger, "Music Editor," was published in November 1941, with an introduction by Archibald MacLeish that praised the Lomaxes for their work in building the archive and developing the nation's awareness of the importance of its own folk music.The criticisms of the first volume had now been addressed with a vengeance: this time they sought the best versions of the songs they chose, and minimized their previous practice of editing together different variants into composite songs. The music was no longer arranged to be sung with piano accompaniment but was transcribed to stay as close to the source's style as possible, making each song less a freestanding artifact than an opportunity to witness a singer's unique aesthetic at work. The songs were threaded together with comments from the singers, most often Aunt Molly Jackson.

In the same year that literary critic John Crowe Ransom published *The New Criticism*—which announced the arrival of a school of criticism that drew a hard line between high and popular art and stressed the unity, independence, and purity of a written text from the life, politics, and intentions of the author and the culture within which it emerged—the Lomaxes had produced a songbook with extensive biographical notes about the singer or the composer, with Aunt Molly Jackson acting as Virgil, to guide the reader through another world of meaning and beauty. The book itself argued for understanding folk art *as* Art: complex, varied, rich in detail, and full of nuance. John and Alan made no attempt to find the oldest or purest versions, and even used songs that had been turned into commercial recordings ("Kitty Kitty Casket," for example, an Alabama children's song that had already reached the public by means of Ella Fitzgerald's 1938 hit recording of "A-Tisket, A-Tasket"). The Lomaxes were saying that folk songs were not artifacts of the past and a subject for historical study, but still alive, and even an important part of modernity. (When Aaron Copland borrowed Ruth Seeger's transcription of Salyorsville, Kentucky, fiddler W. H. Stepp's tune "Bonaparte's Retreat" for "Hoedown" in his ballet *Rodeo*, it was only one of the first of a series of vindications of the Lomaxes' work.)

Despite the friction between Woody Guthrie and Nick Ray, Alan remained close to Woody, and tried to help him whenever he could, passing on to him opportunities to perform and write. When the director of the Information Division of the Bonneville Power Administration in 1941 asked for a recommendation of a folksinger for a film project, Alan knew Guthrie was the one they should have. Bonneville Power was building the Grand Coulee Dam on the Columbia River in the state of Washington and wanted to document the project on film, in part to work against the northeastern power companies by convincing people to vote in favor of rural electrification. Having seen Pare Lorentz's celebrated documentary *The River*, which used bits of folk songs on its soundtrack, it was eager to use a folksinger as the narrator for the film. Woody was signed on to the project for a month, and he drove along the river south from Washington State to Oregon and the Pacific Ocean, writing twenty-six songs in twenty-six days. Some of them, like "Pastures of Plenty" and "Roll On, Columbia" (based on the melody of "Goodnight Irene"), became standards for folksingers for years to come, with lines rich in imagery and poetry that would stand up with the best ("In the misty crystal glitter of the wild and windward spray . . .").

Alan's talk at the Thirteenth Amendment celebration at the Library of Congress caught the attention of black intellectuals and educators, and just as 1941 began he was invited by Horace Mann Bond, the president of the Fort Valley State College of Georgia, to come to the school's folk festival to record the performers and be a judge in the musical competition. Bond, despite being an advocate of Booker T. Washington's no-nonsense black vocational pedagogy (with no time for the arts—too impractical, and maybe too emotional as well), nonetheless promoted the folk festival as a grassroots event in which locals would not be on display but would feel at home. At the same time, it would be a celebration of the arts and culture of working people. This was an idea that was not always appreciated by black music teachers, many of whom thought such music was better left behind in the fields, so Bond sought the help and approval of sympathetic outsiders such as W. C. Handy, who had been a guest the previous year at the first festival. Alan was unable to go, but he recommended to Bond that he invite Sterling Brown, Charles Seeger, Howard Odum, Zora Neale Hurston, his father, and others to be judges for the contests. The festival was an enormous success, winning the praise of the likes of composer William Grant Still, Langston Hughes, and professors of music at Tuskegee and Spelman colleges.

A few weeks later the president of Fisk University in Nashville, the most distinguished black university in the South, invited Alan, Sterling Brown, Josh White, and the Golden Gate Quartet to come to the school on April 29 to repeat their Library of Congress concert as part of the celebration of the seventy-fifth anniversary of the school's founding. Over the previous two years, the Library of Congress music staff and the head of the music department at Fisk had been discussing some kind of joint project on African American music, and this event was a first step in that direction. The day after the performance, Thomas E. Jones, the president of Fisk, offered Alan a one- to two-year appointment at the university "to make Fisk the center for folk song collecting for the Negro in the South." Though he declined the offer, Alan proposed that they talk further, and suggested that if Fisk wanted to develop a folklore center, President Jones might encourage the research being done by their own composer and folk song collector, Professor John Work III. (Work's father, John Wesley Work Jr., was one of the first serious collectors of African American folk songs, and was himself a former professor at Fisk.) Lomax suggested that the university ought to have Work's recording machine repaired and that they lend him a car to continue his travels to record musicians close to Nashville. Since the Library of Congress was building an archive of song state by state, it could duplicate Work's fifty-some field recordings, store them in Washington, and give the professor a set of copies to replace those that were wearing out from replay as he transcribed them. Work would also be given blank records by the library to continue his own recording projects.

Leaving Nashville, Alan and Elizabeth went on to San Antonio for a meeting of the Texas Folklore Society, to Clarksville for his brother's wedding, to Dallas, where he gave some lectures, and then on to Mexico City, where a Latin American conference on educational radio was being sponsored by CBS and the National Defense Council. Even though Alan's *Back Where I Come From* had been canceled, Nelson Rockefeller, the council's coordinator of Latin American cultural and commercial relations, asked to have Lomax, Josh White, and the Golden Gate Quartet give a demonstration of their show. On their way back to Washington, Elizabeth and Alan stopped again at Fisk, where Alan talked further about recording plans with President Jones, Professor Charles Johnson (the head of the Department of Social Science, director of the Institute of Social Research, and later the first black president of Fisk), the heads of the music and drama departments, and Professor Work. Most of the planning was done by Lomax and Johnson, who decided on a joint Library of Congress–Fisk social survey of the folk culture of two Mississippi Delta counties that were familiar to Johnson from his own research for his 1941 book *Growing Up in the Black Belt,* Coahoma and Bolivar (though Johnson later convinced the others that Coahoma County was dense enough that they should limit their work to that area). The Library of Congress would furnish sound equipment, blank records, an engineer, and Lomax as a collector, trainer of fieldworkers, and coeditor of the book, while Fisk would provide fieldworkers from their sociology department under the direction of coeditor Johnson, with the help of John Work and another Fisk sociologist, Professor Lewis Jones. The book that resulted would be underwritten for publication by Fisk.

> The agreed upon study was to explore objectively and exhaustively the musical habits of a single Negro community in the Delta, to find out and describe the function of music in the community, to ascertain the history of music in the community, and to document adequately the cultural and social backgrounds for music in the community. It was felt that this type of study, carried on in a number of types of southern communities would afford: (1) an oral history of Negro music in the South over the past hundred years; (2) describe music in the community objectively, giving all criteria for taste and the relationship of music to the dynamics of social change; and (3) result in a widely varied and completely documented set of basic recorded musical materials.

For both musicology and sociology, it was an intellectually innovative and daring project, the most encompassing study of the social basis of the arts of any community ever attempted. But it was also an unprecedented political act: studies of black people in the South were rare, and, when done at all, were usually carried out by white social scientists alone. It was also the first time that an African American university officially committed itself to the study of folklore.

Alan continued to recommend John Work's own projects to Fisk and the Library of Congress administration, and promised him partial underwriting from the library for a smaller collecting project that Work wanted to carry out in the Nashville area. But as time went by and Alan heard nothing from Work, the two exchanged letters that suggest the beginnings of mutual distrust: for his part, Work wanted assurance in writing that if he shipped his recordings to the archive for copying he would get them back, and that he would receive credit for having collected them. There was also confusion over where Work should be collecting and when.

The plan was for research to begin with a two-week trip in mid-August when Alan was off the air at CBS. He would meet up with Work and some of the Fisk fieldworkers to familiarize themselves with the area, as well as do some preliminary collecting during the season when the religious revival services were taking place out in the country, a project he and Johnson had developed as a preliminary step toward the larger study. But preparations for war were beginning to intrude on every aspect of American life, and Mississippi was no exception: cotton farmers were under pressure to get their crops in, but being short of workers and fearing union organizers, they wanted no outsiders in the area. Wages almost tripled within a few weeks, and everyone—children, cooks, teachers—grabbed sacks and went to work in the fields, leaving the streets empty of activity. With the boom, the research plans quickly shifted. Johnson suggested that as an alternative plan, he would send some of the Fisk researchers ahead into an area to orient themselves before Lomax began collecting, since they would not draw as much attention as a white man and woman would. Alan would come back to Fisk to give seminars to the fieldworkers to teach them about folklore studies and get them ready to be folk collectors, and interviewing and recording would then begin in mid-November when the crop season was winding down. He, Elizabeth, and Work would do the recording in late November.

Alan was now being taken seriously by many of the same academic folklorists who had written his father off as an amateur and a popularizer. In fact, he was one of the first to systematize folk song collecting, and he used his position at the archive to get others to think more seriously about their use of folk songs and how to make their work less academic and more usable for others. Writing to the WPA's Music Division of the Florida Folklife and then to the Florida Writers' Project, for example, he offered some ideas on how the focus of folk song collecting could be widened beyond the text to include the singer, and how the roles of the song and the singer in the community might be better understood:

> It would be worth-while: to ask singers of different types, ages, etc., to recite the words of a song or so for the records, to question them before the mike about their own opinion of their songs, of the factual or moral content of the song; to obtain biographies of singers with large or extensive repertoires.
>
> . . .
>
> The interview technique does seem to run a little slow, but I feel that the workers are in process of learning how to make documentary field recordings. This is an almost unexplored field. Sometimes an interviewer appears to interrupt the performance more often than is necessary, or to have phrased the question so that the informant was supplied with the answer thereby. In general, the objective is to get the informant to talk very freely and sometimes a few stimulating questions or remarks are better than a straight interview technique.

Alan even offered suggestions to his father to improve the value of his work:

> My personal opinion is that it is valuable to get the informant talking eloquently for himself, rather than interrupt him or push him with questions. The recording

> interview can be as significant as the song itself and is valuable as a fresh field document, especially, if the informant does not know that the interview is being recorded, and if he ever learns it. . . . It is very important to record the tunings of all instruments which play a part in the music, to photograph the instruments and get the informant to explain how he plays it. In the case of unusual instruments, it would be worthwhile to make accurate drawings or send the instruments where they could be drawn to scale. If part singing is recorded, it would be a real contribution to record the parts in the harmony separately. This can be done by shifting the singers in front of the microphone. . . . As you know, valuable material is to be had from comparison of different versions of the same song from different regions. So also, are different performances of the same song in the same community by different singers, or the same song by different members of the family, or the same song by the same performers at different times. Therefore, it is not so important to us that material be always rehearsed without a mistake or hesitation. The great beauty of field recordings is that performers take their own time and do things their own way, feeling that if they make a mistake, they can try again. The results are such that no commercial recording company can ever hope to achieve.

To illustrate this social approach to song, Alan began to work on *Listen to Our Story,* a book of first-person narratives based on the lives of people he had recorded, and he submitted twelve pages on Jelly Roll Morton as a sample to Macmillan. He conceived of the book as a new kind of literature and history, with subjects speaking directly to the readers without the outside voice of an editor interpreting them. But the publishers were not impressed and judged it as merely dialect literature, local-color writing that was "flavorful" but nonetheless monotonous. They imagined that it might work better with a proper introduction and with an editor providing connecting passages that would explain the significance of the texts—something more in the spirit of John Dos Passos or John Steinbeck. Alan refused to abandon the idea, however, and continued to work on the book off and on for the next few years.

Archibald MacLeish's goal of having the library use its resources to reach out to the country fit nicely with Alan's work, and MacLeish backed him wherever he could. One of his first acts on being appointed Librarian was to convince the Carnegie Foundation to fund a recording laboratory for the library. The lab was set up by the beginning of summer 1941, and a sound truck was bought for recording in the field. Its initial project was to make copies of recordings in the library to distribute to other libraries for educational purposes, but with hostilities breaking out around the world, these recordings began to seem more valuable for use as part of the State Department's "good neighbor" efforts to influence Latin

American countries to remain friendly to the United States. MacLeish also wanted to use the recording lab to create a series of short radio programs or public-interest spots to be offered free to radio stations for broadcast in the United States and abroad. In a time when fascism was gaining footholds in Europe, there was fear that even the United States could be vulnerable. The Rockefeller Foundation was persuaded to support a library experiment in popular education in which radio programming would be used to remind listeners of the history and traditions of local communities, regions, and their place in the entire nation.

MacLeish also felt that too much power was being vested in a few radio networks, and that news reflected their owners' own biases. What he thought was needed was an alternate medium, a station or a network that expressed the concerns of the country as a whole. Under his plan the library would take to the road and visit small towns, farms, churches, factories, and schools, interviewing people to connect listeners to the speech, songs, and thoughts of their fellow citizens throughout the land. Chief of the project would be Philip H. Cohen, brought in from the Department of Education, with Joseph Liss as script editor, Jerry Wiesner as recordist, and Lomax the music and folklore editor. They formed the core of what was called the Radio Research Project.

Since Alan was the most experienced in the field, he proposed to MacLeish a series of ten programs called *America in the Summer of 1941* that would create "a new function for radio: that of letting the people explain themselves and their lives to the entire nation." The Recording Laboratory's sound truck was sent to places like the Asheville, North Carolina, Mountain Dance and Song Festival, where they recorded the fiddling contest, folktales, songs, and backstage interviews with the singers. They also recorded a white revival service and interviewed Thomas Wolfe's mother, in whose house they stayed. They recorded people's opinions on the war in Europe, asking whether they thought the United States should become involved in it, and documented the Tennessee Valley Authority's work in Union County, Georgia. The TVA was one of the boldest of the New Deal projects, an attempt to develop an entire region by introducing conservation, controlling forest fires, increasing crop yield, and generating massive amounts of electricity to better the lives of the inhabitants of the region and draw industry to the area. An undertaking this big and intrusive guaranteed disruption and conflict. Dams were built and rivers redirected, displacing thousands of families; labor unions were now legally recognized in a region where businesses had previously blocked them; and the top-down, outsider management of the TVA often clashed with local customs and beliefs. The Radio Research group traveled to the heart of the project, moving among those most affected by the changes under way, and let their interviews and field recordings shape the scripts they wrote.

In Union County, Georgia, one of the most isolated counties in the South, they recorded ballads, a church service, a family reunion, and a fox hunt. They interviewed farmers about how the TVA was affecting them, talked to the newspaper editor, the county agent, and the doctor, who spun out stories about bootleggers and midnight buggy rides to sick patients.

"Mister Ledford and the TVA," another program on the same subject, was a drama that wove together interviews with a single farmer and his neighbors and showed their uneasiness as they chatted about the building of the Notterley Dam that would soon flood their farms out of existence. Lomax spared listeners none of the farmers' complaints, nor their mocking of the city folk—their visitors from Washington—who seemed hopeless in the countryside. His script for the program was selected for *Radio Drama in Action*, a collection of the best programs of the early 1940s, which also included scripts by Orson Welles, Arch Oboler, Arthur Miller, Langston Hughes, and Norman Corwin.

Late in the summer, Joseph Liss brought into the group Arthur Miller, a twenty-seven-year-old playwright, to help with the writing. Miller had already written one of their first shows, a program called "Buffalo Bill Disremembered," in which the old man was interviewed. He was now asked to do the field interviewing and write the script for the final show in the series, a documentary on the shipbuilding boomtown of Wilmington, North Carolina, even though Alan had doubts about his ability and thought his previous script was weak. Once the crew was in North Carolina they were almost immediately pulled off the job and put on a new one when the Department of Health decided to do a film in Wilmington on North Carolina mine safety instead. While Miller was interviewing miners and engineers, he also managed to record a strike of black workers at a shirt factory when he heard the marchers outside his hotel window singing strike songs based on old spirituals. Later, Alan wrote MacLeish that Miller's work was "up to now the most stirring program which we have completed."

Come August, Alan and Elizabeth arrived in Nashville on the twenty-fourth for a three-week trip to record revival services in Mississippi for the Fisk project, and then to spend a few days on the way back in western Virginia to find some of the ballad singers who had already been located for them by the Virginia Folklore Society. When they reached Mississippi on August 29 they learned that the revival season was just winding down and they had missed their chance to record. But Alan, Elizabeth, and John Work nonetheless went to Coahoma County for a week to look over the area and do some preliminary recording.

Over the next two weeks they would visit and record services of religious groups in the Church of God in Christ on the Moorhead Plantation in Lula, Mississippi; in the Mt. Ararat Missionary Baptist Church on the King and Anderson Plantation (the singing there was so strong that it overloaded the recording machine); and at the Reverend Ribbins's church in Maple Springs (where, in the middle of a sermon about the reality of hell, the reverend called Alan out of his technological meditation behind the recording machine: "Do you hear me, Brother Lomax? Hell is a place, and not a state!").

Everywhere they went they were asked if they were union organizers, and were sometimes assumed to be something even worse. In Klack's country store in Lake Coromant in Tunica County, Alan and Elizabeth recorded a group of musicians—Fiddling Joe Martin the mandolinist, Leroy Jones on harmonica, Willie Brown, guitarist. At the center was Son House, a preacher turned wandering bluesman whose songs and slide guitar playing made him one of the most passionate and powerful of the Delta guitarists, and who by day was a tractor driver. He had been recorded by Paramount a decade before and claimed to have taught Robert Johnson. When he picked up his guitar he was "no longer the quiet, affable person I had met, but possessed by the song, as Gypsies in Spain are possessed, gone blind with music and poetry. . . . And with him the sorrow of the blues was not tentative, or retiring, or ironic. Son's whole body wept, as with eyes closed, the tendons in his powerful neck standing out with the violence of his feeling and his brown face flushing":

Well, I got up this mornin', jinx all around, jinx all around, 'round my bed
And I say I got up this mornin', with the jinx all around my bed
Know I thought about you, an' honey, it liked to kill me dead

Oh, look-a here now, baby, what you want me, what you want me, me to do?
Look-a here, honey, I say, what do you want poor me to do?
You know that I done all I could, just tryin' to get along with you

You know, the blues ain't nothin' but a low-down shakin', low-down shakin',
achin' chill
I say the blues is a low-down, old, achin' chill
Well, if you ain't had 'em, honey, I hope you never will

There were also moments of revelation on this trip, such as listening in Mound Bayou while Charles Johnson interviewed George Johnson, a musician who recalled the band that Jefferson Davis organized among his slaves and the music they played. Or the pure joy of hearing someone who had the promise of greatness. Such was the meeting on August 31 at Sherrod Plantation, when Alan, Elizabeth, and John Work met McKinley Morganfield, a tractor driver and guitarist who already had a stage name, Muddy Waters, and who twenty years later would change popular music forever. "Waters was bare-footed in raggedy overalls. He was very shy and his house was in the middle of one of those endless cotton fields. He worked all week and played every Saturday night for the little dances in his county. He'd never seen a good guitar before I handed him mine." (The interview with Waters revealed that he seldom had the blues and never had the blues when he played it; that whites couldn't play the blues; that he couldn't dance and had given up trying; and that his favorite radio performer was Fats Waller.)

What particularly impressed Alan was the beauty of his songs: "He was not a composer, but a recomposer—he only made a couple of songs in his life."

> Muddy's song departed from the rigid AAB, three-line blues formula most of his contemporaries used. Instead, Muddy was rhyming variations on the four-phrase song form—ABAB in outline—using syncopations to make eight lines out of four. In two stanzas of hyperbole, he measured his hurt, the moments that turn his thoughts to death, the empty hours and desolate days of longing for his faithless Jenny.
>
> *Yes, minutes seems like hours,*
> *And hours seem like days,*
> *Seem like my baby*
> *Will stop her low-down ways*

On the way back to D.C. on September 11, Alan began filling notebooks with the kinds of questions he wanted the Fisk collectors to ask and hoped to communicate to the fieldwork seminar. His goal was encyclopedic, going far beyond what was understood as folklore protocol. Like an ethnographer, he wanted to know the demographics of the community, sources of income, and the structure of each of the families. As a folklorist, he was interested in the repertoires of individual performers, even the songs that went beyond the traditional, and he made a point of asking about their knowledge of jazz, school songs, classical melodies, patriotic songs, and lullabies; about their favorite performers, national or local; how long had they spent learning their instruments or songs; how they learned them; what the blues meant to them; if they went to dances, listened to the radio, or owned a phonograph; if they preferred Negro or white music. He worked up schedules for interviewing individuals, groups, and members of institutions, made up reading lists and selected examples of field recordings to use as models, and wrote an outline for the seminar that Charles Johnson called "full and fascinating." This was going to be the first ethnography of a community's aesthetics.

Despite some initial misunderstandings between them, Lewis Jones worked closely with Alan, quickly grasped the point of the project, and threw himself into it. He made contact with the most important officials of the county—the plantation owners, teachers, and agricultural officials—preparing the way for the research to come. When the project was delayed by harvest, Jones went out to pick cotton himself in order to inconspicuously learn something of the workers' daily lives. ("Sixteen years have passed since I first picked cotton but I am planning to go out Friday and record a cotton picker's day. I hope I pick enough to pay for the overalls I'll have to buy.") And it was Jones who went to Clarksdale's bars and nightclubs to make lists of the songs on the jukeboxes, a catalog that constituted one of the most important results of the study. The first surprise was that there were very few Delta musicians or singers on any of the jukeboxes, but urban rhythm and blues artists like Lil Green and Louis Jordan were in every bar. Not only were swing bands like Count Basie, Earl Hines, and Jimmie Lunceford popular, but also white bands like those of Artie Shaw, Sammy Kaye, Glenn Miller, Tommy Dorsey, and Woody Herman. As Muddy Waters's own taste revealed, these rural people were already wired into national popular culture, though they still filtered it through their own aesthetic.

Returning to Washington, Alan and Elizabeth stopped at the Galax Fiddlers' Convention in Galax, Virginia, to do some recording, where they were struck by the voice and guitar of Estil C. Ball, a singer with an exceptional knowledge of religious songs, and they followed him home to Rugby, Virginia, to record him. They recorded the fiddling of Emmet Lundy, and Elizabeth interviewed him on record. They also recorded fifteen songs from Texas Gladden of Salem, Virginia. Gladden was not new to Lomax, for her songs had been transcribed by collectors Arthur Kyle Davis and Alfreda Peel in the 1930s, she had been recorded as early as 1935 by folklorist Richard Chase, and Alan himself had recorded her at the National Folk Festival in Washington in 1938. Gladden had grown up in a musical family, and often sang at musical events in rural Virginia. She was an especially fine ballad singer in the old, unaccompanied style that allowed the story of the song to come through clearly and precisely and highlighted her light ornamentation and subtle stylistic touches. "Texas sings her antique ballads in the fashion of ballad singers from time immemorial," Alan said. "The emotions are held in reserve: the singer does not color the story with heavy vocal underscoring; she allows the story to tell itself and the members of her audience to recover and interpret it in accordance with their own emotions." These were songs that made her home audience cry for the beauty of the sadness within them, and her style would come to influence Joan Baez and many other revivalist folksingers in the 1960s. She was equally eloquent in her thoughts about her singing and her songs, and Alan returned to record and interview her several more times over the years.

During that same summer, Pete Seeger was singing at political fund-raisers and strikes with Lee Hays, a singer from Arkansas, and Millard Lampell, a writer from New Jersey, and they were calling themselves the Almanac Singers. Pete wrote to Woody in Oregon, who came back to New York to join them. By the fall they had added to the group Bess Lomax and Sis Cunningham, a labor organizer and music teacher from Oklahoma, and all of them moved into a house in Greenwich Village. Alan was fascinated by their blend of voices, their harmonies, the range of their repertoire, and the spirit with which they approached songs. "Alan had a way of making proclamations and value judgments that could ring down the years," Pete recalled, "and he said of the Almanacs: 'This is the way American folk songs will be introduced to the American people.' " What the public had seen so far was John Jacob Niles dressed up in a suit, giving a very eloquent concert, singing folklike songs he had written himself in a dramatic high voice, maybe also performing the Niles-Merton Song Cycle, his setting of Thomas Merton's poems to music; or they'd seen Richard Dyer-Bennet, a classically trained, pitch-perfect tenor who on other nights might be singing his own translation of Schubert's *Die schöne Mullerin*, wearing a tuxedo; Burl Ives presented songs he'd heard on the road or read in books, much as Carl Sandburg did, though more informally. But they were all actors, in a sense. And Will Geer was in fact an actor, who acted out the songs with great professionalism, even when he took Woody along with him to sing at strikes or union rallies.

The Fisk seminar for folklore fieldworkers began on September 27 and ran day and night for three days. After Alan met and talked with the students, his excitement grew with the certainty that their project might be the most thorough and objective study of an art ever done in the United States. He wrote his father that "naturally the Negro looks at the South with different eyes than the white man, but it seems to me that while neither point of view is exactly right, before a decision can be reached in a democracy both sides must be allowed to have their say, and before the Negro will do the job right he perhaps has to get things off his chest. However, this recording project will not be a propaganda means for anyone, but it is complete and well planned." (Charles Johnson wrote him a few days later that "the seminar yielded, I note, a rich array of materials and a degree of stimulation far exceeding anything expected, although I confess I expected a great deal. You have a genius for hard work as well as for catching, following through and recording a wide range of the most excitingly beautiful as well as culturally significant folk materials.")

Before he ever set foot into the rural Delta that summer, Alan had already accumulated information on local ministers and their denominations, the name of the guard on the local chain gang, and the names and locations of singers and musicians mentioned in W. C. Handy's book *Father of the Blues*. This was the first field trip on which Alan had to take the blues seriously, the music that he and his father had once thought too commercial to be of interest. The record companies had been there at least twelve years before him, and many of the singers they had recorded, advertised, and promoted were still there, either having returned after the Depression crushed their dreams of fame, or never having left at all. Alan knew their names as specters from scarce Okeh and Paramount records—figures like Charlie Patton, who was raised on the Dockery plantation near the crossroads where some said that Robert Johnson had sold his soul to the devil at midnight. Patton himself had been promoted under a shadow of mystery as "the Masked Marvel."

When Alan posed the question "What are the blues? What do they mean to you?" the answers were in part something he sought for himself, to understand this musical form that may have been as ancient as griots in West Africa, or perhaps as recent as the automobile, the airplane, and the phonograph (all of which made guest appearances in the blues). The blues had become a craze, like ragtime, which grew up alongside it, and it leaped from the bottom of the social order to the Astors and the Vanderbilts, who staged blues contests for their own amusement well before the rest of white America came to know them.

John and Alan Lomax arrived in the field just after blues records began to circulate widely, and he and his father had sometimes passed up recording the songs in favor of older ones because they seemed to be everywhere, a part of popular rather than folk culture. Alan, however, came to understand them as another form of folklore, but a recorded form, and therefore one whose origins he might be able to uncover. But he continued to worry: were the blues really folk song? They were not collective or community-based in the usual manner of folk songs. Could they be legitimately considered part of a tradition if they were only, say, forty or fifty years old? Or were they really popular music disguised in overalls, especially when most decent folks wanted nothing to do with juke joint music, those devil's songs? Or were they a form of art song, created by only a very few artists who were trailed by a body of imitators? Lomax eventually solved the problem by coming to regard the blues as an artful response to pain, suffering, and oppression, but one with musical roots in Africa.

The Library of Congress's efforts to expose composers to folk music were beginning to have an effect, and a small body of compositions continued to develop around field-recorded performances, with works by Aaron Copland, Roy Harris, Earl Robinson, and others. Though Alan still scorned it as an out-of-date and elitist approach to art, he did what he could to help composers when asked. Perhaps the most unlikely musician to seek Alan's help was Harry Partch, a writer of experimental music whose attempts to radically rethink the nature of music had been encouraged by Charles Ives, although most of the music establishment treated him as a hopeless eccentric. Like Walt Whitman, Partch was interested in the musical possibilities of American speech and developed the ability to hear minute gradations of pitch in talk. He created extended scales to notate the inflections of the speaking voice and invented his own musical instruments to express these vocal qualities, ultimately constructing his own musical universe. While studying the history of tuning systems in London on a grant, he met W. B. Yeats and convinced him to give his permission to write an opera based on Yeats's translation of Sophocles' *Oedipus the King*. But when he ran out of money, he returned to the United States and hoboed across the country for the next ten years, riding the rails, doing odd jobs, and transcribing onto music paper bits of speech that he had overheard. When he wrote Lomax, he had just completed *Barstow*, a composition for voice built on eight examples of graffiti that he'd seen on a highway railing in California. Written in a forty-three-tone scale, it was intended to be accompanied by Partch's homemade instruments. It may have been an extreme form of art music, but it nevertheless hinted at folk songs, albeit what some would have heard as the folk songs of aliens. Partch later acknowledged that he had been influenced by the singing of Lead Belly and Woody Guthrie.

In his letter to Lomax, Partch talked about *Barstow* and explained that he was broke and hoped that the archive might want to support his work. Alan replied:

> Your work sounds extremely interesting, and I hope some day to hear you talk about it, face to face. Human speech, particularly as spoken by people rather than poets, is in some ways music richer than our musicians can comprehend. I wish you could hear some of the magnificent human documents on records here in our collection. Somehow, though, it seems to me that for the moment we need songs which are simple and direct and courageous, rather than subtly exploratory.

Partch wrote back to say that he thought that was exactly what he was offering.

The news of the Japanese attack on Pearl Harbor reached Washington by radio early in the afternoon of Sunday, December 7, 1941. The shock and anger at the Japanese "dagger in the back of America" spread across the country in the nation's first serious engagement with the wireless conscience that radio was becoming. Three thousand soldiers and sailors were rumored to be dead, and the fear was that if part of America could be attacked without anyone knowing it was coming, what would be next? Alan spent the day thinking about what he might do, what kind of response the library might make, and by evening he had called the people in the Radio Research Project and asked them if they'd support him in recording the reactions of average Americans to what had happened in Pearl Harbor. He reminded them that their unit had been created to offer a counterbalance to an eastern, urban-dominated commercial radio that excluded the voices of most of the country's citizens. Now, of all times, was the moment to give Americans a chance to comment on the attack on their lives by interviewing them and putting them on the radio. The next morning, while Alan was waiting to record the president's response to the attack, the project was approved, and he sent telegrams to folklorists in Nashville, Texas, Denver, Bloomington, Madison, New York City, Boston, and North Carolina asking them to record in their area over the next day or so and mail the results back to Washington. That night, he and two engineers at the library went out into the streets of Washington with a recording machine, visiting a number of African American pool halls and theaters, and standing on the sidewalk so that their microphone could reach the truck with the recording equipment. Later, they edited the interviews down into a fifteen-minute program that was broadcast on the Mutual Broadcasting System, a program that the Library of Congress said was the first documentary broadcast in the United States.

This launch into documentary radio was considered so successful that the Office of Emergency Management commissioned Alan to record a second set of interviews for a program to be called *Dear Mr. President*. This time people were asked to speak directly to the president and explain what they were doing, or wanted to do, in this emergency. Some of the interviewers decided that the "man on the street" designation should also include administrators, politicians, their neighbors, or even members of their own families: the superintendent of the main building at the University of Texas invited the president to come down to see their beautiful campus; the editor of a newspaper assured Mr. Roosevelt that all the papers were supporting the war effort; Alan's old friend Johnny Faulk interviewed his own wife, who asked Mr. Roosevelt to stop the profiteering off the war; and the superintendent of public safety of the city of Pittsburgh assured the president that they had the machine guns and fire trucks to deal with civil defense. Since these recordings were bound for radio, an occasional ringer was brought in by the interviewers to make sure they produced a quality segment: the New York team got Lead Belly to sing "President Roosevelt" and "We're Gonna Tear Hitler Down," and Pete Seeger sang a song about how the Martins and McCoys had ceased feuding in the Kentucky mountains and had joined together to battle the fascists.

Radio had now become such a way of life for Alan that when anthropologist Melville Herskovits, impressed by what Lomax had accomplished in Haiti, offered to make him his field assistant for a study of Brazil, he turned the professor down, thereby closing off a possible entrée into university life: "It was a wonderful opportunity, and the kind of training I would have received would have set me up in the academic world, but I was fascinated by what I thought would be a transformation of American radio into a new and remarkably broad avenue of communication."

CHAPTER 9

The People's War

One spring morning in 1942, Alan received a message asking him to appear at FBI headquarters in Washington. He assumed it was a routine matter—maybe a security check on all government workers during wartime—but when he arrived at the Bureau on April 3 he was put under oath and before a stenographer prepared to take down everything he said. Though he was never given a reason for the summons, it was part of an investigation of federal employees alleged to be members of groups advocating the overthrow of the government. The questioning moved quickly to accusations and denials: he denied membership in the Communist Party, denied that he had ever said he was a member; yes, he had once been a member of the American Youth Congress, but he wasn't sure whether he ever joined the Washington Committee for Democratic Action . . . he had signed so many things. None of the names he was shown on a list were Communists, so far as he knew. By the time they were done he was certain that they saw him as a Communist threat. When he was asked if he had any further comments, he replied:

> I am perplexed as to why I should be investigated because since 1936 when I first came here to work, I have worked so doggone hard at my job—so many hours a day—that it sort of hurts my feelings a little that I should be investigated because I do know that I sure have done my part—as much as I could in my job in the government which has been a source of some unhappiness to me because this thing has come up. I know it came up once before when I sang at the White House for the King and Queen, and my feelings were hurt a little there, and I thought the thing was settled.

When Archibald MacLeish received two reports following the FBI's investigations, he wrote back that he saw no evidence of subversive activities in Lomax, declared him a loyal American citizen, and said he would take no disciplinary action against him. A week later even J. Edgar Hoover himself declared that no action should be taken.

Alan reacted much as he did when he was arrested for protesting in Boston: he was doing what he thought any American should. At the moment he was called in by the FBI, he was working on a national defense songbook that would include patriotic songs, work songs, and recent antifascist songs like Woody Guthrie's "Duck Mister Hitler," "So Long, It's Been Good to Know You," "Round Up the Nazis," "He's On His Last Go 'Round," "Ring Around Hitler," and "You Fascists Bound to Lose." Who, he wondered, among his coworkers, friends, and family might have accused him?

But he was not about to draw back from what he thought was important, and never turned on his friends. He did all he could for Woody Guthrie, especially, and it was on his recommendation that E. P. Dutton agreed to publish Guthrie's *Bound for Glory*. Alan told Woody that he had played the Almanac Singers' records for Eleanor Roosevelt, who enjoyed them, but he also encouraged Woody to rename the Almanacs with a "good old countrified name like 'Oklahoma Rangers' or something of the sort." He also asked for permission to send Guthrie supplies to record new songs that he had written, though Spivacke questioned whether that was a good idea, since Guthrie was becoming a well-known performer and anything he was working on was likely to wind up issued by a recording company. It was something that Alan would run into more and more: either the people he found in his travels had already been recorded commercially, or those he found who were still unknown could easily become the objects of record company interest after he recorded them.

This suggested to him that he should create his own groups and record them. With the backing of his union, the United Federal Workers union of the CIO (Congress of Industrial Organizations), behind him, Alan asked his secretary (and sometime girlfriend of Woody Guthrie) Jackie Gibson to help him find some singers for a vocal group to be modeled on the Almanacs. She located Tom Glazer, a songwriter destined to become a successful folk and pop songwriter, and Edna Neil. Alan added Bernie Ashbel, a follower of the Almanacs who worked at a clerical job in the Library of Congress, and Helen Schneyer, who would ultimately move from being a singing secretary to premiering works for John Cage, and who would join *A Prairie Home Companion* near the end of her career. Alan named the group the Priority Ramblers, taking their name in part from the Prairie Ramblers on the *National Barn Dance* radio show. They sang at local dances, parties, and union affairs, and Alan got them a performance for Mrs. Roosevelt's annual party for the White House guards. In September 1943 he recorded some of their songs at the library, including one of his own, "In Washington," which poked fun at D.C.'s many circles, statues, and disproportionate female-to-male wartime ratio, and then ended with a surprise stanza in praise of the CIO. The following year Alan would create another singing group, the Union Boys, to make records only. It was an all-star folk group along the lines of the *Esquire-* and *Metronome* magazine–sponsored jazz all-star recordings, and gathered together Pete Seeger, Burl Ives, Sonny Terry, Brownie McGhee, Josh White, and Tom Glazer. When he arranged for them to record for Asch Records in March 11, 1944, he joined them in the singing.

One of the first major academic meetings on the study of folklore was the "Conference on the Character and State of Studies in Folklore," sponsored by the American Council of Learned Societies and held at Indiana University on April 11–12, 1942. Alan was one of the youngest speakers in a room full of some of the world's best-known scholars, many of whom thought of folklore as only a means of understanding the past. In his talk he laid out a vision of folklore that was as far from the antiquarian as possible. Folklore, he said, should be understood as the ultimate interdisciplinary subject, one so complex that it required linguists, sociologists, anthropologists, musicians, and scholars of literature; in fact, entire university departments should be devoted to its study. Folklore was the product of both individual artists and the community within which they function, and its proper study should include autobiographies of folklore artists and close readings of their repertoires, as well as community-wide studies of what folklore means to the people and how it functions in their lives. Comparative ethnographic and historical studies across regions, countries, and the world should be the next step, with scholars searching for patterns and discovering the principles that govern folklore. This would constitute a science of folklore. To scholars who were happy to spend their lives classifying and ordering written items of folklore like solitary butterfly collectors, this proposal was a bit frightening.

The seriousness of his talk at that conference was enough to earn him his first invitation to lecture as an academic when Stith Thompson asked him to teach at the newly created Summer Institute of Folklore at Indiana University on June 29–July 11, 1942, along with the likes of John Jacob Niles, Herbert Halpert, and George Herzog. But Alan was not easily flattered, and he reminded Thompson that he was not an academic. When he added that the $150 offered would not cover his expenses and loss of salary, Thompson found the extra money.

Alan headed back to Nashville by way of Bowling Green, Kentucky, on July 12, to resume the Fisk project in Mississippi, but worked largely without the Fisk people for the next six weeks. On July 17, he again visited Son House, who took him to meet Robert Johnson's mother: "She told us of her son, spoke of God, her great maker; got happy as we left—prophesying in the dusty yard." Later he recorded House again, and wrote in his notebook, "Slide guitar, metal body: screams in the night, trains ringing down the tracks, the moans of the lovers and those in pain, a sound that Europe had dreamt of, but never heard." Alan was so moved by his singing that four months later he wrote and asked if he would like to go to New York City to join the Almanacs. It would have changed the direction for the singing group and made a bold public statement, but House was never able to raise the money for the trip.

The session was interrupted by a car horn blowing outside. It was the plantation manager, House's boss, who ordered Alan and Elizabeth to follow him to the sheriff's office. His memory blurred by time and nervousness, Alan later recalled the humiliation of the sheriff doubting his word, disrespecting his government credentials, and accusing them of being foreign agents or, worse, Yankees. (Elizabeth also recalled a pistol jabbed into her kidneys.) Alan was arrested again later for simply putting his foot on a black woman's porch.

In that Delta summer, Alan worked with blind street singers and proud young men in bars, met a middle-class businessman who had studied with W. C. Handy, talked with elderly ladies on their front porches and children playing in the dirt, and took notes on preachers who in their thundering sermons bravely fused the injustices of their small world with those facing an enemy abroad. He recorded hours of prayer meetings, sermons, jokes, field hollers, poems, public occasions, levee songs, minstrel music, soldiers' songs, ballads, cowboy songs, interviews, string band music, and, near the end of the stay, children's songs, dances, and games, and also did some filming.

Even before Alan returned to Washington from Mississippi, Harold Spivacke wrote to tell him that the archive had not been budgeted for any additional money to make recordings for the following year, and any projects that Alan wanted to undertake would have to be related to the library's war efforts—something, say, on the order of record albums to be sent to the USOs, the United Service Organizations that provided entertainment and recreation for the troops and helped with morale. Alan bitterly responded that he thought the democratic heritage of song should not be abandoned because of the war. More than ever, he insisted, a folklore program was crucial "for morale with teachers, musicians, Negroes and people in the minority field," and that was something that the archive could foster. Obviously, no one at the library had faith in him, he said, including Spivacke. In any case, he bemoaned, the army would be calling him up soon.

With the end of the research for the Mississippi project with Fisk near, he asked that his stay there be extended so that he could finish the work, volunteering to do it for free if they couldn't pay him. Lewis Jones had already offered to stay with him to finish up. In his request for an extension, Alan wrote Spivacke:

> I have been in a territory where the Negroes are not reached by the newspapers or the radio, where the whites are quite defeatist in their point of view, where the

> Negroes hear about the war 1) "Hitler is going to kill all the niggers if he wins" (from the whites). 2) "This war is the judgment of God on a wicked world. Only Christianity will win through. Kneel down and pray." (This is the message of the Negro church to the religious Negro.)

The result of this constant message of the uselessness of action was an apathetic black population, he concluded. The whites of the region were threatened and anxious: "I have had more trouble with local whites on this trip than all the rest put together, because of the situation." The best means of changing things, he decided, was to work through the black church, the one institution of the black community that had at least a measure of autonomy and hadn't fallen under the control of whites. He was granted an extension of two weeks.

Leaving Mississippi in late August, Alan and Elizabeth went through Birmingham to attend the annual session of the Alabama Sacred Harp Singing Convention, where they met up with George Pullen Jackson, a professor of German at Vanderbilt University and the leading authority on southern hymn singing. Sacred Harp, which took its name from the hymnbook *The Original Sacred Harp*, was an older form of Anglo-American sacred music, with notes written in shapes different from normal music notation to allow untrained singers to follow the melody in a simpler reading form, and the arrangements were set to allow anyone to sing any part he chose. It was truly otherworldly music, with waves of sound sweeping through the church, especially on the first time through a song, when the singers sang without words.

On his return to Washington, Lomax and John Work remained civil but distant and wary, and were no longer working in league. Word had reached Washington that the Fisk project had come to a virtual standstill, and a Library of Congress memo noted that there was deadlock between the two men "based on professional jealousy" (though that phrase was struck out) that could be broken only if both men were relieved of administrative responsibility for completing the study. Lomax's superiors at the library and President Jones would take over, with the assistance of Charles S. Johnson, by mutual agreement. A further problem was a rivalry between the music department and the social science department at Fisk. The library proposed that John Work clear whatever he did with President Jones, and a plan was set up to complete the book.

The war forced shifts of focus and cuts in budgets at both the library and at Fisk. Key personnel were being drafted, and the book that was to emerge from their project fell into limbo. Lomax continued to look for means to support it, and asked the WPA Writers Project for help, but was astonished when they replied that they had been advised by the director of the Mississippi State Department of

Archives and History that there were no folk songs typical of the Delta, since it had only been settled recently. In addition, they said, they already had too much material to take on any more. Work continued on the project, but slowly, especially as he had lost some of his writing and had to wait for the library to send him copies of their copies, and there was confusion over just what material he had sent them. Work later wrote the library staff that it seemed to him that they were no longer interested in the project, but they responded that there was no one left there to see it through, and a "competent writer" would have to tie all the parts of the report together. President Jones told Harold Spivacke that more would have to be done on Work's manuscript (now titled "In the Bottoms") to make it "readable and attractive to the general public," and that in its current condition it could not be combined with Lomax's and Lewis Jones's parts to make a single book. President Jones said he would come to Washington to talk about the book, but that was the end of the matter.

Five years later Alan started work on his own book about the Fisk/Library of Congress project, and he asked Professor Work if he could make some copies of the recordings that Lomax had made there five years earlier. Work replied that he needed to know why he wanted them copied and whether they would be sold. That was the last contact they had.

It's difficult to know what that 1947 book would have looked like, as nothing remains of his plans, but a paragraph in a report he did in 1969 to the National Institute of Mental Health offers a hint of where he would have gone with at least part of it:

> In 1941 and 1942 when I was assistant in charge of the Archive of American Folk Song in the Library of Congress, I made a conventional functionalist survey of the folk song repertory of one county in the Mississippi Delta. With the help of a research team from the Department of Sociology at Fisk University, I collected and analyzed the entire folk song repertory of the Negroes of this Deep South area in terms of age, class, and economic level, and discovered that during the 100 years from which the survey could account, there had been four major shifts in the musical tastes of this area. However, since I could not control the main stylistic factors that were at work and at war in this area, I could not come to any conclusion about the forces that had produced these shifts of taste.

Alan and Lewis Jones kept in touch over the years, and it was Jones whom he consulted in 1954 when he started work on the manuscript that almost forty years later would became *The Land Where the Blues Began*. In a series of letters back and forth, Alan asked Jones if he knew what had happened to the work they had done toward a book. Jones replied that Charles Johnson had told him that he had organized the materials in the book and had tried to get it published, but it was rejected in the form it was in.

Alan had grown up in Washington's culture, spent his youth in it, and learned how to work the bureaucracy from within, but he had never found a way to completely protect himself within it. Periodic shifts in political alignments in Washington were unpredictable, and if he wasn't alert he could find even his most trusted colleagues suddenly on the other side. With New Deal projects coming under increasing attack from those on the right in Congress, the work of the archive was being seen by some as frivolous, and by others as politically provocative. When he returned to Washington from Mississippi, Alan learned that the Music Division's request for an additional $15,000 to expand the archive's activities had triggered a political battle. A congressman spotted the request in the library's appropriation bill and turned it into the occasion to speak out against the waste of money in a library headed by the "radical poet" Archibald MacLeish, and a House committee cut out the library's entire request for increasing acquisitions, so that nothing could be bought for the following year. Although Alan was not mentioned in the hearings, he felt that the library staff held him to blame. The increase to the budget was ultimately restored, but with a proviso that the archive would receive none of it.

Fearing the end of his run at the library, whether by the draft, cuts in staffing, or a purge, Alan tried to finish as much work as he could and get out as many publications as possible. He and Sidney Robertson Cowell compiled and published *American Folk Song and Folk Lore: A Regional Bibliography* to make the printed material on American folklore available to the public in a way that the scholars never thought to do. The bibliography was divided into the regions of America and by categories such as occupations, dances and games, white spirituals, and even jazz. Also completed were the three volumes of *The Check-List of Recorded Music in the English Language in the Archive of American Folk Songs to July, 1940,* which had been prepared by Charles Seeger with the WPA's support, and edited by Alan. The list was intended as a catalog of the archive's holdings for educational institutions and libraries, so that copies of the most important recordings could be made available to those who were interested. As it turned out, however, the Library of Congress soon began issuing shellac-based recordings for sale to anyone, a development that Alan had hoped for all along.

He wrote Macmillan with a proposal for a book that would summarize his work at the archive, explaining, "The burden of the book might be summed up this way. It is our democratic right to speak to the president and we ordinary Americans speak a language as eloquent and beautiful and distinctive and many-colored as any great writer ever wrote. I expect to make this material move out [*sic*] a more or less personal narrative of my own connection with and impressions of these people." But the publishers showed no interest in the project,

In September he applied for a transfer to some other branch of the government, listing New York City as the place where he most preferred to work. When his application was received, it was passed on to the FBI for clearance, and this time a new report was written about him that again claimed he had admitted to his father that he was a member of the Communist Party. But if the FBI took the allegation seriously, it was not used to block him from government employment.

At President Roosevelt's request, Archibald MacLeish had set up an agency called the Office of Facts and Figures in October 1941, a branch of the library that lasted only briefly before it was turned into the Office of War Information (OWI) in June 1942. MacLeish then resigned from the library to become one of the new office's assistant directors. With no one now at the top of the library to defend him and his work, Alan too resigned on October 10, to follow MacLeish to the OWI as an information specialist in its Bureau of Special Services, where he worked as a producer of radio programs for the Armed Forces Radio Service at a salary of $3,800 a year. The OWI was created to build morale and national spirit to prepare the country for what the war would ask of them. It was staffed with some of the most talented writers, actors, and directors in America: playwrights like Arthur Miller and Norman Corwin; writers of soap operas and radio mysteries such as Orin Tovrov (*Ma Perkins*) and Hi Brown (*Girl Intern* and *Inner Sanctum*); actors Richard Widmark, Mercedes McCambridge, Robert Young, and Frank Lovejoy; artists and literary stars like Arthur Schlesinger Jr., James Reston, and Gordon Parks; and producers and directors John Houseman and Nicholas Ray. Ray was John Houseman's favorite director, and a man who could get soldiers to become actors by encouraging them to improvise and to turn their weaknesses into art, so Houseman made Ray the special projects director for the Western Theater of Operations. (Alan got Bess Lomax a job as Nick's assistant, and she recalled with amusement Alan warning Nick that if he ever laid a hand on her he'd kill him.)

The director of OWI was Elmer Davis from CBS, the most popular radio newscaster in America, well known for delivering the nightly news with a Hoosier accent rather than in Broadcast Standard language. Most of the OWI were New Dealers and leftists of one stripe or another, so the power they had been given to address the nation made some in Congress nervous. Davis, for example, used his position to urge President Roosevelt to allow Japanese Americans to enlist in the military, and tried to persuade him to oppose bills that would deprive them of their citizenship and intern them in camps. In the early days of the war many people were willing to suspend judgment on what increasingly looked to them like an agency for propaganda, but as the spirit that unified the country following the Japanese attack dissipated, many of OWI's programs began to appear a bit too ardent in their support of Roosevelt's administration, and the nationalism they promoted seemed to many to have an internationalist tinge to it. Eventually, some in Congress openly accused the OWI of hiring Communists, and with investigations threatened, over thirty of the staff were forced to resign.

Alan's first task in his new job was to devise a plan to make the meaning of the war clear to minority groups, many of whom were not English speakers. Stories had reached Washington that there were Mexican mothers crying at railroad station platforms with no idea why their sons were being taken from them; and the government feared that many blacks were ambivalent at best over supporting the war. For Lomax, it was a challenge that he was ready for: "All the things I'd learned about as a folklorist were coming into immediate practical use. Folklore was not just for books; it could be a way of changing people's thinking." Two weeks into the job, he had already produced a lengthy proposal, "Plans for Reaching Folk Groups with War Information," which continued and extended ideas he had developed for the Library of Congress. It was a people's war, it said, with information about the conflict that should be provided equally to all, and the principles and aspirations that drove the war and won the peace should be those on which the people agreed. To reach everyone they would have to take account of those whose literacy did not extend to reading a newspaper, and even those whose income did not provide for a radio, those isolated by geography, poverty, or bigotry, the people that "the social scientist, when he is thinking in cultural terms, calls the folk." The way to do it was to understand these people's forms of communication and to locate those they had authorized to speak for them through folk song. This way, it would be possible to create a two-way system of communication:

> It is these folk artists that I hope to be able to motivate. They can assist in distributing war information through the following channels: the phonograph record (in the home and on the juke box), the local radio program, the folk church, the folk theatre (the rep theatre, the medicine show, the Mexican religious play, the foreign minority theatre), the many locales for swapping songs, stories and by-words.

Song was what Alan knew best, and he would start by collecting songs and commercial recordings with war content, surveying hillbilly, black, and Mexican American radio programs, and encouraging the film industry to make short musical films. He planned a two-week trip to the major cities to find the principal singers and composers, work out some new songs with them, then set up the project with the recording, radio, and publishing industries. He'd work to make alliances with several universities, and look for funding with the major foundations. Everything he proposed would take two forms: the local, and the national or international. Alan envisioned local performance settings that would encourage different parts of the community to entertain one another and also strengthen communities. At what he called the "United Nations level"—the nations allied against fascism—he wanted to see more research and collecting among groups like the Mexicans and Eastern Europeans in the United States as a means of connecting to other allies. It was a plan perhaps a bit too grand and novel for his bosses, and they were slow to act on it. Instead, Alan was cast as the house music man, the person you asked about background music for a film or radio show, or if you wanted to know the title of a tune.

The war was already affecting Alan's work and throwing blocks in his path: the shellac used in records was now rationed, as were gasoline, oil, and auto parts; recordings for any purpose were becoming harder to make. But there was also the non-war-related issue of the American Federation of Musicians' ban on recording to stop the use of records on radio in place of live musicians. The ban was in effect between August 1, 1942, and late 1944, and the union was monitoring studios to make sure that no commercial recording took place. In spite of being a government employee who was not engaged in commerce, Alan was unable to do some of the Latin American and Mexican recordings he wanted to make for two programs, "United We Sing" and "Corridos de la Guerra," and he was warned by the union that any recordings sent up from Mexico would be viewed as bootlegging.

When Christmas came around, his father reminded Alan that he had not seen his family for three years. His father had met Elizabeth only once. John had been writing him repeatedly, asking if he had received his letters: "As a final mark of indifference you fail to acknowledge money that I send you . . . until this last failure is repaired I won't send you any more money!"

Alan soon realized he'd transferred into an organization that was even more hierarchic and less flexible than the Library of Congress. OWI was completely occupied with communicating what the war was about to a country that the polls said was not yet convinced of its necessity, trying to assure them that Britain was seriously committed to the conflict, and easing fears of Russia's seeming overly committed to it. Alan found himself having to answer to upper-level management who were in civilian life corporate broadcast executives with little knowledge of the implications of what he called the patchwork of American culture. Their vision of the country was hopelessly East Coast, he thought, with no notion of what their audiences were making of their programs, and for that matter, little idea of who their audiences actually were. At the start of 1943 he wrote proposal after proposal intended to educate his bosses on what he could do. Some of these suggestions read like manifestos; others appeared to be reports on what he was already doing without their approval. Behind them all was the message that he would not be deterred.

Among his plans were two fifteen-minute programs of recordings that would communicate war information to poor whites and blacks: "They will contain topical songs about the enemy, the United Nations, the fighting fronts, rationing, the necessity for sacrifice, etc. These songs will be composed and sung by the leading juke box and Southern radio artists, Negro and White, by Negro ministers, Negro choirs, cowboy singers, etc." He contacted the writers and operators of traveling repertory tent theater groups in hopes of convincing them to produce plays aimed at rural areas and small towns in the Midwest. He proposed that a black newscaster be used on the air in Norfolk, Virginia, as an experiment in integrating the news. Antifascist songs should be recorded in various foreign languages to be used overseas on different fronts of the war, he said, especially the Near East and South Africa. Alan had made a survey of what types of music were popular in these areas and was prepared to find singers in the United States who could record them. He also wanted to compile a songbook of fighting songs, freedom songs, and songs of liberation from all the Allied countries that could be used in schools and communities.

At the same time, he continued to operate as if he were still working at the library, answering letters forwarded to him and pleading for library or foundation help for people he thought were doing good work. He asked the Rosenwald Foundation to support Woody Guthrie's writing and the work of two black scholars, William Harrison Pipes at the University of Michigan and his studies of a black Holiness church in Memphis, and Professor Willis James of Spelman College for his research on folk song in Georgia. He was also lining up experts whom he felt could help with "wartime issues among isolated groups of Americans."

By March it was clear to him that his ideas were not being accepted with much enthusiasm, and even his plans for radio programs for the South were being cut. Instead of his campaign to reach people on the margins of society on their own terms, the OWI was planning to mail out informational bulletins to local media and "to insert 'Buy War Bonds' in the middle of a Camel ad." When he saw what was happening, he wrote William B. Lewis, the deputy director of the Domestic Division of the Office of War Information, a former vice president of CBS:

> I still don't see how you can do the job of reaching underprivileged Americans without (a) budget, (b) planning linked up with the rest of the OWI programs, (c) vigorous administrative backing. Sending out the bulletin you mention to the people whose help we need in reaching these special groups would, I fear, be like throwing into the sea a bottle containing an angry note to Adolf Hitler. In this field one has to work either by example (i.e. transcriptions, church services, etc.) or

> better, by personal contact. What budgetary considerations seem to have pushed us into is a policy of reaching largely those Americans who are already reached by commercial channels, and of giving them information much of which they'd get anyway. . . . My mistake in OWI was that I assumed when I was hired that my plans had been approved in advance and that means for immediate action would be provided. This was awfully naïve of me. The failure of my projects has been due as much as anything to my failure to get a hearing for them. I thought that time was too short. I do not now want to continue to feel useless. If there is nothing in OWI for me to do, I want to get out and get closer to the job of killing Fascists. The problems of the South are still there and something might be done if a group of people like Arthur Raper (FSA [Farm Security Administration]), Lewis Jones (OWI), and Don Young (Army Specialist Corps) got together with us and decided on an action program that would get OWI backing. The Southern local station job remains to be tackled, if you can give me the authority to tackle it. But I don't want to just be kept on. If you are convinced nothing can and will be done, let me know, because in that event I want to resign at once. I know you're busy as hell now and I will be too, for about ten days more. Let me hear from you, if possible, by then.

Despite his misgivings, Alan did succeed in getting on the air more than a hundred hours of radio shows of antifascist and morale-boosting songs featuring Burl Ives, Pete Seeger, Woody, and others in the Lomax circle. He also managed to complete a three-hundred-page mimeographed volume of *Freedom Songs of the United Nations*, a collection of texts and a descriptive bibliography of what he called "democratic songs" that he had developed from materials in the United Nations Information Center in New York with the help of Svatava Pirkova Jakobson, a Czech folklorist and translator and the wife of the émigré linguist and literary theorist Roman Jakobson.

Away from the eight-hour days at OWI, Alan was producing and performing in clubs and concerts, some of which were quite elaborate: "In Time of Battle," for example, at Town Hall on April 18, was a concert that offered music as a weapon in the war. Symphonic works by Ives, Schumann, Brahms, Tchaikovsky, Hindemith, and Shostakovich were performed, Jewish folk songs by the People's Philharmonic Chorus, and songs sung by Alan, Josh White, Lead Belly, and Earl Robinson that ended with an audience sing-along.

Alan's unhappiness at work grew to the point that he applied for a passport, with rather vague plans for touring Europe, and maybe becoming a war correspondent. After he gave his father as a reference, John was asked to come to the State Department to sign papers in support of the application. He did so, but then wrote Alan and chided him about it. Seeing no future left for himself at the OWI, Alan knew he would soon be called up for the draft. While he was waiting he considered returning to his old job at the library, but that would mean that Ben Botkin, his replacement at the archive, a man he liked, would have to be let go just so that he could have his job for the short time before induction.

His dilemma was solved when he got a call from the Columbia Broadcasting System offering him a job that would pay him $8,000 a year ($71,705 in contemporary dollars) and also make him eligible for a deferment. He was to be one of the writers and editors for *Transatlantic Call: People to People,* a program that CBS conceived as a means of building friendly relations with the United Kingdom. CBS and the BBC would each produce its own biweekly programs that would be aired in both the United Kingdom and the United States. The American contributions would be built around subjects such as "American Heroes in Song," "The Indians of New Mexico," or "Lumbering in the State of Washington," and would each originate in a different city. It was a big and high-budget series, and CBS backed it with their best efforts, using Norman Corwin as the lead writer and on-air commentator. Alan and the other writers' job was to arrive two weeks before a broadcast, survey the area, conduct interviews, and then write the scripts in time for them to be approved by the Office of War Information, the Censorship Department of the United States Armed Services, and other oversight groups. As the series progressed, it changed to a more complex format, shifting to a split program, with fifteen minutes from New York and fifteen minutes from London, maybe with both segments describing a wartime Sunday in the two countries' capitals; or a visit to two schools; or backstage in a British music hall and a look at the movie industry in Hollywood.

Because the Office of War Information had a stake in the series, it saw no problem with giving Alan leave and requesting a continuing deferment until December 31, 1943. On May 1 Alan officially went on leave, although the last day he actually worked for the government was April 17; he was scheduled to begin his new job on June 30, and until then he wrote for CBS freelance and borrowed advances on his radio salary. The timing of this new position not only got him out of an unhappy situation, but one that was doomed: by 1944 the budget for the domestic branch of the OWI was cut so deeply that it could barely function, and by September it was closed down.

The first of the new CBS/BBC programs—on Savannah, Georgia—was broadcast on June 6, and Alan wrote his father that "the program, as I hear it, was not very good; but most of that was faulty direction and not my responsibility—though some was due to my amateurish script." It was at this point that Norman Corwin withdrew from the series because of illness, and Alan took his place. After his first two shows as chief writer and on-air commentator, Alan wrote his father about the weight of responsibility he was feeling:

> I had worked for ten days practically continuously on the Spokane show. It was the hardest one to date because I had only four days to find the material and write the script. You see those shows have to be cleared by about 8 or 9 agencies—Censorship, War & Navy, WPIS, CBS, all the local plants involved, etc. And so they have to be done & ready for inspection four or five days ahead of time. I wrote this one in about 36 hours and so high on coffee at one A.M. when I finished I didn't get to sleep until the next night. . . . I continue to have my personal troubles. Two stations have complained about me because I failed to wear my coat into the dining room of some local hotel. I've been fighting about this for the last two days. Two weeks ago I had censorship troubles. These stuff-shirt bastards who are supposed to run the world can't keep their hands off anybody who comes around them. They have kept me in a G-D emotional turmoil for the past three weeks when I should have all my time for my job. The particular s-o-b finally forgave me for the coat deal when he found out I had never belonged to a fraternity in college. The little snob. I wanted to smack him and instead I grinned and took it.

On the other hand, the producer of the BBC portion of the programs, D. Geoffrey Bridson, loved his work: "In the first of [Lomax's] *Transatlantic Call* productions, American actuality came alive: he spoke the same language and sang the same songs as Americans everywhere. More to the point, he was able to help them speak that language into a microphone, and to get the full flavor of their characters across. The shows that he handled came over with the same American impress as the prose of Thomas Wolfe or the poetry of Whitman. He could interpret America because he was so American himself. . . . I never knew any American who more fully embodied the virtues—and the more engaging vices—of all his countrymen."

When he took on the program on the Lower East Side of Manhattan, Alan threw himself into it like an ethnographer who had only three days to learn everything about a very large group of diverse people. He mapped the streets, took notes on people's ages, national origins, jobs, and entertainment, saw what they bought and sold, participated in their street life. He interviewed a lawyer who ran a free legal aid office, listened in on people's opinions about anything and everything, recorded arguments over baseball and politics, women's personal love stories, pushcart peddlers' spiels, and spent a day at the Henry Street Settlement House. When he saw a parade of a marching band, majorettes, faculty, and student body leaving a high school he fell in behind them and followed them to the American Red Cross, where they presented a new ambulance the school had raised the money to buy. While he was in the streets he wrote down what the signs and placards said, and recorded games and children's songs and jokes, many of them on the subject of the war. At Katz's Deli on Houston Street, where they had recently put up a sign in the window that would become part of New York City lore—"Send a salami to your boy in the army"—the manager read him letters from servicemen begging to be put on the list. Alan managed to get most of it into his script, and also admitted that though he had lived in New York for a few years, he had never been on the Lower East Side and wasn't even sure where it began and ended. In the flush of his new discovery he wrote a glowing tribute to a virtual utopia:

> This is a neighborhood of people who have known persecution and poverty and family troubles. This is a neighborhood of friendly people where the Rotary Club label of "self-made man" really fits. This is a neighborhood of night schools and hard jobs and small incomes and dreary walk-up flats. This is a neighborhood that is deeply religious. You'll have to look far and wide before you can find one where there is as much tolerance and warmth and mutual understanding. But out of it has come hundreds and thousands of our leading citizens in all walks of life.

As Alan was leaving OWI, their office's chief investigations officer had requested that the FBI start another investigation of him, and its agents retraced their first inquiries back to Harvard, the University of Texas, and Washington to reinterview people who knew him and to reexamine his records. By the time they forwarded copies of their reports to the OWI on July 17, Alan had been added to the list of alleged Communists drawn up by Texas representative Martin Dies's Committee Investigating Un-American Activities, which declared him to have been a member of the National Student League, the Washington Book Store, and the Washington Committee for Democratic Action, all of them targets of anti-Communist forces.

After conducting their investigation the FBI wrote its own biography of Alan Lomax. He was possessed of an "artistic temperament"; a "Bohemian," "single-mindedly devoted to folk music"; "ornery"; he was not "discreet" in his choice of words; and was slovenly in appearance. He was "intensely interested" in Negro and "underprivileged classes"; was sometimes slow to pay his rent; had several arguments with his father "on the Negro question, wherein he termed his father as a fascist and himself as a communist on this question, his father being anti-Negro minded"; and he was "known to associate with a Negro by the name of 'Lead Belly' who was released from a southern penitentiary."

He was accused of treating the Library of Congress's recording equipment roughly in the field; "tries to live within his means but due to the limited salary he was paid by the Library of Congress and his lack of appreciation of money values, he had a difficult time"; his wife was reported to be more politically liberal than he, but "that the great desire and ambition to collect folk lore music overshadows any political influence his wife may exercise upon him"; he was an outstanding writer; but had no hobbies; was never known to be a drinker, though his father was accused of intoxication and "breaking up the furniture" on weekends; he was "always singing peculiar songs of a Western or Negro type" or reading books. He had "considerable company in his apartment and on three or four nights a week there was a great amount of singing and music emanating from his apartment (the neighbors enjoyed it, but his landlord did not)." Each of the investigators found Lomax to be described by those who knew him as a "rugged individualist" and a loyal American. The investigators had finally accepted that Lomax, like many in what was called the Cultural Front, was too independent and undisciplined to ever be completely loyal to a single party or ideology. The FBI nevertheless continued to quietly trail him for the next sixteen years.

On July 25, 1943, Elizabeth and Alan rented an apartment at 242 East 19th Street in New York City, and Alan commuted back and forth to Washington. With two apartments to maintain, they were now even more behind in rent. Elizabeth was working for the newly organized Office of the Coordinator of Inter-American Affairs on Madison Avenue, a government agency that was created to improve economic and cultural relations between the nations of the Americas, and was headed by Nelson Rockefeller. From the beginning it was a controversial agency, accused of being a haven of Communist operatives, and of funding wildly expensive and eccentric cultural projects such as Orson Welles's doomed Latin American film spectacle *It's All True*. They were said to be infiltrated by Soviet intelligence, and by 1946 the agency's functions had been transferred to the Department of State and elsewhere and it was disbanded. But Elizabeth was still able to be hired by the OWI herself in its last days, at $3,600 a year, and according to Alan she quickly became one of their "top-flight script writers . . . working on an equal basis with Louis Untermeyer & others."

By October, with his deferment ending in less than two months, Alan grew ambivalent about the service. One day his letters to his father might speak of the need to get into the army "and see what needs to be done," and his urge to "kill fascists." On a different day another letter might show a different person:

> And my private opinion is the world's a pretty mad place. The killing is beginning to get under my skin. You can be very reasonable about it, I know, but it's being

> reasonable about unreason. You were lucky in being mature and settled before the First World War hit humanity so hard. I can feel myself changing. I can feel the weariness and bitterness creeping up in everyone I meet. This thing is too much to be endured.

He may have felt that war was the rationalization of the insane, but he was nonetheless resigned to it. He had had two small operations in these two months to have a sebaceous cyst removed from the base of his spine as required for his eligibility to be called to duty.

Meanwhile, *Transatlantic Call* completely engulfed him. He was almost always traveling and away from home, with a schedule that had him working thirteen-hour days. He took to the discipline and the regularity of the production schedule, but over time he found himself living only for the program he was producing. He managed to handle minor disagreements with CBS until a script he wrote on the TVA was returned to him radically changed. "I put the show on in despair, flew back to New York, and found out that the head of public relations for the utilities had been responsible for most of the changes. I resigned and decided to have my draft deferment . . . be cancelled."

His induction notice arrived in January 1944, and he began to fret over what he had not accomplished and might never accomplish. He had completed all of the planning for the projects he had proposed to the OWI, but whether any of them would ever be realized remained a question. "This is strange, selfish talk in the middle of a world where men are dying for liberty every second," he wrote his father. "I realize I have lost a lot of illusions. I think I'll get them back when I get closer to the thing itself. That's only a few weeks away and I wish the time were shorter. I look at my face in the mirror, shaving these cold, smoky mornings—it is the face of a young man who will be crossing a cold, hostile ocean into a world of hate and terror soon. It is a strange face to me. I have sufficient imagination to be a bit scared and admit that."

A week or so later, he wrote John Lomax again:

> Sometimes I wonder what it is that gnaws at the bowels of you and me, makes us restless, discontented, trying to our friends, sad and gloomy. Here I am, with a busy life, lots of people who like me, several who love me, somewhat admired and looked up to by a few, and I am as discontented as if I were a poor bum on the street. Indeed, I really regard myself as a good deal worse off. I know that you sometimes suffer the same way. I wonder what sort of thing it is that bothers us fundamentally. I am really worried about it, and may take the trouble and expense of going to an analyst to find out.

Alan entered the army on April 5, 1944, at Camp Upton, in Yaphank, Long Island, a World War I–era base that had been reopened (and three years later would be closed again and turned into the Brookhaven National Laboratory). Camp Upton was a reception center where inductees were given inoculations and clothing, sworn in, classified, and after a few weeks sent elsewhere for basic training. There was little for him to do there ("the first vacation I'd had in years") but camp maintenance, and Alan volunteered for kitchen work the first week, then worked on the camp newsletter. Radio programs he had written were still on the air, and five days after he arrived at camp, sitting in his barracks, he heard his script "The First Commando" broadcast on *The Cavalcade of America.*

Alan's radio work in New York City in fact had not really ceased. His friendship with the BBC's Douglas Bridson continued, and on weekend leaves from the camp Alan introduced him to folksingers and spent evenings with him in nightclubs in Manhattan. Bridson was fascinated by Lomax's speech, his energy, brashness, optimism, and his principles:

> In Café Society one night I was eating peacefully with a party of friends and talking to Josh [White] over our steaks. Sitting next to me, Alan Lomax suddenly jumped to his feet, seized the man at the table next to me and knocked him clean across his supper. Waiters rushed over, but saying nothing to Alan, threw the body into the street. I asked, in some astonishment, what the hell was going on? "He annoyed me," said Alan, sitting down again. Five minutes later, the man came lurching back, protesting that he wanted to apologize. With a vigilant waiter on either side, he approached our party again and held out his hand: Alan rose, prepared to shake it. "I didn't mean to offend you," said the man, "I only said that I didn't want to sit at the next table to a goddam nigger." Alan hit him again, before the waiters could drag him away.

Bridson hoped to get Alan involved in more of the BBC's projects, such as one from the year before in which he had commissioned Langston Hughes to write a radio play about a black Londoner in the army, *The Man Who Went to War,* with Paul Robeson, Ethel Waters, Canada Lee, Josh White, Brownie McGhee, and Sonny Terry. Bridson had conceived of it as a "ballad opera" in the eighteenth-century tradition of John Gay and Henry Carey's dialogue and song operas about the working classes, and Alan and Elizabeth selected folk songs for the play, with Hughes writing some original pieces. (Lomax and Hughes may have thought of it as being more along the lines of Zora Neale Hurston's folk-song-based *The Great Day,* which had been performed in New York in 1932.)

Hughes's radio play was so popular in Britain that before Bridson returned to

England for a new assignment, he asked Alistair Cooke to see if Alan and Elizabeth were interested in doing another folk opera, this one based on the Martins and the Coys, two fictional southern mountaineer clans engaged in a feud, a humorous, hillbilly *Romeo and Juliet*. It was a legend that had worked its way through pop culture from a nineteenth-century real-life feud between the Hatfields and the McCoys, two extended families in Kentucky, to a 1936 recording of "The Martins and the Coys" that reached the hit charts in both the United States and England. With a substantial budget and a good cast, Bridson felt that they could again draw a big audience, this time perhaps in both countries. Elizabeth (writing under the name of Elizabeth Lyttleton) and Alan agreed to do it, she writing the script, he choosing the music.

The prologue (written for Alan to read) illustrates how she recast the popular story:

> Tonight we bring you a new play, *The Martins and the Coys,* a musical extravaganza, based on the tall stories and the ballads of the southern mountains. These mountains stretch along the Atlantic Coast about two hundred miles inland, and in North Carolina and Tennessee, they reach their full dramatic height in a range named by Indians the Great Smokeys, because of the veil of mist that often hangs over their ragged and heavily timbered heights. Here, in many a walled-in cove and wooded hollow, lives a hearty breed of mountaineers—true descendants of the early American frontiersmen—still clinging to the ways of their ancestors: blood feuding and bear hunting, handicraft making and ballad singing. Poetry and song are as natural to these folk as ordinary speech. Some of their songs have come down to them directly from the Scottish border wars, some were made since 1941. Our play does not attempt to present a factual picture of mountain life, but portrays in a fanciful way the spirit and traditions of the mountaineers, a fighting breed that has been in this war, heart and soul, since long before Pearl Harbor.

Burl Ives, Pete Seeger, and Woody Guthrie were the lead singers, and the rest of the musical cast included Will Geer, Cisco Houston, Sonny Terry, and Alan, with a group of actors added from Broadway and radio to shore up the drama. In Elizabeth's script an isolated mountain community was widened out to include blacks and whites, street singers and soap stars, actors and the acted upon, moving ever outward to hint at the clan wars of Scotland and the battle between fascism and democracy. *The Martins and the Coys* was recorded in the Decca studios in New York in May, broadcast in Britain in June, and then issued for sale in the United Kingdom as a five-disc BBC Records album. This was such a successful production that the BBC later commissioned another ballad opera from Alan and Elizabeth, *The Chisholm Trail*, which was broadcast in the UK in February in 1945.

After the induction process was completed, Alan was sent by train to Camp Crowder, near Neosha, Missouri, southeast of Joplin, on the edge of the Ozarks. The rumor among the troops was that this meant that they were all headed for the Signal Corps. Almost immediately on arriving, Alan came down with a painful case of carbuncles, with boils all over his lower body, and was sent to the camp hospital for almost a week. Next he developed a bad cold and a fever that he thought would lead to pneumonia, but which no one else took seriously. Yet in spite of his health, the disruption in his life, a weak right eye that kept him from being classified as a marksman, partial deafness in one ear, and having been dropped into what most people might think of as nowhere, Alan loved it. The pointless tasks, the instructional films, the sleepy classes, living in absolute equality, listening to the talk of the men—all of it made sense to him. He was one of them, the people, and that was all right. Or so his letters home said. The rumors about the Signal Corps proved to be correct, and as the days of training dragged on he discovered that he was afraid to climb telephone poles and froze whenever he tried it, dooming him to be a telephone operator.

He soon established himself on the base as "the music man." At an evening of entertainment in the recreation hall, Alan sang "Sam Hall" to what he said was "a shocked GI audience":

Oh, my name it is Sam Hall, it is Sam Hall,
Yes, my name it is Sam Hall, it is Sam Hall;
Yes, my name it is Sam Hall, and I hate you one and all,
Yes, I hate you one and all, God damn your eyes.

Oh, I killed a man, they say, so they say,
Yes, I killed a man, they say, so they say;
I beat him on the head, and I left him there for dead,
Yes I left him there for dead, God damn his eyes.
Etc. . . .

"I was billed as the World's Greatest Authority on American Folk Song. That was in a sense, an apology, which I let go by, because I knew they didn't think I could *sing* so that had to excuse [me] somehow."

One day an officer asked him how they could get white soldiers to sing like black soldiers when they drilled. Apparently he had heard that Russian soldiers sang together, and that it made them better fighters. But Alan warned him that they'd never get white soldiers to sing as a group. Shortly afterward he heard black troops counting cadence by using syncopated chants during their drills, and, fascinated by this intrusion of creativity into military procedure, he interviewed a Sergeant Barker about what he called "swing cadence." "We used to sing 'We Gonna Raise a Ruckus Tonight,'" the sergeant said. "We used to drill out from camp, and the boys would put in a lot of mansize verses, and it didn't matter . . . there weren't no ladies around. We'd go on night hikes and everybody be tired, and we begin to sing and hell, man, we'd knock the 27 miles off like anything!"

Alan wanted to find a way to record these drills so that he could send copies back to Washington to the Library of Congress:

> I was at drill one day, the whole camp was being inspected by the general and he said, "I want Private Lomax" so I was pulled out in front of the whole god-damned camp. He said, "What's this I hear about this song that we have here, Lomax?" I said, well sir, it's one of the great songs of my life, and I'm a song collector and I hope it can be recorded for posterity. He turned to the Colonel and he said, "Take charge, get this song recorded." The next day they had the regiment out and the recording machine and we recorded it right there and then. And the General liked the record so much that he wore it out playing it over the camp loud speaker system and it never got to Washington.

This black chanting so enlivened marching that officers were encouraged to let white troops learn it.

Despite his cheerful letters home from camp, Alan was increasingly intensely bored, and had written Harold Spivacke and asked if he knew anyone who could find a place for him in the army where he might be more useful; Harold said that he would ask about military radio broadcasting. Within a month his transfer had been requested to Astoria, Long Island, by Erik Barnouw of the Armed Forces Radio Service, who had worked with Alan and Norman Corwin on several programs in the *Pursuit of Happiness* series for CBS in 1939 and was now in uniform in the military's radio division. Alan wrote his family that he would still like to go overseas and take a greater part in the war effort, but he had just learned that Elizabeth was pregnant, and the move back to New York now "sounded rosier than Homer's rosiest dawn."

By late fall 1944 he was back in the Village with Elizabeth, living at 67 Perry Street, and on November 20, Elizabeth gave birth to a girl, Anne Lyttleton Lomax. Alan's letter to his family radiated with the delirium of a new parent, his helpless joy in the glow of the moment. She was the perfect baby, even more so, and he boasted even about being able to boast. He found similarities between Anne's features and character and those of various family members, and promised pictures by Christmas (they were at the moment "kinda broke").

The sweetness of the new baby was not enough to completely sustain him, however, for within a week or so, he wrote his father that he was "having real soul struggles at the moment":

> Pretty depressed. I haven't got much stimulus in the office. It's sort of sleepy and the people at the top lack courage, imagination and drive. They're just holding down jobs. So I'm lazing along and it really hurts me where I live. There's so much to be done. And in most ways I'd be much happier over the ocean taking what comes with my brother Americans. Also, I'm having a very hard time learning to be a writer. Don't know if I have the stuff. Don't have my folk-lore crutch anymore and I'm worried as hell about that. Go around sick at my stomach half the time because I'm afraid I'm not as good as I thought I was. Bad condition.

His father, meanwhile, was writing him letters that matched his with complaints about illnesses and fears of having reached the end of his life.

Alan's first job for the Armed Forces Radio Service was making network radio shows suitable for overseas rebroadcasting by editing the commercials out and replacing them with messages and short musical selections. "I'm a bit lazy for the first time in my life. I really want to do nothing at all but stay at home and laze around the house. Never felt like that before, but that's what I want to do and it makes work difficult." Elizabeth had gone back to work almost immediately after the baby was born.

> During the day I'm mostly bored and frustrated, but I am told by everyone who's been overseas that I'm a fool for wanting to go. Thing is, my motives are different from those of most guys. Nevertheless I feel out of things and isolated and you know what special service is like. I should be learning to write, but the army life is so lazy and things are so slack I really do little else but sit on my can all day long. Sometimes I wonder whether I'll ever work up energy to work very hard again. Elizabeth is the breadwinner and, I must say, a good deal better provider than I was most of the time. We have a maid and wonderful food and a house full of furniture for the first time in our lives, money in the bank and a steadily growing pile of war bonds. And E. is growing into one of the best writers on OWI payroll, turning out shows which are avidly snatched up by the overseas stations. Things are very nice for her, for the first time in her life and she really blossoms.

"If it weren't for Elizabeth," he wrote his father, "I'd never be able to finish anything. She helps me in every sort of way, but principally by admiring everything I do, or pretending to, so that I have the impetus to go ahead and finish the job."

Since Alan's army pay was only fifty dollars a month, and they had to hire help with the baby while they were both at work, they were not as financially stable as his letter to his father suggested. He felt he had to do more to help with family expenses, and wrote Ben Botkin at the archive to send him copies of all of the Jelly Roll Morton material, because he wanted to turn it into a book. He also picked up a job as a part-time radio scriptwriter for CBS. Now Elizabeth and he were both working six days a week, Alan for the army by day and CBS by night, turning out script after script for his two employers.

The first scripts he worked on for the AFRS were for a series called *Singing America,* morale-building dramatic episodes in American history involving little-known figures in heroic endeavors. "Clipper Ship Sailors," for instance, reenacted the record-breaking voyage of the sailing ship *Flying Cloud* from New York around Cape Horn to San Francisco in eighty-nine days and twenty-one hours. If Alan's previous scripts were small skits written as pretexts to showcase songs, now the songs were often fading back to incidental music.

Then he received notice that he was being transferred, and at the end of July was sent off to Camp Lee, in Petersburg, Virginia, a training school for quartermasters and other odds and ends of military life. "I am in a basic training company, along with a mass of other guys from all over the country. . . . I will be sent to Special Service Training—which I have been trying to avoid since long before I got in the army. Special Service is the entertainment branch of the service—the hide out of all the vaudeville acts, the jazz musicians, the second rate writers, the neurotics, etc., in the army. The generals do not see any point in entertainment. The officers and men are not respected by the fighting branches of the army and their assignment is not taken seriously. Special Service people regard their assignment as a gravy train, the goof-off job in the service."

Once there, however, he got to know the men, and came to see both them and himself in a different light:

> There is much less to do here than at Crowder. Discipline is a good deal more relaxed. The food is better. There is a nice swimming pool. Last night I went to a soldier's round table on "The British Election." The boys, the soldiers are, as always, tougher and more cynical and more knowing than the underworld characters in Villon, in Victor Hugo, in Dos Passos, in Hemingway. In fact the more I listen to the conversation of my fellow-man, the more thoroughly I am convinced that no one has written any realistic literature, with the possible exception

> of Gorki. In my barracks there is every vice and depravity known to mankind, and a few more that have not been recorded; there is a lack of belief in anything; there is more corruption and conflict per square inch than any writer has ever recorded—and yet these are the best boys in the world. Christians, gentlemen, smart, rugged, full of vitality, witty, kind-hearted, friendly, naively loving and full of laughter. It's something terribly hard to describe or explain. And I am convinced that every ship's forecastle, cow camp, prison block, union meeting, pirate gang, and primitive Christian assembly has been just like this—with the small and superficial differences due to the year, the language, the nationality, the historical background of the groups. Here is something eternal, which I feel and appreciate, but do not understand well enough to really write about.

Homesickness soon set in, however, and he again felt lazy and hapless and began living for weekend passes. With the end of the war with Japan in sight, basic training seemed more and more absurd each day, and Alan spent most of his time practicing on his guitar. When he heard that Ben Botkin had resigned from the archive, he suddenly saw a postwar role for himself, and imagined a boom in field recording ahead. He told his father that

> in between and underneath and through everything else I think about these things—a) What I'll do after I get out—I'm still not sure—but I shall and must work up my *own* mind this time instead of having a job *thrust* on me or handed to me. b) How I can get out—appears to be at least a year more of it ahead, unless I can pull some strings. c) What is going to happen in Annie's generation—the Negro problem—equal opportunity—democracy for the weak & oppressed peoples of Africa, Asia, etc.—establishing the four freedoms—keeping the world peaceful. And all around me I hear voices in disagreement—I feel the lines of the conflict already forming—and I begin to decide how I shall be involved, where I'll be most useful. Actually, I struggle hard all day every day to establish some sort of disciplined personal life which will prepare me for the problems of civilian life. And I worry about how & where to begin.

In the long days of waiting at the camp, he wrote many letters to his father, summing up his life to him, expressing his fears about his future, thanking him for what he had given him but also attempting to explain the principles that drove him forward:

> All my concern for the "hoi-polloi" came directly from living with you and hearing about your boyhood in Bosque and the struggles you had and then meeting the "hoi-polloi" in your company and discovering that their songs and stories and

> their strength were more wonderful and inspiring than anything I had hitherto bumped into. Otherwise my poor intellectual notions would have withered on the vine, long ere this, like those of so many people who once believed in the cause of the common man. I'm still very much for [Henry] Wallace [former vice president and then secretary of commerce] and for freedom of opportunity and against poverty and misery and oppression of racial and class and religious minorities. These beliefs I owe, like so much else in my life, not to listening to what you say so much as by watching you and getting to understand what kind of person you are. And I could no more give up those beliefs and feelings now than I could life, itself. Without them my life would completely lose its meaning and I would turn into a lump of shapeless and purposeless clay like so many people have and do every day. After the war is over I shall, if I have the strength and fortitude, concern myself much more directly than I have ever done in my life with the problems and concerns of the common man in this world. At this point I am working, much against my own inclination and with the greatest pain in the world, to make some sort of a writer of myself. If it turns out that I am to be only a mediocre and tepid writer, as I am afraid it will, at least I'll have one tool a bit sharpened for the days of my life that lie ahead—and I know they will be grim days, but at least I'm going to go ahead and do what I think is right.

In the first nine days of August the United States dropped two atomic bombs on Japan, and by August 15 the war was over. The word was that men of Alan's age and at his stage of service might be kept in the service for another six months, maybe a year. Elizabeth's job would be coming to an end now, so they had to find some source of income for the family. Alan wrote Harold Spivacke at the library and asked if he might be requisitioned for a job while he was still in the service, maybe as a song or documentary record specialist. But all that Spivacke would offer was a promise that he would "bear the matter in mind and if anything turns up let you know at once." The first day he had off, Alan made appointments with several people in Washington, the most important of whom was Luther Evans, Archibald MacLeish's replacement as Librarian of Congress. He reminded Evans that by law he was guaranteed his old job after leaving the service, and wondered if the whole process might be hastened by having the library request him from the military. Evans gave him some encouragement, and he went back to Camp Lee to wait.

When no letter came from the library, Alan called Evans and found out that they had decided that he had voided his tenure when he took the job with CBS, and Spivacke already had someone else in mind for the job. All they could offer Alan was a recording trip of six months, or maybe a trip to Russia to study Russian folklore methods. A month later the library announced that they were now issuing albums of selected folk recordings from the archive for sale to the public. Since most of the recordings had been done by John and Alan, all the attendant publicity mentioned the two of them. In an interview for *Time,* Alan described the recordings as "plain and unadulterated folk song, usually about death, sweat, hard work, love. No fancy-pants stuff like *Oklahoma!* Miserable people make the most exciting music I ever heard."

With his plans for the archive dashed, he began looking for an advance on a book, and considered taking the six-month recording offer from the library and then seeing if he could make a living as a writer on the South. Elizabeth had just learned that her job would be secure at least until June, and CBS was now offering her work as writer for an episode of the Helen Hayes radio show.

Alan was ultimately transferred to an army public relations office in New York City in November to wait out the last four months before his discharge. Meanwhile, after years of neglect and little income, his father had completed his book on his work as a folk song collector, *Adventures of a Ballad Hunter,* and Paramount had bought film rights to it; gossip columnists speculated that it would star Bing Crosby as John. Alan also found some work with the movies, as he, Elizabeth, and Nick Ray were offered $2,500 for advising on the music for a film version of Wilbur Daniel Steele's novel *That Girl from Memphis,* a boy-meets-girl story set in the silver boom. The film was never made, nor was the one about his father's life, but their names were now afloat in Hollywood, and RKO approached Alan and Elizabeth about writing some scripts.

Most of this Hollywood buzz was tentative, so as soon as Alan was back in New York he went to Decca Records with a proposal. Decca was headed by Jack Kapp, whom Alan had met while searching out folk songs on commercial recordings. Kapp had created an American branch of the British recording company Decca in the mid-1930s, a period in which many record companies were going out of business. He had shrewdly built up his new company quickly by signing top artists such as Bing Crosby, the Mills Brothers, and the Dorsey Brothers, and at the same time cutting the price of Decca records to thirty-five cents—less than half the cost of the other companies' records. He also created several rural music sublines, and sent his brother Dave to record folk and country artists in what was the record companies' equivalent of a field recording—hotel rooms in southern cities. Alan pointed out to Kapp that Decca and its family of labels—Brunswick, Vocalion, Gennett, and General—owned the rights to a collection of records aimed at country audiences that was second only to the Library of Congress's, and if they hired him he could help them sell folk music not just to rural enclaves but to the entire country. Kapp sensed that the time seemed right to market country recordings on a bigger scale, and gave Alan a part-time job as editor of the Folk Music Series, for which he was paid $300 a month beginning on November 20, 1945.

He was to search through the catalogs of their country recordings to find records that they could reissue, but also bring Decca into the contemporary folk song field by producing recordings for folksingers such as Carl Sandburg and Burl Ives.

As Alan's reputation as a folklorist grew and he sensed success close to hand, his old ambivalence about what he was doing grew with it. Was being a folklorist enough? What of his dream of being a writer? Was he forever to walk in his father's shadow? This new job in the recording business forced him to ponder these questions, and he wrote a lengthy answer to himself. He had become a folklorist because his father had been a folklorist, and he had poured himself into the work:

> There was a cold frenzy in the way I worked. In the field collecting I was never satisfied with what I had found that day—no singer could make me feel that I had gone far enough. No schedule of driving and interviewing and recording, begun no matter how early and continued no matter how late, was enough to make me feel satisfied with the day's work. . . . In the office of the Library, the same thing was true. It seemed to me impossible to quit at the end of the day. When I did get home, I slunk home, with a mountain of worries and anxieties about things undone on my shoulders.
>
> This cloud of anxiety hung so darkly over everything I did, that the work itself suffered. In the field, no matter how hard I tried, I could never keep a systematic notebook. In the office I could never seem to get around to cataloguing or classifying the songs. So behind me year by year, there accumulated an ever-growing black mountain of unfinished and unorganized work. . . . I never had time somehow to look into the books and articles that lay all around me in the Library. I skimmed them, glanced at them, hurried through them or overlooked them with a casual, contemptuous and anxious glance. So, when at CBS they called me a folklore expert, and even today when here at Decca they refer to me as the foremost authority on American folksongs, I get an inward feeling of nausea, due to guilt and what else?
>
> What were my *own* purposes in living this way? What are my reasons for continuing to immerse myself deeper and deeper in this quagmire of folklore? I know objectively that it is a world of beauty and wonder and that within it lie truths and beauties and discoveries about the soul of man that will help this world and the life of man upon it [be] a greener and less sorrowful thing. And yet, unless I meet folk-lore in terms of a living voice—on a record or in a person—something which I can control, I really have no interest in it. I think about only how to use to my own advantage, to the advantage of my friends. . . .
>
> What are my *own* purposes, then? What do I like? What do I think about? What do I want? Why am I born? What path shall my feet follow? All the paths that have opened up before me so far have been the paths of other people—my father,

Dr. Spivacke, Charley Seeger. . . . It's not that I don't know where I stand in my own field of folklore. I stand very much alone, very much in my own place making my own direction, carving a new direction for others to follow. But I am too uncertain of myself to feel strong in this. My *convictions* are strong—there are an earnest of my years of study in college, my firm political emotions, and the confidence that comes from months and months of actual collecting in the field. I know the kind of intellectual, moral and emotional structure that can be made out of folklore. It is a lack of *personal* conviction that is my problem.

CHAPTER 10

The Century of the Common Man

The days crawled by in the army public relations office in New York as Alan waited to be discharged, and he filled the hours with daydreams of making a fresh start and working for himself. He applied for a Guggenheim Fellowship in early 1946, when "post-Service" fellowships were made available to the flood of enlisted people who would be leaving the military. On his application his research plans specified "critical and creative writing in the field of American Folklore," which included "the preparation of a volume titled *Salt of the Earth* and composed of folk biography and folk tales from the recordings of the Library of Congress," and "a series of essays describing and defining the 'functional' approach to American Folklore."

He had already sent off a proposal for *Salt of the Earth* to several publishers, which he envisioned as a large book of around half a million words. It would be in the spirit of James Agee's *Let Us Now Praise Famous Men,* but even more ambitious in scope and free of its pathos and tortured reflexivity. With it Alan would stake his claim as a leading voice of the South by "evaluating a region in a new way—in terms of the creative potentialities of the common people who have made its folk culture":

> I propose to make a book out of these lives, out of the fire that burns in the hearts of these artists of the common man. This book will be, not alone a study of how folk-lore is born, how it grows and changes, but an evaluation of the creative potential, the best seed one can find in the South. The rest is decay, corruption, terror and blind prejudice.
>
> The people who vote for Bilbo, who are swayed by Pappy O'Daniels—the lynchers and the lynched—the Jeeter Lesters and the Porgys—these are the ballad makers, the yarn-spinners, the blues-moaners, the square dancers, the yodelers, the creators of the spirituals and of jazz. Their language and their character gave force and substance to Huckleberry Finn, The Grapes of Wrath, Look Homeward Angel, The People, Yes, Uncle Remus. Their sweat and their conviction

> have transformed the used-up Tennessee Valley into exhibit number one of our American democracy.

"No dialect," he said, "no folksy prose reconstructed from notebooks. But the full-blown prose of the great folk talker. Prose that at times is very close to the best writing of the great novelists. Prose, transcribed and edited for sense and for beauty directly from recordings."

The first section ("White Oak") would contain a series of portraits: Elmer Smith, a Blue Ridge Mountain balladeer and fiddler, and an inheritor of English and Scots ballads and church songs; Roy Acuff, the hillbilly star; and the life story of a Holiness Church preacher. There would be autobiographies of Woody Guthrie and "Kentucky Fireball" Aunt Molly Jackson. He'd tell the story of the "Lintheads," the land-starved mountain people who work in southern mill towns; the epic of the Okies as reflected in their ballads and interviews; and the saga of the TVA and the changes it brought to the people along the Tennessee River. "Black Oak," the second part, would begin with the life of an African American levee camp worker and lead into the story of the blues and Big Bill Broonzy's autobiography. Jelly Roll Morton's portrait of the city of New Orleans and the birth of jazz would be included, and railroad workers' labor and music, the life and poetry of the penitentiaries, and the work of the cotton industry in Coahoma County, Mississippi. There would be accounts of the black Holiness people and of a black Baptist preacher, along with texts of his sermons. The final section ("White Oak and Black") would tell the story of the new industries of the South, where "Negroes and whites are working together and joining unions side by side. This chapter will be the story of unity in the growing labor unions of the South, shown against a background of Ku Klux prejudice."

The other book he planned to write, a collection of essays on folklore, was aimed at "fellow social scientists" and would cover the literature of the nonliterate population of Europe, which was until only recently the lore of the agricultural classes and was the common heritage that crossed national and linguistic borders. Whether the people had created it themselves or merely preserved it from the past, it was a reflection of their values—their problems, ideals, hopes, dreams, and fears—and their acceptance of these values was evident from repetition and re-creation of those stories and songs, even where, he noted, "the neurotic and anti-social patterns of folklore represent part of the adjustment of an oppressed group."

The folklorist's job was to describe and define the system of values in the people's lore, and to show how those values relate to the cultural environments in which they exist. The task was to understand how those values operate in the work and lives of individual carriers and creators of folklore. Folklorists should be interpreters to the world outside the folk communities, but they should also champion these peoples who are subject to the control of the modern world.

Besides, there was something that the larger world could learn from these people and their art: folklore was democratic in its content, and in the social relationships expressed in its narratives. It could only survive with a vote of approval from its audience. And the fact that it had diffused across boundary lines meant that it had the character of international democracy and was in many ways ahead of those with more advanced means of communication.

> Folklore may prove to be, not a romantic and colorful ragbag of the discarded and outworn ideas of humanity, but one of the great well springs of the democratic attitudes that have in the past two centuries begun to make for a more equitable life for all mankind upon this planet.

Folklorists had explored the transmission of British folk songs to the United States and studied the differences between the two traditions. Now Alan was ready to undertake a study of the exchange of stylistic features across southern race lines in folktales, melodies, and dance patterns. This multiracial performance style was the chief characteristic of southern folklore, and something quite unique in the country as a whole. Understanding it might, he thought, put "a quietus, once and for all, upon the absurd notion of 'pure' folklore." Lomax was proposing to turn what had been an antiquarian and literary study into a subject for social scientists (what Zora Neale Hurston called "Literary Science"), and he would do this by showing the degree to which whites and blacks shared a common culture, an idea that was by no means welcomed by most white Americans.

Alan was released from the army with the rank of corporal on March 2. With the help of strong letters of recommendation from Harold Spivacke, Charles Seeger, Harold Thompson, Stith Thompson, and Ben Botkin, he was awarded a twelve-month Guggenheim Fellowship of $3,000 a year, to begin immediately. As soon as he heard he wrote the foundation to ask them to allow him to accept it while he held a part-time job at Decca, and also to delay the award until June, when he would be through with other work that he was still finishing. When June came he delayed it again until September, and then yet again until February 1, 1947.

During this time he was helping finish *To Hear Your Banjo Play*, a twenty-two-minute film history of American folk music that he began writing and doing the narration for while he was still in the OWI. Alan worked with a crew that included three of the most important documentary filmmakers of the time: Irving Lerner, Willard Van Dyke, and a young Ricky Leacock. The film was set in landscapes that suggested WPA films or even Robert Flaherty's, and featured Woody, Pete Seeger, Texas Gladden, Sonny Terry, Brownie McGhee, and Margot Mayo's square dancers.

At the same time, John Lomax asked Alan to help him with a book to be called

The 44 Best Ballads that would be made up of the cream of what he and Alan had collected. Ruth and Charles Seeger would again assist with the music and the arrangements, and he hoped it would sell better than *Our Singing Country*. But as soon as they began work on it, Alan made it clear that even though his father had collected most of the best songs, he wanted this book to be mostly his own: he would write the notes, and Negro spirituals would be the heart of it, since he considered them the best songs that America had produced. Their arguments began as they went forward with the project, and continued to grow with the number of songs selected, from forty-four to fifty-two, then to ninety-nine.

John, who needed the money, knew that America had difficulty ignoring "best of" lists; Alan, on the other hand, saw this as an opportunity to create the first canon of strictly American folk songs. He avoided the ballads identified with England, left out children's game songs and songs in languages other than English, but included political and labor songs, those he called "topical and progressive," none of which would qualify as folk songs among most folklorists for any number of reasons. The methodology was simple: the songs were chosen by the extended Lomax family, and sometimes alternate versions were included where no clear "best" could be agreed upon, or composites of what they thought were the best of different versions. By the time the book that was now supposed to be called *99 Best Ballads* appeared in print in April 1947, it had grown to 111 songs and was entitled *Folk Song U.S.A.* It was later reissued as *Best Loved American Folk Songs*, and again as *Folk Song U.S.A.: 111 Best-Loved American Ballads*. It was intended as a popular book, meant for singing, and the Seegers set aside their skills as accurate transcribers to present the tunes in straightforward arrangements for the average piano player. But it was also unquestionably Alan's book, as the introduction made clear: "This is not calendar art, not escape literature (although there is much fantasy), or yet propaganda put out by some boost-America group advertising ours as the best of all possible lands and our people as generous and gay, well fed and genteel. Folk song, like any serious art, deals with realities—with poor boys a long way from home, with workers killed on the job, with bloody-handed murderers, with children dancing and fighting in the back yards."

For the first time, a songbook included a list of recommended phonograph records that would enable readers to hear the songs performed in the styles of the singers from whom they were collected. Alan's notes on the individual songs drew on a wealth of sources, making it the most interesting and erudite of all the songbooks of its time. When he turned to sacred songs, he accepted Professor George Pullen Jackson's widely accepted claim that most Negro spirituals resemble early white spirituals, but then turned the question around and asked how black singers reshaped white spirituals, and spelled out the stylistic features that ultimately make black song different from that of whites. He then argued that a folklorists' equation that pitted Europe plus white America against black America was unbalanced if not racist: Africa needed to be brought in to rebalance it. Finally, he no longer separated white from black in different chapters, treating all their contributions as American songs.

In this project Alan was writing about folk songs for a public that had never known them as anything more than campfire amusement or local color in Hollywood movies but was beginning to encounter them in Broadway theaters, on the radio, in nightclubs and concert halls. In the Christmas issue of *Vogue* he wrote "The Best of the Ballads" as a shopping list for gifts, drawing up a selection that included recordings by "unsophisticated country singers," "commercial hill-billies" "city-billy ballad singers," and even "art singers" from opera. In "America Sings the Saga of America," an article in the *New York Times Magazine* a year later, he noted that there was a new consciousness of folk song across the country brought about by singers like Burl Ives and Josh White, who were growing in popularity; best-selling books like Ben Botkin's new *Treasury of American Folklore*; and the Walt Disney folklore-based films about Paul Bunyan, Pecos Bill, John Henry, and others that were in the works. He explained that the major areas of American folklore—tall talk and tales, the Negro spiritual, the survival of the British ballad, the American ballad, and the folklore of the minority groups—may all have had roots elsewhere, but each nevertheless demonstrated a unique adaptation to American life. Though folklore is performed by individuals, he said, it is also the expression of the larger social group. It has been "voted on," approved, and so "inherently rejects all authoritarian notions. It allows for the creative rights of the individual at the same time that it is flexible in its response to community sentiment":

> Folklore can show us that this dream ["of democratic and peaceful plenty"] is age-old and common to all mankind. It asks that we recognize the cultural rights of weaker people in sharing this dream, and it can make their adjustment to a world society an easier and more creative process.

In this same spirit of explaining folklore to America, Alan organized a conference with his friends on city folklore at the Elizabeth Irwin High School in New York on May 4, 1946. To most people folklore concerned the past, the nostalgic, the dead and the dying, and no American academic or folklorist had ever before seriously considered city life as a subject for folklore. Yet here were Herbert Halpert, Yiddish collector and singer Ruth Rubin, Ben Botkin, Margot Mayo, Pete Seeger, Woody Guthrie, and Alan presenting the very vital lore of New York City—street cries, folk songs from Harlem, the work of sandhogs (urban miners who dug the tunnels and sewers) and taxi drivers, children's rhymes, Yiddish folk songs, square dances, and other ethnic folklore.

At his job at Decca, Alan had been working on recordings with contemporary singers who he felt should be known by a wider audience, and whom he issued in what he called the Personality Series. Carl Sandburg was the first, recording *Cowboy Songs and Negro Spirituals,* which he followed with an album of poems, *The People, Yes.* Josh White's *Ballads and Blues* was next, then Burl Ives's *Ballads and Folk Songs* and Richard Dyer-Bennet's *Twentieth Century Minstrel.* It was a commercial calculation, a foot in the doorway of American's popular music. Alan intended to follow this series with recordings from the rural folks themselves, and he assumed that listeners would understand his logic. But he was deeply disappointed when Charles Seeger reviewed this first group of recordings without ever mentioning him, and treated the music as a symptom of the hybridization of folk art and fine art that Seeger said had already been under way in Europe for the last hundred years. Seeger pointed to the "prettiness" of the singing, the pretense and affectation of the stage performers, their lack of taste. The irony to Seeger was that these recordings were being released at the same time that contemporary fine art composition was "hybridizing" with folk music:

> During the past 100 years, Anglo-American folk music has been deliberately pushed aside, as "hick-stuff," by protagonists of the fine art of music. The two idioms were technically and culturally opposed in many ways. The richly upholstered romanticism of cosmopolitan concert music could not tolerate the bare, unadorned, almost classic simplicity of folk art—and vice versa.
>
> Now, however, the vanguard of contemporary fine-art composition has come to prize certain factors in music above all others—the strong, bare, almost hard, melodic line, the austere harmonic and contrapuntal fabric, the steady tempo, the avoidance of sentimental dramatization of detail, in short, emphasis upon the very qualities that most distinguish the broad traditions of American folk song. It is not strange that this rapprochement is taking place at the present time. It is strange that it is so rarely recognized.

But Alan continued on with his plan, and once the first "name" records were out, he turned to the project that had been in the planning at least from the time he assembled the RCA *Smoky Mountain Ballads* collection of hillbilly records for his father in 1940. In June and September he issued two anthologies of white country music, *Listen to Our Story—A Panorama of American Balladry* and *Mountain Frolic,* a selection of southern mountain string band tunes and square dances, both on the Brunswick label. Though Alan was limited by what was already available on Decca or the recording labels owned by them, and by what masters for those records still existed, he managed to include Blind Joe Taggart, Uncle Dave Macon, the Tennessee Ramblers, Bascom Lamar Lunsford, Bradley Kincaid, the Crockett

Family, the Reverend Edward W. Clayborn, Mother McCollum, Buell Kazee, Dock Boggs, and a whole array of American folksingers. In a bold move for record companies whose albums typically contained very little printed information on the cover, each of Alan's albums came with a "Sing-Along-Book" containing the melodies and lyrics of the songs along with explanatory material.

Seventy-five more albums were planned, including two anthologies already under way, *Spirituals with Guitar* and *Careless Love*, but sales were apparently not what the company expected, as no more reissues were completed. Alan did manage to get some rural singers their own albums, such as one for Cousin Emmy (Jo May Carver, the lady who preceded Bob Dylan onstage the day he went electric at the Newport Folk Festival of 1965), *Kentucky Mountain Ballads*, and he reissued two 1941 albums recorded by the Almanacs on Commodore Records, the new jazz recording company run by another Decca employee, Milt Gabler: *Sod Buster Ballads: Folk Song of the Early West* and *Deep Sea Chanteys and Whaling Ballads*, both with notes by Alan. He was also obliged to produce albums of folk songs such as *Roustabout Songs* (based on a book of songs collected in the Ohio River Valley by Mary Wheeler) and *Bayou Ballads*, which were performed not in country style but in what Decca called "concert" versions, sung by Conrad Thibault, a popular radio and concert singer, with a full orchestra. Aiming at the current urban fascination with square dance, he produced three albums of dance music with calls: *Quadrilles, Running Set*, and *Longways Dances*. He also wrote the story for a Decca children's record, *Round Up Time in Texas*, performed by Western movie character actor Andy Devine and the Cass County Boys.

When he realized that this venture into mass culture was not turning out the way he had expected, he gave Decca's music director, Gordon Jenkins, a copy of *Folk Song U.S.A.*, hoping that a musician with so many years of production experience behind him would understand. Instead, Jenkins merely thumbed through it and handed it back, saying, "Mark the ones with commercial potential."

Whatever his disappointment with the project, the consequences of Alan's work at Decca would turn out to be important for the folk revival that would begin in the 1950s. Dave Van Ronk, one of the key figures in that revival, recalled finding a copy of *Listen to Our Story* when he was first beginning to play guitar and sing. Then, twelve years after Alan's Decca venture into reissuing country music, Harry Smith, another Greenwich Village dweller, would follow his example by creating a three-volume *Anthology of American Folk Music* for Folkways Records. Using Alan's 1940 mimeographed "List of American Folk Songs on Commercial Records" and the reissued songs on Alan's 1941 *Smoky Mountain Ballads* as a model, Smith created his own anthology on three long-playing records that helped revive older folk music. Smith's reissues have been highly celebrated, and some commentators have used Lomax as his foil, arguing that Alan was opposed to commercial studio recordings, or that his own field recordings were never as interesting or important as the ones chosen by Smith. The first claim ignores his own bibliographies and commercial reissues, limited as they were to his adherence to copyright laws, and the second claim fails to see that in most cases Lomax intended his field recordings for very different purposes than Smith's reissues.

When Pete Seeger returned from the war he was on fire with ideas about changing the world through song. With the help of Alan, John Hammond, Oscar Brand, the remaining Almanacs, and representatives of the CIO, he created People's Songs, Inc., a corporation designed to develop "tens of thousands" of union choruses for strikes, publicity, and as a means for increasing attendance at meetings. ("Just as every church has a choir, why not every union?") "People" captured a certain feel of America at that particular moment. Echoing Marx, Emerson, and Whitman, it also reached back to the German Romantics, Alexander von Humboldt, and finally to the Constitution. The group as Pete conceived it, however, was far from romantic, but organized like a proper corporation, with an elected board and registered with the state of New York. Pete did most of the work of fund-raising, organizing meetings, making connections to unions and political groups, and running a small office in Times Square, and once Pete was in motion he was hard to resist. His energy and enthusiasm drew people in, and within a year there were write-ups in major papers and magazines, several thousand members signed up, fifteen thousand songs on file, and a four-person staff in the office. A monthly bulletin, *People's Songs*, edited by Pete, contained traditional songs (often with new words), labor and topical songs, and news of members, some of whom wrote from jail, where they had wound up after supporting one strike or another. Pete and Earl Robinson set off around the country, singing on picket lines, recruiting members, and opening up branch organizations of People's Songs. They also launched a series of "Hootenannies" to raise money and attract new members. *Time* magazine sent a reporter to a hoot at Irving Place in New York, where he said there were two hundred onstage and a thousand in the audience, some of whom had brought along their guitars.

Alan went up to Columbia University's Teachers College to ask for help from the progressive educators there on getting people to sing, and found Professor Lilla Belle Pitts, famous for her belief in music as a force for change. Her goal was to create a musical culture of collective singing that would bring American communities together in greater tolerance and openness. Alan was quoted by *Time* as saying, "We're going to put more into our songs than June moon croon spoon, and sing Senator Bilbo [the fiery segregationist senator from Mississippi] out of Congress." With the success of this first New York City hoot, they scheduled two more for the following month in the larger Town Hall—a "Union Hoot" and a

"Freedom Hoot." Even with minimal publicity, the turnout for the Union concert was substantial, and the subsequent one was sold out.

Their plans escalated into a proposed national cultural congress, a publishing company, radio programs, recordings. But the times were not with them. Some of the unions saw music as a necessary evil, especially when it was a style alien to their tastes; there was often open disappointment when the performers turned out to be singing hillbilly songs instead of jazz. Several unions dropped their ties to People's Songs, included the CIO, whom they counted as their closest allies. Other radical political groups accused them of being out of date and out of touch. When People's Songs held its first national convention in Chicago, only sixty people turned up, at least some of whom weren't FBI agents. Alan recalled later that he "had the naïve impression that unions might be the best catalyst for creating a revival of American folk music. I tried to sell folk songs to unions as I did to Congress, music educators, and English teachers."

Alan returned to the Folklore Institute at Indiana University in midsummer 1946 to lecture on "Certain Directions in Folklore Studies" and "Techniques of Field Recording," this time with Svatava Jakobson, with whom he was now having an affair, and who joined him in giving the lectures. In New York he returned to producing concerts with a new urgency, raising money, scripting, staging, doing nearly all the work himself. He aimed to present the performers under the best circumstances he could manage and, if at all possible, in support of some cause that he favored. Nothing daunted him, not even the high ground of Carnegie Hall. And why not Carnegie, which from its beginnings had been made available for all kinds of benevolent and partisan causes? Duke Ellington's 1943 premiere of *Black, Brown and Beige*, for example, was staged on behalf of Russian War Relief, a group created to help with the famines that drove many Eastern Europeans into Russia, and one that would be labeled a Communist front organization before the year was up. That spring, Alan organized a People's Songs concert for Russian War Relief, with sponsors such as Mayor Fiorello La Guardia, former New York governor Herbert Lehman, John Hammond, and actress Helen Hayes. Alan was the concert's master of ceremonies, or "narrator," as the radio generation dubbed him.

The success of the concert was such that when he heard that Town Hall could be rented cheaply after the regular repertory was finished for the evening, Alan proposed to People's Songs that they back him for a series of midnight shows built around musical themes. It was a risk, but he was counting on the public's willingness to come out for late Saturday night concerts of musics to which New York had not yet been exposed. He would call the series "The Midnight Special," "the train that would bring folk singers of every race and nationality to New York

City." He knew how to pitch these performances to the press with the passion of an Aimee Semple McPherson and the shrewdness of a P. T. Barnum:

> We plan to cover the whole field of American folk music systematically in these concerts. Most of the people in the first few programs have been heard in New York before, but as quickly as possible we're going to bring in unknown, unrecorded people who sing folk songs naturally just because they like to. . . . Right from the start these concerts are going to be different from anything that's been heard in New York so far. . . . They're going to be sort of conversation pieces. I'll do the narration and explain the songs and the singers will tell stories and their life histories. And they'll say the damndest things in the world on the stage. I know them. They've had experiences in the lost regions of American life. When the audience leaves they'll know these people as human beings.

On November 9, a full house of fifteen hundred people had gathered in Town Hall when the stage lights went up at 11:30 for "Blues at Midnight," the first of the concerts. The performers were Sidney Bechet on clarinet, Big Bill Broonzy, Pete Johnson, Sonny Terry, Billy Taylor on bass, Brownie McGhee, playing with his brother Stick, Roscoe Harris with a washtub bass, Jimmy Braswell on washboard ("with fifty-two attachments, mostly kitchen and garage oddments," according to Alan), and pioneering New Orleans jazz bass player Pops Foster. The musicians played in different configurations throughout the evening, ending with an ensemble version of "Bye Bye Baby."

The *New York Times* reviewer complained that "the adjective 'great' the narrator bestowed so liberally was not justified" by what he had heard that evening. But when composer Virgil Thomson reviewed the show for the *New York Herald Tribune* under the heading of "Differentiated Counterpoint," he was so ecstatic over the performance of the trio of Sidney Bechet, Pete Johnson, and Billy Taylor that he devoted his entire review to just one piece of music, "Saturday Night Blues."

Nine concerts followed over the next few months, mostly on alternate Saturdays, and included "Ballads at Midnight" on November 23, with Susan Reed and Alan Lomax singing, and "Strings at Midnight" on December 7, a wild matchup of flamenco guitarist Carlos Montoya with Pete Seeger playing banjo tunes in alternate sets. Alan wanted to contrast what he called the most distinctive stringed instrument technique in America with the most unusual guitar style that Europe had developed.

The concerts were remarkably successful, and gave audiences the intimate sense of being at smart nightclubs or Greenwich Village coffeehouses. But Alan wanted to push the borders of music even farther beyond the city, and on December 21 he presented "Calypso at Midnight." Calypsos were not entirely new to New

Yorkers, as the music had occasionally appeared on radio in the mid-1930s, and the Village Vanguard and even some clubs in midtown Manhattan were booking calypsonians by 1939. Because he wanted to communicate the sense of a Harlem West Indian social club rather than a downtown nightclub on the stage, Alan recruited singers and musicians—the Duke of Iron, Lord Invader, Macbeth the Great, and the orchestra of Gerald Clark—who had been performing in Harlem for years and had adapted the calypso somewhat to American tastes.

He made an effort to fill the stage behind him with an audience from Harlem who knew the music, the jokes, and the political references in the songs, so that their reactions would clue the audience how to respond and when to sing along. What the concertgoers heard that night were some of the calypsos that had already been turned into pop records (such as "Stone Cold Dead in the Market Place" by Ella Fitzgerald and Louis Jordan from earlier that year, and the Andrews Sisters' hit recording of Lord Invader's "Rum and Coca-Cola") and songs based on well-known historical events, like "Edward VIII," about the Prince of Wales's abdication of the English throne in 1936. Together, singers and narrator guided the audience into the complexities of the history of Trinidad and the musical forms that led to calypso, such as the group work songs, music of the Spiritual Baptists, "Bongo" songs (for waking the dead), hand drumming, and the battles of improvising singers that took place in the Trinidadian Carnival tents. There was even a staged stick fight with accompanying call-and-response music, and a calypso drama in full costume, something never seen outside of Trinidad. At the end of the evening the program was running overtime, but the audience urged the performers to stay.

The "Midnight" series squeezed two more concerts in before the end of the year with Burl Ives and Josh White, and continued in 1947 with "Spirituals at Midnight" and "Mountain Frolic at Midnight." But the biggest success was "Honkytonk Blues at Midnight" on February 15, for which Alan called on performers who represented distinctly different approaches to the genre. One was Big Bill (William Lee Conley) Broonzy, born in Mississippi and raised in Arkansas, a farmer, miner, and redcap whose move to Chicago in 1920 led him to become a singer-songwriter popular among black audiences. Another was Memphis Slim (Peter Chatman), a pianist who found work in the heydays of Beale Street, drifted into rhythm and blues, later moved abroad, and became one of the most influential blues performers in Europe. The third, Sonny Boy (John Lee Curtis) Williamson, also from Tennessee, had traveled to Chicago in the 1930s to become the first widely known blues harmonica player and an important figure in the development of Chicago blues. There were few in the audience that night in New York City who had ever seen working blues musicians, much less those who worked the black club and dance circuits the way these three men did, and their performances were a revelation.

The three musicians stayed with Elizabeth and Alan, and after their Town Hall performance Alan took them to his office at Decca Records to record what started out to be a discussion on the blues, not intended for commercial issue, and not even recorded on studio equipment. (Alan used a Presto, much as he would in the field, a portable recording machine with a single microphone.) Memphis Slim started them off by singing "Life Is Like That," a song about the ironies and trials of life, and for the next several hours the three men conversed while Alan listened. Talk about the blues turned to the causes of the blues, problems of love and work, the tribulations, humiliations, and absurdities of black life in the South, of chain gangs, murderers, lynchings, being tracked by dogs, but also of the pleasures and violence of jukes and barrelhouses, and of the blues as a medium of stories, a record of a way of life, a source of joy and an escape from pain. When they finished, they had produced an unprecedented collective autobiography and a document about the consequences of racism in America in the voices of those who had suffered from it. When Alan played the records back for them, even they were shocked by what they heard themselves saying and asked him to destroy them. After some urging, they finally relented and let him save the documents because of their historic value, but asked him never to reveal who had recorded them, for fear of what might happen to their families who were still in the South.

Alan knew that when Lawrence Gellert published texts of black songs of protest, some folklorists and political activists accused him of having fabricated them—the proletariat could not be that class-conscious, they argued. Even years later, when Gellert's recordings were made public, there were still doubts about their authenticity. But Alan attempted once again to bridge the gap between the culture of working-class blacks and that of all middle-class Americans in a piece he wrote the following year for *Common Ground* based on this recording session, "I Got the Blues." He fictionalized the session, placing it instead in a juke joint in Arkansas, with three musicians under the pseudonyms of Leroy, Sib, and Natchez. The article closely followed the accounts on the recording, but whether for verisimilitude or as a dramatic framing device, Alan inserted himself into the narrative asking questions that portrayed him as completely naïve about black life. In 1957 he produced an LP for United Artists entitled *Blues in the Mississippi Night*, which used fragments of the original recording while still maintaining the speakers' anonymity. The full recording was finally issued in 1990, after all three men were dead and the civil rights movement had opened up the subject of race in America for public discussion.

On the day his Guggenheim Fellowship began, in February 1947, Alan wrote Henry Allan Moe, the president of the foundation, to give him a report on his activities since learning that he had been awarded a fellowship. Promise of the foundation's financial support had liberated him, he explained, to do things he might not otherwise have attempted. By May he had decided to add a recording trip to his schedule, going back to Parchman Farm to determine what changes had occurred in the songs over the last twelve years, and perhaps also to see what he could accomplish alone, free of his father. A reasonably portable paper-backed tape recording machine had just been produced by Magnecord, and he thought that with its greater sensitivity and higher-quality sound he would be able to record the complex layerings in the work songs, and also be the first person to use a tape recorder in the field. With a longer-running recording medium he would be able to interview the prisoners to learn more of the meaning of work songs in their lives.

If he feared that the old-style singing would be on its way out, he was right—at least as a normal practice. But he did find a few exceptional singers who seemed to draw on even older African American traditions than those he and his father had heard in the thirties. "Early in the Mornin'," a song that accompanied woodcutting, had all the elements—choral call and response, polyphony, a backbeat, a passionate, breathless call from "22," the leader (Lomax published only the prisoners' nicknames). Four men stood around a tree with axes, one pair at a time striking from opposite sides of the tree, their efforts timed by the weaving together of their parts (the blows of the axes are marked by slashes [/] below):

/Well, it's early in the mo/r—in the mornin',/
Baby, when I r/ise, Lordy, mama./
Well, it's early every mo/r—in the mornin',/
A-baby, when I r/ise, well-a./
Well-a, it's early every mo/r, in the mornin',/
Baby, when I r/ise, Lordy, baby,/

When Alan attempted to get these prison recordings produced in the late 1940s, there was no interest, possibly because every paragraph of the album's notes that he had written mentioned the brutality of prison life and the need for radical reform. It was not until 1957 that he was able to get Tradition Records to release *Negro Prison Songs from the Mississippi State Penitentiary* and an English edition in the same year from Pye Records, called *Murderer's Home*. The songs were all copyrighted in the names of the performers.

The lives of the people he recorded continued to intersect with his own, sometimes for the rest of their lives. He continued to find work for Lead Belly, though Huddie had not been well and wasn't always able to work. Even though Jelly Roll died in 1941, he was still alive to Alan and many others who valued his contribution to the development of jazz. Art historian and jazz writer Rudi Blesh's boutique record company, Circle, began negotiating with the Morton estate to bring out a limited number of sets of the recordings he had made with Lomax. According to Blesh, Morton had left instructions that certain of the big recording companies were not to have access to his interview with Lomax. An agreement was reached for Circle to issue a "dignified set of all useable sides": "dignified" because some of the recordings were said to be pornographic, others repetitious. Lomax was not in favor of issuing the rougher songs, not so much because of their obscene content but because of their violence.

The Library of Congress resisted selling or giving away any of its recordings to recording companies, but continued public interest in those unheard master recordings led Spivacke to urge Alan to publish something about the Morton interviews to satisfy curiosity. Meanwhile, Circle Records got a court order instructing the library to make the recordings available, and finally in 1947 Circle began pressing some two hundred sets of forty-five twelve-inch 78 rpm recordings culled from the May and June Lomax-Morton sessions only and selling them by subscription under the title *The Saga of Mr. Jelly Lord*. There was no noise reduction or speed correction on the discs, which seemed to have been copied at too slow a speed, and they were edited to shorten and rearrange the spoken sections. Alan then asked the Library of Congress for a copy of his complete typed manuscript of the Jelly Roll Morton interviews so that he could begin work on a book about Morton.

He was still convinced that Woody Guthrie was one of the greatest writers of his time, and figured all Guthrie needed was a few breaks. Woody's first novel, *Bound for Glory*, had appeared in 1943 and had done well enough for him to win the Rosenwald Fellowship for which Alan had nominated him, and now he was to begin work on another novel, *House of Earth*, a mini-epic about life in the Texas Panhandle. The first chapter confirmed for Alan the high praise he had given to Woody's writing. "There was a moment in my life . . . when I considered dropping everything I was doing, and just helping get Woody published. It was, quite simply, the best material I'd ever seen written about that section of the country." But, as was often the case with Woody, he soon dropped the novel and went off in another direction.

When Alan wrote up a proposal for a new radio show, *Hootenanny on the Air*, a "folksong variety show," he put Woody Guthrie and his Oklahoma friend Cisco Houston at its center, with Lomax's old Texas friend John Henry Faulk as host. With the William Morris Agency representing them, they took his idea to CBS. The format was similar to that of *Back Where I Come From*, a jokey, casual exchange of musical ideas, but now with a wider range of music, and this time with Alan behind the scenes as writer and producer.

Alan shopped another show around at the same time, this one with the possible title of *The Daily News*, or *Daily Ballad*, or *Singing the News*. Only four singers would be heard on the program: guitarists Woody Guthrie and Big Bill Broonzy;

pianist Lou Kleinman, a singer of smart cabaret songs; and the Duke of Iron, the calypsonian who also played a mutant instrument called the banjo-ukulele. Each had composed hundreds of songs, and all were quick to improvise lyrics on any subject. The show would simply be the four of them interpreting the news of the day:

> This program will bring these masters of ballad making together into a network office at one o'clock in the afternoon. They will come with ideas and suggestions already developed out of the headlines and the human interest stories in that day's papers. Working with the writer-producer of the program, they will pick out the four or five song ideas for that day's show, and they will develop and polish these ideas. By five o'clock the script will be typed and sent to the script editor's desk. With a break for dinner the performance will be ready to go on the air with DAILY BALLAD by six-thirty or seven.

This was a tough sell: a collectively developed, virtually spontaneous script by performers who had a history of political ideas far from the mainstream, with no time for rehearsal or changes, put on the air live every day? Even Orson Welles's freewheeling Mercury Theatre players would not be trusted with this format.

In December Alan again traveled to Parchman Farm, this time with permission to follow the men into the fields and record them where they accompanied their work with songs, and he was even able to interview some of them away from the other prisoners and the guards. He was again confirmed in his belief that the work songs were beginning to disappear with the coming of a new generation of inmates who considered them "old fogyisms," but a few of the younger prisoners did still sing them, and several of the songs were among the most powerful and complex he had ever heard.

While he was recording, a blizzard struck the farm, and the men stood in the woodyard in six inches of snow "while their axe blades glittered blue in the wintry light, and they bawled out their ironic complaint" to "Rosie," in an old Parchman song led by S.B.:

Be my woman, gal, I'll be your man.
Be my woman, gal, I'll be your man.
Be my woman, gal, I'll be your man.
Every day is Sunday's dollar in your hand.
In your hand, Lordy, in your hand.
Every day is Sunday's dollar in your hand.

The leader's words were responded to by the group singing the last words of each of his lines so that they overlapped with him, with the syncopation shifting throughout and the strong beats—where the hoes or hammers or axes struck—always in the same place. The result was a feeling of urgency, forward motion (some might say "swing"), a powerful oneness in the task, all this within a song about a girl who promised loyalty but failed to wait until a prisoner was set free:

O Rosie,
O lawd gal.
Stick to the promise that you made me.
Wasn gonna marry till I go free.

Choppin in the bottom with a hundred years,
Tree fall on me, I don bit mo care.
O Rosie,
O lawd gal.

Lomax knew that the only way these verses could be appreciated was by hearing them performed, if "performance" was the word for the emotional expression of men sweating their lives away in the fields. Knowing it might be years before they were issued on recordings, he struggled to make his readers grasp their power and significance in print:

> Here is poetry that rings like a hammer on an anvil, that bites the heart, that trills like a bird. Nowhere else in earlier African-American or American folk tradition does one find such disciplined and poignant rhymed couplets. When I transcribe them from field recordings, I am always reminded of the Greek Anthology. Indeed, the fire of the Mediterranean copla and stornello stand in the background of this workman's poesy. And this spare and plangent worksong verse is plainly the main source of the poetry of the blues.

Alan attempted to write up some of the horrors he had seen in the southern prisons and learned about from the inmates in an article called "Burning Hell," but wasn't able to find a magazine to publish it, and it was not until 1993 when he published *The Land Where the Blues Began* that he was able to make these observations public.

John Lomax turned eighty-nine just as he published his autobiography, *Adventures of a Ballad Hunter*, and was invited by an old friend to speak in Greenville, Mississippi, in January 1948. He had not been well, and initially resisted accepting, but finally agreed to it if they could talk Alan, whom he had not seen in over a year, into coming. Alan had already planned to squeeze in more Mississippi fieldwork before his fellowship ran out in January, so it was settled that there would be two days of dinners, talks, and performances on January 23–24. The second day was declared "John Lomax Day" by the mayor of Greenville. The governor would attend, along with local luminaries such as Hodding Carter, the publisher of the *Delta Democrat Times*.

John was met at the train by a local crowd of well-wishers, who took him to his hotel where Alan, local journalists, and old friends were waiting. It turned into a homecoming party and informal press conference, with John talking, drinking, and singing a few songs, when he suddenly fell to the floor with a heart attack and never regained consciousness. The dinner was canceled, but Alan gave the program that he and his father had been scheduled to do together. John died two days later.

The year before Alan had began to undergo what he called "strenuous" psychoanalysis. He had found an analyst, Peter Neubauer, willing to take him on for virtually nothing, and he quickly became a believer in the process and language of analysis. He felt spirited, free from his past, and certain that his work would be better as a result. His conversion was so striking that he urged others, especially folklorists, to undergo analysis to better understand the psychodynamics of the arts of the poor and the marginal. But perhaps the single most important issue he worked on was his relationship with his father, and he hoped that he was at last becoming his own man and taking the study of folk song somewhere his father had never considered.

And yet now here he was, standing in for his father, playing his role. In this moment of crisis, he went back to what he had always done—set off into the field looking for songs. Only a few days later he was sitting in the Rose Hill Baptist Church in Greenville, Mississippi, recording black sermons, hymns, and spirituals. As he worked his way into Texas, he recorded again at the Friendly Will Baptist Church in Austin. When he reached Dallas, it was the True Light Baptist Church. He only ceased to record when he entered the church for his father's funeral.

With his fellowship having run its course, Alan began looking for a job, and in March he briefly became involved with John Steinbeck's film company, World Video, to provide arts programming for television, which was beginning to look like a serious medium. Elia Kazan was contracted to do theater projects with Actors Studio, Ilka Chase would do tours through Paris's haute cuisine, and Lomax would develop folk song projects. Nothing ever came of the company, but on his own Alan tried to convince a television company to give him a series based on folk songs and folksingers. Again there were no takers.

At a time when celebrity disc jockeys were being hired by the networks (bandleaders Paul Whiteman, Duke Ellington, and Tommy Dorsey among them), Alan joined Mutual Broadcasting as the first folk song DJ on a program called *Your Ballad Man*. Mutual gave him a contract for a year, paying $200 a program if they could not find a sponsor and $500 if they were able to sell commercial spots. The best experience he'd ever had in radio is how he described it. He'd walk in off the street with a pile of records and improvise his comments for a half hour. "I have been able to talk about race relations, psychological problems and the oneness of the human family, as well as purely folkloristic matters." Being a DJ was "not nearly as bad as it sounds."

The show gave him the opportunity to draw on everything he'd learned about American music, and every week he strung together an unpredictable set of songs over which he riffed with a fan's passion. On July 24, for example, he played Red Foley's "Freight Train Boogie," Milton Estes's "When the Fire Comes Down," Leroy Carr's "Papa's on the Housetop," the Sons of the Pioneers' "Cool Water," the Selah Jubilee Singers' "It's Cool Down Yonder by the Chilly Jordan," Richard Dyer-Bennet's "Three Ravens," Jo Stafford's "The Nightingale," the Jubilaires' "Jube's Blues," and Sidney Bechet's "Saturday Night Blues."

If there were some who still thought of Lomax as a folk purist, his programming should have disabused them. Burl Ives and Woody Guthrie were weekly favorites, but so were the jazz bands of Woody Herman and Bob Crosby, and also Jo Stafford, the most popular female vocalist of her time. Just as Alan took on the show, she stepped away from pop music and jazz and recorded *American Folk Songs,* becoming the singer that Alan played more than any other. Sometimes he worked the latest trends or recent films into the show, as he did with Robert Mitchum's "Oh He Oh Hi Oh Ho," which Mitchum had sung in that year's film *Rachel and the Stranger.*

Alan continued to seize every opportunity to make appearances, give talks, and organize concerts where he might get across his message of popularizing folk music. When he heard that there was an "Annual Festival of Contemporary American Music" at Columbia University's McMillan Theater, with four days of what they were billing the best music the country had produced, performed by the CBS Symphony Orchestra, the Juilliard String Quartet, and others, he convinced the concert organizers that folk music was part of American music too. They gave him the evening of May 15, 1948, for a program titled "Ballads, Hoe-Downs, Spirituals (White and Negro), and Blues." To get the full variety of American folk song, he brought in Texas Gladden and her brother, Hobart Smith, from Virginia; from Alabama, singer Vera Hall; Jean Ritchie, a young woman from Viper, Kentucky, whom he had met at the Henry Street Settlement School in New York; and Pete Seeger, Brownie McGhee, and Dan Burley. Alan later said it was the most successful concert he'd ever done, even though some of the performers had never been in a concert before: "The audience was academic, young and liberal, refused to leave the theater, they wanted to stay with these people forever. . . . The guards had to clear the place." While the singers were in New York, Alan recorded Gladden and Hobart and introduced them to Moe Asch, who produced albums by each of them for his Disc Record Company, with Alan writing the notes.

In order to draw the press's attention to People's Songs, which was continuing to have financial difficulties, Alan assembled an honorary group of sponsors, though the board thought the idea clashed with the populist ideals of the project. But even with names as luminous as Leonard Bernstein, Aaron Copland, Dorothy Parker, John Hammond, and Oscar Hammerstein II, their financial problems were not to be solved easily. One of their biggest and most expensive projects, *The People's Song Book*, was also struggling. Packed with union and political songs, the songs of American slaves, bitter ballads from poor southern whites, and even songs of freedom from other parts of the world, the book had little relation to what most people understood folk songs to be. In his foreword, Alan made his politics clear:

> At first I did not understand how these songs related to the traditional folk songs, such as those you will sing in the section called Songs That Helped Build America. I began to realize that here was an emerging tradition that represented a new kind of human being, a new folk community composed of progressives and anti-fascists and union members. These folk, heritors of the democratic tradition of folklore, were creating for themselves a folk-culture of high moral and political content. These home-made songs of protest and affirmation shared the permanence of the people's tradition, but were most positive and more sharply critical than the familiar ballads.

He had one idea left to save People's Songs: the presidential campaign of Henry Wallace. Wallace was an Iowan who had served as secretary of agriculture, one of the two Republicans President Roosevelt appointed to his cabinet. A hardworking, dedicated advocate of conservation and modern farming, he was also a believer in civil rights, had created food stamps and lunch programs for poor children, and had attempted to negotiate foreign trade agreements that assured fair pay and safe working conditions. When Roosevelt began planning for his third campaign, he picked Wallace to be his running mate over the objections of many in the Democratic Party. Once Wallace became vice president, he spoke out on his own more and more, drawing the notice of people of every political persuasion and eventually overstepping his role and creating a series of controversies and public feuds within the government. When Roosevelt ran for a fourth term, he chose Harry S. Truman as vice president and made Wallace secretary of commerce, a position he held for barely a year before Truman, now president, replaced him. Four years later, when Truman ran against Thomas E. Dewey for president, Wallace decided to run as a candidate for the Progressive Party, a loose alliance of trade unionists, liberals, veterans, African Americans, socialists, and Communists.

Alan was an early backer of Wallace, having learned of his ideas as they filtered through the Department of Agriculture and the WPA. When word got out that Wallace was thinking of a run for the presidency in 1948, Alan was asked by Lew Frank Jr., Wallace's speechwriter, to plan the music for the campaign. Alan agreed to do so without pay if they would consent to People's Songs' creating a campaign songbook and planning events, to having a song sung for every speech given, and to Pete Seeger accompanying Wallace on his speaking tours.

Once they had an agreement, Alan got Paul Robeson involved in the musical part of the campaign, and solicited the help of Woody, Lee Hays, and E. Y. "Yip" Harburg, a popular songwriter most famous at the time for *The Wizard of Oz* and *Finian's Rainbow*, to write songs and to edit the songbook. Harburg's politics were in line with those of People's Songs, and more importantly, his music was as well. ("Over the Rainbow" was understood by many of those on the left to be a song of liberation, if not of utopian aspirations.) Together they produced cheap paperdisc recordings of songs that could be slipped into booklets or mailed, or played from sound trucks driving through neighborhoods. The songs were spirited and simple—like Alan and Yip's "I've Got a Ballot," set to the tune of "I've Got Sixpence"—but to Woody these frankly agitprop pieces were agonizingly cheap and vulgar. Songs, for him, were not supposed to be speeches; they had to be interesting as well as singable. He wrote a letter to People's Songs complaining, "How a man with such a long road of sensible travels behind him, Alan Lomax, could expect such a shallow jingly and insincere number as 'I've Got a Ballot' to touch the heartstrings and conscience of the hard-hit masses, is a problem beyond me. I never did hear a human being call his vote a 'magic little ballot.' People I have seen call their ballot a number of things, none of which are nearly as cutiepie, as highly polite, as flippant, as sissy nor effeminate as this song." At the same time, Woody had failed to write the songs he could have, according to Pete Seeger.

The Progressive Party's nominating convention was held in Philadelphia in July 1948, and the country had never seen anything like it. The number of delegates was more than double that of any nominating convention previously held, and most of them had never been part of a political campaign. Some were famous or almost famous, film stars or Columbia professors, but most were just folks, a number of them too poor to afford housing and so slept in tents or cars.

When the delegates arrived at Convention Hall on Friday the twenty-third, they were greeted by a string of folksingers who warmed up the crowd by teaching them songs written for the occasion, like Lomax and Seeger's "We Are Building (a People's Party)":

Every new day we grow stronger,
We are black and white together,

Every new man makes us stronger,
Marching on with Henry Wallace.

The crowd finished by singing the rollicking but jingly "Friendly Henry Wallace":

Everyone wants Wallace,
Friendly Henry Wallace,
Friendly Henry Wallace in the White House.

On Saturday afternoon the nominations were completed, interspersed with songs, speeches, snake dancing, and chanting. That night, the whole convention moved up to North Philadelphia's Sheib Park, the home of the Philadelphia Athletics baseball team. The ballpark was packed as Glen Taylor, the vice presidential nominee and a cowboy of sorts, fired up the crowd with his acceptance speech and then played banjo and serenaded the audience with "I Love You as I Never Loved Before." The stadium then went dark and Wallace came out, lit by a single spotlight as he did a slow-walking victory lap.

Even those among the press who opposed all that the Progressives stood for were moved by the singing, the music, and the staging, many describing it as a "revival service." Alan and his friends had created the first of many party-nominating convention spectaculars, and maybe the grandest.

In the last week of the campaign the radio networks offered each candidate a chance to speak on the air one last time before the voting, and ABC was chosen to carry Wallace's program. Alan and Studs Terkel were the producers, and they decided that Wallace, Paul Robeson, and Woody Guthrie would be the only people on the broadcast. But Woody was too sick at the time to be on the show, so Wallace and Robeson went on, each discussing what concerned him most before they talked together informally. It was a daring choice, given the two men's very different styles and priorities, and especially risky was giving that much exposure to Robeson, whose civil rights activities and Communist affiliations had made him a target of the right.

In the end, Wallace was badly beaten, trailing even Strom Thurmond. Most of the Progressives were deeply discouraged, though Alan could still find something positive in the rubble of defeat. "It sure was a singing convention but that singing did not make votes. We did a good public relations job and incorporated into the campaign a friendly and merry element that most left wing movements being somber, do not have." Alan even wrote a song for the next presidential election, "Keep-a Growin'": "When Wallace is elected in '52 / We'll have a fair and happy land."

Together, Pete and Alan wrote up a statement on how the struggle should continue, how People's Songs could get the allegiance of ten million young people who would be old enough to vote the next time around. Their plans were as daring as ever: since they couldn't count on the media to let them get their message through nationally, they would take the fight to the local level. Like modern abolitionists, they would head again to the South, where they would bring working people together to fight Jim Crow. Instead of business meetings and speeches, they would go back to the idea of the Living Newspaper, with local folks reading from a "Report to the People," its script written by highly visible backers of Wallace such as Norman Mailer or Leonard Bernstein. It would be sent out from the national office, but with room left in the script to include local voices and issues. They would build community centers filled with books, magazines, and records in Atlanta, Charlotte, and Richmond, turning them into the only places in town where whites and blacks could meet together on equal terms. People's Songs would support the efforts of black civil rights leaders, especially those in the churches, and provide them with the means to get their message onto radio and records.

But People's Songs was now even more deeply in debt, its funds exhausted by the Wallace campaign. In a last-ditch effort Alan raised the money for a concert at Carnegie Hall on March 4, 1949, "New York: A Musical Tapestry," an audacious production aimed at reaching every level of New York society. The performers were Oscar Brand, Pete Seeger, jazz musician Pee Wee Russell, the Artie Shaw Orchestra with Strings, the Latin band of Miguelito Valdés, and the multi-octave Peruvian singer Yma Sumac. Despite a near-full house, they failed to break even because they had not charged enough for the tickets, and People's Songs went bankrupt a few days later.

Still, Pete would not give up. The world could be changed through song if only he could find an audience big enough to start with. He and several others had been experimenting with Almanacs-type groups, hoping to find a modicum of commercial success. He thought he had found it in a quartet of Lee Hays, Fred Hellerman, Ronnie Gilbert, and himself, who sang a wide repertoire of songs with piercing voices and spirited rhythmic arrangements. They called themselves the Weavers, after the striking workers in a Gerhardt Hauptmann play, a name with some political integrity but one that would not get them in trouble, they hoped, with a government that did not know late-nineteenth-century German theater. But now, after a year of struggle, virtually no one knew their name. "Unions were in disarray," Pete said. "Big unions were taking over the left-leaning weaker ones, and none of them wanted singing groups." Pete had sung at the Village Vanguard, so he asked club owner Max Gordon if the Weavers could appear there for the same money that he had received, plus hamburgers. Just before Christmas they began a two-week run. Alan brought Carl Sandburg in to see them, and when the poet expressed his enthusiasm for them in print, the crowds began to arrive. Gordon Jenkins, the music director of Decca Records, also came, undoubtedly encouraged by Alan, and returned every night afterward, talking to them about recording for him. Jenkins swore that he'd record them even if he had to pay for it himself.

Jenkins did record them in 1950, under both his name and the Weavers', using his arrangements and a large orchestra. Their first two songs were "Tzena, Tzena, Tzena," an Israeli army song, and "Goodnight Irene," one of the songs that Lead Belly sang, but with slightly different words that Pete said he found in a Scots songbook. Both songs went straight up to the top of the charts, and the Weavers were soon rather sheepishly buying tuxedos and evening gowns and playing supper clubs and hotels.

Lomax had been slowly piecing together a book on Jelly Roll Morton based on his interviews. "I later spent five years trying to make my audience and my readers hear him as he talked. It took about five years to polish *Mr. Jelly Roll* from the records into book form." Among other things, this meant finding Morton's relatives, who were spread across the country, then going to New Orleans for several weeks in April 1949 to track down whatever key musical figures remained who could fill in the details of the picture that Morton had given him.

Alan was familiar with the names of New Orleans's jazz musicians, the city's clubs and bordellos, even the names of the madams. What he wanted to know more about was the lives of the musicians; he asked about the origins and meaning of "hot music"; what was the first blues they'd ever heard; who was the first clarinet or trombone or bass player to play hot? He asked about their heroes, especially the unrecorded legendary father of New Orleans jazz, trumpeter Buddy Bolden; or the variety of what they played—mazurkas, schottisches, waltzes, marches, and the blues. He asked for their definitions of syncopation; about songs in French; how the musicians dressed; the difference between those who read music and those who didn't; and about Jim Crow, and how they could tell a Creole from a black person.

Alan began writing the Jelly Roll book in his own words, but increasingly felt that the only way it could be done convincingly was to put the story into the words in which Morton and his contemporaries told it. Finally he settled on a middle ground that suggests both oral autobiography and written biography and subtly manages to bridge his and Morton's roles in the book. The tone of the book would be further defined by the black-and-white line illustrations of David Stone Martin, the former art director of the Tennessee Valley Authority and assistant to Ben Shahn in the Works Progress Administration, whose spidery calligraphic lines were to initiate the stark, noirish look of jazz iconography in the 1940s and 1950s.

Alan's work as a DJ had caught the attention of a number of people in the media. When Dwight D. Eisenhower, then president of Columbia University, announced in 1948 that the university would be cooperating with the Public Health Service to spread the word about the new penicillin drugs for syphilis and gonorrhea, it was decided that public service radio announcements would be the preferred method of communication. Alan's old boss from OWI, Erik Barnouw, now a professor at Columbia, had been picked to develop the programs, and, recalling Alan's proposals for communicating to minorities that had never been acted upon, he brought in Alan to help produce the messages. What Lomax came up with were a series of short radio "ballad dramas" with titles such as "The Lonesome Traveler," "The Worst Enemy," "The Prodigal Son," "Born on a Friday," and "Born to Lose," aimed at persuading people who might be infected to go to local clinics for blood tests. What was extraordinary was the list of people whom Alan convinced to introduce these programs, no easy task in the sexual climate of the times: the Reverend Adam Clayton Powell Jr., the Maddox Brothers, Bill Monroe, Eddy Arnold, the Hall Johnson Choir, the Dixieaires, Woody Guthrie, the Coon Creek Girls, Cisco Houston, and Sister Rosetta Tharpe.

The first program was written for Roy Acuff, one of the biggest names in country music. When Lomax went to see him, he said:

> Acuff told me that he couldn't say the word "syphilis" on the air because he'd lose his entire audience forever. He told me how he felt about syphilis and in the process told me how his whole southern rural folk audience felt about the subject. So it was very easy for me to go back and write a little story using Roy's principal hillbilly songs. When this program was broadcast, the people came in by the hundreds. They were saying, "Roy said it was all right, so I guess I should come in," or—this program was called "Looking for Lester"; Roy was supposed to be looking for a friend who was lost with the disease germ and was going to die—they would come and say, "Wonder what's happened to poor old Lester," and offer their arm for a blood test.

The programs were completely successful, and brought results for years. Erik Barnouw said that it was the first time that a government campaign had enlisted folk figures. "Lomax had some problems with the producers of the shows and with the people who controlled the budgets, but never with the singers themselves."

The hunger for novelty among the rich of New York City provided the impetus behind some odd cultural events in the city. Often in need of money, Alan would sometimes find himself squarely in the midst of some absurd performances. In one instance, he was recruited by Elsa Maxwell to help organize an event announcing the newly redecorated Park Sheraton Hotel. Maxwell was one of those New Yorkers who seemed to come out of nowhere or the Midwest, and she somehow ended up as a kind of professional hostess for royalty and high society, even though her real job was as a gossip columnist. On May 11, a select list of guests were invited to the hotel for an evening of ballroom dancing, a champagne supper, a display of synchronized swimming, a fashion show, Burl Ives singing in the lounge, and, as the invitations said, "Miss Margaret [*sic*] Mayo and Mr. Allan [*sic*] Lomax present American Square Dancing with Eddie Smith & his North Carolina Ramblers and the American Square Dance group." Also included in the show were Ralph Teffyteller, a Tennessee dance caller, Pete Seeger ("the slickest five string banjo picker in the country"), Fred Hellerman on bass, and Eddie Smith on fiddle.

Libby Holman, a torch singer and Broadway actress whose life was more scandalous and tragic than anything she ever sang about, heard about Alan's work through her former cabaret costar Josh White and went down to the Archive of American Folklore at the Library of Congress for two weeks in 1950 to listen to the recordings. "Nobody carried a torch in the early American songs," said Holman, "they didn't feel sorry for themselves." She worked some of them up into a revue called "Blues, Ballads, and Sin-Songs" and took them to Europe.

Popular events and public recognition such as these kept Alan financially afloat and in front of the public, but he was tiring of them. The success of the public service announcements gave him the courage to reconsider what he felt his real vocation should be. In a letter to Yip Harburg he spelled out the differences between Yip's and his approaches to the folk:

> I have been out trying to learn all I could from the people—the only people in our culture who are relatively free from the corrupting cultural influences of big industry art. I've been a big ear for fifteen years. The result is I know something about how to *use* certain of their forms. . . . If only we had a really functional culture in America, I would have a big job in helping to communicate the feelings of the people to the administrators and in helping the people to understand the rapidly changing world in which they live.
>
> So I look at myself as a good deal more than a source of information. I have been an apprentice to the people for fifteen years and now I shall more and more show what can be done creatively with the rich treasures of the people's speech.

Woody and Lead Belly were both struggling with health problems and lack of money. As Guthrie's health and drinking worsened, he wrote sexually charged letters to a woman in California and enclosed news clippings of gruesome murders such as the Black Dahlia slaying. When she took them to the police in Los Angeles, Woody was arrested for sending obscenity through the U.S. Mail, and Alan worked to get his case dismissed by federal attorneys. Through a plea bargain, Woody entered into psychiatric counseling. Though he failed to finish the required number of sessions and was sentenced to six months in prison, his lawyer got him released in a little over a week. Later, while Alan was letting Woody drive his car, he crashed it into a limousine.

Work had become hard to find for Lead Belly in his later years. His fame as both a political singer and a folksinger were fading, but Alan still called him for big concerts and promoted him at smaller folk clubs like the Village Vanguard. Some of the jazz people, especially the traditionalists, accepted him as one of their own, and he was sometimes awkwardly booked in concerts with sophisticated jazz pianist Mary Lou Williams, or with Bunk Johnson's New Orleans band at Stuyvesant Casino in New York. Lead Belly's health had been failing for several years, and in 1948 he was diagnosed as having Lou Gehrig's disease. After a tour of Europe in May, he grew much worse and died of a stroke in Bellevue Hospital on December 6.

On January 28, 1950, "Take This Hammer," a large memorial concert for Lead Belly, was organized by Alan to benefit his wife, Martha. When the audience entered the theater, the first thing they saw was Lead Belly's twelve-string guitar dramatically suspended in the soft glow of a spotlight against a gray curtain at the rear of the stage. Lomax introduced a long list of performers that included Woody Guthrie, the calypsonian Lord Invader, Brownie McGhee and Sonny Terry, Dan Burley, W. C. Handy, Jean Ritchie, street singer Reverend Gary Davis, song collector Frank Warner, the Weavers, jazz musicians Count Basie, Sidney Bechet, Billy Taylor, Sammy Price, and Hot Lips Page, ragtime pianist Eubie Blake, folklorist Harold Thompson, poet David McAdoo, a New Jersey gospel group called the Varieteers, Bill Robinson, and others. The capacity audience included folk fans, intellectuals, and even bebop musicians such as Dizzy Gillespie. "He had come because he heard that a brother musician had died," Alan said. "Burl Ives and Josh White refused to come, it being the McCarthy era," Alan said later, recalling two of the folk musicians who, while under investigation themselves, had cooperated with federal agents pursuing Communists in the entertainment business.

Alan wrote the script for the evening, and he opened by saying, "Lead Belly came before all the rest of us—busting down the doors for us all with his clarion voice, his tiger stride, his merry heart, and his booming twelve string guitar. And what we balladeers thought of him, we will show you in an evening of singing." Toward the end of the night a filmstrip of photos of Lead Belly's life and career was projected on a large screen with a recording of him speaking and singing, followed by an introduction of his family and a sing-along of "Take This Hammer." So ended the first public memorial to an American folksinger.

Elizabeth's and Alan's careers had been overlapping for the last few years, though her fame as a writer independent of him was spreading and her income rising. She was particularly sought out by radio for her adaptations of long novels like

Thomas Wolfe's *Of Time and the River* (1947). Her 1946 script for John Steinbeck's *Pastures of Heaven* was widely praised, as was her radio play based on Wolfe's *Look Homeward, Angel*, which was picked for Joseph Liss's *Radio's Best Plays* in 1947. Her poetry was also regularly published by the *Saturday Review of Literature*, and in 1948 she completed a libretto for Henry Cowell's opera *O'Higgins of Chile* and received a Rosenwald Foundation Fellowship for a novel she was working on.

She and Alan had talked of returning south, of ending their exile in the North to renew their sense of the cadences and pitches of southern speech, recapture that verbal energy that came with living in a society marked by closely observed racial and social lines, a separate history carved away from the rest of the country. Alan continued to imagine himself as a writer. He had heard enough folklore to last him; he knew all those stories, proverbs, and jokes. Faulkner, Welty, the local colorists of the South, they all depended on black speech and lore to carry them to the written word. Like the white folks of the South who didn't write, these southern writers quoted black folks to underscore the truth. Tennessee Williams even went further, saying that he always felt that he was a Negro. But Alan had also read the writers from Europe, especially Russia, with their feeling for the peasantry and the workers. He had read Dos Passos's cinematic prose, the way he used headlines and newspaper clips to thread his way through the times, moving from one character to another, keeping their dialects, shaping their biographies, all toward the creation of a collective American self. Alan now felt he was ready to bring something new to southern modernism.

Meanwhile, Alan become involved with Robin Roberts, an actress and folksinger who often worked in Village clubs and theaters. She had recently graduated from Sarah Lawrence and was now living in Paris. He was determined to see her, and left the country in September 1949 to travel to Europe for the first time. Over the next few weeks he went to Paris, Rome, Florence, Venice, Hungary, and Czechoslovakia. He avoided telling anyone where he was, wrote no letters, and carried no recording machine with him. But in his notebooks he wrote that all his weaknesses and problems were connected to women, and at that moment, Robin was the central point of everything.

Elizabeth's and Alan's work schedules, his long absences, and his need for other women were already wearing their relationship thin. They both wanted to be writers, and they could not afford both writing at the same time. Their marriage had begun to deteriorate rapidly as Alan's affairs piled up on their doorstep, and finally Elizabeth filed for divorce in Harris County, Texas.

CHAPTER 11

Living on the Black List

When *Mister Jelly Roll: The Fortunes of Jelly Roll Morton, New Orleans Creole and "Inventor of Jazz"* was published in 1950, it received over a hundred reviews, all but one of them laudatory. The exception was Leonard Feather's in Britain's *Melody Maker*, which implied that Lomax had been duped by Morton's flash and braggadocio. Louis Armstrong praised the book and Morton's music in the *New York Times*, and promised to buy another copy. Carl Sandburg promoted it rather sensationally in the *Chicago Sun-Times* as "the life story of a wicked and powerful man who was mad about music, a tale interwoven of wild melody and riotous sex." The British playwright and folksinger Ewan MacColl wrote him that *Mister Jelly Roll* was a revelation, a "collaboration with life, and the two of you together have produced a work of art. In short—you have . . . produced the first great work of Socialist Realism." The book sold well, almost reaching the best-seller list.

But Alan was not completely satisfied with the book's reception, as he had hoped it would also be perceived as an important social science document. Deeply hurt to discover that Charles Seeger did not like *Mister Jelly Roll*, he sent a copy to Robert Pehrson, an anthropologist at the University of Chicago, and asked for his opinion. Pehrson replied that he and several of his colleages had read it, and all agreed that it was indeed a success as a "personal history document," and perhaps even as an ethnography, precisely what Alan had hoped for.

The title of the book was carefully crafted. To call Jelly Roll "Mister" was Lomax's insistence on respect for Morton, contrary to the demeaning first-name address then mandatory in the South. "Fortunes" calls up the role of chance in Morton's life, his circumstances and adventures, and the tradition of the picaresque novel. "New Orleans Creole" is a racial identifier, but one that in this case was used for a different purpose, as it called attention to a community of artists. "Inventor," coming as it does after "Creole," may signal that jazz came into being through creolization, the unique process through which historically unrelated cultures come into contact and form a new, emergent culture. By putting "Inventor of Jazz" in quotes, Lomax is not so much slighting Jelly Roll's claim as he is quoting his business cards and posters and offering a nod to his skill at public relations. It is also part of Lomax's effort to present Morton's boasting and self-aggrandizement in a sympathetic light.

In a remarkable passage deep into *Mister Jelly Roll*, Lomax attempted to sum up the meaning of jazz in America and its relation to New Orleans and the Creole community:

> Jazz became many things—frenetic, destructive, hysterical, decadent, venal, alcoholic, saccharine, Lombardish, vapid—it has enriched stuffed bellies; it has corrupted the innocent; it has betrayed and it has traduced; but everywhere and in all its forms, something jazz acquired at the moment of its origin has profoundly touched all its hearers. What was this thing that set folks dancing and smiling from the slums of New Orleans to all the capitals of the earth?
>
> "We had all nations in New Orleans," said Jelly Roll; "But with the music we could creep in close to other people," adds Dr. Bechet. . . . Jazz was the hybrid of hybrids and so it appealed to a nation of lonely immigrants. In a divided world struggling blindly toward unity, it became a cosmopolitan musical argot. This new musical language owes its emotional power to the human triumph accomplished at the moment of its origin in New Orleans—a moment of cultural ecstasy. Two neighborhoods, disjoined by all the sordid fears of our time, were forced to make a common cause. This musical union demanded that there be not merely acceptance and understanding, but respect and love on both sides. In this moment of ecstasy an interracial marriage was consummated, and the child of this union still jumps for joy wherever jazz is hot. Perhaps it is so wherever people share their treasures and a truly fresh stream of culture begins to flow. Such moments of cultural ecstasy may occur prior to all great cultural movements just as seeding precedes birth.

These lines may tell more about Lomax than they do about Morton, as they focus on his desire to put art at the center of humanity and return us to the magic of creation. In doing so, he also joined Morton in making New Orleans a magical city and a metaphor for what America might yet become.

The reception of the Morton book confirmed Alan's belief that he could write in the voices of ordinary people that would capture their intelligence and the artfulness of their speech without condescension. Fired up by the reviews, he planned a series of books to follow. One would be a collection of short autobiographies to be called *From a Great Dark River*, which would include a washerwoman, a preacher, a convict, a race record artist, and "an entire county" of the South. He would edit the spoken prose that he had recorded in interviews, piecing it together so as not to lose the stream: "I believe that this is the beginning of a technique which will make novel writing and biography a profoundly democratic thing. This washerwoman, for example, she speaks of love and it's as glorious as anything I've ever read on love. The convict tells his tale with the passion of a Dostoevsky. It's thorny prose, very thorny, but it has lots of levels. I believe it will help transform writing, which has reached a kind of dead-end."

He also planned to collaborate on a project with Jean Ritchie. The youngest of fourteen children of a Kentucky family with a rich repertoire of stories and songs, Ritchie had a voice as pure Appalachian as any folklorist could dream of, as well as being a guitarist and dulcimer player, a songwriter, collector, and writer. She had grown up in what most Americans would think of as isolation, but her family maintained contact with the outside world, traveled, owned a phonograph and radio, and saw to it that their children received a good education. Jean graduated from the University of Kentucky in 1946 and came to New York City to work at the Henry Street Settlement School, where she met Alan, who would record her songs and stories between 1949 and 1952. Their literary collaboration was her 1955 autobiography *Singing Family of the Cumberlands*, perhaps the best account of Appalachian life and folklore that had been written up to that time. He would also later write a foreword to *Folk Songs of the U.S. Appalachians as Sung by Jean Ritchie* [1965], and their lives would be intertwined for years to come.

But the first book he wanted to write was to be based on the Fisk University/Library of Congress project, a different one than what had originally been planned, to be called *My Heart Struck Sorrow (And the Tears Came Rollin' Down)*. "I felt that without knowing more about the inner emotional lives of the singers, the objective data on social aesthetics would be of slight value," he wrote the Guggenheim Foundation in hopes of getting a second fellowship. "Therefore I recorded long life histories of a singing sister in the Baptist church, a rural preacher, a wandering blues singer, and a convict. These Southern folk poets tell in the most vivid and moving way, and in a style that approaches that of the greatest writers—why they sing and what they're singing about. They make clear the nature of the floodtide of emotion that spilled out of the South and spread across the whole world. . . . I propose now to integrate this material (all of which has been edited and written up)—into [the book]—as the first part of my fellowship plan."

His application to Guggenheim was supported strongly by Geoffrey Bridson and Melville Herskovits, but Goddard Lieberson and Harold Spivacke wrote stressing that Alan was not a scholar, since he approached his work from an "emotional" perspective, and so should be considered a creative writer. Carl Sandburg praised Alan's work, but added that "at one time he had Communist affiliations, whether a party member I don't know." The one folklorist Alan asked to recommend him was Archer Taylor, who criticized him for not displaying knowledge of the German research in musicology, and viewed the proposal as guided by Communists. The application was turned down.

With the publicity behind *Mister Jelly Roll,* Alan's agent easily put together a speaking tour in the Midwest that would earn Alan $1,200. On the long train rides through the countryside he sketched out notes for plays or a musical he might write, short stories or books yet to be published. Robin Roberts was constantly in his thoughts, even as he was tormented by the unbearable idea that Elizabeth might remarry and not come back to him. His dreams were vivid and scrupulously recorded in notebooks, and central to them all was the fear that whatever he did he might end up completely alone. In one of them he announced to an audience that this was to be his last lecture, that a large university had hired him to do more important work.

At Columbia Records the long-playing record had just been perfected, first in a ten-inch version and then a twelve-inch form that allowed some twenty to twenty-five minutes of music to be contained on each side. Though it had been developed to record classical music—no one in the industry believed that ten or twelve pop songs could be sold as an album—Alan thought that the LP would be the perfect means of packaging a folk song collection: one long-playing record could hold as much music as was usually printed in an academic monograph. In those days recordings of ethnic music were hard to find outside of specialty shops, most of which were limited to music of a single language, nationality, or ethnic group. When Alan spoke at the Midcentury International Folklore Conference at Indiana University at the end of July 1950, he proposed that the scholars gathered there form a committee to produce LP records with booklets of notes that would cover the folk songs of all the world's peoples. There had been earlier attempts at such a project—the German ethnomusicologist Erich von Hornbostel's *Musik des Orients*, the Ethnic Series of Folkways Records, and UNESCO's *World Collection of Recorded Folk Music*—but they were either random and unrepresentative in their selections or their creators had abandoned their projects after only a few records were issued. What Alan was proposing was to ask expert musicologists to pick the selections and provide background materials for the countries whose music they knew, to create definitive collections:

> What more people need are just good sets of examples from most of the culture areas. Every folklore center would like to have such samples. If we could agree on some kind of plan for the use of either tape or long-playing records—probably long-playing records—we could make a beginning at this meeting of an international exchange of folksongs between countries. I know that it is possible to get

> about fifty minutes of music from one record at the cost of about three dollars and a half. With two or three records you could get a very great deal of music from Turkey or Pakistan or any particular part of the world. And it could be quite within the realm of possibilities to establish an international exchange on this basis.

For the first time, all the music in the world could be made available to listeners. But there was little interest among the scholars at the conference, and only Charles Seeger supported him. "They made me so mad," he said, "I decided to do it myself."

It was a huge project, and one that an individual would hardly consider undertaking, especially one without money or institutional backing. But something had happened at those meetings in Indiana that led him to risk everything. He had always been frightened by public speaking, and not able to participate in discussions and meetings without anger, impatience, and excess emotion. During his folklore lectures he found "a peculiar sort of outlet":

> At first I started to sing Negro folksongs, all techniques of concealed protest and hidden hostility—always sung in front or at behest of my daddy, and so was almost consciously ridiculing him and defying him, at the same time as I was publicly doing what my mother would have done or would have wished me to do. It was after I lost interest in this particular group of songs (having to do with murder, criminals, mean bosses, etc) and also lost interest in a group of songs that defied and ridiculed Elizabeth that I began to lose interest in singing. . . . My visit to Bloomington was actually like my taking my stand at a rostrum in a public place against *all* warnings of my father not to be an intellectual, not to care about issues.

Later that summer in a coffee shop on Broadway he bumped into Goddard Lieberson, now the president of Columbia Records, and told him about this project. What if he traveled to Europe for a few months to find archives of folk music and then asked for help putting together forty-five or sixty collections that represented the best of each country? And what if he wrote booklets of notes to go with the albums, including photos and maps, and the whole thing could be done cheaply? Would Columbia back him for the project? The answer was yes, but only for thirty LPs, and the notes would have to be part of the covers, not separate books. The series would be called the *World Library of Folk and Primitive Music.* The consulting experts would each be paid an honorarium, and royalties would be arranged for the collectors or archives involved. Lomax was free to negotiate these arrangements on his own, but he would have no advance with which to travel.

Columbia provided a Magnecord tape recorder, tapes, and copying facilities wherever he went, but the rest of his expenses (which eventually amounted to some $20,000) would have to be borne by him. The Jelly Roll book had earned him only $250; he had received $600 for organizing and singing with Woody Guthrie, street singer Reverend Gary Davis, and Pete Seeger at Music Inn, a farmstead in Lenox, Massachusetts; and he had an inheritance of $4,000 from his father's estate, but none of this added up to enough to finance the trip.

Earlier the Weavers' managers had approached Alan for clearance of the song "Goodnight Irene," since it had been published in the Lead Belly book that he and his father had written. By then both John Lomax and Lead Belly were deceased, so Alan proposed an agreement splitting the royalties between the John Lomax and Lead Belly estates. The final agreement gave the song publishing company, World Wide, 50 percent, and the other 50 percent was split between the Weavers and the Ledbetter and Lomax estates. "Goodnight Irene" had been played 100,000 times in one month on radio and TV, and as it was also on most of the jukeboxes in the country, it was heard an estimated two million times a day. From the time of its release on July 3 to October, fifteen versions of it had been recorded, by everyone from Frank Sinatra to Red Foley, and more than two million of those singers' records had also been sold. When Alan's share of the royalties came in, he decided that if he was going to take money from folk song recordings it should only be used to support further research on folklore. The Lomax estate made $6,400 from its 16.7 percent share of the royalties; his stepmother Mrs. Ruby T. Lomax was due half of that. Out of such scraps of money Alan would finance the European trip, which he thought might only last for a year at most.

If this arrangement seemed somewhat tenuous, it would nonetheless turn out to be the way he lived for the rest of his life. He would become a one-man foundation, operating without benefit of the usual academic credentials and support, stepping uneasily between the world of commerce and entertainment and the abstemious, hermetic life of scholars. Anthropologist Margaret Mead, an early admirer of Lomax's, would later say, "One of the reasons that Alan has made enemies is that he has done most of his research on money that he's made himself out of the folk field. That's a fatal thing to do in this country. He not only made money, but he won some fame and prestige and delighted other people. That's even worse."

Although folk songs might have been popular at the time, it was not a good era in which to be a folksinger. The previous December, a New York newspaper carried a story headlined "Red Convictions Scare 'Travelers,'" which told of a dinner held by the Civil Rights Congress earlier that month at the Hotel Fifth Avenue to honor five lawyers who had defended people accused of being Communists. The dinner was sponsored by a number of people, including C. B. Baldwin, the former campaign manager for Henry Wallace, Olin Downes, W. E. B. Du Bois, and Alan Lomax. All of their names were listed in the article, and all were labeled members of Communist front groups. Then, in June 1950, *Red Channels: The Report of Communist Influence in Radio and Television* appeared, a seven-page pamphlet issued by a group of ex-FBI agents who edited the magazine *Counterattack*, and added 151 performers and entertainment figures to the Hollywood blacklist of alleged subversives that had emerged shortly after the end of World War II. The new group of the accused included Orson Welles, Leonard Bernstein, Lena Horne, Gypsy Rose Lee, Dorothy Parker, Aaron Copland, Oscar Brand, Norman Corwin, Richard Dyer-Bennet, Will Geer, Tom Glazer, Yip Harburg, Langston Hughes, Burl Ives, Millard Lampell, Arthur Miller, Earl Robinson, Pete Seeger, Josh White, and Alan Lomax.

At the same time Congress was debating the McCarran Act on internal security, legislation that would require the registration and fingerprinting of all "subversives" in the United States. The House Un-American Activities Committee was given new life by the debate, and had begun to widen its hearings; rumor had it that the FBI was planning mass arrests.

Alan renewed his passport, listing only his stepmother and Carl Sandburg as people to contact if he ran into trouble. In September he went to the office of his agent at the Charles L. Pearson Lecture Management Bureau in Rockefeller Center and canceled his upcoming speaking engagements, explaining that he was concerned about the *Red Channels* listing, that he felt sure the McCarran Act would pass and that he would be ruined. He was leaving for Europe, he said, and would be back in January "if things cleared up." Yet right up to his departure from the United States, Alan kept up his criticism of the reactionary direction of American folklorists, even when he reviewed his friend Ben Botkin's 1949 book *A Treasury of Southern Folklore*. He praised the breadth and scope of Botkin's idea of folklore and his grasp of the distinctiveness of southern lore, but pointed out one dimension missing from the collection:

> He has, however, lost the main theme of the Southern story, which is the exploitation of one group by another, the White exclusion of the Negro from the human family, and the deep and abiding horror of this for both groups. There is no lynching of a Negro described in these pages, and this is and has been the culminating moment in the folk drama of the South. The feelings that produce these moments of terror and violence also motivate the blues, the extraordinary passion of the Southern revival meetings, the flowery concealing phrases of the Southern politician's oratory, the endless aggressiveness that underlies the endless yarn-spinning, the preoccupation with death and whisky, the local pride that a four years' war failed to diminish, and the muttering of that storm of anger

which can be heard in all Negro folk creations and which the folklorist especially should perceive.

As he suspected, the McCarran Act was passed in September, and by October the FBI was again interviewing people who knew Alan, from whom they learned that he had left the country on September 24 on the steamer *SS Mauretania*, en route to Brussels. Elizabeth had tried to keep him from going, in part because it violated their arrangement for raising Anne. She knew that with Alan in Europe, the full weight of parenthood would fall upon her, and she doubted that he would have the hundred dollars a month in child support she had asked for in the divorce. They argued bitterly, with Elizabeth threatening dire consequences if he left. In the end, he offered to pay two hundred dollars a month in child support.

Elizabeth still had a job, but was also working on a novel, writing poetry, and coediting a revision of the Lead Belly book with Alan that would include an interview she had conducted with Martha Ledbetter. She was also recording the life history of Reverend Gary Davis. Alan paid her $1,000 for her work with him, as well as for lengthy interviews she had done with Vera Hall, the Alabama singer, who was to be the subject of the largest portion of his book of autobiographies: "It will now be, because of Elizabeth's contribution, the most moving section of the book. An indictment of the soul of the South from within its tenderest, most loving, and most loveable part." Another of their joint projects was to release the BBC ballad operas *The Chisholm Trail* and *The Martins and the Coys* in the United States on Columbia Records. Alan had negotiated with Mitch Miller of Columbia for Elizabeth and himself to receive advances of $2,000 each to pay the singers and prepare the records, but when the Korean War began Columbia scrapped the project.

Lomax never told his family exactly why he went to Europe, only that he was developing a library of world folk music for Columbia Records. Nor would he ever allow anyone to say that he was forced to leave. In a letter to the editor of the *Record Mirror* of London, he later took a writer to task for claiming that he was a "victim of 'witch-hunting'" and insisted that he was in the UK only to work on the Columbia project.

In the last two weeks before his departure, his anxiety became overwhelming. He not only was leaving everyone he knew and cared for, and the country in which he had invested everything, but was giving up his weekly sessions of psychoanalysis, which he counted on to keep him focused. But as the ship pulled out into the East River he proudly declared himself in his notebook "a comrade of the world, longing to *be* everywhere." He jotted down bits of poetry as they slid out to sea, recalling the sweetness of his daughter's good-byes, realizing that he was the only one on board with flowers, because Anne had given them to him. He noted the cold grayness of the river and the strawberry sun winking through the smog. Looking back to the pier, he spotted a cook from a place where he often had breakfast—the man had come to see a friend off, but now was waving a last good-bye to Alan "out of the universal love that humans have." "And I was proud of my only friend, even if he always burns the bacon. Like meeting your birth doctor at your wake."

Alan wrote Anne a letter as they sailed, filling it with cartoon sketches of the ship, waves, the wind, and himself. He made a note to himself that most of his earthly possessions were on that boat: a trunk, a suitcase, a typewriter, a backpack, an amplifier, tape recorder, guitar, and boxes of tapes. His last New York note, in a Whitmanesque echo, declared, "Farewell Manhattoes / Anne, Anne, Farewell / No more fear now for me."

In Europe, Alan went from Belgium to Rome, where Robin Roberts was staying. The two took a train to Florence and from there went on to Paris. He had been invited to base his project in the Musée de l'Homme by Gilbert Rouget, the director of ethnomusicology, and was granted access to the Phonothèque Nationale to look for recordings. Rouget had heard about Lomax from Claude Lévi-Strauss, the preeminent anthropologist of France; they had met when Lévi-Strauss was at the New School in New York. When Lévi-Strauss returned to Paris, he told Rouget that Lomax was a genius and that he should get to know him.

Yet after only a few days of sitting in his office in the Palais de Chaillot on the hill of the Trocadéro in the 16th arrondissement, across the Seine from the Eiffel Tower, Alan found the charm of Paris to be less than he expected. The October weather had turned grim, he had picked up some form of traveler's indigestion, and instead of strolling the streets of Paris as the flâneur he had imagined, he found himself looking for the shortest way to walk from the office back to his room in the Hôtel l'Universe. He had been granted a place in an institution that many considered the center of world folklore and a position that demanded respect, and had been welcomed into Parisian intellectual circles, but it bothered him to think that he needed those outward signs of honor, and he fought against them. Soon he worked only in his hotel room, writing letter after letter to the collectors and musicologists of the world, and coming in to the office only to get his mail.

Robin was singing folk songs at a club called L'Abbaye, run by two black American expatriates, and Alan was appalled that she enjoyed Parisian nightlife so much. He had doubts about the depth of her feelings for him, which increased the longer they stayed together. When he became ill with the flu and nausea, followed by a sinus infection and an earache, he took to his bed, lying there in resentment of every moment she spent away from him. A doctor was finally summoned. Alan received penicillin and morphine, but then developed facial paralysis, and had difficulty controlling his speech and facial movements. He was hospitalized and operated on for pressure on a nerve, and a mastoidectomy was performed on his ear. Sinking deep into depression, he wrote, "I am a passionate pilgrim and must live at the edge of death and hell."

But he slowly recovered, and then moved to a cheaper room at another hotel, the St. Paul. For the first time in weeks, he felt strong enough to go out to a party given by Alfred Métraux, an anthropologist who had just become a member of UNESCO's Department of Social Science. It was an opportunity for Alan to meet all of the distinguished anthropologists of France. Yet the next day he wrote that "like all anthropologist parties, it was like the gathering of enemy clans at a country funeral. Bad food and liquor, everyone stiff and angular, no conversation. . . . Christ, what a distorted evening."

After two months in Paris with so little accomplished, the money disappearing faster than he'd expected, receiving few promising responses from scholars he had hoped would cooperate with him and discovering that the few archives of folk song he could locate were far from complete, he decided that he would have to do some of the collecting himself. "He told me he was recording the whole world of folk music," Robin recalled. "Where did I want to start? I said, let's go to Ireland." A few years earlier Alan had fallen under the spell of a recording of Marie O'Sullivan singing "The Airy Girl," and thought that it was the kind of voice he had heard about but never actually heard in America. There was "a delicacy of musical line and subtlety in singing we couldn't match in the States."

While he was happy to start with Ireland, he nonetheless knew that he would need help in being introduced to Irish culture and finding the right songs and singers. Since he was still short of money, London would offer the prospect of finding work with the BBC, given the good relations he had developed through his wartime radio shows. If anything, he thought the British appreciated his work more than the Americans, and Geoffrey Bridson, the BBC producer, had often suggested that they work together again. So it was to England that Alan and Robin went on a Cunard boat one cold December night.

The pall of war had not left London. Rationing was still in effect, the skeletons of buildings destroyed by bombing dotted many neighborhoods, travel was difficult, wages were low, nightlife was muted, phonograph records were few, and the city looked back nostalgically to its prewar past instead of developing a popular culture that reflected its times. "Austerity" was what they called it, but the city had the feel of a shabby, underfunded museum. The beginnings of a folk music revival were in the air, but it too looked only backward and was the work of a few scattered individuals who sang in a pub or two, or the occasional workers' group. Yet it was also a time in which West Indian and West African immigration was increasing, bringing with it new cultural elements that would both threaten and energize the country. It was a situation in which Alan imagined that people such as himself might be welcome as cultural brokers who knew the past but could also serve as a link to the future, and might be able to reconnect the country's various regions and traditions and introduce the new citizens moving among them.

Alan's first stop was the BBC, where he laid out his collecting plans for Bridson and explained how the records he would make in Ireland, England, and Scotland could also be used as the basis for radio programs. The BBC had not done much with folk music aside from presenting the folk-music-as-art-song efforts of composers like Ralph Vaughan Williams, or featuring folk songs as fillers on talk shows aimed at farmers, but they nonetheless had a growing archive of recordings. That night at the White Stag pub, Bridson introduced Lomax to Brian George, head of BBC's Central Program Operations, who in 1947 had made a song-collecting trip to Ireland and with Seamus Ennis of Radio Éireann had recorded local singers for a program they called *Songs from the Four Provinces*. George was at the moment lobbying the BBC to fund an expansion of their activities, and he saw in Alan a potential ally. By the end of the evening the three of them agreed to go through the BBC's Irish recordings to see what was usable. But Alan still had the urge to experience Ireland himself, "in spite of the fact that very good recordings already existed and there was no great necessity for my repeating the performance."

Bridson encouraged Alan to apply for a labor permit so that he could be hired immediately to work on his own program, but also to appear on a short series of programs already in development called *Traditional Ballads* that would be aired on the Third Programme, the high-arts broadcast unit of the BBC. Alan appeared on the second of the ballad programs on February 12, 1951, and on the following day his own three-part series, *Adventures in Folk Song*, began to be broadcast on the Home Service, the recently upgraded domestic radio network. The programs were built around the story of his Library of Congress travels, with Robin and him singing songs and playing a few of his field recordings that they found in the BBC library.

A compulsory stop for any folk song collector in London was the English Folk Dance and Song Society, and it was there that Alan met Douglas Kennedy, the man who had replaced Cecil Sharp as its director. Kennedy introduced him to his son Peter, who worked for BBC West Region and at that moment was recording singers in Somerset, Devon, and Dorset for the program *Village Barn Dance*, using his own band to accompany them. Peter shared Alan's belief in the importance of field recording and using the best equipment, and he too had a driven, single-minded vision of his own role in documenting folk music everywhere in England and making the music popular across the country.

In January 1951, Robin and Alan loaded up an old Citroën with guitars, tapes, and the heavy Magnecord tape recorder, took the ferry from St. David to Rosslare, Ireland, and traveled on to Dublin the same day. In Jamestown, north of Dublin, they met with Seamus Ennis, the master singer and piper with whom Brian George had worked in Ireland. After a night of drinking and singing in the Ennis family kitchen the next day, Alan was convinced they could collaborate. There were still songs to be heard that had not been recorded, Seamus said, and he could find the people who were not known outside their own hamlets.

At the Irish Folklore Commission, Alan met with their archivist, Sean O'Sullivan, hoping to get informal permission for collecting from the local folk establishment. "He was perfectly dressed and knew exactly what was worthy and what was not," said Robin. "He showed us a lovely, green-bound collection of the oldest, grandest Irish airs, with translations from the Gaelic. One got the impression that there was very little left to collect. Alan would arrive in his office in unpressed pants, a shirt open at the neck, big smile and homeboy Texas accent. You could almost see O'Sullivan wince."

Before they set out, Alan tested his equipment by recording Seamus's piping, and the tape recorder broke down on the first try. When they took the machine to Radio Éireann for repairs, there was trouble fixing it, and they ended up borrowing a large mobile recording unit and taking radio engineer Jimmy Mahon with them on their travels. On January 23 they motored in a van and two cars to Ballymakeery to look for Elizabeth Cronin, a woman who it was said knew the songs from the Cork area in both English and Irish. She turned out to be elderly and in poor health, but with an enormous repertoire of songs, so many that when singing tired her out they made plans to return to record more later.

On they went, town to town, stopping and asking about this or that person, sometimes finding them, sometimes learning that they were deceased or had moved away. In Macroom they recorded two men who sang "conversation" songs, alternating lines back and forth, then joining together on the chorus; in the villages of Coolea and Ballylickey in County Cork they located several women singers, including Marie O'Sullivan, the one whose voice had so inspired Alan on record, and who sang in a light and fragile voice of fairies and couples who sought to be married against all odds.

Several days were spent in a hotel lobby in Galway with two brothers, drinking, singing, eating, and recording beside a turf fireplace that popped and crackled so loud that it spoiled the record. Although they endured complaints from guests who said they could not sleep with such a racket going on, they got to hear songs so finely filigreed that they seemed almost Middle Eastern. The two singers were "drinking, talking about the devastation of Cromwell's genocidal invasion of Ireland in the 15th century, as if he had been there only two weeks before." When the pain of memory returned, one of the brothers said, "We must forget him now . . . must forget Cromwell."

Donegal was next, to hear fiddler Mickey Doherty, a Traveler (or Tinker), a member of an Irish nomadic group, and then Dundalk, where the "Queen of the Tinkers," Margaret Barry, was selling baskets and singing and playing banjo for coins on a side street. She knew the most ancient of songs, commercially recorded versions of popular older songs like "She Moved Through the Fair," and the latest hits from the United States, such as the Weavers' "Goodnight Irene," which she had heard over Radio Luxembourg, the first of the pirate radio stations. Sometimes recording became impossible without chasing away dogs and chickens, stopping grandfather clocks, or asking curious listeners to be quiet. When records were unusable or the singers were not as good as promised, Alan paid them anyway.

By the end of February they had passed through enough towns and regions of Ireland to have a representative collection of recordings, and when added to those they had selected from other collectors and the BBC library there were more than enough to put together the album of Irish music. It was a remarkable piece of work to have completed in six weeks, especially considering that Lomax was not familiar with Irish culture or the Gaelic language, and the roads were often covered with ice or snow. Despite his freewheeling and improvisatory style, Lomax was sharply disciplined in his work. Perhaps too much so, according to Robin:

> Later, there were those who complained that Alan had roared through Ireland like Attila the Hun, had trod roughshod over other folklorists' special territories. He had not spent enough time with the people to understand them properly, and he did not speak Irish. But he did have the imprimatur of Seamus Ennis, without whom he might easily have been led astray.

Alan could be impatient when he recorded, pushing the singers hard to keep going. If they had forgotten a verse along the way, he could draw them out, looking for complete ballads, sensing that they knew them and could be coached into remembering. Most singers viewed the recording sessions as a kind of social occasion, and wanted to eat and drink as they sang, but Alan tried to keep them focused on singing. A pattern of work developed in which they recorded, then perhaps had something to eat, and then spent the rest of the evening with each singing his own songs from different parts of the world. This song-swapping sometimes led to even more recording. Robin's American versions of songs that were known by the Irish turned out to be a great aid, as they were often heard by her listeners as "wrong," and the singers were then quick to sing the correct version as they knew it.

When they returned to London, Alan and Robin went back to work for the BBC, recording two more three-part programs. In the first, *Patterns in American Folk Song*, songs were introduced by their functions and organized by the themes of "Love," "Violence," and "Work." But it was in the second series of programs that Alan found his voice for an English audience. In *The Art of the Negro*, which included "Jelly Roll from New Orleans," "Trumpets of the Lord," and "Blues in the Mississippi Night," he introduced some of the arts of the black working class in the American South, and at the same time put heavy stress on the conditions under which they were forced to struggle. By the second broadcast, a powerful entrée to the black church, Alan had found a way to weave his voice in and out of the music and other voices, with fades and segues that were the equal or better of film editing. His commentary was often edged with irony, as when he introduced the guitar-playing, jazzy crossover pop star/church singer Sister Rosetta Tharpe:

> *Record: "Up Above My Head"*
>
> LOMAX: "Up above my head, I hear music in the air," that's what Sister Rosetta Tharpe is singing. "Up above my head, I hear trouble in the air," and the brown fingers tear a polyrhythmic accompaniment out of the mother-of-pearl inlaid guitar, and the spotlights glitter on the electric blue evening gown, and in the packed football stadium, the ecstatic Negro crowd yells its approval. For Sister Rosetta is their favorite artist. Marian Anderson and Duke Ellington are all right, in their way; but it takes Sister Rosetta Tharpe, with her sanctified singing to put everybody straight—spirituals with a blues lick, the red hot, but not a bit sacrilegious descendant of "Swing Low Sweet Chariot," and "Go Down Moses." They make Sister Rosetta Tharpe a trumpet of the Lord.

To those who thought folk song was on the way out, Alan would redefine the subject by portraying Sister Tharpe and other religious singers in "streamlined U.S.A.," touring the country "in fast cars, playing to packed Churches, and providing religious entertainment." To make the form of the songs familiar to his English listeners, he first offered a recorded example from his trip to the Hebrides that summer, a hymn in Gaelic lined out, stated by a song leader, and then followed by the congregation, singing the same thing. Then he played a similar way of singing from a black Mississippi church, but drawing attention to a fast pulse being kept by an elderly woman's foot, "like a lead drum." His intention was to show that there were multiple sources to black American music, some European, some African. With taped interviews of a preacher and a church singer, he illustrated how the black church had become the only source of community and sanctuary in a southern town, how the preacher's sermon worked its rhetoric on the congregation, what the songs meant to the singers, and how injustice and terror reigned in the South of the United States.

The last of the three programs was on the blues and used portions of Alan's various trips in the South and some of the "Blues in the Mississippi Night" recordings that he had as yet not been able to make public in the United States. He demonstrated the difference between country blues, pop blues, and George Gershwin's "Rhapsody in Blue," and discussed vocal and guitar techniques, the structure of the songs, and their subject matter. Throughout, he developed a countertheme on the violence of everyday life and the role blues singers played in such a life. At times the series had more political content than the BBC was comfortable with, but it was a success with the public, and Alan received many fan letters for his brave programs. A letter from folksinger Ewan MacColl warned him that when he went back home there would be a committee waiting for him. "Who knows but that some future Librarian of Congress (Folk Song Dep't.) may have the good fortune to visit a state farm or pen with his tape-machine and find prisoner Lomax there just begging to be recorded."

The time and effort that had gone into the trip to Ireland made Alan realize that he would not be able to manage all of the United Kingdom, and that Peter Kennedy was the right choice to put together the record for England, as he had already assembled a wide range of recordings from his own collecting and knew the BBC library and what commercial recordings had been issued. They needed nothing more than a few songs from the north of England and from the cities, so Peter directed Alan to several people he could record from Newcastle and Northumberland and recommended Ewan MacColl and A. L. (Bert) Lloyd for industrial and city songs.

Both men were leftists, Lloyd a sailor, translator (he had translated García Lorca's *Blood Wedding*), amateur folklorist, singer, and journalist whose media connections occasionally got him and folk songs on the BBC, and Ewan MacColl (the pen name of Jimmy Miller) an actor, singer, and playwright who had been praised by George Bernard Shaw as the best in England (other than GBS himself). Lloyd and MacColl had not met until Alan introduced them when he asked them both to sing for the album. MacColl recalled his first encounter with Alan at the BBC studios. "He was at the microphone singing 'Barbara Allen' and filling the room with his own particular kind of excitement":

> I stayed on at the studio until after the broadcast and recorded songs for him until close to midnight. He was the best audience I had ever sung to. Afterwards, in the elevator on the way down to the street, he closed his eyes and appeared to fall asleep. His companion told me that he had been awake for the past thirty-six hours. This was the picture I was to have of him for the next few years: a man given to furious bursts of prolonged activity which only ceased when he was on the verge of collapse. I did not see him again for a couple of months, and then one day he turned up in the heart of the Durham coal-belt where I was on tour with the Theatre Workshop. After the show that night we sat and listened to him sing and talk for some eight hours and felt ourselves catch fire as a new world was opened to us. Up to his time, folk music had been for most of us a pleasant medium of relaxation, but after that night we all became confirmed addicts; in the jargon of the time we were "committed."

MacColl was then part of the Theatre Workshop he had created with his wife, director and actress Joan Littlewood. Together, their travels to small communities, schools, and labor unions with experimental theater and agitprop drama had earned them critical fame and several arrests for disturbing the peace. Alan joined with Ewan to take folk songs to the unions, and for several weeks they went to Executive Committee meetings of the National Union of Railwaymen, making their plea for the union to start an archive of railroad songs. But they had little success with practical people who had a hard time seeing how songs could help their cause. They also worked together on plans to create a Worker's Dance Group that would use Stanislavsky's acting exercises, the movement techniques of dance scholar Rudolf Laban, and the rhythms and actions of laborers to build a new form of modern dance to be used with work songs that Alan would help them collect.

In the spring of 1951 Jean Ritchie came to England with her husband, George Pickow, on a Fulbright Grant to collect folk songs that were the source of her family's Appalachian repertoire. Pickow had brought along a spring-driven Bolex camera to film some folk performances, and when he met up with Alan and Peter Kennedy, Peter suggested they go to the fishing village of Padstow on the Cornish coast to film their May Day festival. On the drive there Peter described the festivities they were going to see while Alan sat in the backseat listening and thinking about how the film could be structured. The documentaries of the time were similar to slide shows with a lecturer, but by the time Peter finished talking, Alan had devised a rough script and had a sense of how the celebration should be filmed. He had done a bit of silent motion picture photography in the southern United States and in Haiti, but only to have a record of pieces of dances, drumming, games, and religious rituals. He had never before had to consider how a film could be made that fit together different images and points of view, how to manage the passing of time or the development of a theme, nor had he ever recorded sound synched to a film. Pickow too had no experience with more complex filmmaking.

The camera crew recorded interviews in which townsfolk described the festival and their reactions to it, which in turn became the basis for the final script. They had arrived with color film, but discovered that some of the most important moments took place in the pub before the celebrations began. This meant they would have to shoot in black and white because of the lack of light, and at the last minute they found two rolls of black-and-white film and a floodlight in a local store. Despite having been shot with a single camera, and at virtually a 1:1 film stock to finished film ratio, the movie was filled with daring angles, quick cuts, and changing perspectives deep within the crowds.

Later there was trouble in synching up sound and image, but Alan solved the problem by using a conversational voice-over added in a London studio, with a "tourist" from London asking a Padstow resident questions about what it all meant. The final cost of the film was $1,000, with none of the crew taking money for their work.

Though they stuck close to the people's view of the festival, the film was not entirely accurate, because local disagreements did not allow them to show that the village was split into two competing factions, with parades in different parts of the town. Nevertheless, *'Oss, 'Oss, Wee 'Oss,* as the film was titled when it was finished in 1953, became something of a milestone in documentary filmmaking, and though it was screened across England for several years and later was presented on television, it was seldom seen for the next fifty years.

After their divorce, Elizabeth and Alan continued to write to each other often. Their letters were open, sometimes confessional, and very affectionate. (Elizabeth called them their "love letters.") They swapped stories from their analysis sessions, discussed Anne (she was not going to school regularly because she was bored, and Elizabeth was looking forward to living in the country, where a better school might be found), and their current lovers. They wrote about Elizabeth's visiting him in England, or Alan's coming home, with each of them urging the other. If he returned to New York, she said, they could again work together on "the great poets of the world," meaning singers such as Reverend Gary Davis. Alan meanwhile promised to show her poetry to British publishers.

Alan sent money for Elizabeth and Anne to join him in Italy for Christmas, but they were not able to make the trip. When Elizabeth's analysis was completed, she considered taking Anne to visit Texas and the Southwest of her own childhood.

The gap between Elizabeth and Alan of time and geography led to much fretting and doubt, but seven months later she ended a relationship she had been involved in and wrote Alan that he was still the only one; if he asked her, she would come to Europe. They planned to meet in England the following Christmas of 1951, but the trip was canceled at the last minute because of passport and other problems and was rescheduled for February.

In his letters to Elizabeth, Alan tried to insist to her that their problem was effectively *his* problem: a clash of ambitions, his desire to go beyond family life to the world, a need for a kind of love that could never be requited. In a letter he wrote to Woody Guthrie after he heard that Guthrie was sick and had parted from his wife, Margie, he spoke of these problems:

> Ever since I left home . . . I've thought about writing to you. In fact I think of you a hell of a lot. . . . People tell me you've been sick a lot and that you and Margie aren't living together any more. The sick part is bad. What is the matter and why in hell don't the doctors cure you. . . . Write and tell me. The Margie part is worse. I reckon it's just not possible for two people to get as close as you and Margie and me and Elizabeth got without separation just about splitting you in two. Maybe our modern system of love—loving the outside—loving the soul—loving the mind—loving the political opinions—loving to be with—loving to have babies by—loving to make love to—all of that may be more kinds of loving than it's safe to have with one person. Here in Spain and in France and in England and in old fashioned countries and out in the country in America and I suspect in old Russia, the people don't expect or get much from love. But in America where love has built up into the thing that will console you for losing your job and losing your roots and having to leave your home town and selling all your friends for money—LOVE, LOVE, LOVE—we're all kind of weakened down and victimized by something that may be impossible anyway. It's happened to me now twice—then I discovered that the beautiful women on whom I had focused all this, never wanted it at all, and ran off looking for something a lot simpler from someone else.

In the midst of his finishing the English folk song disc for Columbia, old doubts returned about the value of the work he was doing, and gloom set in. He was losing interest in folk song and longing to become the serious artist that he had once imagined he could become. In his field notebook he wrote:

> I know it's worth it, but I wonder more and more if I really should be doing this. I really should be writing before I get too old. . . . Why am I traveling? It's all work and anxiety. I see nothing of the countries. Take no pleasure in anything—and I'm lonesome—Today I realized that travel like this of mine is an affectation. To have

> no roots and no love is to be dead—lonely as a gull. . . . The work I do prevents me, at least in London, from talking to ordinary people about ordinary things. My own interests in folklore are now so specialized that I hardly ever have time to follow them out—my sense of reaction to songs is so dulled by the stream that has poured through me these years that I never enjoy anything anywhere—and time is always the shadow of old man John A., to rise and confound any impression I might have that I am doing well something on my own. I keep on and on because it is difficult to stop. . . .
>
> Under the aegis of Bridson and Gillian [of the BBC] I'm beginning a series of ballad operas for April, May, and June which may save my soul. And redeem me from Father, Mother, Elizabeth, Robin, and them all.
>
> Yesterday GD told me the program had been commissioned at 400 pounds. This leaves me free to do other work. Why I'm in radio I don't know—I guess I want to be wanted, to be identified with a big institution. Here in my only year of freedom, instead of wandering and seeing what I can, I'm spending my time in old ways.

When the album was finally completed, Alan wrote that "the vigor and charm of these living English folk songs may surprise most listeners, perhaps most of all the British." Surprise, perhaps, because many assumed there was not much left of folk culture in the first industrialized nation. Alan's and Peter Kennedy's collection may also have been surprising by its very breadth, as it included ballads, sea chanteys, mummers' plays, children's songs, Christmas folk performances, instrumental music from bands, pipes, and concertina, and featured singers they had found in the streets of London, in the archives, and in the theater. Some might have quibbled that the collection defined folk song a bit too freely by casting some professional singers and singing actors. But Alan was hell-bent on making the records he produced be competitive in quality with those produced for pop culture, and if some of the songs could not be presented any other way than by having trained singers perform them, he had no compunction about using them. (He was also fully aware that one of the characteristics of compiling an anthology was that, if carefully done, it could make everyone on the same record seem relatively equal as artists.)

The Stone of Tory: A Ballad Opera from the West of Ireland was the first of several operas that Alan was planning to write using folk songs he had collected in Ireland and Britain, and he and Robin returned to Dublin in the middle of May to record it for BBC. It was planned as a full-scale production with rural Irish singers and a cast from the Abbey Theatre, and would tell the story of how the attempts of a land agent to collect rent by gunboat on the island of Tory had been stopped by magic. Alan worked diligently on the script for the next three weeks, but felt put upon by everyone around him. Robin and he continued what were now long discussions of their future, or lack of one; and he had come to believe that the BBC crew doing the recording were resentful of his "absorption" in her. And indeed, much of the time Alan *was* fretting over Robin, who was now planning to return to the United States.

The work was difficult, but he met the schedule. The project was the first time that professional singers and actors had joined forces with singers who had never performed for audiences other than their own families and neighbors, and it often required great skill to get them to appreciate and make room for each other's very different senses of time, movement, and art. After two days of rehearsal they recorded the opera in the Royal Irish Academy of Music.

Before he arrived in England, Alan had believed that the songs of Scotland could be represented by a small sample that could be included in the English volume of the series. He was not yet aware of the rich history and culture of Scotland, the mix of the very old and the recently invented that constituted its culture, or the split between lowland and highland peoples that dated back centuries. It was at a meeting set up by Ewan MacColl with Hamish Henderson in London in March that Alan was awakened to the complexities and contradictions of English nationhood. He was fascinated by Henderson, an educated Scotsman with a varied and somewhat secretive life, a published poet who had been a part of the "Soho set" of bohemians in London, yet also an expert on rural life; a Scots nationalist, but a socialist as well; a student of Gaelic as spoken by Scots folk, but also a translator of Antonio Gramsci's *Prison Letters*. When they first met, Hamish was employed as the secretary of the Workers' Educational Association in Northern Ireland, but his passion was Scots folk song and poetry. A few hours' discussion with Henderson made Alan realize that Scotland was far more than just another region of Britain, and filled him with the fire he needed not only to collect the songs of Scotland but also to write a Scots ballad opera:

> The conversation was extremely important. . . . Hamish feels that Scotland is the most interesting and important place on earth, with a real live people's culture, now on the march, and I must say, he made me share his feeling. Presbyterians, impoverished Catholic chieftains, the evicted croppers, John McLean, the Scots labor history, the singing masses—all these came very much alive in his talk and, of course, the fact that he is a Marxist made him much more interesting. . . . He also made me sure that the ballad opera job was worth doing in Scotland, as a sort of declaration of Scots independence—giving Scotland the recognition it deserved.

In the summer of 1951 Alan went to Scotland, again backed by the BBC, following the success of the Irish radio programs. His first stop was the newly established School of Scottish Studies at the University of Edinburgh, where he met with collectors and scholars of Scots songs to gather their support for his project and to convince them that recordings were essential to scholarship. In exchange for their help, he promised to store copies of his recordings in the university library. He was given a quick course in Scots geography, history, culture, and language, where he learned just how much Scotland had never completely accepted defeat from the English, and discovered that it maintained different dialects of Gaelic and its own form of spoken English. Perhaps most surprising to a folklorist was the country's high literacy rate, the manner in which "high" forms of poetry were known by the folk, and the degree to which the oral ballads and folk songs were a part of the culture of the learned and those in urban areas.

Hamish offered to be his guide and corecorder for the northeast lowlands of Scotland, and Calum MacLean, another member of the School of Scottish Studies, along with his brother Sorley, themselves from the Hebrides island of Raasay, steered him through Gaelic-speaking west Scotland and wrote to singers they had worked with in the outer Hebrides to prepare them for Alan's visit to those isolated islands.

In the Isle of Lewis area, Alan went beyond collecting to ethnography, interviewing the singers as he recorded them, about their lives and work as summer cattle herders, or as weavers of woolen cloth. Working alone outside of the United States, he now found himself free to listen more closely and without distraction to how they sang: "I felt suddenly at the roots of one major strain of European folk music . . . emotionally open and direct choral singing. I started the recording machine one night and the people around it looked like ordinary shopkeepers, but suddenly, everyone of them joined in on the phrase exactly at the right time. They all knew the emotional nuances of the songs, held back none of their feelings, and sang *together* as well as any Negro congregation I've ever heard." When he recorded the songs that women sang to accompany their collective tweed waulking (the softening of the tweed by pulling and pounding the fabric to shrink the fibers to make it more waterproof and warmer) he heard call and response between leader and singers, with the leader improvising the words (some of which were teasingly at Alan's expense). This was the closest he had come to hearing music with any similarity to the black work songs of the prisons of the southern United States.

Later that summer Alan met with a group of labor unions, arts organizations, and the Communist Party, which had organized a People's Festival in Edinburgh, the latest in a long series of responses to what many artists perceived as the elite nature of the famous Edinburgh Festival founded in the 1940s. MacColl, Henderson, Lomax, and Hugh MacDiarmid, Scotland's leading modernist poet (and another provocative mixture of Scots nationalist and Communist), all discussed the rump festival that was being planned that year and saw it as a means of bringing Scotland's culture back to working-class people. The festival they conceived featured choral performances, poetry readings, art exhibitions, and plays, and ended with a day-long *ceilidh* (a gathering for dancing, singing, and storytelling) in the Oddfellows Hall. No lines were drawn between the literate and nonliterate, and in fact some of the most "authentic" of the folksingers used prompts and notes to remind them of the words, coincidentally reminding their audience of the long literary history of Scotland. After the program ended, the singing and dancing continued informally down the street in another building late into the night.

The festival was declared a success, and would be recalled by some as the day on which the Scottish folk revival became real to many people, connecting Edinburgh to the Highlands and the distant islands of Scotland. Alan documented as much of it as he could, dragging equipment through the streets, struggling to get everything on tape until the last note was sung, and it became part of the twenty-five hours of recordings that he donated to the university. He encouraged the academics to continue his work and suggested that they hire Hamish as their collector. The faculty was suitably impressed, so much so that, as Hamish said, they "disregarded my suspect politics at long last and offered me a job."

Not all the Scots scholars appreciated Lomax's work, however. John Lorne Campbell, the collector who produced *Highland Songs of the Forty-Five* and other folk songbooks, especially, found his collecting an encroachment on Scots specialists. He let it be known that he thought Alan should have sought them out for help, and implied that Lomax planned to benefit financially from the recordings he had made. Alan responded to Campbell that he was sorry he was not able to do the collecting with him, but that he did not know who all the Scots collectors were when he started, and Campbell had not offered him any guidance on how to carry out the project in Scotland. And it was the BBC who had supported him financially so that they could put the songs on the air. He had not copyrighted any of the music, and since the songs were deposited in the library, no one else could either. But, he wrote, "As you know, however, it's possible for any one at any time to copyright his own arrangement of any part of folklore. That's bound to happen, and if the publication of folklore is a good thing, it might even be considered not so bad a thing in this strange world in which we live." None of the singers he recorded had asked to be paid, he said, but all those used on the BBC were paid by them; and those used on the albums that were produced would be paid for their contribution. "All others will be written and thanked for their contributions to folklore." Even the BBC people could find something negative to say about Alan. One executive in Scotland called him the Harry Lime of folk song.

Hamish Henderson, on the other hand, later recalled Alan's work in Scotland as being of the highest quality:

> He brought to the task a ruthless readiness to do things with his bare hands that most orthodox folklorists would not have handled with two thicknesses of kid gloves. For example, when in Northeast Scotland, he got to grips with the social and political set-up, did his best to explore the often grisly reality of hardship and oppression which lay behind the songs, and thus came in conflict with safety-first BBC producers who like to trail a wreath of late roses over the stark cadaver of the old system. Alan did not regard folksong as something "on the side"; he viewed it as an integral part of the life of the community involved, and he enlisted wide reading and lively intellectual curiosity towards the exploring of all its various ramifications. His ruthlessness and intolerance of anything smacking of humbug earned him enemies; he was frequently dubbed a predator and a jungle-cat egotist. Others alleged that he was an oversized humbug himself, and an assiduous organizer of his own legend. However my own feeling is that Alan is, in his own way, a man of genius.

Despite attracting small audiences, the radio programs from Lomax's trip to Scotland had considerable influence in drawing attention to the cultural links between Scotland and Ireland, and to some of the smaller and lesser-known areas of both lands. Once they saw the result of Lomax's collecting, the BBC created a folk music project under the direction of Peter Kennedy and Seamus Ennis. Alan's Scots radio programs also caught the imagination of artists, one of whom was the photographer Paul Strand, another American escaping the Red Scare. Strand arrived in England just before Lomax's radio comments on South Uist, a group of islands in the Outer Hebrides, which suggested to Strand that it might be possible to treat the people on a group of scattered islands in such a way as to represent an entire culture. Shortly afterwards he set to work photographing the people of South Uist, and the results appeared in a book he pubished with Basil Davidson, *Tir a'Mhurain: Outer Hebrides*, a major contribution to the Scottish folk revival.

While he was still in Scotland, Alan learned that Big Bill Broonzy would be performing on September 22 in London at Kingsway Hall, his first appearance in England. Lomax rushed down to London and announced that he would interview Broonzy onstage—a surprise to the bookers and the club—as he knew that there was much the English would not understand about Broonzy and the blues. Though the crowd was not large, it put Alan in touch with London's jazz zealots and musicians, especially Humphrey Lyttleton, a revivalist Dixieland trumpet player who had graduated from Eton, been commissioned at Sandhurst military college, distinguished himself in World War II, and attended art school.

Alan was determined to get Lyttleton into one of his folk productions, and his chance came when he decided to write another ballad opera, this time with a more modern feel to it, set in London and aimed at TV. *Eel's Foot: A Modern Folk Musical* featured dialogue by Ewan MacColl and Alan, who described the setting as "a pub that doesn't exist, but ought to, somewhere along the South Bank of the Thames with a view of St. Paul's. A place where all the folk singers of the world might drop by." The cast would include Lyttleton, playing the role of Pinetop, an Oxford graduate who sleeps on the bar after closing time, and a group of folksingers playing themselves. Alan had in mind creating an updated version of the Eel's Foot, a pub in the tiny village of Eastbridge in East Anglia, where in the 1930s local people gathered one night a week to take turns singing. A historian who lived nearby invited A. L. Lloyd to visit there in 1939, and Lloyd was so impressed by the songs he heard that he convinced the BBC that they merited a program, "Saturday Night at the Eel's Foot," which in turn led to several commercial recordings being made on the spot, and the pub's becoming the kernel of English folk song activities and recordings in the 1940s and 1950s. Alan's reimagining it as a cosmopolitan gathering place cast it as what he called "a musical United Nations, where music, dancing, and ideas would freely be expressed." Though the opera was never produced, he kept promoting it for years, still hoping as late as the 1960s that someone in New York television would be interested.

In December 1951, the Metropolitan Police of London began making discreet inquiries about Lomax at the BBC, having been warned about him by the FBI. It noted that he had been in touch with the Hungarian press attaché in the United Kingdom, but did not see any "sinister significance" to that contact as yet. The American embassy informed the police that Elizabeth and Anne might soon be joining Alan in the UK, as Elizabeth had given that visit as a reason for applying for a passport in New York City, and warned that Alan might be a member of the Communist Party. From then on, his activities in Britain were noted in a file and shared by the American embassy and the London police.

CHAPTER 12

The Grand Tour

Returning to Paris in March 1952, and once again behind his desk in the Musée de l'Homme, Alan thought that he had accomplished very little in the past two years. He was back where he started, only now without Robin, who, despite his pleas, had gone back to the United States. It was supposed to have taken only a year or less to produce the *World Library of Folk and Primitive Music,* but it now seemed years away from completion. The lack of record archives in some countries and the poor quality of the recordings in those that did have them were bad enough. But the failure of some important musicologists to cooperate in the project left him disheartened. A few were loath to let others hear their recordings before their own work on the music was published; others, especially those who were on the staffs of national museums, were slow to respond because of various restrictions on the use of government property. Still others demanded fees before they would even discuss what they could offer. The Soviet authorities never responded to any of his letters. And there were those who just didn't understand what he meant by folk music and sent him recordings of opera singers' interpretations of folk songs. Meanwhile, a pile of disappointing letters had accumulated on his desk informing him in one way or another that the only way he would ever know what was available would be to visit some of the countries himself.

As he was making travel plans, his wallet was stolen or lost, and then he remembered that his passport was running out. He was issued a new one on April 1, good for six months, but this time it barred him from traveling in Eastern Europe, Korea, China, or any militarily occupied areas. Without his being aware of it, the U.S. embassy in Paris had been instructed by Washington to keep track of his movements. The FBI was beginning to cover the same ground at home again, asking for new information, but misspelling his name, getting his age wrong several times (by ten or twelve years), misidentifying his father as a wealthy man still living on an estate near Dallas, and quoting an anonymous source who acknowledged he'd never seen him but remembered his name appearing in a newspaper article along with Burl Ives, who had "admitted his associations" [with Communists].

When Big Bill Broonzy turned up in Paris, Alan set up his equipment in Broonzy's room in the Hôtel Paris on May 13, and for two hours recorded him singing and discussing problems of race in the United States. They covered some of the same subjects that were in the *Blues in the Mississippi Night* recordings, but this time, with only Alan present, Broonzy spoke more directly and less guardedly about his own experiences with white women, and about the failure of American blacks to work together for their own interests. He spoke of his fondness for the French ("the best people I've met in my life. . . . The people of France are just like the Negro of America—they've been pushed around all their lives, they've been in sorrow, they've been in the shape of the blues all their lives"), and how the recording industry had changed the blues to sell it to whites: "I got to forget what I know, and try to do what he [the producer] tells me." Being recorded with bands put an extra strain on players like Broonzy because the musicians were more sophisticated harmonically than many singers. "I got to sing that, or either starve to death in New York or Chicago."

That spring Elizabeth and Anne visited Alan, and the Lomaxes drove south to Lyon, Marseille, and Nice, spending time together on the coast of Corsica, testing their relationship, seeing if they could feel their way toward becoming a family. Back in Paris, they parted with tentative plans for the future, all of which were shadowed by a lack of money and no realistic way of supporting themselves.

Alan made several short trips to Holland and Belgium in the hope of finding musicologists who could be editors for their countries in his survey of the world's music. Spain was a particular problem. He had no luck in finding anyone who could assemble a selection of Spanish music for him, and he had no desire to visit Spain on his own while Franco was in power. But Columbia was insisting on a Spanish volume for the series, since Spanish guitar and flamenco (along with bullfighting posters) were enjoying something of a craze in the United States. Beyond Alan's objections to the political situation in Spain, he could not afford to go there and spend the time needed to locate all of the country's rich musical traditions. It was then that he heard that the BBC was planning a series of programs on Spanish civilization, and he quickly offered to provide them with recordings from every part of that country for their broadcasts if they would help finance the trip and an assistant, Jeannette "Pip" Bell, his girlfriend, to travel with him. They agreed, but would not pay him until they heard the recordings and approved them. He also asked Columbia to give him an advance for the trip, which they provided but asked to be repaid as soon as he returned.

A Romanian musicologist friend, Constantine Brailoiu, had an invitation to speak at the Second International Folklore Competition being held that summer in Palma de Mallorca and needed some way to get there. Alan offered to drive him, thinking that he might find a Spanish scholar at the performances who could serve as editor of the Spanish record, and attending the event himself would also establish him as a serious scholar and allow him to record some of the invited performers. So the Citroën was loaded up with recording equipment, along with Brailoiu, a young Dutchman who specialized in Javanese gamelan music, Pip, and himself, and they set out for Spain.

The first note in his diary of the Spanish trip tells of their arrival:

> Drove from Port Bou to Barcelona. Took pictures of this smoky, dusty, banking city and embarked at 9. In spite of B's [Brailoiu's] constant chatter it was easy to see the poverty of the country—the preponderance of the horse-drawn vehicles, the ragged clothes, the drawn-nervous faces of the people. However, no beggars. The land from Port Bou to Barcelona is as barren as the Pecera country except in patches along the sea. I was still sick from the sun all day and felt nothing. . . . And everywhere are barracks—dusty unkempt—with the announcement over the doors—Todo Por La Patria. It is so nabbed that one wonders without pause "whose patria" and a look around the streets will convince you at once that it is not the patria of the extremely thin men, these truckers driving horses, these swarming lottery tickets salesmen. These damned Franco rules won't work anyhow.

The next day they reached Mallorca, where things went badly from the start. "Shook hands today with my first Fascist—the secretary to the mayor . . . the folklorists are as rude and uncordial as ever. One named [Garcia] Mato[s] lectured me for ordering eggs for breakfast—then at lunch asked B. and myself to move away from the central table." Then Alan encountered Marius Schneider, the most important folklorist and musicologist in the country:

> At that time, I did not know that my Dutch traveling companion was the son of the man who had headed the underground in Holland during the German occupation; but he was recognized at once by the professor who ran the conference. This man was a refugee Nazi, who had taken over the Berlin folk song archive after Hitler had removed its Jewish chief and who, after the war, had fled to Spain and was there placed in charge of folk music research at the Institute for Higher Studies in Madrid. When I told him about my project, he let me know that he personally would see to it that no Spanish musicologist would help me. He also suggested that I leave Spain.

This Alan took as a challenge, and swore that he would do the Spanish recordings himself, no matter how long it took.

The festival that followed the conference's lectures every night was disappointing: the choral groups and dancers seemed coached; the performances took place in a bullring, the Plaza de Toros, to accentuate their Spanishness to visitors. But Alan recorded them anyway, without asking permission, which upset the organizers. Still, a few people he met encouraged him to stay and record as much as possible. Two were the poet and scholar Robert Graves and the writer Beryl Hodge, then living together in Deiâ, Mallorca, and with whom he struck up a long-lasting friendship. Another was Don Juan Uría Riu, a Spanish ethnologist whose museum had just been closed by the Franco government, "which didn't like him." "He gave me a map of Spain . . . and on the basis of that map I did the series."

Once he left the official folklore of the festival and went out into the rural areas, Alan's spirits began to soar:

> This is a great country. Day hot. The sea near. Figs, oranges, plums, pears ripening. The houses old and simple. The towns old and beautiful. The people the most pleasant I have ever met anywhere, I decide to settle for life in every town and marry every sweet young *señorita* I see. Words, movement, ambition are conquered in the Balearics by the sheer pleasure of living. And I would put my whole life off till tomorrow if a lot of people weren't dependent on me. What I want to do is swim, sleep, stare, chat. And if there is anything more pleasant than chatting with a black-eyed girl on the *Rambla,* the shaded promenade in Palma, between 9 and 11:30 I never ran into it.
>
> ---
>
> For a month or so, I wandered erratically, sunstruck by the grave beauty of the land, faint and sick at the sight of this noble people, ground down by poverty and a police state. I saw that in Spain, folklore was not mere fantasy and entertainment. Each Spanish village was a self-contained cultural system with tradition penetrating every aspect of life; and it was in their inherited folklore that the peasant, the fishermen, the muleteers and the shepherds I met found their models for that noble behavior and sense of the beautiful which made them such satisfactory friends. It was never hard to find the best singers in Spain, because everyone in their neighbourhood knew them and understood how and why they were the finest stylists in their particular idiom. Nor, except in the hungry South, did people ask for money in exchange for their ballads. I was their guest, and more than that, a kindred spirit who appreciated the things they found beautiful. Thus, a folklorist in Spain finds more than song; he makes life-long friendships and renews his

belief in mankind. The Spain that was richest in both music and fine people was not the hot-blooded gypsy South with its flamenco, but the quiet, somber plains of the west, the highlands of Northern Castile, and the green tangle of the Pyrenees where Spain faces the Atlantic and the Bay of Biscay. I remember the night I spent in the straw hut of a shepherd on the moonlit plains of Extremadura. He played the one-string vihuela, the instrument of the medieval minstrels, and sang ballads of the wars of Charlemagne, while his two ancient cronies sighed over the woes of courtly lovers now five hundred years in the dust. I remember the head of the history department at the University of Oviedo who, when he heard my story, canceled all his engagements for a week so that he might guide me to the finest singers in his beloved mountain province.

Alan and Pip talked to everyone, from scholars and police to farmers, priests, prostitutes, children, tourists, and intellectuals, making notes on what they said and how they lived. Pip interviewed the women, asking them about matters that Alan didn't dare raise. He critiqued his own notes as he wrote, examining himself like a psychoanalyst for underlying messages and hidden motivations. At the end of a passage describing the people and land of Formentera, for example, he rethought what he had just written:

> Only a few sheep manage to live here. The people work hard piling up their miles of fences, pulverizing the thin soil . . . fine neat little houses in the midst of their rocky fields. It is a battle for water, for food, for life.
>
> The women show in their faces their proud bearing and their somber dress that they are proud that their men and themselves have won the battle.
>
> (I am continually falling back in these sentimental thoughts because it is so easy to say them in Spanish and hard to say the simple thoughtful things.)

The work in Spain was carried out under the worst of conditions. Alan was short of money and recording tape and had little background in Spanish history and ethnography, as well as having only fair ability in the language. Following mountain trails and back roads that led to villages without electricity and water, or wandering through market squares in Spain's winter, Alan encountered the objections of the *curas*, the parish priests, who were suspicious of his recording, and suffered the constant presence of the military police, the Guardia Civil, who under General Franco kept a firm grip on the country towns and rural areas of Spain. "The black-hatted and dreadful Guardia Civil had me on their lists—I will never know why, for they never arrested me. But apparently they always knew where I was. No matter in what God-forsaken, unlikely spot in the mountains I would set up my gear, they would appear like so many black buzzards carrying with them the stink of fear." He was of special concern to the police because he was a foreigner interested in rural customs and music, some of which—like those of the Galicians, Catalonians, and the Basques, districts that had sought independence from the central government before the Spanish civil war—had been repressed for years as threats to national unity.

Folklore was of particular interest to the Franco government because it was perceived as a means of fostering nationalism. Efforts were under way to eliminate non-Spanish languages and to standardize and rewrite local traditions and songs by the Sección Femenina of the Falange, the fascist party that sent teachers to the rural areas to save folklore by reforming it and teaching the "proper" versions. The authorities had also noted that Alan was traveling in Spain with a young Englishwoman, an assistant, but whom he also registered as his wife at their lodgings along the way. (The U.S. embassy in Madrid diligently noted in their records that she was "a slender woman with a British passport, green eyes, 30, blond.") Most of all, the police were interested in Lomax because, unbeknownst to him, the FBI had notified the Spanish authorities that he was a potential threat. Things became even more complicated when the photo provided to the U.S. legal attaché in Madrid was not of Lomax.

Harassment by the police began shortly after they arrived when Alan was stopped and interrogated because they thought the recording machine in the trunk of his car was a radio transmitter. The police in Madrid went through the mail that was being held for them and shared what they found with the U.S. embassy. The aggravation continued everywhere they went, especially when an excuse could be found, as in Granada, where the police rousted them while they were recording Gypsy songs in a hotel room.

Long before the recording in Spain was completed, Alan had begun to revise the map of Spain with which he had started, now seeing broad and very old musical zones rather than political divisions:

> The Spanish musical landscape is divided into three parts. One, monody [solo, unaccompanied singing], south of the Sierra Madre, where the Oriental connection is close. Two, in the middle—familiar to us—the middle-voiced love songs and such which we regard as Spanish music. Three, up the slope, the Catalonian voice, more open and mostly solo—and then, on the high slopes, a natural polyphony. In the pubs in Galicia and the Basque country, the people sing in chorus. The voice drops in pitch, the shape of the song is for singing and dancing in groups. What I found there reinforces an old theory of mine—that European music is naturally polyphonic, and that the usual high-voiced ornamented "folk song" results from contact with the Orient.

As he took note of these variations in musical style, he also saw that there were differences in posture and the physical behavior associated with music, especially the various facial expressions and degrees of tension in the throat. Singers seemed to be acting out strong emotions, sometimes even when the words of the song did not suggest them.

Before he left England, Alan had bought a small Leica camera, and when he reached Spain he began photographing not only singers and musicians, but everything that interested him—empty streets, old buildings, and country roads. His approach to taking pictures was similar to his ideas about recording: he was making records of the past, of ways of life that were still alive but in danger of disappearing. On the back of each of the *World Library of Folk and Primitive Music* albums of European music there was a note that read, "The folk songs of rural Europe and America are linked with the musics of older civilizations and these again with the chants of primitive man. And with every step it becomes clearer that musical style is, perhaps, the oldest, the most unchanging of mankind's creations." Yet now all these musics "are threatened to be engulfed by the roar of our powerful society with its loudspeakers all turned in one direction." Much of Alan's photography was informed by these same concerns, and concentrated on images of peasant farmers and beggars, the people he called "untouched," presumably by the twentieth century. But he also brought to these photos a concern for form and composition that went beyond the ethnographic to the artistic.

In Spain Alan also developed a new approach to recording, bringing the recordist's affect into play with the performer's:

> Recording folk songs works like a candid cameraman. I hold the mike, use my hand for shading, volume. It's a big problem in Spain because there's so much emotional excitement, noise all around. Empathy is most important in field work. It's necessary to be able to put your hand on the artist while he sings. They have to react to you. Even if they're mad at you, it's better than nothing.

Add to this a young English dancer swirling to the music and jumping back and forth to the recording machine as she adjusts the controls, and what a scene they must have created along those Spanish roads.

Despite the constraints and limitations that he faced over the seven months he spent in Spain, Lomax managed to keep copious notes, take hundreds of photographs, track payments to the singers and musicians, file reports to the BBC, and write letters of thanks to all those who performed for him or helped him. A hundred hours of tape were recorded, containing over three thousand items from most of the regions of Spain. There were songs of the Gypsies, shepherds, mule drivers, farm workers, stonemasons, longshoremen, peasants, professional singers in the cafés, mothers' lullabies, children's play songs, national epics, and the private pleas and confessions of love songs. The musical instruments recorded covered the whole of European history: bagpipes, guitars, flutes, pipes, tambourines, tabors, brass mortars rhythmically rattled with pestles, sheep's bells, and Moorish instruments such as the rabel (a fiddle), the dulzaina, a small oboe, and the ximbomba (a friction drum). This music was largely unknown outside of Spain, though not for long: when Columbia Records producer George Avakian gave jazz arranger Gil Evans a copy of the album, Miles Davis and Evans were struck by the beauty of pieces such as the "Saeta," recorded in Seville, and a panpiper's tune ("Alborda de Vigo") from Galicia, and worked both of them into Davis's 1960 album *Sketches of Spain*.

By this point, virtually everything Alan wrote in the field, from letters to diaries to notebooks, made for compelling reading. He seemed to have reached that point where a freelance writer knows the value of every word, and wastes none. Here are Alan's notes for the music from a spring ritual in Galicia:

> Los Mayos . . . sung by a group of 6 ten year old boys.
>
> Some of the most interesting records of the trip were made in Pontevedra, the handsomest and most aristocratic city in the Province. Here every spring bands of school boys go through the streets singing special new topical songs composed by themselves. Their leader walks in the center of the group a conical canopy of straw garlanded held over his body by his five companions. When they find the likeliest street corner he sits down, they lower the little straw tent to the sidewalk and picking up their staves walk round and round him while he sings the song. Then they pass the hat among the passers by. . . . The group of boys that sang for me had made three thousand pesetas in three days in the previous fiesta.

In his notebooks there was also an account of the circumstances under which he came to hear that song:

> [We had been told that] it was absolutely essential for us to record the Mayos. I peered out at the rain, wondering exactly what the Mayos were, and along came the bright-eyed young men fresh from a session at the Juvenile Court and we set the machine inside an electrical shop while the roar of the rain outside subsided to a steady sound like a cement mixer. By this time I had become a complete master at taking over other people's establishments. All the work stopped while I plugged my connections into the one and only light socket, two girls gave up their chairs

to me and the recorder, and all equipment was turned off and activity ceased in that plant. The proprietor stood off in one corner looking rather frightened and when anyone stirred he put his fingers to his lips and said "B.B.C."

In the centre of the room five little school boys of about 11 marched in single file round and round their leader, who stood in the middle singing the Mayo. As they marched they rapped smartly on the floor in time to the tune with broomsticks. I don't remember ever hearing such a dreadful tune, and my young Fascist judge assured me that all the Mayos' poems are equally as bad.

Actually they are so bad they are good, and this has probably helped to keep alive this relic of pagan spring.

Just before Christmas 1952, Alan wrote Elizabeth from Pontevedra, in Galicia, and enclosed his monthly check to her, along with another small check for her to buy presents. He apologized for not having more money for gifts, and for not being able to come home for Christmas or to bring Anne and her to Spain, but things were looking up: residuals from some of the BBC programs were going to pay him $420, which would last them through December, and then he would get $1,500 from the BBC for the Spanish recordings, which would carry them through April or May ("if I'm careful"). He explained that he hadn't written her as often as before because the work had been so intense. He told her about Pip ("my assistant and companion"), whom he said he should have sent home because she was exhausted, but admitted that he didn't want her to leave "for fear of the lonely miles of cold mountains stretching out ahead of me."

Two days later he wrote Woody Guthrie—who he heard had become seriously ill, though Alan did not yet know it was Huntington's disease, the degenerative nerve condition—complaining that the weather, the constant surveillance by the police, and the enormous scope of what he had chosen to do were all weighing him down. "At the front of the town there is a little harbor. Outside is the Atlantic. From there it's a straight shoot to New York. But tomorrow I'm heading the other way. My heart kinda aches about that because in twenty days it'll be my second Christmas away from home and I've been homesick for a long time. But I'm bound and determined not to come back to the States until I've got something to show for my long stay."

Reaching London on April 17, 1953, Alan was able to declare himself reborn, with fresh clarity of insight, and offered himself to Elizabeth as a new man emerging:

I live in a tiny room, a pleasant place to work and unpleasant to sleep. I have only enough money now to keep my work going. I am waiting for BBC to pay me off for my records, and this may or may not come soon. . . . I live in a tiny room that swarms with plans, ambitious plans—for a ballet, for a play, for a book about

> Spain[,] for three television series, for my two books about America, for a book about England, for continuation of my series of records. . . . All the imaginative qualities that were repressed all my life are beginning to merge now for the first time. I can tackle literally anything I choose and understand its insides, not blindly, but somewhat thoughtfully.

Alan went to Rome in September to meet Giorgio Nataletti, the director of the archives at the Centro Nazionale Studi di Musica Popolare in the Accademia Nazionale di Santa Cecilia, the oldest music conservatory in Europe. Nataletti was already at work on a long-term collecting project for Radio Audizione Italiane, the Italian radio and television agency, and he gave Alan access to its archives, where he discovered that there were not enough recordings representative of all areas of Italy for him to be able to put together the Italian record for the Columbia series. Once again he would do all the necessary collecting himself; he "would discover Italy in the spirit of an Italian discovering America. . . . To a Texan, used to driving 500 miles a day, always with the same landscape, Italy seemed small." He approached RAI with the promise that his programs might inspire a folk song revival in Italy, and they agreed to partially support his work. When he returned to London he asked Geoffrey Bridson about the prospect of the BBC's supporting him if he spent eight months to a year in Italy collecting songs, in exchange for which he would produce programs modeled on the Spanish broadcasts he had just done for them, and save them money by recording the shows for both countries in the Italian studios.

Before the BBC would pay him for the Spanish recordings, however, they asked to have them approved by Eduardo Torner, a musicologist who had headed the Folklore Archive of Spain under the Loyalists and was writing some of the series of radio programs on Spain for the British radio network. "I was on the edge of nothing, living in a furnished room [in Chelsea]," Alan said. "Every morning at nine for two weeks, I went to Torner's cold, bare room. He was even poorer than I was, dour, sick, and courteous. He existed mainly by giving Spanish lessons. He listened to the forty-five hours of tape in silence, making marks on a pad of paper. After the last tape was played, the silence was overwhelming. Finally Torner said, 'Mr. Lomax, this is the finest piece of work ever done in the field of Spanish folk music. I will recommend that the BBC buy as much of it as they can afford.'" Alan was so excited by this acceptance of his work that he began making plans to coauthor a book with Torner titled *Folk Music of Spain*, which would be both an introduction to Spanish folk music and an anthology of songs. Torner would do the scholarly notes, and Alan would provide a narrative with "a documentary character." A sizable portion of the manuscript was sent to Oxford University Press in London, but the book was never completed.

Ewan MacColl joined with Alan to work on a series of Saturday morning radio programs called *Ballads and Blues* that were extensions of some club performances Ewan had been promoting. Six episodes were organized around themes of the sea, railroads, crime, work, soldiers, and city life, in each case attempting to reveal some of the roots of American jazz and blues in old English songs. The regular cast of the repertory company was Humphrey Lyttleton's jazz band, A. L. Lloyd, Seamus Ennis, Jean Ritchie, and Isla Cameron, plus visiting guests such as Big Bill Broonzy when he was in town. The programs were intended as entertainment, but Alan also saw them as an opportunity to slip in what was at the time a somewhat radical theory of the connection of folk song to popular culture that crossed the Atlantic.

He had returned to Britain just in time to take part in its early ventures into television, and was offered a six-part series for BBC-TV titled *Song Hunter: Alan Lomax*. The show's producer, David Attenborough, proposed putting both folk and professional singers on live TV, and Alan enthusiastically worked up a list of performers and sketched out a script, and in the process achieved something never before attempted on television. In spite of the troubles such as mixture of performance and musical styles might create, the only problem was getting Ewan on the show because he had been blacklisted by the BBC.

As Attenborough envisioned the shows' format, Alan was to be seated alone in the studio singing "Travelling Along" as it began, and then would introduce two or three guests from different parts of Britain. Without clearing his ideas for the first show with the BBC, however, Alan had already invited a group of women he had recorded in the Outer Hebrides to fly down to London to demonstrate their waulking songs (which Alan contended were as powerful as the blues). "In due course," Attenborough recalled, "the ladies turned up, bringing a huge quantity of tweed with them and sang their songs in Gaelic to, I fear, a somewhat baffled audience." The cost of their airfare alone used up the budget for the first three programs.

It was the first BBC television program to present the music of rural people. "It was also, so far as I know, the first time beer was drunk on television, and the spirit of 'lower class' life from many sections of Britain was given so thorough and free a play. I remember an 82-year-old man from Sussex who had lived on cider and cheese all his life holding up his cider glass, winking every time the camera was on him, and later singing an unbowdlerized version of 'Foggy, Foggy Dew.' " Following early TV practice, the singers were seated stiffly in a half circle, so there would not be much camera movement. Alan was so annoyed by this staging that a third of the way through the last show he "jumped to his feet and led the entire company in a mad procession around the studio, in and out between the two cameras and the sound booms and the lighting stands." The director and camera operators were forced to follow them, and thereafter other shows became more animated.

The Spanish recordings were finally broadcast on BBC Radio's Third Programme production of *The Folk Music of Spain*, a show formatted to closely follow Lomax's own collecting trip through Spain. Then came *Spanish Folk Music*, a six-part series written by Eduardo Torner and based on Alan's recordings. Getting the Spanish material on the air meant that he would be paid, but by then much of that money had already been advanced to him.

The Columbia *World Library* project was stalled, the money was running out, and he knew he would never be able to finish it without help. One day in the spring of 1954 a package arrived from India containing the tapes for India, volume 13 of the Columbia series. It had been assembled by Alain Danielou, a professor of music at the University of Benares, and came with photos, English translations, and transcriptions of scales, melodies, and rhythms. Though it made no attempt to include samples of the vast amounts of music from India Alan had asked for, and settled for the regions of Benares and Madras only, it featured recordings from Indian composers and some of the country's finest musicians. "Unlike several of the other collections I'd received in various states of incompletion and unevenness, there was nothing for me to do with the Indian material but lean back and listen. The music was absolutely beautiful. I cried for an hour. All the torment had been worthwhile, all the nightmare of work."

He then threw himself back into the project, and in December, Columbia was able to announce that the first fourteen volumes had been completed and were for sale: England, Ireland, Scotland, France, Canada, Spain, French Africa, Bantu music from British East Africa, Australia, New Guinea, Indonesia, Yugoslavia, Japan (including the Ryukyus, Formosa, and Korea), and India. (Northern and central Italy, southern Italy, Bulgaria, and Romania were released later.) The albums all received positive reviews, though one reviewer, unaware of the small budget that Lomax was given to produce the series, said that "it is a pity that—in view of the tremendous sums lavished on this project—a few more dollars could have been spent for better pictures, competent make-up and a little careful proof-reading."

Finally having some time to think about writing, Alan sketched out ideas for three books: a journal of his most recent trip to be called *A Summer in Spain* with the best of what he recorded there; *Bonny Bunch of Roses*, a book about the British Isles; and *My Heart Struck Sorrow*, his still unfinished book revisiting the Fisk/Library of Congress project. He wrote for advice to Lewis Jones, the one person in the project he thought understood what it should be about. It would examine the South in the period in which the blues developed in the Delta, one of the areas where the music reached its highest plane. It would begin with ex-slave reminiscences and move to the stories of the bluesmen—"the main theme is the same as in Jelly Roll—rejection, the individual absolutely alone against a hostile world, with his community unable to support and protect him, and disappearing under his feet."

'Oss, 'Oss, Wee 'Oss had just been completed, and Alan now hoped that BBC-TV would find it interesting enough to offer him a chance to create a series of such films. But the odds were slim, and he was becoming aware that he was not likely to make anything more on what he had done in Europe. His best chance for the future was to return to the United States where his European work might create new employment possibilities for him. He wrote his brother, John Jr., for the first time in a year and explained what he had been doing, and that all his savings were gone, but he also expressed the hope that someday they'd be proud of what he had accomplished. He ended by asking him to forward a $90 royalty check that had arrived for him in Texas.

The surveillance of Alan's life was expanding rapidly, but still without his knowledge. The FBI office in New York was again asking for information about him, and the old reports were being recycled, though now in increasingly garbled form, with his name still misspelled in the agents' files. When he asked to have his passport renewed in 1953 so that he could return to Spain and Italy as part of his work for the BBC, the American embassy asked him to sign a statement that he had never been a member of the Communist Party in the United States.

By July, the Metropolitan Police of London had determined that Alan "appeared" to be a Communist, because of the folk song shows he had written for the BBC, and because some of his associates, especially A. L. Lloyd, Ewan MacColl, the people in the Theatre Workshop, and his American friends, such as Joseph Losey and Donald Ogden Stewart (an American actor and screenwriter who had written the script for *The Philadelphia Story*) were already under surveillance. Singers and actors often gathered at Theodore Bikel's house in St. John's Wood, some of whom had been blacklisted in London for their politics, but to Alan it was less a political refuge than a place where he could meet younger folksingers and encourage them to drop what he called their veneer and sing in more authentic styles. He sometimes brought Margaret Barry along to show them how it was done.

The London police had also begun to monitor his radio programs and check on his guests. The conditions for his employment were changed, now requiring him to get permission not only from the Ministry of Labor but also from the U.S. secretary of state, and limiting his stay in the UK to the rest of the year.

Once the BBC agreed to help underwrite his programs, Alan went to Italy and remained there from April 1954 through February 1955. It was a country he would come to think of as "a 20th century museum, not only of art and architecture, but of musical antiquities as well—of important trends that have affected the folk music of Europe for the last 2,000 years." Musically it was "the least spoiled, most vigorous and most varied of all Western Europe."

Italy also offered an opportunity for him to see Anne and Elizabeth again, and in March the three of them met in Paris and stayed for a few weeks. Alan spent his mornings with Gilbert Rouget at the Musée de l'Homme listening to recordings from Asia and Africa. They paid special attention to the music of the Pygmies and the Bushmen of Africa, maybe the oldest peoples in the world, and heard many similarities in their respective musics. Since they had little or no historical contact with each other, Alan speculated that the explanation lay in the parallels between the two cultures' social structure and economic life.

For the Italian trip Alan had replaced the worn-out Citroën with a used VW bus that was also badly in need of repairs, and in mid-April the Lomaxes drove to Italy, heading down the Ligurian coast toward Rome. As they traveled, Alan advised his daughter to keep a diary, to make drawings and maps, and to write down her dreams as soon as she woke up. That was precisely what he was doing, as he intended this to be the best documented of all his collecting trips, as well as the most scientific.

When they reached Rome, he met again with Giorgio Nataletti, who helped him map out the peoples and areas that most needed documentation: the music and song traditions of peasants, shepherds, fishermen, and artisans in over a hundred localities from Sicily to the Alps. An itinerary was developed for him, and letters were written and phone calls made to local officials and important individuls that he should meet before he began recording in each town and district. Since Alan needed help in translation and understanding the different areas and traditions, he agreed to hire Diego Carpitella, a young ethnomusicologist who was an assistant at the Centro, who would accompany him for the first three months of the trip. Carpitella would also coedit the two Columbia LPs that would result from these recordings: southern Italy and the islands, and northern and central Italy and the Albanians of Calabria. This would not only be the first full survey of Italian folk music, but was also intended as a test of his theory that Italy had roughly the same song style orientation as Spain—"a Mediterranean tense-voiced South—a middle ground (near the administrative center) text-oriented song, and an open-voiced choralizing North. It seemed clear from talking to my friend [Alberto] Moravia—that the sexual mores of Italy varied along the same axis—from a South of purdah to a North where sex before marriage was mildly sanctioned if at all."

Alan settled Elizabeth and Anne in two rooms in Positano, a medieval fishing village on the Amalfi Coast in Campania that was then beginning to be discovered by artists and tourists. Here Elizabeth could write, Anne would go to school, and Alan would head off to collect songs. Over the next nine months they would see him only two or three times.

Diego and Alan started out in Sciacca, Sicily, on July 2, recording on the tuna barges off the coast, where very old, very salacious sea chanteys were sung at full force. They later moved on to a puppet theater for children in a park in Palermo, where the *Chanson de Roland* was being recited nearby at epic length. From there they moved north, tracking down harvesting songs, courting serenades, Calabrian *canzoni*, shepherds' songs, bagpipes and polyphonic women's choirs in Abruzzi, folk operatic texts in Umbria, Tuscan marble-cutting songs, Roman *stornelli* and panpipe orchestras from the Piemonte, and the canonic counterpoint of Genoese longshoremen and of tiny Ligurian mountain villages.

> In the mountains above San Remo I recorded French medieval ballads, sung as I believe ballads originally were, in counterpoint and in a rhythm which showed they were once choral dances. In a Genoese waterfront bar I heard the longshoremen troll their five-part tralaleros—in the most complex polyphonic choral folk style west of the Caucasus—one completely scorned by the respectable citizens of the rich Italian port. In Venice I found still in use the pile-driving chants that once accompanied the work of the battipali, who long ago had sunk millions of oak logs into the mud and thus laid the foundation of the most beautiful city in Europe. High in the Apennines I watched villagers perform a three-hour folk opera based on Carolingian legends and called maggi (May plays)—all this in a style that was fashionable in Florence before the rise of the opera there. These players sang in a kind of folk bel canto which led me to suppose that the roots of this kind of vocalizing as we know it in the opera house may well have had their origin somewhere in old Tuscany. Along the Neapolitan coast I discovered communities whose music was North African in feeling—a folk tradition dating back to the Moorish domination of Naples in the ninth century. Then a few miles away in the hills, I heard a troupe of small town artisans, close kin to Shakespeare's Snug and Bottom, wobble through a hilarious musical lark straight out of the commedia del' arte.

Diego and Alan quickly established a mutually comfortable work pattern: they traveled late at night, with Alan driving, reaching their destinations early in the morning, usually sleeping in the van. They depended primarily on their intuition, not paying attention to the authorities to whom the letters and calls had gone out, spending an hour or two in one location, three days in another, talking to people sitting on walls, working in the fields, sweeping the steps, or drinking and gambling, sometimes stopping to speak to people walking along the roads. The authorities, in fact, were shocked by some of the subjects they recorded, and often interrupted to object. But between the two of them, as different as they were, they invariably seemed to find good sources. Diego was short and quiet, with a wry wit, and he thought of Lomax as the professional, the one who knew how to get people to perform and record. Being a foreigner might even be an advantage. But Alan needed Diego to ask "suspicious Sicilian and Calabrian peasants certain rather intimate things I wanted to know about their sex lives, their childhood emotions and their vocal cords," and when he refused they quarreled "violently":

> He told me that he didn't personally care whether Italian peasants made music through their throats, out their ears or blew it out their backsides—he just liked the music. So I have had to give up all but the superficial bagging songs, checking off province by province.

Yet despite their disagreements, their travels together made them lifelong friends, and Alan inluded Diego among the small circle of Ewan MacColl, Peter Kennedy, Nick Ray, and Johnny Faulk as those he could count on.

On their way to Puglie, Diego and Alan stopped back in Positano. Alan had been writing and sending money to Elizabeth regularly, but this was the first time he had seen her and Anne in several months. The work had been intense and exhausting, and complicating things further, Susan Mills, an English girlfriend of Alan's, had come to Italy to visit him. In the letters that went back and forth between him and Elizabeth it became clear they would never remarry: disagreements, Alan's constant work and travel, and the fact that neither of them had prospects for enough money to live on finally put to rest their dreams of a new start together. He stayed in Positano for only a few days, some of which were spent recording the songs of the porters and mule drivers from Monte Pertusi and the fishermen's music down on the beach. He told Anne he would be back in September, but when the fall came he was in Friuli. Elizabeth had meanwhile met Herbert Sturz, a young writer who was freelancing for New York newspapers, and began seeing him. Anne felt abandoned. Alan did return at Christmastime but left again before Christmas Day to record the bagpipers in Abruzzo. Elizabeth was furious with him, and when he returned he took Anne with him to Capri for the New Year's ceremonies. A few days into the new year he again departed, alone, this time for Naples and southern Italy.

> Neither the gaiety of Neapolitan song nor the tarantella can conceal for long the sorrowful voice of Southern Italy, which has been the prey of Rome and Naples for a score of centuries. You will understand this if you allow this razor-edged voice to cut at your heart—a woman, her throat clenched, with the sorrows of a lifetime of oppression and possessive, jealous love, her face a mask of sorrow, rocks back and forth in a straight legged chair and sings a lullaby to her child. . . . Out of the shining olive-groves that overlook the blue Gulf of Salerno comes an answering sound—the drone of the oriental jaw's harp and the voices of two of the men singing what seems to us a lament but is, in fact, a love song—but a love song in the manner of this Saracen colony, lost here in the hills near Naples for 1000 years. . . . Once I had penetrated below its smiling Neapolitan masque, I found in Campania the most varied music of any part of Italy. The culture changes literally from village to village—Saracen to Greek, Greek to Lucanian, Lucanian to Slav. Listen to these folk harvesting chestnuts on the hills near Avellino. Were their ancestors Croats, Bulgars? . . . At the next stopping place in Campania I found a complete contrast. Whereas these Italian-Slavs had rolled up a roar of deep voices, the girls almost singing in baritone, the young women of Lettino made a filigree of pinched silvery tones, singing roundinellas about love. . . . But the true voice of the mysterious hills of Campania is the bagpipe, and its companion, the Moorish oboe, or cirimia. . . . I saw enormous pipes with chanters nine feet long emitting a great baa like a veritable Ram of Derby, and, beyond these, small-size pipes, on down to parlor sets with small, sweet voices. In the Christmas season bands of these pipers invade every town in southern Italy, playing the tunes from house to house, questing for wine and bread and a few lire for their hungry families back in the hills. . . . One cold Christmas afternoon I set up my microphone on the muddy streets of an old Norman fortress town, a band of shepherds in sheepskin trousers and sandals and with two bagpipes, one single and one double oboe come barrel-organing down the street. . . . The shepherd oboe player signals the lady of the house to open her doors, wishes her a happy new year, and then asks permission to play. . . . Meanwhile the shepherds pursue their quest for Christmas money over the next hill.

Postwar Italy faced many problems, some of which Alan had experienced directly. An American entering rural Italy, where poverty and despair persisted after the nation's devastating defeat and occupation, was met with suspicion. When he first came into the country all his clothes were stolen, his camera disappeared, and most of his clothes were taken yet a second time. All of his notebooks were stolen out of the van. He feared being robbed of the money he had to keep on hand to pay singers and musicians, and kept records of each payment for the

BBC. In the town of Caggiano, in Campania, husbands were sometimes so jealous that Alan had to obtain orders from the provincial government for permission to record women, whom the local mayors had to assemble in their offices for recording. On one occasion, a husband burst into the session and dragged his wife out. Sometimes a town official, knowing Alan would be recording there, would announce it to the whole town, and four or five hundred people would turn up, beating on the doors to have their turn. Once when he was recording under a bridge to avoid crowds, local mafiosi threatened to kill him.

Folklore in Italy made him newly aware of the power of tradition to create the character of a people. American folklorists were accustomed to thinking of history in terms of two or three hundred years and describing changes in terms of decades. To encounter cultures that required a two-thousand-year perspective was both exhilarating and overwhelming:

> The regions or localities which did not conform to the south to north pattern . . . were precisely those in which some group of invaders or immigrants, usually coming from the east, had settled down and held to their musical culture. Perhaps the major ethnological find of my trip was to discover that Italian folk song has been subjected to steady influences from across the Adriatic for hundreds of years, for I encountered pockets of Slavic or Greek polyphony from the Carnian Alps all the way down the boot into the northern hills of Calabria.

After traveling for eight months Alan was surviving on a bank loan, dinners from friends, and the occasional royalty check. He was out of tape and film, and the loss of nearly all of his notebooks was a blow from which he never recovered, as he would now be unable to write the detailed book comparing Spain and Italy that he had hoped would be a step toward developing a science of folklore. He took solace in the sheer fact of having driven twenty-five thousand miles and filled sixty miles of tape—enough material to develop the BBC and RAI broadcasts, two LPs for Columbia, and *Music and Song of Italy* for Tradition Records. What gave him the heart to go forward, however, was that the vague ideas he had been pondering for years were beginning to take shape, and the evidence to support them was falling into place. In a letter home just before Christmas, 1954, he laid out the project that would occupy him for the rest of his life:

> Music for most people, not professional musicians, is more than melody, rhythm, and words—it's what kind of voice the singer uses, the way he holds his body, and it's when and how and where the song is sung. All this is learned and transmitted from generation to generation.

The primary function of music is to remind the listener that he belongs to one certain part of the human race, comes from a certain region, belongs to a certain generation. The music of your place stands for everything that has ever happened to you when you were a kid, reminds you of what your family was like, what it was like when you fell in love—in fact is a quick and immediate symbol for all the deepest emotions the people of your part of the world share. (This explains why the saddest songs, like the blues, make the members of that musical family laugh with pleasure. Hearing that sad music gives the members of that group a complete sense of being home again, in the family again.)

So far as I can tell there are between [eight] and a dozen main musical families in the world—styles or ways of making music, I mean. Each of these styles is characterized by a way of placing the voice, a way of moving the body, a relation of the song to the dance, an attitude toward music, a kind of melody, etc.—Each of these families is very widely distributed across the earth. Each is very, very old. In fact, it seems that musical style changes less than any other aspect of human culture—such as religion, language, etc.

Since, as I have pointed out, the primary function of music is to set up a certain atmosphere which corresponds to certain deep patterns of feeling, this means that there are between eight and a dozen main emotional families in the world, each of these families [are] very old, each having had much to do with the coloring and shaping of all culture and all experience.

Naturally the musical style is only the outward manifestation of the deep river of feeling that produces it. This is shown by [the] fact that musical style tends not to alter because of musical reasons, but because of important changes in the lives of people who make the music. So far as I can determine from the music that I have worked with myself, the determining factors seem to be:

—the sexual pattern in the society, especially the position of women, and this is interesting since women tend to be the rememberers of songs, the main song audience, even though the singers are men
—how children are raised
—other sources of security, that vary from culture to culture

Lately I have been thinking about a method of research that would be practical, would make it possible to quickly test these ideas against the available facts. I believe I have found out a pretty good method of study which anyone interested could use. And I'm ready to put it all down on paper as soon as I get settled down.

This means that all this gathering of folksongs, besides putting a lot of good tunes back into circulation, will serve in increasing man's knowledge of himself. It would work like this—if you found musical style A in a community, you would know that a certain family of perhaps deeply hidden emotions was at play in the emotional and aesthetic life of the entire society . . . or in reconstructing the past, you would feel sure that if you discovered style B in the folklore of the community, that aesthetic B had been perhaps operative in the life of the ancient people of that area—in other words, folk music can become a historical touchstone like the radioactive substances studied by geologists. But also folksong can become an index as to what is aesthetically wrong or right about a certain branch of the human family, or even with an individual. . . . This idea has another interesting side to it, too, that it relates music to bodily tensions:

—bodily tensions to inner emotional tensions
—inner emotional tensions to social tensions

therefore it can serve in constructing a proper history of art. Art has always seemed to have a history of its own, dependent but related to the history of the society that produced it. I think my theory explains why. Therefore out of this could grow a proper way of relating art to society, or deciding what kind of art you wanted to have in what kind of world.

In January 1955, Elizabeth, Herbert Sturz, Anne, and Alan all moved to Rome, where Lomax planned to wind up his research in Italy. Alan felt at home among the intellectuals of Rome, people like Alberto Moravia and the American painter Beverley Pepper, freer to speak to them about his ideas than he had been in the United States. His gregariousness and conversation charmed them, and he was welcomed as a different kind of American. But when his Roman friends finally understood what he'd been talking about by listening to what he'd been recording, they were horrified: "That music isn't Italian, it's the barbarous sound of Africa or some such place. Play us the blues!" The political left of Italy, like the right, believed that the masses should be lifted out of their ignorance, enabling them to leave their dialects and folklore far behind. Those attitudes would change later, when Giorgio Nataletti and Alan played folk music and discussed its history on the radio. Soon that same music would appear on film soundtracks, such as Vittorio De Seta's documentaries *Lu tempu di li pisci spata* in 1954 and *Sulfatara* in 1955, and Pier Paolo Pasolini's 1971 *Il Decameron* (though the Pasolini film did not credit Lomax).

Racing against radio schedules, Alan wrote and recorded programs for RAI and BBC, and got the recordings of *The Folk Music of Italy* off to England in time for their first broadcast in March. He gave a set of the field recordings to RAI and copied his records for the library of the Accademia Nazionale di Santa Cecilia, his collection more than doubling its holdings. Anne accompanied Elizabeth and Herbert to Spain, where the two of them were to write *Reapers of the Storm,* an account of life under Franco, fictionalized to protect their sources. In August Anne returned to Italy, and she, Alan, and Susan Mills took a boat from Naples and together spent a month on the island of Ponza. He then sent Anne back to Spain to her mother and returned to England.

Ewan MacColl threw a party in his flat to celebrate Alan's return, and invited London's inner circle of folksingers. The newest face was Shirley Collins, a young singer from Hastings on the south coast of Britain. Collins was born into a family that Alan described as working-class intellectuals: her grandparents were folksingers, her mother had run for local office as a Labor Party candidate, and other relatives were painters and writers who celebrated the life of the southern English in their art. She had grown up listening to Alan's programs on the BBC, learned hundreds of songs from Cecil Sharp's books, and had come to London in 1953 for the opportunity to sing and use the song collections at the English Folk Dance and Song Society. By adapting her five-string banjo playing to pieces that were traditionally unaccompanied, she brought a new spirit to the songs she'd grown up with. But it was her pure, "young girl singing alone in the house or the garden, dreaming of love" quality that attracted Alan's attention—that, and his fantasy of her aging into the maturity of an Aunt Molly Jackson.

To Collins, Alan was a broadcasting star, and an authentic singer in his own right, a Texan with size and speech to match, which made him hard to resist when he asked her to move in with him at his new place in Highgate and be his assistant. It was an awkward situation for her, unmarried and twenty years younger than he, but she went to work on the Columbia world folk music series and the manuscript of a new book, *The Folk Songs of North America*, despite a constant flow of visitors passing through.

On Shirley's twenty-first birthday he arranged a party for her and then failed to show up for it. When he appeared the next day, he told her that he had spent the night with Robin Roberts, who was back visiting in London. Shirley returned home to Hastings, but later forgave him when he asked her to join him on a trip to Paris to work on the world music records and then go on to Mallorca for a vacation, where they would visit Robert Graves and his family.

Alan's struggles to stay afloat in London continued, forcing him to live on tea and cake, as he would say. Without regular work at the BBC, he spent most of his time as a freelance writer, dreaming up ideas and pitching them to media people. He was approached to write a television play for children by the man who owned the drama rights to *Superman*, and with the help of Yola Miller Sigerson, a writer who had worked with Yip Harburg and Joris Ivens, he created a folk play with songs by Woody Guthrie and others. The play was never bought, but at Christmastime 1955, Joan Littlewood staged an expanded version of it, called *The Big*

Rock Candy Mountain, for Theatre Royal at Stratford East. It was what he called a "new American folk musical," though the British audience must have thought of it more as a Christmas pantomime. The play only ran for a week, but the critic at the *Times* of *London* favorably compared the two lead characters with the two tramps of Samuel Beckett's *Waiting for Godot*.

The children's script's success led him to write a musically illustrated book for children, *Harriet and Her Harmonium*, published in London in 1955, which Alan said he wrote for Anne. In it a twelve-year-old girl travels alone across America with her harmonium to meet her fiddle-playing father in San Francisco. On the way she encounters cowboys, sailors on the Mississippi, and Irish travelers, and has various adventures, all while learning American folk songs (with words and music included in the book). Alan also served as an adviser for the folk music used in *the Adventures of Robin Hood* TV series on ITV in Britain (1955–59), produced by Hannah Weinstein, an expatriate leftist journalist who hired blacklisted American writers such as Ring Lardner Jr. whenever she could.

CHAPTER 13

Skiffle: From Folk to Pop

Beyond the music hall ditties, Cockney songs, crooners, and other prewar fare, there was little that was musically unique to the postwar British experience of the early 1950s. Plays and movies were subject to censorship on social and political issues, and BBC Radio regularly barred certain pop and jazz recordings for any number of reasons: the mention of commercial products or God in song lyrics, arrangements of classical melodies for dancing, rhythms that were too "infectious" and threatened workers' daytime routines, songs that implied sexual behavior or drug use. Music from outside the country was seldom heard, as the Musicians Union limited foreign musicians from performing in Britain unless arrangements had been made to send an equal number of British musicians in exchange.

Yet one form of jazz and pop had slipped in and taken hold in certain circles: trad jazz—traditional jazz, in the form of New Orleans or Dixieland music, which had been imported from the United States before the war, following the revival of New Orleans music that occurred about the time Lomax recorded Jelly Roll Morton. By the 1950s this music, which was by then a quaint relic in the United States, was suddenly taken up by labor unions, intellectuals, and student groups in the UK as the art of amateurs and improvisers, and as music for those with disdain for the establishment's arts. So it was that when the Tory government announced in 1956 that it would allow the United States to build a nuclear base at Holy Loch—the same year the UK began to battle with Egypt over the Suez Canal—no one was surprised when trad was the music heard from street bands in Ban the Bomb marches and war resistance parades.

These British bands, like the New Orleans groups of the 1920s that they emulated, had wide repertoires, including hymns, marches, blues, and old pop songs. Though most groups played without vocalists, the Chris Barber Band featured a few songs sung by their guitarist-banjoist, Lonnie Donegan (who had taken his first name from the African American blues guitarist and singer Lonnie Johnson). In 1953 Donegan began to sing Lead Belly songs for his feature spot with the group, sticking close to the original recording, and even repeating Lead Belly's spoken introductions. One of those songs, a sped-up version of "Rock Island Line," was recorded in London on July 13, 1954 (just a week after Elvis Presley recorded a faster version of blues singer Arthur "Big Boy" Crudup's "That's Alright, Mama" in the Sun Record Studios in Memphis), and suggested a parallel to the working-class youth music that was developing in the United States under the name of rockabilly. Donegan sang with just a guitar, bass, and washboard in a scratchy, shuffling, energetic style that was both primitive and new to English ears; "Rock Island Line" became a number one seller in England, and was also the first British recording to reach the American top ten list.

Black American blues singers and folksingers such as Sonny Terry, Brownie McGhee, Big Bill Broonzy, and Muddy Waters had been to the UK in the early 1950s, bringing a vocal style new to most, and making the guitar a centerpiece of their performances. This was a music that British youth would call skiffle, borrowing the name from recordings of early African American performers such as Dan Burley and His Skiffle Boys (a band that included Brownie McGhee), or Jimmy O'Bryant and His Chicago Skifflers. Whatever "skiffle" meant in the United States, in Britain it meant a guitarist or banjo player, usually one who sang, accompanied by a variety of other instruments—bass or clarinet and homemade instruments such as the washboard or a one-string broomstick-handle-and-washtub bass. Suddenly, guitars, not at all a common instrument in the UK, were everywhere. For some, skiffle meant singing Lead Belly songs or blues; for others it was the songs of Woody Guthrie, though some soon became interested in finding songs from their own heritage: Margaret Barry, who was singing at a pub in Camden Town, was a skifflers' source for Irish travelers' songs. Skiffle clubs sprang up, declaring themselves anticommercial, and the music was danced to by Teddy Boys, the Edwardian-dressed gangs, some of whom were also drawn to bluegrass or calypso or jazz.

Alan saw skiffle in broader terms than just the new fad of a new generation. For him, the Scots-Irish-English song tradition, as he called it, took on a particular shape in the United States, where "the melting pot of the American frontier" brought its various threads together and, with the help of African Americans, developed accompaniment for the songs with guitars and banjos and brought new rhythmic sensibilities to these songs and others from the black traditions. Now skiffle was bringing back home local songs of the British Isles, encouraging amateurs to play and sing, something that "Cecil Sharp, Ralph Vaughan Williams, and the British schools were unable to do." (Alan's only fear was that the instrumentalists would "learn too much" and be influenced by "a lot of sophisticated chord progressions from the jazz boys.")

He and Ewan MacColl found skiffle hard to resist, and they formed their own group, the Rounders, with Shirley Collins and others, and performed on Granada TV for fourteen one-hour programs. They then reformed as the Manchester Ramblers, a group they hoped would become the Weavers of Britain. Under the name of Alan Lomax and the Ramblers, in 1956 they made an extended-play single record backed by washboard, bass, guitar, banjo, and jazz clarinet. Their repertoire included black work songs like "O Lula" and "Railroad Man"; MacColl's own compositions such as the Dartmoor prison–inspired "Hard Case," and "Dirty Old Town," a theme he had written for a BBC documentary on Manchester; Scots tunes such as "Rothesay-O" and "Carlton Weaver"; and American songs like "The Water Is Wide." All were collected in a songbook called *The Skiffle Album, Featuring Skiffle and Folk Songs Popularized by Alan Lomax and the Ramblers.*

Skiffle had led Alan into the world of pop music as a performer, but it also drew him into the morass of copyright. Copyright law had not been well understood in the 1930s and 1940s. Few, if any, law schools offered courses on it, and lawyers often depended on the Library of Congress for help on specific cases. The copyright law of 1908 was already out of date, because those who wrote it did not anticipate that the crudely made recordings that began appearing around the turn of the century would ever need protection, given their minimal value. Once the laws *were* extended to cover recordings a flurry of new questions arose: Could an album of songs have the same kind of copyright protection as a book of songs? Did music have to be published to be protected? Folk songs presented their own special problems. If folk songs were passed from person to person by oral tradition, the individuals who created them were likely to have been forgotten, and even if they could be identified, it would be difficult to prove a song was definitively theirs. In the 1940s even the performance of a folk song was not always granted copyright protection. Colonel Clement Bouvé, then the head of the copyright office, declared that "a folksinger could not claim to be an interpretive performer in the same sense that [pop music] performers had made such claims," and the library was thus not obligated to obtain releases from folksingers when records made in the field were issued for sale by the library.

When Alan heard the colonel's interpretation of the law, he responded by insisting that the library did need releases from singers, and that the singers should be paid if the recordings were sold. Since the library did not have a policy of compensating performers early on, when the Lomaxes did manage to pay them the funds had to come out of their expenses or from their own money. But even the act of paying could sometimes be a problem:

> In certain cultures, you have to pay, not because you're a foreigner but because they're professionals. This is true of gypsies of Andalucía and in much of Negro

culture. In a country like Scotland, however, unless the informants are terribly poor, an offer of money would be an insult since the informants sing as a courtesy to a stranger. If their singing is later used on a BBC broadcast, the collector can then send them a contract and pay them, because the music can now become a matter of formal exchange. In American Indian cultures, the singer generally owns his song. If he feels it has magical value, you can't collect it, but he may sell it. The normal practice is to pay small sums of money. When I was in Washington I managed to get the Library of Congress to set up a standard rate for folk informants which was to equal whatever they were earning per hour in their regular work. Now, after my experiences with how tangled the copyright situation can become, I make contracts with the singers whenever I can so that they know if there are royalties from future recordings, they'll receive a share.

Alan was not an expert on copyright, nor was he at that time particularly interested in the need to claim ownership. Neither he nor his father had ever copyrighted individual songs, only their published compilations, a step insisted upon by their publishers for protection against the books being pirated. Even the battle over the rights to the Lead Belly songs was a question of book ownership brought about by the conflict between John and Huddie and the publisher's demands that there be clarity in the matter for their own protection. (Later it would turn out that the claims of copyright in the book were not properly stated by the publisher and none of the parties involved was protected.)

When the Weavers recorded "Goodnight Irene" and it became a worldwide hit, Alan was as surprised as everyone else by the mass popularity of a folk song. He may indeed have hoped that these songs he loved would one day be known by everyone, but "Irene" appearing on jukeboxes in every diner, danced to by dreamy teenagers, and becoming for a few months the soundtrack to an entire country was inconceivable to folklorists and record company executives alike. When Alan received his share of the royalties from the Weavers' hit, he declared it as "unearned income" on his tax return and said that since it came from folklore he would reinvest it in a folklore project. The $3,000 he received paid for the bulk of his first two years in Europe and made the Columbia *World Library of Folk and Primitive Music* possible. Nevertheless, he thought the huge success of "Irene" was a pop culture anomaly not likely to repeat itself.

One day while walking through Piccadilly, Alan passed a music store window where he saw a copy of the sheet music to "Bring a Little Water, Sylvie," composed, it said, by Lonnie Donegan. This was a song he and his father had recorded with Lead Belly. It was the shock of this discovery followed by his learning of Donegan's claim to having written "Rock Island Line" (and the fact that it reached No. 8 on both the UK and American hit charts) that sent Alan off on a quest to find Kelly

Pace, who had taught Lead Belly the song in Arkansas State Penitentiary in 1934, by contacting the superintendent of the prison, the sheriff of Pine Bluff, and the postmasters of several post offices. When he finally located Pace, he sent a letter asking him if he was the composer of "Bring a Little Water, Sylvie," so he could see that Pace was properly remunerated. It was no surprise when Pace affirmed that he, not Donegan, was the author of the song.

"When I looked into the story back of this piece of outright knavery," Alan recalled, "I found myself involved in a tangle of lies, legal chicanery, and outright dishonesty." Lonnie Donegan, he discovered, was copying Lead Belly's songs, along with his performance style and introductory remarks, profiting from both his performances of these songs and his claim to being their composer. The publishing company that had acquired the copyright to "Goodnight Irene" in the United States was also copyrighting Lead Belly's songs and others from the Lomaxes' book under the name of a British affiliate. Alan's first impulse was to sue them, but when he sought legal counsel he was advised that it was far more complicated, difficult, and expensive than he thought to protect the rights to these songs, and probably impossible. A dismayed Alan was persuaded that it would be better to work with this same music publishing company rather than against it.

Alan once sketched out an article in which he stated his view of the issue of copyrighting folk songs, apparently responding to a number of articles and letters that were being exchanged on the subject in *Sing Out!* in 1959–60. He began by reminding readers that folk song collecting took place within a "free enterprise system," and so was more complex than most of those concerned with folk music had understood. The process by which a folk song could reach the public included: (1) the folksinger, "more of a creative figure than most city singers like to remember"; (2) the collector, who located the folksinger, recorded the song, sometimes rearranged or edited it, and found a record company to issue it, or a music publisher to publish it, or a book publisher to print the words and music; (3) the "fine arts or pop arranger," who might find ways to make the songs more palatable to a performer or to a publisher or record company; (4) the performer, who might rerecord the song and possibly change it in doing so; and (5) the publisher and record company. All could make a claim on copyright, depending on how the song was distributed to the public. Alan's view was that the folklorist who recorded a song in the field was obliged to ensure that the singer was paid for his work, but should also have a share of the royalties in consideration for his or her role as a collector if the record was ever sold commercially. Alan's reasoning was that composers of folk songs were not likely ever to be recorded nor ever to earn any money from their songs without the help and guidance of someone devoted to the music and its preservation.

By the late 1950s there was little or no financial support available for folk song collecting and no official encouragement to collect full-time: the Library of Congress had stopped collecting folk songs after Alan left in 1942; the Mexican government had closed down the folklore section of its Department of Fine Arts; the National Museum of France was now limiting folk collecting to one trip a year; and the BBC had ceased supporting folk music, and had even erased many of its existing tapes because it felt they lacked broadcast interest. Much the same was true for Scotland and Italy. Part of the reason for this shift in interest was that the sudden rush of pop hits based on folk songs led governments and foundations to conclude that folk song collecting had "turned into a trashy branch of the pop song business."

But the problem still remained of how to keep people with no connection to the songs from owning them. One solution Alan had proposed was to convince music publishing companies, pop singers, foundations, the composers' protective societies, and folklore organizations to join together to create a foundation to collect monies from folk song copyrights to pay the folk composers (or what Alan more realistically called the "source singers") and to use a portion of the money for research and collecting. But since this did not happen, he returned to the idea that the collector should be paid for his or her work.

Collectors copyrighting folk songs was not that unusual at the time: Carl Sandburg, Zora Neale Hurston, Béla Bartók, Percy Grainger, Ralph Vaughan Williams, Cecil Sharp, even Lawrence Gellert, the most politically leftist of all the collectors, all filed claims for copyright, though none of them shared their earnings with singers. Lomax, however, was the most active and the most publicized collector in the world, and would be criticized by some for what they viewed as his claim that he had written folk songs and, by doing so, denied ownership to the songs' true creators. Those who examined the BMI list of songwriters did indeed see Alan's name on hundreds of songs. There are many kinds of copyright, however—for the writer, the arranger, for the recording or the remaster, for the publishing company, and for the performer, among others—but the BMI list is abbreviated and simplified to read "writer." Alan did not himself file for copyright, but signed Popular Songwriter Contracts that allowed publishers to copyright those songs. On those agreements for folk songs Alan's name, along with the singer's, would come under the title "Writer," but with added language that said, "Collected, adapted, and arranged by." If the song was original with the singer, it might say that it was "by" the singer and "Adapted and Revised by Alan Lomax." Lomax's actual copyrights read, "Traditional song, arranger." Only one or two songs, such as "Old Man" and "My Baby's Gone to Texas," actually read, "Words and Music by Alan Lomax," and they were songs written and recorded by him. Still, even some of those who knew the truth of the situation would not be satisfied. Charles Seeger, for example, argued that the Lomaxes had the right to claim authorship of their books of folk songs or the songs that they had arranged and adapted, but that it was a fraud to label the latter folk songs. On the other hand, Seeger also said that "the folk song is, by definition and, as far as we can tell, by reality, entirely a product of plagiarism," thus reminding us that no one had yet come up with a way to determine who was the creator of a folk song.

After he left the Library of Congress in 1942, Alan made it a rule to pay all of the people that he recorded, and to offer them signed contracts that promised payment of royalties if the recordings were ever commercially issued. He kept account of these finances over the years, though it was difficult to stay current with the recordings, as record companies were sold or went out of business. Doing it himself made it possible to avoid the rough and often sloppy business practices of the record companies, but the downside was constant recordkeeping, checkwriting, unsteady finances, and keeping track of people who were often on the move or had died and had kin who survived them.

By the late 1950s the skiffle craze was over, but not before it could affect the future of British and even world pop music. Amateur guitar-based bands were now everywhere in Great Britain and Ireland, and youth music was permanently in place. John Lennon's skiffle band the Quarrymen was beginning its evolution into what would become the Beatles; Mick Jagger, a member of the Chris Barber–Ken Colyer Skiffle Band, would soon meet Keith Richards, connect with him over a Muddy Waters LP, and end up naming their new band after one of the songs on it. (David Bowie's first band was called the Mannish Boys, after another early Waters song). Graham Nash and Alan Clarke, the core of the Hollies, had both started as a skiffle band called the Two Teens; guitarist Jimmy Page worked in a skiffle band long before he would become part of the Yardbirds and Led Zeppelin; and Van Morrison started his musical career in the Sputniks, a skiffle group that he would revisit in a 1998 session with Lonnie Donegan and Chris Barber. Even Spinal Tap had its beginnings as the Lovely Lads, another washboard and broomstick-and-washtub group.

Alan lived the life of collector, performer, and broadcaster at full tilt, whether or not he was making money. No one around him could match his pace, his conversation, the songs he knew, the hours he kept, his brashness. Paul Oliver, the British blues scholar, recalled Alan as "the only person who could step into Oxford Street and cross the road at the height of the rush hour without looking at the traffic and relying only on his height, his beard and a white raincoat with a tartan lining to get him across safely." His BBC friend Bridson said that Alan's driving on English roads was dreadful: he was often on the wrong side of the road, turned into roundabouts in the wrong direction, and once even bumped into the back of a bobby who was holding back traffic at a light.

Alan summed up his own life at this point in a letter he wrote to Johnny Faulk:

> I lost weight, grew a beard, grew up somewhat, and in the midst of so many real new troubles forgot some of my imaginary ones. . . . This period of being abroad and completely dependent on my own efforts and my own name has been awfully good for me. I've at last almost emerged completely from my father's shadow, which I now realize always hung over me in America. . . . You must all remember that during the last five years I have been really pioneering, doing advanced research without help of any fellowship or the support of any institution, making my way as a freelance, living mostly in cheap hotels and furnished rooms and working like a dog. There's been no time or energy left over, but someday I think you'll all be pleased with how things have turned out.

He requested an extended stay from the Aliens Department of the Home Office on January 13, 1956, in order to remain in the country for twelve more months to do freelance work. Once it was approved, Elizabeth and Herbert Sturz moved into Alan's flat so that the two of them could work together on their book, and Anne could be with both her parents. Because Elizabeth and Herbert had returned from Spain without money, Alan was supporting all five of them. Anne, especially, found the situation difficult. She had been brought to London to live with her father for the first time since she was a baby, and was now effectively a serving girl, caring for adults who were all busy working on their books. Their flat was in a lower-middle-class neighborhood, and when Anne played with other children she was obliged to fabricate to explain their unusual household arrangement to their respectable neighbors: Shirley was Alan's secretary, and Herbert was her mother's brother.

At one point Peggy Seeger also moved in with them, working as one of the editors on his books, and later described his work habits and life in the house:

> His enthusiasm and initiative had spread to record companies, publishing houses, folksong societies, individuals. He talked incessantly. Everything interested him. At the time he was living in a tiny basement flat in Chelsea, the artists' section of London. When I first went into his flat I thought I was in a warehouse. The hall was loaded with tapes from his trips to Spain, Italy, Ireland, Scotland and God knows where else. Tape-ends dribbled from boxes everywhere. Records, books, and coffee cups lay on the floor like underbrush in a forest through which only Alan could find his way.
>
> This is where he worked. Groups crowded in for rehearsals and parties; books and radio programs were begun here; and most inconceivable of all, daily living was carried out amidst the rubble. . . . Later I lived at his home, a half-house, in Highgate. It was more spacious than the Chelsea establishment, but the only

> difference between the two dwellings was that the chaos spread itself further in the larger house. While I was acting as music editor of one of his books [*The Folk Songs of North America*], other people were also involved in the project, each disrupting his neighbor's system of classification, carrying piles of manuscript and typing from room to room, eating meals in whatever was available, all with much laughter, singing and good humor.

When Alan's article on the concept of song style and song families—"Nuova ipotesi sul canto folkloristico italiano"—was accepted by *Nuovi Argomenti*, a journal founded by Alberto Moravia and Alberto Carocci, he was pleased to be published by such distinguished intellectuals, not to mention appearing in the same issue with Moravia and Pier Paolo Pasolini. His article, "A New Hypothesis," was actually packed with many hypotheses. Beginning with a critical analysis of the established musicological approaches, he questioned the value of music notation for understanding the world's musics. Too much was left out with this approach, and the system that notation presented led to false confidence. Instead, he proposed the idea of music style, including in the discussion elements that had seldom been considered by musicologists: the body's role in making and responding to music, its link to the emotions, how such things are learned in making music, the role of music in the life and survival of the individual, the group, and the community. A preliminary mapping of broad families of the world's music making was proposed: Euroasiatic, ancient Euroasiatic, colonial American, Pygmoid, African, Australian, Melanesian, Polynesian, and Amerindian. His classification of these song styles was radically different from those that preceded him: they were not grouped by nationality or race, and even geography was seen to be only loosely connected. (The singing of the Pygmies and the Bushmen of Africa, for example, were grouped together by their use of closely woven hocketing and yodeling, even though there was no apparent history of their having been in contact, and those in the world closest to them in style were not all Africans.) His work on Spain, Italy, and the United States was offered as evidence of how these stylistic features could be studied comparatively, in different musical groupings. In his conclusion he suggested some of the possibilities offered by these concepts:

> First of all, by using the musical style as a diagnostic instrument we can study the emotional and aesthetic story of the nations of the world. Secondly, by using the musical style as an instrument of synthesis we can reconstruct the emotional character of past and ancient societies. Thirdly, we can start to understand the deep emotional factors in the evolutionary processes of cultures. Fourthly, by using the analysis of the musical style as an instrument of prediction, we can start to formulate some hypothesis and to test them in the picture of the current

transformations of the societies around us. Maybe by this way we could reach a technique of cultural planning. Finally, considering that the musical style seems an exterior and symbolic image of extremely deep and ancient formative, emotional and aesthetic currents, it may give us a key to the study of the creative forces which operate in the human society for a time as long as the social, technical and economic forces which we have started to understand in the last two centuries.

Having articulated the foundations of a theory that treated song as a cultural universal, perhaps even a cultural imperative, and that conceived of singing as essentially a social phenomenon, he bravely applied for a grant to the University of London for a study of "The Psychological Patterns of Folk Songs":

> The purpose of this study is to establish the psychological and physiological bases of song. Since song is one of the universal traits of human society, since song is the product of unconscious feeling and subconscious muscular behavior, and since ways of singing are among the most conservative of culture traits, it is hoped that this study will lead toward a science of aesthetics.
>
> The development of modern recording machines and their use by researchers in many parts of the planet have indicated the existence of a number of *styles* of song in the world; these song style families are very old, very slow to change and are continental in their extension. Under the term song style one includes not only melody, rhythm, harmony, etc—the formal musical characteristics—but the tone of voice, the motor behavior, the social organization, the audience response and the inherent emotions that produce the musical whole.

Drawing on the spirit of nineteenth- and early-twentieth-century German musicologists, Alan foresaw a means of moving the study of folklore out of the doldrums of nostalgia and kitsch (and worse, pop culture) by drawing on scientific technology and theories that had never been used the way he intended to employ them.

Lomax wanted to put together a research team that would include an experimental psychologist to study the psychological and physiological bases of song; a cultural anthropologist to identify the cultural patterns associated with the traits of the songs; a psychoanalyst to study the song texts and the anthropologist's data and "seek the main fantasy patterns of culture through interviews"; a musicologist to map the traits of each song style family; a folklorist to choose the people and songs to be studied; along with technicians, cinematographers, and office personnel. It was an ambitious plan that moved far beyond what was known as folklore and took art into the laboratory: devices and instruments would be used to measure different types of vocalizing, patterns of muscular tension in the body during singing, patterns of breathing in songs, variations in electrical current on the skin and in the brain, heart rate. To gather the data they would need music-writing machines, and film and audio recording equipment. The study would take five years, and would all be done at the School of Phonetics at the University of London. And when they were done, they would have "the first mapping of the musical styles of mankind. A scientific method for folk music will be established. New roads will be opened for the history of music. Considerable advances toward a science of aesthetics will certainly have been made."

One can only imagine what the linguists and psychologists at the university thought of this proposal coming from a radio personality. It was an idea that found few advocates, and the reason for the lack of enthusiasm was a familiar one: the methodology was too scientific for the folklorists and the musicologists, and the subject was too humanistic for the scientists. Plus, Alan lacked the proper academic credentials for what he was attempting. Margaret Mead addressed his problem bluntly when she said, "Folklore has always seemed to me a strangely dead field. Alan may animate it with this theory, which makes sense to me. I know Alan tried for a long time to get a foundation grant for further research on the theory, but after all, we mainly give grants to M.A.s and Ph.D.s. We hardly ever give grants to people; we usually give them to degrees."

When the first fourteen of the Columbia recordings of world music were issued, Charles Seeger reviewed them somewhat coolly, hedging faint praise with cautionary remarks: Alan had little experience outside of the United States; the notes were better than those from other collections, but too brief; too many selections were edited for length; the sequencing of selections was too crowded on the record; the record jackets were too flimsy; the editing of the notes was sloppy. Alan was hurt, and wrote Seeger defending his work and accusing him of disloyalty. He feared that Seeger's criticism would mean the end of the series if Columbia ever saw his review, and couldn't believe that Seeger could not appreciate the new ideas and discoveries within it. Although he remained proud that the "richest and most powerful record company in the world" had backed him, he now had to doubt Seeger's friendship. This was more than a scholarly dispute, as Alan had always regarded Seeger as a second father, the father he never had and had always wished for—literate, scholarly, northeastern, radical.

J. Edgar Hoover's office once again requested the New York FBI to prepare an extensive report on Alan, the information to be submitted in better form so that it could be sent out to all the Bureau's offices. This time Hoover was looking for additional assistance from the Boston, Indianapolis, Kansas City, New Haven, San Antonio, and St. Louis offices. He also asked for help from the Central Intelligence Agency.

By June 5, 1956, the sixty-eight-page report was completed—a long, repetitive narrative, still dotted with errors (Alan's name was spelled wrong throughout, and the correct spelling was treated as an alias), incomplete information, hearsay (the Bureau's own word for it), and erroneous and contradictory statements. It reached to connect Alan to the Communists, even going so far as to note that Columbia Record Company president Goddard Lieberson had once published a poem in the *New Masses*. Apparently frustrated with the results, Hoover turned to Louis F. Budenz, a former party member who had become a star anti-Communist by naming many of the individuals singled out by the House Un-American Activities Committee. Yet even he was unable to provide evidence that Alan was a member, though he did recall having "heard" that he was a Communist.

Seven months and a hundred pages of documentation later, the assistant attorney general of the United States declared that given the quality of the evidence against Lomax, it "fail[ed] to disclose sufficient available evidence to warrant prosecution." One office of the FBI after another closed its files on Alan James Lomax, and he remained unaware of the Bureau's interest in him.

Alan, meanwhile, busied himself with new projects. He was back in touch with Zora Neale Hurston, who was now the librarian at Patrick Air Force Base in Florida, where guided missiles were tested, and was writing *A Life of Herod the Great*. Alan asked her permission to publish "O Lula," a railroad workers' song for which they had rewritten the words together. She approved, and suggested that they could work on a few other songs together and perhaps go collecting together again.

He sent Tradition Records the tapes of his 1947 prison recordings, which were issued as *Negro Prison Songs* and in England as *Murderers' Home* in 1958 on Nixa. *Texas Folk Songs* was also issued on Tradition; a version of *Blues in the Mississippi Night* appeared the same year on Nixa. His own singing appeared in 1958 on an HMV recoding, *Alan Lomax Sings Great American Ballads*, accompanied by banjoist Guy Carawan, a young singer who was passing through London on his way to the World Youth Festival in Moscow and then on to China, and Nick Wheatstraw, the pseudonym of guitarist Alexis Korner, one of the founders of British blues and rock. It was Alan's first commercial solo recording, and it included sailing songs, a spiritual, and ballads, almost half of them African American. Also in 1958, *American Song Train* was recorded for Nixa, a collection of railroad songs that included the singing of Peggy Seeger and Guy Carawan, with jazz bassist Sammy Stokes and mouth harpist John Cole.

Alan also approached director Roberto Rossellini about producing a film on Italian or American folk song. He sent him five script ideas, all regionally based, taking advantage of local landscapes and customs. In one script, four different tales of love are spun out from Calabria, Tuscany, Piedmont, and Sardinia, contrasting different styles of courtship and love songs. Rossellini seemed doubtful that these feature films could be made cheaply and with the small crews that Alan had proposed, and turned him down.

With the Metropolitan Police and the Ministry of Labor still listening in on his broadcasts, Alan's freedom to suggest subjects for BBC broadcasts was given closer scrutiny. Although his friends at the BBC cleared the way for him to do a new six-part series for Third Programme, the producer assigned to the series, Ian Grimble, objected to Lomax's theories about song, at first pointing out exceptions to his song family characterization, then insisting that his script compare his findings with those of other ethnomusicologists, and finally asking to see the first script before they went any further. Grimble concluded that Lomax's work was not up to "the standard that this subject requires," and if the programs went forward his scripts would have to be edited to eliminate his use of "potted Marxism" and his "association of 'sexual permissiveness' with happiness and the Christian attitude toward sex with sorrow and suffering." Lomax's programs would also have to be limited to those areas that he knew best—Italy, Spain, and parts of America.

Grimble was ultimately successful in killing the original idea, and Alan was told to write a much narrower series to be titled *Reminiscences of a Folk Song Collector*. When the programs were broadcast in January and February 1957 they were retitled as *Memories of a Folk Collector*, and were another series of audio travelogues with accounts of people and songs he met along the way. Still, Alan knew how to slip in surprises. A newspaper announcement of the first broadcast was headlined to suggest a small scandal in the works: "Rock 'n' Roll on Third Programme." "Listeners," it said, "will be regaled by one of the first rock-'n'-rollers to hit this country; 'Rock Around the Clock.'" It would be offered as an example of "a white hill-billy combination doing its very best to imitate the barrel-house blues popular among Negroes about 20 years ago and reproducing an urbanized folk style." The series went well, and was rebroadcast the following year.

One of the last major radio projects that Alan undertook for the BBC was eight programs for the Home Service called *A Ballad Hunter Looks at Britain*, which was broadcast from October to December 1958. "It took me four months," Alan told journalist Nat Hentoff, "and after summarizing everything that had been done in the field, I tried to set up an image of the main folksong regions of Britain." It was a sweeping survey of recordings from Britain, many of them originally done for BBC's Folk Music and Dialect project, a collecting venture that had lost its funding, and there were some at BBC who hoped that this series might revitalize it. Alan used the best recordings he could find, while also attempting a style survey of Britain similar to those he had done for Spain and Italy.

The very last radio production by Alan appeared at Christmas 1957. Midlands BBC producer Charles Parker, a folk song fan himself, proposed that they prepare a live Christmas morning program on the Home Service that would follow the queen's Christmas address and reach all across the kingdom, presenting folk music from every part of the country. Its theme of Christmas cheer and nostalgia staged on a national platform was hard to resist, and it also presented a daring challenge to eight producers to hook up seven regions of the country, bring in folk musicians—some of whom were not accustomed to performing on tight schedules—and then broadcast the whole program live. But come December 25, all of Britain tuned in to "Sing Christmas and the Turn of the Year" and heard a Texas voice from Birmingham cry out over the air to his colleagues in Wales, Plymouth, Castleton, Scotland, Belfast, and London, each answering back with season's greetings in his own language and dialect.

What followed were choirs, pub orchestras, carol singers, a brass band, children's groups, a Bible reading, poetry recitals, pipers, a flute band, mummers' plays, sword dances, and—when he called on London to perform—a skiffle band, a highlife group from West Africa, Dixieland, and calypso. Even though a few reliables like MacColl and Peter Kennedy appeared, none of it was the standard commercial Christmas fare, and even favorite carols were given older treatments. Alan held it all together from the center, not at all shy about his own singing of American songs, and sharing his memories of Christmas Day in Texas. There were a few gaps in timing, and some things had to be changed in the script as they were broadcasting; when Peggy Seeger failed to appear, having been jailed by immigration authorities in Dover as she returned from the Soviet Union, they replaced her with one of her recordings.

Alan seemed at times to be everywhere in the UK. A cartoon appeared in the July 24, 1957, issue of the British humor magazine *Punch* that captured how a sizable part of the public viewed him. In it a raggedy farmer sitting on the steps of his country shack sings, "I've got those Alan-Lomax-ain't-been-round-to-record-me blues." Yet despite his appearances on the BBC and Granada Television and his book royalties, his income after expenses that year was only £836 ($24,000 U.S. in today's money), which he viewed as a sign that it was time for him to return home. For eight years he had devoted himself to European culture. "In a sense I became more intensely American every year I stayed in Europe, but I was beginning to lose my sense of reality as an American writer. I needed more contact with the sources of my work and myself." His friend John Faulk, who had been blacklisted, left without work in New York, and was now in the midst of what would be a successful lawsuit against CBS, wrote to Alan that the country had changed and McCarthyism was on the run. It was time to come back.

As he began thinking about returning, he decided not to ask Shirley to join him. He would return alone with Anne, as he had been promising to do for years. Just before he informed Shirley he was leaving, he and Peter Kennedy set up a two-day session for her, recording the thirty-seven songs that would make up the first two albums recorded under her name, *Sweet England* and *False True Lovers,* for Argo Records, a subsidiary of Decca. In spite of Shirley's being only twenty-four at the time, Alan took the occasion of writing the notes for the American issue of the second record on Folkways to reflect on the role of maturity in the making of a folk-singer, using Peggy Seeger, Ramblin' Jack Elliott, Muddy Waters, and Jean Ritchie as examples. The first two had started by learning from others' recordings, and later developed a deeper feeling for the style, while Ritchie and Waters were born into their styles of singing, losing none of it in the city but developing ever further. Muddy Waters's voice, Alan said, "had coarsened, he has 'improved' his accent and this has erased some of his early subtlety; he has also learned to work with a band so that his phrasing and his vocalizing are more cut and dried than formerly; yet on the whole he has gained as a singer. He is in complete command of the blues today, and can do whatever he chooses to do in coloring the melodic line to match the flow of the text."

The idea of returning to the United States was almost as frightening to him as had been his departure from it eight years earlier. He had been thinking of entering graduate school again with the support of a Rockefeller Grant, but his anxiety over going back to school was overtaking him:

> I have to pick my way from task to task during this daylight, like an Eskimo leaping from cake to cake in an ice flow [*sic*]. Everything is what I ought to do, not what I want to do. God, when will it be—want to do, have to do, driven to do. Must I always be a schoolboy to my own school master?
>
> I don't really want to apply for more money from Rockefeller. The thought of a long, complex piece of research, the thought of working hard repels me. I am split between the image of myself as a writer and as a researcher. Afraid to discover I am not the first, not willing to settle for the second. The academics are for me terrible poeky [*sic*] and sissy. The campus, the buildings, the gyms, the students with books remind me of my childhood at UT and I swear I became as shy as a girl. All my fears of missing class, of not being prepared, all the whole damn complex is aroused to bite me again.

Even before he left Britain, *Newsweek* had announced his imminent return, stressing that Alan had sought the authentic everywhere and recorded it, in an act of the purest preservation. With Anne, who would now be living with him, he departed by boat on June 29, landing on July 2, 1958. While traveling he had already begun planning a talk on song and sexual repression for the annual meeting of the American Anthropological Association at the invitation of Margaret Mead. A reporter from *Time* was there to greet him on his arrival in New York, and tossed him directly into current controversies by quoting him declaring his newfound enthusiasm for rock and roll, the "furthest intrusion of Negro folksong into U.S. pop music."

CHAPTER 14

The American Campaign Resumed

Despite what his friends had written him about how much America had changed while he had been gone, many things seemed the same to Alan when he returned home in 1958. Some people were still looking for a way into full citizenship, and others were trying to lock them out. The business of the thirties lay unfinished, as he saw it, with new players on the stage in old roles: now an even younger generation was trying to define the nation, and it was still speaking of finding roots, and of justice and freedom.

Some things *were* new: television had found the heart of American popular culture, distracting people from their usual routines and keeping them home. The movies fought back with every weapon of spectacle they could find—wide screens, 3-D, Jell-O-colored pictures, anything bigger than that small screen at home. There was a counterreaction as well, a return to the principles of what film could do that no other medium had managed, "small movies" conceived in realism, even filmed in black and white, and Alan's old friends Elia Kazan, Nick Ray, and Joseph Losey had been building new audiences for their gritty, Method-based visions of America.

In radioland, DJs of every stripe ruled what people listened to, finding ways to elevate singers like Elvis Presley and Chuck Berry, who only a decade before would have been unavailable to those of a different color and class. Even some of the singers that Alan had recorded in the field had dressed up and gone to the city: Sam Cooke and Ivory Joe Hunter, once called "folk," were now rock and roll. High fidelity and stereo had ceased being the toys of the rich and become the symbols of a certain lifestyle, and like the earliest phonographs, they were now part of the furniture of the modern household.

The long dream of some for peaceful racial integration was beginning to lurch toward reality, with Martin Luther King Jr. leading the way. The Beats had made themselves a generational phenomenon, still talking nostalgically about "The People," but now with a hydrogen cloud overhead. Jackson Pollock, whom Alan had known only as a boozy folknik, had spilled and dripped himself into becoming the best-known painter in America. Jazz had splintered into several new directions, some absorbing the lessons of experimental music learned on the GI Bill at conservatories, some retreating from the heat of bebop, others attempting to push bop to higher planes of excitement and speed. What some were calling a second folk revival was under way, this time with black folk music, especially the blues, at its center, along with English-derived or Anglo-American songs. But to hear the music you no longer had to go to the country looking for untutored singers sitting on a cabin porch: the songs were right there in the city, in Washington Square in Greenwich Village, and the pop charts were heavy with folk songs like the Kingston Trio's "Tom Dooley," a ballad from North Carolina; Lloyd Price's "Stagger Lee," the blues ballad that Alan had sought all across the South years before; Wilbert Harrison's one-man-band blues "Kansas City"; and Johnny Horton's "The Battle of New Orleans," an old fiddle tune with words added.

Alan had missed a lot, and found himself having to catch up. The FBI and Congress were still tracking those they perceived as the enemy within—Pete Seeger would be indicted for contempt of Congress within the next two years, and folksinging would be banned in Greenwich Village parks. Coming back when he did would prove to be not particularly easy.

Pete Seeger publicly welcomed Alan's return to the States in the pages of *Sing Out!*, reminding people of his importance and of what he had been achieving in his years abroad. But Pete also offered a stern warning about how things had changed both musically and politically while he was gone: "The folksong revival did grow, and flourishes now like any happy weed, quite out of control of any person or party, right or left, purist or hybridist, romanticist or scientist. Alan Lomax probably looks about him a little aghast." And sure enough, when Alan responded with "The 'Folkniks' and the Songs They Sing," he acknowledged that while "city-billy" singers who were appearing on records and stages had quickly mastered the words, tunes, and accompaniment of rural folksingers, it remained to be seen whether they would be able to learn the authentic singing styles of the various groups from whom they borrowed. Style, he explained, was not only the emotional expression of the song to its singers and community but also the means by which singers learned to create variations on older songs. Many folkniks did not grasp the point of the article, taking "emotion" to be false performance or a showbiz device, and Alan irritated many of them. John Cohen, for example, of the New Lost City Ramblers, a group that based its music on hillbilly recordings of the 1920s and 1930s, answered that Lomax ought to listen more closely, for there were many kinds of responses to songs, and many meanings:

> Lomax has suddenly encountered a folk singing development far different from the social reform movement which he left. . . . The "city-billies" have created

> audiences; some have traveled and engaged in first-hand research; others have studied field recordings and poured [*sic*] through the riches of the Library of Congress and the Public Library. The general level of understanding is higher than it was when Lomax left. . . . The emphasis is no longer on social reform or world-wide reform. The effort is focused more on a search for real and human values. We are not looking for someone to lead us. We are looking within ourselves. In his article, Lomax has presented himself as the "holy ghost" sent from on high to deliver the gospel. He says, in effect, that he will lead us to the "truth" if only we will follow him.

"I began to feel as if I was the grandfather of folk music," Alan said, "and the grandfather had to die. When I first returned, many city-billies asked me to lecture and perform for them, and I consistently turned them down. My refusals were mostly out of shyness and the feeling that they would be judging me. And it still seemed to me that something was being soiled and made into a careerist machine."

Alan had returned from his European travels with a tale to tell. He had heard the world's music, discovered the connection between song and the survival of the world's peoples—between song and the soul, he would say. And what he encountered when he returned to America was folk songs stripped of their social roots and the pain they inscribed and instead turned into fodder for pop artists. When a publisher of a small folk magazine asked him for suggestions for improving it, Alan said "stop publication." He angered black singers Odetta and Leon Bibb by telling them they needed to go deeper into black style to be able to sing the songs he had collected in the South. He told Robin Roberts, who had an actress's ability to project strong emotion, that if she was going to sing white ballads she ought to stand absolutely still when she performed.

To some who followed folk music, Alan seemed a purist who had not listened carefully to the changes that had occurred in music in the eight years that he had been gone. But in fact he had been paying close attention to them, and what fascinated him were precisely these changes. What he had thought of as ethnic and racial styles ten years earlier were now rapidly beginning to influence each other, with singers crossing lines once held in place by custom and even by law. He listened to the radio as if he were collecting in the field, treating the hits as something to treasure and analyze, writing out the words to those he thought were most important: the Cadillacs' "Peek-a-Boo," the Coasters' "Charlie Brown," the Everly Brothers' "Problems" and "Bird Dog," Ricky Nelson's "Gotta Travel On," Ray Charles's "Talkin' About You," Fats Domino's "I Want You to Know" and "The Big Beat." Alan's interests went far beyond their texts, however, for he wanted to know what the words and music triggered in the imaginations of those who heard them on record and radio. When he heard the Drifters' "There Goes My Baby," with its saucy, slow-rolling rhythms that turn into a double-time Latin strut, he said he could see the singer's girl walking away from him, feel the sass and sway of her hips as she left him standing in that street or country road.

In an interview for the *New York Post*, he came out punching for the new pop music:

> "I'm sticking up for Rock 'n' Roll," says Alan Lomax, "because even though some of it is destructive and crude, it is essentially a creative American impulse. It's made by young people for young people. It's a rebellion against the puritan ethic which had decreed from the beginning of our society that Americans are not allowed to have pleasure. . . . . Many of our folk songs . . . are fantasy symbols. 'Barbara Allen,' for instance, is the story of a girl who rejects a suitor. He turns his face to the wall and dies. As simple as that—in hundreds of different lyrics. But what is it really if not the sexual rejection at the moment of climax, the pioneer women punishing their men in the only way they knew how? This was the central drama of a pioneer community which was dominated by that Protestant puritan ethic: 'Thou shalt not have pleasure.'
>
> "I remember . . . when I was recording in rural England. London, of course, maintains a reserve, but rural England is a kind of pagan world, music rolling off the tongue, drink in hand, girl on the knee, hayrollers all—and I said to myself: these were my people, the stock I was descended from. Lord! What happened to us, who took the joy out of the songs, why did our pioneers go sighing through their lives in those songs with the death wish?"

In its blunt way Lomax's reading of these songs was a transvaluation of the pleas and rants of parents and preachers against them. For him, rock and roll was both a sexual and a racial revolution, with white youth finding new meaning in the words of rhythm and blues songs aimed at mature black audiences. He saw rock and roll as part of a tradition of "outlaw music," the music that whites had learned from blacks throughout the history of American music—minstrel shows, vaudeville, blues, even early jazz. His defense caused a stir when two years later he appeared on *Coming of Age*, an FM radio series, with a lecture titled "The Rocking Rebels."

Folk music in New York City, meanwhile, had developed its own conservatism. Alan had returned "to find that New York had gone to sleep around the Peter Seeger banjo picking folknik image, and I was shocked to find that the kids here thought that folk music pretty much began and ended in Washington Square." Folk music was now something one heard at summer camps, in after-school programs, at student clubs at the High School of Arts and Music or the YMHA. "So I decided to show them what America was really like, what urban folk music really was and I put together a concert consisting entirely of urban material." The first program that he sketched out was a blockbuster, the kind of grand staging that John Hammond had accomplished with "Spirituals to Swing," but with a different evolution of music on display, one that led from the farms and small southern towns to urbanized country bands, churches, and pop singers. Balladeers and singing prison crews from the South would represent the origins, while more recent developments and transformations would be illustrated by Bill Monroe's bluegrass group, Muddy Waters's Chicago blues band, a northern gospel choir, Ray Charles, Merle Travis, the Everly Brothers, Fats Domino, Bobby Darin, and Ricky Nelson; and from the urban folk revival, Pete and Mike Seeger, Odetta, Jean Ritchie, and the Kingston Trio. Alan managed to find enough financial backing from promoter Lewis Gordon that for the first time he could do some traveling in search of new artists, hire a press agent, offer recording contracts to some of the musicians, and promise them all a share of the profits depending on the ticket sales—but not enough to hire all the performers he needed for the sweeping tableau he envisioned. He did manage to set off on a few brief field trips, where he found Jimmie Driftwood, an ex–school principal from Arkansas who two years earlier had written and recorded "The Battle of New Orleans," the song that Johnny Horton had since turned into a hit; Alan thought Driftwood had the potential to be another Woody Guthrie. Just across the river in Brooklyn he heard the Selah Jubilee Singers, a gospel quartet, and the Drexel Singers. Mike Seeger led him to Earl Taylor and the Stoney Mountain Boys, a bluegrass band from Baltimore. A group of black girls from Detroit whom no one seemed to have heard of represented rock music. The blues performers were Isaac Washington, Memphis Slim, and Muddy Waters from Chicago, plus a harmonica player from New Jersey.

"Folksong 59" was presented at Carnegie Hall on April 3, 1959. Though some in the audience complained that they failed to see the connection between the different genres, it was an exceptionally well-planned event, with a rationale developed for every act and a script to explain its presence. Alan came on stage with a whoop, "a wild war whoop of the early morning of American History":

> It expresses the way I feel tonight at seeing all you people here in Carnegie Hall tonight . . . and it tells me the way I felt when I returned from Europe a few months ago and discovered what was happening to American music. . . . A stampeding herd of youngsters—hillbillies, citybillies, rockabillies—had broken through the gates and set America singing, dancing, rocking to its own rhythms. The juke boxes were pouring out the wild expressive singing that I once had to hunt for in the Mississippi Delta. I saw geetar and banjo pickers on every subway train. Ballad singers packed the concert halls. . . . I saw rock and roll audiences clapping

> time on the off-beat and watched the kids dancing more expressively than ever in my memory. When I closed my eyes I often couldn't tell a Negro from a white singer. Tin Pan Alley with its stifling snobby European standards was spinning on its pinnacle, the giant amusement industry that had always condescended to our folk songs was hastily signing up every guitar player in sight.

His narrative continued to thread its way through the introductions to each of the performers and their various styles: the devil in the music, song as a means of fathoming the loneliness and fragmented society of an uprooted people, gospel as putting the sinners' music to the service of the Lord, a music that has no regrets and doesn't apologize. Alan worried that his presentation might be too didactic, and near the end of the evening he announced that "the history lesson is over," adding that he'd "stay clear of the track and let this thing run wild on its own." If some in the audience heard it as a rant, it was at least an antipuritan rant, and a declaration of freedom for music in America.

Not as many recordings resulted from that evening as Alan had hoped, but *Alan Lomax Presents Folk Song Festival at Carnegie Hall* (United Artists, UAL 3050, 1959) was a reasonable slice of its blues and bluegrass, and *Earl Taylor and the Stoney Mountain Boys* was a brilliant bluegrass album, confirming all that Alan had said about the music being country jazz, even if Taylor's group never caught the public's attention. One might imagine that Alan would have found bluegrass music too citified, too diluted by jazz, but all those jangling and sliding strings, the odd combination of ballads and minstrel-show songs, those soaring tenor voices grabbed him and fired his poetic imagination. He might on one occasion compare it to the excitement generated by the Eastern European village bands of Romania or Yugoslavia. On another, he'd link bluegrass back to its postwar southern roots: "Folk music in overdrive," a "mountain dixieland combo," he called it, still in the fever of discovery, for an article in *Esquire*:

> The mandolin plays bursts reminiscent of jazz trumpet choruses; a heavily bowed fiddle supplies trombone-like hoedown solos; while a framed guitar and slapped bass make up the rhythm section. Everything goes at top volume, with harmonized choruses behind a lead singer who hollers in the high, lonesome style beloved in the American backwoods. The result is folk music in overdrive with a silvery, rippling pinging sound; the State Department should note that for virtuosity, fire, and speed our best Bluegrass bands can match any Slavic folk orchestra.

Dixieland jazz was his analogy, it should be noted—not the au courant cool jazz of Miles Davis, or the modestly academic music of Dave Brubeck. He had returned home to the Village to find that jazz clubs like Jimmy Ryan's that featured the older jazz were languishing in the face of a new music that he saw as decadent, lost in "the harmonic jungles of Schoenberg and Stravinsky." Jazz had become "high-hat and aging." Yet in bluegrass he heard a new music, fresh, inspired, but nonetheless generated out of its own traditions:

> A century of isolation in the lonesome hollows of the Appalachian gave them time to combine strains from Scottish and English folksongs and to produce a vigorous pioneer music of their own. The hot Negro square-dance fiddle went early up the creek-bed roads into the hills; then in the mid-nineteenth century came the five-string banjo; early in the twentieth century the guitar was absorbed into the developing tradition. By the time folksong collectors headed into the mountains looking for ancient ballads, they found a husky, hard-to-kill musical culture as well. Finally, railroads and highways snaked into the backwoods, and mountain folk moved out into urban, industrialized, shook-up America.

This closing allusion to an Elvis Presley song seems ambivalent, or at best undecided, as if Alan were waiting to see what else might be coming out of the South, for he had already seen a new level of cultural creolization rising, one that demanded documentation. "Many rock 'n' roll recording artists came from church quartets, adapting Negro spiritual elements to a fairly sophisticated musical form. A second influence in rock 'n' roll is the lowdown alley type of jazz, and a third is hillbilly. In other words, it is a music composite of many facets of American popular music."

He was now alert to such intercultural transformations wherever they might occur in southern music. Ed Perl, the founder of the Ash Grove on Melrose in West Los Angeles, the center of the folk revival in L.A., recalls Alan's coming in the club while Bill Monroe and the Bluegrass Boys were appearing. He walked straight up to the stage, and after the second number he asked Monroe where he got the song he'd just played. "I was shocked," Perl said. "Nobody ever did that, let alone to God. Bill responded, 'Is that you, Alan?' and they proceeded to talk about and demonstrate the influence of black music on Bill and bluegrass."

Alan had come back home broke, with no job in sight, and once again had to count on his own creative resources and the projects he was still finishing up as he left Britain. *Salt of the Earth*, the book of southern autobiographies, was coming out at last, though in much reduced form, though now titled *The Rainbow Sign*. From the interviews he and Elizabeth had recorded with Vera Hall and Dock Reed, from Livingston, Alabama, came two virtual novellas, one a love story, the other an account of the making of a holy man, both powerfully told in Deep South rhetoric but without the artificial dialect that had spoiled so many renderings of black thought and experience written by whites. As a sort of appendix, he added a sermon from a revival in northern Mississippi.

In his introduction to the book, Alan was scathing in his account of the systematic debasements of racism, but he also celebrated the strength and discipline that black Americans had found in themselves and in their religions to survive. Then, in a burst of emotion, he wrote, "I have grown almost to detest 'Western civilization.' We are so rigid, so complacent, and so careless of human values that we cannot accept another group on its own terms. We must somehow force them to become like our guilt-ridden, tense, and rather miserable selves." He went on to say that what he called "the relaxed sexual and social mores" of the black working class, their social polyphony, their collective improvisatory abilities had helped them survive, all of which he feared they would lose as they became middle-class Americans with their "solo-voiced 'cool' jazz." It was Lomax's folkloric revision of Freud's *Civilization and Its Discontents*, and it stood to offend many readers—southern whites for his condemnation of them, and blacks for his language, which might have been read as white stereotypical perceptions of life in the underclasses. Yet southern newspapers like the *Chattanooga Times* and the *Richmond Times-Dispatch*, and black magazines like the *Crisis*, the magazine of the NAACP, celebrated the book for its honesty in depicting the lives and travails of people of color. It was selected by the Book of the Month Club, and Alan was invited by TV anchor Dave Garroway to read from it on NBC's *Today* program on May 18.

The eleven LPs of Spanish music he had worked on in England were issued by Westminster Records in late 1959, in the midst of a flamenco craze in the United States, with singers and dancers turning up in nightclubs, dance concerts, and on TV variety programs like *The Ed Sullivan Show*. But Lomax's was the most complete survey of Spanish music that anyone had heard, and it went far beyond the *cante flamenco* that attracted so many. He divided the albums into the music of *Cities of Andalusia*; *Cities of Majorca and Ibiza*; *Jerez and Seville*; *Popular Dances of Majorca and the Jota of Aragon*; *Gypsies of Grenada and Seville*; *The Spanish Basques*; *Eastern Spain and Valencia*; *Galicia*; *Asturias and Santander*; *Castile*; and *Leon and Extremadura*. Though there were too many records in the collection to reach a broad audience, some of the selections from this set and the earlier Spanish album in the *World Library of Folk and Primitive Music* series became influential far beyond folk music circles.

Just as these recordings appeared Alan was asked by RCA Victor to help with the planning of an album of pioneer songs to be called *How the West Was Won*. In April 1959, *Life* magazine had run a series of articles on the history of the West, to which Bing Crosby bought the rights to use to frame a set of records on which he, Rosemary Clooney, and a choir would sing. The project grew larger when Alan suggested that they add Jimmie Driftwood, Texas folksinger Sam Hinton, and some writings by Carl Sandburg to be spoken by Crosby. Lomax prepared a song list and bibliography that would have surprised many Americans had it been used—topics such as drifters after the Civil War, women desperadoes, Indian warfare, and the Mormons. What was used was unusual only in the mix of singers: rough voices and church choirs, Bing crooning cowboy songs and speaking introductory lines that seem to have been written by Alan, all of it capped by a "Farmer's Daughter" photo of Rosemary Clooney pouting against a single bale of hay in a photographer's studio. The concept became further diluted when Crosby convinced MGM to produce a motion picture that would cover the same subject, with leading actors and singers like Debbie Reynolds brought in to sing the songs.

At the same time Alan was also beginning work on several albums for Caedmon Records, a company specializing in poetry and fiction read by their authors. Shirley Collins and he, by overseas mail, assembled two collections of Child ballads from recordings that he and Peter Kennedy had made in England, Ireland, Scotland, and Wales, and with the words of the ballads and notes about them provided, these were the most scholarly collection of these classics on record. There followed *Songs of Seduction*, an unbowdlerized collection of love songs and ballads, the kind of naughty recording that was popular in some circles then, but also one of the first to reveal the degree to which songs of such an open sexual nature existed in Britain. The series continued until they completed ten albums of British songs.

When Alan learned that Elizabeth had married Herbert Sturz, the door closed on that part of his life, and he began to think about another field trip, this time back to the South. He now regretted having left Shirley behind in England. In the spring he asked her to join him for the trip and a series of singing performances for the two of them, and he sent her a boat ticket.

He was living in a fifth-floor walk-up in the Village at 121 West Third Street over a pizza shop, three rooms in which he and Anne were surrounded by his usual hoard of books, tapes, recordings, and sound equipment. Shirley arrived in April, and by late June they set off for Chicago in a used Buick he bought for $250. Eighteen hours later they arrived at Studs Terkel's apartment, had breakfast, appeared on his radio show, and left on a train for California, where Alan was directing the Berkeley Folk Music Festival that year and appearing with Pete Seeger, Jesse Fuller, Sam Hinton, and Jimmie Driftwood. As he introduced the singers, Alan repeated his plea for citybillies to learn the original style of folksingers, but folkniks by then had become a tough and case-hardened crowd and were having none of it.

They flew back to Chicago, picked up the car, and drove to Kalamazoo, where they performed and taught classes at the Circle Pines Center, the center of the Finnish Cooperative Movement and home to various political groups, where Anne was enrolled in summer camp. Five days after their stay at the camp ended, Alan was due in Newport, Rhode Island.

The sudden popularity of folk music caught the entertainment industry by surprise. What had been to most people a light amusement had moved into coffeehouses, then nightclubs and concert halls, and onto popular records. Even if it was not always clear to most what exactly a folk song was, it was recognized, like skiffle in England, as being music of simple melodies and harmonies, homespun imagery, and unamplified string instruments. It was a genre that everyone thought they knew something about. That spring a folk festival was launched at Newport, Rhode Island, by George Wein, a Boston nightclub owner, who a few years earlier had created the Newport Jazz Festival, the most successful outdoor musical event of its time. Wein's idea had been to move jazz out of the confines of the nightclubs that specialized in only one or two styles of jazz, to make all forms of the music available in a single venue, and to build a bigger audience in the process. He had already featured a few folksingers in his clubs, and was just then in the process of staging a folk afternoon at the jazz festival, when, together with promoter Albert Grossman, he decided to expand it to a full-sized festival modeled on the jazz event.

One big difference between the two festivals was that audiences for folk were not as well acquainted with the range of regional and ethnic folk musics as fans of jazz were with its different styles. It was not even clear if a large group would know how to behave at a folk concert. On July 11 a very diverse audience gathered before a mix of New York- and Boston-based revivalist and nightclub folkniks and a scattering of country performers in the very genteel town of Newport. The last group of the evening was the Kingston Trio, a polished act that had developed an ironic distance from the folk material they so carefully arranged, but whose youthful energy and sophisticated patter made them hard to resist. To guarantee that younger audiences would be there to hear them, Wein at the last minute decided to move the trio forward in the evening's schedule. When they came on, they were the success that was expected—so much so, in fact, that when they finished the audience demanded that they keep singing, which they did for so long that the next group, banjoist Earl Scruggs and his bluegrass band, were delayed.

From that moment on, it was clear that a clash between the logic of show business and the low key performance style of many folk musicians would be played out again and again. A Sunday morning panel discussion of collectors and folklorists found Lomax complaining that America had no interest in preserving regional styles of music and dismissing the festival as "a publicity stunt." The festival had established a nonprofit Newport Foundation to give grants to various folk groups across the country, but to Alan it was the same kind of thing he had seen years ago at the National Folk Festival and that he had sought to avoid in the World's Fair events: city singers polishing their country personae, with a few real folksingers presented in such a way that they inevitably seemed like amateurs who were out of place.

Alan convinced Columbia Records to fund a trip south to record two LPs for the company's planned *History of Jazz* series, and while he waited to hear if the project was approved, he began exploring the possibility of starting his own festival. By August he was proposing to the administrators of Sterling Forest in Orange County, New York, that he present a group of "authentic" performers. To locate them, he asked for $1,000 for a scouting expedition to be carried on while he was in the South for Columbia Records.

Columbia, meanwhile, was insisting that Alan take a recording engineer with him, a demand that he felt interfered with the way he worked, so he refused, and the contract was canceled. He turned for help to Atlantic Records' Ahmet and Nesuhi Ertegun and Jerry Wexler, who were flush with money from their hits that summer by the Drifters, Ray Charles, Bobby Darin, the Coasters, LaVern Baker, and Clyde McPhatter. Atlantic had just begun recording in stereo a few months earlier, making it one of the first companies to do so. Both Ertegun brothers were longtime fans of early jazz, so Alan's proposal to find some of the finest musicians and those that influenced them and record them with portable stereo equipment was a project that engaged them personally.

Like all of his field trips, this one often proved to be stressful, but this time it faced the additional burden of not being clearly focused. Was Alan trying to determine if folk song was still alive and developing? Was the trip primarily motivated by the new stereo technology? Or was he doing the one thing he was sure he could do to survive?

He and Shirley left on August 21, and their first stop south was Washington, D.C., to pick up a 601-2 Ampex stereo portable recorder. Passing through Virginia they offered a ride to a hitchhiker, a young black man who declared himself just the performer they were looking for and launched into some painfully sung spirituals. With the car full of equipment, the three of them rode in the front seat, Shirley in the middle with her feet on the gearbox. When she complained that it was becoming too hot to bear, Alan realized that he had been driving in first gear for the last twenty miles.

There was trouble with the new tape recorder before they even could use it, which held them up in Washington for a day, and they didn't reach Norfolk until after dark. Alan headed directly for the black neighborhoods, leaving Shirley in the car while he went into a bar and looked for people who knew sea chanteys and dockworkers' songs.

Their travels took them to Suffolk, Virginia, on a Sunday, where they were guided by a local music booker to a number of church services, and though they were not always welcome, they made plans to return near the end of their trip. Five hours of driving got them to Salem, near Roanoke, to see Texas Gladden and her brothers, Hobart and Preston Smith, for a recording session that lasted for two days and included ballads, dance melodies, and guitar, piano, and fiddle tunes, all interspersed with talk about romance and elopement and an occasional poem. Down in Galax, near the North Carolina border, they recorded Uncle Wade Ward, the banjo-playing son of two singers whom Alan and his father had recorded in 1939. In nearby Hillsville they found the Mountain Ramblers, a bluegrass band with particular strength in spirituals shaped by black barbershop singers.

Continuing along the state's southern border they came to their last stop in Virginia, the home of Estil C. Ball, whom the Lomaxes had recorded several times over the previous two decades. Alan was slowly discovering the changes that had been occurring in the styles and repertoires of such singers. Ball, for example, had been a balladeer when the Lomaxes previously recorded him, and since then he had formed a bluegrass band but now was concentrating on spirituals and playing only in churches.

After recording sermons and singing at several other churches in Kentucky, they went to the tiny town of Fyffe in the northeastern corner of Alabama, to the United Sacred Harp Musical Association convention, and on to Parchman Farm. Though he had the Mississippi Prison Board's permission to enter the prison, there was always the fear that came with entering another world. On their way Alan shaved off his beard.

He was still awed by the power of work songs, and the virtue of stereo recording was that it was now possible to hear each singer's part with clarity, and to understand the weaving and reticulation of the polyphonic vocal lines. Though he found far fewer work song melodies and song leaders than there had been fourteen years before, and less grandeur to the actual performances, they were still deeply moving. On the song "Eighteen Hammers," the leader, Johnny Lee Moore, called his work gang together, Alan said, as though he were "summoning a heavenly group":

Eighteen hammers stand there in a line . . .
Ring like silver and shine like gold.

Yet in the midst of such physical work, he could also express the deepest despair:

Choppin' in the bottom with a hundred years . . .
If a tree fall on me, I don't a bit mo' care.

From the Delta to northern Mississippi they headed in search of Sid Hemphill, a fiddler and "quills" (panpipes) player from Panola County whom Alan had recorded years before. Now ninety-one, he was still active, and Alan recorded him, his daughter, and a guitar-playing friend. Hemphill played the quills in the normal way, blowing over the pipes to get sounds, but he also sang into them and leaned back from them to whoop and shout. It was a style of playing that anticipated early blues harmonica, and continued to be part of black music in the synthesizers of disco and funk of the 1970s and beyond.

At Sid's suggestion, they went to nearby Como, Mississippi, to record Lonnie and Ed Young, who were musicians in a black fife and drum tradition that dated back at least to the late 1700s—living proof that not all drumming had been suppressed during slavery.

As the day was ending and the music winding down, a man in overalls came out of the woods carrying a guitar. Fred McDowell was a neighbor who had just come in from picking his cotton crop, and he had heard the music. He sat down, pulled a bottleneck from his pocket, slipped it over the third finger on his left hand, and began to sing with his guitar weaving in and out of his voice, sometimes with the slide on a string answering him like a chorus or speaking the words for him:

Lord, the 61 Highway,
Is the only road I know
She runs from New York City,
Right down by my baby's door

When he listened to the playback of the recordings, Alan knew they were in the company of a great but almost unknown blues singer:

> The blues, speaking through Fred, sounded like a deep-voiced herald of the loi [ancestral spirits or demigods in Haiti], a silver-voiced heavenly choir answering him from the treble strings. When we played his recording back to him, he stomped up and down on the porch, whooping and laughing and hugging his wife. He knew he had been heard and felt his fortune had been made.

For the next four days they recorded McDowell, sometimes with his wife, Annie Mae, or Sid Hemphill's daughters singing, sometimes with their neighbor Miles Pratcher joining on guitar or Fred's sister Fanny Davis blowing some old-time hokum with a comb-and-tissue-paper "horn." In the years to come McDowell would make a number of commercial recordings and become a regular part of folk festivals.

Alan crossed into Arkansas for all-night recording sessions with Forrest City Joe Pugh and other cotton-gin town blues bands and returned to Memphis for sessions at Pentecostal church services and with barroom singers (the latter of which got Alan arrested again). Then back to Arkansas with Shirley for quick visits to Jimmie Driftwood's Ozark home and Almeda "Granny" Riddle, the only ballad singer who Alan thought could approach Texas Gladden. She had collected songs for years, and he felt that her taste in folk song was as acute as that of a trained critic. She was also a master of songs for children, and when Alan put together his *American Folk Songs for Children* LP her performances made up almost half the album.

Returning east, with their money running out, they recorded Vera Hall again in Alabama, and stopped in St. Simon's Island, Georgia, one of the places that Alan, Barnicle, and Hurston had visited twenty-four years earlier. At a party Alan threw for the community, he met Bessie Jones, an extraordinary singer, raconteur, and teacher who was not a Sea Islander but a mainlander who had married into the community and learned its traditions, and whom Alan would later work with and make known across the country.

A late-night session in Concord, North Carolina, with J. E. Mainer's string band was their final stop in the South. With their last ten dollars, they had yet to travel eight hundred miles home. But after they'd driven only a few minutes on the mainland, the radiator hose burst, and then a rainstorm came up and the windshield wiper fell off. By the time they paid the turnpike toll, bought gas, and paid the Holland Tunnel toll into New York City, they were broke and had to borrow money because two hours later they had to drive to Boston where they were to take part in a concert with Sonny Terry and Brownie McGhee.

The excursion south had lasted two and a half months and eaten up most of the money Alan had left, but it had all been worth it. He had gone south to find out if anything was left from the early days, and now he could declare that "folk music was flourishing wherever there was an institution to support it . . . wherever, that is, a local folk festival, religious group, dance style or broadcasting station gave it an outlet. . . . The South was still a rich area, rich in antiquities and still producing new sounds."

The tapes from the trip still had to be edited, the notes prepared, and the albums sequenced. The stereo recordings were as good as Alan had hoped, capturing the full range of the music, giving the performers a presence and reality that no one had ever heard on a record before. It was folk music with "the bark on it," he said, and the first time it had been treated with the same care that was accorded symphonic, jazz, and popular music. When Atlantic Records issued the records in 1960 and 1961 under the title of *Southern Folk Heritage* ("Recorded in the Field and edited by Alan Lomax, Assisted by Shirley Collins") in seven albums—*Sounds of the South, Blue Ridge Mountain Music, Roots of the Blues, White Spirituals, American Folk Songs for Children, Negro Church Music,* and *The Blues Roll On*—it was the most complete survey of southern music ever recorded for sale. With a leading jazz and rhythm and blues recording company behind them, the albums were assured of getting distribution and attention, and they wound up in the homes of many listeners who might never have bought a recording from one of the smaller, more specialized companies such as Folkways and might never have given a thought to the people or the music they contained.

Alan's work made it possible to grasp something of the history of American vernacular music, especially since the few writers who had attempted to approach it had neither the sheet music nor the recordings on which to build such a history. The rough and powerful origins of white American Protestant music were audible on these recordings, some of which still had traces of eighteenth-century elements. You could hear the mutual influence of black music and white. You could discover instruments and musical techniques derived from Africa, such as gourd banjos, quills, homemade drums, and polyrhythmic clapping, and perhaps understand the influences on jazz and rock and roll; or just experience how witty and complex children's songs and games could be. Alan was particularly proud of the children's anthology, insisting that its tunes and game songs were far warmer and wittier than the Little Golden Books and the confections on children's TV. ("The People's Mother Goose is good and golden, and the Mother Goose of Madison Avenue is, by contrast, vapid and lifeless.")

The reviewers agreed that the recordings were important documents of American history. The *New York Times* marveled at the depth of the collection and the speed with which it had been completed, praising the documentation of African-derived music in America and the quality of the written notes (and suggesting that Lomax had avoided the "social determinism" with which he had interpreted *Best Loved American Folk Songs*). Charles Edward Smith in the *Saturday Review* was equally impressed, but complained about the use of words like "African" (which he seemed to feel was out of place) and "primitive" (a word then still being debated by anthropologists, some of whom, like Alan, were attempting to transvalue it into a positive). Smith also decried "stereotyped descriptions" such as Lomax's use of the term "cooperative labor" within a prison setting.

Despite the breadth of the Atlantic series, there were piles of unused tapes from the trip south, and Alan took them to several companies, most of which did not want what they suspected were Atlantic's leftovers. But they did interest Prestige Records, a shoestring operation built on jazz and famous for its bebop recordings.

In recent years the label had been releasing folk song recordings at low cost, produced by Kenneth Goldstein, a young folklorist who saw the value of making folk music available to the public in its original form. Prestige finally settled on a set of twelve albums to be called *Southern Journey*, which would contain more of the music than on the Atlantic set, but would go deeper into the tradition, often recording the neighbors of the "stars" of the previous albums.

During the work on the second installment of records, Alan came down with another ear infection, this time in his good ear, and he was fearful of losing most of his hearing. He recovered, but was still without money. Westminster Records was going out of business, and he tried to get back the Italian tapes that he had hoped they would bring out. The women to whom he'd sublet his apartment had not paid all the rent, and the landlord was demanding it from Alan. Then one night he and Shirley came home to find that a fire in the pizza shop downstairs had spread through the building and was creeping upwards toward their apartment. But the firemen stopped the flames at the fourth floor, and Alan was able to move everything out and stay with friends until the building was restored after Christmas.

For the second time, he decided that he should end his relationship with Shirley, and he asked her to return home to England in late January. He attempted to soften the blow by giving her a letter that made her his agent to sell the idea of a series of programs for the BBC based on the southern recordings, for which she would receive 10 percent and the artists would receive their fees. (Every song from that trip was copyrighted in the name of the artists singing it.) Shirley was also authorized to use the tapes for any radio shows or lectures of her own.

On his return to New York Alan had attempted to resume analysis with the psychiatrist he had been seeing eight years before, but after a few sessions he was encouraged to stand on his own, and he began a period of self-analysis, keeping copious notes on his dreams and thoughts, sometimes mailing them to his analyst in hopes that he would read them and perhaps agree to see him again. Many of these notes were taken up with ruminations about Shirley, for he was once again having second thoughts. Worrying that it was he who felt rejected by Shirley, he wrote that under analysis he had worked his way through what he had previously thought was hatred for his father, to confronting what he now understood was rejection by his mother, a rejection he had relived through a series of relationships with women who sooner or later rejected him. He was haunted by fear of being inadequate to the tasks he set for himself. Whenever he began new enterprises, such as putting the first words to paper when writing, he said he was frozen by fear of the responses of critics. Finding a new woman to be with seemed to him an "emotionally valid" way of escaping these problems, though he confessed to himself that he had been too hasty and anxious in the relationships he had sought.

When he discovered documentary writing, where he used the words of other people, he felt himself freed of these concerns. "Everything I have written or transcribed has been for me a successful ruse for containing and transmitting my hostility and anger and rebellious feeling. I am always surprised when my enemies don't attack me and blast me harder. . . . I took to folklore with relief and floated on the vast wild Mississippi of American folk fantasy, so much of it loaded with anger and death wish and defiance of authority." Because there were so few folklorists when he began, he said, folklore had given him a sense of freedom from criticism.

But now he was writing page after page in an attempt to prove to himself that Shirley was his perfect mate and that he had been a fool to leave her; they were followed by an equal number of pages refuting himself. When he heard Shirley was to be married, he traveled back to London and asked her to marry him instead, but she turned him down.

One of the visitors to Alan's apartment during this period was Guy Carawan, the folksinger who had stayed with him and recorded with him in London. He spent several nights with Alan talking about music and racial justice and his plans to carry on the cause of the People's Songs by going south. He was moving to the Highlander Folk School that winter, a grassroots political and educational institution in Tennessee, modeled on the nineteenth-century Danish adult schools that built their curriculum on the culture and values of their rural students. Highlander had been founded during the height of the Depression, and at first was dedicated to unionization and the rights of workers in the South. But by the 1950s it had shifted its focus to organizing for desegregation and civil rights and had developed ties to Martin Luther King Jr.'s Southern Christian Leadership Conference. (Rosa Parks was Highlander's most famous student.) Throughout the school's history it had been threatened, investigated, closed down, relocated, and reopened. Just as Guy was settling into life at the school, now newly married to his wife Candie whom he had met there, the school was raided again by the police, and they and dozens of other people were put in jail. It was the dark nights spent in a cell, hearing an old Negro spiritual coming from down the hall, that revealed to them the power of song in maintaining strength and discipline in nonviolent change. Guy knew then that the potential for song as an agent of change in racial relations was far greater than it was in moving the labor movement forward.

The Carawans became documentarians of the civil rights struggle, connecting with the Student Nonviolent Coordinating Committee (SNCC) and recording hundreds of hours of demonstrations and speeches by Ralph Abernathy, Fred

Shuttlesworth, and others. But they also researched the old spirituals and hymns, looking for expressions of the theme of freedom, and printed up songbooks. (Guy helped make "We Shall Overcome" into the most important song of the movement.) Once mass arrests began to be used to threaten the protestors, they turned to prisoners' songs to give them courage. There was a hunger for connecting with the folkways of their ancestors and the struggle they shared, and Guy Carawan was accepted as someone who knew that tradition. When the police began destroying their recordings and songbooks, like the slaveholders had destroyed drums, they knew they were on the winning side.

Recalling all the music that he had heard in black churches and prisons, Alan understood that this was the moment in which those powerful anthems of divine justice and human freedom could be revived by a new kind of folklorist. He kept up a correspondence with Guy throughout the early days of the movement, discussing what could be done to help in the struggle and urging him on. The Carawans were recording at Albany State College in Georgia in 1961–62, where a major confrontation was taking place between students of the black college and the white citizens of the town. Using Vanguard Records' recording studio equipment, Alan edited the materials that they collected—preaching, narration, and songs—into an audio documentary, *Freedom in the Air: A Documentary on Albany Georgia, 1961–63*, issued by SNCC on its own label (as SNCC-101). Alan had written the Carawans a letter urging them on, which was printed on the cover of the recording:

> While I was squirreling round in the past, you were busy with the present, and how I envy you. It must be wonderful to be with those kids who are so courageously changing the South forever. I hope they feel proud of the cultural heritage of their forbears. It was a heritage of protest against oppression, of assertion against hopelessness, of joy in life against death. Tell them that they can search the world over, all the libraries, all the manuscripts, and they will never find a cultural heritage more vital, more noble, more flexible, more sophisticated, more wise, more full of love, more human or more beautiful. Tell them the whole world is shaken by hearing its faint echoes in jazz. Tell them that if they can walk into their free future with the great arts, the great laughter, the wit and the perceptiveness of life that their oppressed but always proud and life-ennobled ancestors possessed—and add to this their own sophistication, that the culture of the American Negro can become the wonder of the civilized world. Tell them that if they lose what is so close at hand, offered them by their fathers and mothers and grandmothers, that their children will have to turn back to it. If they can accept the folk of the South on their own terms, they will build not only an invincible political movement, but a bridge of beauty that all mankind will long to walk across.

CHAPTER 15

The Science of Folk Song

When the American Anthropological Association was holding its annual meeting in 1959, Margaret Mead invited Alan to take several evenings to present his ideas on the relation of song to social organization as part of a series of sessions on the use of media in anthropology. By then folk music outside the United States had become the specialized subject of a new academic discipline called ethnomusicology. Its students aimed to merge the fields of musicology and anthropology to address the neglect of much of the world's music by traditional musicologists, folklorists, and social scientists. In taking his own findings to anthropologists, Alan was declaring that music was too important to the scientific study of humankind to be left to musicologists alone. Music was pan-human and, like language and kinship, one of the few behaviors found wherever humans have attempted to make a way of life. This approach had an appealing ring to anthropologists, who at midcentury had begun to see themselves as the serious students of humanity as a whole, and as true heirs of the Enlightenment.

Although Alan's work was already familiar to a few anthropologists, it was unusual for outsiders to the profession to be invited to their annual meetings, much less to be given several hours to present their work. Alan's old University of Texas roommate Walter Goldschmidt was attending the meetings, and they ran into each other at a hotel bar. "He had come with a big manuscript, the first version of his cantometrics work. Alan oversold what his work could do," Goldschmidt observed, but "that was something you expected of geniuses. His enthusiasm was charming if you liked him, annoying to those who didn't know him well." Goldschmidt was impressed enough by his research that, as editor of the *American Anthropologist,* he asked him to submit a version of his talk for publication, and "Folk Song Style: Musical Style and Social Context" was the result. Though it was anthropologically sophisticated enough to be accepted by the leading journal in the discipline, it was also written clearly, eloquently, and without academic jargon. Once it was published, Alan thought it might reach a bigger audience if given a chance and had it printed as a pamphlet to sell in Greenwich Village.

A few months later Alan took that paper to the meeting of the American Folklore Society. The *New York Times* accurately summarized the most significant part of his talk as saying that his collecting in Europe showed that there were " 'folk-song style families' throughout the world, families whose musical habit patterns 'override the limits of geography, language, religion, culture, and of history itself.' " The folklorists, however, while respecting him for his long years of fieldwork and the importance of what he had collected, were put off by the scientific and anthropological cast to what they considered an art form, and sat there stunned and angry.

The songbook Alan had been working on for the last year or so, *The Folk Songs of North America*, had also just appeared in print, and the folklorists were already saying that it was the biggest and most daring of his popular books. Although he himself called it an anthology of anthologies—a selection of the best that had been gathered—it was more than that: a songbook version of his "Folk Song Style" paper, a summary of his ideas at the moment, but limited to North America, and presented in popular terms. Most reviewers saw it merely as an excellent book for singing folk songs. The *New York Times* treated it as such, leading Margaret Mead to write the editor and complain about the reviewer's "failure to recognize that Alan Lomax's outstanding contribution—a genuine integration between cultural theory, geographical specificity and folklore style—is . . . on the growing edge of our knowledge." The book's endpapers were maps that showed important names and places in North American songs and identified five folk song groups in the United States and Canada (northern, southern, border state white styles, western style, and Negro style). Inside the book each song style was discussed in terms of its characteristic emotions and ethos. The notes Alan wrote for each song quoted freely from regional histories, novels, and poetry, and mentioned collectors, recordings, and scholarly articles and books. There were also psychosocial explanations that treated songs as projections of social life. An Anglo-American nursery song like "Cock Robin," for example, with its detailed account of death and burial, was linked to early childhood training: "Oppressed, humiliated, denied, bullied and talked down to by a race of strong giants, [children's] fantasies have naturally run to violence and death," while their dreams and nightmares are sites for revenge and punishment for their "guilty thoughts." His analysis was partly literary, partly anthropological and psychoanalytic, bringing together ideas that were seldom mentioned in the discussion of folk songs. What he had before only hinted at about American folk song was now laid out boldly. The erotics of British-derived folk song had been largely ignored under the Calvinism of North America, he said, and only the songs that fit its perspective were retained, especially those that dealt with sexual conflict as viewed through women's eyes. The songs were typically sung solo without instrumental accompaniment, with anguish and a "pinched voice":

> In the popular mind a gulf was fixed between pleasure and righteousness, thus inflaming the old wound of guilt and sexual anxiety which has so often characterized our civilization. . . . Their favorite ballads of love were shrouded in gloom, drowned in melancholy and poisoned by sadomasochism.

Meanwhile, just across the tracks was the African American style, more likely than not collectively sung, accompanied by instruments or polyrhythmic handclapping, and "on the whole joyfully erotic, deeply tragic, allusive, playfully ironic."

In January 1960, Alan was awarded an American Council of Learned Societies grant of $6,000 for "Nine months of study and research in the field of folk song . . . aimed at refinement of hypotheses . . . about the importance of vocal style and of behavioral traits to the analysis and classification of folk songs." His plan was to pursue "a study of folksong style, the act of singing being regarded as a whole—a complex of behavioral traits, including its social setting, its physiological and psychological aspects, as well as its aesthetic characteristics."

For several weeks he went looking for an institution that could serve as the base for his work and found encouragement from scholars at the University of Chicago, Northwestern, Harvard, Wesleyan, and Columbia. He also sought out someone in medicine who might help him understand the psychological and physiological sources of vocal tension and the cultural patterning of vocal timbre. At the Hospital for Vocal Disorders in New York he was warned that he would need a great deal of money for a laboratory and the equipment for such a study, but the laryngologists he consulted there were nonetheless encouraging, explaining how the throat and the voice reacted to emotions, and how they worked when crying, laughing, shouting, whispering, and singing. Dr. Paul J. Moses, author of *The Voice of Neurosis*, told him about the psychology of vocal register, and how neurosis could determine how one sang. Lomax also located singing teachers who believed that vocal registers were a function of how one saw oneself.

It was Margaret Mead, again, who was most helpful at the beginning of the project, and who found a way for Alan to enter academia without ever formally becoming part of it. Mead had never hidden her disappointment with the unimaginative work done by many anthropologists who emerged after World War II, those she called the middle-management generation, and had made a point of watching out for those she thought had exceptional talent and interesting ideas—autodidacts and independent thinkers, people like Colin Turnbull, Ray

Birdwhistell, and Lomax—lending them the credibility they needed to make a life as a researcher in the human sciences. She made them part of her salon, guests at her annual Christmas Eve dinners, and provided cover for them in the closely guarded world of the academy. Alan was one of the few successful applicants to the American Council of Learned Societies that year who was not a professor of some kind or another, and the ACLS staff encouraged him to complete his Ph.D. and get out of what they thought of as "the entertainment business." They insisted that he at least be attached to a university, and Mead arranged for the grant to be administered through the Department of Anthropology at Columbia University.

He began his nine months of study by learning what he could about vocal qualities and communications theory. The ACLS suggested that he center his reading, consultation, and research in Philadelphia, where he might also take classes in the University of Pennsylvania's anthropology department or with the several folklorists in the English department. But as he was now almost forty-five years old, he feared that formal study would slow down his work. When he arrived at Penn about a month late for the start of classes, his casual approach annoyed some of the professors, but then Penn's folklore scholars' chief interests were in classifying and ordering collections; they were not prepared for the sweeping study he was proposing. McEdward Leach, professor of English at Penn, recalled that at one point Alan asked who would be examining him for the Ph.D., and when they told him he pointed out that he had had more experience and had published more in folklore than any of them, which they knew to be true.

Alan's passion and urgency likewise did not sit well with most professors, and he had little interest in their kind of scholarly life. As he wrote to Jack Harrison of the Humanities Division of the Rockefeller Foundation to explain why he had not matriculated as a graduate student, "I had come to feel strongly that big institutions often kill good research. Those long corridors, those administrative routines, those bloodless and vicious battles of grades and positions, the weariness of institutional lunches, especially the heavy and puritanical atmosphere that somehow pervades many places—all this combined to stifle the imagination and the impulse to work hard and the freedom to enjoy the work. I resolved to be as unbuttoned as possible during my brief stint of cooperative research and to make the standard of the job that everybody enjoys himself." He eventually returned to New York City and schooled himself by reading ethnographies of the world's people and asking anthropologists—most of whom had never written anything on music—to tell him about the musical practices of the groups they had studied. What he learned was that the social role of music was far more diverse than he or anyone else had ever expected.

At Columbia's anthropology department Alan encountered Conrad Arensberg, a highly respected if atypical anthropologist. Arensberg was open to thinking about human life in broad and general patterns, but at the same time was able to focus on the smallest behaviors. He was a gentleman whose manners and generosity stood out in the overheated competitiveness of university life. Sitting in the only Chinese restaurant close to Columbia University (where Arensberg ordered in Mandarin), their daily conversations revealed to Alan a hidden history of the study of bodily expression, some of which had begun at Columbia. In 1930 Franz Boas and the Russian anthropologist Julia Averkieva made films of Kwakiutl Indian ceremony and daily life, making them the first social scientists to use film to document dance, gesture, and body movement as part of human culture. Later, David Efron, a psychiatrist and a student of Boas's, filmed gesture and social interaction on the streets of ethnic neighborhoods of New York City and on the campus of Columbia in the 1930s. At Harvard, Arensberg himself had studied gesture and motion in human conversations with Elliot D. Chappel, a pioneer in human interaction studies.

When Alan showed him the maps of North American singing styles in his book, Arensberg pulled down from his shelves George Peter Murdock's *World Ethnographic Sample,* the first attempt at creating a crosscultural set of data, coding 565 cultures by thirty-seven variables so that they could be compared. Arensberg suggested that Alan might use this approach for what he had learned about folk songs.

In May 1961, Alan returned to Philadelphia to attend Ray Birdwhistell's seminar at Temple University. For years, Birdwhistell had been working on what he called kinesics, the study of human gesture and the many levels at which human communication operates. The outside participants in the seminar were Alan, the linguist Edith Trager, and Norman Markel, a psychologist who studied conversations. Before the first meeting could take place, however, Birdwhistell became ill, so for the next two weeks Alan worked with Edith Trager, who tutored him in linguistics. He was looking for some way to express an insight he had that the melody of songs followed the patterns of vocal tension in a culture. With the help of a chart developed by Edith's husband, George Trager, and another linguist, Henry Lee Smith, that showed where vowels were formed in the mouth and throat, they began to trace the patterns of movement of vowels in songs. What they discovered was that different styles of singing clearly favored different vowels—from those produced high and in the front of the mouth (*iy* as in "feet") to those that originated low and in the back (*aw* as in "law") to those in between—and different patterns of movement characterized each style. The most typical example of each style's vowel preference pattern seemed to be found in lullabies and in the parts of songs that were called nonsense—the "hey nonny nonnys" and the "fiddle di diddles."

This was not something that the singers or listeners were aware of, although they could quickly recognize a song style as familiar or unfamiliar to them. These patterns confirmed what Alan had heard in Italy and Spain: there was "a marked preference for high front (tense) vowels . . . in Mediterranean lands, where feminine premarital sexual intercourse was forbidden . . . and low back vowels . . . characterized the song styles of areas with more permissive sexual standards, such as northern Italy, northern Spain, and central and eastern Europe." Edith Trager called the form of analysis they had developed "phonotactics."

When Birdwhistell recovered and returned to Temple University to direct his seminar, he devoted all ten meetings to his ideas on communication, which Alan found "both fundamental and a bit terrifying." Birdwhistell taught by example, using his body to show what was impossible to describe adequately in words: the body, and especially the face, sent recurrent signals in interaction with other bodily signals, mostly at a low level of awareness. As one became aware of them and saw how humans interacted through these different levels of communication, they were at once vaguely familiar and shocking, as though watching Birdwhistell perform revealed something deep and hidden in oneself. The combinations of expressions he displayed might show a raised eyebrow, a downturned mouth, eyes blinking, the hairline moving forward, a foot lightly tapping in emphasis, the stomach pushing out very slightly—all these gestures together signifying a change from one state of being to another. Birdwhistell was not acting, and did not depend on words; his signals all took place rapidly, but he insisted that there was much more going on at different levels and moving in a dizzying pattern at even greater speed, with constant repetition of signals. This repetition—or what they called redundancy—revealed the stabilizers that carried messages such as, "We belong to the human race"; "We belong to the same culture"; "I am female and so are you"; "Neither of us is crazy"; "I am receiving—keep sending." Birdwhistell had discovered these exchanges of signals by close analysis of films of conversation, where in slow motion bodies were seen to be moving like dancers in synchrony, and he found that these were the stable baselines that make language and other human messages possible. He had also worked out an elaborate system of analysis by which these gestures and facial expressions could be coded—that is, whereby qualities that were difficult to compare could be turned into quantities or numbers that enabled them to be easily contrasted.

Kinesics was a revelation to Alan. He knew that song was more emotionally charged than speech, which accounted in part for its universality and its endurance. But he had been puzzled by the peculiar relationship between music and speech: music could be enjoyed without words, or even without knowing the language in which the song was sung. If signal redundancy was at the base of all human communication, perhaps it provided a clue to the meaning of music, since music seemed to be the most redundant of all behaviors of which humans are fully aware. Pitch and stress are far more pronounced and repetitive in music than speech, and both are related to the markers that in speech indicate friendliness or hostility, surprise, or simply routine communication. Pitch and stress are learned in early childhood when adults exaggerate when speaking to children. Music, in fact, seems to carry the greatest amount of information in its redundancy of pitch and stress, but even more so in its repetition of words and the use of voice color. In song, words are often distorted by the high repetition of pitch and stress. Speech using the amount of redundancy found in music can only be found in that of children, the mad, or lovers. When these ideas were added to Birdwhistell's method of coding and treating bodily movement, Alan saw a way to rethink what he had spent his life learning: "For the first time I had encountered a system—not so much of social theory, as of how to analyze and organize the bits of cultural material which have been for so long part of my working experience."

What he had been learning resonated with his earliest exposure to folk music. It heightened his awareness of the differences between southern white and black singing. Most of the musicologists and folklorists who came before him had largely dismissed these differences as unimportant, and certainly not a legacy of older traditions of singing. Melville Herskovits's *Myth of the Negro Past* had shown, however, that the loss of African culture among blacks in the United States was far less than had been assumed. Lomax's father's interests in folklore had likewise led him to see the importance of song in work and daily tasks, especially among African Americans. Work songs in Spain, Scotland, and Italy had made Alan further aware of the relationship between vocal tension, sexual restrictions, and socioeconomic development. Reading Freud, Marx, and Emile Durkheim on the relationship between forms of production and social organization and Darwin's writings on emotion in animals and humans, gave him the means to bring together materialism, psychoanalysis, and social and cultural evolution as the foundations of a theory of song. In thinking about song style, he was fully aware of the links between singing, history, the social group, emotions, the physical motions of work, and the production of food. In several of his earliest formulations of the idea of song style, he wrote:

> The main function of musical style seems to be to reestablish for the individual the familial social and psychological climate into which he was born, raised, and seeks to express himself. . . . Song style is the formal elaboration of some instinctive and universally human mode of dramatizing or exteriorizing human feelings. Each song style is dominated by one or the other of these patterns.

> Musical style changes least of all human cultural characteristics. [It] is associated with the first and earliest distributions of mankind across the world. . . . It therefore stands for certain formative, aesthetic processes that operate in human society over long periods of time and in parallel with economic forces.

> Under the term song style one includes not only . . . the formal musical characteristics, but the tone of voice, the motor behavior, the social organization, the audience response and the inherent emotions that produce the musical whole.

To begin his research on comparative musical styles, Alan sought the help of Robert M. Abramson, a well-known teacher of music at Juilliard. Together they worked up a system for characterizing and comparing music, but they soon found that differences in their personalities and work habits made it impossible for them to continue as colleagues. While visiting Wesleyan University in June 1961 to talk with David McAllester, one of the founders of ethnomusicology, Lomax met McAllester's first graduate student, Victor Grauer, and the two spent several weeks together that summer listening to various musics of the world and discussing the most significant features that they might find to help focus the description of styles. What they were looking for was a way to compare different musics without resorting to the Western music notation system, which was not capable of describing other musics accurately. Alan decided in advance that whatever method of coding they developed, it should at least be a pleasure to work with, require no musical knowledge, and be explainable in commonsense terms, so that it "would not become an esoteric object in itself but would stay close to the level of listening and enjoying music of which all human beings are equally capable." This meant, for example, that instead of using Western musicological terms such as "canon," "antiphony," and the like, he would use neutral description terms such as "overlap," "alternation," and "interlock." And when he *was* forced to rely on musicological terminology (such as "unison" and "polyphony"), he would at least widen their meanings to be able to include a greater variety of the world's musics.

Over the rest of the summer Alan and Grauer listened to 2,527 recordings from 233 culture areas, coding each piece, refining their categories as they went along. Because Alan was especially interested in vocal qualities, they decided for the time being to focus on vocal music. Alan and his daughter went to Indiana University to find examples of music in their collections to fill in the missing samples he needed. They also spent ten days at Purdue University, whose experimental speech clinic helped them gather six hundred sonogram samples of vocal timbre.

Alan continued to ferret out the qualities that could be found in all the song style families of the world—the social organization of the performing group; musical organization in terms of musical blend (such as unison, or multi-parted tonal and rhythmic organization, or solo singing); the degree of elaboration of the words; melodic elaboration in terms of length and number of segments and types of elaboration; dynamics; and vocal quality. He finally decided on thirty-seven qualitative measures of style. Each of the samples of song was listened to by two researchers, who then recorded their impressions on rating scales that ranged from 1 to 3 up to 1 to 13, depending on the number of degrees of variations they heard. The results were then compared statistically with the culture traits of the societies from which they came, and conclusions were reached about how a singing style was related to other features of the society. Margaret Mead suggested that the peaks and valleys on the statistical charts could be filled in with color so that their correlations could be viewed as profiles, and therefore be easier to understand by the average person not familiar with statistics.

After his fellowship ran out Alan continued his work, attempting to learn from anyone who might conceivably help him. By this point his central question was how these patterns of aesthetic structure had been operating throughout history. "The special task of folklore," he wrote, "was to examine and clarify the nature of these patterns, to show the role they have played in human evolution and to find out how they can be put to work for the benefit of mankind." The science of folklore was on its way.

In a letter to the Rockefeller Foundation, which he hoped would support the next stage of his research, Alan wrote:

> I have hit upon three ways of describing with a considerable degree of scientific control what goes on whenever a group of people come together to sing in any culture. [There is] a multiple factor coding system for the musical performance, itself, which surveys and rates the organization of the musical group, the structure of the rhythm, the structure of the melody, the musical qualifiers and the vocal characterizers. This code system produces distinct profiles for musical culture areas such as the Indians of North America, Negro Africa, Western Europe, the Near East, Australia, Polynesia, etc. It also shows with considerable clarity what happens when cross-acculturation between any two music style families takes place. It is, I believe, the first successful attempt to describe musical performance in an overall sense.

His Rockefeller proposal was turned into an article, "Song Structure and Social Structure," that urged ethnomusicologists to abandon the study of music in strictly musical terms, and instead see it in context, as a form of human behavior.

Recordings had made transcribing music to paper unnecessary and freed musical analysis from all the errors, limitations, and biases that the traditional Western musicological methods had introduced. The musics of other peoples should no longer be judged on the basis of our own standards of musical value. If formal music analysis was rejected, then what would remain would be the features of musical performance that were available to any "normal listener," who could then describe any music in the world. What was offered in place of traditional musicology he called cantometrics ("a measure of song" or "song as measure").

Alan acknowledged that his system as developed to this point had some areas of "crudeness and ambiguity," but still managed to elicit agreement from a number of listeners. Having examined large numbers of samples of songs from a given area, they found that the same patterns were repeated, so that it was determined that a sample of five to ten songs for each region would be sufficient. Once songs from a given area were coded by listeners, a profile of the preferred song style could be developed and used to compare various features of a musical style with other styles, and to correlate these profiles with other cultural behaviors and social forms. Alan's article offered some preliminary examples of style profiles, which revealed that musical styles were fairly limited in their variety and patterning. The results were "revolutionary":

> The coding system shows that within any given culture area sometimes one, but never more than three or four, performance structures shape all folk songs.... They produce a trait cluster which defines a musical style in an extremely precise way.... When master sheets are made up from the averaging of all the samples from a given area, it then becomes possible to compare musical styles cross-culturally by comparing these master sheets. Heretofore such a thing was completely impossible. One could talk about the melodies of one area or the rhythms of one area or the harmonic system of one area as compared with another, but never about the overall shape of the music as it was performed; that is, as it lived in the culture. This, I believe, is the first time that it has been possible to make anything like a scientific comparison of aesthetic patterns cross-culturally, and this is due to the fact that all music is so highly systematized, no matter how primitive it may happen to be.

Lomax was the first to understand the consequences of audio recording for the study of folk song. Having lived through the transition from transcribing songs to recording them, he could appreciate the limitations of an audio-only medium, but also understood how these limits refocused the way music was received: the body of the singer could now be heard, if not seen, and a physical presence was connected to what had before been only words on paper, or at best, words with a more or less correct musical transcription. The breathing of the singers could be perceived, and where they took breaths could be noted, along with the tension of the throat, the nasality of the singer, the speed of the song, the role of the vowels in sounding the song, the clarity versus the slurring of words. In a work song, one might hear the vocal consequences of muscle strain; if it was a lullaby it was possible to hear sounds that soothed and comforted. Was it a group that sang, or a solo singer? Did they sing together as one, or seem to be unconcerned with blending? A materialist view of song was now possible, and one might think about what could be called the economy of song. The choice of sounds that a people make and the way the body is used to create them might provide a means to consider how they felt about the song and how it related to their lives through a form of musical psychoanalysis.

Unlike the anthropologists and psychologists who studied the microbehavioral level of communication primarily in terms of social interaction, Lomax went one step further, seeing those small and largely out-of-awareness behaviors as being the basis of traditional arts. It was the folk artist's job, he believed, to stay close to the cultural norms and baselines of their societies. Their place in their communities was one of underscoring and reinforcing the norm, rather than attempting, like the avant-garde artists, to expand, improve, or confront the existing aesthetic.

In 1961, Lomax was awarded the one-year Rockefeller Grant he was seeking for the "development of descriptive techniques for folk song." The first task was to collect as many samples of the world's music as possible. This meant writing hundreds of letters and making endless phone calls, and following up again and again when samples were not forthcoming, sometimes even trekking to a collector's or scholar's home to get them himself. Robert Farris Thompson, a professor of art history at Yale, remembered a phone call from Alan asking if he had tapes of Yoruba songs and music. When Thompson said he did, Alan told him that he needed them immediately, and he would take the train from New York to New Haven the following day to copy them himself. Alan arrived looking exhausted just as Thompson was leaving for a dinner party. When Thompson returned hours later he found Alan asleep on the floor, the tapes copied, and the tail of the last reel of tape spinning round and round.

As tapes and discs grew in number and spilled from the shelves of his apartment, maps covering the walls, and song profiles accumulating on every surface, some wondered why a person who had been so close to the singers and the communities that produced this music would step so far back from them and begin high-level comparisons of whole cultures through statistics, of all things. Folksingers listened to his excited accounts of his discoveries and often left puzzled.

Alan patiently explained, as he would have to for the rest of his life, that he was still doing folklore, but a folklore long dreamed of by European scholars and yet never achieved. He was lifting the top off folksinging, looking at its parts, and seeing how it worked—what kept it going for centuries, why so many shared it, and what it was about it that gave them pleasure.

To those who knew him best, what he was attempting was perhaps even more bewildering. After he explained cantometrics to his sister Bess, she asked him why he had come up with the idea. "When you have to sit through a half-hour song in Spanish that you can't understand," he said with a laugh, "you need something else to do." When he tried to interest Geoffrey Bridson at the BBC in his work, Alan told him that he at last had something that television would like: "profiles that look like business curves on performing styles"; "abstract drawings which have to do with the poetics"; and "pictures of timbre, which are rather like fingerprint diagrams."

For years Alan had tried to operate in the old southern tradition of personal management—that is to say, he managed himself. But when his life in New York had grown too complex he found an agent, Paul Rosen, to promote some of his ideas to media companies. The first target was Brad McCuen, the reissue producer at RCA Records, who handled the company's country music. Lomax proposed a series of thematic albums—folk Christmas carols, railroad songs, folk guitar, folk dances, and some eleven other ideas. He also suggested packaging albums of reissues of RCA-owned recordings—a history of the blues, or of hillbilly music, and a collection of ethnic musics from America. RCA showed no interest in his notions, though only four years later they issued some LPs very similar to the ones Alan had recommended. Alan also directed his agent to see if there might still be some opportunities for him in London to write a new play for the Theatre Royal in Stratford, or to develop a TV "spectacular" on folk music, maybe write some documentaries on American life for BBC, select the music for an upcoming documentary on Tuscany featuring the comic actor Terry-Thomas, or write a musical based on the Jelly Roll Morton book.

He developed a proposal to make a series of films on folk song subjects, framing them as a critique of American media for "turning their backs on documentary work." With a crew of three for just a year, he said he could make a series of half-hour films on subjects such as Chicago blues, the songs of *vaqueros*, Lead Belly, the Sea Islands, bluegrass music, Sacred Harp singers, fiddlers, folkniks in Washington Square, and a half dozen other areas of vital and unique musical life. It was how he planned to make these films that would make them distinctive: before they began filming he would interview the singers and musicians and build the story line around what he learned, using them as narrators when possible. While the camera would stay close to the subjects, the "films must not *watch* the folk actors, but give the audience a sense of participation." Everything would be filmed with handheld cameras and portable recording equipment in order to be able to move freely with the performers.

Though no one was willing to support his own film projects at the time, Alan was hired to be one of the musical directors for the film *The Music of Williamsburg*. Its sponsor, the Colonial Williamsburg Foundation, was reacting to criticism of civil rights activists that the reconstructed colonial town had failed to show any black life or culture in its re-creation, and the foundation planned to use the film for classroom and touristic purposes. Lomax's task was to re-create the kind of music that would have been familiar to the town's slaves and might have been performed by them on any given day in 1768, while another music director would do the same for the whites of Williamsburg. Alan explored the earliest writings on the colonies to find authentic songs from the period, and went to work full-time on the project in April 1960. To find performers, he made phone calls to talent agents, to the commissioner of public relations in Nassau, the Bahamian labor commissioner, and to Belle Glade, Florida, where Zora Neale Hurston had located Bahamian dancers and musicians. He went to Warrenton, Virginia, in search of a banjo player, to North Carolina looking for a fiddler, to St. Simon's Island off Georgia for singers, and then to Miami in search of Bahamian drummers (since he could not find black American folk hand drummers). It was a difficult month, filled with dead ends, false leads, and hundreds of miles of driving and auto breakdowns.

His expense sheets listed the tips given to people he asked for help in finding performers, the purchase of food and drinks for parties to audition performers, a musical saw, strings for instruments, a goat hide for drum heads, lime for taking hair off the hide, and a wooden barrel for the drum. He noted that Miami was "an extremely difficult Negro community to enter. It took me five days and many, many contacts before I found [drummer] Nat Rahmings. Actually I bought my way in by handing out odd bits of money to various slum characters who then introduced me down the line." Though keeping the film from becoming anachronistic was a struggle, it was nonetheless one of the early efforts at correcting the television and film image of African Americans as ciphers who had made little contribution to American culture.

Once filming was completed, some singers he had recruited from the Sea Islands stayed on another day so that Alan could record them with fife, drum, and what Alan called a "reconstructed" fretless, bowl-shaped banjo from slavery days (played by Hobart Smith). How authentic this attempt was at getting music from the previous century on record is hard to say, though it surely broke the rules of white-black interaction in the rural South. But Alan took heart when the group enthusiastically approved the addition of the white banjoist and was pleased by the music.

It was during this period that the Friends of Old Time Music was formed by John Cohen and Ralph Rinzler. The name was chosen to avoid the word "folk," which its members thought had already become too identified with commercialism. They sought to associate themselves with all the seriousness that the Friends of Music—an esteemed classical group in New York—would insist on. Cohen and Rinzler thought up the idea of bringing singers and musicians from the hinterlands—the real folks—with the help of Mike Seeger, Margot Mayo, Jean Ritchie, and Izzy Young. (Young was a convert from jazz who had invested in the new Village folk revival by opening the Folklore Center on MacDougal Street, a mixture of a tiny performance space, a folk bibliotheque, and a meeting place for those in the folk movement.) With folk music becoming a national craze and establishing new careers for pop stars who crossed over to folk songs, the Friends decided to return to the kind of performances that Alan had presented in the mid-1940s and again in the 1959 concert at Carnegie Hall and at the Newport Folk Festival. The performers they brought to town for their concerts from 1961 to 1965 were chosen to show the world that there was a difference between folksingers and those who simply sang folk songs. The Friends developed a language and an aura of authenticity to explain these differences, even if they themselves were often not so clear on them. In fact, most of the people they presented turned out to have made commercial recordings or worked in minstrel, vaudeville, and tent shows in the South, and as such were themselves professional folk performers. The Friends of Old Time Music were attempting to turn back musical time at the very moment when the civil rights movement was hitting its peak, and it was not always easy to celebrate southern folk artists gracefully in this climate. John Cohen articulated the larger goals that lay behind their efforts:

> The act of finding linkages between peoples who would otherwise be opposed to one another was interesting and political. We were putting our stamp of approval on these white guys who until that time had been stereotyped as racists, lynchers, and all those nightmarish things about the South. We were trying to turn Ashley and Watson and the Stanleys into real people, and I thought this was a good thing—acknowledging those people and their culture was political. . . . We were looking for deeply human, positive connections rather than confrontations.

When Alan's turn came to produce a show for the Friends, he used performers he knew and had worked with for years, like Hobart Smith, Texas Gladden, Bessie Jones, the Georgia Sea Island Singers, Fred McDowell, and Ed Young.

It was into this mix of musical good intentions and occasional cultural slips that Bob Dylan walked when he arrived in New York City. Carla Rotolo, Alan's assistant in 1961, had a sister, Suze, who was living with Dylan at the time, so he was an occasional visitor to Alan's apartment, where he met many of these singers and heard them perform at Alan's twice-monthly parties—"spiritual experiences," Dylan called them—and where he learned their songs and performance styles firsthand. He later said that Harry Smith's recordings were not as important to him as people thought, because he had seen many of the same people who were on the records perform live. Dylan wanted Alan to include his songs in the next folk song collection that he published, which might well have been a possibility if Alan had prepared another book, for he admired Dylan's work, and even had no objections to his becoming a rock singer. In fact, he said that he saw in Dylan's music what he saw in the best rock and roll: a conscience.

In the spring of 1961 Alan scripted a film for television on folk music in Greenwich Village called *Ballads, Blues, and Bluegrass,* which was shot by George Pickow with one camera (but still without synched sound) in Alan's apartment. It opened with him at the door greeting his guests, and turning to the camera to say, "Well, you're in Greenwich Village now, where people come to get away from America. It's not jazz around here anymore—it's folk music. Jazz is high-hat and aging. Young people have gone mad over ballads, guitar playing, and banjo picking." Dropping by that night were Clarence Ashley, Doc Watson, the Greenbriar Boys, Ramblin' Jack Elliott, Jean Ritchie, Memphis Slim, the New Lost City Ramblers, Peter LaFarge, Roscoe Holcomb, Willie Dixon, and others. It seemed like a miniature version of what Alan had envisioned for the Newport Folk Festival.

On August 26, Alan married Antoinette Marchand, a young woman from a Franco-American family in upstate New York whom he had met while he was consulting with the Tragers in Buffalo. She was twenty-six and had just graduated from the University of Buffalo with a teaching degree. For the wedding he rented a shack in Wellfleet, Massachusetts, where a handful of friends and relations gathered. But it was not too small a wedding for the *New York Times* to ignore, and they noted it was a second marriage for both.

Almost as soon as the newlyweds returned to New York, Bessie Jones turned up at his door and said she was there to get Alan's help starting her career as a singer, storyteller, and teacher and to have him record her biography. She stayed with the Lomaxes for three months and did fifty hours of recording, with Alan and Toni doing the interviewing. "Bessie lived with us and that machine was there, ready to go at any minute, and we never knew when all of a sudden something would start coming."

Though the interviews were never published, Alan wrote letters for Bessie, encouraging various organizations to hire her, and for two years she toured the country playing schools and festivals. Alan's sister Bess, however, did her own interviewing of Jones, which resulted in Bessie Jones and Bess Lomax Hawes's *Step It Down: Games, Plays, Songs, and Stories from the Afro-American Heritage.* It was a very different book from what Alan had planned, though it did draw on portions of his and Toni's interviews. Bessie soon tired of performing alone, however, and wanted to work with a singing group from the Sea Islands the way she had done before. Alan was against the idea, believing that she was such a strong and compelling personality that she needed no one else with her, and he paid for her to take guitar lessons to learn to accompany herself. Without telling Alan, however, she formed her own group, the Sea Island Singers, and was booked on the West Coast by an agent. When he finally heard the group, Alan was convinced she was right, and he had brochures made up, wrote to colleges, and began booking them himself. Bessie and the group moved in with him and worked on how they would present themselves to audiences. They became popular performers at folk festivals, joined in on civil rights demonstrations, and remained together for the next ten years.

CHAPTER 16

To Hear the World in a Grain of Sand

When British decolonization began to accelerate in the Lesser Antilles in the West Indies in the late 1950s, and the governments of Jamaica and Trinidad were seeking to create a federation of all these newly independent islands, Alan recalled his stays in the Caribbean in 1935 and 1937 and the plans he once had for doing comparative studies of how Africans had adapted their music and culture to life in the New World. The islands had been colonized and fought over by the English, French, Dutch, and Spanish, with several different nations sometimes ruling the same small island at different points in its history. But rather than completely surrendering to the cultures imposed by the colonialists, their enslaved African residents used whatever materials they encountered to reshape their own traditions and craft new cultures adapted to their own needs. Some of these local creations had become internationally popular over the last century: in dance alone, there was the habanera, mambo, fire dance, limbo, conga, biguine, rhumba, and calypso, all of which had caught the world's imagination.

Alan, however, felt there were even more engaging and beautiful dances and musics still to be discovered on the smaller, less heralded islands. To him it was the usual story of powerful media determining who would get the attention and rewards. He thought it might be possible to identify the distinctive qualities of each island, but also to determine the characteristics that all the islands shared, and which could form the basis of a new union. So in 1962 he asked the Rockefeller Foundation to extend his funding to allow him to do a summer-long survey of the music of the Caribbean, and Philip Sherlock, a founder of the University of the West Indies and himself a folklorist, gave him permission to base his research there.

The agreement he made with the university provided that he pay singers and musicians a day's wages for recording. Alan listened to each of the prospective contributors for a minute or two and decided whether to record them or not, but they were paid even if they were not chosen. His idea was that all the recordings would be deposited at the university, which would also handle the rights to the songs. Each recorded performer was given a contract turning over his or her West

Indian radio and archive rights but promising an advance plus royalties if the recordings were ever used commercially. The university's policy was to allow the performer, the collector, and the university each a third of any royalties. Vanguard Records had showed interest in issuing four records from the project, and Alan had promised them an opportunity to review the tapes. In addition, he sought out other collectors who had worked in the West Indies, urging them to place their tapes in the university's archive as well and to agree to a similar sharing arrangement, in hopes that the archive would earn enough money to begin its own collecting activities.

Despite all efforts to make the arrangements clear, some confusion over money arose almost as soon as the recording began. A few performers had taken it for granted that their recordings would be sold, and soon began to wonder where their royalty advances where. The Rockefeller Foundation was upset to learn that its money might be used for private gain, even if it was the singers who would benefit. Juggling the interests of all the parties involved became part of every recording project.

Two days after Alan and Toni arrived in Trinidad on April 23 they began to record, and continued for three months. Alan often worked eighteen-hour days in the summer heat of the tropics. To enable people to hear their own performances as quickly as possible, he brought along two large speakers so that they could be set up outdoors, and these had to be dragged from car to beach, through rain forests, and city streets, along with a heavy tape recorder, several mikes, mixer, amplifier, and even batteries, since some of the smaller islands' electricity was unstable and not always available. With so much talent and such a variety of styles and cultures to be covered, and working on such a tight deadline in locations where he had never been, he was forced to resort to the old folklorists' practice of counting on local people to find suitable singers and have them ready when he arrived. In Trinidad and Tobago he relied on J. D. Elder, a man of remarkable abilities who had been a grade school teacher in his youth, and later became a community development officer who organized violent boys' gangs in Port of Spain into steel band players in the early post–World War II days of the oil drum's rise to the status of musical instrument. When these bands became supporters and unofficial bodyguards of Dr. Eric Williams, who was running to be Trinidad's first president following colonial rule, Elder's fame as a politically savvy folklorist and scholar spread and enabled him to organize communities and help develop local cultural events and festivals that raised awareness of the island's history.

Lomax would arrive in a village or small town to see a line of performers whom Elder had found waiting for him. Noise was a problem for recording anywhere in Trinidad, with tropical birds, roosters, and dogs ever present, and any kind of music would instantly draw a crowd. Most of the music of the Caribbean was normally performed for social occasions, and because the etiquette of West Indian music allowed for maximum audience participation, whether supportive or combative, keeping audiences quiet during recording was a constant worry. The sessions were held in dance halls, rum shops, and school buildings, but only where there was neither air conditioning nor fans to interfere. The heat was devastating to both the crew and the performers.

Trinidad at times felt like New York City, at others like Calcutta, Hong Kong, or Lagos, but like the creolized English spoken there, one cultural tradition flowed into the other, often unpredictably. With a population drawn from the Carib Indians, Sephardic Jews, Africa, India, Lebanon, Syria, China, and Europe, cultural interchanges and creolization were standard operating procedure, as the shop signs gave witness: the Bonny Lassie Chinese Restaurant, the Philadelphia Occult Book Store, Blackman, the Bespoke Tailor. Walking down the streets of Port of Spain one might see three men on some steps singing a calypso while one of them kept rhythm with a spoon on a beer bottle. Up the street a steel band could be rehearsing, the leader sporting an RAF flyer's mustache, his back straight, walking between them as they played an aria from *Carmen*, saying nothing but occasionally pointing to the correct note on an errant player's pan.

Alan had already learned a great deal about calypso from Trinidadians in New York, but now he was being led to older people who could connect him to the genre's history—to stick fighters, those who were once considered part of the criminal world, who years ago had songs called *kalindas* sung about their feats, while women's choral songs were sung between the fights called *carisos*, the closest form to the modern calypso. Jacob Elder knew the history of Trinidadian music and the politics that it reflected, and he was aware that behind seemingly carefree songs was a record of slavery and that every song sung publicly was a cry of victory. There were bands and songs of every variety—tamboo-bamboo groups who played tubes of bamboo of different lengths by tapping them on the ground; Spanish string bands influenced by Venezuela and other islands of Spanish heritage; calypsos, with rhythms and melodies similar to the *son* of Cuba; Carnival parade bands; bongo songs for wakes, dancing, and working; and *Hosain* drummers of East Indian background. And then there was the music of the many religious groups—the songs and rhythms of Shango, derived from West Africa, the trancelike foursquare rhythms of Spiritual Baptists, and the hymns of Christian churches that were much like those in the United States.

The work seemed endless, and when Alan began to realize that the recording in Trinidad alone would take at least a month and a half to complete, he knew he would have to work faster and harder. The accelerated pace sometimes left singers grumbling that these sessions were not the social events at which they were used to performing, but rather a form of work. Nor was this the romance of folklore collecting that Toni had likely anticipated, and she, along with the crew working with Alan, had to take orders and keep up the pace that he set. He would later say that he had never wanted her to come on the trip.

While they were still in Trinidad, CBS Television called to tell Alan that they were developing a new show called *Accent*, in which the host, poet John Ciardi, would roam across the United States in search of interesting locations and ideas that would enable him to explore local culture. One of the first episodes was to have as its subject the St. Simons Colored Chanters, a singing group from the Sea Islands that included Bessie Jones. Alan was asked to serve as music coordinator and an onscreen commentator. The pay was good, and it would require only one week of work, so he left an angry Toni in Trinidad and headed for New York and Georgia. The episode in which he appeared aired on June 14, 1962, and he presented the people of the Sea Islands as having the purest folk culture to be found anywhere in the South.

In New York he learned that a review committee from the National Institute of Mental Health, to which he had applied for major funding, wanted to come to the city to talk to him and his working group on June 11. After six hours of questioning he was certain that they would reject his grant proposal, and he caught a plane to meet Toni in Martinique, the next stop in the Caribbean project.

Guadeloupe and Martinique, with their long history of French colonialism, their status as overseas departments of France, and their language of French Créole, were almost as complex and rich with song as Trinidad, and Alan managed to collect a wide sample of Martinique's music in only three days. He recorded the songs that accompanied *danmyé* (or *ladja*), the local form of martial arts that was similar to *capoeira* in Brazil and *mani* in Cuba, songs of collective work groups, and the tales and songs used at wakes and funerals. But dance music ruled on these islands, and two eighteenth-century dances, the *bèlé* and the *kwadril* (both of which had creolized from French court dances and African dances and music), were still performed in the countryside. In Fort-de-France, Martinique's capital, the biguine, a local creation, and the *mazouk* and the *valse Créole*, two nineteenth-century dances with European elements, were popular. The dances were fascinating revelations to those interested in the evolution of black dance in the Americas, but it was the music of the biguine that was the real surprise. With its instrumentation of clarinet, trombone, violin (and sometimes trumpet), and rhythm section, and its improvised weave of polyphonic melody lines, it bore a striking resemblance to Creole jazz in New Orleans, especially as played by bands like those of Kid Ory, Albert Nicholas, and Paul Barbarin. Since boat connections between Martinique and New Orleans ended in 1903 after the Mt. Pelée volcano erupted, the two forms of jazz would have developed independently, which confirmed Alan's view that it was the Caribbean qualities of New Orleans—the mix of African and European cultures, the Catholic calendar with its festivals and parades, the rich bar and gambling life, and the social organizations that underlay Creole life—that enabled the creation of its particular form of jazz in the southern United States.

Most of the rest of June was spent in Dominica, an island with two creolized languages, French and English, but also with a strong Carib Indian tradition. In July he spent a day in Guadeloupe, where he recorded East Indian music, as he had also done in Trinidad. At that time anthropologists and folklorists paid little attention to the East Indian presence, and were seemingly unaware that their population was growing rapidly. St. Kitts, Anguilla, and St. Bartholomew were covered in six days, and then they headed to Nevis, which despite its small size—eight miles by five—had a collective repertoire of music and verbal art without equal anywhere in the Caribbean. They allotted a week to record there with the help of Roger Abrahams, a folklorist who was staying on the island at the time.

As Toni was leaving for New York in July to return for fall graduate study, Anna (Anne was now calling herself Anna) joined her father and the two of them went on to St. Lucia and Carriacou. On tiny Carriacou they experienced a tradition that once again confirmed Alan's belief that the lesser-known islands possessed great musical traditions. There, among a population of only a few thousand, could be found songs that reflected the history of the island and that of the people who came there. The most remarkable part of Carriacou's cultural repertoire was the Big Drum Dance, a ritual practiced by families and fishermen's groups that celebrated and reaffirmed their history, lineage, and relationships by keeping alive songs and dances associated with nine African nations. When Lomax and Anna first came to the island, a fête was arranged for them, and they, too, were integrated into Carriacou life. After spending a week in Grenada, they returned to Trinidad in mid-August to complete arrangements for the storage of the recordings. Alan and Toni were not divorced until 1967, but their marriage was effectively over by the end of 1962.

Everywhere he went in the West Indies, Alan paid special attention to children's games, in part because they played a key role in introducing children to their culture's sense of social life, but also because of the creativity with which they managed to draw elements from various cultures and reassemble the parts in fresh configurations. In a book that came out of this work, *Brown Girl in the Ring: An Anthology of Song Games from the Eastern Caribbean*, Alan noted that the words to girls' game songs provided them lessons for life: they were sung in a language closer to standard English than to the local dialect (what was often called *patois* on most islands), giving the girls the basis for social mobility; they also served as preparation for what they needed to know for courtship to come.

The result of the summer's work was a collection of recordings that made the

West Indies one of the best-documented areas in the world. Alan encouraged J. D. Elder to continue the work they had begun by entering graduate school in the Folklore Program at the University of Pennsylvania, where he earned a Ph.D., then became a professor at Temple University, and went on to be elected a senator of Trinidad and Tobago.

In 1962 Anna entered Bard College as a first-year student. She found herself unhappily in the midst of faculty and students who thought of themselves as bohemians, even though they often came from money. She had lived the bohemian life and wanted more stability, and returned to New York City several months later. Anna continued to live with her father and work in New York for the next three years.

That fall, Alan was given the title of Director of the Cantometrics and Choreometrics Research Project, and Research Associate in the Department of Anthropology and Center for the Social Sciences at Columbia University, a title he would hold for the next twenty-seven years. Impressive as it sounded, it was a job he had only as long as he could financially support his own research. This meant that he would have to spend much of his time fund-raising and would never have the leisure and security that a tenured academic enjoys to conduct and publish his research. He was never assured of having enough money from his grants to even make a living, and often had to return to lecturing and singing in colleges like his father.

As the Rockefeller Grant was ending, he was still hoping that the National Institute of Mental Health would provide him the funds he needed to carry him several years into his project. What he wanted was a team consisting of a folklorist, an ethnologist, a musicologist, a linguist, a laryngologist, and a psychologist, all of whom would analyze a sample of about sixteen hundred tape-recorded songs from two hundred culture areas. Using the Human Relations Area Files (an anthropological database of ethnographies written on hundreds of different societies worldwide, with data on some seven hundred culture traits such as kinship terminology, forms of marriage, and type of economy), they would verify the hypothesis that "music was a simple communications technique which could give information about the emotional shape of a number of extremely important social psychological patterns in any given society." The research group would first test this on smaller and economically less complex societies such as peasants and hunter-gatherers, and then move on to modern societies like the United States. "Indeed," Alan wrote, hinting at future results, "the principal investigator has already made certain experiments in listening to popular songs over the radio. They indicate that singers such as Frank Sinatra, who generally portray love as a source of sadness and frustration, favor the mid-to-high front vowel parameters, whereas Negro rock-and-roll singers prefer a much lower, back-oriented parameter. . . . The indication is that the material is picking the singers and, through them, the audiences. It is planned, during the research period, to apply this technique to the Hit Parade itself, to see whether statistically verifiable traits can be predicted, thus making the vowel and consonant preférence pattern indicator into a thoroughly scientific tool."

He also proposed making serious use of the data folklorists had collected. "The great achievement of folklore up to the present has been the assemblage of an enormous mass of texts, of tunes and tales of folk and primitive sources. Up until the present, very little use has been made of this material for scientific study simply because no set of spinal hypotheses have been available." In *Folk Songs of North America* he had made a start by dividing North American folk music into regions in thematic terms (which translated into stylistic ones—for example the "solo, strident-voiced, high-pitched, tension-filled" singing of the Calvinist backwoods of the South).

Cantometrics would make cross-cultural comparison possible, but "far more significant . . . is the possibility that this objective system will make it possible for musicians and cultural administrators from all over the world to assess the strong and the weak points of their own musical systems in a fairly objective fashion. This should affect the development of educational systems and the patterning of communications systems as far as music is concerned in any given area. Not only that, but it should make it possible for Western European nations to relate their entire cultural framework more positively to the cultural systems they encountered in the non-industrial areas of the world. For these native cultures themselves, the presentation of the objective characteristics of their indigenous music should provide a cultural keel for future planning and development."

There was such boldness and daring in these proposals that some scientists must have thought he was overreaching. But Alan was working like a dynamo, he had early successes to point to, and he presented his work in a hot but eloquent style that suggested he was the next big thing. Plus, he was using advanced statistical methods like multivariant analysis to understand art, something no one had seen before. He was, in other words, the sort of researcher who could waken bored NIMH grant administrators from their muggy Bethesda afternoon drowsiness.

Though Alan was never bashful about what he saw as his successes, he also never ducked criticism from those he trusted, and even sought it out. In a discussion he had with Margaret Mead in October 1963, for example, she bracingly predicted the kind of criticisms to which his study would be subjected: the samples were too small; there were exceptions to the statistical portraits he would be developing; and they had chosen the wrong parameters of music to consider. She suggested that he anticipate them by working in smaller areas, with greater help from specialists in those areas. But it was too late, he explained: he had already decided to go for the whole world, and that meant that he would never have a large sample of musics from everywhere—he would have to count on finding ways to use the samples he had in such a way that they would be truly representative.

When the National Institute of Mental Health awarded him a six-year grant to run from 1963 to 1969, he assembled a staff that included Roswell Rudd, an avant-garde jazz trombonist and graduate of Yale University with roots in Dixieland music who would serve as the archivist; Joan Halifax, who would work with him on the analysis of the verbal content of song; Norman Berkowitz, who would be the computer programmer and statistician; Victor Grauer the ethnomusicologist; Edwin Erickson and Barbara Ayres the anthropologists; and Conrad Arensberg, who would codirect the project with him.

The first findings of their work were published by Victor Grauer in a short article in the journal *Ethnomusicology*. In it they explained that they had hypothesized that characteristic performance traits would be found in most of the songs in the samples from each of the style areas that Alan had sketched out, and in fact they had found these features grouped into distinct clusters that defined European, African, Bardic (the Muslim Mediterranean, India, and high-culture Asia), semi-Bardic, and African style areas. It was a modest and very preliminary finding, Grauer admitted, but it suggested they were on the right path.

Alan never saw any incongruity between his scholarly work and his public persona, and the Newport Folk Festival was at that time the one place where he could bring together his life's work with his political views. When the 1961 jazz festival ended in drunken youth crashing through gates and knocking down fences, both festivals were banned from Newport for the next two years. But George Wein did not give up, and with Pete Seeger's help he got them approved by the city of Newport in time for the 1963 dates. For that year an even larger folk festival was planned, one that would better balance name performers with the folk musicians. The board decided that each of the performers would receive fifty dollars for an appearance, and all of them would be housed in a rented mansion that would serve as a temporary dormitory. But folk musicians, unlike their jazz counterparts, were not accustomed to traveling long distances to perform before big audiences, and were uncomfortable staying in strange houses. Nor were all of them accustomed to being placed on equal terms with members of another race, so that sharing the festival's facilities—such as the seating on a festival bus, when many of them came from areas of the South where people of color sat in the back—became a test for many.

The civil rights movement changed the tone of the festival that year, with singers and organizers from the Student Nonviolent Coordinating Committee present as performers and activists. SNCC was a younger, more assertive wing of the movement, a group whose members had put themselves on the line in the sit-ins and the Freedom Riders. They worked close to the rural black populace—registering voters, running literacy programs, and advising them of their rights under the law—and unlike the Southern Christian Leadership Conference, they were drawn to the expressive power of black folk tradition. On the first night of the festival, their Freedom Singers performed the songs that had seen them through violence and demonstrations in the South, and on the second night SNCC led a march through Newport and staged rallies supporting an upcoming march on Washington. The final night of the festival was brought to a close by Bob Dylan singing some of his most political numbers, followed by Peter, Paul, and Mary with their version of Dylan's "Blowin' in the Wind." Finally, Pete Seeger, Dylan, Joan Baez, Theodore Bikel, and the Freedom Singers all joined together for "We Shall Overcome."

As 1964, the fourth year of the festival, approached, the board added Mike Seeger and Alan, two of the advocates of folk music most concerned with the state of tradition. Alan's first step was to write a long letter to his fellow board members expressing his dissatisfaction with the way the Newport Foundation was dispensing grants. The heart of his complaint was a familiar one with him: the singers of the American folk song revival knew little about performance, and as a result the quality of their singing was still at a very low level. Style is difficult to learn, he granted, because it can't be written down and can only be learned in part from sound recordings. Yet style was where the real meaning of folk song lay, in its verbal, musical, and physical dimensions. It was the reason for song having survived along with the human species. For him it was about more than the survival of an art, it was part of the continuance of the various ways of being human.

He believed that young urban singers would benefit by learning directly from the best performers. This meant searching the entire country for outstanding local singers and musicians, and then preparing them for travel and performance on a scale far greater than they had ever experienced, as well as making sure that they received the respect and care that would enable their artistry to be both understood and appreciated. This was not a task for a talent scout or theatrical agent, since it took a scholar of folklore to find and recognize local artists, some of whom were lonely performers, perhaps ignored even by their own people who had put their traditions behind them in a quest for a better life. Alan's own work with Lead Belly in the house in Connecticut was the model he had in mind. In a note in the 1964 festival program, he seemed to be speaking to the festival's promoters as much as he was to its audience when he wrote that he hoped the festival would be a triumph for these performers:

> For most of them it is their only outlet. Furthermore, despite the fact that they are not all "smooth" entertainers from the point of view of city audiences, they are our only source for learning the art of American folk music, itself. Their more relaxed way of performing, which is sometimes mistaken for lack of accomplishment, is often simply a matter of another style and other standards. Their art lies hidden in these stylistic differences. It consists of more than the words, the tune and the fun of singing. It is, perhaps, our most important, serious and original contribution to world musical culture. These performers are its only carriers and they deserve to be listened to with respect and love and delight.

Lomax also thought that the Newport Foundation should help performers with their own traditions and audiences. The models for this kind of work were Guy Carawan and his wife, Candie, who had recently moved to Johns Island, off of Charleston, South Carolina, where they were helping organize Sea Island singers to present their own local cultural and music festivals. Alan had just returned from a trip there in October 1963, where he and the Carawans had set up weekly get-togethers for local people to explore their local repertoire, sing songs, tell stories, and prepare younger people to carry on their traditions. He would return again at Christmas in 1963 and write an account of the first Sea Island Folk Festival for the *Charleston News and Courier*. One of the first Newport Foundation grants went to the Carawans for that work.

Alan proposed that the festival hire three staff to travel throughout the year to find local artists, work with them, and make it possible for them to perform at home, at regional festivals, and at Newport. There were those on the board who wondered why they themselves weren't considered competent enough to identify such talent when they saw it, and they resisted the idea. But Alan pressed on doggedly until they agreed to hire one person to spend two months a year at the job at a salary of $2,500. At the time, folklore students, blues aficionados, and folkniks were all crisscrossing the country on their own quests to find authentic folk artists, but Alan knew it would be difficult to get anyone of quality to interrupt his or her own life for so little money and under such short notice, so he sought the help of scholars like Charles Seeger and David McAllester to back him, and counted on board members Jean Ritchie and Mike Seeger to support him.

The board eventually gave in and agreed to spend $5,000 to hire Ralph Rinzler, one of the founders of the Friends of Old Time Music and a member of the revivalist group the Greenbriar Boys, to spend three months a year on the road. Rinzler was passionate about folk music and knew local traditions better than almost anyone else in the country. Over the next few months he traveled twelve thousand miles through eight states, Nova Scotia, and French Canada, visiting many of the people with whom Alan had worked, but also finding many new Cajun performers, cowboy singers, and some of the least-known religious singing groups.

The difference that Alan's planning and Rinzler's work made was evident on the 1964 festival's opening night. A "Concert of Traditional Music" introduced the audience to a wide array of traditional performers, and set a tone of discovery that continued throughout the festival. Alan wrote the script and narrated for a stage filled with white and black singers and musicians. "This is an evening of point-counterpoint," he announced, as he began to explain how white and black performers' styles affected one another and shaped the different genres of American folk song. And for the next four hours (most of which were plagued by rain), he held the huge expanse of song together. The performers ranged from Seamus Ennis, brought over to show the Irish style, to Bessie Jones up from the Sea Islands of Georgia; there were hammer dulcimer players, cowboys, Appalachian singers and Cajun musicians, panpipe players, work songs sung to woodcutting, a square dance with fiddlers from different traditions, a jug band, loggers' songs, a frontier playparty demonstration, and rural and urban blues. Mixed in with these performers over the next three nights were Joan Baez, Bob Dylan, Johnny Cash, and other popular stars, and the festival went to some effort to tell the audiences that the singers they had come to see had gotten a lot of their songs from these unknown performers.

But the tension in the festival that year was less between the folk and the media stars than between the public's perception of folk song and what was now being called the protest song. Given the politics of the times, the broadside or topical song workshops attracted a great deal of attention, and Ralph Rinzler was called upon to explain to reporters that protest, too, was traditional, though the examples he cited dated back only to the Depression. Alan, on the other hand, would sometimes add that "every folk song in the Western world was a protest song"—even, and maybe especially, love songs.

That year at the festival Alan met Joan Halifax, a twenty-two-year-old just out of college in New Orleans, who was working with George Pickow's film crew. Alan had just ended an affair with Pamela Gerstman, a relationship that had gotten him into the news five months earlier as a co-respondent in divorce proceedings. Halifax was drawn to the civil rights cause, anthropology, and the work he was doing. They were both involved in the antiwar movement, which was locked together with the struggle for racial justice, and together they participated in demonstrations and rallies.

When it was announced that the International Anthropological and Ethnological Congress would be held in Moscow in 1964, Alan saw an opportunity to gather copies of the recordings he had never been able to obtain when he was assembling the *World Library* recordings in the 1950s. With the help of ethnomusicologist Anna Rudneva, he went through the archives of Moscow and Leningrad and made copies of recordings of some nineteen groups and nationalities. He also managed to record ten hours of artists from Azerbaijan, Georgia, Siberia, and Russia by himself. On his way back from Russia he visited the village of Dragus in Transylvania and recorded some boys and girls and older women singing dance songs, love songs, and lullabies.

The Penguin Book of American Folk Songs, a book that Alan had been working on in England, was published that year with piano arrangements by Elizabeth Poston, a composer and pianist who had studied with Ralph Vaughan Williams, the compiler of *The Penguin Book of English Folk Songs,* with which it was paired. Alan's compilation was largely made up of songs from the previous Lomax books, with an emphasis on how to perform them in the style of the regions from which they originated. When Pete Seeger reviewed it for *Sing Out!,* he praised it and the Lomaxes' good taste in music. ("Collectors were looking for the oldest songs they could find, the Lomaxes were looking for the *best* they could find.")

Ray Birdwhistell had suggested to Alan when they first met that he should begin his studies with dance rather than music, since dance was a more basic component of human communication than music, more primal and preverbal than song, and was more directly connected to everyday work and the social movements of the body. He also recommended that Lomax should use the Laban system in order to compare dance styles. Rudolf von Laban, an early modern dancer, had devised a method of notation that was meant to be free of language and any particular form or school of dance, and could serve as a universal means of describing other forms of motion as well. His system involved the weight, space, flow, time, energy, and effort involved in the motions of dance; it was more concerned with how people moved than it was with what movements they made; and it did not deal with what the dances meant to particular dancers. As Alan got deeper into the comparative study of music he was obliged to pay more attention to differences in the way that singers and musicians used their bodies; dance seemed to be an extension of the same movements.

In 1965 Lomax added two specialists in the Laban method to his staff: Irmgard Bartenieff and Forrestine Paulay, and they set out with him to build an archive of the world's dance films, a far more difficult project than creating a song archive, since fewer of the world's dances had been documented. Once again, there were no archives and world collections of such films, and channels had to be found or made through which to borrow or buy copies of whatever existed. For the next eight years they would write hundreds of letters and travel to distant parts of the world until they eventually amassed 2,138 samples of film. Meanwhile, they would have to code and analyze much of what they found as quickly as possible, because copying everything they borrowed was too expensive. Progress was slow in all of their work because they had to enter data onto punch cards by the thousands and feed them into Columbia's IBM 360 mainframe computer.

After they had watched a number of the films, they realized they needed to add to the Laban system a number of categories that could be quantified and used by nonspecialists to relate body movements to other cultural behaviors and then compare them cross-culturally. The system they devised and named choreometrics was attempting what Margaret Mead called the first ethological study of all the world's peoples, a form of natural history observation before then reserved only for the study of animals.

What they came up with did not chart a step-by-step analysis such that one could use it to learn particular dances. Instead, the coding concerned the levels at which the body signals data to other individuals such as age, gender, occupation, health, and cultural affiliation by means of body attitude or stance, the body parts most often articulated, the shape of the path that movement takes, the patterns that link body and limbs, and the dynamic qualities of dance. Lomax and his staff found that these patterns enabled them to define dance style areas that were analogous to those of song style traditions. The American Indian area, for example, was characterized by the body acting as a single unit, with the whole leg and the whole arm articulated, and by movement in one dimension. Sub-Saharan Africans, by contrast, used their bodies as both one and two units, with the head, face, chest, shoulders, leg, and arm articulated, and by movement in one, two, and three dimensions. It was such characteristics that served to identify an individual with his or her culture and made it possible for members of a culture to act in synchrony.

They quickly expanded the work to include films of representative nondance motions and work patterns of the world's peoples, as it became apparent that all physical behavior in a culture is shaped by standards of behavior that are passed on from generation to generation. Margaret Mead had long before shown that appropriate spatial relations, timing, stance, and the like were learned very early in life, nonverbally, through parents, siblings, and playmates. Dance appeared to be a heightened, more expressive and more conscious form of everyday movement in a culture, much as song seemed to be a heightened form of speech. When the coded profiles of dance were correlated to other cultural domains, the researchers found parallels between the frequency of finger and hand articulation in dance and the complexity of a culture's principal productive activities. The degree and nature of synchrony in dance pointed to the synchrony necessary for community subsistence tasks. They also found that the organization and makeup of dancing groups reflected the nature of gender and social relations in a society. Overall, dance was seen not as a repetition of everyday motions and postures but as a novel and sometimes even distorted rearrangement of them. Dance reinforces human adaptive patterns, and thus is an indicator of social and cultural evolution.

In the summer of 1965 the Newport Folk Festival staged a preview concert in New York City's Central Park. With the pressure increasing within the civil rights movement in response to the death of Malcolm X, the clashes at Selma, Alabama, and mass arrests of demonstrators in Chicago, Alan, who produced and hosted part of the concert, wanted to use it to bring New York audiences closer to the black South and to remind them that there was a long cultural history behind the events they only heard about on nightly TV news reports. The performers included Reverend Gary Davis, the Sea Island Singers, Mabel Hillary, and the Ed Young and Lonnie Young fife and drum band, all of whom were encouraged to take the time onstage to comment and elaborate on their songs and dances.

When the festival opened in Newport the following day, it played to a new kind of audience. Five years earlier, members of Yale's singing clubs might turn up, driving off the ferry in Chrysler Town and Country cars, joining serious students from the University of Michigan's Folklore Society, and any number of Ivy League and Seven Sisters strays, comfortable in their identification with the Kingston Trio's striped summer shirts, chinos, and tidy stage manners. This year, however, it seemed as though refugees and hobos were moving through the land: they came shaggy-haired, with backpacks and sleeping bags, banjos and guitars slung over their shoulders, thumbing their way to the island, every one of them potentially a folk musician, a blues singer, a revolutionary, a rock star, just one of the new folk.

By the time the festival closed, the talk was all about Bob Dylan's turn to amplified, pop-oriented music, but the key event may actually have been the Friday afternoon workshop called "Blues: Origins and Offshoots," featuring Ed and Lonnie Young's fife and drum quartet from Mississippi, a Texas prison work song group, blues singers Son House, Josh White, and Mance Lipscomb, the McGhee Brothers, Bill Monroe and the Bluegrass Boys, and Chicago's Willie Dixon and Memphis Slim representing city blues and boogie-woogie. The daytime workshops had typically never drawn big crowds, but the recent rediscoveries of blues musicians from the 1920s and 1930s assured a large turnout for this one. Alan saw it as a chance both to celebrate the blues as homegrown American art song form in its own right and to place it in the context of the world of folk song that he had discovered outside the United States. But the crowds of young people who had only recently discovered the blues were far more interested in a few of the singers just up from the South and in hearing Mississippi John Hurt sing the naughty "Candy Man" than they were in comparative musicology. Robert Shelton of the *New York Times* reflected the impatience of this nouveau-blues crowd when he described

Alan's role in the workshop as an "articulate, illuminating, fluent, but sometimes maddeningly pedantic host-narrator. Likening the blues to the Italian *stornella*, the Spanish *copla*, and the Mexican *corrido*, Mr. Lomax described the Afro-American blues and its variations as 'our most pervasive popular musical form.'"

Yet it was the conclusion of the workshop that received the most attention. The Paul Butterfield Blues Band, a group of Chicago black bluesmen and young whites, all of whom played amplified instruments, had been late additions to the festival roster, and Alan was not happy with their taking part in this workshop. As they began setting up amps and mikes, he introduced them by musing about whether they would be able to play the blues with all that equipment. When Alan came off the stage, their manager, Albert Grossman, told him that he had given them "a real chicken-shit introduction." Shoves and pushes followed, leading to a rolling-in-the-dirt confrontation between the two big men, who had to be separated by an even bigger man, Sam Lay, the drummer for the band. Later that day the festival board was called into emergency session and voted to ban Grossman from the grounds. It was only when George Wein warned them that if Grossman was ousted the performers he managed—Dylan; Odetta; Peter, Paul, and Mary; the Kweskin Jug Band—might leave, too, that the board backed off their decision.

Bob Dylan's fabled breakthrough into electronics two nights later was not as dramatic as legend would have it, and although some catcalls were mixed with the cheers from the audience, it hardly constituted the makings of an aesthetic riot. Among the older board members—Seeger, Bikel, and Lomax—it was the volume that was objectionable, as it was possibly the loudest sound that they and most of the audience had ever experienced. The story of Pete Seeger's anger reaching the point at which he threatened to cut the cables to the sound system with an axe was apocryphal. That legend may have started when real threats were made against the sound system that afternoon. Alan had asked Texas folklorist Mack McCormick to find a Texas prison gang to bring up to Newport to sing work songs, but the Texas attorney general would not allow it, so McCormick rounded up a group of ex-convicts. Since they had never performed together in front of an audience, much less a microphone, McCormick wanted time to get them used to the stage before the concert. But Bob Dylan's electric band had been rehearsing for some time and refused to leave. "I was trying to tell Dylan, we need the stage," McCormick said. "He continued to ignore me. So I went over to the junction box and pulled out the cords. Then he listened."

For Alan, it was not just the volume of the Dylan band that disturbed him. It was more that, beginning at Newport, Dylan had captured the audience for folk music and then taken it away from the folk. Later Alan would say that Dylan wanted to create a folk music for the urban middle class, which wasn't a bad idea, but just seemed boring to him.

If there were those in the festival who had dreamed of an alternate musical universe, a folk utopia, it had almost reached its end: the country was now awash in the early stages of folk-rock, as it would now be called, and the world of the festival was splintering again, back to those who would ride the pop wave and those who would now learn to survive in coffeehouses and church basements, or just return home to anonymity once again. Some of the performers' salaries were climbing to the breaking point, with administrative costs for a large festival trailing close behind, and what was left for the foundation to spend on grants was slipping away.

After Dylan's shift to pop the festival board once again pledged to draw back from its focus on spectaculars to reaffirm a belief in a program that would treat all the musicians and performers equally. Ralph Rinzler and the Seeger brothers made certain that a 1966 festival would not be limited to music, but would also display the material culture of the folk—crafts, furniture, toys and clothing, anything that brought the daily lives of rural singers to the audience. Dance workshops, a Sunday morning religious program, and food preparation all now contributed to the new meaning of a folk festival.

Alan was the designated writer for many of the scripts for the programs, as well as a producer, and those roles allowed him to bring to the festival the best of the performers he knew from his fieldwork, and also to create a context for the music to help the audience understand the role that music played in their lives. One of his key ideas was to present the musicians in competition with one another, in the belief that it would bring the best out of them. When this idea worked, it worked extraordinarily well, as when the Swan Silvertones met the Dixie Hummingbirds in a battle of gospel quartets, something they had done in Sunday afternoon church challenges across the country. The concept ground to a halt, however, with the "blues contest," its awkward "judges" seated at the side of the stage. The contestants were Son House, Bukka White, and Skip James, three great singers who could not have been more different from one another. Son House resisted engaging in a competition by drinking himself into a semi-stupor, singing one song, getting up, and seating himself at the side of the stage facing away from the audience. The judges carefully avoided declaring any of the three as the winner.

The board permitted Alan to film some parts this festival, including behind-the-scenes activities in some of the festival buildings, and in a simulated "juke joint"—an informal, intimate performance space improvised by Lomax, where he wanted artists to feel at ease so that the music would flow more naturally. Two of these filmed sessions, titled *Devil Got My Woman: Blues at Newport 1966*, and *Delta Blues/Cajun Two-Step*, featured older African American musicians, as well as Cajuns. A third film, *Billy in the Lowlands: Old Time Music from the*

Newport Folk Festival, 1966, focused on older white performers, people like fiddler Clark Kissinger, Kilby Snow, Jimmie Driftwood, the Coon Creek Girls, Tex Logan, and others who were known only to the musicians who brought them along for the trip.

At the end of 1966 Alan and Ralph Rinzler began to object to what they saw as George Wein's dominance in planning the festival. While Wein knew jazz and how to organize a large-scale event, they pointed out, folk music was something new to him and was his limitation. So when a deficit turned up for the year 1966, Ralph and Alan called for an outside audit of the finances, a move that Wein took to be an accusation that he had misspent the money. The outside audit cleared Wein, but Alan's interest in the festival also began to wane as he realized that it would never be what he had imagined it could, and he moved on to other projects.

To those who knew him casually, Alan might have seemed to be prospering, what with research grants, public lectures, and an expanding series of films and recordings. But he was in fact often operating without money. In February 1965, he and Joan moved to an apartment at 207 West 98th Street, where the landlord threatened to force him to leave for using the premises for what the owner asserted was a full-time business. Alan went to court and through a series of charges and countercharges won the right to continue living there. They moved shortly afterwards to 820 West End Avenue, but Alan fell behind several months in rent, for which his landlord had a dispossession notice served. Once again he challenged a landlord in court, and this time it turned out that he had been charged more than the city allowed under rent control laws and he was granted a delay in being evicted. He meanwhile moved his office into an apartment at 215 West 98th Street.

The long-overdue book he and Pete Seeger had put together with Woody Guthrie years before was finally published under the title *Hard Hitting Songs for Hard-Hit People.* But the two volumes of English and American folk songs he had promised Holt, Rinehart and Winston five years before were never finished. He did, however, manage to finish *Folk Song Style and Culture* that year, the first full presentation of the findings of the cantometrics research, a collection and expansion of the talks given at the American Association for the Advancement of Science's meetings two years earlier when he took the staff of the cantometrics project there to present a daylong report entitled "Frontiers of Anthropology: Cantometrics and Culture." Alan had been under pressure to get a major publication out to satisfy those who had funded the research and convince them that the projects were worthy of continued support, and this book was published before he was completely ready. Priced at seventeen dollars, it was too expensive to reach a wide readership, but it did serve as a good introduction to what Alan and his colleagues had accomplished thus far.

When he wrote a proposal to the National Institute of Mental Health for another four years of research support, he explained the importance of the book and showed the directions he next wanted to take the research: to adapt his methods to the study of virtually all the arts, and to make them of practical value.

> The first period of cross-cultural style research showed that: (1) patterns of song and dance behavior vary in orderly ways cross-culturally (2) produced a taxonomy of culture with both evolutionary and historical implications (3) song and dance patterns are correlated with basic features of social structure. These results were summarized in *Folk Song Style and Culture*. . . . In the next phase of research, we will define the main culture style areas of the world in terms of performance variables and social structure variables. We aim toward a minimum set of style factors that will be diagnostic for any given cultural situation. The culture style hypothesis will be tested in studies of two other communication systems: speaking and the visual arts. A cross-cultural library of "speaking style" will be studied by a psycholinguist to produce a cross-cultural typology. The choreometrics team, in collaboration with a scholar of the arts, will attempt a first rating system for the visual arts. Computer techniques will test similarity of cross-cultural variation of dance, song, speaking and design in relation to the variation of culture. The summative and normative patterns of culture style, thus derived, can contribute to an ethology of human culture. . . .
>
> The purpose of our research into cultural style has been to provide a means by which the cultural situation of any human group; can be quickly evaluated. Many governments have been concerned about the future of minority cultures and have attempted to initiate programs in relation to them. Most of these programs have failed because little or nothing was known about the relation of communication style to culture and its function in social change. The problem of cultural equality now stands alongside health, peace, social welfare and political justice, as one of the principal concerns of all people everywhere. The developing nations and the minority cultures within large national frameworks now want to grow in a cultural sense. . . . The human ethology technique will enable scholars, experts and administrators, we hope, to make fruitful plans for the development of this multi-cultural world. Much more importantly, however, we hope that the general dissemination of our methods of analysis of dance, song, speaking style and graphic arts will put these tools into the hands of people everywhere so that they can better evaluate their own social and cultural needs.

Lomax's decision to move into social science was as daring as it was risky. The work he had done with folk and popular music had attracted much attention from anthropologists, who up to that point had little professional interest in this music, so to use social science methodology on that material was bound to seem strange or anachronistic. In retrospect, his interest in the body was years ahead of its rediscovery in the 1980s, and the use of microcultural theory was not yet understood by most social scientists. But at that time comparative analysis had just fallen out of fashion: folklorists were then devoting themselves to single singers or communities, and social scientists were turning to a more radical form of cultural relativism.

Several of the reviews of his work were scathing, and at times seemed to be reviewing Lomax himself. The criticism challenged nearly every aspect of the research: The writing was too romantic for science. The coding process was too subjective, and experts were needed to bring their knowledge to bear on every culture area of the world. The samples were too small. Some countries or territories were not represented at all. The dance films were not representative enough, and new films needed to be made. Yet hidden behind these critiques was the unspoken understanding that there was no folklorist or anthropologist who was willing or able to undertake such projects.

A few of the harshest reviewers admitted that despite their misgivings about methodology, they were nonetheless intrigued by the whole idea. But they, like most others, failed to address the theory that lay behind it. By redirecting the study of music back to culture, Lomax had shown that song could tell us more than we thought about ourselves and others. He had also used the methods of comparative study in a field in which few had ever been interested in comparison before.

Alan wanted to have his work accepted, wanted to be identified with the work and admired for what he had accomplished. The severe and dismissive criticism he received drove him into withdrawal, sometimes retreating to bed for long stretches. But there was no way he could have finessed the work into wider acceptance, for there was no social scientist like Lomax. He could never stay hidden behind the language of positivism and objectivity or the trappings of methodology. Though he often referred to himself as a scientist and declared the scientific method sacrosanct, what he thought and believed were always transparent.

Alan would go on expanding the number of samples used in the study and using new technologies and more sophisticated means of analysis to improve the work and to present their findings in full multimedia form. He also set out to line up support from those he thought would be sympathetic and sent them sets of training tapes, but was often disappointed. When Peggy Seeger and Ewan MacColl said they were too busy to teach the method to others, Alan replied, "Singers are a dime a dozen, but there's only a few working on cantometrics." He thought Pete Seeger was lukewarm to his work after Pete replied that he didn't understand it well enough but would keep at it. Pete added that his father thought Alan hadn't followed scientific procedures. This was just the beginning of years of effort to explain his work to whoever would listen.

Joan Halifax and Alan had now been together for almost four years. They went to conferences and meetings, wrote articles together, and in 1967 did brief fieldwork in the Dominican Republic and Saint Eustatius, two islands that Alan had missed on his Caribbean project in 1962. Later that year they traveled to Morocco for more recordings for cantometrics. When they returned they made plans to be married in Florida, where Joan had grown up and where her family still lived, but Alan never appeared for the wedding. Their relationship ended shortly thereafter.

CHAPTER 17

The Culture War

The violence and public clashes over the Vietnam War and civil rights reached such a pitch in 1967 and 1968 that to Alan it seemed that the country had the same incendiary feel as the early 1930s, only this time the lives lost and the destruction of property made daily life seem far more volatile and precarious. Riots (or mutinies, depending on who was speaking) broke out in over a hundred American cities, with buildings in flames and police and troops occupying black neighborhoods. Martin Luther King was perceived by the CIA as losing control of the movement he had created as ideology began to shift toward Black Power, and planning for full-scale insurrection and mass arrests was under way. To talk about cultural issues in this climate seemed frivolous to some, but Alan persisted. Early in 1968 he wrote his agent with an idea about how the footage he had shot at Newport could be reworked into new films on different topics. Some of the same documentary ideas he had already developed on various aspects of black culture might now reach a national audience through television and film, and in some way could serve the cause of the movement.

> The more I think about it I am sure that I am right about the validity and timeliness for a black heritage program which would be devoted to the whole range of Negro culture, from the African pygmies to the best modern poets on which you would use film inserts liberally and imaginatively. We could have the commenting done by a range of people from the leading Negro entertainers and intellectuals to professionals in African culture, like yours truly. . . .
>
> The guys in the integration movement tell me that a loss of identity, a need to have a clear-cut history, is the problem of the Negro and is the source of more anger than economic conditions. If I can get the SCLC to say that they want to do this, perhaps we could go after Ford money to put the program immediately at work on NET. What I mean is that I think we may have a most direct way to go after tension problems with this series that will win support from many places.

Harry Belafonte had been working on a similar idea at the same time, some of which he presented on television when he substituted for Johnny Carson as host of *The Tonight Show* for a week. Since 1954 Belafonte had been assembling his own recorded history of black music, tracing it from Africa to the slave songs, and on to the music of country and city life. RCA backed the recordings, which featured performers such as Bessie Jones, Danny Barker, Sonny Terry and Brownie McGhee, Leon Bibb, and the Hall Johnson Choir, all of whom Lomax also had in mind. (Belafonte's documentary did not appear until 2001, when Buddah Records issued *The Long Road to Freedom: An Anthology of Black Music*, a more genteel approach to black culture than Alan envisioned.)

When Martin Luther King was murdered on April 4, 1968, violence broke out again in a number of cities, but especially in Washington, where block after block went up in flames and the anger and despair flowed right up to the steps of the White House. Vague threats of some kind of retribution were coming from those in barbershops and the seats of government alike. The Vietnam War dragged on toward no visible end, casualties were rising, and the decay and joblessness in many cities were unrelenting, despite the promises of President Lyndon Johnson's War on Poverty. Alan's own response was a mixture of New Deal solutions, sixties calls for self-determination, and populist stump speeches. In a letter to the *New York Times*, he argued that while the civil rights struggle was slowly gaining ground, cultural equality lagged behind, as black Americans were still being excluded from many of their own cultural resources. The knowledge of scholars of African American culture and history was not reaching schoolchildren, he said, and he called for the media to go beyond "a few token specials and Sunday afternoon shows." He also sent copies of his letter to local politicians, asking them for further suggestions for encouraging and supporting black history and culture. "The American Negro has created the first international musical and dance forms which are popular in every country of the globe," he reminded them, and his research on cantometrics was mentioned as support for the fact that Africa and African America shared many cultural elements.

Such concerns were always part of his work, but now most of his attention was focused on these cultural disparities. He recalled the moment in *Black Boy* where Richard Wright describes the father as seen by his son as he is leaving to go north: "Standing alone upon the red clay of a Mississippi plantation, a sharecropper, clad in ragged overalls, holding a muddy hoe in his gnarled, veined hands . . . we were forever strangers, speaking a different language, living on vastly distant planes of reality." Alan wanted to somehow restore dignity, creativity, and respect to that image of the sharecropper.

Shortly before his death, Reverend King had been aiming his final efforts at the economic structure of American society and the injustices that created it. The Southern Christian Leadership Conference (SCLC) had developed plans for a Poor People's Campaign, and King traveled the country assembling a "multiracial army of the poor" to march on Washington to pressure Congress to enact a bill of rights for lower-income Americans. It would be something of a middle ground between the extremes of rioting and begging for justice, as well as a visible movement that would draw in groups like the Student Nonviolent Coordinating Committee, which was becoming impatient with the pace of King's strategies, and was edging away from nonviolence. The campaign would bring together in Washington several thousand people from across the country to demand a reform of the welfare system, a decent minimum wage, education that would improve their lives, more unemployment insurance, and better distribution of surplus foods among the rural poor. King made a point of involving leaders among Puerto Ricans, poor whites, American Indians, and Mexican Americans. SCLC decided to go ahead with his plans the month after his death and got approval to stage the demonstration. On Mother's Day, May 12, Coretta Scott King led thousands of women into Washington. They were followed by workers who began constructing Resurrection City, hundreds of wooden shacks and tents on the fifteen acres of West Potomac Park between the Reflecting Pool and Independence Avenue, and from the Lincoln Memorial to 17th Street. Nine caravans of cars, airplanes, and trains set out for Washington from different parts of the country, stopping at various cities, picking up people along the way, until there were thousands brought to the site, far more than it could hold. Just after the city was populated, Robert Kennedy was assassinated, and his widow (who had been at the women's march) had his funeral procession pass Resurrection City.

Alan was brought into the planning for the project through the work he did with Guy Carawan and SNCC, and by the young singer of folk and gospel songs, Reverend Frederick Douglass Kirkpatrick, who had moved from King's group to become a SNCC official. Lomax and Kirkpatrick—who had together also performed and recorded with Pete Seeger—sketched out a cultural program for the Washington project, much of it modeled on the Henry Wallace presidential campaign. There was to be a daily gathering of leaders and teachers who could unite the people and prepare them to go back to their homes and teach others. All the local groups sending people to Washington were asked to contribute some of their best singers and musicians. Song sheets were to be prepared with the most important civil rights songs—"We Shall Not Be Moved," "We Shall Overcome," "I Ain't Gonna Let Nobody Turn Me Round." A theater group was to be developed along the lines of the farm workers' Teatro Campesino in California. There would be weekly Sunday revival meetings, sports, dance groups, bands, and discussions. Each large gathering would begin and end with a song, and there would be a song for every speech. Singing games for children would be taught and then performed onstage. Older participants could be gathered together to talk about their past and the history of their people. All of it was to be documented on film and recordings.

Ralph Rinzler committed the Newport Foundation to help support the music and children's programs at Resurrection City, and then negotiated with the Smithsonian Institution to provide a stage and sound system. The list of performers chosen to appear from outside the camp included Bernice and Cordell Reagon, Guy Carawan, Dock Reese, Fanny Lou Hamer of the Freedom Democratic Party, the Sea Island Singers, and a dozen singing preachers. Once the city within a city was functioning, Lomax decided at the last minute that they also needed someone who could bring together the northern ghettos and the Deep South, and called Muddy Waters in Chicago. Alan liked the idea of his band, with its Mississippi Delta roots and its electrically driven message, echoing across the pond and into the Lincoln Memorial as they stood in the same place where Martin Luther King had once spoken and where Marian Anderson had sung. Waters agreed to come, and he and his band drove in from Chicago overnight. Alan found them the next morning asleep in a car near the stage.

Another of the projects on which he and Reverend Kirkpatrick worked was the Mule Train, the only caravan coming to Washington that would not use mechanized vehicles to get there—a plan that was bound to attract media attention and onlookers along the way. Over a hundred people set off from Marks, Mississippi, on May 13, and it took them over a month to travel five hundred miles through Alabama to Georgia. Rain, inexperience with wagons and mules, hostile whites, and equally hostile law officers all worked against them. When they reached Atlanta the carts, mules, and passengers were loaded onto a train to Alexandria, Virginia; they crossed the bridge into Washington on June 19, arriving just days before the closing of Resurrection City.

In the aftermath, many in the movement and the press thought they had not accomplished many of their original goals. Alan, on the other hand, believed he now saw more clearly what would be needed and what he could contribute. He was thinking of a way to present the findings of his research and their implications in a practical and entertaining way that would go beyond the usual tracing of black culture to slavery and its aftermath. He wanted to put black tradition in a more positive perspective, stressing its achievements and global influence and presenting information that could not be found in any history or geography book:

> Like all other humanists during the last five years, we have tried to make a contribution to the resolution of the black crisis in America. Since our style study can pick out social norms in the most evocative of culture's communications and regions of culture, it is possible for us to translate these findings of social

> science directly into educational material for wide audiences, both literate and non-literate. . . . We can offer the same level of fact, of perspective and of healing self-knowledge to other neglected cultural traditions, such as that of the North American Indians. In this way we feel that cantometrics can, on the one hand, become a dependable tool for the social scientist and, on the other, play a therapeutic and educational role in the social theatre.

In a report on his work to NIMH he openly tied his new ideas for research to the political turmoil around them:

> The Black Identity Project was conceived in the spring of 1968 as an answer to an urgent information and education problem in the United States. Blacks were being told and were feeling that they had a separate black tradition, but the range, nature and scope of this tradition was left pretty much undefined. Education in "blackness" in the popular terms that reach the people was a pastiche of many disparate elements—the glories of the West African kingdoms, the politics of the Black Muslims, the teaching of Swahili, the agonies of slavery, the struggle for liberation, the story of successful black Americans and the development of jazz and the blues. Little or nothing was being said about the mainstream of black history as found in the studies of ethnologists, archaeologists, and folklorists. The remarkable unity and integrity of African culture, the story of its spread across the world of the African continent and its almost total survival in the New World was not known to the general black public.

Even before Resurrection City was abandoned, Alan approached the Ford Foundation about supporting a series of projects concerning black culture and identity. He also contacted the J. Walter Thompson Agency, the influential advertising firm, about turning the research materials he was developing into public service radio messages, comic books, pamphlets, children's toys, and television programs. It could all be done, he thought, in three to six months. Faced with the possibility of another long, hot summer of protests and demonstrations, both groups agreed to support him. Ford gave him $50,000 to develop the project, and the Thompson people said they would help him prepare scripts and approach their own clients about underwriting his ideas. Lomax put together an advisory group that included John Henrik Clarke, the historian and editor of *Freedomways*; Raoul Abdul, a concert and opera singer who had been Langston Hughes's secretary; and Alan's cantometrics staff. Reverend Kirkpatrick planned to approach Holiness churches to bring the large body of fundamentalists into the black progressive movement.

Problems soon arose. The advertising agency did not come through with the help Alan expected, and the media people wanted more money than was available.

Characteristically Alan said he would do it himself, and in a big way. Books and pamphlets were to be written and edited, some of which would be distributed through the National Committee of Negro Churchmen; a film would show the contribution of African Americans to world dance and would be shown on television; a book on black cultural style in America would be written. But the first task was to develop what Alan called the *Black Encyclopedia of the Air*: twenty-eight public service spots for radio, each a little over a minute in length, to be narrated by Jack Walker, a popular radio DJ. Some of the spots would relate historical facts unfamiliar to most people (stories about black explorers, liberators, cowboys, inventors, and medical researchers), but most concerned music and stylistic features of African and African American life (large choruses in Africa, the early invention of polyphony by the Pygmies and Bushmen, the African roots of the blues and of Ray Charles's music). Some of the spots made daring sonic links, matching up West African hunting songs with the blues, or comparing Ethiopian military bands to avant-garde saxophonist Albert Ayler's group. The overall point was to show that there were continuities between African and African American culture that were distinctive and had survived the brutal facts of American history.

Alan wrote the scripts for the spots, had them recorded on a twelve-inch LP record, and sent them out free to four hundred radio stations that served minority communities. News releases were mailed to African American newspapers and entertainment trade magazines. The series was popular wherever it was aired, and stations asked for more and longer versions. Requests for copies of the record came in from prisons, schools, hospitals, National Educational Radio, *Jet* magazine, and the National Council of Churches.

By November Alan and Raoul Abdul had also compiled an anthology of what they called "black soul poetry." Titled *3000 Years of Black Poetry*, it was dedicated to Langston Hughes, who had died the previous year. It included verse and song lyrics from a wide range of African peoples: modern African poets like Senghor, Diop, Okara, and Soyinka; texts from ancient and modern Egypt and the Moorish world; black poets of Europe and South America; Creoles of Louisiana and the West Indies; folk poetry from the United States; and a large sampling of American poets and writers from Phyllis Wheatley to Sterling Brown, Amiri Baraka, Bob Kaufman, Ted Jones, Nikki Giovanni, and Martin Luther King Jr. It was a well-chosen and representative collection, and nothing like it had been presented before. But Alan had a greater goal in mind than merely assembling an anthology: he wanted to use what he had learned in cantometrics and phonotactics to identify the poetic principles that characterized all these poets of Africa and the black diaspora. But without having the means to enclose actual recordings in the book to serve as illustrations, he was forced to try to express these stylistic features in words that did not fully convey what he heard in that poetry and speech.

Collecting and publishing texts was no longer enough for him. Being forced to write about the spoken word was frustrating: "It was as if we were back in Bishop Percy's time on the Scots-English border."

Cultural issues continued to surface in the late 1960s and early 1970s as another dimension of the civil rights struggle, both as a way of understanding the differences between social groups and as part of the battle for the right of an ethnic group to celebrate its own cultural heritage. If there ever was an apt time for a folklorist or a social scientist to communicate the meaning and importance of culture to the public or to build research projects around these ideas, it was now. But it was one thing for such ideas to be presented by a person of color; when whites spoke of behaviors that had powerful meanings within the black community but were a source of misunderstanding between races, it became tricky at best, and might be decried as racist, especially by the black middle class.

Yet Alan was not to be dissuaded by what he saw as petty politics by those who did not necessarily have the black masses' best interests at heart. In his search for funding he turned to the National Institute of Mental Health's Center for the Study of Urban and Metropolitan Problems, asking them to help him produce a series of small books on the cultural histories of all American ethnic groups, including those from northern and southern Europe. Though the civil rights movement was the focus of his concern, he felt that the solution to the country's internal crisis lay in some form of multicultural awareness, a process of making all peoples aware of their histories, and creating pride in what America had achieved with its cultural mix. At a moment when some on the left were stressing areas of black cultural and moral superiority, a position that Alan had partially embraced in the past, he now vowed that he wanted no part of a solution that came at the expense of other people's cultural achievements. All Americans had been nurtured within a shared history, albeit an unequal and often violent one.

Lomax proposed a series of two-day conferences that would feature talks by experts on each ethnic group, followed by long discussions, with court stenographers transcribing the proceedings so that chapters could be written and a text created and edited on the spot. They would develop handbooks of the resources of and possibilities for each culture, combined with lists of the best books, articles, recordings, and films, with recommendations for setting up local training programs. Alan had in mind overcoming the bias in the education system that favored northern European cultural heritage, and the corresponding failure to see the importance of the black oral heritage and folkways:

> The present generation are the creators of a rich folk tradition that is virtually unknown to their children. That is the generation that produced jazz, the blues,

> and the popular American dances, but also the folkways, the legends, the web of tradition that lies behind this better known material [that] was largely undocumented and unknown. The value, the life styles, and the lore of this parent generation must be understood and appreciated by white and black alike before any true resolution of the present urban conflict can healthfully take place. At the present moment, in spite of strong interest in black culture, the generation that contributed so much to the building of America is being treated as if what it represents is something to be ashamed of.

In his passion for the cultural history of black America, Lomax appointed himself a watchdog of the arts. He was sometimes offended by young white writers and folksingers who declared themselves one-person archives of black song (those that Amiri Baraka called "keepers of yesterday's blues") and who performed them awkwardly and near to what Lomax regarded as minstrelsy: "Too much tar brush!" When the National Association of Jazz Educators began publication of a journal in 1970 and Alan was asked to be a contributor, he wrote the editor accusing him of continuing the white tradition of taking jazz from blacks and using it as their own. There was not a black face, name, or reference in the issue of the magazine he read: "I hope Jelly Roll and Bunk Johnson and King Oliver haunt you."

He took any number of public issues seriously, often becoming active in political campaigns, as when he and Margaret Mead were asked to help Hubert Humphrey improve his speaking style during the presidential race in 1968. Alan continued to oppose the war in Vietnam, going to demonstrations and writing letters to members of Congress and major newspapers urging an end to it. He and Johnny Faulk hosted a fund-raiser for Students for a Democratic Society, and he testified at the hearings of the Senate Committee on Labor and Public Welfare when the committee was considering placing a newly proposed American Folklore Foundation within the Smithsonian.

Folk song revivals had always been centered in the Northeast, but in the early 1970s Washington, D.C., became the gathering place for those interested in folklore. The arts and humanities endowments were formed in 1965, and though both supported folk arts, it was with little sense of direction. Then in 1967 the Smithsonian began presenting a large folk festival every summer. Alan entered into the spirit of a new national recognition of the vernacular arts when he came to town to arrange "An American Folk Concert," with the help of the Division of Performing Arts of the Smithsonian Institution to accompany the 9th International Congress of Anthropological and Ethnological Sciences on September 1 and 2, 1973. Later his sister Bess came to Washington from her teaching job in California to work on the summer 1975 Smithsonian Folk Festival, and was asked to become deputy director of presentations with Ralph Rinzler for the giant 1976 Bicentennial Festival. She stayed at the Smithsonian until she moved to the National Endowment for the Arts in 1977, as director of the Folk and Traditional Arts Program, a job she virtually created and then held until 1992.

Though Alan had no position in the government, with Bess's D.C. connections and the contacts he made through his various contributions to the Smithsonian festivals he gained some leverage in shaping the national cultural policies that were beginning to emerge. When David Rockefeller Jr. and a committee of the National Endowment for the Arts's Music Policy Conference proposed that a National Institute of Musical Literacy be created to teach everyone to read music and to learn high musical standards, Alan wrote a letter to the *Washington Post* pointing out that the bulk of the world did not read music and yet remained creative. He further claimed that music notation actually restrained creativity because it was intended to serve only a certain kind of music. The Rockefeller proposal was an example of why the endowments needed to be turned away from spending money only on the music that they considered high art.

When he became a consultant to the Smithsonian folk festivals, Alan wrote a fourteen-page report to the festival's organizers in 1975 accusing then of fatal compromises, bad taste, bad food, and lack of seriousness. He especially criticized them for having given in to low-level politics from some of the employees at the Smithsonian:

> I continually find the black diaspora presentations extremely disappointing. It's as if the people in charge were limiting us, the audience, to the things that they themselves approve of and leaving out all the rest of it. We don't have the dancers, the hollers, we don't have the work songs, we don't have the choral spirituals, we don't have the folk tales, we don't have the street corner conversations, we don't have the genuine rituals. When you get through saying all that, what we don't have is the greatest of all American musical traditions, which is the Afro-American creation here. Instead of splendor, we have some bits and pieces. Instead of a program which reaches out and involves the audience in a spirit of passionate joy and outbursts of great emotion, both tragic and life-giving, we have a rather timid and in-turned overall presentation. It's as if the blacks had their backs to us, and that's not African culture, African culture is outgoing and group-involving. There seems to be a wall of censorship here which must be broken down. . . . Because there is political and social tension now between blacks and whites is no possible reason that the Smithsonian Folk Festival, taking the long view and presenting the finest aspects of all the tradition it touches upon, should be affected by this. The persons in charge of this aspect of the Festival must be either replaced or come to

take a new view of their work. . . . Here it seems to me, you should become ferocious impresarios, like the people who run the Met and Lincoln Center, perfectly capable of throwing anyone out of your offices and downstairs who proposes that you do anything that violates the sacred purpose of your Festival and who is willing to impose upon you anything less than the best.

He also wanted to have the festival recorded and filmed by the best cinematographers and archived, but also aired on National Public Radio and PBS, reaching beyond the tourists and Washington residents to the entire country, especially to show those in small towns and distant regions that their people had performed at the highest level of America. In a proposal he circulated to filmmakers and heads of various agencies, he wrote:

> One of the central problems of our culture, a source of sickness and of anomie in our culture and in all the world, is that everything these days happens at the center and is broadcast out from the center to the periphery, to the small places. This makes everyone who is not from megalopolis a hick by inference: he is always cocking his eye on the tube or his ear on the speaker to stay in touch. We have to make culture again grow on the periphery—where culture has always grown. Now that we have artificially brought in the whole American periphery to a national festival, we must show the whole country that our biggest festival was created by the folk from the periphery. Otherwise we can do damage with the festival, instead of using it to right the imbalance that centralized communication and education systems continually bring about.

After many congressional hearings and much infighting among the two endowments, the Library of Congress, and the Smithsonian Institution, Congress passed the American Folklife Preservation Act on January 2, 1976, which created the American Folklife Center in the Library of Congress. Alan had been at the hearings, talking to representatives in Congress and giving testimony before congressional committees, arguing that making such an institution the center for folklore would give Americans an additional means of communication.

In an effort to "revitalize" PBS, he wrote up a statement and sent it to influential figures in the arts and broadcasting. Recalling that PBS had been designed to do what he had long been advocating—decentralize and diversify American media—he argued that public broadcasting had fulfilled the first part of its mandate, bringing high culture and information to the hinterlands, but had failed at the second, celebrating the regional and cultural resources of the country. The local stations were top-heavy with administrators and in need of local talent and local culture and information. It was time for a national talent search to find the

Studs Terkels of every region, the interviewers and commentators deeply rooted in their own territories. Local programs featuring the festivals, shows, and events of every region should be supported by the media. Alan's one specific suggestion was to have every PBS station program the best of their local church music against the worst of the paid religious broadcasts.

When Jimmy Carter was nominated as the Democratic candidate for president in 1976 and gave an acceptance speech that spoke about moral decay, disillusionment, cynicism, and the need for the values of the local, the ethnic, and the small-town, it reawakened Alan's New Deal optimism, and he responded by writing Carter a long letter praising him and promising his support. But the letter was also a cry for help for America, to revitalize cultural life and battle the corruption of Washington and the media. Only the week before, he had sent Carter a proposal titled "Toward a Presidential Commission on Grass Roots Culture," which reached the president-elect through Andrew Young, who passed it on to Stuart E. Eizenstat, of Carter's campaign, and later Carter's chief domestic policy adviser. Lomax once again argued for reversing the monolithic nature of TV, radio, and education, but now using the FCC, PBS, the National Endowments, the National Park Service, the Department of Health, Education, and Welfare, NIMH, the Agency for International Development, the Smithsonian, and the Library of Congress to create cultural equity, offering examples of films that could be made and recommending the creation of regional cultural centers. The document caught the attention of Eizenstat, who wrote him before Carter's inauguration, urging him to apply for a job within the incoming administration. Though Alan never followed up on that sugestion, he did attend Carter's inauguration on January 20, 1977, where he introduced the Georgia Sea Island Singers.

Now that he was well known at the National Endowment for the Humanities through the many grants he had received, Alan met in 1978 with Joseph Duffy, the chairman, to offer his own perspective on what the NEH might accomplish in the non–metropolitan centers of America. They apparently agreed on principles, because a few months later Alan wrote Duffy to say that in spite of their discussion, things were still headed in the wrong direction. The NEH humanities scholars had "organized themselves into elitist cadres," leaving out the "nonprofessional, unorganized culture carriers." Included with his letter were pages of proposals for new ways of documenting and presenting foreign cultures and arts on PBS, ways to refocus the NEH toward the needs of peoples they had never considered, and some detailed and very specific plans for projects that the NEH might fund and that could serve as models: community television developed by the elderly for themselves; an institute for cultural ecology; a field staff whose only function would be to locate and oversee local projects; classroom programs using local artists and craftspeople; and in the wake of the success of Alex Haley's *Roots*, a series of TV and film projects exploring the variety of African American art "enclaves" across America, and reconnecting different facets of the African diaspora. A few months later, Alan wrote Duffy again, since he had not heard back from him, this time including yet another proposal for NEH to consider, a study of America's dance roots, involving film and TV, dance festivals, sending dancers into the schools, developing a "panorama" of American dance history, and promoting a national black folk dance company.

Pete Seeger, who had suffered his share of indignities and blacklisting from television, was also alert to its rising power and its squandering of cultural resources. When he heard that there were plans in the works to blanket the world with American television shows, and to conquer it by exporting reruns of soaps, teen music shows, sports events, political news, and advertising, he became alarmed. *Sesame Street* was already popular in places like Hong Kong, Seeger said, and as much good as it had done, Hong Kong should have its own children's shows. He sent out a letter addressed to "pickers and singers" who he hoped would share his concerns about a new phase of cultural imperialism. When Alan received the letter, he wrote back to Pete, doubling the charges: it was more than content that was a problem with television, it was the nature and use of the technology. It was a one-way, simultaneous, glitzy, loud assault that destroyed cultural styles, exported alien and inappropriate values, and forced people everywhere in the world into passive and potentially hostile and violent reaction. "The result is, in the country where TV operates around the clock, America, we have a rising tide of evil. Evil is absolutely everywhere, in every part of the country and there is an awful feeling that has developed in the country." The tools to fight back with were now available in cantometrics, where cultural styles could be identified and lines of resistance drawn. And, incidentally, *Sesame Street* was far from innocent, he said: it mainstreamed movement, accent, and attitude. "The puppets are great, but the people in it are terrible, and they're teaching the world to be poker-faced Americans or square, clownish Americans." The media, in short, must come to terms with differences in communication systems. "The best thing, of course, would be to turn television clear off, for good."

Alan's life had always been marked with contingencies, doubts, and dependency on a vast range of personal relationships, yet driven by huge, almost utopian ambitions that he would have to realize alone. Nothing got easier as he grew older. He conceived of new projects almost daily—films that he wanted to make to teach the cantometric and choreometric methods were proposed to the National Endowment for the Humanities; he had not given up on TV and film programs for black cultural education, and was asking CBS producer Fred Friendly, then on the faculty of Columbia University's journalism school, to connect him to TV executives to do a special on music and dance, and also help him break into film with what he wanted to call Operation Feedback, making mass communication interactive rather than monological; there was also a series of films he had long wanted to make on various forms of folklore. He had never abandoned his older projects, and he was now regularly corresponding with individual performers he had recorded on the last southern trip, many of whom were sick, old, out of work, and in need of money and counted on that brief engagement they had had in some kitchen or farm field years before to save them.

Since Alan's interest in cantometrics began with his fascination for vocal quality, it was no surprise when he and his colleagues at one point began applying the cantometric methodology to speaking style, a project they called parlametrics. Since all of the style projects he had developed were concerned with the social nature of performance, they sought the data they needed in dialogues and conversations rather than in interviews. Their interest was in how people spoke rather than what they said. Once again they faced the problem of building up an archive where one didn't exist: no one had ever collected conversational samples of speech from a wide range of languages. Without the staff or the money to launch a worldwide field search, they turned to the United Nations for help, and arranged to set up situations in which speakers would be recorded while conversing. Other conversations were contributed to them by the Summer Institute of Linguistics, who drew on its fieldworkers in languages across the world. One hundred and fifty-six speech samples of two to five minutes in length drawn from a large number of the world's languages was the result.

New coding scales had to be developed, using such features as repetition, timing, speech length, spacing, dominance versus sharing, relaxed versus tense speech sounds, and breathiness, and once again they were constructed so that nonspecialists could do the coding. The analysis of the data was preliminary to a larger study that never occurred, but the results seemed to suggest that music, dance, and speech all evolve in parallel with socioeconomic systems.

At the invitation of his own therapist, Alan addressed the American Group Psychiatry Association's meetings in New Orleans, where he met Carol Kulig, who worked for the association and had a background in language study. She became his companion and coworker for the next twenty-three years.

Though he ran out of money for the choreometrics project in late 1968, Alan continued to work on it, convinced that someone would appreciate the value of his work. He and his colleagues spent a great deal of time making decisions about what parts of each film on dancing could be used for coding and analyzing, since camera placement, movement, and editing are typically not helpful for close observation of dance. The difficulties of having to search for dance films and then struggle to locate the characteristics of the dances spurred him to write several articles over the next few years about the limits and possibilities of film as a research source. His chief concern was the same as it had been for song—namely, the rapid disappearance of the great variety of dances around the globe—and he urged filmmakers, professional and amateur, to set to work immediately to rescue them:

> One of the greatest opportunities and most urgent tasks of this century is to film the full range of human culture while we can: With the new portable sound equipment, the job would require no more than a generation of concerted international effort. . . . There is little time left, the overwhelming success of the urban-industrial system in controlling and exploiting the biosphere has temporarily blinded the majority of mankind to other values. The entertainment industry, operating a one way communication system, now threatens to obliterate national cultures as it has long shamed into silence neighborhood, peasant and primitive cultures. . . . Unless we take action now, what remains of human cultural variety will vanish.

He had been using motion picture equipment for years, but had not attempted to make a film since *Ballads, Blues, and Bluegrass* in 1961. Margaret Mead had been encouraging him to become a filmmaker for the last ten years, however, and now that he was creating the world's largest archive of dance and work films he was sharply conscious of how thin the film record of everyday human life was and what it would take to produce films that fulfilled their promise of being the most honest medium for capturing its reality.

As excited as he was about motion pictures, when he wrote about the potential of film he nonetheless focused on the defects that were deeply ingrained in the conventional practices, especially the editing style of the West. "Dramatic editing, shifts of perspective, and all the tricks of montage simply destroy the value of the film document for the scientist. He requires the whole event, the full contest, the whole body and action, the entire group—and above all, long continuous, undisturbed shots, so that the overlay of patterns in the interaction itself will have time to emerge":

> It is a common experience in screening film to see movements cut off in mid-phrase or interactions sliced in two as they are unfolding. The length and spatial dimensions of movement phrases and segments of interaction vary profoundly among cultures. West Europeans, for example, use linear, punchy, abrupt, moderately long phrases. These factors strongly affect the way they shoot our films. Cultures with a different sense of timing and phrasing are often visually chopped

> to pieces by Western filmmakers. . . . Western filmmakers can take great liberties with Western material because they know the fit of everything in the behavior of their fellows. Lacking that intimate acquaintance where they deal with unfamiliar kinetic and social systems, they are likely to miscut.

A new kind of filmmaking would have to be developed to create the consciousness needed to offset these problems, and documentary makers would have to be sensitized to microbehavioral observation and nonverbal behavior. Lomax offered a set of suggestions that would help to make documentaries free of the clichés, conventions, and biases that made most films of limited use for research. Filmmakers should start with an overview of the context of the event being filmed; continue with medium and long shots and not change focus or angle; keep the principal actors in the frame in the longer and more important parts; avoid close-ups of one person or one person's face or isolated body parts; and always keep a complete, unedited copy of the original filming. He also called for the filmmaker to involve the people in the film, especially by showing them the work as it progressed and then listening to their opinions of what they'd seen. If camera operators, directors, and editors objected to these constraints as the very things they avoided because they would put an audience to sleep, Alan's retort was that it was the nervous cutting, zooming, and refocusing that made documentaries fatiguing to watch, and more often than not it was not the audience's taste that was driving the nervous, busy camerawork, but rather something that the camera operators didn't want to watch that led them to cut away.

As new and cheaper communication technologies began to appear, he persistently tried to convince UNESCO to give money to talented people in each of the great cultural families of the world to enable them to make films that would show their cultural traditions and their unique cultural style to their own people and to the world, and to store these films in archives around the world, forming a global network of archives. It was again his idea of cultural feedback, but now at a global level. UNESCO, however, never seemed to understand how this would work. He tried to interest influential people such as Rudolf Nureyev, Yehudi Menuhin, and Jean Rouch, the great French ethnographic filmmaker, in becoming involved with the project, and to get Time-Life interested in making films. He wrote to Sony to persuade them to put portable cameras into the hands of every "tribe in the world for the purpose of documenting their own culture." When in the early 1970s the Society for Visual Anthropology was created, a group of social scientists that shared many of Lomax's beliefs, Alan argued with them about their priorities, telling them that they were narrow and self-serving by wanting to make their own films when they ought to be finding ways to help others make films.

With the support of Margaret Mead, he sought funding to build up an archive of film, and hundreds of personal letters were again sent out across the world for help in finding dance films. But as with the library of the world's folk music, many of his requests went unanswered, especially those sent to Russia. In May 1972 the National Science Foundation gave him $119,000 to continue the search for dance footage and to produce two pilot films that would teach choreometrics. It was not enough, but sufficient to make him redouble his efforts.

Dance and Human History was the first of four films on dance he would write and direct, all of them produced by the University of California Extension Media Center at Berkeley. It opened with a long, visually stunning montage of the variety of the world's dances, most of which had never before been seen by even the best of the dance specialists, and was followed by a demonstration of two of the scales used in choreometric research, for arm and body trunk movements, and their variations that existed across cultures. The rest of the film provided directions for coding dances and analyzing them in relation to social structure, climate, and forms of tool use and level of subsistence of the society. Unlike most anthropological and ethnographic films, this one was both a research report and a set of directions for its viewers on how to conduct the research themselves. It was also one of the most cinematic of anthropological films, as it counted on images more than words to communicate. It was awarded a Cine Golden Eagle Award in 1976.

Two more choreometric films followed in 1980—*Step Style* and *Palm Play*, the former devoted to the legs and feet in dance and their relation to work movements and sports, and the latter to the openness or closure of the palm in dance and the cultural symbolism of these gestures. Both films once again won Cine Golden Eagle Awards. *The Longest Trail*, made in 1986 and the last of the dance films, followed the settlement of the New World by Native Americans and showed more than fifty different dances. Alan's theories of the relation between environment, economy, culture, and dance were all brought to bear on the history of these dances, explaining their continuity and spread from Asia to South America.

Three months before NASA launched Voyager I and II into space in 1978, Carl Sagan wrote Alan and asked him to join a committee that would be advising the part of the project that would place a gold-plated copper disc containing ninety minutes of earth's music in each spacecraft. The two ships would pass by Jupiter, Saturn, Uranus, and Neptune and continue on into interstellar space at a million miles a day, capable of surviving for an estimated billion years, giving them a probable life greater than any human artifact, greater than the life of most of the continents on earth. Whatever music was chosen to be fired into space would become the ultimate mix tape, each selection becoming a classic by virtue of being granted immortality. Lomax's study of the evolutionary history of the earth's music made him the most influential member of the committee, so when the final choices were made, half of the selections were his. While the music included works by Bach, Stravinsky, Mozart, Debussy, and Beethoven, there was far more music from the Solomon Islands, Bulgaria, the Navajo, Peru, India, Japan, Mexico, Australia, and Java. There were no American classical composers, but Blind Willie Johnson, Louis Armstrong, and Chuck Berry were included.

But Alan was unhappy with the way things were organized and he perceived himself as being treated like just another media hack. He wrote Sagan to instruct him on the years of work that lay behind the choices he had made and to chastise him for not treating his role in the enterprise more seriously, as scientist to scientist, rather than just someone in the recording business. Sagan apologized and assured him of his importance to the project.

The two spacecraft were launched with their sonic payloads, and shortly after, a letter arrived from Moe Asch of Folkways Records asserting that certain recordings for which he held copyrights—the Navajo, Blind Willie Johnson, and the Pygmies—had been launched and written about without his permission, and he was concerned about abridgement of his rights on earth and presumably in space as well.

The excitement about documentary filmmaking in the 1970s was partly the result of a rediscovery of the power of documentaries, enhanced now by improvements in quality, along with the drop in the cost of the necessary equipment. After so much writing and giving talks about the potential of film, Alan wanted not only to show folklorists and anthropologists what they could accomplish with it, but also to get such works aired on television. In 1978 he convinced PBS to back another trip into the South, this time to focus on the blues and the musics that contributed to it, and to make a pilot for a projected series of folklore films. This one was to be called *The Land Where the Blues Began*, but with the rapid spread of television itself, and his not having been in the South for a while, Alan wasn't certain that there was any folk music left there. Still, if everything else failed, he thought they could at least interview some of the older people about the past.

For assistance Alan turned to Worth Long, a SNCC folklorist and photographer, to point the way to the best singers and musicians, and to John Bishop, whom he had just engaged as a photographer at the Newport Folk Festival. NEH gave them a small grant, and because PBS couldn't offer them a great deal of money, they videotaped instead of filming. When Bishop arrived in Mississippi, Alan and Long had already been there for ten days, looking around and making arrangements to work with a camera crew from Mississippi ETV.

Over the next month they found their way into Arkabutla, Bentonia, Bolton, Canton, Como, Greenville, Hollandale, Independence, Lexington, Sardis, Senatobia, and Vicksburg, all shrines of the blues lover's world. Alan had to adapt his recording style to film: what he didn't know about cameras, editing, and how a film was put together he made up for in his mastery of microphones and their placement. He wanted to catch all the parameters of singing style on film, but there was no time to train camera operators in the method. Despite the summer heat, when the sun went down they rigged up lights and sweated while the bugs burned up as they hit the bulbs; or they set up the lights in bars and juke joints, turning them into ovens. They filmed singers and musicians such as R. L. Burnside, Sonny Boy Nelson, Napoleon Strickland, and Sam Chatmon of the Mississippi Sheiks, famous for "Corinna, Corinna" and "Sitting on Top of the World." There were interviews with workers in the field and tractor drivers, talking about their youth spent picking cotton by hand, or men who had built the levees recalling working for white men on horseback who had one hand on the horse's reins and the other on a gun. They walked the tracks with railroad men, filming them straightening rails, laying ties, and singing so loudly that they failed to hear a train coming at them and barely were able to save the cables and cameras.

Postproduction work was started back in Boston without money to pay for equipment and labor, and somehow they managed to get the program finished by September 1979. It was first aired in Mississippi and then nationally on PBS in 1980. The film was given a Gabriel Award in 1980 from the Catholic Broadcasters Association; a Houston International Film Festival Gold Medal, also in 1980; and a Blue Ribbon at the American Film Festival in 1985. The success of the pilot got Alan the money he needed from the National Endowment for the Arts to make a series of films for PBS called *American Patchwork*, and between 1978 and 1985 he would make field trips to Mississippi, Alabama, Georgia, Louisiana, Virginia, North Carolina, and Arizona to videotape regional American culture—*Jazz Parades, Cajun Country, Appalachian Journey,* and *Dreams and Songs of the Noble Old.*

Two of the most important people in Alan's life died within a few months of each other between 1978 and 1979. Margaret Mead was the first. When he spoke at her memorial service at Columbia University, Alan told the gathering that he had not met Mead until she located him while he was working in the UK in the mid-1950s. She invited him to hear her speak in London, and afterwards told him that she had seen his film *'Oss 'Oss, Wee 'Oss* and wanted to tell him that he had interpreted it wrong. Nonetheless, she admired the film, and insisted that he come back to the United States and get a grant for research. She actually applied for a grant for him to make sure he obtained it, and introduced him to her inner circle. She and Alan worked together more often when she organized and pushed for the creation of the American Film Research Institute, sometimes jointly applying with him for various film projects. "In our last conversation, Margaret said, 'Is anybody making trouble? If so call me and I'll deal with it.' And she would have."

Nick Ray died in June 1979, and his memorial was held at Lincoln Center, with Alan as master of ceremonies. They had stayed in contact over the years, and when the jagged trajectories of their lives intersected they found they still shared the same dreams and aspirations they had developed together some forty years earlier in Washington. During the long illness that led to his death, Ray had been teaching at Harpur College in New York State, and often stayed with Alan when he was in the city. In his eulogy Lomax said that Nick had become a playboy in Hollywood, "the perfect camouflage for a man who was making socially significant pictures in the 1950s." But the speakers at the memorial were not the moguls, the actors, the bankers, those for whom he had made money, but Will Lee, a blacklisted actor who remained close to Ray and who ended his career as Mr. Hooper on *The Muppet Show*, and film students like Jim Jarmusch. Alan said at one point that Nick was forced to go to Europe to find work, but he was never comfortable there because American culture and American character were his subjects. If it had not been clear before this that Alan was also speaking about himself, it became so when he turned to the vision Nick had of America: "The world which Nick [and] his contemporaries knew was full of injustice, poverty, tyranny, and above all the threat of Fascism—Nick worked and fought, covertly, with every weapon he had, his whole life to change these conditions, to expose the evils of his time."

CHAPTER 18

The Global Jukebox: "Got the World in a Jug, the Stopper in My Hand"

Alan had passed his sixty-fifth birthday, and though he had been diagnosed as having arrhythmia of the heart and was taking Ritalin, he had no thoughts of retiring. He was deep into unfinished research—no one else knew the material well enough to take over and complete it—the grants were running out, and government funding agencies were reluctant to continue backing projects without tangible results. In any case, Alan could hardly afford to retire, given that his total income for 1981 was $41,218—a figure that included the sale of stock his father left him, worth $36,088. Over the next two years he would have problems with late payment of taxes, and the IRS attached his wages. He would need to work harder, come up with new research proposals, or find a way to sell some of the work he had done in the past, work with which he was identified and that no one else could do.

In a letter to the president of the Carnegie Foundation in January 1981, Alan reminded him that it was his organization that had helped create the Archive of American Folk Song at the Library of Congress, and that the most serious purpose of his and his father's work was "to give a new basis for growth to America's finest and most important indigenous tradition—the folk music of the black people of the South. . . . [But] this our most beautiful music has, for a variety of reasons, fallen into disuse . . . this break in cultural continuity represents a serious threat to the future development of American culture and its music." What he was asking for now was funds to create the *Recorded Treasury of Black Folk Music,* fifty to one hundred records that would survey black folk music of the United States and the Bahamas (the latter because of its ties to people of the southeastern coastal United States):

> This Treasury will present one of the most remarkable of mankind's cultural achievements. The blacks, brought here as slaves, deprived of their languages

> and their material culture, and learning a new system of musical and linguistic communication, combined these traditions to create a new river of song and dance which has, in the last two or three hundred years, swept the whole world into its currents. Nothing quite like this had ever happened before. Having just surveyed the music of the whole world on the Cantometric Project, I can say that no song style exists anywhere that can beat this material for sheer variety, originality and charm. Yet its most genuine aspects are little known today and are fast fading out of currency, under the pond of the media. It would be possible to put the whole back into circulation, to start this mighty river flowing again with the stimulus of the Recorded Treasury.

Though his claims for the reissue of black folk music might have seemed exaggerated, the *Southern Journey* recordings of 1960 had in fact become extraordinarily significant. When they were issued by a major recording company they found their way into every corner of the country and began to influence both the folk revival and popular music in general. The Carnegie Foundation decided not to fund the project in 1981, but a decade later the National Endowment for the Humanities would underwrite it.

Despite the label of "folk purist" that was hung on him later in his career, Alan had spent years thinking about pop music and its power to affect the lives of Americans from birth to old age. He tracked the changes in the content of pop songs, such as the switch from the nineteenth century's pain and sorrow at the loss of one's mother and the old homestead to the twentieth century's heartbreak and anguish over the loss or the lack of a lover. But the most striking difference was the way in which Euro-American and African American singing styles had radically affected each other in spite of a long history of racial censorship that kept each group's recordings and performances separate from the other (race records, rhythm and blues, the ban against blacks in popular radio DJ programs and in the early days of *American Bandstand*, and even MTV, which was then still refusing to feature black performers). Alan applied to the National Endowment for the Humanities for a grant to study the development of American popular music, and in 1982 was awarded $50,000 for a project he called "The Urban Strain: A Cross-Cultural Interpretation of American Performance Styles." According to Roswell Rudd, one of his associates on the grant, "Alan began the Strain project because he was criticized for not including the development of urban society into his system." Some skeptics insisted that while cantometrics might work on isolated or very old societies, it would be unable to deal with the vast and complex hybrid or creolized modern musics of North America.

To enable the coding system of cantometrics to include these newer musics, Rudd added electronics, overdubbing, and new forms of musical instruments to the categories, along with novel stylistic features such as "strict temperament," "blue notes," "speaking quality like Louis (Armstrong)," "screaming," "sprechstimme," "imitating singers," and "imitating animals or environmental sounds."

The survey covered a full range of singers, right up to Michael Jackson, Bob Dylan, Elvis Presley, and Frank Sinatra. Alan and Forrestine Paulay examined changes in dance and analyzed their relation to dance music. In films of the early white pop singers, such as Bing Crosby, they noticed that the performers' head motions did not match the phrasing of their singing; only later in their careers were the two synchronized. An African American performer like Fats Domino, in contrast, phrased not just with his head but with his whole body. Members of Domino's band also phrased with their entire bodies, though not necessarily in the same manner or at the same time, but in a complex synchrony with the singer's. As the researchers worked their way forward in time to white performers like Pat Boone, they saw the beginnings of new physical phrasing emerging.

By pulling pop music out of the language of fashion that surrounded it and placing it into a historical context, then comparing it to other musics without the use of musical transcriptions, the Urban Strain project aimed to demystify the music, chart its growth and its spread across the world, and then offer explanations for its success. Unlike those in the music business who looked for novelty everywhere, it sought the traditional elements within the new. What Alan found was that American pop had tapped some of the richest and farthest-reaching of the world's style structures—the folk and the art musics of West and Central Africa, and those of Northeastern, Eastern, and Middle Europe. The Western European ballad, African hocketing and orchestral form, and the Eurasian brass band and concert orchestra traditions had all come together in the United States.

The scope of the project was huge: an entire country's popular music and dance were to be assessed and analyzed, including musical ads, Broadway dances, and movie scores, and then reduced to a final sample of 321 songs and a hundred dances. Under the pressure of the size of the task facing him and the limits of staff and money, Lomax departed from cantometrics and choreometrics methods, and most of the work was done in discussion and debate; all of it was recorded, but without codings and statistical analysis. The real work of the project was in Lomax's mind: he knew the musical and social background of American pop song better than anyone else, but lacked the time to put together what they had discovered in the research with the knowledge he had already accumulated over a lifetime, and even though he had written several hundred pages for a book, he never had time to finish it. Instead, he planned to use what they had discovered for a later effort.

With the retirement or passing of several of Alan's key supporters at Columbia University and more of his time being spent in film and public media, his future at the school seemed less secure. In 1983 he decided to incorporate his various preservation, research, and media activities and founded the Association for Cultural Equity, a nonprofit corporation with which to support his various projects and to develop methods of assuring "cultural feedback," the means by which equity could be assured for the people whose music had been recorded as part of ethnographic and folkloric studies. The idea of "return" was then circulating in cultural circles—the restoration of cultural artifacts or documented materials to their originators, making it possible for them to receive royalties for their works. Lomax took this idea a step further by urging that people should also have the means to document their own cultures by setting up recording and filming centers in third-world countries "to give them media status, the educational standing, and the sense of professional competence in the arts that will enable them to face the pressure of the media and to grow from their own roots." Those outsiders doing field research among them should take along tape recorders, a tape duplicator, a video camera, and a videotape duplicator, all of which they would leave behind after they had been used cooperatively with the people who were documented.

The fieldwork and filming for *the American Patchwork* films funded by the National Endowment for the Arts would preoccupy him for the next few years. In 1983 alone he was shooting film in Tucson, rural Georgia, Kentucky, Louisiana, North Carolina, Tennessee, Virginia, Williamsburg in Brooklyn, and the Smithsonian Folklife Festival in Washington. Alan had enough money for the five one-hour films he had planned, but he had shot enough footage in a number of places that he also hoped to make several more: *The Harp of a Thousand Strings*, on shape-note singers in Georgia and Alabama, with comparisons to black Sacred Harp singers in the Carolinas, long-meter singing among Baptists in Kentucky, psalm singing in the Hebrides, and Holiness spirituals in the Tennessee mountains; the stories and songs of the Papago, Mountain Apache, and Yaqui Indians and Mexican Americans in *Desert Folk: The Most Civilized Americans*; and *Festa Italiana*, a comparative study of the Giglio festival, the feast of Saint Paulinus, in Neapolitan communities in Italy and the United States.

When he finally received funding for the *Recorded Treasury of Black Folk Music* from the National Endowment of the Arts, Alan hired folklorist, collector, and record company owner Peter Lowry to work with him at the Library of Congress. He had estimated that the project would take two months, but even with a research fellowship at the Smithsonian to support him it took Alan ten months of working six ten-hour days a week to listen to all the black American folk recordings in the archive, then organize them by region and occupation. He stayed in Bess's apartment while Lowry took the copies home with him to upstate New York and spent several more months assembling the master tapes. Alan's plan was to shop the recordings to record companies, but it was not until the 1990s that the black song collection would be released by Rounder Records, because he was distracted by the postproduction work on the *American Patchwork* film series and a half dozen other efforts: a book on dance for the University of Nebraska Press; *The Hot and the Cool*, a one-hour film mapping sub-Saharan African dance style; a four-hundred-page rough draft of a book for the Urban Strain project; and another songbook, one that would expand his *Folk Songs of North America* to seven hundred selections.

At the same time, he was being forced out of his office because the building in which it was located was being turned into co-op apartments. When Columbia University failed to offer him space so that he could continue his research under their name, he made a desperate attempt to sell his collections and papers to some university that would also allow him to continue working, on salary, so that he would be able to finish the work and have something to leave to his family. But he had no takers. At the last second he was introduced to Joseph S. Murphy, the chancellor of the City University of New York, a former labor organizer who spoke Yiddish and Gaelic, had worked in Africa and the Caribbean, and was seeking to open the city's universities up to more minority and working-class students. He offered Alan an unpaid position of research associate in the Department of Anthropology at Hunter College, and office space near one of Murphy's own offices on the west side of Manhattan; in exchange, Alan would give the college a percentage of whatever grants he received.

When President Reagan awarded the National Medal of the Arts on July 4, 1986, Alan was surely the financially poorest recipient of that honor: his tax return for the previous year showed that his adjusted gross income was $11,531.

The Grateful Dead's Rex Foundation gave him a grant that kept him at work on the archives' databases, and he was able to borrow enough equipment from the Smithsonian Institution and the Massachusetts Institute of Technology to begin digitizing the song collection, but research money was becoming harder to find. To keep the foundations interested in his work he still had to take his research results to various academic conferences to demonstrate the validity of the methodology of his various projects. Many of the older folklorists and ethnomusicologists had never fully accepted his later work, and had warned some of the younger ones away from it. Alan knew too much, had done too much, had been there before anyone else, and was too hot for the cool eighties. At one of the annual folklore meetings, someone printed up buttons that showed his picture with a bar across it, the universal sign of "no." At gatherings where he tried to win over some of the young scholars who were now committed to an extreme form of cultural relativism and narrowly defined research projects, they often found his old-school passion to defend the forgotten people of the world a bit embarrassing, and he was mockingly referred to by a few as "The People's Republic of Me." As he saw his influence fading and the support of foundations shifting elsewhere, the energy and vision that had driven him for a lifetime began to waver. He resolved not to publish any more until he could fully respond to his critics. Falling out of touch with even the colleagues who did support him, he retreated.

But Lomax was not done yet. The move from Columbia to a Hunter College building near the Hudson River was an awakening to how much he had accomplished. The boxes and crates, weighed down with more than 8,000 tapes and recordings from the United States, the Caribbean, and Europe, 300,000 feet of film from Africa and Asia, hundreds of hours of dance on film and videocassettes, 400 volumes of printouts, maps and charts, and piles of electronic equipment, were testament to the hours in the field and at the computer, and the sheer human cost of what had been accomplished and what remained to be done. But his work was still stored away in an archive, without the money or facilities for it to be made available to the public. He was beginning to realize, however, that with the rise of personal computers, CD-ROMs, and the digital compression of music and film, all that he had seen and done might now be made accessible to everyone in the world. What was needed was an "intelligent museum," an easy-to-use, interactive computerized audiovisual system that would allow anyone to access the databases he was still developing. It would be called a global jukebox, and "jukebox" was the perfect word for what he had in mind, as it was the electrical playback device that first brought music created in distant places to groups of people in small towns and big cities alike, a machine that Alan and his father had once feared would destroy local and regional styles and bury folk song.

The databases from the cantometrics, choreometrics, parlametrics, and phonotactics projects, along with other musical and ethnographic data, would be the heart of the Global Jukebox, so that musical, dance, and speech styles of single performances, whole cultures, or regions of the world could be called up by the user. The microbehaviors that underlay cultural styles but were virtually impossible to see and difficult to demonstrate could be made visible. Descriptions of cultural styles could be read on the screen as text. Maps of peoples and styles would be used to locate and trace cultural patterns. Statistical comparisons could be made; migrations and settlement patterns might be traced. Every occurrence of a particular feature of style throughout the world could be located. Observations of behavior and their interpretation could be made directly by the individual, as well as the expert. The evolution of culture and the conditions under which it occurred could be reconstructed. A user could code her own examples of performance, enter them in the computer, and locate them globally. Everyone could find his own place in the cultural world, locate his roots, and trace his links to peoples and cultures never imagined.

Alan himself was no computer expert, but he had been working innovatively with communications technology ever since the early 1940s, when he and Jerry Weisner were editing records and experimenting with multitracked recordings in the Library of Congress. If this new idea seemed utopian in the pre-Web, pre-Google days of digital enthusiasm, Lomax was in fact dreaming up what later would be called metadata, huge banks of data from which other data could be derived; in conceiving of discrete features of music as predictors of style, he was imagining the concept of predictive algorithms; and in foreseeing that average people could make reliable judgments about complex style systems, he was anticipating the digital concept of folksonomy—collaborative categorization and indexing. All he needed were some smart young people to work on these ideas, and he found them in Michael Del Rio, Gideon D'Arcangelo, Michael Naimark, and others, who contributed fresh musical, technical, and aesthetic ideas. Once again Lomax was attracting the interest of people with money and equipment: Apple, the MacArthur Foundation, and Interval Research Corporation (headed by Paul Allen, who with Bill Gates had created Microsoft) all helped, and were then followed by the National Science Foundation, which gave him a grant of a million dollars. He was back in business.

An Apple Macintosh IIcx with CD-ROM and laserdisk players constituted the hardware for the Global Jukebox; HyperCard was used as a data management program, and four thousand songs and one thousand dances were selected for its software database. For demonstration of the device there was an LCD projector, a low-resolution LCD panel, and a high-luminosity overhead projector. A prototype was constructed, and Alan, now seventy-six years old, was once again on the road, dragging bulky electronic equipment with him as he demonstrated it to the world. It excited everyone who saw it, with corporate executives spinning out ideas for their own uses on the spot or rushing to the phone to call their colleagues. They had never seen such masses of data organized electronically, and it fired their imaginations. But in the end none of them followed through. Michael Naimark concluded that their failure to invest in the Global Jukebox was part of a central problem of the multimedia industry:

> The Global Jukebox has fallen into an abyss between academic and pop culture, between world-saving and money-making, and between content and technology. And in the new media industry, the technology folks seem to drive the content, rarely the other way around . . . it's too bad, since most of the planet's cultures have the content but not the technology.

In the late 1970s, stage productions built around black composers' works, such as *Ain't Misbehavin'* (1978), *One Mo' Time* (1979), and *Sophisticated Ladies* (1981), had become very successful, and Alan might have found in them a hopeful sign of the integration of long-segregated musical and dance styles. Instead, he was sadly disappointed, dismissing them as travesties, crude misrepresentations of period productions that resulted in stereotypes. Lomax had long dreamed of a production based on Jelly Roll Morton's life, and feared that if he didn't move quickly to shape it himself, it might be done by someone who would turn it into another historical distortion like the *Leadbelly* film. He had already sold the motion picture rights to *Mister Jelly Roll* to Harry Belafonte and Harold Leventhal when he was in need of the money, and Belafonte had since bought Leventhal out when they were unable to interest Hollywood in the idea. But Alan had kept the theatrical rights because he wanted to develop a musical around Morton's life, and had even discussed the idea with jazz saxophonist Bob Wilber and others. Now he proposed to Belafonte that the time was right for the two of them to work on a theatrical musical, with words added to Morton's instrumental compositions. But Belafonte was leaving on a lengthy world tour just as Alan's letter arrived, and nothing came of it.

Years later, producers Margo Lion and Pamela Koslow set out to stage their own musical based on Jelly Roll's life, and they approached Alan with a proposal to make him a partner with a small share in the show. But Alan wanted a part in writing the show, or at the very least wanted an acknowledgment that the musical had been adapted from *Mister Jelly Roll*, neither of which the producers were willing to do. When he learned that they were thinking of August Wilson to write the book for the show in order to bring a black perspective to it, he was sorely torn, as he considered Wilson America's greatest playwright and *Ma Rainey's Black Bottom* a great work of art. Yet he could not bring himself to be involved. Wilson asked to meet with Alan, but when Lomax explained that he wanted a collaborative relationship, a relationship acknowledged by contract, Wilson directed his attorneys to write him that nothing from his book would be used in the musical, and that in the future Alan should communicate with him only through his lawyers. It was the end of their relationship.

Shortly afterwards Wilson's script was rejected by the producers, and George C. Wolfe was brought in to rewrite it. With the recent successes of his satirical revue *The Colored Museum*, and *Spunk*, his adaptation of some short stories by Zora Neale Hurston, Wolfe seemed ideally poised to save the production. But to Wolfe the story of Jelly Roll was that of a man who so hated the "black" side of his heritage that he destroyed himself and everyone close to him—in short, his story was a tragedy, not a romance. The show went forward as *Jelly's Last Jam* and opened in New York in 1992 starring dancers Gregory Hines and Savion Glover as the older and younger Jelly Roll (*this* Jelly Roll was also a tap dancer), with script and direction by Wolfe. Alan was erased from the story, along with most of

Morton's life. The spirit of Morton's music was gone as well. To Lomax the show was another example of the corny Dixieland clichés and raucous laughter and singing of all Broadway shows set in the 1920s. It ignored the efforts of Katherine Dunham and Zora Neale Hurston in the 1930s to free Harlem musicals from the conventions of Broadway theater by bringing in the music and dance of black America and the Caribbean. By turning Morton into a dancer, it obscured the circum-Caribbean rhythms of his music and substituted the more straightforward 4/4 meter of East Coast tap. And in order to accommodate a shallow sense of jazz history, Alan complained, Morton was portrayed as taking part in jam sessions, a practice that he disliked. In his preface to the 1993 edition of *Mister Jelly Roll*, Alan criticized Wolfe bitterly for condemning Morton for race prejudice on slim evidence, as if Morton were the only person of color to hold such views. But *Jelly's Last Jam* had nonetheless gone on to win the cheers of critics, three Tony awards, and six Drama Desk awards in 1992.

Many of the issues Alan raised against the musical were on his mind because at that time he was writing *The Land Where the Blues Began*, a summary of his experiences with African American culture and the South that was published in 1993. The book represented something of an odyssey of what he had seen and done, his memories of preachers, storytellers, blues singers, church congregations, the levee and railroad builders, prisons and chain gangs, the police, Big Bill Broonzy, and Chicago blues. Included were sections of "Burning Hell," the article on prisons he had never been able to sell, a history of the blues; a part of the book that the Fisk/Library of Congress team never completed; and pieces of an autobiography. It also accommodated sections of another book he never finished, *My Heart Struck Sorrow*, which if it had been completed back in the 1940s would have been an exposé, a racial bombshell, and an introduction to a music and a people's existence of which most of his readers were unaware.

Among those who read *The Land Where the Blues Began* were many who did not recall the full extent of the horrors of the caste/class system of the South in the 1930s and 1940s. Nor did they recall the tales of the blues collectors of the 1960s who fanned out across the South in search of what was left of the great black troubadours whose songs were passing quickly into the voices of blues-based rock and roll. When Lomax wrote about what he saw in the South by saying, "My heart struck a depth of sorrow and hurt such as I had never imagined," and described the wonder of finding those great bards driving tractors or picking cotton, he faced an audience many of whom were made uncomfortable by his witness. Instead of praising his work, they judged him as a type, an exploitative white southerner, and took pains to point out the shortcomings in his account—he collapsed two Tennessee trips into one; he wasn't up on recent blues scholarship; and was that really Robert Johnson's mother to whom he spoke?—or looked for a crack in his outrage at naked injustice and rejected the romanticism of his account of discovery as crypto-racism. He was vindicated, however, when *The Land Where the Blues Began* won the National Book Critics Circle Award in 1993.

Then Luigi Cavalli-Sforza, the originator of the Human Genome Diversity Project, and other geneticists became interested in his projects. Things were once again looking brighter, but just as his health began to deteriorate. When doctors recommended surgery of the carotid artery, he was operated on in mid-1994 and emerged from the first stage of his surgery successfully. Yet after the second operation at the end of 1995, he had a stroke. He was kept for five months in Beth Abraham, a rehabilitation facility in the Bronx, and made great strides in recovery. When he was released, an apparent overdose of blood thinner caused a brain hemorrhage, and he became unable to speak or write or care for himself. He fell into depression, living in a small house in Long Island, with only $9,000 left in the bank, $800 a month retirement from Columbia University, and $1,100 a month from Social Security, while the IRS was still attaching his income. In order to get the money for the care he would need, Anna reopened negotiations with Rounder Records to bring out recordings of most of the music he had collected. She moved him to Tarpon Springs, Florida, where for the next seven years he lived quietly with her and her son, Odysseus.

Alan Lomax died on July 19, 2002, at age eighty-seven.

After his death, the obituaries noted that Alan Lomax had been a musicologist, archivist, singer, DJ, filmmaker, photographer, author of books, producer of dozens of radio, TV, video, and concert programs and hundreds of recordings, in addition to being the world's most famous folklorist. Still, they might have also added that he was an anthropologist, political activist, lobbyist, and, in his later years, something of a social theorist. This was a remarkable achievement for a man who never held an academic post or a high government position, nor received an international or even a national award for his work until the very end of his life. But Lomax was arguably one of the most influential Americans of the twentieth century, a man who changed not only how everyone listened to music but even how they viewed America.

Lomax was part of the group of competing yet intertwined interests defining the cultural landscape of the first half of the twentieth century—a group that included the New England Brahmins, the labor movement, the exclusivity and cultural conservatism of a Henry Ford or a Bascom Lamar Lunsford, the folklore scholars, and the entertainment and communications industries, all of them contending to set the agenda for American identity. It was a time when race and social class were given new status and visibility through popular culture, an epoch in which new electronic media brought the social pariah and the rejected into everyone's living room. (George Clooney's character in the folk-song-soaked film *O Brother, Where Art Thou?* says of the coming of electricity in the South, "Things will never be the same.")

Lomax had begun his career with an early-twentieth-century folklorist's aesthetic, the belief that a song was a thing, an object to be collected, labeled, and put on display as a text that was evidence of a community's collective cultural creation. Yet as he tramped through canefields and visited prisons, he became aware of the astonishing creativity and artistry of individual folk performers, something not discernible in the frozen words of songbooks. He believed his own collection could function not as a display of relics from the old worlds of Europe and Africa, but rather as proof of the vitality and the richness of the living traditions of people. Folklore could show what it meant to be an American. At the same time, Lomax was convinced that every village and town had its own stars, singers and composers who captured the spirit of their people. If these artists were presented properly, they could attract an audience as large as America itself. Folk culture could become pop culture.

In Washington he was given the opportunity to document all of America's folk artists, even to present them in popular recordings and on national radio. When he moved to New York City he transported the southern idea of the local music festival there, eventually filling Town Hall every few weeks with an eclectic mix of black and white folksingers. Thereafter, nothing excited him more than acting as impresario for the whole country, bringing unknown rustics to venues like Newport or Carnegie Hall and seeing them win over crowds of urban sophisticates.

As the poet laureate of the folk, he was viewed by some as a kindly, benign guide to a nostalgic return trip to simpler times. But he was also the pied piper of the Other America, the common people, the forgotten, the ethnic, those who always came to life in troubled times—in the Great Depression, in the storms of World War II, during the postwar anti-Communist hysteria, and in the chaos of the era of civil rights and counterculturalism—those who with their resentment and unpredictability could provoke the deepest fears in the more privileged. At such times folk songs seemed not so much charming souvenirs as ominous and threatening portents.

In his later years, travel abroad exposed Lomax to a greater variety of song styles and content and set him to wondering about the deeper functions of song in all societies. He recalled the rhythms of the rattle and flap of pulleys and sails aboard ship, and the grunting and singing of deckhands; the thwack of axes against wood and the cries of the prison work team leaders; and the tears and pinched faces of singers in the southern Mediterranean. Eventually he turned to the cross-cultural techniques used by anthropologists and drew on insights derived from his own experience with psychotherapy to work out a complex vision of song and, later, dance and speech, as part of the apparatus of cultural adaptation and survival. Lomax now asked us to listen more closely to recordings, to the sounds that revealed a depth of emotions previously undisclosed, in light of what amounted to his theory of an auditory unconscious. His later work in photography of dance and body motion demystified elements of human nature far beyond what Edweard Muybridge's pioneering freeze-frame photographic studies of animal and human movement had accomplished before him.

One of the last pieces of writing that Alan did before he fell ill was the notes for what he was calling a "general theory," his first steps toward a synthesis of his life's work. He began by reaffirming well-established anthropological knowledge, and then adding his own findings: Cultures are systems of adaptation that shape and motivate the behavior of those within their borders, and they over time vary with survival needs and environment. The main features of culture—the means of subsistence, population size, nature of government, level of social stratification, solidarity of social groups, technology, methods of childrearing, family size and type, sexual division of labor, severity of sexual sanctions—all take symbolic form in music, dance, and speaking styles, all of which reflect and support each other in a tradition. So powerful are these symbolic functions that within a few seconds of hearing a particular piece of music or seeing a dance, audiences accept or reject the performance because it clearly states its cultural allegiance to some form of social structure, some type of adaptation, that is or isn't important to the audience. Every cultural system has affinity for some other cultures, and the world is made up of twelve to fourteen cultural regions with some sixty subregions. Despite the differences in these cultural systems, Lomax thought they were all ultimately traceable to two ancient and primal sources—the African gatherers and the hunters of North Asia.

These were big ideas, and he saw there was much left to do to support them. Lomax wanted to apply his theories to folktales, and the stories and pop songs that derive from them, and then turn his attention to the visual arts. He was especially concerned with the vanishing of some cultural systems under the spread of modernity, seeing musical diversity as akin to biodiversity: every song style that disappeared was potentially as serious a tragedy as the loss of a species. He was also seeking out new forms of communication and education to create tolerance and appreciation for the diversity of cultures in the world. (Much of this work—which involved the physical return of works of art and the means to document and analyze them to their originators; the payment of royalties; the development of teaching materials; and the use of the Web to make the databases available to the world—was continued and expanded by his daughter, Anna Lomax Wood, through the Association for Cultural Equity.)

While Alan's public influence reached its peak between 1940 and 1960, when he was the single greatest force in bringing folk songs to American awareness, it continues today in any number of cultural domains: in the music used for Alvin Ailey's dance "Rainbow 'Round My Shoulder"; in the soundtrack of *Gangs of New York*; in his persona as played by an actor in the film *Cadillac Records*, or as animated in *RiP: A Remix Manifesto*, or in the spirit of the PBS children's show *Lomax the Hound of Music*; in his field recordings as remixed by Moby on *Play*, or by the Italian sound collagists Fabio Orsi and My Cat Is an Alien's recording *For Alan Lomax*; and even in the street names of McGill's Common in Columbia, Maryland, that were taken from Alan's *Folk Songs of North America*.

At times his influence can be seen in the distortions of the funhouse mirror of American culture, where a hard-fought idea can be perverted through the countervailing forces of social and technological interests and the discourse of fashion. Though he never had the time or the funding to make the Global Jukebox fully operational to the public, the idea nonetheless migrated into various commercial ventures, most notably Pandora.com, an online project developed by the Music Genome. In Pandora, more than four hundred "musical measures" ("breathiness," "depth of bass," and the like) are used to analyze each song in a database, and users can enter either a song or several musical characteristics that in turn are used to find other songs that are similar, then fed into a personal "radio station" that plays nothing but examples of that type of music for the listener. A request for, say, "Barbara Allen" sung solo by a woman might lead to Texas Gladden's recording of that folk song, then to Hazel Dickens's "Pretty Bird," Dorothy Elliott's "Adieu to Judges and Juries," "Whirling Whorl" by Anne Briggs, and on to many others with similar characteristics. But where Lomax's Global Jukebox took the listener beyond his or her own tastes, beyond his own culture, leading to new worlds of music, Pandora's recommendations based on personal taste tend to lead sideways, apparently staying closer to production style than to deeper principles of cultural and musical organization. It creates a musical identity specific to the personal-taste parameters entered, closing the listener into a sonic world of her or his making.

Throughout his lifetime of struggle with commercial media, Lomax anticipated the misunderstanding of his ideas, though he was not always able to prevent it. Following the disappointment he felt when the captains of the information technology industry could not see the uses he proposed for the Global Jukebox, he drew on his own cultural theories to explain to himself the source of this misunderstanding: "The romantic tradition has long provided a needed emotional balance to the practical, operational forces in North-West-European culture. It is crucial that we gain some perspective on this very unusual—in the eyes of most humans, rather outlandish—cultural tradition." He then traced the history of the cattle herders and fishermen of Scotland, Ireland, Norway, and Spain, with their solo ballads and dances, single-family farms, deep-sea fishing and boat building, to factory systems in Great Britain, the Low Countries, and northern France.

> When I hear the moralists of the present era bemoaning the materialism of the electronic-industrial system, accusing it of lacking in a value system, I wish to remind them that the value profile of modern American culture is a reworking of this ancient North-east European tradition. It was present in the court of Beowulf, who was no less self-aggrandizing than the overseas market manager of Ford and Sony. The inventive flair of a group of programmers tackling a problem in Silicon Valley replicates the team-work of a boat-building crew in the Norwegian fiords or in the Chesapeake, where the clipper ship was designed and launched. Such teams bring together the talents of a peer group of equal experts, each one listened to in his turn respectfully and with the absorbed attention given to a singer in the Scottish ballad circle.
>
> The driving force is ancient—the sure knowledge of the lone fisherman, herdsman, and crofter that if he doesn't manage his affairs on his own, his family will starve and his generation will disappear. This powerful and ancient incentive, fostered in the cold latitudes, is now focused with equal intensity on the bottom-line as a commercial solution for the solution of all human problems. Its shibboleths are total independence for the individual and free trade. But we may question whether this primeval Northwest European solution to human affairs, which is now summed up in the doctrine of the bottom line, can apply to corporations like General Motors and General Magic, and have much relevance for other adaptive cultural systems with other goals and other techniques for arriving at them.

Yet in the end, it was those very commercial and bureaucratic bodies he struggled with who recognized him for his achievements. After the film awards, the National Medal of the Arts, and the National Book Critics Award, he was named a "Living Legend" at the Library of Congress's bicentennial celebration in 2000. He received an honorary doctorate of philosophy from Tulane in 2001 and a Trustees Award of the National Academy of Recording Arts in 2003 for his lifelong contributions to music. It was all far more than his folklorist and anthropologist colleagues were willing to grant him.

ACKNOWLEDGMENTS

This book began with discussions I had with Bess Lomax Hawes and Roger D. Abrahams, two friends of many years back, who encouraged me to write it. Bess, whom I had known almost as long as I knew her brother, was an inspiration and a great help, even while she was writing her own autobiography. Roger has supported me on any number of projects, often as my coauthor, and his help on this one was essential: in addition to being the most important folklorist in the United States, he had known and worked with Alan Lomax. If the dice had been rolled differently, Roger would have been my coauthor of this book. Once I began the research, Anna Lomax Wood, Alan's daughter, helped me in countless ways, and has been tolerant of my often awkward forays into her family's life. I have also benefited enormously from her own brilliant interpretations and extensions of her father's work. These three people above all made this book possible.

Biographers depend on letters, manuscripts, published materials, and interviews for their work, and in writing this book I was blessed with an exceptional archive that Alan Lomax built throughout his life. This collection filled several large rooms in the office of the Association for Cultural Equity at Hunter College in New York City, with 5,000 hours of sound recordings, 400,000 feet of motion picture film, 2,450 videotapes, 2,000 books and journals, hundreds of photographic prints and negatives, several databases concerning portions of the archive, and more than 120 linear feet of manuscripts, letters, field notes, files, program scripts, indexes, and book and article manuscripts. To find my way through that collection, I, like many others before me, counted on the courtesy and help of its staff: Odysseus Chairetakis, Bertram Lyons, Nathan Salsburg, Molly W. Sirignano, John M. Tan, and others. To each of them I offer my thanks. But I want to single out Don Fleming and Ellen Harold for special praise. For years they put up with my endless requests for scraps of paper, tapes, images, explanations, and guidance, and did so cheerfully and expertly.

When the Lomax archive was moved to the American Folklife Center of the Library of Congress in Washington, D.C., and was added to the very large Lomax collection that institution already had, I followed its migration there and again was given help and guidance by its wonderful staff of scholar/librarians. My thanks to Peter Bartis, Peggy Bulger, Jennifer Cutting, Judith Gray, Nancy Groce, Joe Hickerson, Fabian Holt, Guha Shankar, Michael Taft, Stephen Winick, and others, and most especially to Todd Harvey, the man whose role it is to oversee the Alan Lomax Collection. His knowledge of the materials and his commitment to their preservation and use is exemplary. In another part of the Library of Congress, the Music Division, I was especially fortunate to have the aid and advice of Larry Appelbaum and Matt Barton, two individuals whose knowledge extends over vast territories.

I'm pleased to have a chance to state my gratitude to other libraries and librarians: the Chicago Historical Society, The Woody Guthrie Foundation and Archives, The Briscoe Center for American History at the University of Texas at Austin, the Indiana University Library, the Stanford University Library, Diana Cary at the Schlesinger Library of Radcliff College, Elizabeth Davis of the Music & Arts Library of Columbia University, James Moske of the New York Public Library Archives, Karl Schrom, the Recordings Collection supervisor of the Irving S. Gilmore Music Library of Yale University, Bruce Boyd Raeburn of the William Ransom Hogan Archive of New Orleans Jazz of Tulane University, and Dan M. Morgenstern and his staff of the Institute of Jazz Studies, Rutgers University, Newark.

Profound thanks to those who worked with Lomax or knew him well and helped steer my efforts. Pete and Toshi Seeger, who have always been open to writers, fans, and musicians, treated me with great kindness. Their long memories were invaluable. Others who were close to Alan and became saints of this book were John Bishop, Shirley Collins, Gideon D'Arcangelo, Michael Del Rio, Victor Grauer, Carol Kulig, Joan Halifax, Robin Roberts, and Roswell Rudd.

Scholars who have written on Lomax's work in various parts of the world were essential to this book, and I thank them for their industry and care: Judith R. Cohen for her work on Lomax's Spanish travels, E. David Gregory for his publications on Lomax in the UK, Goffredo Plastino's writings on the years in Italy, Nolan Porterfield's biography of John A. Lomax, and Robert Hemenway's research on Alan Lomax and Zora Neale Hurston. I also owe a great debt to Sara Villa for her support and her expert Italian translations.

A special thanks to Nat Hentoff, who is the most generous writer I've ever known, and who gave me permission to quote from his excellent but unpublished *New Yorker* profile of Alan Lomax. A thousand thanks and cheers to George Avakian, Gage Averill, Robert Baron, Erika Bourguignon, Oscar Brand, Dave Burrell, John Cohen, Hal Conklin, Alistair Cooke, Steve Feld, Grey Gundaker, Billy Joe Harris, Edward Hirsch, Bill Knowlin, Michael McLaughlin, Mike Meddings, Jon Meltzer, James Napoli, Roz Payne (daughter of Edith Berkman), Brian Priestley, Irwin Silber, Studs Terkel, and Izzy Young.

Anita Hoyvik, Sarah Lash, and Matt Sakakeeny assisted in the research, although "assisted" doesn't cover the resourcefulness and creativity each of them brought to this project. Anita was especially helpful in her close readings of the various Jelly Roll Morton documents and in her knowledge of documentary photography and cinematography; Sarah steered through the complexity of libraries with the resourcefulness of a true scholar; and Matt read his way through stacks of Lomax publications and letters with the discernment of a world class ethnomusicologist and media specialist. Rita Putnam provided unique musical and editorial advice, for which I am eternally grateful.

My day job at Yale University and then Columbia University made this book financially possible; the Griswold Research Fund of the Whitney Humanities Center at Yale University gave me support in the early days of the research. My students and colleagues at both institutions were always inspirations.

Among the other saints of the book is my editor at Viking, Rick Kot, a man of infinite patience, optimism, and life-saving editorial eyes. My thanks also to Laura Tisdel, Kate Griggs, Carla Bolte, Roland Ottewell, and Patti Pirooz. And high in the pantheon of the book's deities is my agent, Sarah Lazin, also blessed with patience and the long view, thank God, and who sticks by her clients even in the face of natural (and unnatural) disasters. Kudos also to her worthy assistant, Rebecca Ferreira.

Finally, there are those to thank who have sustained and tolerated my projects for years: Nick Spitzer, Robert Farris Thompson, and Dan Rose, without whom my life wouldn't be the same. And as always, thankfully, there were Marilyn Sue Szwed, Matt Szwed, and now Heather Szwed to forgive and even aid my literary obsessions.

Among the [illegible] of the [illegible].

[illegible] there are [illegible] to [illegible] who have [illegible] and [illegible] [illegible] [illegible] [illegible] [illegible] [illegible] [illegible] [illegible] [illegible] [illegible] [illegible] [illegible] [illegible] the same [illegible] [illegible] [illegible] [illegible] [illegible] [illegible] [illegible] [illegible] [illegible] [illegible] [illegible] [illegible] [illegible].

NOTES

Most of the research for this book was conducted when the bulk of the Lomax materials were located in the Alan Lomax Archive at the Association for Cultural Equity in New York City. Since that time most of these materials have been moved to the Alan Lomax Collection in the American Folklife Center at the Library of Congress. Materials labeled AL here were among those in New York City and have since been reorganized in the Alan Lomax Collection. Those labeled LC were always in the Alan Lomax Collection at the Library of Congress and remain there. The other major source of Lomax documents is the Center for American History at the University of Texas at Austin (UTA).

For more photographs of Alan Lomax, visit http://www.culturalequity.org/pubs/ce_pubs_books_szwed.php.

Chapter 1: From Chisholm Trail to Harvard Yard

5 **Two years after the end of the Civil War:** This account of John Lomax and his family is indebted to Nolan Porterfield's excellent biography of John Lomax, *Last Cavalier: The Life and Times of John A. Lomax* (Urbana and Chicago: University of Illinois Press, 1996).

9 **"tawdry, cheap and unworthy":** John A. Lomax, *Adventures of a Ballad Hunter* (New York: Macmillan, 1947), 32.

9 **"a nervous collapse":** Porterfield, 501.

9 **"a general breakdown":** Ibid., 138.

14 **"Our house was a two-story building":** Nat Hentoff, "Profile: Alan Lomax—Surprising the Folk Song," January 18, 1960, 35, unpublished, *The New Yorker Records, c. 1924–1984,* New York Public Library, Manuscripts and Archives Division, Box 1506, folders 7–8.

15 **"In addition to being a talent scout for the university":** Ibid., 36.

15 **"successfully completed a course of study":** Ibid., 38.

15 **"I was given an absurd notion":** Ibid.

16 **"I've always had an oppressive sense":** Ibid., 39.

16 **"I've always been afraid of being rejected":** Ibid., 40.

17 **"I decided not to die":** Ibid., 49.

17 **"He was everything Father wanted":** Bess Lomax Hawes interviewed by John Szwed, California, 2005.

17 **Alan called the first ten years:** Anna Lomax Wood interviewed by John Szwed, 2008.

18 **"At thirteen I was a junior":** Alan Lomax to Bess Lomax, April 1934, AL.

18 **The headmaster and his wife became so concerned:** Cora St. John to Mrs. Lomax, February 1, 1930.

19 **He had to be instructed how to use a knife and fork:** Nat Hentoff, "Profile: Alan Lomax," 40.

19 **Alan apologized and promised:** Alan Lomax to John A. Lomax, February 19, 1930, UTA.

19 **His mother followed with her own thirteen-page letter:** Bess Brown Lomax to Alan Lomax, undated, UTA.

19 **But Alan was not to be threatened:** Alan Lomax to Ruby Lomax, April 20, 1930, UTA.

20 **"brought me to the brink of the greatest enjoyment":** Alan Lomax to John A Lomax, April 26, 1930, UTA.

20 **"frighteningly smart"**: Walter Goldschmidt quoted in Nat Hentoff, "Profile: Alan Lomax," 39.
21 **"Race and culture were central topics"**: Ibid., 39.
21 **"It wasn't a matter of folklore"**: Ibid., 44.
21 **"a woman who played blues guitar"**: Ibid., 44.
21 **"In visiting Ruby's place"**: Alan Lomax, untitled, undated manuscript, AL.
22 **"I was numb"**: Nat Hentoff, "Profile: Alan Lomax," 41.
23 **"warped by their environment"**: Alan Lomax to John A. Lomax, n.d., ca. 1932, UTA.
24 **"For your own good and happiness"**: Alan Lomax to John A. Lomax, n.d. ca. December, 1932, UTA.
24 **Alan found himself sitting through Kittredge's class:** Alan Lomax to Peter (his psychiatrist), n.d., AL.
24 **Alan was now the head of a student organization:** Nat Hentoff, "Profile: Alan Lomax," 41.
25 **"By that time I shall be partially soaked"**: Alan Lomax to John A. Lomax, undated, ca. April 1932.
25 **"Dear Father"**: Alan Lomax to John A, Lomax, n.d., ca. April 1932, AL.
27 **"In dealing with me for the last two years"**: John A. Lomax to Alan Lomax, n.d., ca. April 1932. AL.
27 **There had been previous demonstrations:** Robert A. Bakeman, "Lawrence Decides," *Nation* 132, no. 3432 (April 15, 1931): 404–6.
28 **Later he said that he expected half of Boston:** Alan Lomax FBI files, April 3, 1942, 9–19.
28 **The officials assumed that Alan's bail had been paid:** Nat Hentoff, "Profile: Alan Lomax," 42.
28 **The *Boston Traveler* wrote about his arrest:** *Boston Traveler*, May 10, 1932.
28 **"It is . . . simple truth"**: John A. Lomax to Alan Lomax, n.d., ca. June, 1932, AL.
29 **"They know nothing of the future"**: Nat Hentoff, "Profile: Alan Lomax," 43.
29 **"First, it is imperative"**: Alan Lomax, untitled, undated paper, UTA.
29 **"had Mr. Lomax not had pneumonia"**: Untitled, undated letter, AL.
30 **"A year at Harvard has just run away from me"**: Alan Lomax to Ruby Terrill, 1932, AL.

Chapter 2: Road Scholars

32 **When John Jr. left them in July:** Nolan Porterfield, *Last Cavalier: The Life and Times of John A. Lomax* (Urbana and Chicago: University of Illinois Press, 1996), 285.
33 **"he was living like a hippie"**: Bess Lomax Hawes, interviewed by John Szwed, California, 2005.
33 **"spend your years in folk-song work"**: Alan Lomax to John A. Lomax, April 1933, AL.
34 **Walter Goldschmidt could not believe:** Quoted in John Bishop, "Alan Lomax (1915–2002): A Remembrance," *Visual Anthropology Review* 17, no. 2 (Fall–Winter 2001–2002): 15.
34 **"Our cook, Ethel"**: Nat Hentoff, "Profile: Alan Lomax—Surprising the Folk Song," January 18, 1969, 43, unpublished, *The New Yorker Records, c. 1924–1984*, New York Public Library, Manuscripts and Archives Division, Box 1506, folders 7–8.
34 **"the prettiest girl I had ever seen"**: Alan Lomax, untitled, undated manuscript. AL.
36 **"The voice of the skinny little black woman"**: Alan Lomax. "From a Great Dark River," *Radio Times*, November, 23, 1951, 6, AL.
37 **"Poor farmer"**: Alan Lomax, "Alan Lomax," in *Decade of Destiny*, ed. Judith L. Graubart and Alice V. Graubart (Chicago: Contemporary Books, 1979), 311.
37 **"Now, Mr. President"**: "Folk Music in the Roosevelt Era," transcription of interview by Ralph Rinzler, in *Folk Music in the Roosevelt White House: A Commemorative Program* (Washington, DC: Office of Folklife Programs, Smithsonian Institution, 1982), 14–17.
37 **"When the record was over"**: Lomax, in *Decade of Destiny*, 311–12.
38 **"The Negro in the South"**: John A. Lomax, *Adventures of a Ballad Hunter* (New York: Macmillan, 1947), 129.
39 **"They were very polite"**: Lomax, in *Decade of Destiny*, 312.
40 **"They were slow-dragging"**: Alan Lomax, "From a Great Dark River," *Radio Times*, November 23, 1951, 6, AL.
42 **But for John the true thrill of the place:** John A. Lomax, *Adventures of a Ballad Hunter*, 119.
42 **Alan was annoyed by what he saw as his father's excessive romanticism:** Alan Lomax, " 'Sinful' Songs of the Southern Negro," *Southwest Review* 19 (Winter 1934): 16.
42 **"I'm goin' tell you somethin' "**: Ibid., 15.

43 **On hearing his own voice in playback:** "Who's Here: Alan Lomax," *Dan's Papers*, July 27, 1990, 17, AL.
44 **In a letter he wrote from Angola:** John A. Lomax, *Adventures of a Ballad Hunter*, 121.
44 **But then, just as they were leaving:** Huddie Ledbetter's nickname is here written as Lead Belly, the spelling preferred by his family and heirs.
46 **"I knows what you wants":** Lomax, " 'Sinful' Songs," 12.
47 **"a barren field for collection":** Alan Lomax to Carl Engel, August 1, 1933, LC.
47 **"Were it possible for the world to listen":** Lomax, *Adventures of a Ballad Hunter*, 124.
48 **"When the men finished with work":** Nat Hentoff, "Profile: Alan Lomax," 70.
49 **"The people who sang for us were in stripes":** Lomax, in *Decade of Destiny*, 313.
50 **Alan wanted to help pay for the girl's education:** L. C. Henderson, Principal, Harlan Kentucky High School, to Alan Lomax, August 31, 1933, AL.
51 **"So, for the first time":** Lomax, in *Decade of Destiny*, 314.
51 **His father was beginning to see Alan's success:** Porterfield, *Last Cavalier*, 304–5.
51 **Herbert Putnam agreed:** Ibid., 305.
52 **"part of the ceremonies":** Ibid., 307.
54 **Carnegie then offered him money:** Ibid., 314–15.
56 **The leader's part is short:** Alan Lomax, Notes to *Cajun & Creole Music 1934/1937, Vol. 2*, Rounder 1843 CD, 5.
57 **She called herself "the ghetto girl":** Walter Goldschmidt interviewed by John Bishop, July 2001.
57 **"Why do you isolate yourself":** Becky Machanofsky to Alan Lomax, June 4, 1934, AL.
58 **"started to sing Negro worksongs":** Alan Lomax to Peter Neuman, psychiatrist, no date, AL.

Chapter 3: The Saga of Lead Belly

59 **Alan and his father may nonetheless have felt:** *American Roots Music*, "Oral Histories: Alan Lomax," http://www.pbs.org/americanrootsmusic/pbs_arm_oralh_alanlomax.html. A year after Lead Belly's release from prison John wrote the warden and learned the conditions of his release. See letter to John A. Lomax in Wilton, CT, from R. L. Hines, General Manager of the Louisiana State Penitentiary, Baton Rouge, LA, Mary Elizabeth Barnicle Papers, Schlesinger Library, Radcliffe College, 1/15/35. John did acknowledge Hines's letter and the reason for Lead Belly's release in a footnote to *Negro Folk Songs as Sung by Leadbelly*, 33.
60 **"If you get there":** Nolan Porterfield, *Last Cavalier: The Life and Times of John A. Lomax* (Urbana and Chicago: University of Illinois Press, 1996), 322.
60 **Alan wanted desperately for Lead Belly to be his friend:** Bess Lomax Hawes interviewed by John Szwed, California, 2005.
61 **His article also contained song texts:** Henry Smith to Alan Lomax, February 6, 1934, AL.
61 **It was Sandburg who first encouraged John:** Carl Sandberg to Alan Lomax, November 3, 1934, AL.
62 **Alan did find bookings for him:** Carl Sandburg to Alan Lomax, March 1, 1935, AL.
64 **"For Father I continue to be a source of disappointment":** Alan Lomax to Dr. Chris Mansell, December 21, 1934, AL.
65 **"I can beat Calloway singin' every time":** *New York Herald Tribune*, as quoted in Charles K. Wolfe and Kip Lornell, *The Life and Legend of Leadbelly* (New York: HarperCollins, 1992), 140.
66 **"Lead Belly," John wrote his wife:** John A. Lomax to Ruby Terrill, January 1935, quoted in Wolfe and Lornell, *Life and Legend of Leadbelly*, 144.
66 **"Up to now this experiment has been a sort of nightmare":** John A. Lomax to Ruby Terrill, January 6, 1935, AL.
66 **Despite his ambivalence:** Wolfe and Lornell, *Life and Legend of Leadbelly*, 147.
67 **The deal granted the publisher the right:** John, in fact, never copyrighted individual songs, but did copyright them when they were anthologized as part of a book.
67 **"We retired to the country":** *American Roots Music*, "Oral Histories: Alan Lomax," http://www.pbs.org/americanrootsmusic/pbs_arm_oralh_alanlomax.html.
68 **"We went over Lead Belly's repertory with him":** Ibid.
68 **"We asked Lead Belly how his songs came to be":** Frederick Ramsey in *Playback* magazine, 1950, 4.
69 **"He sang, he was very pleasant socially":** Alan Lomax, "Alan Lomax," in *Decade of Destiny*, ed. Judith L. Graubart and Alice V. Graubart (Chicago: Contemporary Books, 1979), 314–15.

70 **In February, for example, they were visited:** John A. Lomax to Oliver Strunk, March 16, 1935, AL.

71 **But he also claimed:** Wolfe and Lornell, *Life and Legend of Leadbelly*, 195.

71 **Some of the guitar accompaniments:** Ibid., 183; "Appendix on Lead Belly's Music by George Herzog," unpublished manuscript, in AL.

71 **"We present this set of songs":** John A. Lomax and Alan Lomax, *Negro Folk Songs as Sung by Leadbelly* (New York: Macmillan, 1936), xiii.

72 **"Beyond the doggerel":** Lawrence Gellert, *New Masses*, December 11, 1934, 21–22.

72 **A few years later, Richard Wright:** Richard Wright, "Huddie Ledbetter, Famous Negro Folk Artist, Sings the Songs of Scottsboro and His People," *Daily Worker*, August 12, 1937.

73 **"Have you got a pistol?":** *March of Time* newsreel, No. 2, 1935.

73 **Stripes were the visual identifier of prisoners:** Al Rose and Edmond Souchon, *New Orleans Jazz: A Family Album* (Baton Rouge: Louisiana University Press, 1984), 244.

73 **Alan also detested:** Some forty years after the events had occurred, Alan commented on Parks's film, and on the media's development of the Lead Belly narrative:

> Whoever was responsible [for this film], they made a creampuff out of a tiger of a man. They turned the tough and rancid landscape of Texas and Louisiana into the "perpetual spring of the downs of southern England." None of the prisoners were shown to sweat, whereas in actuality it was so hot that sweat poured off them in sheets. . . . The baby-faced, smooth-muscled actor playing Lead Belly doesn't begin to do justice to Lead Belly's genius. When Lead Belly first sang as a complete unknown before an audience of 3,000, the purity of his thrilling tenor voice drew a standing ovation.
>
> The prison farms of the American South were living hells of violence, evil, and despair. They were American Dachaus, where inmates worked from before sunrise to dark of night, supervised by trusties with shotguns. A surly look or even a reluctant move could get you killed by the guards, no questions asked. The existence of these prisons inspired a terror that kept the population in line throughout the South. There was one way and one way only to respond and that was through accommodation. Yet in the film, Lead Belly is shown grabbing the whip out of a guard's hand and indignantly protesting injustice like a 1960s civil rights leader.
>
> By sentimentalizing Lead Belly and making him into a contemporary black man openly protesting injustice, the filmmakers missed an opportunity to tell the grimmest, strangest, important American story of the camps that kept blacks in line for 100 years. There was no way for an individual to survive if he fought back. Lead Belly played it the other way. He smiled and kowtowed and came out stronger than ever. Lead Belly was made of indestructible steel, "a piece of human carborundum." When the filmmakers ignored this authentic character and made up a pastiche, a softie, a protester, they turned an American story into treacle. The prison camp was turned into a 1960s era TV-comedy Nazi prisoner of war camp. It was not hot. The sukey jump was choreographed like an Alvin Ailey ballet. Lead Belly and Blind Lemon Jefferson are shown playing North Carolina mountain-style blues in front of a Confederate flag while dancers do a 1965 white hop.
>
> Alan Lomax, untitled, unpublished note, ca. 1976.

74 **When Lomax returned he was furious:** Porterfield, *Last Cavalier*, 356.

74 **"I found some of my color":** Wolfe and Lornell, *Life and Legend of Leadbelly*, 171.

75 **As they were leaving he gave Martha $298.94:** Porterfield, *Last Cavalier*, 361, 365; Wolfe and Lornell, *Life and Legend of Leadbelly*, 179.

Chapter 4: Travels with Zora Neale Hurston and Mary Elizabeth Barnicle

78 **"The oaths of secrecy":** Alan Lomax, "Zora Neale Hurston—A Life of Negro Folklore," *Sing Out!* 10 (October/November 1960): 12.

78 **"she was no reserved scientist":** Ibid.

78 **"Lead Belly that all of us":** Alan Lomax to Robert Hemenway, November 17, 1976, courtesy of Robert Hemenway.

79 **Early in 1935:** Zora Neale Hurston to Carl Van Vechten, January 5, 1935; Zora Neale Hurston to John A. Lomax, January 5, 1935, AL.

80 **"You can't just sit down and ask people":** Langston Hughes, *The Big Sea: An Autobiography* (New York: Hill and Wang, 1993 [1940]), 196–97.

81 **"And if he asks you what's my Union":** Alan Lomax, Woody Guthrie, and Pete Seeger, *Hard Hitting Songs for Hard-Hit People* (New York: Oak Publications, 1967), 84–85.

81 **"My Dostoievskyan weight of guilt":** Nat Hentoff, "Profile: Alan Lomax—Surprising the Folk Song," January 18, 1969, 51–52, unpublished, *The New Yorker Records, c. 1924–1984*, New York Public Library, Manuscripts and Archives Division, Box 1506, folders 7–8.

81 **"I can't tell you that you can't live there":** Ibid., 52.

82 **"Day by day now":** Zora Neale Hurston, *Their Eyes Were Watching God* (1937), 196, quoted in Bruce Bastin, *A Tribute to Zora Neale Hurston*, notes to Flyright-Matchless Library of Congress Series, vols. 3 and 4 (SDM 257 and SDM 258), 1974.

83 **Alan had to write his father:** Alan Lomax to John A. Lomax, June 22, 1935, AL.

83 **Hurston tried to eke out a little funding:** Zora Neale Hurston to Ruth Benedict, June 28, 1936, *Zora Neale Hurston: A Life in Letters*, ed. Carla Kaplan (New York: Anchor, 2003).

83 **"Miss Hurston . . . is ambitious":** Alan Lomax to John A. Lomax, n.d., AL.

83 **"Miss B. and Miss H. were raging":** Alan Lomax to John A. Lomax, June 22, 1935, AL.

83 **"Miss Hurston, who had been":** Alan Lomax to Oliver Strunk, August 3, 1935, AL.

84 **"Negro Songs there are probably":** "Folk Lore Student Plans Tour of Bahamas in Search of Songs," unidentified news clip, AL.

84 **"energy patterns and social [work] roles":** Alan Lomax, Notes to *Deep River of Song: The Bahamas 1935*, Rounder Records 11661-1822-2, 1999.

84 **"There were story sessions every night":** Alan Lomax, "Tracking Tradition," *Folk Roots* 127/128 (February 1994): 56–57.

85 **By the middle of July:** Alan Lomax to John A. Lomax. July 15, 1935, AL.

85 **"It was an evening out of long ago":** Alan Lomax to John A. Lomax, n.d., AL.

85 **"see further than the surface of things":** Zora Neale Hurston to John A. Lomax, August 30, 1935, in Carla Kaplan, *Zora Neale Hurston: A Life in Letters*, 357.

86 **"When she proposed that I go on this trip":** Zora Neale Hurston to John A. Lomax, September 16, 1935, ibid., 359.

86 **"she was attracted to him":** Ibid.

87 **"the neighbors had asked her to leave":** Nat Hentoff, "Profile: Alan Lomax," 61.

88 **Charles Seeger had already been exposed to hillbilly music:** Judith Tick, *Ruth Crawford Seeger: A Composer's Search for American Music* (New York: Oxford University Press, 2000), 346.

88 **The next day, there was Aunt Molly's picture:** *New York Times*, November 21, 1935.

89 **"Put any good, 'authentic,' traditional singer":** Charles Seeger, "The Folkness of the Nonfolk," in *Folklore and Society: Essays in Honor of Ben Botkin* (Hatboro, PA: Folklore Associates, 1966), 5.

89 **she replied that she was writing a book:** Aunt Molly Jackson to Alan Lomax, September 2, 1939, reprinted in Shelly Romalis, *Pistol Packin' Mama: Aunt Molly Jackson and the Politics of Folksong* (Urbana and Chicago: University of Illinois Press, 1999), 155.

89 **When they later did reach an agreement:** The recordings Aunt Molly made for Lomax in New York are described in Shelly Romalis's *Pistol Packin' Mama* as being a source of discord between them, since Aunt Molly claimed she was never told that the recordings were being made for the Library of Congress and assumed they were for Barnicle's use only. Romalis also accepts Aunt Molly's statement that she never made a record for Alan Lomax. But Jackson knew who the recordings were for, as Lomax had recorded her for the library six months before, and she continued to record for him for several years after, in November 1937 and again in May 1939. She also appeared on at least one of his radio programs in 1941, and corresponded with him for the rest of her life.

90 **"If you aren't well enough for a while":** Alan Lomax to John A. Lomax, n.d., ca. 1935, AL.

90 **"I'm going to disobey you straight out":** Alan Lomax to John A. Lomax, n.d., ca. 1935, AL.

91 **It was that spring that Alan met Elizabeth Harold Goodman:** Bess Lomax Hawes interviewed by John Szwed, California, 2005.

92 **When he learned that no one was willing to back him:** Alan Lomax to Herbert Halpert, July 11, 1936, AL.

92 **"It is much the nicest gift I ever had"**: Alan Lomax to John A. Lomax, July 9, 1936, AL.
92 **"After all we had been together"**: Alan Lomax to John A. Lomax, September 17, 1936, AL.
92 **But by September it was clear**: Alan Lomax to John A. Lomax, September 8, 1936, AL.

Chapter 5: Honeymoon in Haiti

94 **By November 1936**: The most complete account of Lomax's Haitian trip is contained in *Alan Lomax in Haiti, 1936–1937: Recordings for the Library of Congress* (Harte Records, 2009).
94 **The letters to the Haitians**: The most complete account of Lomax's Haitian trip is contained in *Alan Lomax in Haiti 1936–1937: Recordings for the Library of Congress*, Harte Records, 2009.
94 **Hurston had applied for a Guggenheim Fellowship**: In her work on hoodoo Hurston would have encountered *The Sixth and Seventh Book of Moses*, a collection of texts widely used by hoodoo practitioners and Pennsylvania Dutch hex workers that is said to explain the magic Moses used in his Old Testament feats.
94 **She wrote Alan from Kingston**: Zora Neale Hurston to Alan Lomax, June 7, 1936, AL.
95 **She did not speak to either one of them for the rest of their stay**: Harold Courlander, "Recollections of Haiti in the 1930s and '40s," *African Arts* 23, no. 2 (April 1990): 60–70.
95 **pianist-composer Ludovic Lamothe**: A little more than a year later, Lomax would be recording the music of Jelly Roll Morton, whose name at birth was apparently also Lamothe.
96 **She had become the toast of the Haitian army**: Alan Lomax interviewed by John Szwed, New York, 1970.
96 **"Zora is hard enough to fathom by herself"**: Alan Lomax to Elizabeth Harold, n.d., ca. December 20, 1936, AL.
96 **he had to submit a request to the library**: "Itemized Schedule of Travel and Other Expenses," January 11, 1937, AL.
96 **"Five or six radios going very loud"**: Alan Lomax, field notes, December 20, 1936, AL.
97 **"We had not walked twenty yards"**: Ibid., December 20, 1936, AL.
97 **"This country is, so far as my experience goes"**: Ibid., December 21, 1936, AL.
98 **"The banana and cane plantations"**: Ibid., 1936, AL.
98 **It was a short step to adapting his abilities**: Katherine Dunham, *Island Possessed* (Chicago: University of Chicago Press, 1994 [1969]), 18–20.
98 **"I am so nervous I can scarcely write"**: Alan Lomax, field notes, December 29, 1936, AL.
98 **"everything is so new here"**: Alan Lomax to John Lomax Jr., January 18, 1937, LC.
99 **"This land is literally all folklore"**: Ibid.
99 **"This is the first place I have ever visited"**: Alan Lomax to Charles Seeger, January 16, 1937, LC.
100 **"Haitian Journey"**: *Southwest Review* 23, no. 2 (January 1938): 125–147.
100 **"I am in a rather desperate mess"**: Alan Lomax to John A. Lomax, February 7, 1937, AL.
101 **"I come to you with an unusual request"**: Alan Lomax to Estenio Vincent, February 13, 1937, AL.
101 **Living in a hut**: *Current Biography*, September 1941, 46.
102 **"In Haiti it is not a good policy"**: Alan Lomax, "Pantheon of Vaudou (Plaisance)," n.d., AL.
102 **The owner of an American yacht**: Alan Lomax to Doc Reiser, May 15, 1937, AL.
103 **"It was characteristic of me then to let my father's work come first"**: Nat Hentoff, "Profile: Alan Lomax," 63.
104 **In early April John tried again**: John A. Lomax to Alan Lomax, April 10, 1937, AL.
105 **"Tell all the colored folks to listen to me"**: "Bourgeois Blues," words and music by Huddie Ledbetter, edited with new additional material by Alan Lomax. Copyright 1959, Folkways Music Publishers, Inc.
106 **"Everything local and native"**: Alan Lomax to Richard Reuss, n.d., 1971, Indiana University.
106 **"The New Deal"**: Alan Lomax quoted in Bernard Eisenschitz, *Nicholas Ray: An American Journey* (London: Faber and Faber, 1996), 40.
107 **"It was Tugwell's idea"**: Ibid., 39.
108 **"When I met Nick"**: Ibid., 44–45.
110 **Bess recalled Alan complaining**: Bess Lomax Hawes, "Reminiscences and Exhortations," *Ethnomusicology* 39, no. 2 (Spring/Summer 1995): 180.

111 **By 1940, three years into her part of the project:** Ruth Seeger's essay was finally published in complete form in 2001 as *The Music of American Folk Song,* edited by Larry Polansky with Judith Tick (Rochester, NY: University of Rochester Press).
111 **A few weeks later a letter arrived:** Archive of American Folk Song memo, August 12, 1937.
112 **"The shortest and best road to Harlan":** Alan Lomax to the Acting Chief of the Music Division, Library of Congress, August 16, 1937, AL.
113 **"one has to make friends of the people everywhere":** Alan Lomax to Harold Spivacke, September 30, 1937, LC.
113 **What should he do?:** Alan Lomax to Harold Spivacke, September 19, 1937, LC.
113 **"Try to remember":** Harold Spivacke to Alan Lomax, September 23, 1937, LC.
113 **"The young people were so shy":** Alan Lomax to Harold Spivacke, September 23, 1937, LC.
113 **At the end of October, Alan told the library:** Alan Lomax to Harold Spivacke, October 20, 1937, LC.
114 **"The mountains have always been poor":** "From the Report of the Assistant in Charge, Mr. Alan Lomax," in Annual Report of the Librarian of Congress for the Fiscal Year Ended, June 30, 1938, 183–189, LC.

Chapter 6: Doctor Jazz

116 **At the end of 1938, for instance:** Review of Arthur Palmer Hudson, *Folk Songs of Mississippi and Their Backgrounds* (Chapel Hill: University of North Carolina Press, 1936), in the *Journal of American Folk-lore* 51, no. 200 (April–June, 1938): 211–213.
118 **But Alan thought the event was of poor quality:** Alan Lomax to Harold Spivacke, April 1, 1938. Later, in a report on this era, he gave a much more sanguine account of the festival and the help given him. See Carl Engel, "Archive of American Folk-Song: A History, 1928–1939," Library of Congress Project, Work Projects Administration, 1940, 58–59.
118 **"It was the usual uncritical hash":** Alan Lomax to John A. Lomax, May 26, 1938, AL.
119 **"a partial idea of what happened":** Alan Lomax to Harold Spivacke, June 8, 1938, AL.
119 **"In sounding folk-lore resources":** Ibid.
119 **"job, union duties, teaching":** Alan Lomax to John A. Lomax Jr., n.d., AL.
120 **"The whole thing still seems a little bit churlish":** Alan Lomax to John A. Lomax, July 2, 1938, AL.
120 **"Modern folksongs are as important as old ones":** Quoted in Jean Fagan Yellin, "Remembering Kay," *Melus* (Fall–Winter 2004), 546.
120 **In the foreword to Katherine Dealy Newman's 1995 *Never Without a Song*:** Katherine Dealy Newman, *Never Without a Song: The Years and Songs of Jennie Devlin* (Urbana and Chicago: University of Illinois Press, 1995), xiii–xvi.
122 **Among his visitors was William Russell:** *"Oh, Mister Jelly": A Jelly Roll Morton Scrapbook,* compiled by William Russell (Copenhagen: JazzMedia Aps., 1999).
122 **Alistair Cooke, a young British reporter:** From *An Evening with Alistair Cooke at the Piano,* Columbia Records, ML 4970.
122 **"He was trying to make a living":** Alan Lomax, "Jelly Roll Morton Symposium," Dixon Hall, Tulane University, May 7, 1982, unpublished transcript in the Hogan Archives, Tulane University, 37.
123 **"I looked at him with considerable suspicion":** Ibid.
123 **Alan had intended to make only a few records:** Ibid., 37–38.
124 **"As I listened to it":** "The Art of the Negro: Mr. Jelly Roll Morton from New Orleans," BBC Third Programme, October 3, 1951.
124 **"I later came to call this process":** Alan Lomax, "Jelly Roll Morton Symposium," pt. 3, May 7, 1982, 40.
125 **Recorded interviews such as Morton's:** Harvey Breit, "Talk with Alan Lomax," *New York Times,* July 23, 1950, Book Review, 7.
126 **"Jelly Roll had been deeply hurt":** Alan Lomax, "Jelly Roll Morton Symposium," pt. 3, May 7, 1982, 40.
127 **"the most purely Irish colony in the United States":** Alan Lomax to Harold Spivacke, August 27, 1938, AL.
127 **Among other things:** James P. Leary, "Fieldwork Forgotten as Alan Lomax Goes North," recording from the Thirty-Third Annual Association for Recorded Sound Collecting Conference, May 30, 1999.

128 **He and Nick Ray had also sketched out a play:** Alan Lomax to John A. Lomax, November 7, 1938, LC; Alan Lomax to Bess Lomax, November 22, 1938, LC. Orson Welles, possibly inspired by the Morton sessions, was also planning to interview musicians and write and direct *The Story of Jazz*, a project that was ultimately sidetracked by other films.

128 **On his own, Jelly Roll wrote out short accounts:** See Danny Barker in Nat Shapiro and Nat Hentoff, *Hear Me Talkin' to Ya: The Story of Jazz as Told by the Men Who Made It* (New York: Rinehart, 1955). Barker describes the dress and games of New Orleans people, and the stylized ways they walked.

128 **When Morton laid out his theory of jazz:** The Morton recordings were licensed not by the Library of Congress, but by his estate. Jelly Roll had blacklisted a number of record companies and individuals through his executor before he died, so that none of them would be able to issue any of his recordings after his death. Rudi Blesh's boutique company Circle was the twelfth recording company to ask for permission to bring out the Library of Congress recordings, and it was the one approved by Morton's estate. See Rudi Blesh, "An Open Letter to *Jazz Record* Readers," *Jazz Record*, no. 60 (November 1947): 17–18.

128 **"Today, however, the divine right":** Blesh, notes to *The Saga of Mr. Jelly Lord*, Circle Records, 1947.

128 **Nick Ray and Alan set to work together:** Nick Ray and Alan Lomax to Olin Downes, May 19, 1938, 2, AL.

130 **"We suggest these techniques":** Alan Lomax to Olin Downes, June 18, 1938, 3, AL.

131 **"the stage [should be] a raised dais":** Ibid., 3–4.

132 **"Driven into the back woods":** Ibid., 5.

132 **"People come to the fair":** Ibid., 6.

132 **"In [folk] festivals a genuine folk singer":** Ibid., 7.

132 **One of his suggestions:** Ibid., 8.

133 **"You may not agree with me":** Alan Lomax to Olin Downes, May 26, 1938, AL.

133 **In the end, a series of bureaucratic tangles and turf wars:** David Robertson, *W. C. Handy* (New York: Alfred K. Knopf, 2009), 214.

134 **When Morton talked about his problems with Lomax:** George W. Kay, "Basin Street Stroller," *Jazz Journal* 4, no. 6 (June 1951): 1–3; nos. 7 and 8 (July–August 1951): 1–2; and no. 9 (September 1951): 1–2.

135 **The concert was an unqualified success:** "Music: Spirituals to Swing," *Time*, Jan. 2, 1939. My thanks to Andrew Horowitz for his suggestions.

135 **Alan came up from Washington for the 1938 concert:** Alan Lomax interviewed by Nick Spitzer, July 25, 1990, for his radio program *American Routes*.

136 **Danny Barker was one of Morton's staunchest defenders:** Alan Lomax, "Jelly Roll Morton Symposium," pt. 4, 13–14.

137 **"I realized that Jelly was telling me the history of jazz":** "The Art of the Negro: Mr. Jelly Roll Morton from New Orleans," BBC Third Programme, October 3, 1951.

137 **"There was as yet no serious jazz criticism":** Alan Lomax, "Jelly Roll Morton Symposium," pt. 4, 10.

137 **It was not so much the corruption of entertainment:** Ibid., pt. 1, 32–34.

138 **"New Orleans was the only place in America":** Ibid.

139 **"a sort of musical dictionary": Alan** Lomax to Bill Russell, May 16, 1957, AL.

139 **"In just a few years":** Preston McClanahan interview of Alan Lomax for a film on New Orleans bassist Chester Zardis, May 5, 1990, AL.

Chapter 7: Bohemian Folklorist

140 **In return, he offered an ambitious plan:** Alan Lomax to Harold Spivacke, fall 1938, LC.

141 **"You'll get some idea of what TAC would like to do":** "Concert and Opera," *New York Times*, February 3, 1939.

142 **This way he would develop a discography:** Alan Lomax to Harold Spivacke, April 8, 1939, LC.

142 **Spivacke informed him:** Harold Spivacke to Alan Lomax, February 24, 1939, LC.

142 **Spivacke begged Alan to at least listen:** Harold Spivacke to Alan Lomax, April 14, 1939, LC.

143 **He also talked with J. Mayo "Ink" Williams:** Alan Lomax to Harold Spivacke, n.d., ca. March 1939, LC.

143 **"My opinion is that the commercial recording companies"**: Alan Lomax to Harold Spivacke, March 8, 1939, LC.
143 **He had already discussed the prospect**: Alan Lomax to Harold Spivacke, March 26, 1939, and April 17, 1939, LC.
143 **When he approached the Musicraft Record Company**: Alan Lomax to Harold Spivacke, March 26, 1939, LC.
144 **After this find, he wanted to go out**: Alan Lomax to Harold Spivacke, April 17, 1939, LC.
145 **"When we were walking around New York"**: Pete Seeger interview with John Szwed, New York, 2008.
145 **"He wanted me to listen to banjo pieces"**: Ibid.
145 **Alan's long trek through the lists**: "List of American Folk Songs on Commercial Records," in *Report of the Committee of the Conference on Inter-American Relations in the Field of Music* (Washington, DC: William Berrien, Chairman, Department of State, September 3, 1940), 126–46.
146 **"But I have come away from this listening experience"**: Unnumbered p. 1 of untitled mimeograph, AL.
146 **On March 5, Lead Belly fought over Martha**: Nat Hentoff, "Profile: Alan Lomax," 48.
146 **"from Huddie's hand to the lawyer's pocket"**: News clipping reprinted in Tiny Robinson and John Reynolds, eds., *Lead Belly: A Life in Pictures* (Göttingen: Steidl, 2008), 101.
146 **His actions got him a lighter sentence**: Charles K. Wolfe and Kip Lornell, *The Life and Legend of Leadbelly* (New York: HarperCollins, 1992), 212–14.
147 **He wrote Spivacke with these suggestions**: Alan Lomax to Harold Spivacke, April 17, 1939, AL.
147 **Spivacke was astonished by Lomax's ambitious plans**: Harold Spivacke to Alan Lomax, April 22, 1939, LC.
147 **But Alan and Hammond had become wary of each other**: Alan Lomax to Harold Spivacke, May 28, 1939, AL.
148 **"As you probably know by the papers"**: Ibid.
148 **Charles Seeger was put in charge**: Rob Neufeld, "Mountain Music and Dance Grown from Many Roots," *Asheville Citizen-Times*, July 27, 2002.
148 **"You will have to 'open cold' "**: Harold Spivacke to Alan Lomax, June 1, 1939, LC.
148 **"Young Alan Lomax threw back his head"**: "Ballad of Old Chisholm Trail Drowns New York's Subway Roar as Texas Singer Practices for White House Date with King," *Dallas News*, June 4, 1939, AL.
149 **The usual protocol was of little help**: John Szwed interview with Alan Lomax, 1970.
149 **"One of the young men who had been asked to sing"**: Eleanor Roosevelt, *This I Remember* (New York: Harper and Brothers, 1949), 191.
150 **She told them that he had been arrested**: Alan Lomax FBI files, June 30, 1941; February 26, 1942.
150 **When they failed to reply**: Alan Lomax FBI files, July 15, 1941; October 3, 1941.
150 **But no one they interviewed said he was a Communist**: Ibid.
150 **There was not much that could top an appearance at the White House**: "Writers' Congress," *Time*, June 19, 1939.
150 **Alan put music to it**: Langston Hughes to Alan Lomax, December 8, 1939; Langston Hughes to Alan Lomax, n.d., ca. 1939; Alan Lomax to Langston Hughes, February 7, 1940, Langston Hughes Papers, Beineke Library, Yale University; *Our Singing Country*, 328–30. My thanks to Billy Jo Harris.
152 **It would be the most costly production**: Lanfranco Rasponi, "Radio in Education," *New York Times*, November 17, 1940.
152 **"I thought this was a joke"**: Bernard Eisenschitz, *Nicholas Ray: An American Journey* (London: Faber and Faber, 1996), 52.
153 **"I recall the day"**: Alan Lomax, "Saga of a Folk Song Hunter," *HiFi/Stereo Review* 4, no. 5 (May 1960). Reprinted in *Alan Lomax: Selected Writings 1934–1997*, ed. Ronald D. Cohen (New York: Routledge, 2003), 178.
154 **"They didn't even listen to me sing"**: *Four Symposia on Folklore*, Indiana University Publications Folklore Series No. 8, 1953, 171.
154 **"I specified that I could have so and so many guests"**: Alan Lomax, "Alan Lomax," in *Decade*

of Destiny, ed. Judith L. Graubart and Alice V. Graubart (Chicago: Contemporary Books, 1979), 316.

155 **By some people's standards Ives was not an authentic folksinger:** Pete Seeger, *The Incomplete Folksinger* (New York: Simon and Schuster, 1975), 9–12.

155 **"We cut past the fancy ballads:** Alan Lomax, in *Decade of Destiny*, 316.

155 **"Lomax, 24-year-old assistant in charge":** *CBS Pix* 1, no. 13 (August 14, 1939): 1.

155 **But now here he was, standing alone:** The orchestra was later conducted by Howard Barlow.

156 **his speaking voice was ragged:** John A. Lomax to Alan Lomax, October 2, 1939, AL.

156 **his choice of singers completely wrong:** John A. Lomax to Alan Lomax, May 4, 1939, AL.

156 **His job description at the archive:** "Duties of Alan Lomax in Connection with his work in the Archive of American Folk Song," n.d., LC.

156 **As he prepared to leave:** Nancy-Jean Ballard Seigel, "Helen Hartness Flanders: The Green Mountain Songcatcher," *Voices* 29 (Fall–Winter 2003).

157 **"Woody was on the show":** *American Roots Music*, "Oral Histories: Alan Lomax," http://www.pbs.org/americanrootsmusic/pbs_arm_oralh_alanlomax.html.

158 **"Woody came up in a frontier place":** Ibid.

159 **Once when he came into Alan's apartment:** Bess Lomax Hawes interview by John Szwed, California, 2005.

159 **"Their music has grabbed the attention of the world":** *American Roots Music*, "Oral Histories: Alan Lomax," http://www.pbs.org/americanrootsmusic/pbs_arm_oralh_alanlomax.html.

159 **"The guy in back of the glass there":** Ibid.

161 **It was not purity of tradition that he wanted:** Alan Lomax interviewed by Richard Reuss, August 29, 1966, Indiana University Library.

161 **"When did you make that one up, Woody?":** "Chain Around My Leg," in *Woody Guthrie*, Library of Congress Recordings, vol. 2, Rounder Records 1041/2/3, 1988, track 7.

161 **After a night at a borrowed typewriter:** Alan Lomax interviewed by Michael O'Rourke, July 7, 1987, AL.

161 **Woody could write out all the songs he knew:** Alan Lomax to Woody Guthrie, July 26, 1940, LC.

162 **"a testament to an unknown America":** Alan Lomax, Woody Guthrie, and Pete Seeger, *Hard Hitting Songs for Hard-Hit People* (Lincoln: University of Nebraska, 1999 edition), 366.

162 **The keystone of the albums:** Alan Lomax interviewed by Michael O'Rourke, July 7, 1987, AL.

163 **"These albums are not a summer sedative":** Quoted in Joe Klein, *Woody Guthrie: A Life* (New York: Ballantine, 1982 [1980]), 163–64.

163 **Even though they crossed into popular and blues territory:** R. P. Wetherald to Alan Lomax, April 4, 1940, LC.

163 **"learned these songs from Lead Belly by rote":** Alan Lomax quoted in notes to *The Midnight Special and Other Prison Songs*, RCA P-50, reprinted in the notes to *Take This Hammer*, Bluebird 82876-50957 CD, 2000.

164 **They hoped to get the Rockefeller Foundation:** John A. Lomax to Archibald MacLeish, April 4, 1940, AL.

165 **"a commercial possibility":** Alan Lomax to John A. Lomax, n.d., ca. July 1940.

165 **"We had Adam, we had Noah":** Bernard Eisenschitz, *Nicholas Ray*, 56.

165 **"Hear you fellas talk":** http://www.geocities.com.Nashville/3448/dustyold2html (no longer available).

166 **"When a woman's blue she hangs her little head and cries":** "Back Where I Come From," September 25, 1940, 1–2, AL.

166 **From there the cast went on to sing:** Ibid.

166 **The subject might be anything:** Bernard Eisenschitz, *Nicholas Ray*, 58.

167 **Alan managed to talk Nick into a compromise:** Alan Lomax to Woody Guthrie, November 1, 1940, LC.

167 **He chatted with Sam Goldwyn:** Alan Lomax to John A. Lomax, October 12, 1940, AL.

Chapter 8: A Bourgeois Town

168 **"I need not overstress my opinion":** Alan Lomax to Harold Spivacke, August 1940, LC.

169 **And why not have them recorded by pop singers:** Ibid.

169 **Archibald MacLeish loved the idea:** Archibald MacLeish to Alan Lomax, August 30, 1940.

170 **"I hope you will be ready now to listen":** Alan Lomax, "Reels and Work Songs," in *75 Years of Freedom: Commemoration of the 75th Anniversary of the Proclamation of the 13th Amendment to the Constitution of the United States* (Washington, DC: Library of Congress, 1943), 27–36; Ronald Cohen, ed., *Alan Lomax: Selected Writings 1934–1997* (New York: Routledge, 2003), 76; *Freedom: The Golden Gate Quartet and Josh White at the Library of Congress,* Bridge CD 9114, 2002.

170 **"Alan was pretty hard-hitting":** Quoted in Nat Hentoff, "Profile: Alan Lomax—Surprising the Folk Song," January 18, 1969, 16, unpublished, *The New Yorker Records, c. 1924–1984,* New York Public Library, Manuscripts and Archives Division, Box 1506, folders 7–8.

171 **It was an event that John Lomax would not soon forget:** The "Spirituals to Swing" concert had been dedicated to Bessie Smith by John Hammond.

171 **John doubted the story:** Later research confirmed John Lomax's account. See Chris Albertson, *Bessie,* rev. and exp. ed. (New Haven, CT: Yale University Press, 2003), 265–67; and Sally Grimes, "The True Death of Bessie Smith," *Esquire* 71, no. 6 (June 1969): 112–13.

171 **Alan and Brown apparently met to talk about it:** Alan Lomax to Sterling Brown, October 16, 1941, LC.

171 **But even fifty years later:** Alan Lomax, *The Land Where the Blues Began* (New York: Pantheon, 1993), 61.

171 **Alan was sent to talk with Mrs. Roosevelt:** "Folk Music in the Roosevelt Era," transcription of interview by Ralph Rinzler, in *Folk Music in the Roosevelt White House: A Commemorative Program* (Washington, DC: Office of Folklife Programs, Smithsonian Institution, 1982), 14–17.

172 **The next day MacLeish asked Alan to prepare a memo for him:** Ibid.

172 **With the war in Europe intensifying:** Archibald MacLeish to Alan Lomax, February 24, 1941, AL.

172 **"He'd get so excited":** Hentoff, "Profile: Alan Lomax," 3.

173 **Next, the publishers announced that because manufacturing costs had gone up:** Nolan Porterfield, *Last Cavalier: The Life and Times of John A. Lomax* (Urbana and Chicago: University of Illinois Press, 1996), 438–39.

173 **The book itself argued for understanding folk art *as* Art:** This section was aided by Judith Tick's introduction to the Dover edition of *Our Singing Country: Folk Songs and Ballads* (Mineola, NY, 2000), "Rediscovering Our Singing Country," xiii–xviii; and Judith Tick, *Ruth Crawford Seeger: A Composer's Search for American Music* (New York: Oxford University Press, 2000).

174 **Alan's talk at the Thirteenth Amendment celebration:** "The History of the Fort Valley State College Folk Festival," *The Peachite* 2, no. 2 (March 1944): 1.

175 **The day after the performance:** Alan Lomax to Harold Spivacke, n.d., ca. May 1941; Alan Lomax memorandum, n.d., ca. mid-September 1941, 1, LC. The Fisk/Library of Congress project was the basis of a book edited by Robert Gordon and Bruce Nemerov, *Lost Delta Found: Rediscovering the Fisk University–Library of Congress Coahoma County Study, 1941–1942* (Nashville: Vanderbilt University Press, 2005), which gathered together several parts of the project that never reached print. However, the editors never found, or chose not to use, all of the relevant correspondence and documentation from this project available in the Library of Congress and the Alan Lomax Archive in New York City, and consequently developed a very different narrative from the one presented here. Gordon and Nemerov see Lomax as having downplayed or perhaps even hidden the work of his black colleagues. A number of articles and reviews of their book found irresistible this story of a southern white man who built a career in part by using his black coauthors' work. For other commentaries and reviews challenging the book's research and conclusions, see Matthew Barton's review in *Western Folklore,* Summer 2007, and John Cowley's "Commentary" in *Blues & Rhythm,* March 2006.

175 **Even though Alan's *Back Where I Come From* had been canceled:** "South of the Border," *New York Times,* August 10, 1941; Alan Lomax to Harold Spivacke, n.d., ca. May 1941, LC.

176 **The Library of Congress would furnish sound equipment:** Alan Lomax to Charles Johnson, July 7, 1941, AL.

176 **"The agreed upon study":** Alan Lomax Library of Congress memorandum, September 18, 1941, LC.

176 **But as time went by and Alan heard nothing from Work, the two exchanged letters:** Alan Lomax to John W. Work III, July 17, 1941; John W. Work III to Alan Lomax, July 24, 1941; Alan Lomax to John W. Work III, July 30, 1941, LC.
176 **He would meet up with Work:** Charles Johnson to Alan Lomax, August, 11, 1941, LC.
176 **But preparations for war were beginning to intrude:** "Report on Preliminary Work in Clarksdale, Mississippi," 1941, AL.
177 **Johnson suggested that as an alternative plan:** Charles Johnson to Alan Lomax, September 18, 1941, LC.
177 **"It would be worth-while: to ask singers":** Alan Lomax to Chief of the Music Division of Florida Folklife, August 31, 1939. LC.
177 **"The interview technique does seem to run a little slow":** Alan Lomax to Carita Doggett Corse, [Florida] Statewide Writers' Project, October 15, 1939, LC.
177 **"My personal opinion":** Alan Lomax to John A. Lomax, July 17, 1940, LC.
180 **"Mister Ledford and the TVA":** Alan Lomax, "Mister Ledford and the TVA," in *Radio Drama in Action: Twenty-Five Plays of a Changing World*, ed. Eric Barnouw (New York: Rinehart, 1945), 47–58.
180 **Later, Alan wrote MacLeish:** Matthew Barton, "Arthur Miller—A View from the Field," *Folklife Center Notes*, nos. 1–2 (Winter/Spring 2005): 5.
181 **When he picked up his guitar:** Alan Lomax, *The Land Where the Blues Began*, 18.
181 **"And with him the sorrow of the blues":** Ibid.
181 **"Well, I got up this mornin' ":** Son House, "The Jinks Blues," Library of Congress CC08-A3.
181 **"Waters was bare-footed in raggedy overalls":** "The Art of the Negro: "Blues in the Mississippi Night," BBC, November 20, 1951, 3/1.
182 **"He was not a composer":** Alan Lomax, undated, untitled field note, LC.
182 **"Muddy's song departed from the rigid AAB":** Alan Lomax, *The Land Where the Blues Began*, 407.
182 **"full and fascinating":** Charles Johnson to Alan Lomax, September 18, 1941, LC.
183 **"Sixteen years have passed since I first picked cotton":** Lewis Jones to Alan Lomax, n.d., AL.
184 **"Alan had a way of making proclamations and value judgments":** Pete Seeger interviewed by John Szwed, 2006.
184 **"Naturally the Negro looks at the South with different eyes":** Alan Lomax to John A. Lomax, October 3, 1941, LC.
184 **"the seminar yielded, I note":** Charles Johnson to Alan Lomax, September 29, 1941, LC.
186 **"Your work sounds extremely interesting":** Alan Lomax to Harry Partch, October 24, 1941, LC.
188 **"It was a wonderful opportunity":** Nat Hentoff, "Profile: Alan Lomax," 64.

Chapter 9: The People's War

189 **"I am perplexed as to why":** Alan Lomax FBI files, April 3, 1942.
189 **When Archibald MacLeish received two reports:** Alan Lomax FBI files, July 2, 1942.
189 **A week later even J. Edgar Hoover:** Alan Lomax FBI files, July 11, 1942.
190 **"good old countrified name":** Alan Lomax to Woody Guthrie, January 21, 1942, LC.
190 **He also asked for permission:** Alan Lomax to Harold Spivacke, January 20, 1942, LC; January 22, 1942, LC.
191 **One of the first major academic meetings on the study of folklore:** The proceedings of the conference were published as "Conference on the Character and State of Studies in Folklore," *Journal of American Folklore*, October–December 1946, 495–527.
191 **But Alan was not easily flattered:** Alan Lomax to Stith Thompson, November 12, 1941, LC; July 14, 1941, LC.
191 **"She told us of her son":** Alan Lomax, Mississippi notebooks, AL.
192 **It would have changed the direction:** Alan Lomax to Son House, December 24, 1941; January 28, 1942; February 10, 1942; Son House to Alan Lomax, January 4, 1942, AL.
192 **His memory blurred by time and nervousness:** Alan Lomax, *The Land Where the Blues Began* (New York: Pantheon, 1993), 18–23.
192 **Elizabeth also recalled a pistol:** Undated, untitled note, AL.
192 **Alan was arrested again later:** Boris Weintraub, "The Folklore of Alan Lomax: Library Marks Anniversary of Archive of Folk Song," *Washington Star*, undated clipping from AL.

192 **Even before Alan returned to Washington:** Harold Spivacke to Alan Lomax, July 11, 1942, LC.
192 **"for morale with teachers, musicians, Negroes":** Alan Lomax to Harold Spivacke, n.d., AL.
192 **"I have been in a territory":** Alan Lomax to Harold Spivacke, August 7, 1942, LC.
193 **"I have had more trouble with local whites":** Ibid.
193 **a Library of Congress memo:** Ben Botkin to Harold Spivacke, October 27, 1942, LC.
193 **The library proposed that John Work clear whatever he did:** Ibid.
194 **In addition, they said:** Memo from Eri Douglass to Jeroma Sage, WPA: "Data for Mr. Lomax," October 30, 1942.
194 **Work later wrote the library staff:** John W. Work III to Ben Botkin, November 5, 1943, LC; and Ben Botkin to John W. Work III, November 10, 1943, LC.
194 **President Jones told Harold:** President Thomas E. Jones to Harold Spivacke, n.d., ca. October or November 1943, LC, AL.
194 **President Jones said he would come to Washington:** President Thomas E. Jones to Duncan Emrich, December 26, 1943, LC, AL.
194 **Work replied that he needed to know:** John W. Work III to Alan Lomax, December 28, 1947; Alan Lomax to John W. Work III, January 2, 1948, AL.
194 **"In 1941 and 1942":** Alan Lomax, "Report to NIMH," 1969, AL.
194 **In a series of letters back and forth:** Alan Lomax to Lewis Jones, February 10, 1954, AL.
194 **Jones replied that Charles Johnson:** Lewis Jones to Alan Lomax, February 16, 1954, AL.
195 **The increase to the budget:** Alan Lomax, "Saga of a Folksong Hunter," 177.
195 **The bibliography was divided into the regions of America:** Alan Lomax and Sidney Robertson Cowell, *American Folk Song and Folk Lore: A Regional Bibliography* (New York: Progressive Education Association, 1942).
195 **Also completed were the three volumes:** *The Check-List of Recorded Music in the English language in the Archive of American Folk Songs to July, 1940* (Washington, DC: Library of Congress, 1942).
195 **"I expect to make this material":** Alan Lomax to James Putnam, The Macmillan Company, December 26, 1942.
196 **When his application was received:** Alan Lomax FBI files, May 28, 1943.
197 **"All the things I'd learned about as a folklorist":** Nat Hentoff, "Profile: Alan Lomax," 65.
197 **"It is these folk artists that I hope":** Memo, "Plans for Reaching Folk Groups with War Information," from Alan Lomax to Bryson and Hinsaker, October 27, 1942, AL.
198 **At what he called the "United Nations level":** Ibid.
198 **"As a final mark of indifference":** John A. Lomax to Alan Lomax, ca. December 1943, AL.
199 **"They will contain topical songs":** Alan Lomax to Lewis Cowan, January 25, 1943, AL.
199 **He also wanted to compile a songbook of fighting songs:** Alan Lomax to Lewis Cowan, Robert Blakely, Douglas Meservey, and Archibald MacLeish, January 25, 1943; Alan Lomax to Alan Cranston and Lee Falk, February 4, 1943, AL.
199 **Instead of his campaign to reach people:** Nat Hentoff, "Profile: Alan Lomax," 65.
199 **"I still don't see how you can do the job":** Alan Lomax to William B. Lewis, March 21, 1943, AL.
200 **Symphonic works by Ives, Schumann, Brahms:** *New York Times*, April 19, 1943.
201 **Alan and the other writers' job:** CBS to Alan Lomax, May 12, 1943, May 18, 1943, AL.
201 **On May 1, Alan officially went on leave:** CBS to Alan Lomax, May 18, 1943, AL.
201 **The timing of this new position:** Howard Blue, *Words at War: World War II Era Radio Drama and the Postwar Broadcasting Industry Blacklist* (Lanham, MD: Scarecrow Press, 2002), 101–37.
201 **"the program, as I hear it":** Alan Lomax to John A. Lomax, July 20, 1943, AL.
202 **"I had worked for ten days practically continuously": Ibid.**
202 **"In the first of [Lomax's] *Transatlantic Call* productions":** D. G. Bridson, *Prospero and Ariel: The Rise and Fall of Radio* (London: Victor Gollancz, 1971), 101–2.
203 **"This is a neighborhood of people":** Alan Lomax, "Description of the Lower East Side," n.d., AL.
203 **After conducting their investigation:** Alan Lomax FBI files, July 23, 1943.
204 **But Elizabeth was still able to be hired:** Alan Lomax to John A. Lomax, October 6, 1943, AL.
204 **"see what needs to be done":** Ibid.
204 **"And my private opinion is the world's a pretty mad place":** Alan Lomax to John A. Lomax, October 13, 1943, AL.

205 **"I put the show on in despair"**: Nat Hentoff, "Profile: Alan Lomax," 68.
205 **"This is strange, selfish talk"**: Alan Lomax to John A. Lomax, ca. late January 1944, AL.
205 **"Sometimes I wonder what it is"**: Alan Lomax to John A. Lomax, February 6, 1944, AL.
206 **"In Café Society one night"**: D. G. Bridson, *Prospero and Ariel*, 193.
207 **"Tonight we bring you a new play"**: Notes to *The Martins and the Coys*, Rounder 11661-1819 CD.
207 ***The Martins and the Coys* was recorded**: Though Americans never got to hear any of these performances, they were so successful in England in 1944 that the BBC later commissioned another ballad opera, *The Chisholm Trail*. Alan was in the army by then, so the program was scripted by Elizabeth, the music arranged by Bess Lomax, and the singing was done by Woody, Burl Ives, Lee Hays, the Coon Creek Girls, and others. It was broadcast in the UK in February 1945.
208 **"I was billed as the World's Greatest Authority"**: Alan Lomax to John A. Lomax, n.d., ca. early 1944, AL.
208 **One day an officer asked him**: Bess Lomax Hawes interviewed by John Szwed, California, 2005.
209 **"We used to sing 'We Gonna Raise a Ruckus Tonight'"**: Alan Lomax, Army diaries, AL.
209 **"I was at drill one day"**: "Folk Music in the Roosevelt Era," transcription of interview by Ralph Rinzler, in *Folk Music in the Roosevelt White House: A Commemorative Program* (Washington, DC: Office of Folklife Programs, Smithsonian Institution, 1982), 14–17.
209 **Despite his cheerful letters home**: Harold Spivacke to Alan Lomax, August 29, 1944, LC.
209 **"sounded rosier than Homer's rosiest dawn"**: Alan Lomax to John A. Lomax, n.d., ca. early 1944, AL.
210 **He found similarities between Anne's features**: Alan Lomax to Family, November 20, 1944, AL.
210 **"Pretty depressed"**: Alan Lomax to John A. Lomax, n.d., AL.
210 **"I'm a bit lazy"**: Alan Lomax to John A. Lomax and family, December 22, 1944, AL
210 **"During the day I'm mostly bored"**: Alan Lomax to John Lomax Jr. and family, n.d., AL.
211 **"If it weren't for Elizabeth"**: Alan Lomax to John A. Lomax, n.d., AL.
211 **"I am in a basic training company"**: Alan Lomax to John A. Lomax, July 31, 1945, AL.
211 **"There is much less to do here"**: Ibid.
212 **"in between and underneath and through everything else"**: Alan Lomax to John A. Lomax, August 20, 1945, AL.
212 **"All my concern for the 'hoi-polloi'"**: Alan Lomax to John A. Lomax, n.d., AL.
213 **Alan wrote Harold Spivacke at the library**: Alan Lomax to Harold Spivacke, undated, AL.
213 **But all that Spivacke would offer**: Harold Spivacke to Alan Lomax, September 11, 1945, AL.
213 **All they could offer Alan was a recording trip**: Alan Lomax to John A. Lomax, October 1, 1945, AL.
214 **"No fancy-pants stuff like *Oklahoma!*"**: "Miserable but Exciting Songs," *Time*, November 26, 1945, 52.
214 ***That Girl from Memphis***: *That Girl from Memphis*, one-page film treatment, AL.
214 **The film was never made**: Alan Lomax to John A. Lomax, November 19, 1945, AL.
214 **Kapp sensed that the time seemed right**: Alan Lomax to John A. Lomax, November 20, 1945, AL.
215 **"There was a cold frenzy in the way I worked"**: Alan Lomax, untitled, ca. 1946, AL.

Chapter 10: The Century of the Common Man

217 **"I propose to make a book out of these lives"**: Alan Lomax, undated *Salt of the Earth* proposal, AL.
218 **"No dialect," he said**: Ibid.
218 **"Negroes and whites are working together"**: Ibid.
219 **"Folklore may prove to be"**: Alan Lomax, proposal to the Guggenheim Foundation, AL.
219 **"a quietus, once and for all"**: Ibid.
220 **But as soon as they began work on it**: John A. Lomax to Alan Lomax, January 17, 1946, AL.
220 **Their arguments began as they went forward**: Alan Lomax to John A Lomax, February 6, 1946, AL.

220 **"This is not calendar art"**: John A. Lomax and Alan Lomax, *Folk Song U.S.A.* (New York: Signet, 1966 [1947]), viii–ix.

221 **"unsophisticated country singers,"**: Alan Lomax, "The Best of the Ballads," *Vogue*, December 1, 1946, 208, 291–96.

221 **"Folklore can show us that this dream"**: Alan Lomax, "America Sings the Saga of America," *New York Times Magazine*, November 26, 1947.

221 **In this same spirit of explaining folklore to America**: "Folklore Meeting Set," *New York Times*, April 20, 1956; "All-Day Meeting of Folklore Held," *New York Times*, May 5, 1946.

222 **At his job at Decca**: Carl Sandburg, *Cowboy Songs and Negro Spirituals*, Decca A-356, 1945; *The People, Yes*, Decca A-273, 1949; Josh White, *Ballads and Blues, Vol. 1*, Decca A-447, 1946; Josh White, *Ballads and Blues, Vol. 2*, Decca A-611, 1947; Burl Ives, *Ballads and Folk Songs, Vol. 1*, Decca A-407, *Ballads and Folk Songs, Vol. 2*, Decca A-431, 1947; Richard Dyer-Bennett, *Twentieth Century Minstrel*, Decca A-573, 1947. See "Americana on Records," *Newsweek*, September 22, 1947.

222 **"During the past 100 years"**: Charles Seeger, "Reviews of Recordings," *Journal of American Folklore* 62, no. 243 (January–March 1949): 68–69.

222 **Though Alan was limited by what was already available**: *Listen to Our Story—A Panorama of American Ballads*, American Folk Music Series, Brunswick B-1024, 1947; *Mountain Frolic: Square Dance Pieces and Hoedowns*, American Folk Music Series, Brunswick B-1026, 1947.

223 **Seventy-five more albums were planned**: *Newsweek*, "Americana on Records," September 22, 1947.

223 **Alan did manage to get some rural singers their own albums**: Cousin Emmy, *Kentucky Mountain Ballads*, Decca A-574, 1947.

223 **he reissued two 1941 albums**: *Sod Buster Ballads: Folk Song of the Early West*, Commodore Records (Decca Records) CR-10 album no. B-1025, 1947; *Deep Sea Chanteys and Whaling Ballads*, Commodore Records (Decca Records), album no CR-11, 1947. The reissues were under Woody Guthrie's, Lee Hays's, Millard Lampell's, and Pete Seeger's names, and not the Almanacs'. Other albums mentioned in this paragraph: *Roustabout Songs*, Decca A-451; *Bayou Ballads*, Decca A-583; *Quadrilles, Decca A-617; Running Set*, Decca A-275; *Longways Dances*, Decca A-274; *Round Up Time in Texas*, Decca K-24.

223 **"Mark the ones with commercial potential"**: Alan Lomax interviewed by John Szwed, New York, 1970.

223 **Using Alan's 1940 mimeographed "List of American Folk Songs"**: John Cohen, "*Sing Out*, Vol. 19, No. 1, 1969," in *Think of the Self Speaking: Harry Smith—Selected Interviews*, ed. Rani Singh (Berkeley, CA: Cityful Press, 1998).

224 **"Just as every church has a choir"**: David Dunnaway, *How Can I Keep from Singing? The Ballad of Pete Seeger* (New York: Villard/Random House, 2008), 117.

224 **"We're going to put more into our songs"**: "Hootenanny," *Time*, April 15, 1946.

225 **Even with minimal publicity**: Edwin Gordon, "Cultivating Songs of the People," *New York Times*, May 26, 1946.

225 **When People's Songs held its first national convention**: David Dunnaway, *How Can I Keep from Singing?*, 125.

225 **"had the naïve impression"**: Nat Hentoff, "Profile: Alan Lomax," 68.

225 **Alan returned to the Folklore Institute at Indiana University**: Roger D. Abrahams interviewed by John Szwed, 2008.

226 **"We plan to cover the whole field of American folk music"**: John S. Wilson, "Lomax Brings in the Roots," *PM*, November 4, 1946.

226 **"the adjective 'great'"**: "Blues Featured at Midnight Concert," *New York Times*, November 11, 1946.

226 **But when composer Virgil Thompson reviewed the show**: Virgil Thomson, "Differentiated Counterpoint," *New York Herald Tribune*, November 11, 1946.

226 **Alan wanted to contrast**: John S. Wilson, "Lomax Brings in the Roots," *PM*, November 4, 1946.

227 **But the biggest success was "Honkytonk Blues at Midnight"**: In *The Land Where the Blues Began* (New York: Pantheon, 1993), 459, Lomax mistakenly recalled this concert as occurring the year before.

228 **But Alan attempted once again to bridge the gap**: Alan Lomax, "I Got the Blues," *Common Ground* 8 (Summer 1948): 38–52.

228 **In 1957 he produced an LP for United Artists:** *Blues in the Mississippi Night,* Rykodisc RCD 90155.
228 **On the day his Guggenheim Fellowship began:** Alan Lomax to Henry Allan Moe, February 1, 1947, AL.
229 **"/Well, it's early in the mo/r—in the mornin',/":** *Prison Songs, Vol. 1,* Rounder Records CD 1714.
229 **It was not until 1957 that he was able:** In 1987 Rounder Records released a two-volume set of these recordings produced by Alan's daughter, *Prison Songs: Historical Recordings from Parchman Farm 1947–48,* Rounder Records CD 1714 and CD 1715.
230 **There was no noise reduction:** LC Office Memorandum from HS to Roy P. Basler, Director of the Reference Department, June 13, 1958. The Morton interviews were kept in print for the next thirty years, and then completely restored and issued unedited by Alan's daughter and Jeffrey Greenberg of the Alan Lomax Archive on Rounder Records in 2005.
230 **Alan then asked the Library of Congress for a copy:** Alan Lomax to Duncan Emrich, March 11, 1946.
230 **"There was a moment in my life":** Alan Lomax quoted in Joe Klein, *Woody Guthrie: A Life* (New York: Delta, 1980), 332.
231 **"This program will bring these masters of ballad making together":** Lomax proposal, March 19, 1947, AL.
231 **While he was recording, a blizzard struck the farm:** Alan Lomax, "Saga of a Folksong Hunter," 178.
231 **"Be my woman, gal, I'll be your man":** *Prison Songs, Vol. 1: Murderers' Home.* Rounder Records 1714, 1997.
232 **"O Rosie, O lawd gal":** Alan Lomax, *The Land Where the Blues Began,* 265.
232 **"Here is poetry that rings like a hammer on an anvil":** Alan Lomax, *The Land Where the Blues Began,* 265; anthologized on Tradition in 1958 as *Negro Prison Songs,* and in the UK as *Murderers' Home* on Nixa Jazz Today LP, and released in 1997 in two volumes of *Prison Songs* in the Alan Lomax Collection, Rounder 1714 and 1715.
233 **Elia Kazan was contracted to do theater projects:** "Video vs. Housework," *Time,* July 19, 1948, 65.
233 **Nothing ever came of the company:** Jackson T. Brown, *John Steinbeck, Writer* (New York: Penguin, 1990), 611.
234 **"I have been able to talk about race relations":** Untitled report of work done under his Guggenheim Fellowship, 1948.
234 **"The audience was academic, young and liberal":** Alan Lomax interviewed by Nick Spitzer, June 25, 1990.
235 **"At first I did not understand how these songs related":** Alan Lomax, foreword, *The People's Song Book* (NY: Boni and Gaer, 1948), 3.
236 **Harburg's politics were in line with those of People's Songs:** Pete Seeger interviewed by John Szwed, 2007.
236 **Songs, for him, were not supposed to be speeches:** Bess Lomax Hawes quoted in Ed Cray, *Ramblin' Man: The Life and Times of Woody Guthrie* (New York: W. W. Norton, 2004), 328.
236 **"How a man with such a long road":** Joe Klein, *Woody Guthrie,* 347.
236 **At the same time, Woody had failed to write the songs:** Pete Seeger interviewed by John Szwed, New York, 2008.
236 **"Every new day we grow stronger":** *Songs for Wallace,* 2nd ed., n.d., 12.
237 **It was a daring choice:** Studs Terkel, *Touch and Go* (New York: New Press, 2007), 136–37.
237 **"It sure was a singing convention:** People's Songs National Staff Meeting minutes, November 5, 1948, AL.
237 **Alan even wrote a song for the next presidential election:** Joe Klein, *Woody Guthrie,* 347.
238 **People's Songs would support the efforts of black civil rights leaders:** Untitled document from People's Songs and Alan Lomax, ca. 1948.
238 **"Unions were in disarray":** Pete Seeger interviewed by John Szwed, New York, 2008.
240 **What was extraordinary was the list of people:** *New York Times,* October 6, 1948.
240 **"Acuff told me that he couldn't say the word 'syphilis'":** Nat Hentoff, "Profile: Alan Lomax—Surprising the Folk Song," January 18, 1969, 65, unpublished, *The New Yorker Records, c. 1924–1984,* New York Public Library, Manuscripts and Archives Division, Box 1506, folder 7–8.

240 **"Lomax had some problems with the producers":** Ibid., 65–66.
241 **On May 11, a select list of guests were invited:** Shortly afterwards, Alan recorded Burl Ives for the album *The Wayfaring Stranger* on Stinson Records, issued in 1949.
241 **She worked some of them up into a revue:** Jon Bradshaw, *Dreams That Money Can Buy: The Tragic Life of Libby Holman* (New York: William Morrow, 1985), 294.
241 **"I have been out trying to learn all I could":** Alan Lomax to Yip Harburg, ca. March 1949, Yale Music Library.
241 **Through a plea bargain, Woody entered into psychiatric counseling:** Ed Cray, *Ramblin' Man*, 330–32; Robin Roberts interviewed by John Szwed, 2006.
242 **"Burl Ives and Josh White refused to come":** Alan Lomax interviewed by Richard Reuss, August 20, 1966, 2, Indiana University Library.
242 **Alan wrote the script for the evening:** Ibid.
243 **Her 1946 script for John Steinbeck's *Pastures of Heaven*:** Joseph Liss, ed., *Radio's Best Plays* (New York: Greenberg, 1947).

Chapter 11: Living on the Black List

244 ***Mister Jelly Roll*:** Alan Lomax, *Mister Jelly Roll* (New York: Duell, Sloan and Pierce, 1950).
244 **The exception was Leonard Feather's:** Leonard Feather, "The Ananias of Jazz," *Melody Maker*, 1950.
244 **British playwright and folksinger Ewan MacColl wrote him:** Ewan MacColl to Alan Lomax, June 1950, AL.
244 **a "personal history document":** Robert Pehrson to Alan Lomax, December 29, 1950, AL.
245 **"Jazz became many things":** Alan Lomax, *Mister Jelly Roll*, 99–100.
245 **"I believe that this is the beginning":** Harvey Breit, "Talk with Alan Lomax," *New York Times*, July 23, 1950, Book Review, 7.
246 **"I felt that without knowing more":** Alan Lomax, "Application and Work Plan for a Guggenheim Fellowship, 1950," AL.
246 **His application to Guggenheim was supported strongly:** Ibid.
247 **His dreams were vivid:** Alan Lomax, 1950 notebooks, AL.
247 **Though it had been developed to record classical music:** Alan Lomax, "Saga of a Folksong Hunter," 178, AL.
247 **"What more people need are just good sets of examples":** Stith Thompson, ed., *Four Symposia on Folklore* (Bloomington: Indiana University Press, Folklore Series No. 8, 1953), 141. See also 135–54.
248 **"They made me so mad":** Nat Hentoff, "Profile: Alan Lomax," 73.
248 **"At first I started to sing Negro folksongs":** Alan Lomax to his therapist from the ship SS *Mauretania*, n.d., AL.
249 **Earlier the Weavers' managers had approached Alan for clearance:** Later, he made Lead Belly's estate half owner of all the songs in the Lead Belly book. Alan Lomax to Mr. Boros, June 5, 1975, AL.
249 **From the time of its release on July 3:** Gilbert Millstein, "Very Good Night," *New York Times*, October 15, 1950.
249 **When Alan's share of the royalties came in:** Alan Lomax FBI files, July 7, 1952.
249 **"One of the reasons that Alan has made enemies":** Nat Hentoff, "Profile: Alan Lomax," 74.
249 **The previous December, a New York newspaper:** Howard Rushmore, "Red Convictions Scare 'Travelers,'" December 15, 1949, unidentified news clipping in AL. Rushmore was also editor of *Confidential* magazine.
250 **rumor had it that the FBI was planning mass arrests:** The rumors were correct: J. Edgar Hoover planned to have habeas corpus suspended and to arrest twelve thousand Americans and hold them in military prisons, but it was never approved by the White House. See Tim Weiner, "Hoover Planned Mass Jailing in 1950," *New York Times*, December 23, 2007.
250 **He was leaving for Europe, he said:** Alan Lomax FBI files, October, 39, 1950.
250 **"He has, however, lost the main theme of the Southern story":** *New York Folklore Quarterly*, Summer 1950, 126–27.
251 **Elizabeth still had a job:** Alan Lomax, field notes, 1951, AL. Portions of Elizabeth Lomax's interviews with Davis can be read in the booklet included in the CD *Lifting the Veil: The First Blues Guitarists, Rev. Gary Davis & Peers*, World Arbiter Records, 2008.

251 **In a letter to the editor of the *Record Mirror* of London:** Alan Lomax to Isodore Green, Editor, *Record Mirror*, undated clipping in AL.

251 **"a comrade of the world":** Alan Lomax, 1950 notebook, AL.

253 **"like all anthropologist parties:** Alan Lomax diary, AL.

253 **"He told me he was recording the whole world:** Robin Roberts interviewed by John Szwed, New York, 2006.

253 **There was "a delicacy of musical line":** Alan Lomax, "A Ballad Hunter Looks at Ireland: Dublin to Donegal," radio script broadcast, December 13, 1957.

254 **But Alan still had the urge to experience Ireland himself:** Alan Lomax to Stith Thompson, May 7, 1951, AL.

255 **In January, 1951, Robin and Alan loaded up an old Citroën:** Nicholas Carolan, unpublished notes for forthcoming CDs of Alan Lomax's Irish recordings.

255 **"He was perfectly dressed":** Notes to *World Library of Folk and Primitive Music: Ireland*, Rounder CD, unpaginated.

256 **Later, there were those who complained:** Robin Roberts interviewed by John Szwed, New York, 2006.

257 **When they returned to London:** Broadcasts on Third Programme, August 15, 20, and 30, 1951. For my discussion of Lomax's time in London, I am indebted to the hard work and fine research of E. David Gregory in "Alan Lomax: The European Years, 1950–58, *B.C. Folklore*, no. 16 (February 2002): 9–35, and especially for his "Lomax in London: Alan Lomax, the BBC, and the Folk Song Revival in England," *Folk Music Journal* 8, no. 2 (December 2002): 136–69.

257 **But it was in the second series of programs that Alan found his voice:** Broadcasts on Third Programme, October 3 and 31 and November 28, 1951.

257 **"Up Above My Head":** "The Art of the Negro: Trumpets of the Lord," BBC script, 1, AL.

257 **To those who thought folk song was on the way out:** Ibid., 2.

258 **"Who knows but that some future Librarian of Congress":** Ewen MacColl to Alan Lomax, November 7, 1951, AL.

258 **"He was at the microphone singing 'Barbara Allen'":** Nat Hentoff, "Profile: Alan Lomax," 75.

259 **But they had little success with practical people:** Ewan MacColl, *Journeyman* (London: Sidgwick and Jackson, 1990), 272.

259 **Pickow had brought along a spring-driven Bolex camera:** John Bishop, notes to *'Oss, 'Oss, Wee 'Oss*, included on the DVD *OssTales*. (Portland, OR: MediaGeneration, 2007).

261 **"Ever since I left home":** Alan Lomax to Woody Guthrie, December 5, 1952, AL.

261 **"I know it's worth it":** Alan Lomax, field notebook, March 1951, AL.

262 **"the vigor and charm of these living English folk songs":** Alan Lomax, *England*, Rounder 1741.

263 **Robin and he continued what were now long discussions:** Alan Lomax, field notebook, May 1951, AL.

263 **"The conversation was extremely important":** Alan Lomax, field notebook, March 1950, AL.

264 **"I felt suddenly at the roots":** Nat Hentoff, "Profile: Alan Lomax," 76.

264 **This was the closest he had come to hearing:** *Gaelic Songs of Scotland: Women at Work in the Western Isles*, Rounder 1785.

265 **The faculty was suitably impressed:** Alec Finlay, ed., *The Armstrong Nose: Selected Letters of Hamish Henderson* (Edinburgh: Polygon Press, 1996), 59.

265 **And it was the BBC who had supported him:** Lomax continued to record some of the singers and get their autobiographies on tape as late as 1953 and 1957. See the *World Library of Folk and Primitive Music*, vol. 3: *Scotland*, Rounder 1743; *1951 Edinburgh People's Festival Ceilidh*, Rounder 1786; *Portrait of Jeannie Robertson*, Rounder 1720; *Portrait of Davie Stewart*, Rounder 1833; *Portrait of Jimmy MacBeath: Tramps and Hawkers*, Rounder 1834; *Portrait of John Strachan: Songs from Aberdeen*, Rounder 1835; and *Two Gentlemen of the Road: Jimmy MacBeath & Davie Stewart*, Rounder 1793.

265 **"As you know, however":** Alan Lomax to John A. Lomax, September 15, 1951, AL.

266 **"He brought to the task a ruthless readiness to do things":** Nat Hentoff, "Profile: Alan Lomax," 77.

266 **Once they saw the result of Lomax's collecting:** Paul Strand and Basil Davidson, *Tir a'Mhurain: Outer Hebrides* (London: MacGibbon and Kee, 1962). See Fraser MacDonald, "Paul Strand and the Atlanticist Cold War," *History of Photography* 28, no. 4 (Winter 2004): 357–74, esp. 369.

267 **From then on, his activities in Britain were noted in a file:** National Archives, catalog reference KV/2/2701, available from the Library of Congress.

Chapter 12: The Grand Tour

268 **The FBI was beginning to cover the same ground at home again:** Alan Lomax FBI files, October 13, 1952, and October 22, 1952.
269 **He spoke of his fondness for the French:** Unissued recordings of Big Bill Broonzy recorded by Alan Lomax, Paris, May 13, 1952, http://research.culturalequity.org/rc-b2/audio-ix-recording.jsp?d-446288-p=2.
270 **A Romanian musicologist friend, Constantine Brailoiu:** Lomax misremembered this trip date as beginning in 1953 in his "Saga of a Folksong Hunter," 181.
270 **So the Citroën was loaded up with recording equipment:** Martin Mayer, "Recordings," *Esquire*, October 1959, 42–43.
270 **"Drove from Port Bou to Barcelona":** Alan Lomax, Mallorca notebook, AL.
270 **"At that time, I did not know":** Alan Lomax, "Saga of a Folksong Hunter," 181.
271 **"This is a great country":** Alan Lomax, Mallorca notebook, AL.
271 **"For a month or so, I wandered erratically":** Alan Lomax, "Saga of a Folksong Hunter," 181.
272 **"Only a few sheep manage to live here":** Alan Lomax, Mallorca notebook, AL. I am also indebted here to Antoni Pizâ, "A Passionate Visual Curiosity: Alan Lomax's Leica in Mallorca, Ibiza, and Formentera," in *Alan Lomax: Mirades, Miradas Glances*, ed. Antoni Pizâ (Barcelona and Madrid: Lunwerg Editores, 2006), 134–42.
272 **"No matter in what God-forsaken, unlikely spot":** Alan Lomax, "Saga of a Folksong Hunter," 182.
273 **Efforts were under way to eliminate non-Spanish languages:** See Judith R. Cohen's essay "The Spanish Recordings," in the notes to all of Rounder Records' Spanish recordings on CD.
273 **Most of all, the police were interested in Lomax:** U.S. embassy records, October 30, 1952, quoted in the Alan Lomax files of the Metropolitan Police (British) National Archives.
273 **Things became even more complicated:** Alan Lomax FBI files, July 2, 1953.
273 **The police in Madrid went through the mail:** U.S. embassy records, October 30, 1952.
273 **"The Spanish musical landscape is divided into three parts":** Alan Lomax, quoted in Martin Mayer, "Recordings."
274 **"The folk songs of rural Europe and America are linked":** Antoni Pizâ, "A Passionate Visual Curiosity."
274 **"Recording folk songs works like a candid cameraman":** Martin Mayer, "Recordings."
274 **A hundred hours of tape were recorded:** Judith Cohen, "Spain: Lomax Remembered," *Canadian Folk Music* 36, no. 4 (Winter 2002): 22.
275 **This music was largely unknown outside of Spain:** "Alborda de Vigo" was retitled as "Toques de Chifro" in *The Spanish Recordings: Galicia*, Rounder 1761, in 2001.
275 **"Los Mayos . . . sung by a group of 6 ten year old boys":** Manuscript sent to "Mr. Frank," Music Division, Oxford University Press, n.d., AL.
275 **"[We had been told that] it was absolutely essential":** Alan Lomax, Galician notebooks, n.d., AL
276 **Just before Christmas 1952, Alan wrote Elizabeth:** Alan Lomax to Elizabeth Harold, December 3, 1952, AL.
276 **"At the front of the town there is a little harbor":** Alan Lomax to Woody Guthrie, December 5, 1952, AL.
276 **"I live in a tiny room":** Alan Lomax to Elizabeth Harold, unsent, ca. 1953, AL.
277 **"would discover Italy":** Alan Lomax, "Ascoltate, le colline cantano!" ("Listen, the Hills are Singing!"), *Santa Cecilia*, anno V, no. 4 (1956): 84–85, quoted in Goffredo Plastino, "Un sentimento antico," in *Alan Lomax L'anno più felice della mia vita Un viaggio in Italia 1954–1955*, ed. Goffredo Plastino (Milano: il Saggiatore, 2008), 3. For help with understanding the Lomax Italian project, I am indebted to Goffredo Plastino, both for his advice and for his excellent book *Alan Lomax L'anno più felice della mia vita Un viaggio in Italia 1954–1955*, which also includes Anna Lomax Wood's memoir, "Il doppio solittario" ("Double Solitaire"), 8–15. I also thank Sara Villa and Luca Formenton for their help and kindness in translating this book.

277 **"I was on the edge of nothing":** Alan Lomax, unpublished and partly finished book on the Spanish journey, AL.

278 **True enough, the folksingers turned out not to be problems:** Peter Kennedy, Notes to *Folk Songs of England, Ireland, Scotland, and Wales* CDs, Rounder 11661-1775-2, 11661-1776-2, and 11661-1778-2, 2000.

278 **In spite of the troubles:** Peter Cox, *Set into Song: Ewan MacColl, Charles Parker, Peggy Seeger and the Radio Ballads* (Cambridge, UK: Labatie Books, 2008), 45.

278 **"In due course," Attenborough recalled:** David Attenborough, *Life on Air: Memories of a Broadcaster* (London: BBC, 2002), 28.

278 **Alan was so annoyed by this staging:** Ibid., 30.

279 **The director and camera operators were forced to follow them:** Nat Hentoff, "Profile: Alan Lomax—Surprising the Folk Song," January 18, 1969, 81, unpublished, *The New Yorker Records, c. 1924–1984,* New York Public Library, Manuscripts and Archives Division, Box 1506, folders 7–8.

279 **"Unlike several of the other collections I'd received":** Ibid., 80–81.

279 **The albums all received positive reviews:** Howard LaFay, "To Fourteen Corners of the World with Alan Lomax," *High Fidelity,* March 1955.

280 **It would begin with ex-slave reminiscences:** Alan Lomax to Lewis Jones, February 10, 1954, AL.

280 **He wrote his brother, John Jr.:** Alan Lomax to John Lomax Jr., n.d., AL.

280 **The surveillance of Alan's life was expanding rapidly:** Alan Lomax FBI files, May 5, 1954.

280 **The American embassy asked him to sign a statement:** Alan Lomax FBI files, September 2, 1953.

280 **He sometimes brought Margaret Barry along:** Theo Bikel, *Theo: The Autobiography of Theodore Bikel* (New York: HarperCollins, 1964), 83–90.

280 **The London police had begun to monitor his radio programs:** Metropolitan Police report, July 3, 1954 (British) National Archives.

280 **The conditions for his employment were changed:** Ibid.

281 **"a 20th century museum":** Tradition Records notes, quoted by Nat Hentoff, "Profile: Alan Lomax," 82.

281 **"a Mediterranean tense-voiced South":** Alan Lomax, notes for untitled, undated talk in Italy, AL.

282 **"In the mountains above San Remo":** Alan Lomax, "Saga of a Folksong Hunter," 183.

283 **Being a foreigner might even be an advantage:** Goffredo Plastino, *Alan Lomax,* 36.

283 **"He told me that he didn't personally care":** Alan Lomax to "Dear Family," n.d., ca. November 1954, AL.

284 **"Neither the gaiety of Neapolitan song nor the tarantella":** Alan Lomax, script for "Italy: Puglia to Genoa," part of "Memories of a Ballad Hunter," February 5, 1957, quoted in E. David Gregory, "Alan Lomax: The European Years, 1950–58," *B.C. Folklore,* no 16 (February 2002): 21–22.

285 **In the town of Caggiano:** Nat Hentoff, "Profile: Alan Lomax," 82–84.

285 **To encounter cultures that required a two-thousand-year perspective:** Alan Lomax, "Italy: Puglia to Genoa," 21.

285 **"The regions or localities which did not conform":** Ibid.

285 **"Music for most people":** Alan Lomax to "Dear Family," n.d., ca. November 1954, AL.

287 **But when his Roman friends finally understood:** Alan Lomax, notes for untitled, undated talk in Italy, AL

287 **"Soon that same music would appear on film":** Later Alan found himself losing control over the work he had done in Italy. He discovered that Diego had sold the rights to Alan's Sicilian tapes to be used as the music for the second half of Pier Paolo Pasolini's 1971 film, *II Decameron,* though Alan would receive no credit or money and Ennio Morricone would be listed as the music consultant. It caused a rift between them, but such was their relationship that Alan quickly forgave him. There was also trouble later, after the death of Diego, when the professorial committee that directed the ethnic music archive of the Accademia Santa Cecilia urged the Accademia to sue Alan and Rounder Records for using the recordings Alan and Diego had made.

287 **Anne accompanied Elizabeth and Herbert to Spain:** Elizabeth Lyttleton and Herbert Sturz, *Reapers of the Storm* (New York: Thomas Y. Crowell, 1958).

289 **The play only ran for a week:** Script and handbill; review in the *Times* of London, December 28, 1955, 5, AL.

289 **The children's script's success:** Alan Lomax, *Harriet and Her Harmonium* (London: Faber and Faber, 1955).

Chapter 13: Skiffle: From Folk to Pop

291 **"the melting pot of the American frontier":** Alan Lomax, "Skiffle: Why Is It So Popular?" *Melody Maker,* August 31, 1957, 3.

291 **"learn too much":** Alan Lomax, "Skiffle: Where Is It Going?" *Melody Maker,* September 1957, 5.

292 **All were collected in a songbook:** Published by Chappell & Co. in 1957, and republished in 1963 as *The Folk Song Album.*

292 **"a folksinger could not claim to be an interpretive performer":** Col. Bouvé to V. W. Clapp, June 18, 1942, LC.

292 **When Alan heard the colonel's interpretation of the law:** One of two memos from Lomax responding to Ben Botkin on this matter is missing from the Library of Congress, though the second memo concerning releases exists. But both Lomax memos are summarized in another memo from Harold Spivake to V. W. Clapp, LC.

292 **"In certain cultures, you have to pay":** Nat Hentoff, "Profile: Alan Lomax—Surprising the Folk Song," January 18, 1969, 83–84, unpublished, *The New Yorker Records, c. 1924–1984,* New York Public Library, Manuscripts and Archives Division, Box 1506, folders 7–8.

293 **Neither he nor his father had ever copyrighted individual songs:** Harold Spivacke, "Copyright," in "Conference on Character and State of Studies in Folklore," *Journal of American Folklore* 59, no. 34 (October–December 1946): 324–30.

293 **When Alan received his share of the royalties:** It may have indeed been "unearned" by all parties involved, since the Weavers' version of the song was different from Lead Belly's.

293 **The $3,000 he received:** As he wrote the IRS from England in 1951, "You can see by my bank statements that I have already spent the entire sum in getting the project going." Alan Lomax to "Mr. Income Tax Man," ca. spring 1951, AL.

293 **Nevertheless, he thought the huge success of "Irene" was a pop culture anomaly:** My thanks to Don Fleming for guiding me through the thickets of copyright.

293 **This was a song he and his father had recorded with Lead Belly:** It's more likely that he knew about Donegan's use of these recordings earlier than this: "Rock Island Line" had been recorded by Donegan a year earlier, a song that Lead Belly had learned from inmate Kelly Pace in the Arkansas State Penitentiary in 1934.

294 **It was no surprise:** Alan Lomax to Kelly Pace, January 14, 1958; Kelly Pace to Alan Lomax, March 23, 1958, and April 22, 1958, AL.

294 **"When I looked into the story back of this piece of outright knavery":** Alan Lomax, "On the Subject of Copyrights," ca. 1960, unpaginated, unpublished article, AL.

294 **A dismayed Alan was persuaded:** Alan Lomax to Denton, Hall & Burgen, April 17, 1956; L. Kirby of Denton, Hall & Burgen to Alan Lomax, April 18, 1956, AL. The Lead Belly songs continued to be a copyright problem for years. When planning for Gordon Parks's *Leadbelly* film was beginning in the mid-1970s, Alan learned that the same publishing company with which he had been working had discovered that he had let the copyright to the Lead Belly book expire without renewing it, and they had copyrighted the book in the name of Lead Belly's deceased widow as their coauthor without informing Alan. Paramount, the film's producers, then made a deal with the music publisher and Lead Belly's heir for film rights to the book. Alan only became aware of this when Paramount gave him a fee to see if the script contained anything offensive in the characterization of his father and himself. When he retained a lawyer to help him regain his rights, he was informed that since he had not renewed the copyright and had accepted money from the film's producers he was in no position to sue. Finally he was given a small screen credit and a "minuscule" percent of the film's royalties.

294 **Alan once sketched out an article:** Alan Lomax, "On the Subject of Copyrights," undated manuscript, ca. 1950–51, AL.

295 **Charles Seeger, for example:** Charles Seeger, "Who Owns Folklore—A Rejoinder," *Western Folklore* 21, no. 2 (April 1962): 98.

296 **On the other hand, Seeger also said:** Ibid., 97.
296 **"the only person who could step into Oxford Street":** Nat Hentoff, "Profile: Alan Lomax," 66.
296 **His BBC friend Bridson said:** Ibid., 88.
297 **"I lost weight, grew a beard, grew up somewhat":** Alan Lomax to John Faulk, November 13, 1955, AL.
297 **Once it was approved, Elizabeth and Herbert Sturz moved into Alan's flat:** Elizabeth Lomax to Alan Lomax, March 4, 1956, and March 19, 1956, AL.
297 **She had been brought to London to live with her father:** Anna Lomax Wood interviewed by John Szwed, 2009.
297 **"His enthusiasm and initiative had spread":** Nat Hentoff, "Profile: Alan Lomax," 87–88. Alan also wrote with Peggy's help *American Folk Guitar*, an instruction book on playing guitar. It was published by Robbins in London in 1957.
298 **When Alan's article on the concept of song style and song families:** "Nuova ipotesi sul canto folkloristico italiano," *Nuovi Argomenti* 17/18 (November/February 1955–56): 109–35.
298 **"First of all, by using the musical style as a diagnostic instrument":** Alan Lomax, "The Psychological Patterns of Folk Songs," proposal for a grant from the University of London, 1957, AL.
299 **"The purpose of this study is to establish the psychological and physiological bases of song":** Ibid.
300 **"the first mapping of the musical styles of mankind":** Alan Lomax, "The Psychological Patterns of Folk Songs."
300 **Margaret Mead addressed his problem bluntly:** Nat Hentoff, "Profile: Alan Lomax," 92.
300 **Alan was hurt, and wrote Seeger defending his work:** Alan Lomax to Charles Seeger, May 3, 1956, AL.
300 **This time Hoover was looking for additional assistance:** Alan Lomax FBI files, May 11, 1956, May 15, 1956, August 6, 1956.
301 **Yet even he was unable to provide evidence:** Alan Lomax FBI files, June 6, 1956.
301 **Seven months and a hundred pages of documentation later:** Alan Lomax FBI files, December 13, 1956.
301 **She approved, and suggested that they could work on a few other songs:** Zora Neale Hurston to Alan Lomax, February 4, 1957, AL.
302 **Rossellini seemed doubtful:** Alan Lomax to del Papa, January 9, 1957, AL.
302 **When the programs were broadcast:** E. David Gregory, "Lomax in London," *Folk Music Journal* 8, no. 2 (2002): 154–55.
302 **"It took me four months," Alan told journalist Nat Hentoff:** Nat Hentoff, "Profile: Alan Lomax," 93.
303 **There were a few gaps in timing:** *Sing Christmas and the Turn of the Year*, Rounder 11661-1850 CD.
303 **Yet despite his appearances on the BBC and Granada Television:** Financial statement from Baker, Todman Ltd, London, December13, 1957. AL.
303 **"In a sense I became more intensely American":** Nat Hentoff, "Profile: Alan Lomax," 93.
304 **It was time to come back:** John Faulk to Alan Lomax, June 6, 1958, AL.
304 **Muddy Waters's voice, Alan said, "had coarsened":** Album notes to Shirley Collins, *False True Lovers*, Folkways Records FG 3564, 1, 1958.
304 **"I have to pick my way from task to task":** Alan Lomax, undated note to himself, AL.
304 **Even before he left Britain:** "Folk Song as It Is," *Newsweek*, April 14, 1958, 80.
305 **A reporter from *Time* was there to greet him:** "Just Folk," *Time*, September 22, 1958, 70.

Chapter 14: The American Campaign Resumed

307 **But Pete also offered a stern warning:** Pete Seeger, *The Incomplete Folksinger*, 185 (originally published in *Sing Out!*, Winter 1958–59).
307 **"The 'Folkniks' and the Songs They Sing":** *Sing Out!* 9, no. 1 (Summer 1959): 30–31.
307 **"Lomax has suddenly encountered a folk singing development":** John Cohen, *Sing Out!* 9, no. 1 (Summer 1959): 32–33.
308 **"I began to feel as if I was the grandfather of folk music":** Nat Hentoff, "Profile: Alan Lomax—Surprising the Folk Song," January 18, 1969, 95, unpublished, *The New Yorker Records, c.*

1924–1984, New York Public Library, Manuscripts and Archives Division, Box 1506, folders 7–8.

309 **"There Goes My Baby"**: Alan Lomax interviewed by John Szwed, New York, 1970.

309 **"I'm sticking up for Rock 'n' Roll"**: Joseph Wershba, "Daily Closeup," *New York Post*, March 30, 1959, 18.

309 **His defense caused a stir**: "The Rocking Rebels," broadcast May 29, 1961; see also Bob Rolantz, "Alan Lomax Jr. [*sic*] Interprets R & B," *Billboard* clipping in AL, ca. 1961.

309 **"to find that New York had gone to sleep"**: Alan Lomax interview by Nick Spitzer, July 25, 1990.

310 **"It expresses the way I feel tonight"**: Script for "Folksong 59" show, AL.

311 **He might on one occasion compare it**: Robert Shelton, "Bluegrass Style," *New York Times*, August 30, 1958.

311 **"Folk music in overdrive"**: Alan Lomax, "Bluegrass Background: Folk Music with Overdrive," *Esquire* 52 (October 1959): 108.

311 **He had returned home to the Village**: Alan Lomax, unpublished notes, AL.

312 **"high-hat and aging"**: Alan Lomax, *Ballads, Blues, and Bluegrass*, TV film, 1962, AL.

312 **"A century of isolation in the lonesome hollows"**: Alan Lomax, "Bluegrass Background," 108.

312 **"Many rock 'n' roll recording artists"**: Alan Lomax, quoted by Ara Piastro and Harry Altschuller in "The Big Change: He's International. What Will Happen to Elvis?" *Mirror*, January 27, 1960, AL.

312 **Ed Perl, the founder of the Ash Grove on Melrose in West Los Angeles**: "Alan Lomax," message on Yahoo! Groups, http://groups.yahoo.com/group/SocEcJustice/message/620.

313 **"I have grown almost to detest 'Western civilization'"**: Alan Lomax, *The Rainbow Sign* (New York: Duell, Sloan and Pierce, 1959), 10–11.

313 **Yet southern newspapers like the *Chattanooga Times:*** Christine Noble Govan, "Negro Music," *Chattanooga Times*, September 20, 1959; Harry L. Smith, "Two Accounts of Negroes in the South," *Richmond Times-Dispatch*, August 30, 1959; R. Henderson Shuffler, "Excursion into Negro Lore Found Authentic, Instructive," *Houston Chronicle*, September 20, 1959; Marguerite Cartright, "Rural Southern Folk Character," *The Crisis*, August–September 1959.

313 **Just as these recordings appeared Alan was asked by RCA**: *How the West Was Won*, RCA Living Stereo LSO-6070, 1960.

314 **The concept became further diluted**: *How the West Was Won*, film, 1962.

314 **The series continued until they completed ten albums**: All of these recordings were issued by Caedmon in the United States in 1961, and later by Topic records in the UK.

314 **He now regretted having left Shirley behind in England**: This account owes much to Shirley Collins, *America, Across the Water* (London: SAF Publishing, 2004), and Anna Lomax Wood.

315 **When they came on, they were the success that was expected**: Lester Flatts, the co-leader of the group, refused to appear when their time slot was changed.

315 **A Sunday morning panel discussion**: Israel G. Young, "Newport Folk Festival," *Caravan*, no. 18 (August–September 1959): 26.

317 **Though he found far fewer work song melodies and song leaders**: Shirley Collins, *America*, 127.

317 **On the song "Eighteen Hammers"**: Alan Lomax's notes and transcribed texts to *Sounds of the South*, Atlantic Records, 1993.

318 **It was a style of playing that anticipated early blues harmonica**: Hear, for instance, Herbie Hancock's electronic introduction to "Watermelon Man."

318 **"Lord, the 61 Highway"**: Shirley Collins, *America*, 135.

318 **"The blues, speaking through Fred"**: Alan Lomax, notes to *Deep South: Sacred and Sinful*, Prestige International 25001, 1960.

319 **"folk music was flourishing"**: Nat Hentoff, "The Man They Sing To," *Reporter*, 1961, 48, 50.

320 **Alan was particularly proud of the children's anthology**: Alan Lomax, notes to *American Folk Songs for Children*, Atlantic 1350, 1960.

320 **The *New York Times* marveled at the depth of the collection**: Robert Shelton, "Guide to the Southern Folk-Song Maize [*sic*]," *New York Times*, June 4, 1961.

320 **Charles Edward Smith in the *Saturday Review* was equally impressed**: Charles Edward Smith, "Cross-Seeding in Southern Songs," *Saturday Review*, February 11, 1961, 74.

320 **Smith also decried "stereotyped descriptions"**: Ibid.

321 **Prestige finally settled on a set of twelve albums to be called *Southern Journey***: The notes and editing for this series were done by Alan, his daughter Anne, and his assistant Carla Rotolo (wrongly identified as "Carlo" on the records). Though these recordings were recorded in stereo, they were issued only in mono by Prestige.

321 **Shirley was also authorized to use the tapes**: Alan Lomax, "To Whom It May Concern," January 26, 1960, reprinted in Shirley Collins, *America*, 181.

322 **"Everything I have written or transcribed"**: Alan Lomax, self-analysis notes, September 21, 1960, AL.

323 **"While I was squirreling round in the past"**: Alan Lomax to Guy Carawan, 1960, printed in the album *Freedom in the Air*, SNCC-101, 1962.

Chapter 15: The Science of Folk Song

324 **"He had come with a big manuscript"**: Walter Goldschmidt interviewed by John Bishop.

324 **Goldschmidt was impressed enough**: Alan Lomax, "Folk Song Style: Musical Style and Social Context," *American Anthropologist* 61, no. 6 (December 1959): 927–54.

325 **The *New York Times* accurately summarized the most significant part**: *New York Times*, February 9, 1959.

325 **The *New York Times* treated it as such**: Margaret Mead, *New York Times*, Letters to the Editor, February 5, 1961.

325 **An Anglo-American nursery song like "Cock Robin"**: Alan Lomax, *Folk Songs of North America* (Garden City, NY: Doubleday, 1960), 168–70, 181.

326 **"In the popular mind a gulf was fixed between pleasure and righteousness"**: Ibid., xviii.

326 **Meanwhile, just across the tracks**: Ibid., xx.

326 **"a study of folksong style"**: Alan Lomax, ACLS grant proposal, January 6, 1960, AL.

326 **Dr. Paul J. Moses**: Paul J. Moses, *The Voice of Neurosis* (New York: Grune and Stratton), 1954.

327 **As he wrote to Jack Harrison**: Alan Lomax to Jack Harrison, March 14, 1962, AL.

328 **Arensberg suggested that Alan might use this approach**: Alan Lomax, "The Best Things in Life," *AnthroWatch* II, no. 2 (October 1994): 12–13.

328 **In May 1961, Alan returned to Philadelphia**: See Alan Lomax, "The Adventure of Learning, 1960," *American Council of Learned Societies Newsletter* 13 (February 1962): 10–14.

329 **Edith Trager called the form of analysis they had developed "phonotactics"**: Their work was published as "Phonotactique du chant populaire" in *L'Homme*, Tome IV, no. 1 (January–April 1964): 5–55.

330 **"For the first time I had encountered a system"**: Alan Lomax, "The Adventure of Learning, 1960," 13.

330 **"The main function of musical style"**: Alan Lomax's notes written from 1954 to 1961, from Anna Lomax Wood.

331 **"Musical style changes least of all"**: Ibid.

331 **"Under the term song style"**: Ibid.

331 **Alan decided in advance**: Alan Lomax to Jack Harrison, Rockefeller Foundation, March 14, 1962, AL.

332 **The results were then compared statistically**: Victor Grauer, "Cantometrics: Song and Social Culture—A Response," *Musical Traditions*, no. 159 (July 24, 2006).

332 **"The special task of folklore"**: Alan Lomax, "The Adventure of Learning, 1960," 13–14.

332 **"I have hit upon three ways of describing"**: Alan Lomax to the Rockefeller Foundation, ca. 1961, AL.

332 **His Rockefeller proposal was turned into an article**: Alan Lomax, "Song Structure and Social Structure," *Ethnology* 1, no. 4 (January 1962): 425–52.

333 **"The coding system shows"**: Alan Lomax to Jack Harrison, Humanities Division of the Rockefeller Foundation, March 14, 1962, AL.

334 **Robert Farris Thompson, a professor of art history at Yale**: Robert Farris Thompson interviewed by John Szwed, New Haven, CT, 2008.

335 **"When you have to sit through a half-hour song"**: Bess Lomax Hawes interviewed by John Szwed, California, 2005.

335 **When he tried to interest Geoffrey Bridson at the BBC:** Alan Lomax to Geoffrey Bridson, September 22, 1961, AL.

335 **RCA showed no interest in his notions:** Brad McCuen to Paul Rosen, March 15, 1960, AL.

336 **Everything would be filmed with handheld cameras:** Alan Lomax, "American Folk Song Films," January 1960, AL.

336 **Its sponsor, the Colonial Williamsburg Foundation:** A *Teachers Manual for Music of Williamsburg* was developed in cooperation with the National Educational Association in 1962.

336 **"an extremely difficult Negro community to enter":** Expense sheets for Williamsburg film, 1960, AL.

336 **Though keeping the film from becoming anachronistic:** Carol J. Oja, "Filming the *Music of Williamsburg* with Alan Lomax," *Institute for Studies in American Music* 33, no. 1 (Fall 2003).

337 **But Alan took heart:** Alan Lomax, notes to *Georgia Sea Island Songs*, New World Records, NW 278, 1977.

337 **"The act of finding linkages":** Alan Lomax quoted in Ray Allen, "Staging the Folk: New York City's Friends of Old Time Music," *Institute for Studies in American Music* 35, no. 2 (Spring 2006), 2.

338 **But it was not too small a wedding for the *New York Times* to ignore:** *New York Times*, August 27, 1961.

338 **"Bessie lived with us and that machine was there":** Alan Lomax, from the transcript of an unnamed and undated conference in Detroit, November 26, 1961, AL.

339 **Though the interviews were never published, Alan wrote letters:** The interviews can be heard at http://research.culturalequity.org/get-audio-ix.do?ix=recording&id=10812&idType=sessionId&sortBy=abc.

339 **Alan's sister Bess, however, did her own interviewing:** Bessie Jones and Bess Lomax Hawes, *Step It Down* (New York: Harper and Row, 1972).

339 **They became popular performers at folk festivals:** Alan Lomax, liner notes to *Georgia Sea Island Songs*, New World Records, NW 278, and *Southern Journey: Georgia Sea Islands*, vols. 1–2, Rounder CDs 1712 and 1713; and Bessie Jones, *For the Ancestors: Autobiographical Memories*, collected and edited by John Stewart (Urbana: University of Illinois Press, 1983), 137–46.

Chapter 16: To Hear the World in a Grain of Sand

342 **Nor was this the romance of folklore collecting:** Alan Lomax to Lee Hazen, September 26, 1966, AL.

343 **While they were still in Trinidad, CBS Television called:** "Local Singers Perform for CBS Television Show," clipping in AL, no author, source, or date.

343 **After six hours of questioning:** Alan Lomax to John Lomax Jr. and Family, July 1, 1962, AL.

344 **In a book that came out of this work:** Alan Lomax, J. D. Elder, and Bess Lomax Hawes, *Brown Girl in the Ring: An Anthology of Song Games from the Eastern Caribbean* (New York: Pantheon, 1997), xi–xii.

345 **"Indeed," Alan wrote, hinting at future results:** Alan Lomax, NIMH 1963–69 grant proposal, AL.

346 **In *Folk Songs of North America* he had made a start:** Ibid.

346 **"far more significant . . . is the possibility":** Ibid.

347 **But it was too late, he explained:** Transcript of discussion between Margaret Mead and Alan Lomax, October 13, 1963, AL.

347 **It was a modest and very preliminary finding:** Victor Grauer, "Some Song Style Clusters—A Preliminary Study," *Ethnomusicology* 9, no. 3 (September 1965): 265–71.

349 **"For most of them it is their only outlet":** Newport Folk Festival program, 1964, AL.

349 **He would return again at Christmas in 1963:** Alan Lomax, *Charleston News and Courier*, January 19, 1964, reprinted in *Moving Star Hall Singers and Alan Lomax: Sea Island Folk Festival*, Folkways FS 3841, 1965.

349 **Alan proposed that the festival hire three staff:** Alan Lomax to Newport Folk Foundation, November 5, 1963, AL.

349 **At the time, folklore students:** Alan Lomax to Charles Seeger, January 21, 1964, AL.

349 **Over the next few months he traveled twelve thousand miles:** George Wein with Nate Chenin, *Myself Among Others: A Life in Music* (New York: Da Capo, 2004), 325.

350 **The performers ranged from Seamus Ennis:** Robert Shelton, "Newport Begins Its Folk Festival," *New York Times*, July 24, 1964; Ted Holmberg, "Exotic Sounds Waft Over Freebody Park," *Providence Journal*, July 24, 1964.

350 **"every folk song in the Western world":** Alan Lomax on Studs Terkel's radio show.

350 **Alan had just ended an affair:** "Sued Mate Says Wife Is Folklorn," *New York Post*, February 28, 1964, 36.

351 **"Collectors were looking for the oldest songs they could find":** Pete Seeger, "The Incomplete Folksinger," 275 (originally published in *Sing Out!*, July 1965).

353 **Dance reinforces human adaptive patterns:** Alan Lomax, "Choreometrics and Ethnographic Filmmaking," *Filmmakers Newsletter* 4, no. 4 (February 1971): 1–14.

354 **Likening the blues to the Italian *stornella*:** Robert Shelton, "Folklorists Give Talks at Newport," *New York Times*, July 24, 1965, 12.

354 **The story of Pete Seeger's anger:** Joe Boyd, *White Bicycles: Making Music in the 1960s* (London: Serpent's Tail, 2006): 98–100, 103–8; Pete Seeger interviewed by John Szwed.

354 **"I was trying to tell Dylan":** Michael Hall, "Mack McCormick Still Has the Blues, *Texas Monthly*, April 2002, reprinted in *Da Capo Best Music Writing 2003*, ed. Matt Groening and Paul Bresnick (Cambridge, MA: Da Capo, 2003), 107–121 (quote on 115).

355 **Two of these filmed sessions:** *Devil Got My Woman: Blues at Newport*, Vestapol DVD 13049, 2002; *Delta Blues/Cajun Two-Step: Music from Mississippi & Louisiana, Newport Folk Festival, 1966*, Vestapol VHS 13050, 1997.

355 **A third film:** *Billy in the Lowlands: Old Time Music from the Newport Folk Festival, 1966*, Vestapol VHS 13051, 1997.

356 **So when a deficit turned up for the year 1966:** George Wein, *Myself Among Others*, 335–36.

356 **He did, however, manage to finish *Folk Song Style and Culture*:** Alan Lomax, *Folk Song Style and Culture* (Washington, DC: American Association for the Advancement of Science, Publication no. 88, 1968).

357 **"The first period of cross-cultural style research":** Application to extend an NIMH grant for a further four years, 1970–74, AL.

358 **A few of the harshest reviewers admitted:** See, for example, Elli Köngäs-Maranda, "Deep Significance and Surface Significance: Is Cantometrics Possible?" *Semiotica* 2, no. 2 (1970): 173–84; and Steven Feld, "Sound Structure and Social Structure," *Ethnomusicology* 28, no. 3 (September 1984): 393–409.

Chapter 17: The Culture War

360 **"The more I think about it":** Alan Lomax to Paul Rosen, February 2, 1968, AL.

361 **"a few token specials and Sunday afternoon shows":** Alan Lomax to Editor, *New York Times*, April 13, 1968, not published.

361 **He recalled the moment in *Black Boy*:** Richard Wright, *Black Boy* (New York: Harper Perennial Modern Classics, 2008 [1945]), 35.

363 **Alan liked the idea of his band:** Alan Lomax, *The Land Where the Blues Began* (New York: Pantheon, 1993), 431.

363 **"Like all other humanists during the last five years":** Alan Lomax, "Progress Report" prepared June 1969 for an NIMH 1963–69 final report, AL.

364 **"The Black Identity Project was conceived in the spring of 1968":** Alan Lomax, "Narrative Report on the Black Identity Project," n.d., AL.

365 **Titled *3000 Years of Black Poetry*:** Alan Lomax and Raoul Abdul, eds., *3000 Years of Black Poetry* (NY: Dodd, Mead and Co.), 1970.

366 **"It was as if we were back in Bishop Percy's time":** Nat Hentoff, "Profile: Alan Lomax—Surprising the Folk Song," January 18, 1969, 68, unpublished, *The New Yorker Records, c. 1924–1984*, New York Public Library, Manuscripts and Archives Division, Box 1506, folders 7–8.

366 **"The present generation are the creators":** Alan Lomax, "Application to the Center for the Study of Urban and Metropolitan Problems at NIMH," December 3, 1969, AL.

367 **"I hope Jelly Roll and Bunk Johnson and King Oliver haunt you":** Alan Lomax to Matt Vetton Sr., July 15, 1970, AL.

367 **he testified at the hearings of the Senate Committee on Labor and Public Welfare:** *Washington Post*, May 18, 1970.

368 **The Rockefeller proposal was an example:** Alan Lomax, "Presenting America's Musical Heritage," *Washington Post*, February 11, 1975.

368 **"I continually find the black diaspora presentations extremely disappointing":** Alan Lomax, "Report and Recommendations from Alan Lomax Subsequent to His Observations of the '75 Festival and His Continuing Relation as a Folklore Consultant," ca. 1975, AL.

369 **He also wanted to have the festival recorded and filmed:** The Smithsonian did film and record the festival, but for a long time it was done in a haphazard way in poor quality.

369 **"One of the central problems of our culture":** Alan Lomax, "Filming the Smithsonian Folklife Festival," ca. 1976, AL.

369 **Alan had been at the hearings:** Hollie I. West, "American Folklife Foundation Endorsed," *Washington Post*, May 16, 1970, B2.

370 **But the letter was also a cry for help for America:** Alan Lomax to Jimmy Carter, July 16, 1976, AL.

370 **Only the week before, he had sent Carter a proposal:** Alan Lomax, "Toward a Presidential Commission on Grass Roots Culture," July 6, 1976, AL.

370 **The document caught the attention of Eizenstat:** Stuart E. Eizenstat to Alan Lomax, December 1976, AL.

370 **They apparently agreed on principles:** Alan Lomax to Joseph Duffy, February 28, 1979, and March 16, 1979, AL.

371 **Pete Seeger, who had suffered his share of indignities:** Seeger had already appeared on *Sesame Street* a number of times, and in 1974 had recorded *Pete Seeger and Brother Kirk Visit Sesame Street* ("Brother Kirk" being Rev. Frederick Douglass Kirk). Alan Lomax, "P.S. to 'Pickers and Singers,'" 1975, AL.

371 **"The best thing, of course, would be to turn television clear off":** Alan Lomax to Pete Seeger, February 26, 1976, AL.

371 **Alan's life had always been marked with contingencies:** Alan Lomax to Fred Friendly, February 11, 1971, AL.

372 **The analysis of the data was preliminary to a larger study:** Alan Lomax with Norman Berkowitz, Dorothy Peng, Carol Kulig, and Norman Markel, "A Stylistic Analysis of Speaking," *Language in Society* 6 (1977): 15–36.

373 **"One of the greatest opportunities":** Alan Lomax "Cinema, Science, and Culture Renewal," *Current Anthropology* 14, no. 4 (October 1973): 174.

373 **"Dramatic editing, shifts of perspective":** Ibid., 479.

373 **"It is a common experience in screening film":** Ibid., 477.

374 **A new kind of filmmaking would have to be developed:** Alan Lomax, "Choreometrics and Ethnographic Filmmaking," *Filmmakers Newsletter* 4, no. 4 (February 1971): 13.

374 **Alan argued with them about their priorities:** Alan Lomax to Sol Worth and Jay Ruby, March 22, 1972, AL.

375 ***Dance and Human History* was the first of four films:** The Media Extension Center also brought out *Cantometrics: An Approach to the Anthropology of Music* in 1977, a manual and a set of training tapes for cantometrics.

375 **The rest of the film provided directions for coding dances:** The relationship between tool type and use, subsistence level, dance, and social evolution was a key element in Lomax's choreometrics project, though it is seldom commented upon by those who write about his work. For an extensive discussion of social evolution and subsistence levels (though without concern for music or dance), see Alan Lomax and Conrad M. Arensberg, "A Worldwide Evolutionary Classification of Cultures by Subsistence Systems," *Current Anthropology* 18, no. 4 (December 1977): 659–708.

376 **But Alan was unhappy with the way things were organized:** Carl Sagan to Alan Lomax, June 6, 1977, September 26, 1977; Alan Lomax to Carl Sagan, March 26, 1978; Carl Sagan to Alan Lomax, April 8, 1978; Alan Lomax to Carl Sagan, April 9, 1978, AL.

376 **a letter arrived from Moe Asch:** Moses Ash to Carl Sagan et al., November 20, 1978, AL.

377 **Postproduction work was started back in Boston:** Alan Lomax, "Interim Report on the American Patchwork Series," n.d., AL.

378 **"In our last conversation, Margaret said, 'Is anybody making trouble?'":** Alan Lomax, "Margaret Mead of Columbia: A Memorial," n.d., AL.

378 **"The world which Nick [and] his contemporaries knew"**: Alan Lomax's notes for his talk at Nick Ray's memorial, n.d., AL.

Chapter 18: The Global Jukebox: "Got the World in a Jug, the Stopper in My Hand"

379 **In a letter to the president of the Carnegie Foundation:** Alan Lomax to Alan Pfeiffer, Carnegie Foundation, New York, January 14, 1981, AL.
379 **"This Treasury will present"**: Ibid.
380 **"Alan began the Strain project"**: Roswell Rudd interviewed by John Szwed, New York, 2007.
381 **In films of the early white pop singers:** Notes from Alan Lomax and Forrestine Paulay reviewing video performances of singers, April 24, 1986, AL.
382 **"to give them media status"**: Alan Lomax to Burt Feintuch, March 20, 1980, AL.
382 **Those outsiders doing field research among them:** Robert Baron, "'All Power to the Periphery'—The Public Folklore Thought of Alan Lomax," unpublished, 2009.
385 **"The Global Jukebox has fallen into an abyss"**: http://www.naimark.net/writing/lomax.html.
386 **Now he proposed to Belafonte that the time was right:** Alan Lomax to Harry Belafonte, July 1, 1981, and Harry Belafonte to Luis Sanjurjo, May 20, 1981, AL.
386 **It was the end of their relationship:** August Wilson to Alan Lomax, AL.
386 **The show went forward as *Jelly's Last Jam*:** Marty Bell, "That's the Way We Do Things in New Yawk," *Theater Week*, November 8–14, 1993, 24–31.
387 **In his preface to the 1993 edition of *Mister Jelly Roll*:** Alan Lomax, *Mister Jelly Roll*, p. viii.
387 **Many of the issues Alan raised against the musical:** Alan Lomax, *The Land Where the Blues Began* (New York: Pantheon, 1993).
387 **"My heart struck a depth of sorrow"**: Ibid., 63.
391 **"The romantic tradition has long provided a needed emotional balance"**: Alan Lomax, "A General Theory," 1993, unpaginated, AL.
392 **"When I hear the moralists of the present"**: Ibid.

INDEX